McGraw-Hill Accounting 10/12 Series

ACCOUNTING

SYSTEMS AND PROCEDURES · FOURTH EDITION

David H. Weaver, Ph.D.
Vice President, Director of
Editorial Planning and Research
McGraw-Hill Book Company

Edward B. Brower, Ed.D.
Professor, Department of
Vocational Education,
Business Education
Temple University
Philadelphia, Pennsylvania

James M. Smiley, Ph.D.
Professor of Accounting
and Information Sciences
Morehead State University
Morehead, Kentucky

Anthony G. Porreca, Ed.D.
Professor of Education
The Ohio State University
Columbus, Ohio

Gregg Division
McGraw-Hill Book Company
New York Atlanta Dallas
St. Louis San Francisco
Auckland Bogotá Guatemala
Hamburg Johannesburg
Lisbon London Madrid
Mexico Montreal New Delhi
Panama Paris San Juan
São Paulo Singapore
Sydney Tokyo Toronto

Sponsoring Editors: Marie Orsini and Susan Schornstein
Editing Supervisor: Elissa Pinto
Production Supervisor: Frank Bellantoni
Design Supervisors: Karen Tureck and Caryl Spinka
Photo Editor: Mary Ann Drury

Cover Photographer: Martin Bough, Corporate
Studios Communications, Inc.

Part Opening Photographs
Part 1
Joseph Neumayer (top)
Kip Peticolas/Fundamental Photographs (bottom; right)
Part 2
Kip Peticolas/Fundamental Photographs (all)
Part 3
Ray Ellis/Kay Reese & Associates (top)
Courtesy Mohawk Data Sciences (bottom)
Kip Peticolas/Fundamental Photographs (right)
Chapter Opening Photographs
Chapters 1, 2, 3, 4, 6, 8, 9, 10, 11,
12, 13, 14, 15, 16, 18, 19, 20, 22
Kip Peticolas/Fundamental Photographs
Chapter 5
Courtesy Ohio Scientific
Chapter 7
Joseph Neumayer
Chapter 17
Richard Megna/Fundamental Photographs
Chapter 21
Courtesy National Association of Mens Sportswear Buyers

Library of Congress Cataloging in Publication Data
Main entry under title:

Accounting, systems and procedures.

   (McGraw-Hill accounting 10/12 series)
   Includes index.
   1. Accounting.   I. Weaver, David H., date
II. Series
HF5635.A222   1982   657   81-12336
ISBN 0-07-069320-X   AACR2

    4 5 6 7 8 9 0 DODO 8 9 8 7 6 5 4 3

ISBN 0-07-069320-X

Chapter 1   The Language of Business   **4**
TOPIC 1   The Elements of Accounting   **5**
TOPIC 2   The Accounting Equation   **14**

Chapter 2   An Accounting Cycle Using Increases and Decreases   **20**
TOPIC 1   Increasing and Decreasing Permanent Accounts   **21**
TOPIC 2   Increasing and Decreasing Temporary Owner's Equity Accounts   **30**
TOPIC 3   Proving the Accounting Equation   **39**

Chapter 3   An Accounting Cycle Using Debits and Credits   **51**
TOPIC 1   Form of Accounts   **52**
TOPIC 2   Debiting and Crediting Permanent Accounts   **61**
TOPIC 3   Debiting and Crediting Temporary Accounts   **70**
TOPIC 4   Proving the Ledger   **77**

Chapter 4   Summarizing the Accounting Cycle Activities   **83**
TOPIC 1   The Trial Balance and the Income Statement   **84**
TOPIC 2   The Balance Sheet   **91**
TOPIC 3   Updating the Owner's Equity Accounts   **98**

Chapter 5   Origination and Input of Accounting Data   **114**
TOPIC 1   Originating Data   **115**
TOPIC 2   Journalizing Data   **126**

Chapter 6   Processing Accounting Data   **142**
TOPIC 1   Posting Data to the Ledger   **143**
TOPIC 2   Preparing Accounting Proofs   **156**

Chapter 7   Output of Accounting Data   **166**
TOPIC 1   Preparing the Financial Statements   **167**
TOPIC 2   Updating the Owner's Equity Accounts   **173**
TOPIC 3   Interpreting Financial Information   **184**
TOPIC 4   Financial Statements for Partnerships and Corporations   **192**

Project 1   Fortune Bus Line   **207**

Chapter 8   Banking Activities   **209**
TOPIC 1   Paying by Check   **210**
TOPIC 2   Depositing Cash   **217**
TOPIC 3   Verifying the Cash Balance and the Bank Balance   **221**
TOPIC 4   Petty Cash   **230**

Chapter 9   Payroll Activities   **240**
TOPIC 1   Computing Gross Earnings   **241**
TOPIC 2   Deductions From Gross Earnings   **246**
TOPIC 3   Payroll Records and Procedures   **256**

[PRO-LAWN SERVICE Accounting Application]

NOTE: Students are taken through the accounting cycle three times in Part 1: in Chapter 2, in Chapters 3–4, and in Chapters 5–7.

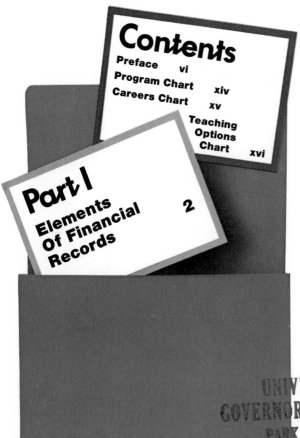

Contents

Preface   vi
Program Chart   xiv
Careers Chart   xv
Teaching Options Chart   xvi

Part I
Elements Of Financial Records   **2**

Chapter 10   Accounting Systems   276
TOPIC 1   Information Processing   277
TOPIC 2   Visualizing the Accounting
System   287

**Chapter 11   A Cash Receipts
Subsystem**   295
TOPIC 1   Controlling Cash Receipts   296
TOPIC 2   Processing Cash Receipts   302

**Chapter 12   A Cash Payments
Subsystem**   314
TOPIC 1   Controlling Cash Payments   315
TOPIC 2   Processing Cash Payments   318
TOPIC 3   Proving Cash   324

**Chapter 13   A Purchases
Subsystem**   333
TOPIC 1   Controlling Purchases: Ordering,
Receiving, and Accounting for Merchandise   334
TOPIC 2   Controlling Purchases: Storing
Merchandise   344
TOPIC 3   Processing Purchases on Credit   348
TOPIC 4   Controlling the Accounts Payable
Ledger   354
TOPIC 5   Controlling Net Purchases   360
TOPIC 6   Controlling Cash Payments on
Account   371

Chapter 14   A Sales Subsystem   381
TOPIC 1   Controlling Sales of Merchandise   382
TOPIC 2   Processing Sales on Credit   390
TOPIC 3   Controlling Net Sales   402
TOPIC 4   Controlling Cash Received on
Account   413
TOPIC 5   Controlling Accounts Receivable   419

**Chapter 15   A Personnel and
Payroll Subsystem**   426
TOPIC 1   Controlling Personnel and Payroll   427
TOPIC 2   Processing the Payroll   432
TOPIC 3   Paying the Payroll   441
TOPIC 4   Preparing Payroll Tax Returns   444

**Chapter 16   A General Accounting
Subsystem**   457
TOPIC 1   Controlling Internal Transactions   458
TOPIC 2   Updating the Trial Balance   461
TOPIC 3   Completing the Worksheet   472
TOPIC 4   Preparing Financial Statements   482
TOPIC 5   Adjusting and Closing the Ledger   491
TOPIC 6   Interpreting Financial Information   497

Project 2   Reno Appliances   509

[JEANS-PLUS Accounting Application]

[SUN-N-SKI Accounting Simulation]

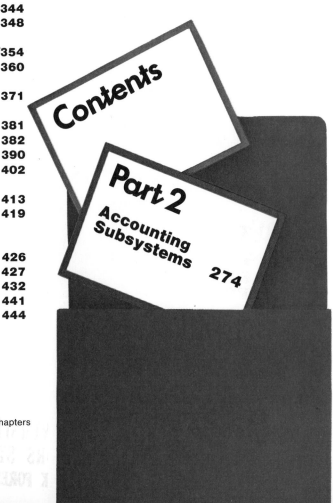

Contents

Part 2

Accounting
Subsystems   274

NOTE: Chapter 10 describes accounting systems. Chapters
11–16 describe accounting subsystems.

Contents

Chapter 17   Updating Accounts/Uncollectible Accounts and Depreciation   **516**
TOPIC 1   Updating Accounts Receivable   **517**
TOPIC 2   Estimating and Writing Off Uncollectible Accounts   **525**
TOPIC 3   Updating Plant and Equipment Accounts   **531**

Chapter 18   Updating Accounts for Accruals and Deferrals   **546**
TOPIC 1   Unrecorded Expenses and Liabilities   **547**
TOPIC 2   Unrecorded Revenue and Assets   **554**

[KENNA'S CARPET MART
Accounting Application]

Chapter 19   Manual Accounting Systems   **567**
TOPIC 1   The Combination Journal   **568**
TOPIC 2   Direct-Entry Records/Pegboards   **577**

Project 3   Georgia Appliance Center   588

Chapter 20   Automated Accounting Systems   **591**
TOPIC 1   Computers and Word Processors   **592**
TOPIC 2   Components of a Computer   **598**
TOPIC 3   Common Language Media   **605**
TOPIC 4   Computer Applications   **611**

Chapter 21   A Perpetual Inventory Subsystem   **616**
TOPIC 1   Inventory Management   **617**
TOPIC 2   The Inventory Ledger   **636**
TOPIC 3   Automated Inventory Procedures   **649**

Chapter 22   A Credit Card Subsystem   **660**
TOPIC 1   Credit Card Sales   **661**

Index   **673**

Part 3
Special Accounting Systems and Procedures   514

NOTE: Chapters 21–22 describe accounting subsystems.

Preface

Accounting
SYSTEMS AND PROCEDURES
Fourth Edition

Take another look at the cover of this textbook. *Break through* is its theme. Why? Because the *Accounting: Systems and Procedures*, Fourth Edition, program is a breakthrough in accounting instruction, both for teachers and for students.

The new edition builds upon the successful aspects of the previous edition of the *Accounting 10/12 Program* and continues *breaking through* the deceptive approaches so commonly used. For example, the equation/cycle approach and the systems approach to teaching accounting help students and teachers break through into the true world of accounting where microcomputers and minicomputers play vital roles in processing data. In addition, the emphasis placed on interpreting financial information helps students and teachers break through to understanding the connection between procedures presented in the program and those actually used in accounting today and in the future.

Teaching Methodology

The *Accounting: Systems and Procedures* program consists of this series as well as the *Accounting: Systems and Procedures, Advanced Course* series. The entire program is based on up-to-date accounting methodology, systems, and procedures. It can be used as a semester, year, two-year, three-year, or shorter course of instruction. It can also be used in vocational, avocational, or general education courses of instruction. (See the Teaching Options Chart on page xvi.) The complete program is best described as holistic in its presentation. That is, it emphasizes the importance of the whole teaching system as well as the independence of its parts, which are described below.

Short Learning Units. The learning sequence is structured in a building-block arrangement. Each learning unit—a reading section followed by one or more exercises (activities)—leads logically to the next. Related units make up a topic.

Related topics make up a chapter. Related chapters make up a part. The basic program is made up of three parts.

Learning Reinforcement and Immediate Feedback. Each topic and chapter, like each learning unit, is followed by appropriate exercises, so that at each stage learning is reinforced. Students move on to the next learning unit, topic, or chapter only after they have mastered the present one. The reinforcement exercises also provide students with immediate feedback, so that they can check what they have learned at every stage.

Learning Evaluation. The evaluation strategy includes performance goals for every topic, which state what students are expected to learn, and progress and comprehensive tests to measure the achievement of those goals. This evaluation strategy enables both the student and the teacher to assess whether the student is ready to proceed to the next topic or chapter.

Recycling. The teaching methodology also includes a recycling strategy. That is, students restudy the particular concepts or topics they have failed to master. There are ample problems of all levels of difficulty and complexity, so that teachers can assign materials appropriate to the needs of the student until mastery is achieved.

Career Information. Instruction in this program is based on a hierarchy of skills and knowledge. The vocational skills and knowledge associated with various accounting, computing, and related office jobs are presented in a progression from the simple to the complex. A photographic scenario introduces each part and each chapter's content of the textbook. The scenario uses a personal approach. Emphasis is on the aspects of accounting in that part or chapter that involve people, forms, procedures, and/or equipment. Other career education information is included from the *Dictionary of Occupational Titles*. (See the Careers Objectives Chart on page xv.)

Vocabulary. All accounting terms are in bold print in the textbook and are defined at that point. Then, they are listed at the end of the chapter under "The Language of Business" section in the order in which they appear in the chapter. In this way, students can easily locate the word in the chapter. In addition, such a listing gives a brief outline of the content covered in the chapter. Accounting terms which have general, everyday usage but also have special meanings in accounting are discussed separately in selected chapters under the heading "Language." (See page 8.) Various vocabulary building activities, such as crossword puzzles, are included in the *Working Papers and Chapter Problems*.

Accounting Concepts, Principles, and Controls. The program teaches students the fundamental accounting concepts, principles, and controls. The text is based on generally accepted accounting principles, Accounting Principles Board (APB) Opinions, and statements of financial accounting standards. These are accounting principles accepted by the accounting profession. Accounting concepts and accounting principles are included in the topic of the textbook where they are relevant.

The subsystems in Part 2 emphasize internal controls in an accounting system. Students are taught that subsystems are designed to include internal controls for safeguarding assets, checking accuracy, promoting honesty, and encouraging efficiency and speed in processing data.

Equation/Cycle Approach. This approach emphasizes the importance of the three basic accounting elements and then presents accounting content following the sequential steps of the accounting cycle. It presents the analysis of transactions using the common language of increases and decreases.

The equation/cycle approach overcomes the disadvantages and shortcomings of the balance sheet/equation approach, which introduces the financial statements out of sequence and fails to cover the complete accounting cycle. The equation/cycle approach takes students through the entire accounting cycle in sequence, up to closing the ledger. Thus students' difficulty understanding closing is greatly reduced since they are presented with the reasoning behind closing the ledger before having to record the closing entries.

This approach also presents the concept of accounts much earlier, including extending accounts into revenue and expenses and the Income Summary prior to encountering debits and credits. Thus the equation/cycle approach presents the complete picture of closing entries and accumulating net income in the accounting cycle.

Systems. The entire program follows an accounting systems approach. This approach traces the flow of data in a continuous sequence from its origin to its ultimate use. Flowcharts are used to show this sequence and flow of data. No business activity is treated as an isolated event. Coverage is from source documents to financial statements.

The concept of an accounting system is developed throughout. In Part 1, systems are presented in a service business using the equation with increases and decreases, as well as a journal-ledger system. In Part 2, the accounting system involves special journals and subsidiary ledgers in a merchandising business. In Part 3, systems are presented using combination journals, journalless accounting, ledgerless accounting, and one-write procedures.

Subsystems. Most accounting systems have a number of subsystems to process specific kinds of data. Six subsystems are presented in Part 2. Cash receipts, including coverage of bank cards; cash payments; purchases on credit; sales on credit; personnel and payroll (new to this edition), including computation of state income tax; and general accounting, emphasizing the interpretation of financial statements and including coverage of control of internal transactions, statement of changes in financial position, cash-flow statement, ratios, and budgeting are covered. In Part 3, two special subsystems are presented. Perpetual inventory and credit card sales are discussed.

Financial Statements. All pertinent financial statements are covered. These include the income statement, schedule of cost of goods sold, statement of owner's equity, balance sheet, statement of changes in financial position, and cash-flow statement. While the cash-flow statement is extremely important as a mangerial tool, the latest statements of the Financial Accounting Standards Board require that certain corporations must publish a statement of changes in financial position. Thus this program includes coverage of that statement.

Interpretation of Financial Information. The interpretation of financial information is emphasized throughout the program. In Part 1, students first learn to interpret accounting data within the accounting cycle, as well as to interpret the results between two accounting periods. Students learn that accounting cycle activities are continuous from one accounting period to the next. As a result, they study the closing procedures for one accounting period and begin work for the next accounting period. In addition, interpretation of financial information is expanded to include comparative financial statements.

Integrating Data Processing. In accounting practice, little if any accounting work is done using only manual data processing methods. Therefore, the *Accounting: Systems and Procedures* program takes accounting students through both the accounting cycle and the data processing cycle. Automated data processing and the data processing cycle are introduced in Part 1 and are emphasized throughout the program. For example, the equation/cycle approach introduces processing financial data both by computer and by hand. Special journals and batch process-

ing are part of the coverage of automated data processing. In addition, automated procedures are discussed within each subsystem. Further coverage of automated accounting systems includes word processors (including nontechnical discussions of electronic mail and electronic funds transfer); computer components, common-language media, and computer applications (including nontechnical discussions of automated data processing in payroll, accounts receivable, and perpetual inventory).

Components of the Program

Accounting: Systems and Procedures consists of several components that complement the basic textbook by reinforcing cognitive, affective, and psychomotor learning. Each component is designed to correlate with teaching and learning stages throughout the instructional period. The components supplementing this textbook are described below and are summarized in the chart on page xiv.

Textbooks. The textbook is divided into three parts, each of which is available in a separate, soft-cover version. Having both hard-cover and soft-cover textbooks available enables teachers to choose the materials best suited to their classroom needs.

Part 1, Elements of Financial Records, uses the accounting equation/cycle approach to teach students basic accounting theory and applications. Two accounting periods are used to illustrate the steps of the accounting cycle. The Globe Travel Agency, a single proprietorship, is used as an example of a service business. The role of accounting in business and the economic, social, and consumer aspects of accounting are described. Banking activities, petty cash, and payroll activities are also included to help students prepare for employment and to help them in their personal financial management.

Part 2, Accounting Subsystems, introduces six accounting subsystems. This is done using a merchandising business, the House of Sound. Cash receipts, cash payments, purchases on credit, sales on credit, personnel and payroll, and general accounting are covered. The worksheet and end-of-period adjustments are shown in relation to the complete accounting cycle. Each subsystem describes the people, forms, procedures, and equipment used to control the subsystem. Career titles and *Dictionary of Occupational Titles* reference numbers and descriptions are included. Flowcharts for each subsystem are included so that students can visualize the accounting subsystem.

Part 3, Special Accounting Systems and Procedures, covers uncollectible accounts, depreciation, accruals and deferrals, manual and automated accounting systems, a special perpetual inventory subsystem, and a special credit card subsystem. Coverage of a manual accounting system includes the combination journal, one-write systems, and direct-entry records for sales. Coverage of an automated accounting system includes a nontechnical description of computers and word processors with examples of nontechnical computer applications. As a continuation of the automated accounting content of Chapter 20, a new chapter, Chapter 21, describes inventory management, the inventory ledger, and automated-inventory procedures. This chapter is useful for students who are interested in careers in marketing and distribution. Work in business, whether in the office, in sales, or in private enterpreneurship, requires an understanding of a credit card subsystem. Therefore, a new chapter, Chapter 22, includes coverage of controlling credit card sales.

Working Papers and Chapter Problems. There are three workbooks, one for each part of the textbook. These workbooks contain the working papers needed to complete the activities, topic problems, and projects found in the textbook. They also contain chapter problems to supplement the extensive problem material in the textbook. The workbooks also include "Check

Your Reading" exercises and exercises on accounting concepts and principles.

Each *Working Papers and Chapter Problems* workbook has a teacher's edition, which is an exact copy of the workbook with the solutions printed in bright red.

Learning Guides. There are three self-instruction workbooks, one for each part of the textbook. They include performance goals, step-by-step instructions, all working papers, and self-check answers at the back of each learning guide. The self-check gives students immediate feedback and helps them pinpoint which areas they need to study further. There is a comprehensive teacher's edition, which, in one volume, is an exact copy of all three learning guides, with the solutions in a second color.

Accounting Applications. There are four accounting applications. Three are practice sets to be used by the students individually. The fourth is a simulation to be used by several students working together. *Pro-Lawn Service* is an accounting application involving a service business and includes banking, petty cash, and payroll procedures. It is intended to be used after Part 1. *Jeans-Plus* is an accounting application involving a merchandising business and includes subsystems for cash receipts, cash payments, purchases, sales, payroll, and general accounting. It is intended to be used after Part 2. *Kenna's Carpet Mart* is an accounting application involving procedures for uncollectible accounts, depreciation, accruals, and deferrals. It is intended to be used after Chapter 18 of Part 3. All three applications have separate teacher's manuals and keys which include teaching suggestions, progress sheets, solutions to the practice set, and suggested solutions to the management cases.

The *Sun-n-Ski* simulation involves a merchandising business that sells athletic equipment. It covers the complete accounting cycle for a merchandising business, special journals and ledgers, and payroll procedures. In the last week of the simulation, the books are closed and financial statements prepared. The accounting information is interpreted and applied in making the decisions called for by the management cases in the simulation. The number of students working in the *Sun-n-Ski* group is flexible and can vary from five to nine. Any number of groups can work on *Sun-n-Ski* in a classroom. *Sun-n-Ski* is intended to be used after Chapters 11–16 of Part 2 have been studied. *Sun-n-Ski* has a separate teacher's operating manual.

Microcomputer Applications. At least three integrated microcomputer programs are available with the *Accounting: Systems and Procedures* program. One deals with accounting applications, a second with review and testing, and a third with interpreting financial data and decision making. The programs present a universal view of accounting concepts and procedures. In addition, each is designed so that generic microcomputer applications can be used. A teacher's operating manual is available for each program.

Transparencies. Color transparencies are available for use with an overhead projector. Correlated with the topics in the textbook, these can be used to preview new material, reinforce the presentation of a topic, or review material taught previously. The transparencies are in two colors. They are made up in such a way to enable concepts to be explained step by step as each transparency is placed in position. Students see a journal or ledger, for example, being built up just as they would see it if they themselves were preparing the accounting form. Included with the transparencies are guide notes that give text references, points for discussion for each transparency and other information and suggestions for presenting the transparencies most effectively. Having the guide notes as an integral part of each transparency is especially convenient for teachers, since everything needed for presenting each transparency is immediately at hand.

Evaluation Manual. An *Evaluation Manual* (performance goals, progress tests, and comprehensive tests) is available. The evaluation model begins with competencies, with the instructional aspects broken down by performance goals. Each performance goal is represented by some activity or problem in the textbook. The tests are then used to evaluate the student's performance against these goals. Solutions to the tests are included in the *Source Book and Key.*

Source Book and Key. The *Source Book and Key,* or teacher's manual, provides a comprehensive guide to organizing and teaching the accounting course. It includes a general section on organizing the accounting course, methods of teaching accounting, and use of special features of the textbook and supplementary materials. Visual materials are described, particularly the transparency masters of the most commonly used accounting forms and of accounting content. There are discussions of performance goals, testing, and grading. Lesson plans, teaching suggestions, time schedules, and solutions to management cases, chapter questions, and tests for each chapter are also included.

Other Teacher's Aids. These include, as already mentioned, teachers' editions of each of the three *Working Papers and Chapter Problems,* one comprehensive teacher's edition of the three *Learning Guides and Working Papers,* teachers' manuals and keys for each of the three practice sets, a teacher's operating manual for each of the three microcomputer programs, and a teacher's operating manual for *Sun-n-Ski.*

Special Features

Included in the special features of *Accounting: Systems and Procedures* Fourth Edition, are the following.

Readability. The authors have used a simple, direct style of writing. All technical accounting vocabulary terms are printed in bold print and are defined at that point. Margin notes and illustrations are used to review, illustrate, and provide additional detail to text discussions. Color is used schematically to improve readability.

Vocabulary. The authors believe that understanding accounting terms is essential for success in accounting. Therefore, as previously described, there are several new features in this program to highlight vocabulary study. These include having accounting vocabulary shown in bold print in the text and defined at that point, as well as being listed in "The Language of Business" sections at the end of each chapter. In addition, a special "Language" feature is used intermittently throughout the book to distinguish vocabulary having both general usage and accounting usage.

Marginal Notes and Illustrations. The marginal notes identify key terms, ideas, rules, controls, and formulas. These notes provide a valuable aid for reinforcing reading, completing problems, and reviewing for tests. Students and teachers report that marginal notes are often used to refresh their memories about an accounting control, concept, principle, or procedure. The marginal illustrations visually reinforce the content without interrupting the student's reading of the text. In many instances, marginal illustrations highlight specific areas of larger illustrations, serving as a reference to illustrations previously shown. As a result, students do not have to turn back and forth among pages.

Accounting Concepts and Accounting Principles. The basic concepts of accounting and the generally accepted accounting principles from the FASB are included at the end of each topic in the textbook.

"Think Metric." The United States is gradually converting to the SI System (metric) of measurement. In anticipation of this changeover, *Accounting: Systems and Procedures,* Fourth Edition, gives the approximate metric equivalents of the U.S. Customary units used in the text. Thus students are helped to become familiar with a different system of measurement by relating the unfamiliar to what they already know.

Projects. Three projects are provided at appropriate intervals throughout the textbook. These projects enable students to integrate and apply the concepts, principles, and procedures they have learned in preceding chapters. The projects are longer than topic and chapter problems but shorter than the practice sets.

Chapter Problems. Chapter problems are in the *Working Papers and Chapter Problems.* Chapter problems are designed to show business operations as a continuous process. As students learn new accounting concepts and procedures, chapter problems are assigned which tap previous learning and build on earlier chapter problem experiences. This unique feature prepares students to work on projects, practice sets, and the accounting simulation.

Management Cases. As a further check of mastery, but especially to enable students to understand the purpose of what they have learned, management cases are provided at the end of every chapter. These cases require students to apply their knowledge in a realistic business situation. Students must analyze and interpret financial information and then make a critical decision, in the same way business managers must. These cases also underscore how managers use accounting information to direct and control the operations of a business. Because these cases are sufficiently detailed, answers will usually vary, just as they would in actual business situations.

Working Hints. There is a working hint at the end of each chapter. These hints help students develop better work and study habits. The working hints reflect current accounting practices and techniques in the real world of accounting.

Acknowledgments

Accounting: Systems and Procedures is the culmination of years of research and input from classroom teachers and students, accounting and data-processing practitioners, professional leaders, and learning theorists. Many people have helped make *Accounting: Systems and Procedures,* Fourth Edition, possible. Certified public accountants from business, cooperatives, government, and educational institutions have assisted us in developing the program. We are deeply grateful especially to Domenic Nascenzi, Assistant Fiscal Officer and Budget Analyst, Surface Warfare Officers School Command, United States Navy, Newport, Rhode Island; Pat Pace of Richard P. Dubuque, Certified Public Accountants, Torrance, California; George Stealy, Manager, Credit Customer Relations, Midwestern Territory, Sears Roebuck, Inc., Chicago, Illinois; Mark Thomson, CPA, Lawrence and Lawrence, Certified Public Accountants, Mobile, Alabama; and Dr. Donald Zook, CPA and CMA, Professor of Accounting, Messiah College, Grantham, Pennsylvania. We also want to express our thanks to the many users of the previous editions, especially to those who offered the helpful comments and suggestions which we have incorporated into the present edition. Special thanks go to the following users of the program who have also served as consultants to the *Accounting: Systems and Procedures,* Fourth Edition, program: David E. Gynn, COE Coordinator, Kent Roosevelt High School, Kent, Ohio; Ralph Heatherington, formerly Chairperson of the Business Department of Wheaton Central High School, Wheaton, Illinois; Scott Peterson, Teacher of Business Education, Columbia Heights High School, Columbia Heights, Minnesota; Virginia Rose, Columbus, Ohio public school system; Dr. Ralph Ruby, Jr., Associate Professor and Coordinator of Vocational Business Education, Arkansas State University, Jonesboro, Arkansas; and Connie M. Stubbe, formerly of the Department of Business Education, Workman High School, City of Industry, California.

David H. Weaver
Edward B. Brower
James M. Smiley
Anthony G. Porreca

ACCOUNTING: SYSTEMS AND PROCEDURES, FOURTH EDITION PROGRAM CHART

	PART 1	PART 2	PART 3
HARD-COVER TEXT	Elements of Financial Records	Accounting Subsystems	Special Accounting Systems and Procedures
SOFT-COVER TEXT	Elements of Financial Records	Accounting Subsystems	Special Accounting Systems and Procedures
WORKING PAPERS AND CHAPTER PROBLEMS	Elements of Financial Records	Accounting Subsystems	Special Accounting Systems and Procedures
LEARNING GUIDES AND WORKING PAPERS	Elements of Financial Records	Accounting Subsystems	Special Accounting Systems and Procedures
ACCOUNTING APPLICATIONS (PRACTICE SETS)	Pro-Lawn Service	Jeans-Plus	Kenna's Carpet Mart
ACCOUNTING APPLICATION (SIMULATION)		Sun-n-Ski	
ACCOUNTING APPLICATIONS (MICROCOMPUTER)		Microcomputer Software	
TRANSPARENCIES	Elements of Financial Records	Accounting Subsystems	Special Accounting Systems and Procedures
EVALUATION MANUAL (TESTS AND PERFORMANCE GOALS)	Elements of Financial Records	Accounting Subsystems	Special Accounting Systems and Procedures
SOURCE BOOK AND KEY	Elements of Financial Records	Accounting Subsystems	Special Accounting Systems and Procedures
TEACHER'S EDITION FOR WORKING PAPERS AND CHAPTER PROBLEMS	Elements of Financial Records	Accounting Subsystems	Special Accounting Systems and Procedures
TEACHER'S EDITION FOR LEARNING GUIDES AND WORKING PAPERS	Elements of Financial Records	Accounting Subsystems	Special Accounting Systems and Procedures
TEACHER'S MANUAL AND KEY FOR ACCOUNTING APPLICATIONS (PRACTICE SETS)	Pro-Lawn Service	Jeans-Plus	Kenna's Carpet Mart
TEACHER'S KEY FOR ACCOUNTING APPLICATION (SIMULATION)		Sun-n-Ski	
TEACHER'S AIDS FOR ACCOUNTING APPLICATIONS (MICROCOMPUTER)	Instructions and Key for Microcomputer Software		

NOTE: Dotted rule between parts indicate that material is found in one volume.
Solid rule between parts indicates separate volumes.

CAREERS OBJECTIVES CHART*

	PART 1 — ELEMENTS OF FINANCIAL RECORDS									PART 2 — ACCOUNTING SUBSYSTEMS							PART 3 — SPECIAL ACCOUNTING SYSTEMS AND PROCEDURES					
CHAPTERS / ACCOUNTING CAREERS	1 THE LANGUAGE OF BUSINESS	2 AN ACCOUNTING CYCLE USING INCREASES AND DECREASES	3 AN ACCOUNTING CYCLE USING DEBITS AND CREDITS	4 SUMMARIZING THE ACCOUNTING CYCLE ACTIVITIES	5 ORIGINATION AND INPUT OF ACCOUNTING DATA	6 PROCESSING ACCOUNTING DATA	7 OUTPUT OF ACCOUNTING DATA	8 BANKING ACTIVITIES	9 PAYROLL ACTIVITIES	10 ACCOUNTING SYSTEMS	11 A CASH RECEIPTS SUBSYSTEM	12 A CASH PAYMENTS SUBSYSTEM	13 A PURCHASES SUBSYSTEM	14 A SALES SUBSYSTEM	15 A PERSONNEL AND PAYROLL SUBSYSTEM	16 A GENERAL ACCOUNTING SUBSYSTEM	17 UNCOLLECTIBLE ACCOUNTS AND DEPRECIATION	18 UPDATING ACCOUNTS FOR ACCRUALS AND DEFERRALS	19 MANUAL ACCOUNTING SYSTEMS	20 AUTOMATED ACCOUNTING SYSTEMS	21 A PERPETUAL INVENTORY SUBSYSTEM	22 A CREDIT CARD SUBSYSTEM
PAYROLL CLERK	▬	▬	▬	▬	▬	▬	▬	▬	▬	•					•					•		
GENERAL OFFICE CLERK	▬	▬	▬	▬	▬	▬	▬	▬	▬	•						•			•	•		
CASH RECEIPTS BOOKKEEPER	▬	▬	▬	▬	▬	▬	▬	▬	▬	▬	▬											
CASHIER, OFFICE	▬	▬	▬	▬	▬	▬	▬	▬	▬	▬	▬	▬								•		
CASH PAYMENTS BOOKKEEPER	▬	▬	▬	▬	▬	▬	▬	▬	▬	▬	▬	▬										
CASH POSTING CLERK	▬	▬	▬	▬	▬	▬	▬	▬	▬	▬	▬	▬										
PURCHASING AGENT	▬	▬	▬	▬	▬	▬	▬	▬	▬	▬	▬	▬	▬							•	•	
INVENTORY CLERK	▬	▬	▬	▬	▬	▬	▬	▬	▬	▬	▬	▬	▬				•			•	•	
PURCHASING CLERK	▬	▬	▬	▬	▬	▬	▬	▬	▬	▬	▬	▬	▬							•	•	
RECEIVING CLERK	▬	▬	▬	▬	▬	▬	▬	▬	▬	▬	▬	▬	▬							•	•	
ACCOUNTS PAYABLE CLERK	▬	▬	▬	▬	▬	▬	▬	▬	▬	▬	▬	▬	▬					•		•		
ACCOUNTS PAYABLE BOOKKEEPER	▬	▬	▬	▬	▬	▬	▬	▬	▬	▬	▬	▬	▬					•		•		
ORDER CLERK	▬	▬	▬	▬	▬	▬	▬	▬	▬	▬	▬	▬	▬	▬					•	•		
CREDIT CLERK	▬	▬	▬	▬	▬	▬	▬	▬	▬	▬	▬	▬	▬	▬								•
STOCK CONTROL CLERK	▬	▬	▬	▬	▬	▬	▬	▬	▬	▬	▬	▬	▬	▬						•	•	
SHIPPING CLERK	▬	▬	▬	▬	▬	▬	▬	▬	▬	▬	▬	▬	▬	▬						•	•	
BILLING CLERK	▬	▬	▬	▬	▬	▬	▬	▬	▬	▬	▬	▬	▬	▬					•	•		•
ACCOUNTS RECEIVABLE CLERK	▬	▬	▬	▬	▬	▬	▬	▬	▬	▬	▬	▬	▬	▬			•			•		•
ACCOUNTS RECEIVABLE BOOKKEEPER	▬	▬	▬	▬	▬	▬	▬	▬	▬	▬	▬	▬	▬	▬			•			•		•
ACCOUNTING CLERK	▬	▬	▬	▬	▬	▬	▬	▬	▬	▬	▬	▬	▬	▬	▬	▬	•	•		•		
AUDIT CLERK	▬	▬	▬	▬	▬	▬	▬	▬	▬	▬	▬	▬	▬	▬	▬	▬	•	•				
FULL-CHARGE BOOKKEEPER	▬	▬	▬	▬	▬	▬	▬	▬	▬	▬	▬	▬	▬	▬	▬	▬	•	•	•	•	•	•

*Based on *Accounting: Systems and Procedures,* Fourth Edition. Accounting careers based on the *Dictionary of Occupational Titles.*
NOTE: The chart shows the accounting skills and knowledge needed for jobs listed at the left of the red bars. The chart also shows which chapters students should study to be prepared for these jobs. For example, the scope of Chapter 14 is the sales subsystem. If students complete Chapter 14, they will be prepared for the job of credit clerk because they will have completed all the units of study relating to sales on credit. They will also be prepared for the jobs of payroll clerk, general office clerk, office cashier, purchasing agent, purchasing clerk, receiving clerk, accounts payable clerk, order clerk, credit clerk, stock-control clerk, billing clerk, and accounts receivable clerk. Solid bar (▬) indicates minimum competency for the career. Bullet(•) indicates competencies beyond the minimum recommended for the career.

TEACHING OPTIONS CHART*

OPTIONS	PART 1 ELEMENTS OF FINANCIAL RECORDS	PART 2 ACCOUNTING SUBSYSTEMS	PART 3 SPECIAL ACCOUNTING SYSTEMS AND PROCEDURES
VOCATIONAL Option A	Chapters 1–9	Chapters 10–16	Chapters 17–22
Option B	Chapters 1–9	Chapters 10–16	Chapters 20–22
Option C	Chapters 1–9	Chapters 10–16	
AVOCATIONAL Option D	Chapters 1–9	Chapters 10–12 and 15	Chapter 20
Option E	Chapters 1–9	Chapters 10–12	
GENERAL Option F	Chapters 1–9	Chapter 15	Chapter 20
Option G	Chapters 1–9		

*Based on *Accounting: Systems and Procedures,* Fourth Edition. Can be used in traditional accounting classes, block accounting programs, integrated office education block programs, cooperative office education programs, and data processing programs. Note that Chapters 17 and 18 may be taught at the beginning of Part 3 or may be omitted entirely, depending on the time available and the career objectives of the students.

Accounting is the language of business. It is used to exchange financial information of all kinds throughout the world.

A knowledge of accounting helps citizens understand complex issues like inflation and taxes, and helps them make more informed decisions when they vote on these issues.

Part I
Elements of Financial Records

People who work in business offices and who handle financial information profit from an understanding of accounting. These people include bookkeepers, clerks, typists, and those who prepare and analyze accounting records.

The Language of Business

Accounting terms, concepts, and principles are the common language used to communicate financial information. This is why accounting is often called the language of business. You will now learn how the elements of accounting and the accounting equation are used to provide this information.

A = L + OE
$20,000 = $12,000 + $ 8,000

Accounting terms and concepts are used in preparing financial records for businesses. These same terms and concepts are also used in reporting and analyzing the financial results from operating the businesses. In fact, accounting terms and concepts are the common language used to communicate financial information from one person to another. Thus **accounting** is often called the language of business.

Some accounting terms have certain meanings in general usage. Yet the terms have very specific meanings in accounting. Sometimes the accounting meaning may be different from its general usage. In this textbook, accounting terms are highlighted to help you learn the language of business.

A profit-making organization is known as a **business.** There are three main types of businesses. A **merchandising business** sells goods (such as food markets and automobile dealers). A **service business** sells services (such as beauty salons, dry cleaners, and airlines). A **manufacturing business** produces goods (such as automobile manufacturers). Some organizations are nonprofit. A **nonprofit organization** supplies certain benefits to society. Examples of nonprofit organizations are churches, governmental agencies, schools, and hospitals.

Financial information is presented in the same terms regardless of the size or kind of business or type of ownership. Information for large corporations such as Exxon and General Motors is presented in the same terms as information for medium or small businesses such as your local sporting goods store. The terms and concepts you learn in accounting can be applied to any business.

Accounting also plays a role in our personal and social lives. Each of us must keep records for income taxes. Our social organizations, such as clubs, schools, and universities, must also have financial information to operate successfully. Citizens are asked to vote on issues that involve accounting terms and concepts. As a result, it is important for everyone to understand the language of business.

Accounting is the language of business.

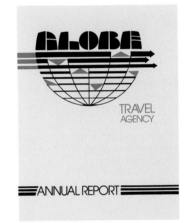

The same accounting terms and concepts are used for all sizes and kinds of businesses.

Topic 1
The Elements of Accounting

A *What are the elements of accounting?* Accounting is based on three elements: assets, liabilities, and owner's equity. These three elements are explained in this topic.

Every business needs economic resources to operate. **Economic resources** is a general term that describes the items needed to start and operate a business. (These items might include money, buildings, equipment, and trucks.) In accounting, the term for economic resources is *assets.*

Businesses get their economic resources (assets) from two sources. The owner may invest personal money or goods, such as furniture. Or

Elements of Accounting
• Assets
• Liabilities
• Owner's Equity

the owner may borrow money from others. In accounting, the term *owner's equity* refers to that portion of the economic resources contributed by the owner. The term *liabilities* refers to that portion of the economic resources obtained by borrowing.

You will learn more about assets, liabilities, and owner's equity in the following discussion.

Assets

What is the meaning of assets, the first accounting element? **Assets** are anything of monetary value that a business owns. The assets that a business owns depend on the nature of the business. For example, a delivery company would own assets such as trucks needed to deliver goods. A department store's assets would include counters, racks, and shelves needed to store and display the goods it has to sell.

Although there are many kinds of assets, accountants classify them into several general categories. These categories are cash, receivables, inventories, plant and equipment, natural resources, and intangible assets. Each type of asset is described in the following pages.

Categories of Assets
- Cash
- Receivables
- Inventories
- Plant and Equipment
- Natural Resources
- Intangible Assets

Cash. One of the most common assets is cash. **Cash** includes not only coins and currency but also checks and money orders that have been received from others. Cash also includes money deposited in bank accounts.

Receivables. Another common business asset is receivables. **Receivables** are amounts of money to be collected in the future. Many businesses do not immediately receive all or part of the money owed to them. Until a receivable is collected, the business has a legal right or claim against someone else's assets. As a result of this claim, all receivables are assets.

All receivables are assets.

RECEIVABLES. Amounts to be collected in the future.

The most common types of receivables are accounts receivable and notes receivable. **Accounts receivable** are the total amount to be collected from customers to whom goods and services are sold on credit. In accounting the term **credit** means buying, selling, or borrowing with a promise to pay within a period of time. Thus **selling on credit** means that goods or services are given to the customer but the seller will not receive payment until a future date.

Each account receivable is an asset because it is a claim against the customer's property until the customer pays the amount owed. For the same reason, notes receivable are assets. A **note receivable** is a written promise signed by the customer to pay the business a sum of money at a future date.

Inventories. Other forms of assets are the goods a business has on hand to sell, goods that will be used to manufacture other goods, or goods that will be used to operate the business. These goods are called **inventory.**

In accounting, the goods a merchandising business has on hand to sell are called **merchandise inventory.** Ten-speed bicycles, blue jeans, and roller skates are examples of merchandise available for sale in department stores.

A manufacturing business has three types of inventory: raw materials, work in process, and finished goods.

Raw materials are the goods a business starts with to manufacture its products. For example, in manufacturing blue jeans, the business uses cloth, thread, zippers, and buttons. These are its raw materials. Another type of manufacturing inventory is partially completed goods called **work in process.** In manufacturing blue jeans, fabric cut or partially stitched is work in process. The third type of manufacturing inventory is **finished goods,** which are goods completely finished and ready for sale. These are the ready-to-sell blue jeans in our example.

Materials that a business has on hand to be used to operate a business make up an inventory called **supplies.** Supplies are used by all three types of businesses—service, manufacturing, and merchandising. Paper and pens are office supplies. Cartons and packing materials are shipping supplies. Waxes and cleaning liquids are custodial supplies. All these supplies on hand are assets until they are used.

Plant and Equipment. Some assets, such as merchandise inventory, are intended to be sold to customers. Other assets, like plant and equipment, are not. **Plant and equipment** (sometimes referred to as *fixed assets*) are assets used over a long period of time to operate the business. Examples of plant and equipment assets are buildings, furniture, land, machinery, office equipment, and trucks.

Natural Resources. **Natural resources** (sometimes referred to as *wasting assets*) refer to assets held in their natural state until converted (changed) into products to be sold in the future. Examples of natural resource assets are coal mines, oil fields, and standing timber. Until the coal and oil are removed from the ground or the timber is cut, they are natural resource assets.

When the businesses convert the natural resources into products, the natural resource assets become inventory assets. For example, standing timber in a forest is a natural resource asset. As soon as the standing timber is cut, the logs and lumber become inventory assets, such as raw materials.

Intangible Assets. Assets that are used in the operation of a business but have no physical characteristics are called **intangible assets.** These assets are used over a long period and have a monetary value to the business. In accounting, these items are intangible assets only if

Inventories in Merchandising Businesses
• Merchandise inventory

Inventories in Manufacturing Businesses
• Raw materials
• Work in process
• Finished goods

Courtesy Ford Motor Company

Martin Bough / Studios, Inc.

INVENTORY. Goods on hand to be sold, to be used in making finished goods, such as those used to assemble a car, or to be used in operating a business.

Courtesy U.S.D.A. Forest Service

NATURAL RESOURCES. Assets held in natural state for future conversion into goods to be sold. These become inventory assets when changed into products.

A cost must have been incurred in buying or developing an intangible asset.

© 19X3 by Lambert, Inc., New York

Courtesy Gino's, Inc.

Courtesy A.T.&T. Company

INTANGIBLE ASSETS. Assets of value that are used in operation of business but that have no physical characteristics.

the business incurred a cost in buying or developing the asset. Examples of intangible assets are copyrights, franchises, trademarks, and patents.

A **copyright** gives the owner the exclusive legal right to reproduce and sell a particular literary or artistic work or object for a specific period of time. For example, a published song is given a copyright date that is printed on one of the first pages of the song. The owner of the copyright has exclusive rights to that song for a period of time from that date.

A **franchise** is an agreement between a supplier and a distributor that gives the distributor the right to handle a product under certain conditions. Fast-food establishments, such as Gino's, McDonald's and Burger King, are examples of businesses that operate under franchise agreements.

A **trademark** is a symbol used by a company for identification. Examples of trademarks are those used by American Telephone and Telegraph (Bell Telephone companies) or the Coca-Cola Company. When a business owns a trademark, only that business has the right to use it.

A **patent** gives the owner the exclusive right to make, use, or sell an invention for a specified number of years.

As you know, people are needed to run a business. However, people are not considered to be accounting assets. In accounting, people are viewed as employees. How people are paid for their efforts is explained in Chapters 9 and 15 on payroll.

Language:

Asset. *Asset* is one of the words that has a specific meaning in accounting. In general usage, people use *asset* to mean advantage. In accounting usage, however, an asset must have monetary value *and* the business must own it.

Asset Accounts

Every business needs to keep records about each of its assets. For example, a separate record is kept to show how much cash the business has. The record also shows, as is discussed in later chapters, that the amount of cash changes. It will increase and it will decrease. All these changes are recorded in an account. An **account** is a record of the financial details for each asset, liability, or owner's equity item.

In accounting, similar items are grouped together in a single account. For example, a record of all the coins, currency, money orders, and checks the business has on hand plus the money it has deposited in banks is recorded in the Cash account. Desks, chairs, and tables are assets that are recorded in the Furniture account. Typewriters, adding

EXAMPLES OF ASSET ACCOUNT TITLES

Cash	Receivables	Inventories	Plant and Equipment	Natural Resources	Intangible Assets
Cash	Accounts Receivable Notes Receivable	Merchandise Inventory Raw Materials Work in Process Finished Goods Supplies on Hand	Buildings Furniture Land Machinery Office Equipment Trucks	Coal Mines Oil Fields Timber	Copyrights Franchises Trademarks Patents

machines, and duplicating machines are recorded in the Office Equipment account.

The different types of assets are summarized in the chart shown above. Examples of asset accounts are also shown for each type of asset. For example, Accounts Receivable and Notes Receivable are accounts called *receivables*. Buildings, Furniture, Land, Machinery, and Office Equipment are accounts called *plant and equipment*.

Assets are only one element of accounting. As you learn more about assets and the other two elements, you will see that accounts are kept for each element.

You are going to learn about the elements of accounting through the activities of a small business—the Globe Travel Agency. The business does not produce or sell goods. It sells services. The Globe Travel Agency plans and makes travel arrangements for customers who want to travel on business or vacation. The trips will be made by air, rail, bus, or ship.

The assets of the Globe Travel Agency are shown in four accounts. The Cash account totals $8,000, the Accounts Receivable account $1,000, the Furniture account $2,000, and the Office Equipment account $9,000. The monetary value of the total assets the business owns on September 1 is $20,000, as shown in the margin.

Globe Travel Agency Assets	
Cash	$ 8,000
Accounts Receivable	1,000
Furniture	2,000
Office Equipment	9,000
Total Assets	$20,000

Accounting Concepts

In studying accounting, you will learn the *terms* (vocabulary) used in accounting. But to get a broad understanding of accounting, you must also learn the *concepts* (general ideas) behind these accounting terms. Let's review the three concepts that you have learned thus far.

Accounting Concepts:
Economic Resources. Every business, regardless of type, size, or ownership, needs economic resources to operate. In accounting, these economic resources are called *assets*.

Accounting Concepts (continued):
Borrowing Economic Resources. Some economic resources are obtained through borrowing from others.
Investing Economic Resources. Some economic resources are obtained through investment by the owner or owners.

Activity A-1. Indicate which of the following items are business assets. Some of the following items are business assets and some are not.

EXAMPLE: *Furniture—Yes*

1. Tools
2. Supplies
3. Good weather
4. Trademarks
5. Employees
6. Furniture
7. Deposits in bank
8. Goods for sale
9. Good reputation

Activity A-2. Classify each of the following assets as either cash, receivables, inventories, plant and equipment, natural resources, or intangible assets.

EXAMPLE: *Furniture—Plant and Equipment*

1. Money order
2. Accounts receivable
3. Timber
4. Office equipment
5. Franchises
6. Partially completed goods
7. Oil fields
8. Goods for sale
9. Display tables

Liabilities

Some economic resources are obtained through borrowing from others.

B *What is the meaning of liabilities, the second accounting element?* **Liabilities** are debts that a business owes. Some of a business's assets may be obtained by borrowing from others. For example, a business may borrow money from a bank and then use the money to buy assets, such as trucks. When the business borrows the money, it incurs a liability for the amount of the loan.

Borrowing can also take place in other ways. A business may buy a typewriter from a dealer on credit and promise to pay for the typewriter sometime in the future. **Buying on credit** means that goods or services are received by the buyer but the buyer will pay for them later.

The one to whom the debt is owed is called the **creditor.** In the examples just given, the bank and the typewriter dealer are the creditors. Each creditor has a legal claim against the assets of the business until the business pays its debts. The business in turn has incurred liabilities for the amount of the loan from the bank and the amount it owes to the typewriter dealer.

Most businesses have liabilities. They frequently find it easier to buy on credit than to pay cash immediately. For example, most new-car dealerships have liabilities for the cars they hold for sale. Very few dealers could pay cash immediately for the cars before they sell them.

The Globe Travel Agency has liabilities. It bought $3,000 of office equipment from Bell Products. It could have paid cash for the equipment or bought the equipment on credit. Let's say that this time the Globe Travel Agency bought the equipment on credit. Bell Products provided the office equipment. It accepted the Globe Travel Agency's promise to pay the $3,000 in the future.

The Globe Travel Agency now owes Bell Products $3,000 for office equipment bought on credit. Until the Globe Travel Agency pays this debt, Bell Products has a claim of $3,000 against Globe Travel Agency's assets. The Globe Travel Agency has incurred a liability of $3,000.

Liability Accounts

In accounting, liabilities are identified by the word *payable*. **Payables** are amounts owed (debts) to be paid in the future. For example, an amount borrowed from a bank is called a **loan payable.** The amounts owed to creditors for goods or services bought on credit are called **accounts payable.** A written promise to pay a creditor a specific amount in the future is called a **note payable.**

In some cases, a business may find it necessary to borrow large sums of money for long periods of time, such as 20 or 30 years. This usually happens when land and buildings are bought. These long-term debts are usually secured with a legal document called a mortgage. A **mortgage** is a written promise in which the buyer pledges property as security for the payment of the debt. A long-term debt secured by mortgages is known as a **mortgage payable.**

Accounts are used to keep a record of each liability. When the Globe Travel Agency bought the office equipment on credit, the liability of $3,000 was recorded in an Accounts Payable account.

All payables are liabilities.

Globe Travel Agency
Liabilities
Accounts Payable $3,000

Language:
Liability. *Liability* is another word that has a specific meaning in accounting. In general usage, *liability* is sometimes used to mean disadvantage. In accounting usage, however, a liability is a debt that the business is obligated, or liable, to pay.

Accounting Concept:
Claims of Creditors. Economic resources that are obtained by borrowing result in claims of creditors against the economic resources of the business. In accounting, claims of creditors are called *liabilities.*

Activity B. Classify each of the following items as an asset or as a liability. Refer to the text and margin notes on pages 10 and 11.
EXAMPLE: Note Receivable—Asset
1. Note payable
2. Gold mine
3. Plant and equipment
4. Accounts payable
5. Amounts due from customers
6. Loans payable
7. Furniture
8. Amounts payable to creditors
9. Mortgage payable

Owner's Equity

C *What is the meaning of owner's equity, the third accounting element?* **Owner's equity** is the financial interest of the owner in a business. In other words, owner's equity is the claim against the assets by the owner.

Some economic resources are invested by the owner.

Creditors, as you learned earlier, have legal claims against the assets of a business. The owner has a legal claim against the remaining assets. Thus, owner's equity in a business is the difference between the total assets owned and the total liabilities owed.

If there is more than one owner of the business, the term *owner's equity* changes to identify the form of business ownership. How the meaning changes is shown in the following discussion of the four forms of business ownership: single proprietorship, partnership, corporation, and cooperative.

Types of Owner's Equity
Single
Proprietorship → Owner's Equity
Partnership   → Partners' Equity
Corporation   → Stockholders'
                 Equity
Cooperative   → Members' Equity

Single Proprietorship. The **single proprietorship** is a business owned by one person. For example, the Globe Travel Agency is a single proprietorship owned by Mark Nero. **Owner's equity** here means the financial interest of the owner in a single proprietorship.

Partnership. In a **partnership,** ownership of a business is divided among two or more persons. In this case the term partners' equity is used instead of owner's equity. **Partners' equity** is the financial interest of owners in a partnership.

Corporation. A **corporation** is a business chartered under state law that has the legal right to act as a person. Usually a corporation is owned by many people. Owners of a corporation are known as *stockholders* or *shareholders*. In this case the term stockholders' equity is used. **Stockholders' equity** is the financial interest of owners in a corporation.

Cooperative. A **cooperative** is a special form of corporation that is owned by its customers. Owners of a cooperative are called *members.* In this case the term **members' equity** is used for the financial interest of owners in a cooperative.

Owner's Equity Accounts

**Computing
Owner's Equity**

Assets $20,000
Less: Liabilities   3,000
Owner's Equity $17,000

Globe Travel Agency
Owner's Equity
Mark Nero, Capital . . . $17,000

Let's look at the owner's equity of the Globe Travel Agency—a single proprietorship owned by Mark Nero. The total assets are $20,000, and the total liabilities are $3,000. The total liabilities of $3,000 are subtracted from the total assets of $20,000. The remaining $17,000 is the owner's equity.

The owner's equity account used to show the owner's investment in the business is called **capital.** Therefore, Mark Nero's investment in the Globe Travel Agency is $17,000. This is written as "Mark Nero, Capital $17,000," as shown in the margin.

Language:

Capital. *Capital* is another word that is often misunderstood by accounting students. In general usage, *capital* is sometimes used to mean cash. At this point in your study of accounting, however, the meaning of *capital* is limited to mean investment.

Accounting Concept:

Claims of Owner. Economic resources that are invested by the owner or owners result in claims of the owner or owners against the economic resources of the business. In accounting, the claim of the owner against the assets of a business is called *owner's equity.* (The term differs according to the form of business ownership.)

Activity C. Classify each of the following items as an asset, a liability, or owner's equity. Refer to the text, margin notes, and illustrations on pages 11 to 13.
EXAMPLE: *Office Equipment—Asset*
1. Land
2. Mortgage payable
3. Standing timber

4. Loan payable
5. Merchandise inventory
6. Louis Rosario (owner's investment)
7. Money on deposit with banks
8. Maria Sanchez (a customer)
9. Ronald Jones (partner's investment)
10. Now Hifi, Inc. (a creditor)

Topic 1 Problems

1-1. Edward's Clothing Store has the assets, liabilities, and owner's equity shown below. Compute the total assets and total liabilities. The total owner's equity is given.

Assets		Liabilities		Owner's Equity	
Cash	$5,000	Loans Payable	$1,400	Edward Miller, Capital	$13,100
Accounts Receivable	400	Accounts Payable	1,200		
Merchandise	6,300				
Store Equipment	4,000				
Total Assets	$?	Total Liabilities	$?		

1-2. Marcia DelFrate, a dentist, has the assets, liabilities, and owner's equity shown below. List the assets in one column and the liabilities in another column. Compute the total assets and total liabilities. The total Capital amount is given.

Cash	$ 5,000	Dental Equipment	$25,000
Notes Payable	500	Land	20,000
Accounts Receivable	8,000	Office Equipment	3,000
Building	30,000	Mortgage Payable	28,000
Accounts Payable	1,000	Supplies	500
		Marcia DelFrate, Capital	62,000

Total Assets $?   Total Liabilities $?   Total Owner's Equity $?

Topic 2
The Accounting Equation

A *How are assets, liabilities, and owner's equity related to each other?* Assets represent the things of monetary value that a business owns. Liabilities are the claims of the creditors against those assets. (Creditors always have a claim against the assets of a business until the liabilities are paid.) Owner's equity is the claim of the owner against the remaining assets of the business. What is not claimed by the creditors is claimed by the owner.

Relationship of the Elements of Accounting

The relationship among accounting elements can be summarized as follows. The total assets always equal the total claims against those assets—creditors' claims and owner's claims. This relationship is expressed in the **accounting equation**:

$$\text{Assets} = \text{Liabilities} + \text{Owner's Equity}$$

ASSETS	=	CLAIMS AGAINST ASSETS
Total Assets	=	Claims of Creditors + Claim of Owner

The accounting equation states that the total assets equal the total liabilities plus the total owner's equity. Accountants frequently shorten this statement by showing the equation as A = L + OE. Assets (A) are shown on the left side of the equation. Liabilities (L) and owner's equity (OE) are shown on the right side of the equation. Mathematically the total of the left side of the equation must always equal the total of the right side. If no liabilities exist, then the owner's equity equals the total assets.

Left Side		Right Side
A	=	L + OE

The accounting equation for the Globe Travel Agency on September 1 is as follows.

	Assets				=	Liabilities	+	Owner's Equity
	Cash	Accounts Receivable	Furniture	Office Equipment		Accounts Payable		Mark Nero, Capital
Accounts →								
Amounts →	$8,000 +	$1,000 +	$2,000 +	$9,000	=	$3,000	+	$17,000
Equality →		→ $20,000			=		$20,000	

Assets	=	Liabilities	+	Owner's Equity
A	=	L	+	OE
$20,000	=	$3,000	+	$?
$20,000	=	$3,000	+	$17,000

The accounting equation shows Mark Nero's equity in the Globe Travel Agency as $17,000. The total assets of the business are $20,000. The total liabilities are $3,000. Thus the owner's equity is $17,000 because the total liabilities and total owner's equity must equal the total assets.

The accounting equation has three elements. If you know any two, you can easily compute the amount of the missing element.

COMPUTING THE AMOUNT OF A MISSING ELEMENT

Cases	Computation							Proof of Equation				
								A	=	L	+	OE
Know all three elements	A	=	L	+	OE							
	$20,000	=	$ 3,000	+	$17,000			$20,000	=	$3,000	+	$17,000
Know liabilities and owner's equity	L	+	OE	=	A							
	$ 3,000	+	$17,000	=	$___?___			$20,000	=	$3,000	+	$17,000
Know assets and liabilities	A	−	L	=	OE							
	$20,000	−	$ 3,000	=	$___?___			$20,000	=	$3,000	+	$17,000
Know assets and owner's equity	A	−	OE	=	L							
	$20,000	−	$17,000	=	$___?___			$20,000	=	$3,000	+	$17,000

Accounting Concept:
Accounting Equation. There is always a relationship between assets and the claims against those assets. This relationship is expressed by the accounting equation *assets equal liabilities plus owner's equity* (A = L + OE).

Activity A. When the amounts of any two of the accounting elements are known, the third can be computed. Compute the missing amounts in the following accounting equations.

Assets	=	Liabilities	+	Owner's Equity
Ex. $1,000	=	$ 300	+	$ 700
1. $ 700	=	$ 50	+	$___?___
2. $ 300	=	$ 200	+	$___?___
3. $ 900	=	$___?___	+	$ 500
4. $ 750	=	$ 340	+	$___?___
5. $___?___	=	$ 98	+	$ 1,200
6. $12,340	=	$8,340	+	$___?___
7. $10,400	=	$___?___	+	$ 900
8. $___?___	=	$ 970	+	$11,450
9. $ 8,765	=	$ 0	+	$___?___
10. $ 7,000	=	$___?___	+	$ 3,000

Equality in the Equation

B *Why do total assets equal the total of liabilities plus owner's equity?* The totals on the two sides of the accounting equation are always equal because these two sides are two views of the same business. Assets on the left side show what the business owns. Liabilities and owner's equity on the right side tell who supplied the assets and the amount each group supplied. Creditors and the owner have supplied everything that a business owns.

The order in which the elements are listed in the equation is important. For example, liabilities come before owner's equity. This emphasizes that the claims of the creditors are recognized before the claims of

The creditor's claim on the assets comes before the owner's claim.

A	=	L	+	OE
$20,000	=	$3,000	+	$17,000
$20,000	=		$20,000	

The equality of the equation should be verified at regular intervals.

the owner or owners. If a business cannot pay its debts when they become due, the business may be declared bankrupt. In this case the assets would be sold and the claims of the creditors would be paid before the owner(s) would receive any money.

In accounting, a **proof** is used to "prove" or "check" that the work is accurate. The accounting equation provides one such proof. You recall learning that the total of the left side of an equation must equal the total of the right side of the equation.

The equality of the left- and right-side totals is a proof or check that the totals are mathematically correct. The equality of left- and right-side totals is used as a proof in all accounting work.

Notice, however, that the proof shows only that the totals are mathematically correct. It does not prove that the amounts are in the correct place in the equation. For example, suppose the amounts of the liabilities and owner's equity are switched. That is, liabilities are shown as $17,000 and owner's equity as $3,000. These amounts still equal $20,000 even though the amounts are under the wrong element.

In balance: amounts agree.

There is another expression used for equality in accounting. When two amounts agree, they are said to be **in balance.** Having the equation in balance means that the total of the amounts on the left side equals the total of the amounts on the right side of the equation. When two amounts do not agree in accounting, the amounts are said to be **out of balance.** Thus if the two sides of the equation do not agree, the equation is said to be out of balance.

Out of balance: amounts do not agree.

Accuracy and Legibility

Only accurate and legible work is acceptable in accounting. **Accuracy** means that all records are without error. **Legibility** means that the accounting records can easily be read. Many problems in accounting are caused by numbers that are not written neatly and legibly. Accounts may be misspelled and amounts may be recorded incorrectly. Legibility would decrease the possibility of these errors.

Accounting Concept:
Proving the Equation. The equality of the total assets to the total liabilities and owner's equity in the equation should be verified at regular intervals.

In the following topics, the accounting concepts and principles are given at the end of the topic instead of at the end of each reading segment. However, the formation which the accounting concepts and principles are given is exactly the same as here.

Activity B. Compute the proof of the following accounting equations. Compute the left-side total and then compute the right-side total. Show the equality check.

Assets			=	Liabilities	+	Owner's Equity	Equality Check		
Cash	Accounts Receivable	Supplies		Accounts Payable		Capital	A	=	L + OE
Ex.: $ 50 +	$ 20 +	$ 10 =		$ 20 +		$ 60	$ 80 =		$ 80
1. $500 +	$400 +	$300 =		$200 +		$1,000	$?		$?
2. $400 +	$500 +	$ 25 =		$370 +		$ 555	$?		$?
3. $520 +	$ 80 +	$ 20 =		$ 40 +		$ 580	$?		$?
4. $700 +	$ 50 +	$ 20 =		$ 30 +		$ 740	$?		$?
5. $900 +	$200 +	$ -0- =		$ -0- +		$1,100	$?		$?
6. $680 +	$250 +	$300 =		$500 +		$ 730	$?		$?
7. $650 +	$ -0- +	$ -0- =		$ -0- +		$ 650	$?		$?
8. $750 +	$560 +	$150 =		$200 +		$1,260	$?		$?
9. $720 +	$ -0- +	$200 =		$150 +		$ 770	$?		$?
10. $888 +	$222 +	$111 =		$221 +		$1,000	$?		$?

Topic 2 Problems

1-3. Spring's Health Center, owned by Ruth Spring, has the following assets and liabilities on September 15, 19—. Arrange the assets, liabilities, and owner's equity in an accounting equation. Compute the owner's equity amount. Prove the equality of the accounting equation.

Accounts Payable.	.$500
Cash	750
Accounts Receivable.	400
Supplies	300

1-4. The National Service Center has the amounts in the accounting equation on October 3, as shown below. Work through the equation to check for accuracy.
a. Correct any errors.
b. Prove the equality of the equation.

Assets			=	Liabilities	+	Owner's Equity	Equality Check		
Cash	Accounts Receivable	Supplies		Accounts Payable		Sid Moore, Capital	A	=	L + OE
$1,500 +	$590 +	$950 =		$40 +		$3,000	$2,680 =		$3,040
	Total Assets		=	Liabilities	+	Owner's Equity			
	$?		=	$? +		$?	$? =		$?

The Language of Business

Here are some basic terms that make up the language of business. Do you know the meaning of each?

accounting
business
merchandising business
service business
manufacturing business
nonprofit organization
economic resources
assets
cash
receivables
accounts receivable
credit

selling on credit
note receivable
inventory
merchandise inventory
raw materials
work in process
finished goods
supplies
plant and equipment
natural resources
intangible assets
copyright

franchise
trademark
patent
account
liabilities
buying on credit
creditor
payables
loan payable
accounts payable
note payable
mortgage
mortgage payable
single proprietorship

owner's equity
partnership
partners' equity
corporation
stockholders' equity
cooperative
members' equity
capital
accounting equation
proof
in balance
out of balance
accuracy
legibility

Chapter 1   Questions

1. What is meant by the statement, "Accounting is the language of business"?

2. Name four assets for a department store. For a bakery. For a pizza parlor. For a beauty salon.

3. What is the difference between a receivable and a payable?

4. Give five examples of merchandise inventory.

5. Describe the six major categories of assets. Give two examples of each.

6. Give three examples of liabilities.

7. Who has first claim against the assets of a business? Who has second claim?

8. In what way does the equity section of the equation vary according to the form of business ownership?

9. What is the accounting equation? Why must it always be in balance?

10. Why do total assets equal the total of liabilities plus owner's equity?

Chapter 1   Problems

Problems for Chapter 1 are given in the *Working Papers and Chapter Problems for Part 1*. If you are using the workbook, do the problems in the space provided there.

Chapter 1   Management Cases

Starting a Business. Many businesses fail because the owner does not have enough money to operate while the business is getting started. The owner needs to have enough money to cover items, such as rent and salaries, until the business becomes a thriving operation. If more money is needed, the owner must decide how much money can be borrowed and how much money must come from the owner's own investment.

Case 1M-1. A brother and sister, Charles and Sharon, are starting separate businesses. Charles has learned furniture building, repair, and refinishing. For the past three years, he has worked for a furniture refinishing shop. In six months, Charles plans to open a small business—Chuck's Don't-Chuck-It Shop. His business will repair and refinish furniture and will also build furniture on special order.

Sharon has passed the certified public accountant's examination and plans to open an accounting office. She will serve as an accountant for small businesses, prepare and file tax returns, and provide consulting services.

Who will need more assets to open a business, Charles or Sharon? Explain.

Case 1M-2. David Valance plans to open his own men's clothing shop. He has worked for five years as a salesclerk in Max's Men's Shop. In addition to gaining sales experience, Mr. Valance learned about men's fashion trends and how to work well with people. Max Shole, the owner of the shop, also taught Mr. Valance how to keep accounting records. Under Mr. Shole's guidance, David Valance gained valuable experience.

a. What advantages does David Valance have as an employee that he will not have when he becomes the owner of his own shop?

b. Why might David Valance prefer to own a business rather than be an employee?

c. What assets will David Valance need when he starts his own men's clothing shop?

Working Hint

Checking Addition and Subtraction Answers.
Here are some ways for you to verify the accuracy of your mathematics.

Manually. To check the accuracy of a total in addition, re-add the column in the opposite direction. To check the accuracy of subtraction, add the remainder to the subtrahend. The sum of the two must equal the minuend.

Add down.	$ 24.85 ↑ 9.62 75.15 38.10 4.55 15.46 ↓ $167.73	Add up to check.	$43.81 minuend −27.47 ↑ subtrahend ⎫ $16.34 remainder ⎭	Add up to get the minuend.

With a Calculator. If a display calculator is used, add the amounts from the top down. Then check the total by re-adding the amounts from the bottom to the top. Check the subtraction the same way you would in manual subtraction.

If the calculator has tape, you can re-add the amounts as described previously and compare the tapes, or you can simply check the amounts on the tape with the original amounts. This is done for both addition and subtraction.

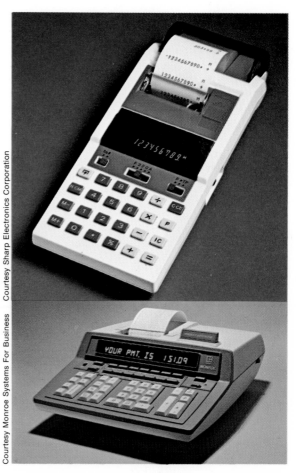

Courtesy Sharp Electronics Corporation

Courtesy Monroe Systems For Business

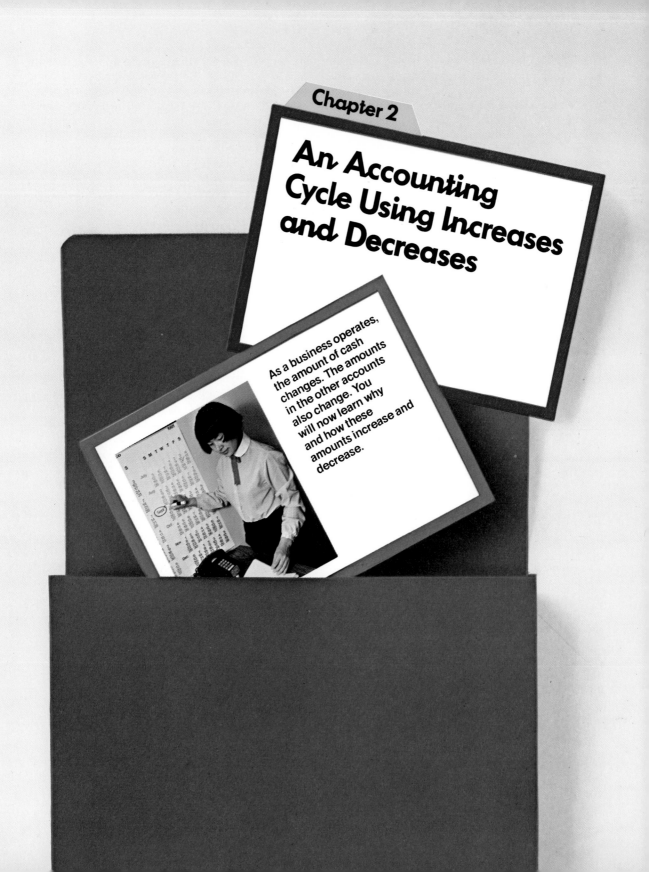

Chapter 2

An Accounting Cycle Using Increases and Decreases

As a business operates, the amount of cash changes. The amounts in the other accounts also change. You will now learn why and how these amounts increase and decrease.

Topic 1
Increasing and Decreasing Permanent Accounts

A | *Why do the amounts in the accounting equation change?* The amounts increase and decrease as a result of business transactions. A **transaction** is a financial event that affects one or more of the elements in the accounting equation. The term **financial** here means that the transaction must be expressed in monetary terms (in dollar amounts). Due to the unique nature of accounting, each transaction affects the amounts of two or more accounts in the accounting equation. Also, the accounting equation remains in balance after each transaction is recorded.

Transactions cause the accounts in the equation to change amounts.

Accounting Periods

In accounting it is assumed that a business will have an ongoing life. This is the going concern concept. A **going concern** is a business that operates from year to year. In other words, the business does not expect to stop operating in the foreseeable future.

Transactions cause the accounting equation to change throughout the life of a business. The amounts in the accounts are continuously increasing and decreasing. Periodically, however, managers and owners want the data in the accounts summarized. To **summarize** means to condense data in order to emphasize its main points. For example, the assets, liabilities, and owner's equity of the Globe Travel Agency are summarized on September 1, as shown here. The total of each account is given without details. Thus the data is summarized because it provides brief information.

			Assets				=	Liabilities	+	Owner's Equity		
Cash		Accounts Receivable		Furniture		Office Equipment		Accounts Payable		Mark Nero, Capital	←	Accounts
$8,000	+	$1,000	+	$2,000	+	$9,000	=	$3,000	+	$17,000	←	Amounts
			$20,000				=			$20,000	←	Equality (Balance)

The accounting equation on September 1, the beginning of the accounting period.

Each business decides when it is best to summarize its accounting information. Some businesses want a summary every month. Other businesses prefer the summary every three months. The period of time for which the accounting information is summarized is called an **accounting period.**

An accounting period covers a period of time for which accounting information is summarized.

Monthly accounting periods usually cover the calendar month.

Quarterly accounting periods cover any three consecutive months.

JAN. FEB. MAR.
APR. MAY JUNE
JULY AUG. SEPT.
OCT. NOV. DEC.

Calendar year accounting periods run from January 1 to December 31.

Fiscal year accounting periods cover any 12 consecutive months.

An accounting period may cover any period of time. A period covering three months is referred to as a **quarter** (one quarter of a year). For example, an accounting period beginning on January 1 and ending March 31 is a quarterly accounting period. Any 12-month period beginning on a given day and ending 12 months later is called a **fiscal year.** An accounting period that begins on July 1 and ends on June 30 is an example of a fiscal year accounting period. A 12-month period that begins on January 1 and ends on December 31 is also known as a **calendar year.** All these types of accounting periods are illustrated here.

A business may choose any accounting period to summarize its data. But the Internal Revenue Service and some other agencies require a business to report the results of its operations at least once a year. The year does not have to cover a calendar year. It may cover any fiscal year.

It is important to note that once a business selects a specific accounting period, that period of time must be used in all following accounting periods. By using the same time period, managers and owners can compare the results of one accounting period with the results of another accounting period.

The Globe Travel Agency uses an accounting period of one month. The accounting equation on September 1 is shown on page 21. The equation shows the amounts in each account at the beginning of the accounting period for September (September 1). The business transactions during the accounting period affect the amounts in this equation.

Permanent Accounts

The accounts in the accounting equation at the beginning of the accounting period are permanent accounts. An account is called a **permanent account** because it produces data continuously from one accounting period to another. For example, asset accounts, liability accounts, and the owner's equity Capital account are permanent accounts.

Some accounts gather data for one accounting period only. An account which gathers data for one accounting period only is called a **temporary account.** This is discussed in Topic 2.

Activity A. Answer the following questions about the accounting equation. Refer to the accounting equation for the Globe Travel Agency shown on page 21.
1. What is the date of the accounting equation?
2. Name the asset accounts.
3. What is the title of the liability account?
4. What is the title of the owner's equity account?
5. What is the amount of total assets?
6. What is the amount of total liabilities?
7. Do the total assets equal the total of liabilities plus owner's equity? Why or why not?

Asset Transactions

B *Which transactions affect only assets?* Two transactions that affect only assets are buying an asset for cash and collecting an account receivable.

Buying Assets for Cash. When cash is paid for another asset, only one accounting element is affected—assets. On September 5, the Globe Travel Agency decides to buy office equipment for $4,000 in cash. Determining which accounts are affected and how they are affected by a transaction is called **analyzing a transaction.** This transaction is analyzed in the illustration shown below. The asset received, Office Equipment, increases by $4,000 because the business now owns more equipment. The asset given, Cash, decreases by $4,000 because the business now has less money.

Transaction	Analysis
September 5: The Globe Travel Agency buys additional office equipment from the Eagle Office Corporation and gives a check for $4,000 in payment.	• The asset *Office Equipment* increases by $4,000 because the business now owns more office equipment. • The asset *Cash* decreases by $4,000 because the business now has less money.

	Assets				=	Liabilities	+	Owner's Equity	
Cash	Accounts Receivable		Furniture	Office Equipment		Accounts Payable		Mark Nero, Capital	
$8,000 +	$1,000	+	$2,000	+	$ 9,000 =	$3,000	+	$17,000	Previous balance
−4,000					+ 4,000				Effect of transaction
$4,000 +	$1,000	+	$2,000	+	$13,000 =	$3,000	+	$17,000	New balance
		$20,000			=		$20,000		Equality of equation

Buying assets for cash.

When one asset is exchanged for another asset, the total amount of the assets does not change. The Globe Travel Agency now has more office equipment but less money. The left side of the equation still totals $20,000. The liabilities and owner's equity accounts are not affected. Thus the right side of the equation still totals $20,000. The accounting equation is in balance.

Collecting Accounts Receivable. A business is said to have received cash on account when a customer pays all or part of a debt. **Cash received on account** means that cash is received from a customer in full or partial payment of a debt.

Cash received on account affects only one accounting element—assets, as shown here. On September 6, the Globe Travel Agency received $1,000 from Karen Louis. This was received in payment of an account receivable. The asset Cash increases, and the asset Accounts Receivable decreases.

Transaction	Analysis
September 6: The Globe Travel Agency receives a check for $1,000 from Karen Louis on account. The money is to be applied against the amount that Karen Louis owes the Globe Travel Agency.	• The asset *Cash* increases by $1,000 because the business now has more money. • The asset *Accounts Receivable* decreases by $1,000 because the business now has less money to be received from its customers.

	Assets				=	Liabilities	+	Owner's Equity
	Cash	Accounts Receivable	Furniture	Office Equipment	=	Accounts Payable	+	Mark Nero, Capital
Previous balance / Effect of transaction	$4,000 +	$1,000	$2,000 +	$13,000	=	$3,000	+	$17,000
	+1,000	−1,000						
New balance	$5,000 +	$-0- +	$2,000 +	$13,000	=	$3,000	+	$17,000
Equality of equation		$20,000			=		$20,000	

Collecting accounts receivable.

Activity B. The assets, liabilities, and owner's equity for the Reed Insurance Service on March 1 are shown in the accounting equation below. The equality check is shown in the margin.

Show what happens to the equation as a result of each of the listed April transactions. Use this procedure for each transaction: First record the transaction. Then add or subtract to determine the new balance for each account. Then prove the equality of the two sides of the equation. Refer to the accounting equation below.

EXAMPLE: Bought equipment for $100 in cash.
1. Received $300 from customer on account.
2. Bought supplies for $100 in cash.
3. Returned equipment bought for $100 in cash.
4. Returned supplies bought for $50 cash.
NOTE: Save your equation for further use in Activity C.

Equality Check		Assets				=	Liabilities	+	Owner's Equity
A = L + OE		Cash	Accounts Receivable	Equipment	Supplies	=	Accounts Payable	+	Carol Reed, Capital
$6,500 = $6,500		$600 +	$400 +	$5,000 +	$500	=	$3,000	+	$3,500
	EX.:	−100		+ 100					
$6,500 = $6,500		$500 +	$400 +	$5,100 +	$500	=	$3,000	+	$3,500

Liability Transactions

C *Do liability transactions affect only one element?* Liability transactions usually affect more than one accounting element. In the following transactions, both assets and liabilities are affected.

Buying Assets on Credit. Assets bought on credit are received at the time of purchase but are not paid for until a future date. Buying an asset on credit creates a liability. This kind of transaction affects two accounting elements—assets and liabilities. Both elements increase, as shown in the analysis of the transaction for September 7.

Transaction	Analysis
September 7: The Globe Travel Agency buys additional furniture for $1,500 on credit from Bell Products. The creditor allows the Globe Travel Agency 30 days to pay this amount.	• The asset *Furniture* increases by $1,500 because the business now owns more furniture. • The liability *Accounts Payable* increases by $1,500 because the business now owes more money.

		Assets			=	Liabilities	+	Owner's Equity	
Cash		Accounts Receivable	Furniture	Office Equipment		Accounts Payable		Mark Nero, Capital	
$5,000	+	$-0-	+	$2,000	+	$13,000	=	$3,000	+	$17,000	← Previous balance / Effect of transaction
				+1,500				+1,500		
$5,000	+	$-0-	+	$3,500	+	$13,000	=	$4,500	+	$17,000	← New balance
		$21,500			=	$21,500			← Equality of equation

Buying assets on credit.

With this increase in furniture, the total assets are now $21,500. The claim against these assets by the creditor (Bell Products) has increased to $4,500. The $4,500 liability is made up of $3,000 from the September 1 balance plus $1,500 for furniture bought on September 7. Owner's equity, which is not affected, is still $17,000. Thus the Globe Travel Agency now has total liabilities and owner's equity of $21,500. The accounting equation is in balance.

Returning Assets Bought on Credit. When a business returns assets bought on credit and not yet paid for, two accounting elements are affected—assets and liabilities. Both elements decrease. Assets decrease because the business now has less assets. Liabilities decrease because the creditor has less claim against the assets. The accounting equation is still in balance.

Transaction	Analysis
September 8: The Globe Travel Agency returns furniture (one cabinet) bought for $500 on credit from Bell Products because it arrived in damaged condition.	• The asset *Furniture* decreases by $500 because the business now owns less furniture. • The liability *Accounts Payable* decreases by $500 because the business now owes less money.

	Assets				=	Liabilities	+	Owner's Equity
	Cash	Accounts Receivable	Furniture	Office Equipment		Accounts Payable		Mark Nero, Capital
Effect of transaction	$5,000 +	$-0- +	$3,500 + − 500	$13,000 =		$4,500 + − 500		$17,000
New balance	$5,000 +	$-0- +	$3,000 +	$13,000 =		$4,000 +		$17,000
Equality of equation			$21,000		=		$21,000	

Previous balance — Effect of transaction — New balance — Equality of equation

Returning assets bought on credit.

Paying Liabilities. When a business pays all or part of a debt, the cash is said to be **cash paid on account.** Paying a liability affects two accounting elements—assets and liabilities. Both elements decrease.

Transaction	Analysis
September 12: The Globe Travel Agency writes a check for $3,000 to Bell Products on account. The payment is to be applied against the total amount owed to Bell Products.	• The asset *Cash* decreases by $3,000 because the business now has less money. • The liability *Accounts Payable* decreases by $3,000 because the business now owes less money.

	Assets				=	Liabilities	+	Owner's Equity
	Cash	Accounts Receivable	Furniture	Office Equipment		Accounts Payable		Mark Nero, Capital
Effect of transaction	$5,000 + − 3,000	$-0- +	$3,000 +	$13,000 =		$4,000 + − 3,000		$17,000
New balance	$2,000 +	$-0- +	$3,000 +	$13,000 =		$1,000 +		$17,000
Equality of equation			$18,000		=		$18,000	

Previous balance — Effect of transaction — New balance — Equality of equation

Paying liabilities.

Language:
Account. The term *account* has several meanings in accounting usage. *Account* refers to the record of financial details for each asset, liability, or owner's equity item. *Cash paid on account* means to pay all or part of a debt. *Cash received on account* means that cash is received for all or part of a debt.

Activity C. Continue with the accounting equation from Activity B. Show what happens to the equation as a result of the following transactions. Prove the equality of the equation. Refer to the accounting equation on page 24.

5. Bought equipment for $600 on credit.

6. Returned equipment bought for $300 on credit.
7. Bought supplies for $200 on credit.
8. Paid $800 to a creditor on account.
9. Returned supplies bought for $100 on credit.
NOTE: Save your equation for further use in Activity D.

Owner's Equity Transactions

D *Can owner's equity be increased and decreased at any time?* Yes, owner's equity can be increased and decreased at any time in the accounting period. To illustrate how owner's equity increases and decreases, we now analyze transactions that affect the owner's investment.

Increasing Owner's Investment. When the owner increases his or her investment in the business, two elements are affected—assets and owner's equity. Both elements increase. For example, as shown in the analysis of the transactions for September 14, Mark Nero withdraws $13,000 of his personal savings to invest in the Globe Travel Agency.

Transaction	Analysis
September 14: Mark Nero decides that the Globe Travel Agency needs more cash for additional office equipment and furniture. He withdraws $13,000 from his personal savings account and deposits the cash in the business checking account.	• The asset *Cash* increases by $13,000 because the business now has more money. • The owner's equity *Mark Nero, Capital* increases by $13,000 because the owner now has increased his investment in the business.

	Assets				=	Liabilities	+	Owner's Equity	
Cash	Accounts Receivable	Furniture	Office Equipment			Accounts Payable		Mark Nero, Capital	
$ 2,000 + +13,000	$-0- +	$3,000 +	$13,000	=		$1,000 +		$17,000 +13,000	← Previous balance ← Effect of transaction
$15,000 +	$-0- +	$3,000 +	$13,000	=		$1,000 +		$30,000	← New balance
	$31,000			=		$31,000			← Equality of equation

Increasing owner's investment.

This transaction increases assets because the business now has more money. Owner's equity increases because the additional investment increases the owner's claim against the total assets. Liabilities are unchanged. The accounting equation is in balance.

Decreasing Owner's Investment. When the owner decreases his or her investment in the business, two elements are affected—assets and owner's equity. Both elements decrease. For example, on September 21 Mark Nero withdraws $5,000 for his personal use.

Transaction	Analysis
September 21: Mark Nero withdraws $5,000 from the Globe Travel Agency checking account.	• The asset *Cash* decreases by $5,000 because the business now has less cash. • The owner's equity *Mark Nero, Capital* decreases by $5,000 because the owner now has decreased his investment in the business.

	Assets				=	Liabilities	+	Owner's Equity
	Cash	Accounts Receivable	Furniture	Office Equipment		Accounts Payable		Mark Nero, Capital
Previous balance / Effect of transaction	$15,000 − *5,000*	+ $-0-	+ $3,000	+ $13,000	=	$1,000	+	$30,000 − *5,000*
New balance	$10,000	+ $-0-	+ $3,000	+ $13,000	=	$1,000	+	$25,000
Equality of equation		$26,000			=		$26,000	

Decreasing owner's investment.

This transaction decreases assets and owner's equity by the same amount. The accounting equation is still in balance.

Summarizing the Analyses of Transactions

Transactions must do the following.
• The effects of each transaction must be stated in dollar amounts.
• Each transaction must affect at least two accounts.
• The accounting equation must be in balance after each transaction is recorded.

Accounting Entity

In accounting, the financial affairs of a business must be kept separate from the owner's personal financial affairs. For example, when Mark Nero invested his personal money in the business on September 14, only the amount of his investment ($13,000) was included in the assets of the Globe Travel Agency. When he withdrew money from the business on September 21, the amount of his withdrawal ($5,000) was subtracted from the assets of the business.

The accounting equation for the business does not include any of Mr. Nero's other personal assets, such as his home, car, and other cash. Also, the accounting equation does not include his personal liabilities. The individual business for which accounting records are kept is called an **accounting entity** (also referred to as a *business entity*).

The accounting records for the business must be separate from the owner's personal records.

Activity D. Continue with your accounting equation from Activity C. Show what happens to the equation as a result of each of the following transactions. Prove the equality of the equation. Refer to the equation on page 24.

10. Carol Reed invested an additional $2,000 in the business.

11. Carol Reed paid $800 to a creditor on account.

12. Carol Reed withdrew $50 from the business for personal use.

Accounting Concepts:

Accounting Entity. Each business must maintain a set of accounting records separate from other businesses and from the personal affairs of the owners.

Going Concern. A business is expected to operate from one year to the next. It is not expected to stop operating in the foreseeable future.

Accounting Periods. The life of a business is divided into a series of accounting periods. The length of these accounting periods varies from business to business.

Transactions. Transactions are financial events which cause the amounts in the accounting equation to change. Each transaction has an effect on one or more of the elements.

Accounts. A record of the changes in the elements is kept in an account. A separate account is kept for each asset, liability, and owner's equity item.

Permanent Accounts. Amounts in permanent accounts are carried forward from one accounting period to another.

Measuring Unit. The effects of business transactions are expressed in monetary terms. Thus the results of business operations in the United States are reported in dollar amounts.

Recording Transactions. The dollar amount of each transaction affects at least two accounts.

Equality of the Equation. A direct relationship exists between the accounts and the accounting equation. The total of the accounts on the left side of the equation must equal the total of the accounts on the right side of the equation. This keeps the equality of the equation.

Topic 1 Problems

2-1. Colonial TV Service is a single proprietorship owned by John LePage. The accounting equation for the business showed the information below.

Show what happens to the accounting equation for Colonial TV Service as a result of each of the January transactions on page 30. Follow this procedure for each transaction: First record the effects of the transaction. Then determine the account balance. After completing these tasks, then check the equality of the accounting equation.

	Assets		=	Liabilities	+	Owner's Equity		Equality Check	
Cash	Accounts Receivable	Shop Equipment		Accounts Payable		John LePage, Capital		A = L + OE	
$2,000 +	$100 +	$23,900	=	$6,000	+	$20,000		$26,000 = $26,000	

a. Owner withdrew $500 from the business.
b. Bought shop equipment for $100 in cash.
c. Bought shop equipment for $1,000 on credit.
d. Paid $500 to a creditor on account.
e. Owner invested an additional $5,000 in the business.
f. Returned shop equipment bought for $50 in cash.
g. Returned shop equipment bought for $300 on credit.
h. Received $100 cash from a customer on account.

2-2. Each of the accounting equations below was prepared after the completion of a transaction by Gram Trucking Company. Explain what happened in each transaction.

EXAMPLE: Mary Gram started the business with a cash investment of $30,000.

	Assets			=	Liabilities		+	Owner's Equity
	Cash	Delivery Equipment	Shop Equipment		Accts. Pay./ City Garage	Accts. Pay./ Town Motors		Mary Gram, Capital
EXAMPLE:	+$30,000							+$30,000
Trans. a		+$14,000				+$14,000		
New balance	$30,000 +	$14,000 +		=		$14,000 +		$30,000
Trans. b	− 1,000		+$1,000					
New balance	$29,000 +	$14,000 +	$1,000	=		$14,000 +		$30,000
Trans. c		+ 3,000			+$3,000			
New balance	$29,000 +	$17,000 +	$1,000	=	$3,000 +	$14,000 +		$30,000
Trans. d	−10,000					−10,000		
New balance	$19,000 +	$17,000 +	$1,000	=	$3,000 +	$ 4,000 +		$30,000
Trans. e	+ 8,000							+ 8,000
New balance	$27,000 +	$17,000 +	$1,000	=	$3,000 +	$ 4,000 +		$38,000
Trans. f		− 1,000			−1,000			
New balance	$27,000 +	$16,000 +	$1,000	=	$2,000 +	$ 4,000 +		$38,000
Trans. g	− 4,000							− 4,000
New balance	$23,000 +	$16,000 +	$1,000	=	$2,000 +	$ 4,000 +		$34,000
Trans. h	− 2,000				−2,000			
New balance	$21,000 +	$16,000 +	$1,000	=	$ -0- +	$ 4,000 +		$34,000
Trans. i	+ 300		− 300					
New balance	$21,300 +	$16,000 +	$ 700	=	$ -0- +	$ 4,000 +		$34,000
Trans. j	− 500	+ 2,500				+ 2,000		
New balance	$20,800 +	$18,500 +	$ 700	=	$ -0- +	$ 6,000 +		$34,000

Topic 2
Increasing and Decreasing Temporary Owner's Equity Accounts

A Is owner's equity affected only when the owner increases or decreases the amount of the investment? No, owner's equity also is affected when a business makes a profit or suffers a loss. The main reason for operating a business is to increase owner's equity by earning a profit. In this topic, you will see how owner's equity is affected by transactions related to earning a profit.

Income

When a business sells goods or services, it receives cash or accounts receivable from its customers. Sales transactions cause the left side of the accounting equation to increase. This happens because either the asset Cash or the asset Accounts Receivable increases. When the left side of the equation increases, the right side of the equation must increase by the same amount.

On September 26 the Globe Travel Agency receives $2,000 in cash from the sale of travel services. The asset Cash increases by $2,000 because the business now has more money. This transaction is shown here. An element, however, is also affected on the right side of the equation.

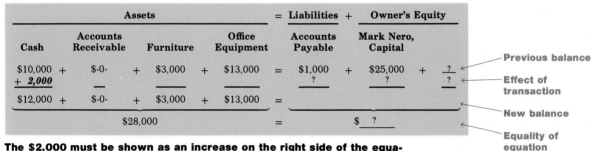

	Assets			= Liabilities +	Owner's Equity	
Cash	Accounts Receivable	Furniture	Office Equipment	Accounts Payable	Mark Nero, Capital	
$10,000 +	$-0- +	$3,000 +	$13,000 =	$1,000 +	$25,000 +	?
+ 2,000				?	?	?
$12,000 +	$-0- +	$3,000 +	$13,000 =			
	$28,000			=	$?	

Previous balance

Effect of transaction

New balance

Equality of equation

The $2,000 must be shown as an increase on the right side of the equation. Which element is affected?

Liabilities are debts of the business. They are not affected by the sales transaction. Thus owner's equity must increase. But what owner's equity account is affected?

The Capital account is a record of the claims of the owner from investments. Thus the Capital account is not affected at this time since this is not an investment by the owner.

This brings us to the profit incentive. The **profit incentive** means that a person risks investment in a business in hopes of increasing owner's equity by earning a profit.

People hope to make profits from investments in businesses.

In accounting, the term *income* is used instead of profit. **Income** is the difference between the revenue received from the sale of goods and services and the expenses incurred in operating the business and making those sales. To explain these terms, we will first look at how revenue is earned in a service business. Then we will look at how expenses are incurred in operating the business.

Language:
Income. In general usage, the term *income* is used for anything coming in. In accounting usage, income is the difference between revenue and expenses. People frequently think income means the same thing as revenue. In accounting, the terms do not have the same meaning.

Revenue Transactions

Revenue is the increase in owner's equity caused by the inflow of assets from the sale of goods and services. The asset Cash is increased by revenue from cash sales. The asset Accounts Receivable is increased by revenue from sales on credit. Other assets, such as Notes Receivable, may also be increased by revenue from sales.

The cash sales and sales on credit made by the Globe Travel Agency during September are now analyzed. These transactions show how revenue transactions increase both assets and owner's equity.

Receiving Revenue From Cash Sales. Two elements are affected when a business sells services for cash—assets and owner's equity. Both elements increase. For example, on September 26 Globe receives $2,000 from September's sale of travel services. This transaction is illustrated here.

Revenue From Sales for Cash and on Credit

Assets = Liabilities + Owner's Equity

$+$ 0 $+$

Assets increase.
Liabilities not affected.
Owner's Equity increases.

Transaction	Analysis
September 26: The Globe Travel Agency receives $2,000 in cash as revenue from the sale of travel services during September.	• The asset *Cash* increases by $2,000 because the business now has more money. • The owner's equity *Income Summary* (Revenue) increases by $2,000 because the business now has earned revenue.

	Assets				= Liabilities +	Owner's Equity	
	Cash	Accounts Receivable	Furniture	Office Equipment	Accounts Payable	Mark Nero, Capital	Income Summary (Revenue)
Previous balance	$10,000 +	$-0- +	$3,000 +	$13,000 =	$1,000 +	$25,000	
Effect of transaction	+ 2,000						+ $2,000
New balance	$12,000 +	$-0- +	$3,000 +	$13,000 =	$1,000 +	$25,000 +	$2,000
					$1,000 +	$27,000	
Equality of equation		$28,000			=	$28,000	

Receiving revenue from cash sales.

Inflow of Cash

From Investment   From Sales

Increases   Increases

Capital account   Revenue account

Increases
Owner's Equity

In this transaction, cash increases by $2,000. Thus the left side of the accounting equation now shows total assets of $28,000. The total claims against the assets must always equal the total assets. Thus the right side of the accounting equation must also increase by the same amount. Since liabilities are not affected by this transaction, owner's equity must increase by $2,000.

The sale of services is not an additional investment. Thus the Capital account is not used. Instead a new owner's equity account titled "Income Summary" is used to increase owner's equity.

Receiving Revenue From Sales on Credit. The sale of services on credit affects two accounting elements—assets and owner's equity. Both elements increase. This is illustrated in the analysis of the transaction here. On September 27 the Globe Travel Agency sells $1,700 of travel services on credit.

Transaction	Analysis
September 27: The Globe Travel Agency sells travel services on credit to Karen Louis for $1,000 and to Rose Shops for $700.	• The asset *Accounts Receivable* increases by $1,700 because the business now has more money to be received from its customers. • The owner's equity *Income Summary* (Revenue) increases by $1,700 because the business has now earned revenue.

	Assets			=	Liabilities +	Owner's Equity		
Cash	Accounts Receivable	Furniture	Office Equipment	=	Accounts Payable	Mark Nero, Capital	Income Summary (Revenue)	
$12,000 +	$-0- +*$1,700*	+ $3,000 +	$13,000	=	$1,000 +	$25,000 +	$2,000 +*$1,700*	Previous balance Effect of transaction
$12,000 +	$1,700 +	$3,000 +	$13,000	=	$1,000 +	$25,000 +	$3,700	New balance
					$1,000 +		$28,700	
		$29,700		=			$29,700	Equality of equation

Receiving revenue from sales on credit.

The sale on credit increases the left side of the accounting equation because the asset Accounts Receivable increases. The right side of the accounting equation increases by the same amount. Liabilities are not affected. Thus it is owner's equity that increases. The revenue from sales on credit is added to the Income Summary account. The total revenue is now $3,700 ($2,000 from cash sales plus $1,700 from sales on credit).

Liabilities are still $1,000. The owner's equity is now $28,700. Thus the right side of the equation totals $29,700. The accounting equation remains in balance.

In accounting, revenue is recorded when the service is performed or when the goods are sold to the customer. The asset received—either cash or the customer's agreement to pay in the future—is also recorded at that time.

Revenue is recorded at time service is performed or goods are given to customer.

Activity A. Goodwin's Repair Service is a single proprietorship owned by Paul Goodwin. The assets, liabilities, and owner's equity for the business on July 1 are shown in the accounting equation on page 34. Indicate what happens to the accounting equation as a result of the following July transactions. Prove the equality of the two sides of the equation after each transaction.

A = L + OE	Assets			= Liabilities +	Owner's Equity	
	Cash	Accounts Receivable	Equipment	Accounts Payable	Paul Goodwin, Capital	Income Summary (Revenue)
$5,000 = $5,000	$3,000 +	$600 +	$1,400 =	$500 +	$4,500 +	
EX.: + 200					+	$200
$5,200 = $5,200	$3,200 +	$600 +	$1,400 =	$500 +	$4,500 +	$200

EXAMPLE: Received $200 for the sale of services.
1. Paid $500 to a creditor on account.
2. Paul Goodwin invested an additional $3,000 in the business.
3. Received $500 for the sale of services.

4. Paul Goodwin withdrew $1,000 from the business.
5. Sold services for $600 on credit.

NOTE: Save your equation for further use in Activity B.

Expense Transactions

B   *Are goods and services needed to operate a business?* Yes, goods and services are needed to operate a business and obtain revenues. The cost of the goods and services used in the operation of a business are called **expenses.** Salaries, advertising, supplies used, telephone, fuel, and electricity are common business expenses. Since expenses are the costs of goods and services used by the business, they are also known as **expired costs.**

To see how expenses affect owner's equity, let's look at the expense transactions of the Globe Travel Agency for September. Note that the term *expense* is used under Income Summary in the accounting equation. This shows that amounts paid as expenses are subtracted directly from the amounts received as revenue.

Paying Expenses With Cash. When a business pays cash for an expense, two accounting elements are affected—assets and owner's equity. Both elements decrease. The left side of the accounting equation decreases because the asset Cash has decreased, as illustrated in the margin.

The right side of the equation decreases by the same amount. Since no debt is incurred by this expense, no liability account is affected by this cash transaction. Thus owner's equity must decrease.

Expenses Paid by Cash

Assets = Liabilities + Owner's Equity

−   0   −

Assets decrease.
Liabilities are not affected.
Owner's Equity decreases.

The Capital account is not affected at this time since no investment is involved. Revenue is not affected since revenue involves the inflow of assets (cash or accounts receivable). Expenses are affected. Expenses are expired costs that decrease owner's equity. The accounting equation is in balance.

The accounting equation for September 28 shows that the Globe Travel Agency pays cash for an expense of $2,100. Expenses can be viewed as decreases in owner's equity caused by an outflow of assets. In this case cash is paid immediately.

Transaction	Analysis
September 28: The Globe Travel Agency pays an expense of $2,100 for salaries.	• The asset *Cash* decreases by $2,100 because the business now has less money. • The owner's equity *Income Summary* (Expense) decreases by $2,100 because the business has incurred an expense.

Assets				=	Liabilities +	Owner's Equity	
Cash	Accounts Receivable	Furniture	Office Equipment		Accounts Payable	Mark Nero, Capital	Income Summary (Revenue − Expense)
$12,000 + − 2,100	$1,700 +	$3,000 +	$13,000 =		$1,000 +	$25,000 +	$3,700 ← − 2,100 ←
$ 9,900 +	$1,700 +	$3,000 +	$13,000 =		$1,000 +	$25,000 +	$1,600 ←
					$1,000 +		$26,600
		$27,600		=		$27,600 ←	

- ② Previous balance
- ① Effect of transaction
- New balance
- Equality of equation
- ③

Paying expenses with Cash.

Notice these changes to the accounting equation.

1 Expense shows the cost of operating the business. The expense is recorded under owner's equity.
2 A minus sign is used between "Revenue" and "Expense" to show that the amounts must be subtracted.
3 The heading "Income Summary" is used to show how much owner's equity has been increased by income, which is the difference between revenue and expenses.

The total owner's equity is now $26,600 (Capital of $25,000 plus Income Summary of $1,600). Liabilities of $1,000 and owner's equity of $26,600 total $27,600. The cash payment of $2,100 decreases the asset Cash. The assets now total $27,600.

The heading "Income Summary" is used in the equation to show the revenue and expense amounts used to compute income. The word "Summary" following "Income" indicates that it shows the main ways (revenue and expenses) of how the income was earned.

Incurring Expenses on Credit. A business may incur an expense but promise to pay for it in the future. In this case, two accounting elements are affected—liabilities and owner's equity. Liabilities increase and owner's equity decreases. This is illustrated in the margin.

Expenses Incurred on Credit

Assets	=	Liabilities	+	Owner's Equity
0		+		−

Assets not affected.
Liabilities increase.
Owner's Equity decreases.

On September 29 the Globe Travel Agency incurs an additional expense of $200 on credit. Instead of paying cash, the Globe Travel Agency gives its promise to pay. This promise to pay is a liability. (This expense will represent an outflow of assets when the liability is paid.) The equation shows:

1 The amount of Mark Nero's investment.
2 The amount of net income.
3 The amount of owner's equity.

Transaction	Analysis
September 29: The Globe Travel Agency receives a bill for repairs expense of $200 from the Royal Service Shop for repairing a copying machine. The creditor allows the Globe Travel Agency 30 days in which to pay this amount.	• The liability *Accounts Payable* increases by $200 because the business now owes more money. • The owner's equity *Income Summary* (Expense) decreases by $200 because the business has now incurred an expense.

	Assets				= Liabilities +	Owner's Equity	
	Cash	Accounts Receivable	Furniture	Office Equipment	Accounts Payable	Mark Nero, Capital	Income Summary (Revenue − Expense)
Previous balance	$9,900 +	$1,700 +	$3,000 +	$13,000 =	$1,000	+ $25,000 +	$1,600
Effect of transaction					+ 200		− 200
New balance	$9,900 +	$1,700 +	$3,000 +	$13,000 =	$1,200	+ $25,000 +	$1,400
					$1,200 +		$26,400
Equality of equation			$27,600		=		$27,600

Incurring expenses on credit.   ① ③ ②

Revenue	$3,700
Less: Expenses	−2,300
Net Income	$1,400

As the equation shows, the Globe Travel Agency incurred an expense of $200 on credit for repairs. The difference between the revenue and expenses is $1,400, as shown in the margin. Accountants usually call this amount *net income*. **Net** means that all deductions have been made. Therefore, net income indicates that all the related expenses have been deducted from the revenue.

Expenses are recorded when costs are incurred to generate revenue. What is given—cash or an agreement to pay in the future—is also recorded at the same time.

Temporary Owner's Equity Accounts

In this topic, an Income Summary account was added to the accounting equation. This account is used to summarize all revenues and expenses for the accounting period. It is a temporary account. An account used to compute the net income for an accounting period is called a *temporary account*. Temporary accounts gather data for one accounting period only. Permanent accounts, however, provide data from one accounting period to the next. The permanent accounts, as you recall from Topic 1, are asset accounts, liability accounts, and the owner's equity capital accounts. In Topic 3, you will learn that temporary accounts are used to compute net income for each accounting period.

Activity B. Continue with your accounting equation from Activity A. Show what happens to the equation as a result of each of the following transactions. Prove the equality of the equation after each transaction. Refer to the equation on page 34.

6. Paid $100 for advertising expense.

7. Bought equipment for $300 on credit.
8. Paul Goodwin withdrew $1,000 from the business.
9. Owes $250 for equipment repair.
10. Received $400 from the sale of services.
11. Paid $500 for rent.
12. Sold services for $300 on credit.

Accounting Concepts:
Profit Incentive. Every individual who invests in a business risks the investment in the hope of making a profit and must make a profit to survive.
Changing Owner's Equity. Owner's equity is affected not only by changes in the investment but also by revenues and expenses.

Accounting Principles

Accounting records are kept and interpreted according to generally accepted accounting principles (GAAPs). These principles are broad, general statements accepted by the members of the accounting profession. The current principles are issued by the Financial Accounting Standards Board (FASB). This group issues Statements of Financial Accounting Standards. In this text, you will learn about some of these accounting principles. Three such principles involve revenue, expenses, and net income.

Accounting Principles:
Recording Revenue. The generally accepted accounting principle is that *revenue* is recorded at the point of sale of goods or as the services are rendered.
Expenses. The generally accepted accounting principle is that *expenses* represent the cost of the goods and services used up in the process of generating revenue.
Revenue and Net Income. The generally accepted accounting principle is that *revenue* is used to indicate receipts (in the form of cash and accounts receivable) from the sale of goods and services, and that *net income* is used to refer to the amount remaining after all expenses have been deducted.

Topic 2 Problems

2-3. On August 31 Dr. Lee Lanski had the following assets, liabilities, and owner's equity in his dental practice. Refer to the accounting equation and equality check below. Show what happens to the equation as a result of the following transactions, which took place in September. Prove the equality of the two sides of the equation after each transaction.
a. Bought equipment for $5,000 on credit.
b. Received $600 for the sale of services.
c. Returned equipment bought for $1,000 on credit.
d. Paid $60 for telephone expense.
e. Received $200 from a patient on account.
f. Owner invested an additional $2,000 in the business.
g. Paid $300 for rent.
h. Sold services for $550 on credit.
i. Paid $300 to a creditor on account.
j. Owner withdrew $1,000 from the business for personal use.
k. Bought additional equipment for $1,000 in cash.
l. Owes $100 for repair expense.
m. Returned equipment bought for $800 in cash.

Equality Check	Assets			= Liabilities	+	Owner's Equity	
	Cash	Accounts Receivable	Equipment	Accounts Payable		Lee Lanski, Capital	Income Summary (Revenue – Expense)
A = L + OE							
$7,000 = $7,000	$2,000 +	$500 +	$4,500 =	$1,200 +		$5,800 +	$0

2-4. Sarah Levine opened Plaza Bowling Lanes. Each equation below was done after the completion of a transaction. Explain what happened in each transaction.

EXAMPLE: Sarah Levine started the business with an investment of $75,000 in cash and $40,000 in equipment (total capital of $115,000).

	Assets			= Liabilities +		Owner's Equity	
	Cash	Accounts Receivable	Equipment	Accounts Payable	Sarah Levine, Capital		Income Summary (Revenue – Expense)
EXAMPLE:	$75,000 +	$-0- +	$40,000 =	$-0- +	$115,000 +		$-0-
Trans. a			+40,000	+40,000			
New balance	$75,000 +	$-0- +	$80,000 =	$40,000 +	$115,000 +		$-0-
Trans. b		+$300					+300
New balance	$75,000 +	$300 +	$80,000 =	$40,000 +	$115,000 +		$300
Trans. c	– 100						–100
New balance	$74,900 +	$300 +	$80,000 =	$40,000 +	$115,000 +		$200
Trans. d	+ 50	– 50					
New balance	$74,950 +	$250 +	$80,000 =	$40,000 +	$115,000 +		$200
Trans. e	+ 500						+500
New balance	$75,450 +	$250 +	$80,000 =	$40,000 +	$115,000 +		$700
Trans. f	–20,000			–20,000			
New balance	$55,450 +	$250 +	$80,000 =	$20,000 +	$115,000 +		$700
Trans. g				+ 400			–400
New balance	$55,450 +	$250 +	$80,000 =	$20,400 +	$115,000 +		$300
Trans. h	– 5,000				– 5,000		
New balance	$50,450 +	$250 +	$80,000 =	$20,400 +	$110,000 +		$300
Trans. i	– 800		+ 800				
New balance	$49,650 +	$250 +	$80,800 =	$20,400 +	$110,000 +		$300
Trans. j			– 2,100	– 2,100			
New balance	$49,650 +	$250 +	$78,700 =	$18,300 +	$110,000 +		$300
Trans. k	+ 200		– 200				
New balance	$49,850 +	$250 +	$78,500 =	$18,300 +	$110,000 +		$300
Trans. l	+ 3,000				+ 3,000		
New balance	$52,850 +	$250 +	$78,500 =	$18,300 +	$113,000 +		$300

2-5. Indicate what happens to each of the three accounting elements as a result of the following transactions. For each element, write in the answer column + for increase, − for decrease, or 0 for no effect.

EXAMPLE: *Bought truck on credit.*

Assets	Liabilities	Owner's Equity
+	+	0

a. Bought equipment on credit.
b. Returned equipment bought on credit.
c. Owner invested additional cash.
d. Received revenue from sales on credit.
e. Paid cash for an expense.
f. Incurred an expense on credit.
g. Received cash from a customer on account.

h. Paid cash in payment of a liability.
i. Bought equipment for cash.
j. Owner withdrew cash from business.
k. Returned equipment bought for cash.
l. Received revenue from cash sales.
m. Owner withdrew equipment from the business.
n. Bought building with cash and a mortgage payable.
o. Owner gave two office desks as an investment in the business.
p. Gave a note payable in place of an account payable.

HINT: Transactions m to p involve expanding on the concepts you learned in this topic.

Topic 3
Proving the Accounting Equation

A *Are transactions from one accounting period separated from other accounting periods?* Yes, the transactions from one accounting period are separated from those of another accounting period. During the accounting period, transactions are recorded as they occur. Then at the end of the accounting period, the data is sumarized and the net income (or net loss) for the period is transferred to the Capital account. After this transfer, the Income Summary account will have a zero balance.

This procedure summarizes the transactions of a business for each accounting period. Thus the accounting equation, like the life of the business, is separated into accounting periods..

Proving the Equality of the Equation

During the accounting period, the amounts in the accounts may be totaled after each transaction is recorded. An increase (+) is added and a decrease (−) is subtracted. In accounting, the difference between the increases and the decreases in an account is called a **balance,** instead of a total. Thus, as shown here, the balance of the Cash account for the Globe Travel Agency on September 6 was $5,000. The balance of the Accounts Receivable account on September 5 was $1,000. On September 6, however, the Accounts Receivable account had a zero balance.

The transactions that were analyzed in Topics 1 and 2 are shown in the equation on page 40. Note the following items.

1 The account balance was computed after each transaction.
2 The equation was not proved until the end of the accounting period.

	Assets	
	Cash	Accounts Receivable
Sept. 1 balance	$8,000	$1,000
Sept. 5	−4,000	
balance	$4,000	$1,000
Sept. 6	+1,000	− 1,000
balance	$5,000	$ -0-

Add pluses and subtract minuses to compute account balance.

	Assets				=	Liabilities	+	Owner's Equity	
	Cash	Accounts Receivable	Furniture	Office Equipment		Accounts Payable		Mark Nero, Capital	Income Summary (Revenue − Expense)
Sept. 1 balance	$ 8,000 +	$1,000 +	$2,000 +	$ 9,000 =		$3,000 +		$17,000 +	$ -0-
	− 4,000			+ 4,000					
Sept. 5 balance	$ 4,000 +	$1,000 +	$2,000 +	$13,000 =		$3,000 +		$17,000 +	$ -0-
	+ 1,000	− 1,000							
Sept. 6 balance	$ 5,000 +	$ -0- +	$2,000 +	$13,000 =		$3,000 +		$17,000 +	$ -0-
			+ 1,500			+ 1,500			
Sept. 7 balance	$ 5,000 +	$ -0- +	$3,500 +	$13,000 =		$4,500 +		$17,000 +	$ -0-
			− 500			− 500			
Sept. 8 balance	$ 5,000 +	$ -0- +	$3,000 +	$13,000 =		$4,000 +		$17,000 +	$ -0-
	− 3,000					− 3,000			
Sept. 12 balance	$ 2,000 +	$ -0- +	$3,000 +	$13,000 =		$1,000 +		$17,000 +	$ -0-
	+ 13,000							+ 13,000	
Sept. 14 balance	$15,000 +	$ -0- +	$3,000 +	$13,000 =		$1,000 +		$30,000 +	$ -0-
	− 5,000							− 5,000	
Sept. 21 balance	$10,000 +	$ -0- +	$3,000 +	$13,000 =		$1,000 +		$25,000 +	$ -0-
	+ 2,000								+ 2,000
Sept. 26 balance	$12,000 +	$ -0- +	$3,000 +	$13,000 =		$1,000 +		$25,000 +	$2,000
		+ 1,700							+ 1,700
Sept. 27 balance	$12,000 +	$1,700 +	$3,000 +	$13,000 =		$1,000 +		$25,000 +	$3,700
	− 2,100								− 2,100
Sept. 28 balance	$ 9,900 +	$1,700 +	$3,000 +	$13,000 =		$1,000 +		$25,000 +	$1,600
						+ 200			− 200
Sept. 29 balance	$ 9,900 +	$1,700 +	$3,000 +	$13,000 =		$1,200 +		$25,000 +	$1,400
Sept. 30 Equality of equation			$27,600		=	$1,200 +		$26,400	
					=			$27,600	

Transactions of Globe Travel Agency for monthly accounting period ending September 30.

Summarizing Accounting Information

Each transaction must be recorded so that the accounting equation will show the effects of that transaction. Owners and managers, however, are usually not interested in having the details about each transaction. Instead, they want the results of the transactions summarized for them. Thus managers and owners are more interested in knowing the account balances, especially at the end of the accounting period. For example, Mark Nero wants to know the balance of the Cash account. He might want this information on a daily basis. He certainly wants to know whether the business earned a net income for the accounting period.

Net Income and Net Loss

Whether a business has a net income or a net loss depends upon whether the revenues are more or less than the expenses for the same accounting period. A **net income** results when revenues are greater than the expenses. A **net loss** results when the expenses are greater than the revenues.

An accounting principle, called the **matching principle,** requires that the revenue earned in one accounting period be matched against the expenses incurred in earning that revenue. The expenses must be matched against the related revenue to state accurately the fair amount of net income (or net loss) earned by the business during the accounting period.

Expenses must be matched against revenue.

The Globe Travel Agency has a net income of $1,400 for the accounting period ending September 30. This is shown in the margin. This net income is obtained by matching total revenues of $3,700 ($2,000 + $1,700) against total expenses of $2,300 ($2,100 + $200). The $1,400 is a net income because total revenues are greater than total expenses. This information is very important for managers and owners.

COMPUTING NET INCOME FOR ACCOUNTING PERIOD ENDED SEPTEMBER 30,19—

Revenue	Expenses
$2,000	$2,100
+1,700	+ 200
$3,700	$2,300

Total Revenue	$3,700
Less: Total Expenses	−2,300
Net Income	$1,400

Activity A-1. Answer the following questions about proving the equality of the accounting equation. Refer to the Globe Travel Agency's equation on page 40.
1. What is the amount of the total assets on September 1?
2. What is the balance of the Accounts Payable account on September 8?
3. What is the balance of the Mark Nero, Capital account on September 14?
4. What is the balance of the Accounts Receivable account on September 28?
5. What is the amount of total liabilities plus owner's equity on September 29?

6. What is the amount of owner's equity on September 30?
7. How many transactions affected the Cash account during the accounting period ending September 30?

Activity A-2. Compute the net income (or net loss) for each of the companies below. Show the change in the Income Summary and the change in owner's equity. The first computation is done as an example. Refer to the table below.

Company	Revenue	Expenses	Income Summary		Amount	Owner's Equity	
			Net Income	Net Loss		Decrease	Increase
EXAMPLE: A	$15,000	$ 5,000	✓		$10,000		✓
B	$20,000	$ 7,000			$_____		
C	$14,000	$15,000			$_____		
D	$10,000	$ 8,000			$_____		
E	$19,900	$20,000			$_____		

Transferring Net Income (or Net Loss) to the Capital Account

 What happens to the net income (or net loss) at the end of the accounting period? The net income (or net loss) is transferred to the Capital account at the end of the accounting period. During the accounting period, revenue transactions increase the Income Summary account. Expenses decrease the Income Summary account. Thus the revenue and expenses are matched in the Income Summary account for the accounting period. The result of this matching is a net income (or net loss) for the period.

The **Income Summary account** is a temporary account whose balance is transferred to the permanent Capital account at the end of each accounting period. As you know, temporary accounts gather data for one accounting period only. Therefore, the temporary account balance must be zero at the end of each accounting period. This is done by adding a net income to the Capital account or by subtracting a net loss from the Capital account. After this is done, the total liabilities plus the owner's equity still equal the total assets. The accounting equation is proved and is in balance.

Transferring a Net Income. During the accounting period ending September 30, the Globe Travel Agency had a net income of $1,400. The Income Summary account balance must be zero on October 1 so that the new revenue and expense data for the next accounting period (October) may be collected. Starting each accounting period with a zero balance in the temporary accounts prevents getting the revenue and expense data for one accounting period mixed with the data of another accounting period. The following procedure is used to get a zero balance in the temporary account.

At the end of each accounting period, the net income amount is transferred to the Capital account. The amount of the net income is subtracted from the Income Summary account ($1,400 − $1,400), as shown in the following table. Thus the Income Summary account is now zero. The net income is added to the Capital account. Thus the

	Owner's Equity		
	Mark Nero, Capital	**Income Summary (Revenue − Expense)**	
Net income	$25,000	+	→$1,400
Total owner's equity		→$26,400	
Transfer net income	→+ 1,400 ←		− 1,400
Total capital investment	$26,400	+	$ -0-
Total owner's equity		→$26,400	

Transferring net income to the Capital account.

Capital account will increase by the amount of the net income ($25,000 + $1,400 = $26,400). Since the Income Summary amount is zero, the account is ready to have data recorded for the next accounting period.

The following equation shows that the net income for the Globe Travel Agency is transferred to the Capital account on September 30, the end of the accounting period.

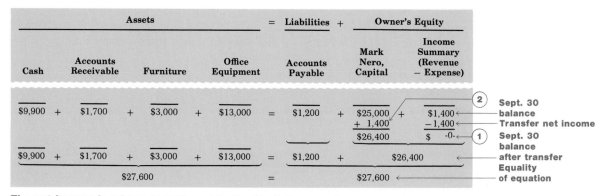

Assets				=	Liabilities	+	Owner's Equity		
Cash	Accounts Receivable	Furniture	Office Equipment		Accounts Payable		Mark Nero, Capital	Income Summary (Revenue – Expense)	
$9,900 +	$1,700 +	$3,000 +	$13,000	=	$1,200	+	$25,000 / + $1,400 $26,400	$1,400 ← – 1,400 ← $ -0- ←	② Sept. 30 balance Transfer net income ① Sept. 30 balance
$9,900 +	$1,700 +	$3,000 +	$13,000	=	$1,200	+	$26,400		after transfer
		$27,600		=			$27,600		Equality of equation

The net income has been transferred to the Capital account.

Notice how this transfer of net income affected the accounts.
1 The Income Summary account balance is now zero.
2 The Capital account has been increased by the amount of the net income ($1,400).
Only one element is affected—owner's equity. The equation is still in balance.

Transferring a Net Loss. If a business suffers a net loss for the accounting period, its expenses must have been greater than its revenue. Expenses decrease owner's equity. Therefore a net loss decreases the capital account.

Suppose the Globe Travel Agency had suffered a $2,000 loss during September as shown in the table in the margin. (In accounting, parentheses or a circle around an amount means minus.) The net loss is also transferred to the Capital account. However, the net loss is subtracted from the Capital account since a net loss decreases owner's equity.

This is done by subtracting $2,000 from the Capital account and adding the amount to the Income Summary account. The amount is added because the Income Summary account must be zero at the end of the accounting period.

Again only one element—owner's equity—is affected. The equation is still in balance.

Transferring a net loss to the Capital account.

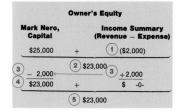

1 Net loss
2 Total owner's equity
3 Transfer net loss
4 Total capital investment
5 Total owner's equity

Language:
Data and Information. In accounting usage, *data* means unorganized facts. *Information* refers to data organized so that it is meaningful. Therefore, use *data* when referring to things that need to be processed. Use *information* when referring to a summary of the data.

Activity B-1. Answer the following questions about transferring net income (or net loss) to capital. Refer to the accounting equations on pages 42 and 43.
1. What is the amount of the owner's equity before the net income is transferred on September 30?
2. What amount is transferred to the capital account?
3. What is the balance of the Income Summary account after the net income is transferred on September 30?

4. What is the amount of the owner's equity after the net income is transferred on September 30?
5. Does the total liabilities plus owner's equity equal the total assets at all times?

Activity B-2. Show the transfer of the Income Summary account balance in the Owner's Equity section of the equation. Use a form similar to the one illustrated here.

Owner's Equity **April 30, 19—**		
Ellen Terry, **Capital**		**Income Summary** **(Revenue** **– Expense)**
$15,000 + 3,000	+	$3,000 –3,000
$18,000	+	$ -0-
$18,000		

Owner's Equity **May 31, 19—**		
Ellen Terry, **Capital**		**Income Summary** **(Revenue** **– Expense)**
$20,000 ?	+	$6,000 ?
$?	+	$?
$?		

Owner's Equity **June 30, 19—**		
Ellen Terry, **Capital**		**Income Summary** **(Revenue** **– Expense)**
$28,000 ?	+	($4,000) ?
$?	+	$?
$?		

Interpreting Accounting Information

C *Why do owners and managers need accounting information?* People use the summarized accounting information to make decisions. Mark Nero, for example, knows that the business has $9,900 in cash on September 30. If he wanted to buy an automobile for the agency, could he pay $7,000 cash for it?

Before Mark Nero can answer that question, he will need to consider such questions as: What expenses will he have in October? When does he have to pay his liabilities? Approximately how much cash will be received from cash sales in October? To make the decision to buy an automobile for the agency, Mr. Nero will need to interpret the accounting information given to him.

To **interpret** accounting information means to clarify the meaning of the information.

For example, to report that the Globe Travel Agency earned a net income of $1,400 for the accounting period ending September 30 implies that all the expenses incurred in making the sales during September have been recorded. Suppose an expense for $400 had been incurred but not recorded in September. The net income would then show $1,800 rather than the correct amount of $1,400. Thus it is important that the revenues and the related expenses be matched for the same time period covered by the accounting period.

Remember also that a net income (or net loss) is computed for an accounting period. Therefore it is important to know that the Globe Travel Agency earned that net income in one month. A different meaning would be conveyed if the Globe Travel Agency's accounting period were three months.

Interpreting accounting information is covered in the later chapters of this textbook.

Accounting Cycle

Businesses follow a standard set of procedures in keeping their accounting records. The sequence of procedures or steps repeated in each accounting period to process the accounting data is known as the **accounting cycle.** In this chapter you learned how to analyze transactions and use the equation to process the accounting data.

The procedures in this chapter covered the accounting cycle in its simplest form. Here is a summary of what happened.

STEP 1. Each transaction was recorded.

STEP 2. A chronological record was kept of each transaction. (**Chronological** means by date.)

STEP 3. The changes caused by the transactions were available for each account, and the account balance was updated. (**Update** means to bring up to date.)

STEP 4. The equality of the equation was proved at the end of the accounting period.

STEP 5. The accounting information was summarized by account balances at the end of the accounting period.

STEP 6. The revenue and expense data was summarized in the Income Summary account transferred to the Capital account at the end of the accounting period.

STEP 7. The equality of the equation was proved again after the net income was transferred from the Income Summary account to the Capital account.

STEP 8. The accounting records provided financial information for managers and owners to make decisions.

Activity C. Answer the following questions about interpreting accounting information. Refer to the text on pages 44 to 45 and the equations on page 46.
1. How many steps are described as the accounting cycle?

2. Describe the transactions that affect the Capital account.
3. What procedures are followed to transfer the net income of $1,400?

		Assets				=	Liabilities	+	Owner's Equity	
		Cash	Accounts Receivable	Furniture	Office Equipment		Accounts Payable		Mark Nero, Capital	Income Summary (Revenue − Expense)
Sept. 1 balance		$ 8,000 + −4,000	$1,000 +	$2,000 +	$ 9,000 + 4,000 =		$3,000 +		$17,000 +	$ -0-
Sept. 5 balance		$ 4,000 + + 1,000	$1,000 + −1,000	$2,000 +	$13,000 =		$3,000 +		$17,000 +	$ -0-
		$ 9,900 +	$1,700 +	$3,000 +	$13,000 =		$1,000 + + 200		$25,000 +	$1,600 − 200
Sept. 29 balance		$ 9,900 +	$1,700 +	$3,000 +	$13,000 =		$1,200 +		$25,000 +	$1,400
Sept. 30 Equality before transfer				$27,600		=	$1,200 +			$26,400
				$27,600		=			$27,600	
Sept. 30 Transfer of Net Income									+ 1,400 $26,400	− 1,400 $ -0-
Sept. 30 Balance after transfer		$ 9,900 +	$1,700 +	$3,000 +	$13,000 =		$1,200 +			$26,400
Sept. 30 Equality after transfer				$27,600		=			$27,600	

Circled reference numbers: 1, 3, 2, 5, 4, 6, 7

The theory behind accounting is illustrated in these procedures.

(8) **Owners and managers use this information to make decisions.**

Accounting Concepts:
Temporary Accounts. Amounts in temporary accounts are not carried forward from one accounting period to the next.
Accounting Cycle. A sequence of procedures, or steps, called the accounting cycle, is followed in doing accounting work in each accounting period.

Accounting Principle:
Matching Revenue and Expenses. The generally accepted accounting principle is that revenue must be matched against the expenses incurred in obtaining that revenue. The result of matching revenue and expenses is net income (or net loss) for the accounting period.

Topic 3 Problems

2-6. On November 1 Gerald Brown had the assets, liabilities, and owner's equity in his law practice shown on the next page. Refer to the accounting equation and equality check on the next page.

a. Show what happens to the accounting equation as a result of the following transactions taking place during the accounting period ending November 30.
b. Prove the equality of the equation after the last

transaction but before the transfer of the Income Summary account balance.

c. Transfer the Income Summary account balance to the Capital account.

d. Prove the equality of the equation after transfer.

Nov. 1 Owner started the business with an investment of $10,600 in cash and $3,400 in office equipment, which equals capital of $14,000.

15 Bought equipment for $75 on credit.
18 Sold services for $550 on credit.
25 Received $400 for the sale of services.
28 Paid $235 for rent.

NOTE: Save your equation for further use in Topic Problems 2-7, 2-8, and 2-9.

Equality Check	Assets			=	Liabilities	+	Owner's Equity	
A = L + OE							Gerald Brown, Capital	Income Summary (Revenue − Expense)
$14,000 = $14,000	Cash	Accounts Receivable	Office Equipment		Accounts Payable			
Nov. 1 Balance	$10,600 +	$-0- +	$3,400	=	$-0- +		$14,000 +	$-0-

2-7. Gerald Brown continued his law practice during the next accounting period beginning December 1. The account balances as of December 1 are shown in the equation below.

a. Show what happens to the accounting equation as a result of the following transactions, which took place during the accounting period ending December 31.

b. Prove the equality of the equation after the last transaction but before the transfer of the Income Summary account balance.

c. Transfer the Income Summary account balance.

d. Prove the equality of the equation after the transfer.

Dec. 1 Owner started the new accounting period with $10,765 in cash, $550 in accounts receivable, and $3,475 in office equipment. These assets equal the total of liabilities of $75 plus owner's equity of $14,715.

5 Returned equipment bought for $50 on credit.

12 Received $500 for sale of services.

28 Paid $235 for rent.

NOTE: Save your equation for further use in Topic Problem 2-8.

	Assets			=	Liabilities	+	Owner's Equity		Equality Check
		Accounts Receivable	Office Equipment		Accounts Payable		Gerald Brown, Capital	Income Summary (Revenue − Expense)	A = L + OE
	Cash								$14,790 = $14,790
	$10,765 +	$550 +	$3,475	=	$75 +		$14,715 +	$-0-	Dec. 1 Balance

2-8. Gerald Brown continued his law practice during the next accounting period beginning January 1. The account balances as of January 1 are shown in the equation on page 48.

a. Show what happens to the accounting equation as a result of the following transactions, which took place during the accounting period ending January 31.

b. Prove the equality of the equation after the last transaction but before the transfer of the Income Summary account balance.

c. Transfer the Income Summary account balance to the capital account.

d. Prove the equality of the equation after the transfer.

Jan. 1 Owner started the new accounting period with an investment of $11,030 in cash, $550 in accounts receivable, and $3,425 in office equipment. These assets equal the total liabilities of $25 plus owner's equity of $14,980.

10 Received $575 for the sale of services.
15 Paid $45 for repair expense.
22 Paid $25 on account.
28 Paid $235 for rent.

NOTE: Save your equation for further use in Topic Problem 2-9.

	Assets			=	Liabilities	+	Owner's Equity		
Cash		Accounts Receivable	Office Equipment	=	Accounts Payable	+	Gerald Brown, Capital	Income Summary (Revenue − Expense)	
$11,030	+	$550	+ $3,425	=	$25	+	$14,980 +	$-0-	Jan. 1 Balance

2-9. Gerald Brown continued his law practice during the next accounting period beginning February 1. The account balances as of February 1 are shown in the January 31 accounting equation from Topic Problem 2-8. Carry the January 31 balances forward to the February 1 equation, which is shown below.

a. Show what happens to the accounting equation as a result of the following transactions, which took place during the accounting period ending February 28.

b. Prove the equality of the equation after the last transaction but before the transfer of the Income Summary account balance.

c. Transfer the Income Summary account balance to the capital account.

d. Prove the equality of the equation after the transfer.

Feb. 12 Sold services for $465 on credit.
21 Owed $35 for repair expenses.
26 Paid $235 for rent.
27 Received $200 for sale of services.

		Assets			=	Liabilities	+	Owner's Equity	
	Cash	Accounts Receivable	Office Equipment		Accounts Payable		Gerald Brown, Capital	Income Summary (Revenue − Expense)	
Feb. 1 Balance	$11,300 +	$550	+ $3,425	=	$-0-	+	$15,275 +	$-0-	

The Language of Business

Here are some basic terms that make up the language of business. Do you know the meaning of each?

transaction
financial
going concern
summarize
accounting period
quarter
fiscal year

calendar year
permanent account
temporary account
analyzing a transaction
cash received on account
cash paid on account

accounting entity
profit incentive
income
revenue
expenses
expired costs
net
balance
net income
net loss

matching principle
Income Summary account
data
information
interpret
accounting cycle
chronological
update

Chapter 2 Questions

1. What is the difference between a fiscal year accounting period and a calendar year accounting period?

2. How does a transaction affect at least two elements in the accounting equation? How does a transaction affect only one element?

3. Is net income the same as the total revenue? Why or why not?

4. Name four different businesses or professions and the major source of revenue for each.

5. Give examples of five transactions for each business you named in question 4. Describe the effect that each transaction might have on the elements of the accounting equation.

6. Which transactions increase owner's equity?

7. Why does revenue increase owner's equity?

8. Why do expenses decrease owner's equity?

9. Which accounting principle is violated when an expense incurred on December 28 is matched against revenue for the period starting January 1? The accounting records for how many accounting periods would be wrong? Explain.

10. Accounting information can tell owners and managers what has happened in the past. It can also help them make plans for the future. Which use of accounting information is more important—to tell what *has happened,* or to help predict what *will happen?* Explain.

Chapter 2   Problems

Problems for Chapter 2 are given in the *Working Papers and Chapter Problems for Part 1.* If you are using the workbook, do the problems in the space provided there.

Chapter 2   Management Cases

Comparing Information. One feature of accounting is that it provides information in such a way that each business is uniquely described. One business does not look exactly like another. Each business entity has its own assets, liabilities, and owner's equity. As a result, accounting data provides information to help owners, managers, and others to make informed decisions about a business or businesses.

Case 2M-1. Gayle Stevens and Peter Lubbeck own separate businesses. Gayle's Card Shop is in its third year of profitable operation. Peter's Gift Shop just opened last summer. Each owner uses a monthly accounting period.

Ms. Stevens and Mr. Lubbeck decide to form a business partnership by combining their businesses.

a. Based on the data below, what are the differences in the assets of the card shop and of the gift shop?

b. Compare the net incomes for the month ended November 30.

c. Why do you think Gayle's Card Shop is earning a larger net income than Peter's Gift Shop?

d. What can Mr. Lubbeck do to increase his net income? (*HINT:* Look at his Cash balance.)

Gayle's Card Shop, November 30, 19—

Assets			=	Liabilities	+	Owner's Equity	
Cash	Merchandise for Sale	Display Equipment		Accounts Payable/ Marcall Cards		Gayle Stevens, Capital	Income Summary (Revenue − Expense)
$5,000 +	$8,000 +	$12,000 =		$2,000	+	$20,000 +	$3,000 Net Income

Peter's Gift Shop, November 30, 19—

Assets			=	Liabilities	+	Owner's Equity	
Cash	Merchandise for Sale	Display Equipment		Accounts Payable/ Navaho Gifts		Peter Lubbeck, Capital	Income Summary (Revenue − Expense)
$15,000 +	$1,000 +	$6,000 =		$500	+	$21,000 +	$500 Net Income

Case 2M-2. Opal Natal, the owner of the Brilliant Jewel Shop, examines the information below and sees that the business has $2,500 in cash. This is more cash than she believes the business needs. She is considering withdrawing $2,000 in cash to invest in another business. Refer to the equation below.

a. In anticipating the amount of money that the business will need in the near future, what items should Ms. Natal consider?

b. How much money can Ms. Natal expect the business to receive in the near future?

c. Do you feel that Ms. Natal can make a cash withdrawal of $2,000 without placing the business in a difficult financial situation? Why or why not? Include all of the reasons why Ms. Natal should or should not make this cash withdrawal.

Assets			=	Liabilities	+	Owner's Equity	
Cash	Accts. Rec./ Kay Macao	Merchandise for Sale		Accounts Payable/ Rouen Jewelers		Opal Natal, Capital	Income Summary (Revenue − Expense)
$2,500 +	$1,000 +	$11,800 =		$6,500	+	$6,500 +	$2,300 Net Income

Working Hint

Writing Legible Numbers. Many errors in accounting are caused by people not writing numbers legibly. Here are a few hints to help you improve your writing of numbers.

• Take time to form each number. Hastily written numbers are usually difficult to read.
• Draw a line through the stem of sevens to distinguish them easily from ones, nines, and fours.

• Draw a diagonal line through zeros to distinguish them easily from eights and the letter O.
• Slant each number slightly to the right.

```
1 2 3 4 5 6 7 8 9 Ø
```

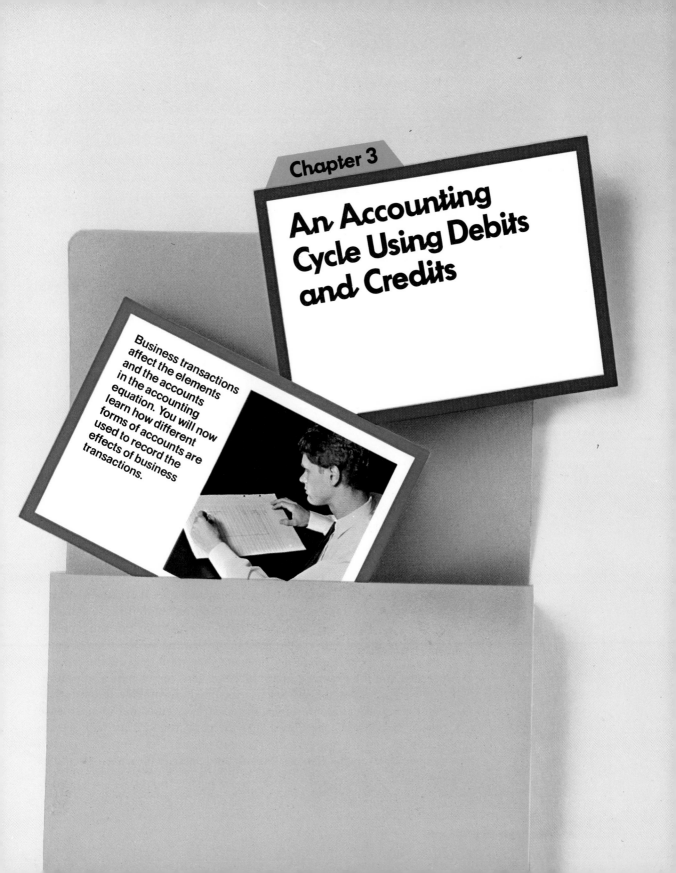

Chapter 3

An Accounting Cycle Using Debits and Credits

Business transactions affect the elements and the accounts in the accounting equation. You will now learn how different forms of accounts are used to record the effects of business transactions.

Cash
One-Column Account
increases and decreases are
recorded in same column.

$8,000
−4,000
$4,000
+1,000
$5,000
−3,000
$2,000
+13,000
$15,000
− 5,000
$10,000
+ 2,000
$12,000
− 2,100
$ 9,900

Topic 1
Forms of Accounts

A *Is only one form of account used in business?* No, several different forms of accounts are used. In Chapter 2 you saw a one-column account, as shown in the margin. Increases were added to the account balance and decreases were subtracted from the account balance in the same column. In this chapter, a two-sided, or two-column, account is used. Increases to the account balance are put on one side of the account, and decreases to the balance are put on the other side.

Accounts

The accounting equation for the Globe Travel Agency has only seven accounts: Cash; Accounts Receivable; Furniture; Office Equipment; Accounts Payable; Mark Nero, Capital; and Income Summary.

Using many accounts in an accounting equation is awkward.

Assets				=	Liabilities	+	Owner's Equity	
Cash	Accounts Receivable	Furniture	Office Equipment		Accounts Payable		Mark Nero, Capital	Income Summary

Most businesses, however, have many more accounts. For example, the Globe Travel Agency has only one Accounts Receivable account, even though more than one customer could have purchased its services on credit. Likewise, the Globe Travel Agency has only one Accounts Payable account, even though it could have purchased things on credit from more than one business. Most businesses want a separate account for each person who owes it money and for each creditor to whom it owes money. Businesses also have many other asset accounts and liability accounts; for example, Delivery Equipment and Loans Payable.

Also, an Income Summary account was used in the equation for the Globe Travel Agency. But most managers and owners want to know more than the amount of net income. They want to know the revenue earned and the expenses incurred. Managers and owners also want to know what *types* of expenses are incurred. To provide this information, a separate account is set up for each revenue and each expense item. Since the Globe Travel Agency has revenue from only service sales, it can use one revenue account—Sales. However, at least two expense accounts—Repairs Expense and Salaries Expense—should be used.

It is awkward to use many accounts in an equation. As a result, a different set of accounts is generally used in accounting records.

T Accounts

A **T account** is the simplest form of an account with two sides. It looks like a large T, as shown in the margin. All increases to the account are written on one side. All decreases to the account are written on the opposite side.

A T account has four parts.

1 Account title and usually an account number
2 Debit, or left, side
3 Credit, or right, side
4 Account balance (can be either a debit or a credit balance)

The T account does the following:

- It keeps a record of each transaction by account title.
- It separates the increases and decreases to the account balance.
- It stores the amounts for future use.
- It shows the account balance.

There is one important difference between the one-column account and the T account. The T account separates the increases and decreases to the account. The one-column account does not.

A separate T account is set up for each account in the accounting equation. Thus a T account is set up for each asset, each liability, and each owner's equity account.

Account Title and Number. Each T account is given a title that clearly identifies that account. The **account title** is the specific name of the account. Examples are Cash; Furniture; or Mark Nero, Capital. The account title is written on the top line of the T account, as shown in the margin.

In addition to a title, accounts are usually assigned account numbers. The **account number** is the specific number assigned to an account. The account number is a code. **Coding** is a means of abbreviating (shortening) data. The numbers are used to code accounts so that it is easier and quicker to locate a specific account. For example, the Cash account can be assigned an account number, such as 101. It would be easier to find account number 101 than it would be to look randomly through a group of accounts. The account number is written at the right along the top line of the T account. This is also shown in the margin.

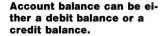

T account separates increases and decreases to an account.

1		Account Title	Account Number	3
2	Debit side (left)		Credit side (right)	
4	Debit Balance	or	Credit Balance	4

Account balance can be either a debit balance or a credit balance.

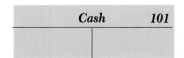

Cash 101

Account title is written in the center. Account number is written at right.

Plan for a Chart of Accounts

Account	Number
Asset accounts	101 through 199
Liability accounts	201 through 299
Owner's Equity accounts	301 through 399
Revenue accounts	401 through 499
Expense accounts	501 through 599

Globe Travel Agency Chart of Accounts

Assets
101 Cash
102 Accts. Rec./Karen Louis
103 Accts. Rec./Rose Shops
111 Furniture
112 Office Equipment

Liabilities
201 Accts. Pay./Bell Products
202 Accts. Pay./Royal Service Shop

Owner's Equity
301 Mark Nero, Capital
399 Income Summary

Revenue
401 Sales

Expenses
501 Repairs Expense
502 Salaries Expense

Debit side (Dr.)	Credit side (Cr.)
200	50

The $200 is a debit. The $50 is a credit.

Account numbers are assigned to each account according to a chart of accounts. A **chart of accounts** is a listing of all account titles and numbers used by a certain business. The account numbers and titles identify the accounts as asset, liability, or owner's equity accounts. The Globe Travel Agency uses a three-digit plan for numbering its accounts. The plan is shown in the margin. Other numbering plans may call for more digits, but in general, they operate the same way.

The first digit in any account number indicates the group to which that account belongs. For example, account numbers beginning with 1 designate asset accounts. The Globe Travel Agency's Cash account, an asset, was previously illustrated. Those beginning with 2 designate liability accounts, and a 3 designates owner's equity accounts. Note that revenue accounts are assigned numbers beginning with 4, and expense accounts are assigned numbers beginning with 5. Revenue and expense accounts are temporary owner's equity accounts and are given separate numbers.

The next two digits in the account number indicate the sequence of the account within its group. Refer to the chart of accounts for the Globe Travel Agency in the margin. Note that a gap has been left after the Accts. Rec./Rose Shops account. The gap from 103 to 111 will allow new Accounts Receivable accounts to be inserted. Most businesses leave gaps in the sequence of numbers assigned to accounts so that in the future new accounts can be inserted within the sequence later on.

Using alphabetic abbreviations is another form of coding. "Accts. Rec.," for example, is the abbreviation for "Accounts Receivable." "Accts. Pay." is the abbreviation for "Accounts Payable." These abbreviations also keep account titles as short as possible. Note that "Accts. Rec." comes before the name of each customer in the account title. Also, "Accts. Pay." is used before the name of each creditor.

Debit Side. The left side of a T account is always called the **debit side.** An amount on the debit side of an account is called a **debit,** or abbreviated as **Dr.** Recording data on the debit side is known as **debiting the account.** In the T account illustrated in the margin, the $200 is a debit.

Credit Side. The right side of the T account is always called the **credit side.** An amount on the credit side of an account is called a **credit,** or abbreviated as **Cr.** Recording an amount on the credit side is known as **crediting the account.** The $50 illustrated in the margin is a credit.

Account Balance. The **account balance** is the difference between the total debits and the total credits in an account. The procedures for computing the balance of a T account are shown on the next page.

Computing an Account Balance			
Account Not Showing Balance		**Account Showing Balance**	

Cash	101	Cash	101
90	50	90	50
10	20	10	20
		③ 30 ① 100	② 70
		Debit	
		④ *Balance*	

1 Total all debits ($90 + $10 = $100).
2 Total all credits ($50 + $20 = $70).
3 Subtract the smaller amount from the larger amount. The difference is the account balance ($100 − $70 = $30).
4 Show the balance on the side of the account with the larger total.

In the Cash account above, the debit total ($100) is larger than the credit total ($70). Therefore, the Cash account has a debit balance ($30). When the credit total is larger than the debit total, the account has a credit balance, as illustrated in the margin. Notice that the balance is written to the left of the totals.

The terms *debiting* and *crediting* should not be confused with *increasing* and *decreasing*. *Debiting* simply means entering an amount on the left side of an account. *Crediting* means entering an amount on the right side of an account. As you will see later, a debit will increase some accounts and will decrease others. Likewise, a credit will increase some accounts and decrease others.

Accts. Pay./Bell Products	201
50	70
10	20
60	30 90
	Credit Balance

The credit total is greater than the debit total. Thus the account has a credit balance.

Language:
Debit. In general usage, *debit* means something unfavorable or not good. This general usage has no relationship to the accounting usage. In accounting, *debit* simply means left side.

Credit. In general usage, *credit* may mean favorable or good. In accounting, as you know, *credit* has more than one meaning. As you learned earlier, *buying on credit* means that you buy goods or services, receive them, and agree to pay for them later. *Selling on credit* means that you sell goods or services, the customer receives them, and he or she will pay you for them later. In referring to an account, *credit* simply means right side.

Activity A-1. Open T accounts for the accounts listed in the chart of accounts for Globe Travel Agency shown on page 54. Write the account titles and account numbers.

EXAMPLE:	Cash	101

Activity A-2. Compute the account balances for the following T accounts. Refer to the text, margin notes, and illustrations on pages 52 to 55. An example is done below.

EXAMPLE:

Accts. Rec./Now Stores 103

100	*25*
50	
75	
200 *225*	

Dr. Balance 200 or Cr. Balance ___

Furniture 111

200	*250*
300	
500	

Accts. Pay./Glass Shop 201

200	*750*
	300
	200

Gregg Beete, Capital 301

1,000	*5,000*

Sales 401

	700
	500

Delivery Expense 501

300	
50	
75	

Rules for Debiting and Crediting

B *Are all accounts decreased on the same side?* No, some accounts are increased on the debit side. Others are increased on the credit side. The reason *why* one account is increased on the debit side and another account is increased on the credit side is based on the position of the elements in the accounting equation. Refer to the accounting equation below as you read the rules for debiting and crediting.

Assets = Liabilities + Owner's Equity

Assets appear on the left side of the equation. Liabilities and owner's equity appear on the right side of the equation. As a result, asset accounts increase and decrease differently than liabilities and owner's equity accounts. The three basic rules for debiting and crediting accounts are as follows.

- The balance of an account normally appears on the same side of the account as the element appears in the accounting equation.
- The balance of an account is *increased* on the same side of the account as the element appears in the accounting equation.
- The balance of an account is *decreased* on the opposite side of the account as the element appears in the accounting equation.

Rules for Debiting and Crediting

- To increase an asset, debit the account.
- To decrease an asset, credit the account.
- To increase a liability, credit the account.
- To decrease a liability, debit the account.
- To increase owner's equity, credit the account.
- To decrease owner's equity, debit the account.

Showing Opening Balances. All accounts begin with amounts shown on the same side of the accounts as the element appears in the accounting equation. The beginning amount is called an **opening balance.** Since assets appear on the left side of the accounting equation, the opening balance of an asset account is shown on the debit, or left, side of the account. For example, the opening balance of the Cash account shown in the margin is a debit of $90.

Liabilities and owner's equity appear on the right side of the accounting equation. Thus the opening balances of liability accounts and the owner's equity capital account are shown on the credit, or right, side of the accounts.

Increasing Accounts. An increase to an account is recorded on one side of the account only. Since assets appear on the left side of the accounting equation, any increase to the balance of an asset account is recorded on the debit, or left, side of the account. For example, a transaction occurred that increased the Cash account by $10. This increase is recorded by debiting the account for $10.

Since liabilities appear on the right side of the accounting equation, all liabilities are increased on the credit, or right, side. Thus liability accounts are increased by crediting the accounts.

Owner's equity also appears on the right side of the accounting equation. Thus owner's equity accounts are increased on the credit side.

Decreasing Accounts. A decrease to an account is recorded on the opposite side of the account as the element appears in the accounting equation. As a result, asset accounts are decreased on the credit side because that is the side opposite to where assets appear in the accounting equation. For example, a transaction occurred that decreased the Cash account by $50. This decrease is recorded in the Cash account by crediting the account.

Since liabilities appear on the right side of the equation, liability accounts are decreased on the opposite side. Thus liability accounts are decreased on the debit side. The debit side is the side opposite to that in which the liability element appears on the accounting equation.

Owner's equity also appears on the right side of the equation. Thus owner's equity is decreased by debiting the owner's equity accounts.

Showing Normal Balances. The difference between the two sides of an account is the account balance. The account balance normally appears on the same side as the element appears in the accounting equation. Thus asset accounts normally have debit balances. Liability accounts and owner's equity accounts normally have credit balances.

| Assets | = | Liabilities + Owner's Equity |
| A | = | L + OE |

Asset Accounts		Liability Accounts	
+	−	−	+
Increase on the debit side.	Decrease on the credit side.	Decrease on the debit side	Increase on the credit side.

Owner's Equity Accounts	
−	+
Decrease on the debit side.	Increase on the credit side.

The rules for debiting and crediting are based on the accounting equation.

Cash			101
Opening		Decrease	50
Balance	90	Decrease	20
Increase	10		
$30	100		70
Debit			
Balance			

Asset accounts are increased by debits and decreased by credits.

Account balance normally appears on same side as element appears in accounting equation.

| Assets | = | Liabilities + Owner's Equity |
| Debit Balance | | Credit Balance |

Activity B-1. Find the balance for each of the following T accounts. Then show the debit balance or credit balance using a form similar to the one shown in the example at the right.

EXAMPLE:
Cash 101

	Balance	
	Dr.	Cr.
	1,750	

Cash	101		Accts. Rec./Jo Lynn	102		Furniture	112		Supplies	113
1,550	30		200	250		300	300		30	
50	20		300			20			200	
200			500			100				

Truck	114		Accts. Pay./Rita Spinto	201		Roger Huber, Capital	301
3,200			10	400		20	5,680

Activity B-2. Indicate which of the following items would appear on the debit side and which would appear on the credit side of an account.
EXAMPLE: Balance of a liability account—Credit
1. Balance of an owner's equity account.

2. Increase to an asset account.
3. Decrease to an asset account.
4. Increase to a liability account.
5. Decrease to a liability account.
6. Increase to an owner's equity account.
7. Decrease to an owner's equity account.

Opening the Accounts

C *Is a separate account opened for each asset, liability, and owner's equity item?* Yes, a separate account is used for each asset, liability, and owner's equity item. The T accounts shown on the next page were opened for the Globe Travel Agency. All the data was taken from the September 1 accounting equation.

The following procedure is used to open an account.
1 Write the account title at the center and the account number at the right.
2 Enter the date and the opening balance on the same side as the account is shown in the accounting equation.

Asset accounts have debit balances.

Opening Asset Accounts. Assets appear on the left side of the accounting equation. Thus asset account balances are recorded on the debit (left) side of the T accounts. The first asset listed in the accounting equation is Cash, which has a balance of $8,000. Thus the Cash account is debited for $8,000. The second asset in the equation is Accounts Receivable. A separate account is opened for each business or individual who owes a debt. The business or individual who owes a debt is called a **debtor.** A separate account is opened for each debtor so that the amount that each owes is shown separately and can be found quickly. Karen Louis is the debtor who owes $1,000 to the Globe Travel

		Assets		=	Liabilities + Owner's Equity		
Cash	Accounts Receivable	Furniture	Office Equipment		Accounts Payable	Mark Nero, Capital	
$8,000 +	$1,000 +	$2,000 +	$9,000	=	$3,000 +	$17,000	

$20,000 = $20,000

① ② Cash   101

```
19—
Sept. 1    8,000 |
```

Accts. Rec./Karen Louis   102

```
19—
Sept. 1    1,000 |
```

Furniture   111

```
19—
Sept. 1    2,000 |
```

Office Equipment   112

```
19—
Sept. 1    9,000 |
```

Accts. Pay./Bell Products   201

```
              | 19—
              | Sept. 1    3,000
```

Mark Nero, Capital   301

```
              | 19—
              | Sept. 1    17,000
```

Assets	=	Liabilities + Owner's Equity	
$20,000	=	$3,000 +	$17,000
(Total Debits = $20,000)	=	(Total Credits = $20,000)	

Accounting equation as of September 1.

To open an account: write the title at the center and the number at right. Enter the date and the opening balance on the proper side.

The account balance appears on the same side of the account as the account appears in the accounting equation.

Agency. Therefore, an account is opened for Accts. Rec./Karen Louis. The account is debited for $1,000.

Opening Liability Accounts. Liabilities appear on the right side of the accounting equation. Thus liability account balances are recorded on the credit (right) side of the T accounts. The first liability is Accounts Payable. A separate account is opened for each creditor (business or individual to whom a debt is owed) so that the amount owed to each can be found quickly. The Accts. Pay./Bell Products account is credited for $3,000.

Liability accounts have credit balances.

Opening Owner's Equity Accounts. Owner's equity also appears on the right side of the accounting equation. Therefore, owner's equity account balances appear on the credit (right) side of the T accounts. Since the total owner's equity on September 1 is $17,000, the Mark Nero, Capital account is credited for $17,000.

Owner's equity Capital account has credit balance.

Ledger

A group of accounts is called a **ledger.** The Globe Travel Agency ledger on September 1 is made up of the six accounts shown on page 59.

The asset accounts have debit balances. The debit side of the accounts in the Globe Travel Agency ledger totals $20,000. The liability and owner's equity accounts have credit balances. The credit side of the accounts also totals $20,000. According to the accounting equation, the total debit balances (assets) in the ledger must always equal the total credit balances (liabilities and owner's equity). Thus the equality of the accounting equation is maintained in the ledger.

Activity C. Open a T account for each asset, liability, and owner's equity item listed in the following accounting equation. Enter the account title, the account number, the account balance, and the date. Refer to the chart of accounts at the right and to the accounting equation for April 1 below.

Chart of Accounts

Assets	**Liabilities**
101 Cash	201 Accts. Pay./
102 Accts. Rec./	Road Motors
Grant Mellin	
103 Accts. Rec./	**Owner's Equity**
John Olive	301 Gary Ross,
111 Truck	Capital

	Assets				=	Liabilities	+	Owner's Equity
	Cash	Accts. Rec./ Grant Mellin	Accts. Rec./ John Olive	Truck		Accts. Pay./ Road Motors		Gary Ross, Capital
April 1 balances	$900 +	$510 +	$115 +	$8,000 =		$2,000	+	$7,525

Accounting Concepts:

Ledger. Records of the changes caused by transactions should be available by account title and number. These records are kept in a *ledger*.

Equality of Ledger. A direct relationship exists between the accounts and the accounting equation. The accounts for items on the left side of the equation have debit balances. The accounts for items on the right side of the equation have credit balances. The total of the debit balances must equal the total of the credit balances, thus keeping the equality of the accounting equation in the ledger.

Accounting Principles:

Balance of an Account. The generally accepted accounting principle is that the balance of an account normally appears on the same side as the element appears in the accounting equation.

Increasing an Account Balance. The generally accepted accounting principle is that the balance of an account is increased on the same side as the element appears in the accounting equation.

Decreasing an Account Balance. The generally accepted accounting principle is that the balance of an account is decreased on the side opposite which the element appears in the accounting equation.

Topic 1 Problems

3-1. Open a T account for each asset, liability, and owner's equity account listed in the chart of accounts at the right. Enter the account title, the account number, the date, and the account balance. If there is no account balance, do not record the date or an amount. Check that the total debit balances equal the total credit balances in the ledger. Refer to the accounting equation below.

Chart of Accounts

Assets	Revenue
101 Cash	401 Sales
102 Accts. Rec./Judy Holt	
	Expenses
Liabilities	501 Rent Expense
201 Accts. Pay./Alan Park	

Owner's Equity
301 Eric Kohr, Capital
399 Income Summary

Assets			=	Liabilities	+	Owner's Equity		
Cash		Accts. Rec./Judy Holt		Accts. Pay./Alan Park		Eric Kohr, Capital		Income Summary (Revenue − Expense)
$3,260	+	$120	=	$190	+	$3,190	+	-0-

Aug. 1 balances

3-2. Open a T account for each asset, liability, and owner's equity item for the following accounts. Use appropriate account numbers according to the chart of accounts at the right. Check that the total debit balances equal the total credit balances. The May 1 balances are as follows:

Accts. Pay./West Corporation	.$ 7,000
Cash	4,750
Shop Equipment	17,000
Walter Yielman, Capital	14,750
Repairs Expense	-0-
Sales	-0-
Income Summary	-0-

Chart of Accounts

Assets	Revenue
101 Cash	401 Sales
111 Shop Equipment	
	Expenses
Liabilities	501 Repairs Expense
201 Accts. Pay./ West Corporation	

Owner's Equity
301 Walter Yielman, Capital
399 Income Summary

Topic 2
Debiting and Crediting Permanent Accounts

A *Must all transactions be recorded in accounts?* Yes, the accounts must show all the increases and decreases that occur from transactions. For example, the Cash account is used to keep a record of the money a business has available. All transactions that change the amount of money available must be shown in this account so that it will always provide current data. Thus whenever cash items are received, the increase in cash must be shown in the Cash account. Whenever cash is paid out, the decrease in cash must also be shown in the Cash account.

Double-Entry Accounting

Remember that business transactions are financial events that cause the amounts in the accounting equation to change. Transactions occur whenever a business uses or exchanges something of monetary value. The accounting system used to record the effects of transactions is based on the double-entry accounting principle.

Double-entry accounting requires debit total to equal credit total for each transaction.

Double-entry accounting means that each financial transaction has a double effect. That is, each transaction affects two or more accounts and is recorded so that the total of the debit amounts is always equal to the total of the credit amounts.

The theory behind double-entry accounting was first published by Luca Paciolo in 1494. What he wrote almost 500 years ago is the basis for the double-entry accounting followed today in both manual and automated accounting systems.

Accountants follow three basic rules of the double-entry theory to analyze all transactions. (You learned these rules in Chapter 2.) The first rule of double-entry accounting is:

- Each transaction must affect at least two accounts.

For example, on September 5 the Globe Travel Agency buys additional office equipment for $4,000 in cash. Cash is exchanged for office equipment. In this transaction, two accounts—Cash and Office Equipment—are affected. The asset Office Equipment increases and the asset Cash decreases.

The second rule of double-entry accounting is:

- The effect of each transaction must be stated in dollar amounts.

Transaction	Analysis
September 5: The Globe Travel Agency buys additional office equipment from the Eagle Office Corporation and gives a check for $4,000 in payment.	• The asset *Office Equipment* increases by $4,000 because the business now owns more office equipment. • The asset *Cash* decreases by $4,000 because the business now has less money.

	Assets				=	Liabilities	+	Owner's Equity
	Cash	Accounts Receivable	Furniture	Office Equipment		Accounts Payable		Mark Nero, Capital
Previous balance								
Effect of transaction	$8,000	+ $1,000	+ $2,000	+ $ 9,000	=	$3,000	+	$17,000
	−4,000			+4,000				
New balance	$4,000	+ $1,000	+ $2,000	+ $13,000	=	$3,000	+	$17,000
Equality of equation			$20,000		=		$20,000	

When an asset is bought, the amount of money transacted is the agreed-upon price between the buyer and seller. In the September 5 transaction illustrated on page 62, the agreed-upon price for the office equipment is $4,000. Thus the Globe Travel Agency (the buyer) records the office equipment at $4,000. The Eagle Office Corporation (the seller) also records the sale at $4,000.

The third rule of double-entry accounting is:

• The accounting equation must be in balance after each transaction is recorded. The total debit amounts in each transaction must be equal to the total credit amounts.

The September 5 transaction affected the Cash account and the Office Equipment account. Each account changed by $4,000. As you will see, one of the accounts will be debited and the other will be credited. As a result, the total debit ($4,000) will be equal to the total credit ($4,000). The equation will still be equal after the transaction is recorded.

The accounting equation must remain in balance, and so each transaction has a double effect—a debit and a credit—which is the basis for double-entry accounting.

Activity A. Decide whether the account is increased or decreased in each of the following.
EXAMPLE: The Cash account is debited— Increased
1. Accts. Pay./Peter Moore is credited.
2. Mortgage Payable account is credited.
3. Accts. Rec./Helen Peters is debited.
4. Accts. Pay./Olson Supplies is debited.
5. Capital account is credited.
6. Equipment account is credited.
7. Mortgage Payable account is debited.
8. Furniture account is credited.

Analyzing Business Transactions

B *What is a good way to analyze business transactions?* An accountant studies each business transaction to determine what happens, which accounting rules apply to what happened, and what accounting entry is to be made. The following questions will help you to analyze the changes caused by a transaction.

• *What happens?* For each business transaction, name all accounts affected, classify the accounts, determine whether the accounts are increased or decreased, and determine what the amounts are.
• *Which accounting rules apply?* Apply the accounting rules of debiting and crediting to each part of the transaction. Use the summary of accounting rules for increasing and decreasing accounts shown in the margin.
• *What entry is to be made?* State the business transaction as an

Accounting Rules

Assets:	Debits increase
	Credits decrease
Liabilities:	Credits increase
	Debits decrease
Owner's Equity:	Credits increase
	Debits decrease

accounting entry. An **accounting entry** is (1) the date of the transaction, (2) the debit account title and the amount, and (3) the credit account title and the amount. The debit part of the entry is always stated before the credit part.

Assume that the Globe Travel Agency buys additional office equipment for $4,000 in cash. "What happens?" would be answered as follows. The asset *Office Equipment increases* by $4,000, and the asset *Cash decreases* by $4,000.

The accounting rules that apply to this transaction are the following. *To increase an asset, debit the account. To decrease an asset, credit the account.* Thus the accounting entry is this: Debit the *Office Equipment* account for $4,000, and credit the *Cash* account for $4,000.

Activity B. Analyze the following transactions in a sentence form. Use the example as a guide.
EXAMPLE: The Harbold Company received $500 from Keith Shoes on account.

The asset account Cash is increased; therefore, it is debited for $500. The asset account Accts. Rec./Keith Shoes is decreased; therefore, it is credited for $500.

1. Pet World Lovers Company bought additional equipment for $300 on credit from Pet Store Suppliers.
2. Cohen and McDonald Law Partners returned office furniture bought for $200 on credit from Benski's Furniture.
3. Janice Bovard invested an additional $3,000 in her single proprietorship, Bovard's Boutique.

Recording Changes in Asset Accounts

C *How are changes in asset accounts recorded?* To answer this question, we will enter the September transactions of the Globe Travel Agency in the T accounts already opened. The beginning balances were taken from the accounting equation of September 1. Each transaction will be analyzed to show the following.

• Which asset account is increased or decreased.
• Which rules of debiting and crediting apply to these increases or decreases.
• What the accounting entry should be.

The following transactions illustrate the accounting rules for increasing and decreasing asset accounts.

The Globe Travel Agency buys additional office equipment from the Eagle Office Corporation and issues a check for $4,000 in payment.

The asset account Office Equipment is increased. Therefore, it is debited for $4,000. The asset account Cash is decreased. Therefore, it is credited for $4,000.

September 5: The Globe Travel Agency buys additional office equipment for $4,000 in cash.

What Happens	Accounting Rule	Accounting Entry
The asset *Office Equipment* increases by $4,000.	To increase an asset, debit the account.	Debit: Office Equipment, $4,000
The asset *Cash* decreases by $4,000.	To decrease an asset, credit the account.	Credit: Cash, $4,000

Cash		101		Office Equipment		112
19— Sept. 1	8,000	19— Sept. 5	4,000	19— Sept. 1	9,000	
				5	4,000	

Buying assets for cash.

The Globe Travel Agency receives a check for $1,000 from Karen Louis on account. The asset account Cash is increased. Therefore, it is debited for $1,000. The asset account Accts. Rec./Karen Louis is decreased. Therefore, it is credited for $1,000.

September 6: The Globe Travel Agency receives $1,000 from Karen Louis on account.

What Happens	Accounting Rule	Accounting Entry
The asset *Cash* increases by $1,000.	To increase an asset, debit the account.	Debit: Cash, $1,000
The asset Accts. Rec./Karen Louis decreases by $1,000.	To decrease an asset, credit the account.	Credit: Accts. Rec./ Karen Louis, $1,000

Cash		101		Accts. Rec./Karen Louis		102
19— Sept. 1	8,000	19— Sept. 5	4,000	19— Sept. 1	1,000	19— Sept. 6	1,000
6	1,000					

Collecting an account receivable.

Activity C-1. For each of the transactions on page 66, determine: (1) what happens to the basic elements, (2) which accounting rule of debiting or crediting applies, and (3) what accounts should be debited and credited. Use the signs A+ to indicate increases and A— to indicate decreases in the asset accounts.

EXAMPLE: *Received $460 in cash from a customer on account.*

1. Bought a typewriter for $700 in cash.
2. Returned tools bought for $40 in cash.
3. Received $125 from a customer on account.
4. Received $15 from sale of an asset, equipment.
5. Bought tools for $500 in cash.
NOTE: Save your form for further use in Activity D-1.

What Happens	Accounting Rule		Accounting Entry	
	Debit	Credit	Account Debited	Account Credited
Example A+	✓		Cash	
A−		✓		Accounts Receivable

Activity C-2. Analyze each of the following transactions. Then record the debit amount and the credit amount in the appropriate T accounts.
EXAMPLE: *Bought supplies for $20 in cash.*

1. Bought office equipment for $400 in cash.
2. Received $75 from Harry Peer on account.
3. Bought shop equipment for $200 in cash.
4. Returned shop equipment for $100 in cash.

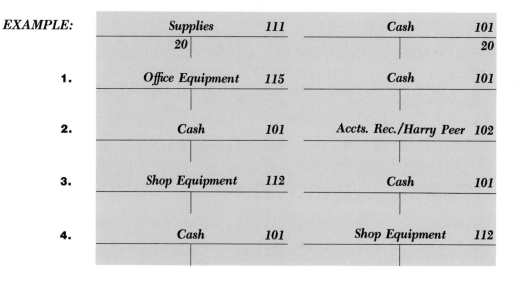

EXAMPLE:

| *Supplies* | 111 | | *Cash* | 101 |
| 20 | | | | 20 |

1.

| *Office Equipment* | 115 | | *Cash* | 101 |

2.

| *Cash* | 101 | | *Accts. Rec./Harry Peer* | 102 |

3.

| *Shop Equipment* | 112 | | *Cash* | 101 |

4.

| *Cash* | 101 | | *Shop Equipment* | 112 |

Recording Changes in Liability Accounts

D *How are changes in liability accounts recorded?* The steps used to record changes in liability accounts are the same as those for making changes in asset accounts. The rules for increasing and decreasing liability accounts, however, differ from those used for changing asset accounts. Remember that liability accounts increase on the credit side and decrease on the debit side.

The Globe Travel Agency buys additional furniture for $1,500 on credit from Bell Products. The asset Furniture account is increased. Therefore, it is debited for $1,500. The liability Accts. Pay./Bell Products account is also increased. Therefore, it is credited for $1,500.

September 7: The Globe Travel Agency buys additional furniture for $1,500 on credit from Bell Products.

What Happens	Accounting Rule	Accounting Entry
The asset *Furniture* increases by $1,500.	To increase an asset, debit the account.	Debit: Furniture, $1,500
The liability *Accts. Pay./Bell Products* increases by $1,500.	To increase a liability, credit the account.	Credit: Accts. Pay./Bell Products, $1,500

Furniture	111		Accts. Pay./Bell Products	201
19—			19—	
Sept. 1 2,000			Sept. 1 3,000	
7 1,500			7 1,500	

Buying assets on credit.

On September 8 the Globe Travel Agency returns furniture (one cabinet) to Bell Products because the cabinet arrived damaged. Bell Products gives the Globe Travel Agency $500 credit. The liability Accts. Pay./Bell Products account is decreased. Therefore, it is debited for $500. The asset Furniture account is decreased. Therefore, it is credited for $500.

September 8: The Globe Travel Agency returns furniture bought for $500 on credit from Bell Products.

What Happens	Accounting Rule	Accounting Entry
The liability *Accts. Pay./Bell Products* decreases by $500.	To decrease a liability, debit the account.	Debit: Accts. Pay./Bell Products, $500
The asset *Furniture* decreases by $500.	To decrease an asset, credit the account.	Credit: Furniture, $500

Furniture	111		Accts. Pay./Bell Products	201
19— 2,000	19—		19— 500	19—
Sept. 1 2,000	Sept. 8 500		Sept. 8 500	Sept. 1 3,000
7 1,500				7 1,500

Returning assets bought on credit.

The transaction for September 12 illustrates the rule for decreasing a liability account when a liability is paid. On September 12 the Globe Travel Agency writes a check for $3,000 to Bell Products on account.

September 12: The Globe Travel Agency pays $3,000 to Bell Products on account.

What Happens	Accounting Rule	Accounting Entry
The liability *Accts. Pay./ Bell Products* decreases by $3,000.	To decrease a liability, debit the account.	Debit: Accts. Pay./Bell Products, $3,000
The asset *Cash* decreases by $3,000.	To decrease an asset, credit the account.	Credit: Cash, $3,000

	Cash		101		Accts. Pay./Bell Products		201
19—		19—		19—		19—	
Sept. 1	8,000	Sept. 5	4,000	Sept. 8	500	Sept. 1	3,000
6	1,000	12	3,000	12	3,000	7	1,500

Paying liabilities.

The liability Accts. Pay./Bell Products account is decreased. Therefore, it is debited for $3,000. The asset account Cash is decreased. Therefore, it is credited for $3,000.

This topic has explained how changes are recorded for two types of permanent accounts—assets and liabilities. In Topic 3, you will see how changes are recorded for owner's equity accounts—the permanent Capital account and the temporary revenue and expense accounts.

Activity D-1. Use your form from Activity C-1 to analyze the following transactions. For each transaction, determine (1) what happens to the basic elements, (2) which accounting rule of debiting or crediting applies, and (3) what accounts should be debited and credited. Use the signs A+, A−, L+, and L− to indicate increases and decreases in the asset and liability accounts.

6. Bought tools for $100 on credit.
7. Returned tools bought for $50 on credit.
8. Bought tools for $50 in cash.
9. Bought supplies for $35 on credit.
10. Paid $80 to a creditor on account.

Activity D-2. Set up two T accounts for each of the following transactions. Give an appropriate title and account number to each account. Then record the amount on the correct side of each account.
EXAMPLE: Bought equipment for $150 on credit from the Manor Company.

EXAMPLE:

Equipment 111		Accts. Pay./Manor Company 201	
150			150

1. Bought equipment for $500 in cash.
2. Returned equipment bought for $80 in cash.
3. Returned equipment bought for $90 on credit from Manor Company.
4. Paid $200 to the Manor Company on account.
5. Bought supplies for $45 on credit from Astro Supplies.
6. Received $75 from the Niles Bakery on account.
7. Borrowed $5,000 from Federal Savings Bank as a loan to be paid in 90 days.
8. Bought adding machine for office for $150 on credit. Gave a note to Best Office Machine Company.
9. Bought land for $9,000 on credit and gave mortgage to Bank One Savings.
10. Bought a chair for $150 in cash.
HINT: Transactions 7 to 9 involve expanding on the concepts you learned in this topic.

Accounting Concept:
Analyzing Transactions. Each transaction affects at least two accounts, is stated in dollar amounts, and has total debit amounts equaling the total credit amounts.

Accounting Principle:
Double-entry Accounting. The generally accepted accounting principle is that the dollar results of each financial transaction are recorded in the form of a double entry.

Topic 2 Problems

3-3. Set up two T accounts for each of the following transactions. Give an appropriate title and number to each account, and record the amount on the correct side of each account.
a. Received $800 from Ruth Zota on account.
b. Bought a second-hand truck for $3,000 on credit from the City Motors.
c. Bought a desk and chair for $400 on credit from the Desk Makers Company.
d. Paid $600 to City Motors on account.
e. Bought two tables for $200 cash.
f. Received $300 from Nancy Rossi on account.
g. Returned the chair bought for $50 on credit from the Desk Makers Company.
h. Paid $50 to the Desk Makers Company on account.

3-4. The T accounts below show the results of seven transactions for Daniel Evans' business. Explain what happened in transactions **a, b, c, d, e, f,** and **g.** The debit and credit entries for a transaction are identified by the same letter. The first transaction is done as an example. Refer to the T accounts below.

EXAMPLE: a. Daniel Evans started a business with an investment of $5,500 in cash, $700 in accounts receivable, $6,000 in equipment, and $400 in accounts payable.

	Cash		101		Accts. Rec./ Peter Christoff		102		Supplies		103
a.	5,500	c.	800	a.	700	g.	700	c.	800	e.	200
e.	200	d.	400								
g.	700	f.	500								

	Equipment		111		Accts. Pay./Ann Fields		201		Accts. Pay./Alert Stores		202
a.	6,000			d.	400	a.	400	f.	500	b.	2,000
b.	2,000										

	Daniel Evans, Capital		301
		a.	11,800

3-5. Set up two T accounts for each of the transactions below. Give an appropriate title and account number to each account. Then record the amount on the correct side of each account.

a. Borrowed $1,500 from First Savings Bank as a loan to be paid in 90 days.

b. Bought adding machine for office for $375 on credit. Gave a note to Crown Office Machines promising to pay in 30 days.

c. Paid $500 to First Savings Bank as part payment of its loan.

d. Paid $10,000 to Trust Savings in full payment of mortgage.

HINT: Transactions a and d involve expanding on the concepts you learned in this topic.

3-6. Set up two T accounts for each of the transactions below. Set up all accounts to be debited in Column A. Set up all accounts to be credited in Column B. Give an appropriate title and account number to each account. Then record the amount on the correct side of each account.

a. Bought truck for $5,000 in cash.

b. Borrowed $9,000 from Mutual Savings Bank as a loan.

c. Paid $300 to Star Supplies on account.

d. Received $150 from Mayes Company on account.

e. Paid $350 to James Martlow on account.

f. Returned shop equipment bought for $300 on credit from Star Supplies.

g. Bought shop equipment for $800 in cash.

h. Returned tools bought for $25 in cash.

i. Paid $1,000 on loan.

j. Bought supplies for $150 on credit from Lenox Co.

k. Returned shop equipment bought for $350 cash.

l. Bought shop equipment for $900 on credit from Elmer Storage Company.

m. Paid $150 to Lundberg Sons on account.

n. Bought tools for $425 on credit from Makita Tool Company.

HINT: Transactions b and i involve expanding on concepts you learned in this topic.

Topic 3
Debiting and Crediting Temporary Accounts

A *Which accounts are used to record changes in owner's equity?* The capital, revenue, and expense accounts are used. The permanent Capital account is used when the owner makes additional investments or withdrawals. The temporary revenue accounts are used when the business obtains revenue. The temporary expense accounts are used when the business incurs expenses. In all cases, two basic rules govern the increases and decreases in owner's equity.

Mark Nero, Capital	301
Record withdrawals on the debit side.	Record investments on the credit side.

• To increase owner's equity, credit the account. Additional investments and revenues increase owner's equity. Therefore, credit the Capital account when investments are made, and credit the revenue accounts when revenue is earned.

• To decrease owner's equity, debit the account. Withdrawals of investment and incurring expenses decrease owner's equity. Therefore, debit the Capital account when investments are withdrawn, and debit the expense accounts when expenses are incurred.

Recording Changes in the Capital Account

The Capital account shows the owner's investment in the business. This account balance increases when the owner makes an additional investment. The Capital account decreases when the owner withdraws an asset, such as cash or equipment. The Mark Nero, Capital account had a balance of $17,000 on September 1. During September the following transactions caused changes in the Capital account.

On September 14 Mark Nero invested more money in the Globe Travel Agency. The asset Cash account is increased. Therefore, the Cash account is debited for $13,000. Owner's equity is also increased. Thus, the Mark Nero, Capital account is credited for $13,000.

September 14: Mark Nero invests an additional $13,000 in the Globe Travel Agency.

What Happens	Accounting Rule	Accounting Entry
The asset *Cash* increases by $13,000.	To increase an asset, debit the account.	Debit: Cash, $13,000
The owner's equity *Mark Nero, Capital* increases by $13,000.	To increase owner's equity, credit the account.	Credit: Mark Nero, Capital, $13,000

Cash			101	Mark Nero, Capital			301
19—		19—				19—	
Sept. 1	8,000	Sept. 5	4,000			Sept. 1	17,000
6	1,000	12	3,000			14	13,000
14	13,000						

Increasing owner's investment.

On September 21 Mark Nero decides to withdraw money from the Globe Travel Agency. Owner's equity is decreased. Therefore, the Mark Nero, Capital account is debited for $5,000. The asset Cash also decreases. Thus, the Cash account is credited for $5,000.

September 21: Mark Nero withdraws $5,000 from the Globe Travel Agency.

What Happens	Accounting Rule	Accounting Entry
The owner's equity *Mark Nero, Capital* decreases by $5,000.	To decrease owner's equity, debit the account.	Debit: Mark Nero, Capital, $5,000
The asset *Cash* decreases by $5,000.	To decrease an asset, credit the account.	Credit: Cash, $5,000

Cash			101	Mark Nero, Capital			301
19—		19—		19—		19—	
Sept. 1	8,000	Sept. 5	4,000	Sept. 21	5,000	Sept. 1	17,000
6	1,000	12	3,000			14	13,000
14	13,000	21	5,000				

Decreasing owner's investment.

Activity A. The T accounts below show the results of six transactions for Swatek's Accounting Service. Indicate whether each transaction increases or decreases the accounts. Then explain what happened in each transaction.

EXAMPLE:

EXAMPLE: 1. *Cash account increases. Jane Swatek, Capital account increases. Jane Swatek started the business with an investment of $6,000 in cash.*

	Cash		101
1.	6,000	2.	2,000
5.	8,000	6.	600

	Office Equipment		102
3.	800	4.	200

	Jane Swatek, Capital		301
2.	2,000	1.	6,000
4.	200	3.	800
6.	600	5.	8,000

Recording Changes in Revenue Accounts

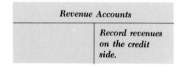

Revenue Accounts	
	Record revenues on the credit side.

To increase owner's equity, credit the account.

B *What transactions increase owner's equity?* Owner's equity increases when the owner makes an additional investment and when revenue is received. Most businesses obtain their revenue from sales of goods or services.

The amount of a sale is recorded in a revenue account called Sales. Since revenue increases owner's equity, the Sales account is credited for the amount of the sale. The Globe Travel Agency sold services for cash and on credit during the September accounting period.

On September 26 the Globe Travel Agency received $2,000 cash as revenue from the sale of travel services during September. The asset Cash increases. Therefore, the Cash account is debited for $2,000. The revenue also increases owner's equity. Therefore, the owner's equity Sales account is credited for $2,000.

September 26: The Globe Travel Agency receives $2,000 in cash from the sale of services during September.

What Happens	Accounting Rule	Accounting Entry
The asset *Cash* increases by $2,000.	To increase an asset, debit the account.	Debit: Cash, $2,000
The revenue *Sales* increases owner's equity by $2,000.	To increase owner's equity, credit the account.	Credit: Sales, $2,000

	Cash		101
19—		19—	
Sept. 1	8,000	Sept. 5	4,000
6	1,000	12	3,000
14	13,000	21	5,000
26	2,000		

	Sales	401
	19—	
	Sept. 26	2,000

Receiving revenue from cash sales.

In the transaction for September 27, sales are made on credit to two customers. As a result, two accounts receivable accounts are affected—an account for Karen Louis and an account for Rose Shops.

The asset Accts. Rec./Karen Louis account is debited for $1,000. The asset Accts. Rec./Rose Shops account is also debited for $700. The owner's equity Sales account is credited for $1,700. Although this transaction involves two debits ($1,000 + $700) and one credit ($1,700), the total of the debits equals the total of the credits. Any transaction involving more than one debit or more than one credit is called a **compound transaction.**

September 27: The Globe Travel Agency sells services on credit to Karen Louis for $1,000 and to Rose Shops for $700.

What Happens	Accounting Rule	Accounting Entry	
The asset *Accts. Rec./ Karen Louis* increases by $1,000, and the asset *Accts. Rec./ Rose Shops* increases by $700.	To increase an asset, debit the account.	Debit: Accts. Rec./Karen Louis, $1,000 Accts. Rec./Rose Shops, $700	
The revenue *Sales* increases owner's equity by $1,700.	To increase owner's equity, credit the account.	Credit: Sales, $1,700	**Receiving revenue from sales on credit.**

Accts. Rec./Karen Louis	102			Accts. Rec./Rose Shops	103		Sales	401
19—		19—		19—			19—	
Sept. 1	1,000	Sept. 6	1,000	Sept. 27	700		Sept. 26	2,000
27	1,000						27	1,700

Activity B-1. For each of the transactions below, determine (1) what happens to the basic elements, (2) which accounting rule of debiting or crediting applies, and (3) what accounts should be debited and credited. Use the signs A+, A−, L+, L−, OE+, and OE− to indicate increases or decreases in the accounts. Use a form like the one shown at the right.
EXAMPLE: Edward Martino started the business with $6,000 in cash.
1. Received $200 from the sale of services.
2. Edward Martino withdrew $100 from the business.
3. Sold services for $500 on credit to Larry McDale.
4. Bought tools for $80 in cash.
5. Received $20 from sale of services.
6. Edward Martino invested an additional $3,000 in the business.
7. Sold services for $700 on credit to Otto Stein.
8. Received $200 from Larry McDale on account.

What Happens	Accounting Rule		Accounting Entry	
	Debit	Credit	Account Debited	Account Credited
A+	√		Cash	
OE+		√		Edward Martino, Capital

9. Sold services for $400 on credit to the Viking Company.
10. Received $10 from sale of tools.
11. Edward Martino withdrew $500 from the business.
NOTE: Save your form for further use in Activity C.

Activity B-2. Analyze each of the following transactions. Then record the debit amount and the credit amount in the appropriate T accounts.

EXAMPLE: Anna Saltzwick started the business with $27,000 in cash.

Cash 101	Anna Saltzwick, Capital 301
27,000	27,000

1. Sold services for $380 in cash.

1.	Cash 101	Sales 401

2. Sold services for $350 on credit to Thomas Albaugh.

2.	Accts. Rec./Thomas Albaugh 102	Sales 401

3. Owner withdrew $200 from the business for her personal use.

3.	Anna Saltzwick, Capital 301	Cash 101

4. Owner invested another $2,500 in the business.

4.	Cash 101	Anna Saltzwick, Capital 301

5. Sold services for $480 on credit to Max Mueller.

5.	Accts. Rec./ Max Mueller 104	Sales 401

6. Bought office equipment for $275 cash.

6.	Office Equipment 111	Cash 101

7. Received $280 from Thomas Albaugh on account.

7.	Cash 101	Accts. Rec./Thomas Albaugh 102

8. Owner withdrew $30 of office equipment from the business.

8.	Anna Saltzwick, Capital 301	Office Equipment 111

Recording Changes in Expense Accounts

Expense Accounts	
Record expenses on the debit side.	

To decrease owner's equity, debit the account.

C *What transactions decrease owner's equity?* Owner's equity decreases when the owner makes a withdrawal of an asset for his or her personal use. Owner's equity also decreases when expenses are incurred to operate the business. A business normally has many different types of expenses, such as rent, salaries, and utilities. A separate account is usually opened for each kind of expense. Since an expense decreases owner's equity, the amount is recorded as a debit to the expense account. Expenses can either be paid in cash or they can be paid on credit.

The first transaction illustrates an expense paid with cash. The second transaction illustrates an expense incurred on credit.

On September 28 the Globe Travel Agency paid salaries to its employees. The salaries are an expense of $2,100 to the business. The expense decreases owner's equity. As a result, the Salaries Expense account is debited for $2,100, thus decreasing owner's equity. The asset Cash account is also decreased. Therefore, the Cash account is credited for $2,100. The effect of this transaction is shown in the table at the top of the next page.

September 28: The Globe Travel Agency pays an expense of $2,100 for salaries.

What Happens	Accounting Rule	Accounting Entry
The expense *Salaries Expense* decreases owner's equity by $2,100.	To decrease owner's equity, debit the account.	Debit: Salaries Expense, $2,100
The asset *Cash* decreases by $2,100.	To decrease an asset, credit the account.	Credit: Cash, $2,100

Cash		101		Salaries Expense		502
19—		19—		19—		
Sept. 1	8,000	Sept. 5	4,000	Sept. 28	2,100	
6	1,000	12	3,000			
14	13,000	21	5,000			
26	2,000	28	2,100			

Paying expenses.

On September 29 the Globe Travel Agency receives a bill for $200 from the Royal Service Shop for repairing a copying machine. The Repairs Expense account is debited for $200, thus decreasing owner's equity. The liability Accts. Pay./Royal Service Shop account is credited for $200, thus increasing liabilities.

September 29: The Globe Travel Agency owes a repairs expense of $200 to the Royal Service Shop for repairing a copying machine.

What Happens	Accounting Rule	Accounting Entry
The expense *Repairs Expense* decreases owner's equity by $200.	To decrease owner's equity, debit the account.	Debit: Repairs Expense, $200
The liability *Accts. Pay./Royal Service Shop* increases by $200.	To increase a liability, credit the account.	Credit: Accts. Pay./Royal Service Shop, $200

Accts. Pay./ Royal Service Shop	202		Repairs Expense		501
	19—		19—		
	Sept. 29	200	Sept. 29	200	

Incurring expenses on credit.

Activity C. Analyze the following transactions, using your form from Activity B-1. For each transaction, determine (1) what happens to the basic elements, (2) which accounting rule of debiting or crediting applies, and (3) what accounts should be debited and credited. Use A+, A−, L+, L−, OE+, and OE− to indicate increases and decreases.

12. Paid $200 for rent.
13. Sold services for $300 on credit to Jane Starr.
14. Paid $50 for telephone expense.

15. Edward Martino withdrew $225 from the business.

16. Owes $40 to Lane Station for gasoline.

17. Received $75 from sale of services.

Accounting Concept:
Owner's Equity Accounts. Owner's equity is divided into three kinds of accounts—capital, revenue, and expense.

Topic 3 Problems

3-7. Set up two T accounts for each of the following transactions. Give an appropriate title and number to each account. Record the amount on the correct side of each account.

EXAMPLE: Henry Webb started a business with $4,500 in cash.

Cash	101		Henry Webb, Capital	301
4,500				4,500

a. Bought equipment for $2,000 on credit from Sunshine Cabinets.

b. Sold services for $560 on credit to Nina Westin.

c. Henry Webb withdrew $900 from the business for his personal use.

d. Returned equipment bought for $400 on credit from Sunshine Cabinets.

e. Received $375 from Nina Westin on account.

f. Paid $250 for rent.

g. Sold services for $450 in cash.

h. Paid $250 to Sunshine Cabinets on account.

i. Sold services for $700 on credit to Augusto Smith.

j. Paid $45 for utilities.

k. Henry Webb invested an additional $1,000 in the business.

l. Bought additional equipment for $150 in cash.

3-8. Earl Teague bought the National Detective Agency on April 1. Complete the following accounting activities for the business.

a. Open the following T accounts: Cash; Accts. Rec./Coy Stores; Automobile; Office Fixtures; Accts. Pay./Superior Auto; Earl Teague, Capital; Fees; Automobile Expense; and Rent Expense.

b. Record the transactions for April 1–3 in the appropriate T accounts. Enter both the date and the amount of each transaction.

c. Prepare an accounting equation on April 3 from the data in the T accounts.

d. Record the remaining transactions for April in the T accounts. Enter both the date and the amount of each transaction.

e. Determine the balance of each T account. Indicate whether each balance is a debit balance or a credit balance.

f. Prepare an accounting equation for April 30.

April	1	Earl Teague bought the following asset of the National Detective Agency: Office Fixtures, $18,000.
	2	Earl Teague invested an additional $5,000 in the business.
	3	Bought an automobile for $8,000 on credit from Superior Auto.
	4	Sold services for $5,000 on credit to Coy Stores.
	5	Paid $455 for rent.
	10	Paid $3,000 to Superior Auto on account.
	15	Sold services for $1,500 in cash.
	18	Received $300 from Coy Stores on account.
	18	Bought an office lamp for $85 in cash.
	24	Owes $30 to Superior Auto for gasoline expense.
	28	Sold services for a fee of $1,800 in cash.
	29	Earl Teague withdrew $2,000 from the business for his personal use.

Topic 4
Proving the Ledger

A *Is there a way to check that the ledger is in balance after the transactions are recorded?* Yes. One way is to make sure that for each transaction, the total debits equal the total credits. Then at regular intervals make a proof to show that the total debit balances in the ledger equal the total credit balances. (The term *proof* means a test to show that something is true.) The proof that the ledger is in balance is called a **trial balance.**

Computing Account Balances

Before a trial balance can be prepared, the balance of each account must be determined. As you recall from Topic 1, an account balance is the difference between the total debits and the total credits in an account.

If entries appear on both sides of the account, draw a single rule under the last amount in the column with the most entries. Then draw a single rule directly across in the other column. Enter the totals of each column below the single rule. Then record the account balance to the left of the total in the column with the larger total. See the Cash account on page 78.

If all the entries are on one side of the account, draw a rule and record the total. Also, draw a rule directly across in the other column and enter a zero below the rule. Write the balance, which is the same as the total, in the appropriate column. (See the Office Equipment account and the Sales account on page 78.)

If an account has only one entry, no total needs to be written because the amount of the entry is the total and also the account balance. (See the Accts. Rec./Rose Shops account on page 78.)

As you recall, each type of account usually has a "normal" balance. For example, an asset account, such as Office Equipment, should have a debit balance. Likewise, a liability account, such as Accounts Payable/Bell Products, should have a credit balance. Capital and revenue accounts normally have credit balances and expense accounts normally have debit balances. The types of accounts and their normal balances are listed in the margin.

The process of computing account balances is referred to as **balancing the accounts.** The ledger on page 78 shows the accounts for the Globe Travel Agency at the close of business on September 30. *Remember that the balance of an account normally appears on the same side as the account appears in the accounting equation.* Expense accounts have debit balances because they decrease owner's equity.

Computing an Account Balance
- Total all debits.
- Total all credits.
- Subtract the smaller amount from the larger amount.
- Show balance on side of account with larger total.

Account	Normal Account Balance
Asset	Debit
Liability	Credit
Capital	Credit
Revenue	Credit
Expense	Debit

Globe Travel Agency Ledger

Assets	=	Liabilities	+	Owner's Equity

Cash   101

19—		19—	
Sept. 1	8,000	Sept. 5	4,000
6	1,000	12	3,000
14	13,000	21	5,000
27	2,000	28	2,100
9,900	24,000		14,100

Accts. Rec./Karen Louis   102

19—		19—	
Sept. 1	1,000	Sept. 6	1,000
27	1,000		
1,000	2,000		1,000

Accts. Rec./Rose Shops   103

19—	
Sept. 27	700

Furniture   111

19—		19—	
Sept. 1	2,000	Sept. 8	500
7	1,500		
3,000	3,500		500

Office Equipment   112

19—	
Sept. 1	9,000
5	4,000
13,000	13,000	-0-

Accts. Pay./Bell Products   201

19—		19—	
Sept. 8	500	Sept. 1	3,000
12	3,000	7	1,500
	3,500	1,000	4,500

Accts. Pay./Royal Service Shop 202

19—	
Sept. 29	200

Mark Nero, Capital   301

19—		19—	
Sept. 21	5,000	Sept. 1	17,000
		14	13,000
	5,000	25,000	30,000

Sales   401

		19—	
		Sept. 26	2,000
		27	1,700
	-0-	3,700	3,700

Repairs Expense   501

19—	
Sept. 29	200

Salaries Expense   502

19—	
Sept. 28	2,100

Activity A-1. Answer the following questions about the Globe Travel Agency's accounts. Refer to the account balances shown above.

1. What is the Cash account balance?

2. Does the Cash account balance represent the total amount of cash received during the month? Explain.

3. What is the balance of the Karen Louis account on September 15? On September 30?

4. Does the Sales account have a debit or credit balance? Why?

5. Why is the balance of the Bell Products account on the credit side?

6. What does the balance in the Office Equipment account represent?

7. Does the Salaries Expense account have a debit balance or a credit balance? Why?

8. What is the total amount of cash paid out during the month?

9. What is owed to Bell Products on September 8?

10. What is Mark Nero's investment on September 1? On September 15? On September 30?

Activity A-2. Compute the debit total and credit total for the following accounts. Then show the debit balance or credit balance. Use a format similar to the one shown in the example.

EXAMPLE: Cash
Debits: $300, $500, $700, $250, $50
   Credits: $625, $35, $45

Debit Total $1,800   Credit Total $705
Debit Balance $1,095   Credit Balance _____

a. Rent Expense
   Debits: $345
     Credits: $0
b. Accts. Pay./Lake Motors
   Debits: $43, $422, $80, $10
     Credits: $175, $63
c. Fees
   Debits: $0
     Credits: $100, $160, $170, $85

d. Equipment
   Debits: $3,000, $7,000
     Credits: $4,000
e. Loans Payable
   Debits: $0
     Credits: $5,500
f. George Simpson, Capital
   Debits: $3,000; $2,000; $1,000
     Credits: $20,000

Preparing a Trial Balance

B *When is a trial balance prepared?* A trial balance may be prepared at any time to ensure that the accounts are in balance. Generally, a trial balance is prepared at the end of each month. One must be prepared at the end of each accounting period.

You recall from Chapter 2 that we proved the equality of the accounting equation as each transaction was recorded. However, when T accounts are used, the equation is not generally proved as each transaction is recorded. Instead, a proof is made after several transactions have been recorded.

A trial balance can be prepared in several ways. In this topic, we use what accountants call a quick trial balance. A **quick trial balance** is a listing of the account balances to check the equality of the debits and credits in the ledger. The account titles and account numbers are not shown. The next chapter uses a formal trial balance. A **formal trial balance** is a summary that lists the account titles and account numbers in addition to the debit and credit balances.

A trial balance may be prepared on an adding machine or a calculator with a tape. Simply add all the debits and get a total. Then add all the credits and get a total. The two totals must be equal for the ledger to be in balance.

There is another way of doing a quick trial balance. Each account balance is entered in the calculator in the order in which the account appears in the ledger. Each debit balance is added. Each credit balance is subtracted. When the last account balance has been entered, the final total should be zero. Since the total debits (amounts added) must equal the total credits (amounts subtracted), the final result must be zero. If the total is zero, the ledger is in balance. If the total is not zero, an error has been made. The calculator tape can be used to check the amounts back to the accounts to find the error.

The above procedure is called a zero proof. A **zero proof** is a test in which the difference is zero if two amounts are equal. Therefore, the difference between the total debit amounts added and the total credit amounts subtracted must be zero.

Globe Travel Agency
Trial Balance
September 30, 19–

```
        0.00T
    9,900.00
    1,000.00
      700.00
    3,000.00
   13,000.00
      200.00
    2,100.00
   29,900.00T

        0.00T
    1,000.00
      200.00
   25,000.00
    3,700.00
   29,900.00T
```

Quick trial balance of total debits and total credits.

Globe Travel Agency
Trial Balance
September 30, 19 –

```
        0.00T
    9,900.00
    1,000.00
      700.00
    3,000.00
   13,000.00
    1,000.00 –
      200.00 –
   25,000.00 –
    3,700.00 –
      200.00
    2,100.00
        0.00T
```

Quick trial balance with zero proof.

If a calculator is not available, the amounts can simply be written on a sheet of paper and computed manually.

Whether the proof is written on a sheet of paper or is prepared on a calculator tape, the proof should be identified by writing a heading on the paper. Answer these three questions: WHO? (the name of the company), WHAT? (the name of the accounting proof), and WHEN? (the date as of when the proof was made).

Summarizing the Use of T Accounts

This chapter covered the procedure for using T accounts for recording the changes caused by transactions. The procedure made no change to the accounting cycle that is discussed in Chapter 2. Here is a summary of the accounting cycle through Step 4.

STEP 1. Each transaction was recorded.
STEP 2. A chronological record was kept of each transaction.
STEP 3. The changes caused by the transaction were available for each account, and the account balance was updated.
STEP 4. The equality of the equation was proved at the end of the accounting period.

The next chapter discusses different ways for completing Steps 5 through 8 of the accounting cycle.

Accounting Concept:
Trial Balance. The equality of the total debits and the total credits in the ledger should be verified at regular intervals.

Activity B. Take a quick trial balance of the accounts for the Fashion Hair Company and of the Huntington Machine Repair Company. Total all debits. Total all credits. State if there is equality of debits and credits.
1. Accounts for the Fashion Hair Company: Leslie Hunt, Capital, $4,933; Cash, $3,500; Accts. Rec./Ann Johnson, $24; Accts. Rec./John Loomis, $14; Equipment, $2,750; Accts. Pay./Hair Supplies, $150; Loans Payable, $1,200; Rent Expense, $250; Salaries Expense, $375; Utilities Expense, $55; Sales, $685.
2. Accounts for the Huntington Machine Repair Company: Equipment, $1,500; Utilities Expense, $55; Accts. Pay./Stanford's Supplies, $900; James Huntington, Capital, $2,155; Cash, $1,000; Supplies, $2,500; Accts. Rec./Kenny Auto Service, $600; Sales $3,000; Rent Expense, $400.

Topic 4 Problems

3-9. Prepare a quick trial balance for the Tec-Com Company on November 30 for the data given at the top of the next page. Check that the total debits equal the total credits.

Account No.	Account Title	Balance		Account No.	Account Title	Balance
101	Cash	$ 5,000		201	Accts. Pay./Radio Supplies	6,000
102	Accts. Rec./Tanner Stores	8,000		202	Accts. Pay./Sound Company	-0-
103	Accts. Rec./Boulder Stores	3,500		301	David Tallent, Capital	20,700
104	Accts. Rec./Soller Company	-0-		401	Sales	9,000
111	Furniture	3,000		501	Rent Expense	1,000
112	Office Equipment	4,300		502	Repairs Expense	-0-
113	Radio Supplies	10,900		503	Salaries Expense	-0-

3-10. Prepare a trial balance for Lawn Care Service on December 31 from the following data. List the accounts by account number as they would appear in the chart of accounts. Check that there is a zero proof.

Account No.	Account Title	Balance		Account No.	Account Title	Balance
101	Cash	$ 7,500		103	Accts. Rec./Ann Benton	100
111	Lawn Equipment	15,000		301	Phillip Powell, Capital	19,650
118	Office Equipment	3,000		401	Sales	11,000
102	Accts. Rec./Joseph Tello	50		502	Salaries Expense	5,000

The Language of Business

Here are some basic terms that make up the language of business. Do you know the meaning of each?

T account
account title
account number
coding
chart of accounts

debit side
debit (Dr.)
debiting the account
credit side
credit (Cr.)

crediting the account
account balance
opening balances
debtor
ledger
double-entry
  accounting

accounting entry
compound transaction
trial balance
balancing the accounts
quick trial balance
formal trial balance
zero proof

Chapter 3 Questions

1. What are the three basic rules of the double-entry accounting system used to analyze all transactions?
2. What are accounts? What are T accounts?
3. Name the four parts of a T account.
4. List the rules for debiting and crediting.
5. Does debit always mean increase and credit always mean decrease? Why or why not?
6. Name two revenue accounts. Name three expense accounts.
7. What is the normal balance of asset accounts? Lia-

bility accounts? Owner's equity capital account? Revenue accounts? Expense accounts?
8. What are the three steps to analyzing business transactions?
9. Why are revenue accounts credited to increase owner's equity? Why are expense accounts debited to decrease owner's equity?
10. Describe the comparison that is made on the trial balance. What principle does the trial balance use?

Chapter 3 Problems

Problems for Chapter 3 are given in the *Working Papers and Chapter Problems for Part 1*. If you are using the workbook, do the problems in the space provided there.

Chapter 3 Management Cases

Fitting Records to the Business. The information needed by a business varies according to the type of business. No two businesses will have the same number of accounts or use the same account titles. The kind of information that is needed by the management determines what accounts are used.

Case 3M-1. Thomas and Harriet Uclid operate an automobile service station along with an attached diner. Mr. Uclid sells gasoline, oil, tires, batteries, and other automobile supplies. He also fixes flat tires, lubricates cars, and does mechanical repair work. Mrs. Uclid operates the diner. She has a breakfast and luncheon menu, and she keeps the diner open the same hours as the service station—from 8 A.M. to 5 P.M.

Mr. Uclid had enough time in the past to do the repair work and to handle other customer services. When Mrs. Uclid had extra time, she helped out in the service station with customer services while Mr. Uclid did the repair work. Recently, business has increased. Mr. Uclid now finds that he cannot do the repair work, and also attend to customer services. Mrs. Uclid's diner has become a favorite place for breakfast and lunch. They must decide whether they should employ a full-time helper, limit the repair work, reduce customer services, or close the diner.

No separate record of revenue from the various phases of the business is kept. All revenue from customer service and repairs, as well as from the diner, is shown in one revenue account. How can the records be organized to help Mr. and Mrs. Uclid decide what to do?

Case 3M-2. The Clockwise Repair Company cleans and repairs antique clocks. Olive Lorelei is the owner and manager of the business, and she has two employees. The Clockwise Repair Company cleans and repairs clocks in the shop and also provides a pickup and delivery service to businesses and residences. Customers like the pickup and delivery service.

Ms. Lorelei keeps her own accounting records. The business uses one revenue account to record all revenue. It uses one expense account to record all expenses. However, she believes that her system is not giving her the information needed about revenues and expenses.

a. What are the various expenses that such a business might have?

b. Why would it be useful to Ms. Lorelei to know the amount received from each source of revenue and the amount spent for each type of expense?

c. What plan would you suggest to make the financial records show the total of each major item of revenue and expense?

Working Hint

Ruling. Always use a ruler to draw rules (lines). The ruler should be slanted on one side (rather than being perfectly flat). Place the ruler so that the slanted side faces the paper. This leaves space between the ruling edge and the paper. When you are using ink, this space prevents ink from running underneath the ruler and smudging the paper. Spread your fingers on the ruler and press firmly so that the ruler will not slip and spoil your work.

Double rules are made in the same way as single rules. When you draw the second rule, do not move the ruler. Tilt the pen slightly from the position where you made the first rule. The lines of the double rules should be close together.

Summarizing the Accounting Cycle Activities

The accounting equation, double-entry accounting, and T accounts are different ways to process data through Steps 1 to 4 of the accounting cycle. You will now learn different ways for completing Steps 4 to 8 of the accounting cycle.

Topic 1
The Trial Balance and the Income Statement

A *How is the accounting data in the ledger summarized for managers and owners?* The data in the ledger is summarized in two financial statements: the income statement and the balance sheet.

The statements are prepared at the end of each accounting period. Many businesses also prepare statements more frequently to keep their financial information up to date. But financial statements must be prepared at least once a year. They are prepared after the trial balance.

The Formal Trial Balance

Formal trial balance lists the account titles and account numbers in addition to the debit and credit balances.

At the end of each accounting period a formal trial balance must be prepared. In a formal trial balance, the account titles and numbers as well as their debit and credit balances are listed. The accounts are listed in the order in which they appear in the ledger.

The formal trial balance for the Globe Travel Agency at the close of business on September 30 is shown at the bottom of the next page. The balances were obtained from the ledger.

Purpose of the Formal Trial Balance

Accounting Cycle
STEP 4: Prove equality of ledger at end of accounting period.

The trial balance serves several important purposes.

- It proves that the ledger is in balance.
- It summarizes the balance of each account in the ledger.
- It sorts the accounts according to the sequence of the chart of accounts. Thus, assets are listed first, followed by liabilities and owner's equity capital. Next comes revenue and expenses.

STEP 5: Summarize accounting information at end of accounting period.

STEP 6: Transfer net income (or net loss) to Capital account at end of accounting period.

- It supplies the data needed to compute the net income or net loss for the accounting period. The revenue accounts (400s) and expense accounts (500s) are shown.
- It provides the data needed to transfer the net income or net loss to the Capital account at the end of the accounting cycle (Step 6 of the accounting cycle).

As a result, the trial balance plays an important role in performing Step 4, Step 5, and Step 6 of the accounting cycle.

Preparing the Formal Trial Balance

A trial balance is usually prepared in pencil because it is not a formal statement. However, it can also be prepared in ink. The procedure for preparing a formal trial balance is as follows.

Globe Travel Agency Ledger

Assets	=	Liabilities	+	Owner's Equity

Assets

Cash — 101

19—		19—	
Sept. 1	8,000	Sept. 5	4,000
6	1,000	12	3,000
14	13,000	21	5,000
26	2,000	28	2,100
9,900	24,000		14,100

Accts. Rec./Karen Louis — 102

19—		19—	
Sept. 1	1,000	Sept. 6	1,000
27	1,000		
1,000	2,000		1,000

Accts. Rec./Rose Shops — 103

19—	
Sept. 27	700

Furniture — 111

19—		19—	
Sept. 1	2,000	Sept. 8	500
7	1,500		
3,000	3,500		500

Office Equipment — 112

19—			
Sept. 1	9,000		
5	4,000		
13,000	13,000		-0-

Liabilities

Accts. Pay./Bell Products — 201

19—		19—	
Sept. 8	500	Sept. 1	3,000
12	3,000	7	1,500
	3,500	1,000	4,500

Accts. Pay./Royal Service Shop — 202

		19—	
		Sept. 29	200

Owner's Equity

Mark Nero, Capital — 301

19—		19—	
Sept. 21	5,000	Sept. 1	17,000
		14	13,000
	5,000	25,000	30,000

Sales — 401

		19—	
		Sept. 26	2,000
		27	1,700
	-0-	3,700	3,700

Repairs Expense — 501

19—	
Sept. 29	200

Salaries Expense — 502

19—	
Sept. 28	2,100

The trial balance proves that the total debits equal the total credits in the ledger.

Globe Travel Agency
Trial Balance
September 30, 19—

Heading { WHO WHAT WHEN

ACCOUNT TITLE	ACCT. NO.	DEBIT	CREDIT
Cash	101	9 900 00	
Accts. Rec./Karen Louis	102	1 000 00	
Accts. Rec./Rose Shops	103	700 00	
Furniture	111	3 000 00	
Office Equipment	112	13 000 00	
Accts. Pay./Bell Products	201		1 000 00
Accts. Pay./Royal Service Shop	202		200 00
Mark Nero, Capital	301		25 000 00
Sales	401		3 700 00
Repairs Expense	501	200 00	
Salaries Expense	502	2 100 00	
		29 900 00	29 900 00

Single rule shows totals.
Totals must equal.
Double rule shows completion.

Heading. Center the heading at the top of the trial balance. The heading answers these questions: WHO? (the name of the company), WHAT? (the name of the accounting proof), and WHEN? (the date as of when the proof was made).

ACCOUNT TITLE	ACCT. NO.	DEBIT	CREDIT
Cash	101	9,900 00	
Accts. Rec./Karen Louis	102	1,000 00	
Accts. Rec./Rose Shops	103	700 00	
Furniture	111	3,000 00	
Office Equipment	112	13,000 00	
Accts. Pay./Bell Products	201		1,000 00
Accts. Pay./Royal Service Shop	202		200 00
Mark Nero, Capital	301		25,000 00
Sales	401		3,700 00
Repairs Expense	501	200 00	
Salaries Expense	502	2,100 00	

List of Accounts. List the accounts in numeric order, just as they appear in the ledger. Write the account title in the first column and the account number in the second column. Write the account balance in the appropriate money column, Debit or Credit. Then, beginning each word with a capital letter, list all accounts whether or not they have balances. This will ensure that you have not missed an account. Some accountants, however, prefer to list only accounts with balances.

Dollar Signs and Decimal Points. When the trial balance is prepared on ruled accounting paper, dollar signs, commas, and decimal points are not used with amounts in money columns. The vertical lines in the money columns take the place of commas and decimal points. The money columns also show that you are working with dollars. Therefore, it is not necessary to use dollar signs ($). Use dollar signs, commas, and decimal points when writing amounts in columns other than ruled money columns.

Proving a Trial Balance Prepared in Pencil. After all the account balances have been entered, the trial balance is totaled and ruled. Complete the trial balance as follows when it is prepared in pencil.

		29,900 00	29,900 00

- Draw a single rule across both money columns.
- Add the amounts in the money columns.
- Record the totals on the line below the single rule.
- Check that the total of the Debit column equals the total of the Credit column. If the total debits do not equal the total credits, then there is an error. All errors must be corrected before the trial balance can be completed.
- Draw a double rule across both money columns beneath the totals when the totals balance. The double rules indicate that the columns are completed.

In general, rules are drawn across all columns except explanation columns on accounting paper. In the trial balance, the account title and account number columns are considered explanations. In accounting, single rules indicate computations (addition or subtraction). Double rules across columns mean that the work is accurate and completed. Single and double rules are always drawn with a ruler. For a practical tip on how to draw rules, see the Working Hint on page 82.

Proving a Trial Balance Prepared in Ink. After all the account balances have been entered, complete the trial balance as follows when it is prepared in ink.

- Add the amounts in the money columns.
- Record the totals in small *pencil* figures directly under the last entry in the money columns. This small pencil total is called a **pencil footing.** The pencil footing is used to double-check the additions and the equality of the debit total and credit total before the amounts are written in ink.
- Draw a single rule across both money columns, after the totals agree.
- Record the totals on the line below the single rule.
- Draw a double rule across both money columns beneath the totals.

Salaries Expense	502	2,100 00	
		29,900 00	29,900 00
		29,900 00	29,900 00

Pencil-footings check the equality before totals are written in ink.

When you prepare a trial balance in ink, it is important to pencil foot the columns to ensure that the totals balance before writing the totals in ink.

Activity A. Prepare a trial balance for Yellow Taxi, Inc., on May 31. The account balances are given below. Assign appropriate numbers to the accounts. Follow the chart of accounts on page 54. (Capital stock is a stockholders' equity account.)

Accts. Pay./College Motor . . . .$ 900	
Accts. Rec./Rock Corporation 1,275	
Cash 4,500	

Vehicles . . . .$ 9,500
Fare Revenue 3,000
Rent Expense 425
Salaries Expense 1,540
Maintenance Expense. 155
Capital Stock 13,780
Gas and Oil Expense 285

The Income Statement

B The **income statement** is a financial statement reporting the revenue, expenses, and net income or net loss of a business for a specific period of time. It is sometimes referred to as a *statement of profit and loss,* a *statement of revenue and expenses,* a *statement of earnings,* or a *statement of operations.* The preferred title, however, is *income statement.* The word *income,* as you recall, means the difference between the revenue received from the sale of goods and services and the expenses incurred in operating the business and making those sales.

The income statement explains the Income Summary section of the accounting equation. In other words, it summarizes in detail the accounts that affect the net income (or net loss) for the accounting period.

		Assets			=	Liabilities	+	Owner's Equity	
	Cash	Accounts Receivable	Furniture	Office Equipment		Accounts Payable		Mark Nero, Capital	Income Summary (Revenue – Expense)
Sept. 30 balance	$9,900 +	$1,700 +	$3,000 +	$13,000 =		$1,200 +		$25,000 +	$1,400 ←
Transfer net income						$1,200	+	$26,400	
Equality of equation		$27,600			=			$27,600	

Globe Travel Agency
Income Statement
For the Month Ended September 30, 19–

Revenue Section	Revenue:	
	Sales	3 7 0 0 0 0
Expense Section	Expenses:	
	Repairs Expense	2 0 0 0 0
	Salaries Expense	2 1 0 0 0 0
	Total Expenses	2 3 0 0 0 0
Net Income or Net Loss Section	Net Income	1 4 0 0 0 0 ←

Income statement explains the Income Summary section in the accounting equation.

Purpose of the Income Statement

The income statement provides the following information.
- It gives the accounting period covered by the statement.
- It summarizes all sources of revenue for that accounting period.
- It reports all expenses that are matched against the reported revenues for the period.
- It reports fairly the net income (or net loss) for that accounting period.

The length of the accounting period is an important part of the income statement. If "For the Month Ended September 30, 19—" were not included in the heading, it would not be known whether the net income was earned in one week, one month, one quarter, or one year. The heading of the income statement for the Globe Travel Agency shows that the business earned a net income of $1,400 in one month—the month of September.

Activity B. Answer the following questions on the income statement. Refer to the Globe Travel Agency income statement on page 88.
1. What is the length of the accounting period?
2. What is the source of the revenue?
3. What is the total revenue?
4. What are the total expenses?
5. What kinds of expenses were incurred?
6. What is the net income for the accounting period?

Preparing an Income Statement

C *How is an income statement prepared?* An income statement is a permanent record. It can be written in ink, typewritten, or printed on a press or by a computer. It is for the use of managers, owners, and outsiders, such as creditors. The income statement, as you know, is prepared at the end of each accounting period, or more frequently. It is prepared by using data from the trial balance as follows.

Income statement is prepared from trial balance.

Heading. Center the heading at the top of the income statement, as shown in the margin. The heading answers these questions: WHO? (the name of the company), WHAT? (the name of the statement), and WHEN? (the accounting period the statement covers).

Remember that an accounting period can cover a period of time, such as one month, three months, a calendar year, or a fiscal year. The third line of the heading on the income statement would then read as follows.

Globe Travel Agency
Income Statement
For the Month Ended September 30, 19—

- For one month: "For the Month Ended September 30, 19—" (use the last day of the month).
- For three months: "For the Quarter Ended March 31, 19—" (use the last day of the third month).
- For a calendar year: "For the Year Ended December 31, 19—".
- For a fiscal year: "For the Year Ended July 31, 19—" (use the last day of the twelve-month period).

Revenue Section. After the heading is written, the revenue information must be entered on the income statement. Write the title "Revenue" followed by a colon on the first line at the left margin, as shown. Indent one-half inch (1.25 centimeters) and list the revenue items beneath the title. Begin each word with a capital letter. When there is only one revenue account, as in the example in the margin, enter the amount in the second money column. If there are several accounts, the individual amounts are listed in the first money column and the total amount in the second money column. (Notice that the money columns are not indicated as debit or credit columns.)

Revenue:
Sales 3,700 00

Expense Section. Next, the expenses information must be entered. At the margin on the line beneath the last entry in the Revenue section,

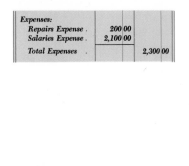

Expenses:		
Repairs Expense .	200 00	
Salaries Expense .	2,100 00	
Total Expenses .		2,300 00

| Net Income . . . . | | 1,400 00 |

write the title "Expenses" followed by a colon. Indent one-half inch and list the expenses beneath the title. List the accounts in the order in which they appear in the ledger. Begin each word with a capital letter. The illustration in the margin shows how the expenses should be listed. The individual amounts are listed in the first money column. The total amount is entered in the second money column. Write the words "Total Expenses" immediately following the last expense listed. If there is only one expense account, enter that amount in the second money column.

Net Income or Net Loss Section. Finally, the net income or net loss must be entered. Draw a single rule across the money column under the amount of total expenses, as shown. Subtract the total expenses from the total revenue, and enter the difference on the next line in the second money column. Write either "Net Income" or "Net Loss" on the same line at the left margin. Then draw a double rule across both money columns to show that the money columns are completed.

The accounts listed in the lower portion of the trial balance are those that appear on the income statement. The expense and revenue accounts are temporary accounts frequently called *income statement accounts* or *nominal accounts*.

The completed income statement for the Globe Travel Agency at the end of its September accounting period shows the relationship of the trial balance to the income statement.

Globe Travel Agency
Trial Balance
September 30, 19—

ACCOUNT TITLE	ACCT. NO.	DEBIT	CREDIT
Cash	101	9,900 00	
Accts. Rec./Karen Louis	102	1,000 00	
Accts. Rec./Rose Shops	103	700 00	
Furniture	111	3,000 00	
Office Equipment	112	13,000 00	
Accts. Pay./Bell Products	201		1,000 00
Accts. Pay./Royal Service Shop	202		200 00
Mark Nero, Capital	301		25,000 00
Sales	401		3,700 00
Repairs Expense	501	200 00	
Salaries Expense	502	2,100 00	
		29,900 00	29,900 00

Globe Travel Agency
Income Statement
For the Month Ended September 30, 19—

Revenue:		
Sales		3,700 00
Expenses:		
Repairs Expense	200 00	
Salaries Expense	2,100 00	
Total Expenses		2,300 00
Net Income		1,400 00

The income statement accounts (numbers 400s and 500s) are listed in lower portion of trial balance.

Activity C. The All-Night Parking Garage had the following revenue and expenses between January 1 and December 31. Prepare an income statement for the year ended December 31, 19—.

Utilities Expense . . . .$ 800

Advertising Expense . . . .$ 600
Salaries Expense 4,000
Parking Fees (revenue) 30,500
Rent Expense 6,500
Miscellaneous Expense 1,500

Accounting Concept:
Income Statement. Revenues, expenses, and net income or net loss for an accounting period are summarized in a financial report called an *income statement*.

Accounting Principle:
Matching Revenue and Expenses. The generally accepted accounting principle is that revenue must be matched against the expenses incurred in obtaining that revenue. The result of matching revenue and expenses is net income (or net loss) for the accounting period.

Topic 1 Problems

4-1. The Dallas Cinema had the following revenue and expenses during the month of November. Prepare an income statement for the month ended November 30, 19—.

Paid for advertising . . . .$	600
Film rental expense	8,000
Admissions (revenue)	15,000
Rent expense	2,000
Food sales (revenue)	1,500
Miscellaneous expense	15
Salaries paid	5,300
Paid for heat and light (utilities)	150

4-2. Michael Barlow owns the Hair Design Barber Shop. On June 30 the business's financial records show the data given below. Set up an accounting equation like the one on page 88 to classify the financial data for this business. Then prepare an income statement for the three-month period ended June 30, 19—.

Shop equipment owned	$5,500
Sales to customers	8,000
Utilities expense	250
Michael Barlow, Capital (April 1)	5,900
Advertising costs	75
Salaries paid	4,300
Cash in bank	5,200
Due from customers	75
Rent expense	500
Owed on equipment	2,000

Topic 2
The Balance Sheet

A *How do managers and owners learn about the financial position of a business?* Another financial statement, the balance sheet, provides this information. A **balance sheet** (also known as a *statement of financial position*) is a financial statement reporting the assets, liabilities, and owner's equity of a business for a specific date.

Balance sheet is prepared from trial balance after income statement has been prepared.

The balance sheet is prepared after the income statement because the net income or net loss will change owner's equity.

A balance sheet, like the income statement, must be prepared at the end of each accounting period. Depending on the length of the accounting period, the balance sheet may be prepared more often, such as at the end of each month.

Purpose of the Balance Sheet

The balance sheet does the following.

- It states the name of the accounting entity. This means that the amounts reported are only those of the business and do not include the personal assets and liabilities of the owner or owners.
- It summarizes the assets of the business and the claims of creditors against those assets.
- It shows the owner's claims against the assets of the business.
- It provides information about the business's financial position.

Analyzing a Balance Sheet

The balance sheet is based upon the accounting equation. The accounting equation shows the relationship among the accounting elements, and the balance sheet reports that relationship.

	Assets				=	Liabilities	+	Owner's Equity	
Cash	Accounts Receivable	Furniture	Office Equipment			Accounts Payable		Mark Nero, Capital	Income Summary (Revenue – Expense)
Sept. 30 balance									
$9,900	+ $1,700	+ $3,000	+ $13,000		=	$1,200	+ $25,000	+	$1,400
Transfer net income						$1,200		$26,400	
Equality of equation		$27,600			=			$27,600	

WHO WHAT WHEN } Heading

Globe Travel Agency
Balance Sheet
September 30, 19—

Liabilities Section
Assets Section
Owner's Equity Section
Proof of Equality Section

① Assets			① Liabilities		
Cash		990000	Accounts Payable:		
Accounts Receivable:			② Bell Products $1,000.00		
② Karen Louis $1,000.00			Royal Service Shop 200.00		
Rose Shops 700.00	170000		Total Liabilities	120000	
Furniture	300000		③		
Office Equipment	1300000		① Owner's Equity		
			Mark Nero, Capital $25000.00		
			Net Income 140000		
			Total Owner's Equity 2640000		
④ Total	2760000		④ Total	2760000	

Note the following on the balance sheet.

1 Center titles.
2 Indent and list debtors and creditors.
3 Skip a line between sections.
4 Center "total" on same line.

The balance sheet shown is in the account form, which looks like a large T account. In later chapters, you will learn about another type of balance sheet, the report form. In the **account form balance sheet,** the assets are listed on the left side and liabilities and owner's equity are shown on the right side. Both the income statement and the balance sheet are prepared from the trial balance data. The accounting equation as of September 30 for the Globe Travel Agency is shown on page 92 together with the balance sheet.

The balance sheet consists of five sections.

- A heading, which answers the questions: WHO? (the name of the business), WHAT? (the name of the statement), and WHEN? (the date of the statement). The date is extremely important because the statement shows the financial position of the business on that day.
- The assets, which are reported on the left side. The kinds and amounts of assets owned are listed.
- The liabilities, which are reported at the top part of the right side. The kinds and amounts of liabilities owed are listed.
- The owner's equity, which is reported on the lower part of the right side. The Owner's Equity section shows two items: the capital (investment) and the net income (revenue minus expenses for the accounting period). The net income links the income statement to the balance sheet at the end of the accounting period.
- The Proof of Equality section, which shows that the total assets equal the total liabilities plus owner's equity.

Activity A. Answer the following questions on the balance sheet. Refer to the Globe Travel Agency's balance sheet on page 92.
1. Who is the owner of the business?
2. The balance sheet shows the financial position of the business for what date?
3. How much cash does the business have?
4. Who owes money to the business? How much money is owed by each customer?

5. What equipment does the business own?
6. What is the recorded cost of the furniture?
7. What is the total amount of all the assets owned by the business?
8. To whom does the business owe money?
9. What is Mark Nero's equity in the business?
10. Using Globe's balance sheet, solve the accounting equation.

$$\$\underline{\ \ ?\ \ } = \$\underline{\ \ ?\ \ } + \$\underline{\ \ ?\ \ }$$

Preparing a Balance Sheet

B *How is a balance sheet prepared?* A balance sheet, like an income statement, is a permanent record. It can be written in ink, typewritten, or printed on a press or by a computer. The balance sheet is prepared using the data from the trial balance after the income statement has been prepared.

Heading. Center the heading at the top of the balance sheet as shown in the margin. The heading answers these questions: WHO? (the name of the company), WHAT? (the name of the statement), and WHEN? (the specific date of the statement). Notice that the date is reported differently on the balance sheet than on the income statement. The income statement states that the net income was earned *over a period of time.* The balance sheet states the assets, liabilities, and owner's equity *on a specific date.*

Assets Section

Center the title "Assets" on the first line of the left side of the balance sheet. Then list each asset along the left margin, starting with Cash. Begin each word with a capital letter. Record the amount of each asset in the left money column.

Accounts receivables and other assets.

One Account Receivable		
Assets		
Cash	*9,000*	*00*
Accounts Receivable:		
Karen Louis	*1,000*	*00*
Furniture	*3,000*	*00*
Office Equipment	*13,000*	*00*

Several Accounts Receivable			
Assets			
Cash		*9,000*	*00*
Accounts Receivable:			
Karen Louis	*$1,000.00*		
Rose Shops	*700.00*	*1,700*	*00*
Furniture		*3,000*	*00*
Office Equipment		*13,000*	*00*

If there are several accounts receivable, list them alphabetically with their balances in the Assets section. Since the amounts are not written in the ruled money columns, use dollar signs, commas, and decimal points. Draw a single rule below them. Then list the total in the left money column, as shown above. If there is only one account receivable, list the debtor's name and enter the amount in the money column.

Assets are usually listed in the order in which they are expected to be exchanged for cash or used. The ease with which assets can be exchanged for cash is called **liquidity.** Cash is the most liquid of all assets and is therefore listed first. Receivables—accounts receivable and notes receivable—usually follow cash because the money is expected to be received shortly. Then the other assets, such as buildings, furniture, and office equipment, follow, listed alphabetically. These assets are not normally converted into cash.

When preparing the balance sheet, list cash and receivables first, then the other assets in the order found on the trial balance.

The data given below shows the financial position of the Grand-Slam Tennis Company on December 31. Complete the heading and Assets section of a balance sheet in account form.

Cash . . . .$ 5,250
Accounts Receivable, Brenda Wells. 55
Building. 7,000
Equipment 5,000

Land $11,000
Accounts Payable, Joel Company 4,000
Accounts Payable, Debolt Company 6,000
Helen Strauss, Capital 16,305
Net Income 2,000
NOTE: Save your balance sheet for further use in Activities C and D.

Liabilities Section

C *How is the Liabilities section prepared?* Center the title "Liabilities" on the first line of the right side of the balance sheet, as shown on the balance sheet on page 92. Liabilities are listed before owner's equity because the claims of creditors come before the claims of the owner.

List each liability at the margin, beginning each word with a capital letter. Start with Accounts Payable, unless there are loans payable. If there are any loans payable, they are listed before accounts payable. Record the amount of each liability in the money column at the right. Note that there are several ways of presenting the Liabilities section.

One Account Payable	
Liabilities	
Accounts Payable:	
Bell Products	1,000 00

Several Accounts Payable			Accounts payable only.
Liabilities			
Accounts Payable:			
Bell Products . . . $1,000.00			
Royal Service Shop 200.00			
Total Liabilities	1,200 00		

Liabilities		
Liabilities		
Loans Payable	600 00	
Accounts Payable:		
Bell Products	1,000 00	
Mortgage Payable	25,000 00	
Total Liabilities	26,600 00	

Liabilities			Accounts payable and other payables.
Liabilities			
Loans Payable	600 00		
Accounts Payable:			
Bell Products . . . $1,000.00			
Royal Service Shop 200.00	1,200 00		
Mortgage Payable	25,000 00		
Total Liabilities	26,800 00		

Liabilities are usually listed in the order in which they must be paid. That is, debts that must be paid first are listed first.

Accounts Payable are usually listed after Loans Payable because the conditions of paying the debt are more flexible than those for paying a bank loan. Debts that must be paid over long periods of time, such as a Mortgage Payable, are listed last in the Liabilities section.

Activity C. Complete the Liabilities section of the balance sheet you began for the Grand-Slam Tennis Company in Activity B.

NOTE: Save your balance sheet for further use in Activity D.

Owner's Equity Section

Single Proprietorship
• Owner's Equity
Partnership
• Partners' Equity
Corporation
• Stockholders' Equity

D *How is the owner's equity section prepared?* Skip a line after the Liabilities section is completed. Then center the title "Owner's Equity" on the next line, as shown on the balance sheet on page 92. The title of the section identifies the type of business ownership. For example, a single proprietorship uses Owner's Equity, a partnership uses Partners' Equity, and a corporation uses Stockholders' Equity. The Globe Travel Agency is a single proprietorship, therefore it uses Owner's Equity.

On the line after the title, write at the margin "Mark Nero, Capital." Write the amount of the capital as shown on the balance sheet on page 92. Since the amount is not written in a ruled money column, use a dollar sign, comma, and decimal point. This quickly identifies the numbers as dollar amounts.

On the next line, write "Net Income" and then the net income amount under the capital amount. Draw a single rule under the net income amount. On the next line, indent one-half inch (1.25 centimeters) from the margin and write the word "Total Owner's Equity." Total the capital amount and net income amount, and write the total in the money column on the same line as total owner's equity.

In a single proprietorship, like the Globe Travel Agency, the name of the one owner appears in the Owner's Equity section. As you recall from Chapter 1, there are other forms of business ownership. If Globe were a partnership, financial interest of each owner would be shown. If Globe were a corporation with hundreds or thousands of owners, the total stockholders' equity would be shown. The ways of handling the equity section of the balance sheet for other forms of business ownerships are illustrated in Chapter 7.

Proof of Equality. After all items are entered on a balance sheet, the amounts must be totaled and ruled to prove the equality of the statement.

Draw a single rule across both money columns, as shown in the balance sheet on page 92, and total the amounts in the columns. Center the word "Total" and enter both totals (which must be equal) on the line immediately below the single rule. Draw a double rule across both money columns beneath the totals to indicate that the columns are equal and complete.

The balance sheet is prepared from the trial balance data. The accounts listed in the upper portion of the trial balance are those that appear on the balance sheet.

1 The permanent accounts are called **balance sheet accounts** or real accounts.

2 The temporary revenue and expense accounts are the **income statement accounts.**

The completed trial balance, income statement, and balance sheet for the Globe Travel Agency at the end of its September accounting period shows the relationship between the trial balance and the financial statements.

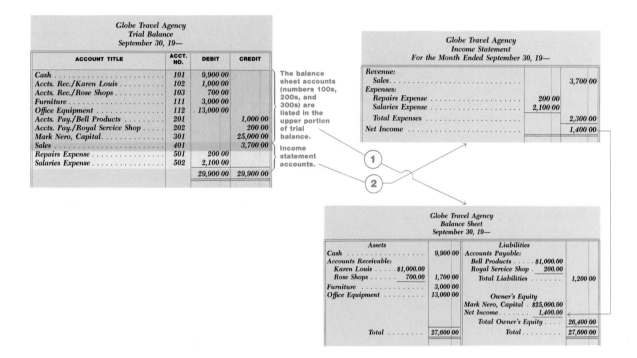

The balance sheet accounts (numbers 100s, 200s, and 300s) are listed in the upper portion of trial balance.

Income statement accounts.

Globe Travel Agency
Trial Balance
September 30, 19—

ACCOUNT TITLE	ACCT. NO.	DEBIT	CREDIT
Cash	101	9,900 00	
Accts. Rec./Karen Louis	102	1,000 00	
Accts. Rec./Rose Shops	103	700 00	
Furniture	111	3,000 00	
Office Equipment	112	13,000 00	
Accts. Pay./Bell Products	201		1,000 00
Accts. Pay./Royal Service Shop	202		200 00
Mark Nero, Capital	301		25,000 00
Sales	401		3,700 00
Repairs Expense	501	200 00	
Salaries Expense	502	2,100 00	
		29,900 00	29,900 00

Globe Travel Agency
Income Statement
For the Month Ended September 30, 19—

Revenue:		
Sales		3,700 00
Expenses:		
Repairs Expense	200 00	
Salaries Expense	2,100 00	
Total Expenses		2,300 00
Net Income		1,400 00

Globe Travel Agency
Balance Sheet
September 30, 19—

Assets		Liabilities	
Cash	9,900 00	Accounts Payable:	
Accounts Receivable:		Bell Products $1,000.00	
Karen Louis $1,000.00		Royal Service Shop . 200.00	
Rose Shops 700.00	1,700 00	Total Liabilities	1,200 00
Furniture	3,000 00		
Office Equipment	13,000 00	Owner's Equity	
		Mark Nero, Capital . $25,000.00	
		Net Income 1,400.00	
		Total Owner's Equity	26,400 00
Total	27,600 00	Total	27,600 00

Financial Position

The balance sheet provides managers, owners, and other interested people with information about the business's financial position.

Financial position means a business's ability to pay its debts. The Globe Travel Agency, for example, has $9,900 in cash. Its debts are $1,200. Thus its financial position is very good, and it can easily pay its debts and have cash left over to cover its business operations.

As you saw in this chapter, the accounting information is summarized in financial statements at the end of the accounting period. The income statement summarizes the results of the business's operations for a period of time. The balance sheet summarizes the business's financial position on a specific date.

Activity D. Complete the balance sheet you began in Activity B for the Grand-Slam Tennis Company.

> **Accounting Concepts:**
> **Financial Statements.** An income statement summarizes the revenues and expenses for a period of time. A balance sheet summarizes an accounting equation on a given date.
> **Financial Position.** The financial position of a business or individual is expressed through its assets, liabilities, and owner's equity.
> **Balance Sheet.** The accounting equation is summarized in a financial statement called a *balance sheet.*

Topic 2 Problems

4-3. Indicate whether each of the following items appears on the income statement, the balance sheet, or both. Use IS for income statement and BS for balance sheet. If the item appears on both statements write IS and BS.

a. The total revenue.
b. The amount owed to the business by customers.
c. The net income.
d. The amount owed to creditors by the business.
e. The accounting period.
f. The total liabilities.
g. The net loss.
h. The financial position of the business on a specific date.
i. A list of the assets owned by the business.
j. A list of the expenses.
k. The owner's investment.
l. The capital account amount.
m. Total assets.
n. Name of the statement.
o. Name of the company.
p. Proof of equality.

4-4. The following data shows the financial position on June 30 of Swan Cleaners, owned by John Goodman.
Has $5,000 in cash.
Owns equipment that cost $20,000.

Owes $1,500 to A-Z Machinery.
Charles O'Brien owes him $200.
Net Income $3,500.

a. Set up an accounting equation like the one on page 88 to classify this financial data. Once you have determined the kind and amount of each asset and liability, use the equation to determine the capital.
b. When the accounting equation is in balance, prepare a balance sheet.

4-5. The following assets and liabilities are for Nancy's Beauty Salon on March 31, 19—. The shop is owned by Nancy Wilson. Set up an accounting equation to determine the capital. Prepare a balance sheet to present this information.
Has $5,000 in cash.
Lisa Poll owes her $30.
Owns building that cost $30,000.
Owes $800 to Bell's Beauty Supply.
Owns land that cost $5,000.
Owes mortgage of $20,000.
Owns shop equipment that cost $8,000.
Owns supplies that cost $400.
Owes $2,000 to Mars Corporation.
Ann Sellers owes her $50.
Net Income $1,500.

Topic 3
Updating the Owner's Equity Accounts

A *What happens to the temporary account balances after the financial statements have been prepared?* Step 5 of the accounting cycle is to summarize the accounting information in financial statements at the end of the accounting period. Step 6 of the accounting cycle is to transfer the revenue and expense data to the Capital account. The revenue and expense data is transferred for two reasons.

Accounting Cycle
STEP 6: Transfer net income (or net loss) to Capital account at end of accounting period.

• The temporary accounts (revenue and expense) must be prepared at the end of the accounting period to collect the new revenue and expense data for the next accounting period. The net income was computed on the income statements. Thus the temporary accounts are no longer needed for this accounting period.
• The permanent Capital account balance must be updated to agree with the total owner's equity amount shown on the balance sheet. The net income from the income statement was added to the Capital account on the balance sheet. Thus the same thing must be done in the ledger.

After all temporary account balances have been transferred to the Capital account, the ledger will show the following.

• The temporary accounts will have zero balances.
• The Capital account will contain the owner's investment plus the net income or minus the net loss for the accounting period.

Transferring a Net Income or a Net Loss

In Chapter 2, the transactions are recorded in accounts in an equation. The net income (or net loss) in the accounting equation is transferred from the Income Summary account to the Capital account. The following equation reviews how the net income for the Globe Travel Agency was transferred to the Capital account on September 30. (You may want to refer back to Chapter 2, Topic 3 to review the entire procedure.) Note the following.
1 Income Summary balance is now zero.
2 Capital account has increased by amount of net income.

Assets				=	Liabilities	+	Owner's Equity		
Cash	Accounts Receivable	Furniture	Office Equipment		Accounts Payable		Mark Nero, Capital	Income Summary (Revenue − Expense)	
$9,900 +	$1,700 +	$3,000 +	$13,000	=	$1,200	+	$25,000 + 1,400	+	$1,400 −1,400	② Sept. 30 balance
							$26,400	$ -0-	① Transfer net income
					$1,200	+		$26,400	Equality of equation
		$27,600		=			$27,600		

In Chapter 3, the transactions are recorded in T accounts in a ledger instead of in an equation. On September 30 the T accounts in the ledger for the Globe Travel Agency appear as follows.

Globe Travel Agency Ledger

Assets			=	Liabilities			+	Owner's Equity		
	Cash	101		Accts. Pay./Bell Products		201		Mark Nero, Capital		301

Cash 101

19—		19—	
Sept. 1	8,000	Sept. 5	4,000
6	1,000	12	3,000
14	13,000	21	5,000
26	2,000	28	2,100
9,900	24,000		14,100

Accts. Pay./Bell Products 201

19—		19—	
Sept. 8	500	Sept. 1	3,000
12	3,000	7	1,500
	3,500	1,000	4,500

Mark Nero, Capital 301

19—		19—	
Sept. 21	5,000	Sept. 1	17,000
		14	13,000
	5,000	25,000	30,000

Accts. Rec./Karen Louis 102

19—		19—	
Sept. 1	1,000	Sept. 6	1,000
27	1,000		
	1,000	2,000	1,000

Accts. Pay./Royal Service Shop 202

19—	
Sept. 29	200

Income Summary 399

Accts. Rec./Rose Shops 103

19—	
Sept. 27	700

Sales 401

19—	
Sept. 26	2,000
27	1,700
-0-	3,700 3,700

Furniture 111

19—		19—	
Sept. 1	2,000	Sept. 8	500
7	1,500		
	3,000 3,500		500

Repairs Expense 501

19—	
Sept. 29	200

Office Equipment 112

19—	
Sept. 1	9,000
5	4,000
	13,000 13,000	-0-

Salaries Expense 502

19—	
Sept. 28	2,100

Globe Travel Agency ledger on September 30.

Transferring the net income in a ledger differs from transferring the net income in the equation. Note these differences for the Globe Travel Agency.

- The revenue is recorded in a Sales account. (See Account 401.)
- The expenses are recorded in various expense accounts. (See Accounts 501 and 502.)
- The Income Summary account has not been used yet. (See Account 399.)
- The net income amount does not appear in the ledger.

- The total owner's equity in the Capital account does not yet equal the total amount shown on the balance sheet. (The balance sheet shows total owner's equity of $26,400; the Capital account balance shows $25,000.)

Before illustrating how to transfer the net income to the capital account, it may help you to learn how to transfer *any* amount from one T account to another.

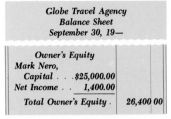

Globe Travel Agency
Balance Sheet
September 30, 19—

Owner's Equity		
Mark Nero,		
Capital . . .	.$25,000.00	
Net Income . .	1,400.00	
Total Owner's Equity .		26,400 00

Capital account does not show the total owner's equity in the ledger.

The Transfer Process

An amount is transferred from one account to another by means of a debit entry in one account and a credit entry in another account. Remember that the double-entry accounting principle requires that the debits must equal the credits for each transaction.

Transferring a Debit Amount From One Account to Another.
Debit the account to which you want to transfer the amount. Credit the account containing the amount you want to transfer. Suppose you want to transfer a $100 debit from Account A to Account B. You debit Account B for $100 and credit Account A for the same amount.

1 Account A now has a zero balance. A **zero balance** occurs when the debits equal the credits in an account. The zero balance in Account A shows that the amount was transferred out of the account.
2 Account B has a debit balance of $100 showing that the amount was transferred to this account.

The $100 debit amount has been transferred from Account A to Account B.

An account that has a zero balance is called a **closed account.**

A	B
100	

Before transfer.

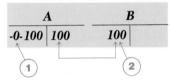

A	B
-0- 100 | 100	100 |

After transfer.

Transferring a Credit Amount From One Account to Another.
Debit the account containing the amount you want to transfer. Credit the account to which you want to transfer the amount. The following is done to transfer a $300 credit from Account C to Account D. Debit Account C for $300 and credit Account D for $300.

1 Account C now has a zero balance.
2 Account D has a credit balance of $300.

The $300 credit amount has been transferred from Account C to Account D.

C	D
| 300	

Before transfer.

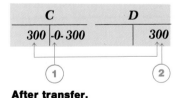

C	D
300 | -0- 300	| 300

After transfer.

Transferring Amounts

There are several reasons for transferring an amount from one account to another.

- *Correcting an error.* An amount may have been entered in the wrong account. To correct the error, the amount must be transferred to the correct account. For example, a $500 debit may have been entered in the Furniture account instead of the Office Equipment account. To correct this error, the Office Equipment account is debited for $500 and the Furniture account is credited for $300.

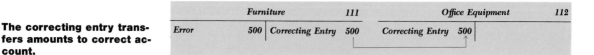

Furniture		111	Office Equipment		112
Error	500 | *Correcting Entry*	500	*Correcting Entry*	500 |	

- *Transferring the revenue and expense data to the Capital account.* This process is explained in the next segment.

Activity A. Which accounts would be debited and credited to *transfer* the following amounts?
1. Transfer the balance of Account A to Account B.
2. Transfer the balance of Account C to Account D.
3. Transfer the balance of Account F to Account E.
4. Transfer the balance of Account H to Account G.

Account A	Account B	Account E	Account F
800 |	|	200 |	| 500

Account C	Account D	Account G	Account H
300 |	|	500 | 300	600 | 1,000
200 |		200 |	100 |

Closing the Temporary Accounts

B *Is the revenue and expense data transferred directly to the capital account?* No, the balances of the revenue and expense accounts are transferred to the Income Summary account. The Income Summary account will then summarize the revenue and related expenses in the ledger. The balance of the Income Summary account will be the net income or net loss for the accounting period. The net income or net loss will then be transferred from the Income Summary account to the Capital account. Three entries are required to transfer the revenue and expense data to the capital account.

1 The revenue account balances are transferred to the Income Summary account.
2 The expense account balances are transferred to the Income Summary account.
3 The balance of the Income Summary account (net income or net loss) is transferred to the Capital account.

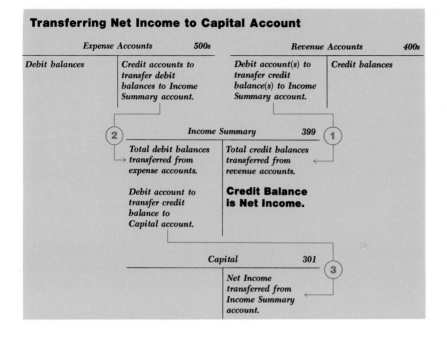

Transferring Net Income to Capital Account

Expense Accounts	500s		Revenue Accounts	400s
Debit balances	Credit accounts to transfer debit balances to Income Summary account.		Debit account(s) to transfer credit balance(s) to Income Summary account.	Credit balances

②   Income Summary   399   **①**

Total debit balances transferred from expense accounts.	Total credit balances transferred from revenue accounts.
Debit account to transfer credit balance to Capital account.	**Credit Balance is Net Income.**

Capital   301   **③**

Net Income transferred from Income Summary account.

Purpose of the Income Summary Account

The Income Summary account is a temporary account and is used only at the end of each accounting period. It serves several purposes.

• It summarizes the revenue and expense data in the ledger. That is why the title "Income Summary" is used.
• It summarizes the total revenue and the total expenses for each accounting period.
• It shows the net income or net loss for each accounting period in the ledger.
• It allows one amount (the net income or net loss) to be entered in the Capital account. As a result the Capital account shows only investments, withdrawals, and net incomes or net losses.

Transferring a Net Income

Remember that amounts are transferred from one account to another account by means of debit and credit entries. Also remember that the total debits must equal the total credits for each entry.

1 *Transferring Revenue Account Balances.* The first step in transferring the net income is to transfer the revenue for the accounting period from the revenue account(s) to the Income Summary account. This is done by debiting the revenue accounts and crediting the Income Summary account. On September 30, the revenue account Sales has a credit balance of $3,700. (The Globe Travel Agency uses only one revenue account.) This credit balance is transferred by debiting the revenue account for $3,700 and crediting the Income Summary account for the same amount.

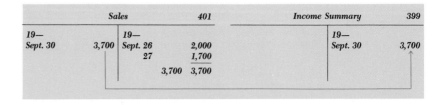

First closing entry transfers revenue account balances.

    Notice that the revenue account Sales now has a zero balance. The Income Summary account has a credit balance. Thus, the revenue of $3,700 for the accounting period has been transferred to the Income Summary account.

2 *Transferring Expense Account Balances.* The second step is to transfer the expenses from the expense accounts to the Income Summary account. The expense accounts have debit balances. Therefore, the expense accounts are credited and the Income Summary account is debited. This transfers the expense account balances.

    On September 30, the Repairs Expense account has a $200 balance and the Salaries Expense account has a $2,100 balance. The debit balances are transferred by crediting each expense account and debiting the Income Summary account for the total expenses.

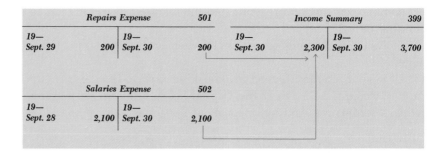

Second closing entry transfers expense account balances.

    Notice that the expense accounts now have zero balances. The expenses for the accounting period have been transferred to the Income Summary account.

    In this entry, the debits to the expense accounts ($200 + $2,100) equal the total credit ($2,300) to the Income Summary account. As a result, the ledger will still be in balance.

3 *Transferring the Income Summary Account Balance.* The third step is to transfer the balance of the Income Summary account to the permanent capital account.

Note that in the Income Summary account the total expenses ($2,300) are listed on the debit side. The total revenue ($3,700) is listed on the credit side. The revenue is greater than expenses. Therefore, the business earned a net income for the accounting period ending September 30.

If the expenses had been greater than the revenue, the balance would be on the debit side. This would be a net loss.

Net income, as you know, increases owner's equity. The net income of $1,400 must be added to the Mark Nero, Capital account to update owner's equity. The net income is, therefore, transferred from the Income Summary account to the Mark Nero, Capital account. The credit balance in the Income Summary account is transferred by debiting the Income Summary account for $1,400 and crediting the Mark Nero, Capital account for the same amount.

Mark Nero, Capital			301	Income Summary			399
19—		19—		19—		19—	
Sept. 21	5,000	Sept. 1	17,000	Sept. 30	2,300	Sept. 30	3,700
		14	13,000	30	1,400		1,400
	5,000		25,000	30,000			
		30	1,400				
			26,400				

Third closing entry transfers Income Summary account balance.

The Income Summary account now has a zero balance. In fact, after the net income or net loss is transferred to the Capital account, all the temporary accounts will have zero balances. The Mark Nero, Capital account now has a balance of $26,400. The Capital account now contains the net income for the month of September. Thus the Capital account shows the total owner's equity at the end of the September accounting period: the investment plus the net income.

Transferring a Net Loss

If the business suffers a net loss, the Income Summary account shows a debit balance at the end of the accounting period. To transfer a debit balance, you would credit the Income Summary account and debit the capital account. The debit to the Capital account would then decrease the owner's equity by the amount of the net loss.

A review of the transferring process is helpful here. The revenue and expenses have been transferred to the Income Summary account. Now suppose the Income Summary account for the Globe Travel

Agency had shown a net loss of $500 instead of a net income of $1,400. The balance of the Income Summary account would have been transferred as follows. The $500 debit balance would be transferred by crediting the Income Summary account for $500 and by debiting the Mark Nero, Capital account for the same amount.

Mark Nero, Capital				301		Income Summary				399
19—		19—				19—		19—		
Sept. 21	5,000	Sept. 1	17,000			Sept. 30	4,200	Sept. 30		3,700
		14	13,000				500	30		500
	5,000		25,000	30,000						
30	500		24,500							

Transferring a net loss from the Income Summary account.

The net loss would be subtracted from the balance of the Capital account. The Mark Nero, Capital account would now have a balance of $24,500 ($25,000 − $500).

Closing the Ledger

Transferring the net income (or net loss) to the Capital account closes the temporary Income Summary account.

In accounting, the procedure of transferring the net income from the temporary accounts to the capital account is called **closing the ledger.** At the end of the accounting period, the temporary accounts (revenue, expense, and Income Summary) need to have zero balances so that they can be used to collect the data for the next accounting period. An account with a zero balance is said to be a closed account. Thus the process of reducing the account balances to zero by transferring the balances to another account is known as **closing the accounts.** The entries to transfer the balances from the temporary accounts are frequently called **closing entries.**

Activity B-1. Indicate which of the following is a permanent account and which is a temporary account that is closed.
EX.: Delivery Expense   Temporary—Closed
1. Accts. Pay./Marcia Henning
2. Sales
3. Equipment
4. Income Summary
5. Fees (Revenue)
6. Electricity Expense
7. Henry Carlton, Capital
8. Salaries Expense
9. Postage Expense

Activity B-2. Analyze each of the transactions below and on page 107. Then record the debit amount and the credit amount in the appropriate T accounts.
1. Close the Sales account.
2. Close the expense accounts.
3. Close the revenue and expense accounts.
4. Close the Income Summary account.

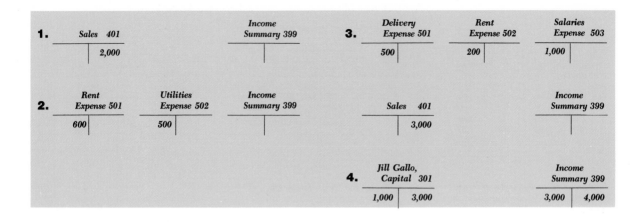

The Postclosing Trial Balance

C *Is the equality of the ledger checked after the net income has been transferred to the capital account?* Yes, the equality is checked again to ensure that the ledger is still in balance. All temporary accounts in the ledger now have zero balances. The permanent accounts still have their balances. The ledger is considered "closed" for the accounting period.

Even though the ledger appears to be in balance, an additional step is necessary to prove that the figures are correct. Errors could have occurred after the trial balance was prepared. Thus another trial balance is prepared. This second trial balance, the proof that the ledger is in balance after all the temporary accounts have been closed, is called a **postclosing trial balance.** (The prefix *post* means *after*.) Thus the postclosing trial balance is the check that is made after the accounts have been closed. Proving the closed ledger is the seventh step that you must perform in the accounting cycle.

Accounting Cycle
STEP 7: Prove the closed ledger.

Updating Account Balances

Before a postclosing trial balance can be prepared, the account balances must be updated. The transferring entries did not affect the permanent asset and liability accounts. Therefore, these account balances did not change.

The permanent Capital account and the temporary accounts, however, have been affected and must be updated. The illustration on page 108 shows the updated accounts.

Globe Travel Agency Ledger

Assets = Liabilities + Owner's Equity

Assets

Cash — 101

19—		19—	
Sept. 1	8,000	Sept. 5	4,000
6	1,000	12	3,000
14	13,000	21	5,000
26	2,000	28	2,100
9,900	24,000		14,100

Accts. Rec./Karen Louis — 102

19—		19—	
Sept. 1	1,000	Sept. 6	1,000
27	1,000		
1,000	2,000		1,000

Accts. Rec./Rose Shops — 103

19—	
Sept. 27	700

Furniture — 111

19—		19—	
Sept. 1	2,000	Sept. 8	500
7	1,500		
3,000	3,500		500

Office Equipment — 112

19—			
Sept. 1	5,000		
5	4,000		
13,000	13,000		-0-

Liabilities

Accts. Pay./Bell Products — 201

19—		19—	
Sept. 8	500	Sept. 1	3,000
12	3,000	7	1,500
	3,500	1,000	4,500

Accts. Pay./Royal Service Shop — 202

	19—	
	Sept. 29	200

Owner's Equity

Mark Nero, Capital — 301

19—		19—	
Sept. 21	5,000	Sept. 1	17,000
		14	13,000
	5,000		25,000 30,000
		30	1,400
	5,000	26,400	31,400

Income Summary — 399

19—		19—	
Sept. 30	2,300	Sept. 30	3,700
30	1,400		
	3,700		3,700

Sales — 401

		19—	
		Sept. 26	2,000
		27	1,700
19—	-0-		3,700 3,700
Sept. 30	3,700		
	3,700		3,700

Repairs Expense — 501

19—		19—	
Sept. 29	200	Sept. 30	200

Salaries Expense — 502

19—		19—	
Sept. 28	2,100	Sept. 30	2,100

Account balances updated after closing temporary accounts.

Here are situations involving a permanent and a temporary account. To update the account balances, do the following.

• *Update the Capital account with an entry following the balance computed for the trial balance.* (See the Mark Nero, Capital account.) Draw a single rule under both money columns. Total the amounts and compute a new account balance.

• *Update a closed account with two or more entries on either side of the account.* (See the Income Summary account.) Draw a single rule across both money columns and total the columns. Then draw a double rule across both money columns. Remember that a double rule means that the amounts equal and the work is completed.

• *Update a closed account with only one debit and one credit amount.* (See the Repairs Expense account.) Draw a double rule across both money columns.

Purpose of the Postclosing Trial Balance

The postclosing trial balance does the following. Refer to the postclosing trial balance for Globe Travel Agency shown below.

• It lists only open permanent accounts. The accounts not closed are the balance sheet accounts (assets, liabilities, and owner's equity capital accounts).

• It contains no temporary accounts. The temporary accounts have been closed.

• It contains the accounts and the balances that agree completely with the items on the balance sheet. As a result, the balance of the Mark Nero, Capital account is now identical with the total owner's equity shown on the balance sheet.

• It verifies that the ledger is now ready to receive the entries for the new accounting period.

Owner's Equity

Mark Nero, Capital   301

19—		19—		
Sept. 21	5,000	Sept. 1	17,000	
		14	13,000	
	5,000	25,000	30,000	
		30	1,400	
	5,000	26,400	31,400	

Updated Capital account.

Globe Travel Agency
Postclosing Trial Balance
September 30, 19—

ACCOUNT TITLE	ACCT. NO.	DEBIT	CREDIT
Cash	101	9 9 0 0 00	
Accts. Rec. / Karen Louis	102	1 0 0 0 00	
Accts. Rec. / Rose Shops	103	7 0 0 00	
Furniture	111	3 0 0 0 00	
Office Equipment	112	1 3 0 0 0 00	
Accts. Pay. / Bell Products	201		1 0 0 0 00
Accts. Pay. / Royal Service Shop	202		2 0 0 00
Mark Nero, Capital	301		2 6 4 0 0 00
		2 7 6 0 0 00	2 7 6 0 0 00

Globe Travel Agency
Balance Sheet
September 30, 19—

Assets			Liabilities		
Cash		9,900 00	Accounts Payable:		
Accounts Receivable:			Bell Products	$1,000.00	
Karen Louis	$1,000.00		Royal Service Shop	200.00	
Rose Shops	700.00	1,700 00	Total Liabilities		1,200 00
Furniture		3,000 00			
Office Equipment		13,000 00	Owner's Equity		
			Mark Nero, Capital	$25,000.00	
			Net Income	1,400.00	
			Total Owner's Equity		26,400 00
Total		27,600 00	Total		27,600 00

The account balances on the trial balance now agree with the balances shown on the balance sheet.

Mark Nero, Capital			301
19— Sept. 21	5,000	19— Sept. 1 14	17,000 13,000
	5,000	25,000 Sept. 30	30,000 1,400
	5,000	26,400	31,400

Owner's Capital account shows investment plus retained income.

An important concept is emphasized by the way that the Capital account appears on the postclosing trial balance. The owner's Capital account shows the amount invested plus retained income. **Retained earnings** is net income less any amount distributed to the owner. As Mark Nero's Capital account shows, he has an investment of $25,000 plus he has retained income of $1,400. Retained earnings is also known as *retained income*.

Preparing the Postclosing Trial Balance

A postclosing trial balance is prepared like a formal trial balance but only permanent accounts are listed. The balance for each account is listed in the order in which it appears in the ledger. A quick postclosing trial balance can be prepared with an adding machine. A postclosing trial balance, like a formal trial balance, is usually prepared in pencil. It may, however, be prepared in ink. The postclosing trial balance prepared for the Globe Travel Agency on September 30 is shown on page 109.

Activity C. Arrange the following accounting activities in the correct order. The accounting period is for the month ending on December 31, 19—. Refer to the text, margin notes, and illustrations on pages 107 to 110.

1. Update owner's equity
2. December 31 trial balance

3. Enter transactions for the December accounting period
4. December 1 account balances
5. Prove equality—postclosing trial balance
6. January 1 account balances
7. Prepare balance sheet
8. November 30 postclosing trial balance
9. Prepare income statement

Interpreting Accounting Information

Accounting Cycle
STEP 8: Interpret financial information.

D *Do owners and managers use the accounting information only at the end of the accounting period?* No, to operate a business successfully, owners and managers require a constant flow of information. Much of this information is provided by financial statements such as those that have been discussed.

Interpreting (or using) accounting information is often considered the last step in the accounting cycle. This is because people often think of the income statement and the balance sheet as being the only sources of accounting information for owners and managers.

Actually, accounting information must be interpreted constantly and must often be obtained from other sources besides the financial statements. For example, suppose Mark Nero wants to know the details of the total revenue he received from sales from September 1 to September 26. He will have to look at the Sales account in the ledger. The income statement shows the revenue for the entire period from September 1 to September 30 and not for parts of the period.

Suppose that on September 14 Mr. Nero wants to know the amount of cash he has available. He must look at the Cash account in the ledger. The balance sheet will not be prepared until September 30. When it is prepared, the balance sheet will show the amount of cash available on September 30 only. Similarly, if Mr. Nero wants to know to whom he sold services for $700 on credit on September 27, he must look at the ledger, not the income statement, for that information. Thus while you learned that the interpretation of accounting information is the eighth step of the accounting cycle, remember that it is a process that goes on constantly.

Management interprets financial information on a continuous basis.

The Accounting Cycle

The eight steps of the accounting cycle can be reviewed as follows.

STEP 1. *Record each transaction.* The data for each transaction is recorded in the accounting equation and in the ledger.

STEP 2. *Keep a chronological record of each transaction.* The transactions are shown by date in the equation and in the ledger.

STEP 3. *Store the changes caused by the transactions to each account, and update the accounts.* In the equation, the increases and decreases are recorded for each account. In the ledger, the debits and credits are recorded for each account in T accounts.

STEP 4. *Prove the equality of the accounts.* In the equation, the total assets equal the total liabilities plus the owner's equity. When a ledger is used, a trial balance is prepared to prove the equality of the debits and credits in the T accounts.

STEP 5. *Summarize the accounting information at end of accounting period.* The accounting information is summarized by account balances at the end of the accounting period. Two financial statements— an income statement and a balance sheet—are prepared.

STEP 6. *Transfer net income (or net loss) to the Capital account at the end of the accounting period.* The revenue and expense data is transferred to the Capital account at the end of the accounting period. This is done by the closing entries, which close the temporary accounts.

STEP 7. *Prove the equality of the accounts after the net income (or net loss) has been transferred.* A postclosing trial balance is prepared to prove the equality of the closed ledger.

STEP 8. *Interpret the accounting information.* The financial information is used to make business decisions.

Activity D. Indicate in which step of the accounting cycle each of the following activities is performed. Refer to the accounting cycle steps on page 111.
EXAMPLE: 1: Step 1.
1. Recording the original data.
2. Preparing a statement showing total assets, liabilities, and owner's equity.
3. Proving that the closed ledger is in balance.

4. Closing the revenue and expense accounts.
5. Using the accounting data to make decisions.
6. Proving that the ledger is in balance before preparing the financial statements.
7. Updating the Capital account with Income Summary data.
8. Preparing a statement showing total revenue, expenses, and net income or net loss.

Accounting Concepts:
Closing the Ledger. The revenue and expense data for one accounting period must be clearly distinguished from that of another accounting period.
Postclosing Trial Balance. The equality of the total debits and the total credits in the ledger should be verified after the ledger has been closed.

Topic 3 Problem

4-6. The T accounts for the revenue accounts, expense accounts, Income Summary account, and Capital account of the David Hays Company are shown below. Transfer the amounts to close all revenue accounts and expense accounts. Close the Income Summary account. These end-of-accounting period activities occur on March 31, 19—. Refer to the illustration on pages 103 and 108.

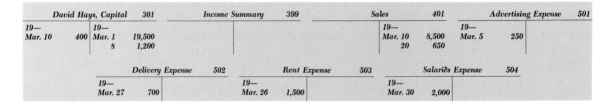

The Language of Business

Here are some basic terms that make up the language of business. Do you know the meaning of each?

pencil footing
income statement
balance sheet

account form balance
    sheet
liquidity

balance sheet accounts
income statement
   accounts
financial position
zero balance
closed account

closing the ledger
closing the accounts
closing entries
postclosing trial
   balance
retained earnings

Chapter 4 Questions

1. What are the two major financial statements? What is the purpose of each? Why does an owner need both?

2. Describe how the information that is included on an income statement is arranged. Describe the arrangement of information on the balance sheet.

3. What item appears on both the income statement and the balance sheet? Why?
4. What does a single rule drawn across a money column indicate? What does a double rule indicate?
5. The total owner's equity of a business on December 31 is $4,000 less than it was on December 1. Give two possible reasons for the decrease.
6. How does the equity section of the balance sheet vary according to the type of business ownership?

Chapter 4 Problems

Problems for Chapter 4 are given in the *Working Papers and Chapter Problems for Part 1*. If you are using the workbook, do the problems in the space provided there.

Chapter 4 Management Cases

The Need for Information. Each day a manager must make important business decisions. Examples include paying a bill in full or buying new equipment or granting a loan to an applicant. Information for these decisions can come from the records either of the manager's business or of other businesses. All of these records must provide accurate information quickly.

Case 4M-1. Carolina Williams has been giving ceramic lessons in her home to family and friends. Recently, Carolina decided to go into business and advertised to give lessons for a fee. She seeks your help in setting up accounting records. What financial information would you need from her to determine the business's assets, liabilities, and owner's equity? What accounts would you suggest? What other advice would you give her? Where can she find additional information?

Case 4M-2. Donald LaPaz owns a successful restaurant. Since new housing is being built nearby, he ex-pects an increase in business. He wants to add more seating and a larger kitchen so that his customers will not have to wait. In order to expand, Donald wants to borrow $50,000 from a bank and makes an application for a loan. With the application he includes a letter saying that his business is estimated to be worth $150,000. The bank replies that it cannot make a decision about the loan. It needs information about the revenue and expenses of the business and a list of the assets and liabilities of the business.
a. Why would the bank want a list of the assets and liabilities of the business before making a decision about the loan?
b. What financial statements should Donald have sent with his loan application?
c. Why would the bank be interested in the income statement?
d. What factors other than those shown on the financial statements do you think the bank will consider in determining whether or not to approve the loan?
e. What other factors should Donald consider before he decides whether or not to expand?

Working Hint

Making Corrections. When writing in ink on ruled paper, write each word and amount so that it will take up slightly less than one-half the space between the lines. When you make an error, draw a neat horizontal line through the entire word or amount and write the complete correct word or amount in the space *above* the incorrect one. If a word or amount is written in ink, you must *not* correct an error by erasing or by writing the correct word or amount over the incorrect one. Such corrections give the impression that the data might have been changed to hide the mishandling of funds.

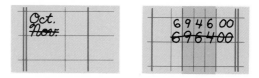

Origination and Input of Accounting Data

The accounting vocabulary, elements of accounting, types of ownership, accounting equation and records, analyzing and recording transactions in a T account ledger, what financial statements show, and the accounting cycle steps make up much of accounting theory. To see how this theory is used to supply information, you will now study again the accounting cycle steps.

Topic 1
Originating Data

A *What is the first step in the accounting cycle?* The first step in the accounting cycle, as you learned, is to record the data about each transaction. In accounting terms, the initial recording of data about a business transaction is called **originating data.**

In the next three chapters, the accounting cycle is examined in greater detail. Each step of the accounting cycle examines actual business forms and procedures. First, the step of originating data is covered.

Accounting Cycle

Source Documents

In previous chapters, the transactions were given in a narrative form. That is, the details of the transactions were described in words. You were told that on a certain date a certain transaction took place. For example, on page 25 a transaction for the Globe Travel Agency is given as follows.

September 7 The Globe Travel Agency buys additional furniture for $1,500 on credit from Bell Products. The creditor allows the Globe Travel Agency 30 days to pay this amount.

In actual practice, the details of this transaction would usually be recorded on a business form. In this way, a separate record of each transaction is available. For example, the details of the transaction to purchase the additional furniture on credit would be recorded on a business form called a *purchase invoice,* or *bill.* The details of a sale are recorded on a sales invoice.

Look at the purchase invoice at the top of page 116, and note the following information. The purchase invoice lists the details of the transaction on September 7 described above.

1 The number of the invoice. Note that the number is preprinted on the purchase invoice.
2 The date of the transaction.
3 The name of the seller (creditor).
4 The name of the purchaser (debtor).
5 The terms of the credit granted by the creditor.
6 The quantity, stock number, and description of the items or service purchased.
7 The dollar amount of the transaction. Note that all extensions appear in the Amount column. An **extension** is the product of multiplying the quantity by the unit price. The extensions are then totaled.

To the seller, this is a sales invoice. To the purchaser, this is a purchase invoice.

The accounting clerk receives this purchase invoice, and it becomes the source document for recording the transaction. The clerk must then analyze the transaction and determine the debit entry and the credit entry. Since the transaction can be traced back to this purchase invoice, the invoice is a source document for the transaction. It originates the data and supplies evidence that the transaction took place.

A **business form** is a printed piece of paper that provides blank spaces for entering data. The invoice above shows the data filled in the spaces: the invoice number, the date, the name of the purchaser, the terms on how long the customer has to pay the invoice, the items purchased, the total amount of the transaction, and other items that the business wants to know.

Business forms are used extensively in business. When a business form is used to record the data about a business transaction, the form is called a source document. A **source document** is a business form containing data about a transaction.

A source document provides information and evidence about a transaction.

Use of Source Documents

The term *document* is frequently used in accounting. A **document** is a written or printed paper that is used to provide evidence or information. A source document gives evidence that a transaction occurred. Also, the source document will provide the information needed to analyze the transaction. Source documents usually consist of paper forms with data written on them. The purchase invoice on the previous page is a source document.

Chapters 2 and 3 give the transactions for September in narrative form. The transactions for October are now listed on pages 118 to 121. An example is given of a source document that would be used for each transaction.

Once a source document is prepared, it will be used to communicate the data about a transaction through additional steps in the accounting cycle. It is also used to communicate the data to other parts of the business. For example, a salesclerk in the store writes out a sales invoice for a sale on credit. This is step one of the accounting cycle—originating the data. The salesclerk then sends the sales invoice to the accounting clerk in the accounting office. The sales invoice is the source document that provides the accounting clerk with the data needed to record the transaction in the accounting records. This is Step 2 of the accounting cycle—journalizing the transactions.

Another reason for communicating data is that frequently the salesclerk will be located in a store in one city and the accounting clerk will be located in an accounting office in another city. The important accounting details of the transaction must be communicated from the store to the office.

In some cases there is more than one business form to support a transaction. For example, the Globe Travel Agency issues a check for $1,800 to pay salaries. In this case there are more details to the transaction than are recorded on the checkbook stub. As you will learn later, a payroll summary is prepared to summarize the payroll data for all employees. Thus the complete details of this transaction are supplied by the checkbook stub and the payroll summary. It is good accounting practice to have a source document support each check that is written. In this way the source telling why the check was issued can be traced back to the invoice or other authorization.

Some other terms used in place of *source documents* are *business papers*, *original papers*, and *supporting documents*.

Language:

Invoice. In general usage, the term *bill* is used. However, in accounting usage, the term *invoice* is preferred.

OCTOBER TRANSACTIONS FOR THE GLOBE TRAVEL AGENCY

Narrative Transactions	**Source Documents**
October 1: The Globe Travel Agency started a new set of records.	Balance Sheet: A financial statement reporting the assets, liabilities, and owner's equity for a specific date.

Globe Travel Agency
Balance Sheet
September 30, 19—

Assets			Liabilities		
Cash		9,900 00	Accounts Payable:		
Accounts Receivable:			Bell Products	$1,000.00	
Karen Louis	$1,000.00		Royal Service Shop	200.00	
Rose Shops	700.00	1,700 00	Total Liabilities		1,200 00
Furniture		3,000 00			
Office Equipment		13,000 00	Owner's Equity		
			Mark Nero, Capital	$25,000.00	
			Net Income	1,400.00	
			Total Owner's Equity		26,400 00
Total		27,600 00	Total		27,600 00

October 5: The Globe Travel Agency received a check for $1,000 from Karen Louis on account.

Remittance Slip: A record listing details of cash received.

October 6: The Globe Travel Agency bought additional office equipment from the Eagle Office Corporation and issued a check for $500 in payment.

Checkbook Stub: A record in a checkbook giving details of each check issued.

OCTOBER TRANSACTIONS FOR THE GLOBE TRAVEL AGENCY

Narrative Transactions	Source Documents

October 7: The Globe Travel Agency bought additional furniture for $600 on credit from Bell Products. The creditor allows the Globe Travel Agency 30 days to pay this amount.

Purchase Invoice: A bill listing the items or services purchased, the amounts, the terms, and the date.

Bell Products
9190 Lincoln Parkway
Niles, Illinois 60606

Invoice No. 9822

Sold to: Globe Travel Agency
3010 South Fifth Street
Chicago, Illinois 60612

Date: October 7, 19--

Ship to: Same

Sales Clerk B. Bliss	Customer Order No. 4375	Shipped Via Truck	Terms Net, 30 days

Quantity	Stock No.	Description	Unit Price	Amount
3	4398	Conference tables	200.00	600.00
		TOTAL AMOUNT		600.00

October 8: The Globe Travel Agency returned furniture (one table) bought for $200 on credit from Bell Products because it arrived in damaged condition.

Credit Memorandum: A form granting credit to the purchaser for a purchase return or allowance.

Bell Products
9190 Lincoln Parkway
Niles, Illinois 60606

CREDIT MEMORANDUM
Copy 1: Customer

No. **CM-67**

To: Globe Travel Agency
3010 South Fifth Street
Chicago, Illinois 60612

Date: October 8, 19--
Sold on Invoice No. 9822
Your Order No. 4375

We have credited your account as follows:

QUANTITY	DESCRIPTION	PRICE	AMOUNT
1	Conference table, Model 4398	200.00	200.00

October 12: The Globe Travel Agency issued a check for $1,000 to Bell Products on account.

Checkbook Stub: A record in a checkbook giving details of each check issued.

NO. 6 $1,000 00/100
DATE Oct.12, 19—
TO Bell Products
FOR Paid on account

	DOLLARS	CENTS
BALANCE	10,400	00
AMT. DEPOSITED		
TOTAL	10,400	00
AMT. THIS CHECK	1,000	00
BALANCE	9,400	00

Narrative Transactions	Source Documents

October 12: Mark Nero invested an additional $5,000 in the Globe Travel Agency. He withdrew $5,000 from his personal savings account and deposited the cash in the business checking account.

Remittance Slip: A record listing details of cash received.

Globe Travel Agency
3010 South Fifth Street
Chicago, Illinois 60612
REMITTANCE SLIP 105

NAME: Mark Nero

AMOUNT RECEIVED	CHECK NUMBER	CHECK DATE
$5,000.00	552	10/12/—

EXPLANATION:
Additional investment.

DATE RECEIVED	RECEIVED BY
10/12/—	EA

No. 552   2-816 / 710
October 12, 19 —
$ 5,000.00
DOLLARS
Chicago, Illinois 60612
For: Additional investment   Mark Nero
⑆0710⑆0816⑈ 02894⑆87113⑆0552⑈

October 21: Mark Nero withdrew $2,000 from the Globe Travel Agency checking account and deposited it in his personal savings account.

Checkbook Stub: A record in a checkbook giving details of each check issued.

NO. 7 $2,000.00
DATE Oct. 21, 19 —
TO Mark Nero
FOR Cash withdrawal

	DOLLARS	CENTS
BALANCE	9,400	00
AMT. DEPOSITED	5,000	00
10/12 TOTAL	14,400	00
AMT. THIS CHECK	2,000	00
BALANCE	12,400	00

October 26: The Globe Travel Agency received $1,200 in cash from the sale of travel services during October.

Sales Invoice: A bill listing the items or services sold, the amounts, the terms, and the date.

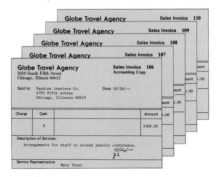

OCTOBER TRANSACTIONS FOR THE GLOBE TRAVEL AGENCY

Narrative Transactions	**Source Documents**

October 27: The Globe Travel Agency sold travel services on credit to Karen Louis for $1,000 and to Rose Shops for $800.

Sales Invoice: A bill listing the items or services sold, the amounts, the terms, and the date.

Globe Travel Agency
3010 South Fifth Street
Chicago, Illinois 60612

Sales Invoice 112
Accounting Copy

Sold to: Rose Shops
14 Second Avenue
Chicago, Illinois 60614

Date: 10/27/--

Charge	Cash		
X			

Description of Services:
Arrange florist convention tours.

Service Representative: Andrew Brodsky

Globe Travel Agency
3010 South Fifth Street
Chicago, Illinois 60612

Sales Invoice 111
Accounting Copy

Sold to: Karen Louis
34 South Street
Chicago, Illinois 60616

Date: 10/27/--

Charge	Cash		Amount
X			$1,000.00

Description of Services:
Arrange All-American tour.

10/27/--
JL

Service Representative: Andrew Brodsky

October 28: The Globe Travel Agency paid an expense of $1,800 for salaries.

Checkbook Stub: A record in a checkbook giving details of each check issued.

NO. 8 $1,800 00/100
DATE Oct. 28, 19 --
TO Salaries Expense
FOR October payroll

	DOLLARS	CENTS
BALANCE	12,400	00
AMT. DEPOSITED	1,200	00
10/26 TOTAL	13,600	00
AMT. THIS CHECK	1,800	00
BALANCE	11,800	00

October 29: The Globe Travel Agency received a bill for repairs expense of $100 from the Royal Service Shop for repairing a typewriter. The creditor allowed the Globe Travel Agency 30 days in which to pay this amount.

Purchase Invoice: A bill listing the items or services purchased, the amounts, the terms, and the date.

ROYAL SERVICE SHOP
126 Mountain Road
Lakeville, Illinois 60610

Invoice No. 212

Date: 10/29/--

To: Globe Travel Agency
3010 South Fifth Street
Chicago, Illinois 60612

Terms: Net, 30 days

Repair to typewriter	$100.00

Sources of Transaction Data

Some source documents are originated inside the business. Data collected inside the business is called **internal data.** Sources of internal data for the Globe Travel Agency are its checkbook stubs and its sales invoices. The data comes from business forms originated by someone in the Globe Travel Agency.

Other source documents are originated outside the business. Data that comes from outside the business is called **external data.** Sources of external data for the Globe Travel Agency are the checks from customers, the owner's personal checks, purchase invoices, and credit memorandums. The data from these transactions comes from business forms originated by someone outside of the business.

In some cases the business forms that come from outside businesses cannot be used as source documents (for example, when a customer gives a check). That check will be deposited in the business's checking account. The business will no longer have possession of the check. Thus, when a check is received, the business records the details of the cash transaction on a receipt form called a *remittance slip.* The remittance slip will become the source document for the transaction. A **remittance slip** is a record listing the details of cash received. The remittance slip shows the *amount* received, *from whom* the amount was received, *why* the amount was received, *the date* that the amount was received, and *by whom* the amount was received.

A business form may be a source of internal data for one business and a source of external data for another.

Some source documents provide internal data to one business and external data to another. For example, the invoice from Bell Products to Globe Travel Agency serves both purposes. To Bell Products, which originated the invoice, it provides internal data. To the Globe Travel Agency, which received the invoice from Bell, it provides external data. Bell Products considers the invoice a sales invoice because it documents a sale of goods. The Globe Travel Agency considers the invoice a purchase invoice because it documents a purchase of goods.

Purpose of the Source Documents

A source document is important for these reasons.
- It provides evidence that the transaction occurred.
- It communicates the transaction data from one person or place to another.
- It allows one person to record the transaction data and another person to analyze the transaction into its debit and credit entry.
- It makes it possible to trace the transaction through the accounting cycle.
- It provides the essential details to record the transaction in a journal, the next step of the accounting cycle.

Activity A. Decide which of the following is a source document. Write "Yes" or "No" after the item, as appropriate.

EXAMPLE: *Sales invoice—yes*

1. Telephone conversation
2. Employee's conversation
3. Checkbook stub
4. Purchase invoice
5. Cash register receipt

Methods of Processing Data

B *How does a business process data?* A business may use manual and/or electronic or automated methods of processing its accounting data. **Manual data processing** is a method of processing data manually (by hand) with the use of some equipment, such as calculators and cash registers. **Automated data processing (ADP)**, or **electronic data processing (EDP)**, is a method of processing data using a computer. The computer operates electronically and processes data at a very rapid speed.

The same basic accounting concepts and principles you learned apply to either method of processing data. However, the procedures, or ways of doing things, vary. For example, both methods rely on source documents for the origination of data. But the source documents may look somewhat different. In manual data processing systems, for example, the source documents are usually paper business forms with preprinted information and blank spaces on them. In certain automated data processing systems, the source documents consist of paper cards or tapes with holes punched in them, magnetic tapes with magnetized spots on them, or paper forms with magnetic ink characters imprinted on them.

Accounting concepts and principles apply to both manual and automated data processing.

Manual Data Processing

Several different business forms are used as source documents in manual data processing, as shown here.

Recorded Data in Manual Data Processing

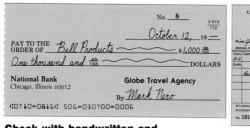

Check stub with handwritten data.

Check with handwritten and printed data.

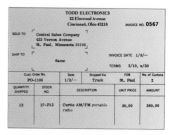

Paper form with typewritten data.

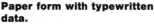

Paper form with handwritten data.

Keyboard with CRT.

Courtesy Haworth, Inc.

Data recorded on magnetic discs.

Courtesy IBM Corporation

Magnetic tape with data in the form of invisible magnetized spots.

Automated Data Processing

Source documents used in automated data processing may be paper forms with magnetic ink characters, punched tapes, or punched cards. The source documents may be magnetic tapes or disks. Special printing, such as optical type font and the universal product code, may be used. These are shown on the next page. In some instances, a console typewriter with a cathode-ray tube (CRT) display, similar to a television screen, is used. In such a case, data about a transaction is keyed into the computer through a computer terminal. A computer terminal is similar to a typewriter keyboard. In the computer, the data is stored on a storage device, such as a magnetic disk. The source documents may be printed out on paper forms immediately or at a later time.

You may be familiar with several business forms designed for use with automated data processing equipment. Several examples are shown on the next page. These forms utilize the following special printing.

- Optical type font.
- Magnetic ink characters.
- Universal product code.

These forms contain all the data about a business transaction. Such data is read and processed automatically by automated data processing equipment. For example, some electronic cash registers can read universal product codes, which consist of numbers and lines of various thicknesses. At the checkout counter, the salesclerk passes the coded label on the product over an optical scanner. The data is automatically entered into the cash register, which is connected with a computer to process the data.

Electronic Cash Register

Courtesy NCR Corp.

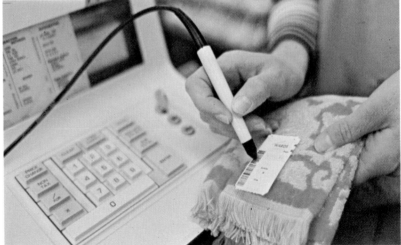

Tag Reader

Courtesy Montgomery Ward

SOME BUSINESS FORMS USED IN AUTOMATED DATA PROCESSING

Optical Type Font

Data is printed in optical type font.

Magnetic Ink Characters

Precoded check with bank identification number and depositor's account numbers.

Punched Card Code

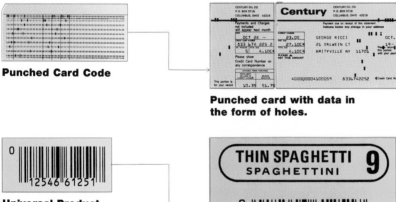

Punched card with data in the form of holes.

Universal Product Code

Data printed in Universal Product Code.

The computer relays the price back to the cash register. The cash register then prints the data on a cash register tape. One copy of the tape is given to the customer, and another remains locked inside the cash register. The cash register tape becomes the source document.

A variety of source documents are used in business. Each source document is designed to fit the specific needs of a business as well as the way the business processes data.

```
WAYNE DEPARTMENT STORES
10-05---
07    20.00X
10     4.00X
      24.00TCa
THANK YOU CALL AGAIN
```

Receipt Tape

Activity B-1. Match the automated data processing items in column A with the business forms items in column B.

Column A		Column B	
1	Universal product code	A	Check from a checkbook
2	Magnetic ink characters	B	Credit card account
3	Punched card code	C	Bill from the telephone company
4	Optical type font	D	Label on a grocery can

Activity B-2. Following are listed ways of processing data. Identify the method being used in each item. *EXAMPLE: Checks written by hand—Manual data processing*
1. Report cards printed by a computer.
2. Sales recorded on a cash register.
3. Amounts recorded as holes in cards.
4. Invoices typed on a typewriter.
5. Checks prepared on punched cards.
6. Amounts added on an adding machine.
7. Amounts added by a computer.
8. Invoices written by hand.

Accounting Concept:
Source Document. A record of the original data about each transaction should be available. This record is commonly called a *source document*.

Topic 1 Problems

5-1. Carolyn Jones is a new employee in the accounting department. Her supervisor asks her to select all the source documents from a stack of forms, correspondence, and other records. Only list the items that are accounting source documents. The stack includes the following items.

 5 invoices
 1 electric bill
10 letters to be signed
20 checks that came in the morning mail
 4 telephone messages
 2 memos from the company president
 1 telephone bill
 2 grocery lists
45 sales slips

5-2. For each of the following transactions, name an appropriate source document.
a. Henry Keller started a new set of accounting records on January 1.
b. Bought a new truck from American Motors for $12,000, Check 256.
c. Sold services to Donna Webber for $600 on credit.
d. Received a check for $200 from Elm Real Estate on account.
e. Issued a check for $39 to Mountain States Telephone Company for monthly services.
f. Sold services for $600.
g. Returned a power drill that was purchased on credit.

Topic 2
Journalizing Data

A *Is it practical to enter debits and credits directly into accounts?* In Chapter 3, the debits and credits for each transaction are entered directly into T accounts in the ledger. This may be done easily when there are only a few transactions. However, entering debits and credits directly into accounts is not practical when many transactions are involved.

There are several reasons why data from source documents are not recorded directly into the ledger.

• It is difficult to locate a complete transaction in the ledger. The record of each transaction exists in the form of a debit entry in one or more accounts and a credit entry in one or more different accounts. The debits and credits for a transaction do not appear together. Thus you would have to search throughout the entire ledger to locate all parts of a specific transaction.

• It is difficult to compare the volume of transactions by day. Debits and credits of transactions for a specific date are not stored in one account in the ledger. Instead, the transactions are scattered throughout the ledger by account title. Thus you again would have to search throughout the entire ledger to determine the volume of transactions for a specific date.

• It is difficult to locate an error in an entry. The debits and credits for each transaction do not appear together. Again you would have to tediously search throughout the entire ledger to check that the debits equal the credits for each entry.

These difficulties can be avoided by recording the transactions from source documents into a record called a *journal* before transferring the debits and credits to the accounts in the ledger.

Journals

A journal is a daily record of the important facts and amounts of every transaction. In a journal, the transactions are recorded in chronological order. That is, transactions are recorded according to the date on which they occurred. This makes it quite easy to trace any transaction. A **journal** is, therefore, a chronological listing of all transactions analyzed in terms of the accounts to be debited and credited.

A journal is sometimes referred to as a *register* or simply a *listing*. The most common term, however, is *journal*, which comes from the French word *jour*, meaning *day*. The journal is, in fact, a daybook of transactions. It is the diary of a business.

After the data about a transaction is originated, it is recorded in a journal. **Journalizing** is the recording of transactions in a journal. Journalizing is the second step in the accounting cycle.

Several items should be emphasized before showing you how to journalize transactions.

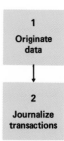

Accounting Cycle

• There are many different types of journals used in business. The first journal that will be described is the two-column journal, which is the basic type of journal. It is illustrated here.

The two-column journal has one money column for debits and one column for credits.

JOURNAL Page

DATE	ACCOUNT TITLE AND EXPLANATION	POST. REF.	DEBIT	CREDIT

• Journalizing does not change the accounting rules of debiting and crediting. The only difference between this procedure and the one followed in Chapter 3 is that a transaction is recorded in the journal before it is stored in the accounts.
• The transaction will be journalized in a traditional manual (pen-and-ink) method. The manual method is still used in many businesses today. Also, the same details are present whether the transactions are recorded manually or by some machine or computer.
• The details of the transactions are obtained from source documents.

Purpose of the Journal

Using a journal to record transactions offers these advantages.

• It provides a chronological listing of all transactions. Thus only the date of the transaction needs to be known to locate any transaction. It does not matter how many months, years, or accounting periods ago the transaction occurred.
• It provides a record of the transactions by day. As a result, the volume of transactions for any day can be obtained and compared with the volume of other days.
• It shows the debits and credits for each entry. Thus the equality of the debits and credits can be quickly checked for each transaction. Errors, such as entering the wrong debit or credit amount, can be discovered before the transactions are transferred to the ledger.
• It shows all the data about a transaction (including an explanation) in one place, and it provides an audit trail to locate the data.
• It provides proof of the business's transactions, in case a source document gets lost, stolen, or destroyed.

Activity A. Answer the following questions about the journal. Refer to the text and illustrations on pages 126 to 128.
1. What are the first two steps in the accounting cycle?
2. How can the difficulties of entering debits and credits directly into accounts be avoided?
3. In what order are transactions recorded in journals?
4. What does the French word *jour* mean in English? How does this meaning relate to the accountant's use of the journal?
5. What are three reasons why data from source documents are not recorded directly into the ledger?

The Journalizing Procedure

B *What must be done before a transaction can be journalized?* Before the data from a source document is recorded in a journal, the transaction must be analyzed. **Analyzing a transaction** means determining the effects the transaction has on the various asset, liability, and owner's equity accounts. This analysis determines the journal entry to be recorded. A **journal entry** is a recording in a journal of a transaction showing the date, accounts and amounts to be debited and credited, with, if necessary, an explanation. A journal entry contains the following data.

- The date.
- The title of the accounts to be debited and credited.
- The amounts of the debits and the credits.
- The source document number and/or a brief explanation.

The basic guidelines for making a journal entry will be illustrated by using the October 5 transaction. On October 5 the Globe Travel Agency receives a check for $1,000 from Karen Louis on account.

Mark Nero prepared a remittance slip as a record of the transaction. The remittance slip becomes the source document because it is a record of the amount of cash received from each customer.

Here are the basic guidelines to follow in recording the journal entry.

Analyzing the Transaction. Analyze the effects of the transaction in the usual way. Determine what happens, the accounting rule to apply, and the debit entry and the credit entry. You may find it helpful to use T accounts in determining the entry. (When using T accounts to analyze transactions, you do not have to write the date. You are just analyzing the debits and credits of the transaction and checking the equality of the debits and credits.)

Check received from debtor.

Remittance slip is source document.

Cash	101	Accts. Rec./Karen Louis 102	
1,000			1,000

T accounts help in analyzing transactions.

The year and month are written at the top of a page.

The month is written when the month changes.

The year and the month are written when the year changes.

Recording the Date of Transaction. Record the date of the transaction in the Date column. When starting a page of a journal, write the year in small figures at the top of the page in the left part of the divided Date column, as shown in the margin. Abbreviate the month, and enter it below the year. Then write the day of the month in the right part of the Date column. Write the date when recording the first debit of each journal entry. Do not repeat the date for other debits and credits of the same journal entry.

For the next transaction, record only the day of the month. Do not repeat the month and the year. Write the year and month only in these three instances: when starting a new page, when the month changes, or when the year changes.

Recording the Debit Entry. Record the debit entry. Write the title of the account that is to be debited in the next column. Use the same line as the date. Start writing the title at the vertical rule of the Account Title and Explanation column. Then enter the amount of the debit in the Debit money column, on the same line. Since this is a ruled form, it is not necessary to use dollar signs, commas, or decimal points.

Recording the Credit Entry. Record the credit entry on the line below the debit entry. Indent about a half inch (1.25 centimeters) from the Date column, and write the title of the account that is to be credited. On the same line, enter the amount of the credit in the Credit money column.

The credit entries are indented so that they can easily be distinguished from the debit entries. Remember that *debit* means left and *credit* means right. Thus the debit is written to the left and the credit to the right.

Writing an Explanation. On the line below the credit entry, indent about an inch (2.5 centimeters) and record an explanation of the transaction. The source document number, if one is available, should be entered as part of the explanation.

When the account titles or the source documents reveal the reason for an entry, a further explanation is frequently omitted. Explanations are used when transactions are unusual, complicated, or additional data is needed. The explanations should be short but clear.

The type of source document should be identified, such as an invoice (Inv.), check (Ck.), remittance slip (RS), or credit memorandum (CM). Note that these words have been abbreviated in the journal in order to save space.

In the illustrations in this chapter, explanations have been included for all journal entries. However, they will be omitted in later chapters except where the journalized transaction is unusual or complicated in nature.

Posting Reference. The Posting Reference (Post. Ref.) column is not used in journalizing. This column is used when the data is transferred from the journal to the ledger. This procedure is known as posting, and is explained in Chapter 6.

The following illustration shows how the October 5 transaction would be recorded in the journal. This example shows a transaction in which the Globe Travel Agency receives $1,000 in cash from Karen Louis on account.

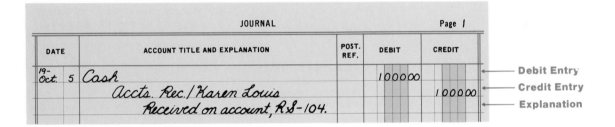

Cross-Referencing. The date of the transaction and the journal page number are entered on the source document. This cross-references the source document and the journal.

Cross-referencing involves entering the date and journal page number on the source document and the source document number, if one is available, in the journal. Through this procedure, anyone can readily trace an entry from the source document to the journal. Cross-referencing also allows anyone to readily locate the source document from the journal entry.

Journalizing Typical Transactions

The following transactions are the October transactions for Globe Travel Agency. In Chapter 3, similar transactions are entered directly in the T accounts for the month of September. The journal entries illustrate how the October transactions would be recorded in the journal.

Oct. 1 Account titles and balances for the opening entry are taken from the September 30 balance sheet.

Oct. 5 Received $1,000 from Karen Louis on account.

Oct. 6 Bought office equipment (display racks) for $500 in cash.

Oct. 7 Bought furniture (conference tables) for $600 on credit from Bell Products.

Oct. 8 Returned furniture (conference table) bought for $200 on credit from Bell Products.

Oct. 12 Paid $1,000 to Bell Products on account.

Oct. 12 Received $5,000 from Mark Nero as an additional investment.

Oct. 21 Paid $2,000 to Mark Nero as a withdrawal from the business.

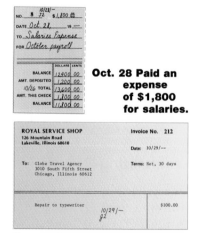

Oct. 26 Received $1,200 cash for sale of services.

Oct. 27 Sold services on credit to Karen Louis for $1,000 and to Rose Shops for $800.

Oct. 28 Paid an expense of $1,800 for salaries.

Oct. 29 Recorded an expense of $100 for repairing office equipment owed to the Royal Service Shop.

	JOURNAL				Page 1	

DATE	ACCOUNT TITLE AND EXPLANATION	POST. REF.	DEBIT		CREDIT	
19— Oct. 1	Cash		9900 00			
	Accts. Rec./Karen Louis		1000 00			
	Accts. Rec./Rose Shops		700 00			
	Furniture		3000 00			
	Office Equipment		13000 00			
	Accts. Pay./Bell Products				1000 00	
	Accts. Pay./Royal Service Shop				200 00	
	Mark Nero, Capital				26400 00	
	Opening entry, Sept. 30 balance sheet.					
5	Cash		1000 00			
	Accts. Rec./Karen Louis				1000 00	
	Received on account, RS-104.					
6	Office Equipment		500 00			
	Cash				500 00	
	Bought display racks, Ck. 5.					
7	Furniture		600 00			
	Accts. Pay./Bell Products				600 00	
	Bought conference tables, Inv. 9822.					
8	Accts. Pay./Bell Products		200 00			
	Furniture				200 00	
	Returned table, CM-67.					
12	Accts. Pay./Bell Products		1000 00			
	Cash				1000 00	
	Paid on account, Ck. 6.					
12	Cash		5000 00			
	Mark Nero, Capital				5000 00	
	Additional investment, RS-105.					
21	Mark Nero, Capital		2000 00			
	Cash				2000 00	
	Cash withdrawal, Ck. 7.					
26	Cash		1200 00			
	Sales				1200 00	
	Cash sales, Inv. 106-110					
27	Accts. Rec./Karen Louis		1000 00			
	Accts. Rec./Rose Shops		800 00			
	Sales				1800 00	
	Credit sales, Inv. 111-112		40900 00		40900 00	

Journal does not have enough lines remaining for a complete entry.

DATE	ACCOUNT TITLE AND EXPLANATION	POST. REF.	DEBIT	CREDIT
19— Oct. 28	Salaries Expense		1800 00	
	Cash			1800 00
	October payroll, Ck. 8.			
29	Repairs Expense		100 00	
	Accts. Pay./Royal Service Shop			100 00
	Repair of typewriter, Inv. 212.			

Page is numbered consecutively. Year, month, and date are entered in date column.

An audit trail involves cross-referencing each step of the accounting cycle.

Audit Trail

When data is recorded, a reference is usually given to show the source of the data. The reference can be a date, a name and address, or a number such as the journal page number. These references form an audit trail. An **audit trail** is a cross-referencing of items that makes it possible to trace the details of a transaction from the source document to the financial statements.

Making the audit trail involves cross-referencing the source documents and the journal. Anyone can then trace the entry from the source document to the journal, or the source document can be traced from the journal.

A cross-referencing number on the source document shows that the entry has been journalized. If you are interrupted while journalizing, you can tell from the cross-reference numbers on the source document which ones have been journalized. If a cross-referencing number were omitted after a source document had been journalized, you might journalize the transaction a second time by mistake. Thus it is very important to record all cross-referencing numbers on the source documents during the journalizing procedure.

Summarizing the Journalizing Procedure

Here are some points to remember in journalizing.

- The data actually originates on source documents.
- The first entry is an opening entry. An **opening entry** opens the accounts in a new set of books. The source document for the Globe Travel Agency's opening entry is the balance sheet. If the Globe Travel Agency were a new business and the owner invested only cash, the Cash account and the owner's Capital account would be the only accounts shown.

The Globe Travel Agency opens a new set of books on October 1. Therefore, the opening entry records the permanent account balances as of October 1. The source document for the opening entry is the September 30 balance sheet. The balance sheet is prepared after all transactions for September 30 are recorded. Thus, the balance sheet for September 30 and the accounts in the ledger would be the same.

• No blank lines are left between entries. Since the explanation is indented an inch, each journal entry clearly stands out.

• Within any one entry, there is at least one debit and one credit. However, there may be more than one debit and more than one credit. In such a case, this entry is called a compound journal entry. A **compound journal entry** is an entry that contains more than two accounts. For example, the journal entry dated October 1 requires more than one debit and more than one credit. In every compound journal entry, the total debits for the transaction must always equal the total credits.

• Each source document is cross-referenced to the journal page so that an audit trail is available.

• Only complete journal entries are recorded on a journal page. Do not begin recording a transaction at the bottom of a page unless there are enough lines to journalize the complete entry. Note that in the journal on page 133, only two blank lines remain at the bottom of the page. The pages of the journal are numbered consecutively. That is, the pages are numbered in numeric sequence. The year and the month are repeated at the top of the Date column on each page. In each entry, the debits are always recorded before the credits.

• The journal form illustrated on page 133 is a two-column journal. A **two-column journal** is a journal that has two money columns—one for debits and one for credits. The two-column journal helps to prevent errors because the equality of the debits and credits for each transaction can be checked at a glance. The **journal proof** is the equality of the total debits and total credits. This is shown with pencil footing on page 1 of the journal. (See the Working Hint on page 141.)

• Listing transactions in chronological order makes it quite easy to locate any specific transaction. The complete entry is located in one place. It is easy to compare the volume of transactions from day to day.

Activity B-1. Answer the following questions about journalizing. Refer to the Globe Travel Agency's journal on pages 133 and 134.
1. What assets are recorded on October 1?
2. Is office equipment bought with cash or on credit on October 6?
3. What is the source of the $5,000 cash received on October 12?
4. Which customer paid on October 5? How much?

5. From whom is furniture purchased on October 7?
6. For what item is $1,800 in cash spent on October 28?
7. To whom are sales on credit made on October 27?

Activity B-2. The journal on page 136 contains the entries for the first two weeks of February for Electric Tool Supply Company.

DATE		ACCOUNT TITLE AND EXPLANATION	POST. REF.	DEBIT	CREDIT
19—					
Feb.	1	Cash..........................		1,500 00	
		Tools		2,500 00	
		Accts. Pay./Jay Hanels...........			600 00
		Karen Shultz, Capital............			3,400 00
	2	Utilities Expense		45 00	
		Cash			45 00
	3	Equipment		450 00	
		Accts. Pay./Jay Hanels...........			450 00
	4	Cash........................		550 00	
		Accts. Rec./Gregg McAndrew			550 00
	5	Tools		75 00	
		Cash			75 00
	7	Accts. Rec./Gregg McAndrew		700 00	
		Sales			700 00
	8	Cash........................		955 00	
		Sales			955 00
	9	Accts. Pay./Jay Hanels		35 00	
		Equipment....................			35 00
	11	Karen Shultz, Capital		400 00	
		Cash			400 00
	14	Accts. Pay./Jay Hanels		340 00	
		Cash			340 00

On a form like the one below, analyze each journal entry in terms of an increase or decrease in the accounting elements. State what occurred in each transaction. Use the signs A+, A−, L+, L−, OE+, and OE− to show the increases and decreases.

Date	Debit	Credit	Transaction That Took Place
Feb. 1	A+	L+, OE+	Karen Shultz started the business with an investment of $1,500 in cash, $2,500 in tools, and an account payable of $600.

Other Methods of Keeping the Journal

A journal is a chronological listing of transactions that can be prepared in a variety of ways.

C *Are all journal entries recorded in a paper-based journal?* No, a journal can be a bound book, it can be a group of loose-leaf sheets, or it may not be a paper form at all. The journal can be maintained by computers. In this case transaction data may be entered into the computer from a keyboard or directly from a cash register connected with the computer. The data does not have to be printed on a business form. Instead, it may be entered in the computer and stored on cards, magnetic disks, magnetic tapes, or other forms of electronic storage. The journal may be printed later or may not be printed at all. Data may remain stored in the computer until it is needed. Today businesses frequently use machines to make listings of transactions instead of doing so by hand.

The method of preparing a journal varies from business to business. The form of the journal also varies. Businesses may use journals with only one money column or more than two money columns. These types of journals are explained in future chapters. Regardless of the method or the form, the function of the journal is the same in all businesses. It provides a chronological record of the transactions.

Various automated data processing methods are discussed in Topic 1. These can be used to journalize transactions and originate data.

Data Processing Cycle

Every business processes data to provide information that will meet the needs of managers and owners who use accounting information to make business decisions. Their need for information is called an **internal need.** The need for accounting information from outside is called **external need.** Some of the information comes from accounting data and some does not. However, before any data is processed, a business must decide on what information is needed, where to get the information, and how to process it. Managers and owners make decisions concerning needed information in logical order similar to the following.

• *What information is needed?* In data processing, *output* is the term used for information needed. It has the same meaning in accounting. Managers and owners need information shown on financial statements, such as the income statement and the balance sheet. This information in accounting is called output.

• *What data is required to supply output?* In accounting and data processing, data needed to supply output is called *input.* Transactions recorded in a journal are input into the accounting system.

• *Where is the input data collected?* In accounting, input data is collected on source documents. All accounting information originates on some sort of source document. This data enters the accounting cycle as transactions in a journal. Transactions, therefore, become input data for the needed output.

• *What should be done to the input data to provide the needed output?* Specific procedures are used to process input to get the desired output. This is called *processing data.* In accounting processing input data involves these activities: journalizing, updating the accounts, proving the ledger, preparing financial statements, closing the ledger, and proving the ledger after closing. You are learning about these activities. You know that these accounting cycle activities can be processed through manual data processing or through automated data processing. In either instance, the same accounting cycle activities, accounting concepts, and principles are used. But the data is manipulated differently in a manual process versus an automated process. This is because of the differences in materials and equipment used, such as the use of paper and pen versus the use of computers.

These four questions are called the accounting cycle. The **data processing cycle** is the series of steps taken to process data and provide information.

Now we compare the first two steps in the data processing cycle with the steps in the accounting cycle. (Note that the order in which data is processed is different from the order in which the questions are asked.)

STEP 1. *Origination of Data.* The origination step involves collecting the data. The data is collected on source documents. This step usually does not involve a computer. As a result, this is sometimes not considered to be the first step in data processing.

STEP 2. *Input of Data.* After the data has been collected, it must be entered into the system so that it can be processed. The data to be processed is called **input data.** In accounting, the input data is taken from source documents and arranged in the manner needed for processing. When a computer is used, this is the step where the input data is put into the computer. The form on which input data is arranged is called the **input medium.** The device used to transfer and arrange input data is called the **input device.**

Now apply this data processing vocabulary to accounting. The data is always collected on some form of source document. Then the *input data* (data to be processed) is taken from the source documents and is entered into a journal. The journal is the *input medium* because this is where the data is entered into the accounting system. If a pen is used, for example, the pen is the *input device.* Another input device is a console typewriter with a cathode-ray tube (CRT) display.

It is very important that you learn data processing terms when studying accounting. Accounting systems and procedures use a variety of data processing equipment to complete accounting activities. However, as you learned earlier, the same accounting concepts and principles are used both in manual and automated data processing. The title of this chapter is "Origination and Input of Accounting Data." Thus you can begin to see from this discussion how accounting relates to data processing.

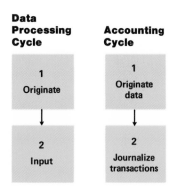

Data Processing Cycle

1
Originate

↓

2
Input

Accounting Cycle

1
Originate data

↓

2
Journalize transactions

Activity C-1. Answer the following questions about journalizing in accounting and data processing. Refer to the text, margin notes, and illustrations on pages 136 to 138.

1. Is there only one way to keep a journal? Explain.
2. What are the four questions used to make decisions about needed information?
3. Name the first two steps of the data processing cycle.

Activity C-2. Listed below are people, businesses, and government agencies from whom the Ready-Built Trucking Company, Inc. needs accounting information. Indicate whether Ready-Built's need is an external or internal need for accounting information.

EXAMPLE: Banks—external need

1. Customers
2. Employees union
3. Company president
4. Consumer agencies
5. State government
6. Sun Company, creditor
7. Marketing department
8. Trucking Association
9. Florida Orange Co., debtor
10. Purchasing department
11. Payroll department

Accounting Concepts:

Journal. A record of all transactions should be available in chronological order. This record is commonly called a *journal.*

Audit Trail. References should be provided so that data can be traced from its origination (beginning) to its use (end).

Topic 2 Problems

5-3. The Midwest Data Service, owned by William Carrington, had the following transactions during November and December. Journalize these transactions. Provide a brief explanation for each journal entry.

Nov. 1 William Carrington started the business with $10,000 in cash.
    14 Bought office equipment (adding machine and calculator) for $1,200 in cash (Check 101).
    21 Bought office equipment (typewriter) for $800 on credit from Delta Supplies (Invoice 321).
    28 Sold services for $565 on credit to Dolores Inski (Invoice 001).
Dec. 3 Paid $35 for telephone bill (Check 102).
    5 Returned office equipment (adding machine) bought for $250 in cash (Check 732).
    15 Received $300 from Dolores Inski on account (Remittance Slip 001).
    17 Sold services for $910 in cash (Invoice 002).
    18 Paid $75 to Delta Supplies on account (Check 103).
    29 Paid $150 to William Carrington as a withdrawal for his personal use (Check 104).

NOTE: Save your journal for further use in Topic Problem 6-1.

5-4. Tremont Cleaners, owned by Janet Muski, had the following transactions during January. Journalize these transactions. If the account titles do not reveal the reason for an entry, provide a brief explanation for the entry. Always include source document numbers.

Jan. 2 Janet Muski started the business with an investment of $30,000 in cash and $4,000 in cleaning equipment.
    5 Bought used cleaning equipment for $12,000 on credit from the Swan Company.
    8 Bought office equipment (cash register and typewriter) for $1,100 in cash.
    9 Sold services for $350 on credit to Mt. Pleasant High School for cleaning uniforms.
    11 Paid $500 for January rent.
    12 Returned cleaning equipment (presser) bought for $1,750 on credit from the Swan Company.
    14 Paid $755 to Janet Muski as a withdrawal from the business.
    18 Returned office equipment (typewriter) bought for $550 in cash.
    19 Paid $2,000 to the Swan Company on account.
    20 Received $200 from Mt. Pleasant High School on account.
    25 Owes $150 to *Citizen Press* for advertising during January.
    30 Sold services for $1,500 in cash.

NOTE: Save your journal for further use in Topic Problem 6-2.

The Language of Business

Here are some basic terms that make up the language of business. Do you know the meaning of each?

originating data
extension
business form
source document
document
internal data
external data

remittance slip
manual data
   processing
automated data
   processing (ADP)
electronic data
   processing (EDP)

journal
journalizing
analyzing a transaction
journal entry
cross-referencing
audit trail
opening entry
compound journal
  entry

two-column journal
journal proof
internal need
external need
data processing cycle
input data
input medium
input device

Chapter 5 Questions

1. Name four different types of source documents.
2. Describe the data contained in a journal.
3. What are the differences between a journal and a source document?
4. Describe the procedure followed in journalizing a transaction.
5. Give reasons why data from source documents are not recorded directly in the ledger.
6. Compare the origination of data in manual data processing with that of automated data processing.

7. How can the equality of debits and credits be proved in the two-column journal?
8. Why is an audit trail necessary in accounting?
9. What are the first two steps in the data processing cycle? Briefly describe the first two steps.
10. What are the differences between internal and external data?

Chapter 5 Problems

Problems for Chapter 5 are given in *Working Papers and Chapter Problems for Part 1*. If you are using the workbook, do the problems in the space provided there.

Chapter 5 Management Cases

Keeping Appropriate Records. When starting a business, owners often decide to keep their own accounting records. Sometimes they will not have had a course in accounting. Even if they have, they may not recall exactly the procedures to follow. Thus owners may be getting inaccurate information and missing information that they need.

There is no single way of keeping accounting records. However, accurate records must be kept to provide the information that is needed for making decisions.

Case 5M-1. Donald Yuan owns and operates a jewelry store. He keeps a bank account into which he deposits cash received and from which he pays invoices. His checkbook is the only accounting record he maintains. If there is a larger balance in the bank account at the end of the year than at the beginning, he assumes that his business has had a net income. If there is a smaller balance in the bank account, he assumes that his business has had a loss. For example, at the beginning of last year the bank account had a balance of $5,000. At the end of the year the balance was only $2,300. Thus, Mr. Yuan assumed that his business had lost $2,700 during the year.
a. Do you agree that the business had a net loss for the year?

b. Would it be possible for the bank account to have decreased and yet for the business to have had a net income during the year? Explain.

c. What information would Mr. Yuan need in order to learn whether or not the owner's equity actually increased or decreased during the year?

d. What types of transactions are not shown in the checkbook?

e. Does Mr. Yuan need a journal? Give your reason.

Case 5M-2. Barbara Ashley has excellent accounting knowledge. She is the accountant for Grandview Auto Services, a gas station and auto repair shop. Her work involves all phases of accounting processes using manual data processing.

Grandview Auto Services is expanding its repair services in January. As a result of the expansion, the present manual method of processing accounting data is inadequate. Ms. Ashley, recognizing the need to keep appropriate accounting records, recommended to the owner that automated data processing equipment should be purchased. As a result, Ms. Ashley was given approval to purchase the automated accounting equipment and to make any changes in business forms.

a. Would the accounting concepts and principles change when automated data processing equipment is used? Why?

b. Which step in the accounting cycle (originating data or journalizing) would show the greatest change in business forms? Explain your answer.

c. Is an opening entry necessary when Grandview Auto Services converts to automated data processing equipment for accounting records? Why?

Working Hint

Check the Journal for Mathematical Accuracy.
The double-entry principle holds true in the journal as well as the ledger. Each transaction must have equal amounts recorded in the Debit column and the Credit column. Several procedures are followed to ensure that the journal is in balance before the amounts are transferred to the ledger. An adding machine or calculator is frequently used to check this equality.

- Clear the machine; check for the clear symbol.
- Add the debits and total the amounts.
- Add the credits and total the amounts.
- Check that the two totals agree.

Journal Proof
Page 1
October 27, 19—

```
        0.00T
    9,900.00
    1,000.00
      700.00
    3,000.00
   13,000.00
    1,000.00
      500.00
      600.00
      200.00
    1,000.00
    5,000.00
    2,000.00
    1,200.00
    1,000.00
      800.00
   40,900.00T✓

        0.00T
    1,000.00
      200.00
   26,400.00
    1,000.00
      500.00
      600.00
      200.00
    1,000.00
    5,000.00
    2,000.00
    1,200.00
    1,800.00
   40,900.00T✓
```

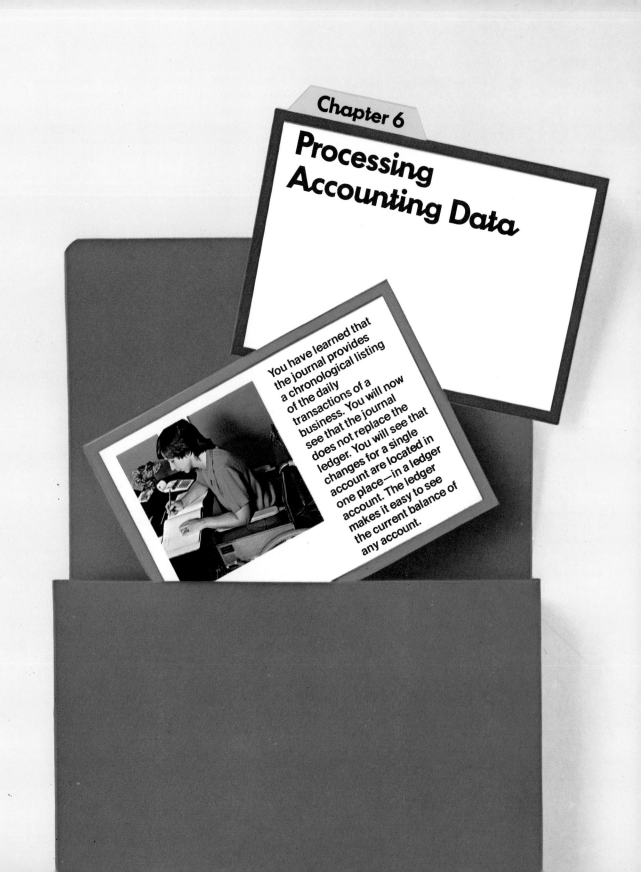

Chapter 6

Processing Accounting Data

You have learned that the journal provides a chronological listing of the daily transactions of a business. You will now see that the journal does not replace the ledger. You will see that changes for a single account are located in one place—in a ledger account. The ledger makes it easy to see the current balance of any account.

Topic 1
Posting Data to the Ledger

A *What is the third step in the accounting cycle?* The third step in the accounting cycle is to transfer the accounting data from the journal to the ledger. This procedure is called posting. **Posting** is the process of transferring data from one medium to another. (A **medium** is an object on which something is recorded.) In this case posting to the ledger means that the entries are transferred from the journal to the ledger.

In posting, data is classified according to account titles, and the amounts are sorted according to debits and credits. Each amount listed in the Debit column of the journal will be posted to the Debit money column of an account in the ledger. Each amount listed in the Credit column of the journal will be posted to the Credit money column of an account in the ledger.

Accounting Cycle

Forms of Ledger Accounts

As you know, a **ledger** is a group of accounts. In Chapter 3 you used T accounts in a ledger. The T account is only one of many different forms of accounts. Any account used to show the increases and decreases for each asset, liability, and owner's equity item is called a **ledger account.**

T accounts are useful when learning accounting and when analyzing transactions. However, businesses need more information than the T account provides.

Some of the disadvantages of a T account are:

Cash			101
19—		19—	
Oct. 1	9,900	Oct. 6	500
5	1,000	12	1,000
14	5,000	21	2,000
26	1,200	28	1,800
11,800	17,100		5,300

Balances are not constantly available in T accounts. Also, it is time-consuming to obtain the balances.

• The balance of the account is not readily available. To obtain the balance, first the debit amounts have to be added. Next the credit amounts have to be added. Then the smaller total must be subtracted from the larger total.
• It is very time-consuming to balance the accounts at the end of the accounting period and to indicate where one accounting period ends and another starts.

Four-Column Balance Ledger Form. In this chapter a four-column balance ledger form will be used. The form is called a four-column form because it has four money columns. The form of ledger account used most commonly today is the balance ledger form. The **balance ledger form** is an account form that shows the current balance of the account after each entry is posted.

The four-column balance ledger form has a heading section, a Date column, an Explanation column, a Posting Reference column, and four money columns. The first two money columns are used to record the amounts for the entries. The last two money columns are used to record the account balance as each entry is posted.

Balance ledger form shows the current account balance.

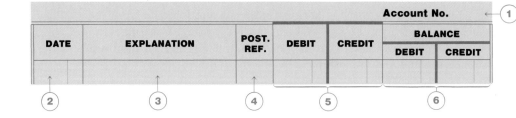

			Account No.				①
DATE	EXPLANATION	POST. REF.	DEBIT	CREDIT	BALANCE		
					DEBIT	CREDIT	

② ③ ④ ⑤ ⑥

1 *Heading:* When a ledger account is opened, the title of the account is written at the top left of the account and the account number is written at the top right. Numbers are assigned to each account in the order in which the account is listed in the chart of accounts.

2 *Date column:* The date the transaction was recorded in the journal.

3 *Explanation column:* An explanation of the transaction may be given.

4 *Posting Reference (Post. Ref.) column:* The page number of the journal in which the transaction is recorded is listed.

5 *Debit and Credit columns:* The amount of each debit or credit entry is listed in the appropriate money column.

6 *Balance (Debit and Credit) columns:* The current balance of the account is listed in the appropriate balance money column.

The money columns for the entries follow the T account format. The Debit column is the left money column. The Credit column is the right money column. The money columns in the Balance section also follow this format. A debit balance is recorded in the left balance column. A credit balance is recorded in the right balance column.

When a ledger is opened, a heading and account number are entered for each account listed in the chart of accounts. The chart of accounts for the Globe Travel Agency is shown in the margin. An account is opened for each of these items, regardless of whether it has a balance or not. If this is done, an account will be available when it has to be used.

Globe Travel Agency Chart of Accounts

Assets
101 Cash
102 Accts. Rec./Karen Louis
103 Accts. Rec./Rose Shops
111 Furniture
112 Office Equipment

Liabilities
201 Accts. Pay./Bell Products
202 Accts. Pay./Royal Service Shop

Owner's Equity
301 Mark Nero, Capital
399 Income Summary

Revenue
401 Sales

Expenses
501 Repairs Expense
502 Salaries Expense

An account is established for each account on the chart of accounts.

Cash						Account No.	101	
DATE	EXPLANATION	POST. REF.	DEBIT	CREDIT	BALANCE			
					DEBIT	CREDIT		
19— Oct. 1	Opening entry	J1	9 9 0 0 00		9 9 0 0 00			

Activity A. Answer the following questions about the balance ledger form. Refer to the balance ledger form on page 144.
1. What two items identify an account?
2. What type of account is commonly used in learning accounting and in solving problems?
3. How many money columns are there on a balance ledger form?
4. What date is posted to the ledger?
5. What number is in the Posting Reference column?
6. What amounts are recorded in the first two money columns?

The Posting Procedure

B *What is the procedure followed for posting data from the journal to the ledger?* The procedure for posting from the journal to the ledger accounts can be illustrated by posting the October 1 entry for the Globe Travel Agency. The journal entry and the accounts to which it is posted are illustrated. Refer to this illustration as you study the following steps for posting from the journal to the ledger.

1 Locate the ledger account for the first debit listed in the journal entry.

2 Record the date in the Date column. The date is the date of the journal entry. Thus the date in the ledger should be the same as the date in the journal. For the first line only, record the year, the month, and the day of the first entry. In following entries, post the day of the month only. Do not repeat the month or the year except when either changes or when the account is continued on another page.

3 Enter an explanation if one is needed to explain the entry. In the ledger accounts shown here, the words "Opening entry" are written as the explanation. This means that this is an opening balance and not a change caused by a transaction. In later accounts we show the source document written out. To save time, these are often abbreviated. Explanations, other than source document numbers, are seldom used. To find a complete explanation of the entry, the entry is traced back to the journal or to the source document.

4 Enter in the Posting Reference column of the ledger the letter "J" (for "journal") and the number of the journal page from which the entry is being posted. This cross-references the journal with the ledger. Thus an audit trail exists.

5 Record the amount in the correct Debit or Credit money column. In the transaction illustrated, Cash has been debited in the journal. Thus the amount is recorded in the Debit column of the Cash account.

6 Compute and record the balance in the correct Balance money column. Since there is only one debit amount in the Cash account and no previous balance, the debit amount is the balance. Thus the debit amount is repeated in the Debit Balance column.

7 Enter in the Posting Reference column of the journal the number of the ledger account to which the journal entry has been posted.

8 Locate the ledger account for the next entry. If the next entry is a debit, repeat the same procedure. If the next entry is a credit, apply this procedure, but record the amount in the Credit money column and the Credit Balance column.

Additional debits will be added to the Cash account balance, and additional credits will be subtracted. In this way the current balance of the Cash account is always shown.

Other ledger accounts after October 1 entry is posted.

Accts. Rec./ Rose Shops   Account No. 103

DATE	EXPLANATION	POST. REF.	DEBIT	CREDIT	BALANCE DEBIT	BALANCE CREDIT
19— Oct. 1	Opening entry	J1	700 00		700 00	

Furniture   Account No. 111

DATE	EXPLANATION	POST. REF.	DEBIT	CREDIT	BALANCE DEBIT	BALANCE CREDIT
19— Oct. 1	Opening entry	J1	3000 00		3000 00	

Office Equipment   Account No. 112

DATE	EXPLANATION	POST. REF.	DEBIT	CREDIT	BALANCE DEBIT	BALANCE CREDIT
19— Oct. 1	Opening entry	J1	13000 00		13000 00	

Accts. Pay. / Bell Products   Account No. 201

DATE	EXPLANATION	POST. REF.	DEBIT	CREDIT	BALANCE DEBIT	BALANCE CREDIT
19— Oct. 1	Opening entry	J1		1000 00		1000 00

Accts. Pay. / Royal Service Shop   Account No. 202

DATE	EXPLANATION	POST. REF.	DEBIT	CREDIT	BALANCE DEBIT	BALANCE CREDIT
19— Oct. 1	Opening entry	J1		200 00		200 00

Mark Nero, Capital   Account No. 301

DATE	EXPLANATION	POST. REF.	DEBIT	CREDIT	BALANCE DEBIT	BALANCE CREDIT
19— Oct. 1	Opening entry	J1		26400 00		26400 00

Income Summary   Account No. 399

DATE	EXPLANATION	POST. REF.	DEBIT	CREDIT	BALANCE DEBIT	BALANCE CREDIT

Sales   Account No.   401

DATE	EXPLANATION	POST. REF.	DEBIT	CREDIT	BALANCE	
					DEBIT	CREDIT

Repairs Expense   Account No.   501

DATE	EXPLANATION	POST. REF.	DEBIT	CREDIT	BALANCE	
					DEBIT	CREDIT

Salaries Expense   Account No.   502

DATE	EXPLANATION	POST. REF.	DEBIT	CREDIT	BALANCE	
					DEBIT	CREDIT

Account	Normal Balance
Asset Accounts	Debit Balance
Liability Accounts	Credit Balance
Capital Accounts	Credit Balance
Revenue Accounts	Credit Balance
Expense Accounts	Debit Balance

Computing New Balances. Computing and recording the new balance in the Cash account was simple because there was no previous balance. When there is a previous balance, however, you must compute the new balance. Remember that the balance of an account normally appears on the same side as the account appears in the accounting equation.

Computing Debit Balances. The Cash account will be used to illustrate how to compute the account balance after posting amounts to an account with a debit balance. Refer to the Cash account on page 149.

1 The opening entry on October 1 shows a debit balance of $9,900. The balance is identified as a debit by entering the amount in the Debit Balance column.

2 The second posting is on October 5. This shows a debit of $1,000 from the receipt of cash on Remittance Slip 104. The account previously had a debit balance of $9,900. The debit entry of $1,000 must be added to the previous debit balance. The new balance is $10,900 ($9,900 + $1,000). Since this is still a debit balance, the amount is again entered in the Debit Balance column.

3 The third entry is a credit posted on October 6. The Globe Travel Agency issued Check 5 for $500. Since this payment decreases the

Cash   Account No.   101

DATE		EXPLANATION	POST. REF.	DEBIT	CREDIT	BALANCE	
						DEBIT	CREDIT
19—							
Oct.	1	Opening entry	J1	9,900 00		9,900 00	
	5	Remittance Slip RS-104 . . .	J1	1,000 00		10,900 00	
	6	Check 5	J1		500 00	10,400 00	
	12	Check 6	J1		1,000 00	9,400 00	
	12	Remittance Slip RS-105 . . .	J1	5,000 00		14,400 00	
	21	Check 7	J1		2,000 00	12,400 00	
	26	Invoices 106–110	J1	1,200 00		13,600 00	
	28	Check 8	J2		1,800 00	11,800 00	

① ② ③ ④

Debits are added to a debit balance. Credits are subtracted from a debit balance.

amount of cash, the Cash account is credited and the new balance must be computed. The credit entry of $500 is subtracted from the previous debit balance. The new balance is $10,400 ($10,900 − $500). Since the account still has a debit balance, the amount is again entered in the Debit Balance column.

4 Additional debits are added to the previous debit balance. Additional credits are subtracted. In this way the current balance is always shown in the account.

Computing Credit Balances. Computing the new balance for an account with a credit balance is basically the same. Additional credits are added to the previous credit balance. Additional debits are subtracted from a previous credit balance. The Accts. Pay./Bell Products account will be used to illustrate how to compute credit balances.

Accts. Pay./Bell Products   Account No.   201

DATE		EXPLANATION	POST. REF.	DEBIT	CREDIT	BALANCE	
						DEBIT	CREDIT
19—							
Oct.	1	Opening entry	J1		1,000 00		1,000 00
	7	Invoice 9822	J1		600 00		1,600 00
	8	Credit Memorandum CM-67	J1	200 00			1,400 00
	12	Check 6	J1	1,000 00			400 00

① ② ③ ④

Credits are added to a credit balance. Debits are subtracted from a credit balance.

1 The first entry shows a credit balance of $1,000. This balance is identified as a credit balance by being placed in the Credit Balance column.

2 The second entry is a credit of $600 on October 7 from Invoice 9822. This credit amount is added to the previous Credit Balance because it increases the account balance. The new balance is $1,600 ($1,000 + $600). It is recorded in the Credit Balance column.

3 The third entry is a debit of $200 on October 8 from Credit Memorandum 67. Since a debit decreases liabilities, the debit is subtracted from the previous credit balance. The new balance is $1,400 ($1,600 − $200). The balance is still a credit balance.

4 Additional debits are subtracted. Additional credits are added to the previous credit balance. Thus the current balance is always shown.

Computing Zero Balances. In some instances the computation results in a zero balance. When there is no balance, a dash and zeroes are written in the last balance column used. The Accts. Rec./Karen Louis account, for example, has a zero balance after her remittance on October 5 was posted.

Accts. Rec./Karen Louis					Account No.	102	
DATE	EXPLANATION	POST. REF.	DEBIT	CREDIT	BALANCE		
					DEBIT	CREDIT	
19—							
Oct. 1	Opening entry.........	J1	1,000 00		1,000 00		
5	Remittance Slip RS-104 . . .	J1		1,000 00	— 00		
27	Invoice 111...........	J1	1,000 00		1,000 00		

A dash and zeros are written in last balance column used.

• The first entry shows a debit balance of $1,000.
• The second entry is a credit of $1,000 from Remittance Slip 104 on October 5. A credit reduces a debit balance. Thus the new balance is $0 ($1,000 − $1,000). To show a zero balance, write a dash and zeros in the Debit Balance column—the last balance column used.
  If a zero balance occurs in an account with a credit balance, enter the dash and zeros in the Credit Balance column.
• Additional debits and credits are added or subtracted. The current balance is always shown.

Summary. In general, debit entries are added to a previous debit balance. Credit entries are deducted from a previous debit balance.
  Credit entries are added to a previous credit balance. Debit entries are deducted from a previous credit balance.

Activity B. Answer the following questions about the procedure for posting from the journal to the ledger. Refer to the text and illustration on pages 145 to 150.
1. Is the debit or the credit part of the journal entry posted first?
2. What date is used in posting a transaction?

3. In the ledger account, what data is written in the Posting Reference column?
4. What data is written in the Posting Reference column of the journal?
5. Is a debit entry added to or subtracted from a debit balance? From a credit balance?

Audit Trail

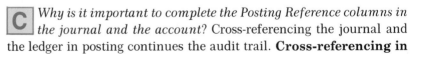

Why is it important to complete the Posting Reference columns in the journal and the account? Cross-referencing the journal and the ledger in posting continues the audit trail. **Cross-referencing in**

posting is the entering of the journal page number in the ledger and the ledger account number in the journal. The journal page number and the ledger account number are called **posting reference numbers.** There are two advantages to cross-referencing the journal and the ledger.

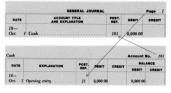

- It allows anyone to easily trace an entry from the journal to the ledger.
- It allows anyone to easily locate the journal entry from which an item was posted to the ledger. Thus you can easily go back to the complete journal entry to obtain more information about the transaction.

If the audit trail is continued, an entry can be traced from the source document, to the journal, to the ledger. Or it can be traced from the ledger, to the journal, to the source document.

It is very important to show all posting reference numbers in the journal and in the ledger. A posting reference number in the journal shows that the journal entry has been posted to the ledger. If you are interrupted while posting, you can identify your last posting by the posting reference numbers in the journal. If a posting reference number is omitted after an entry has been posted, you could post the entry a second time by mistake.

The Ledger After Posting

After the October transactions are posted from the journal, the ledger for the Globe Travel Agency should appear as follows. Remember that the account number is entered in the Posting Reference column of the journal after each entry is posted.

LEDGER

Cash   **Account No.**   *101*

DATE		EXPLANATION	POST. REF.	DEBIT	CREDIT	BALANCE DEBIT	BALANCE CREDIT
19—							
Oct.	1	Opening entry	J1	9,900 00		9,900 00	
	5	Remittance Slip RS-104 . . .	J1	1,000 00		10,900 00	
	6	Check 5	J1		500 00	10,400 00	
	12	Check 6	J1		1,000 00	9,400 00	
	12	Remittance Slip RS-105 . . .	J1	5,000 00		14,400 00	
	21	Check 7	J1		2,000 00	12,400 00	
	26	Invoices 106–110	J1	1,200 00		13,600 00	
	28	Check 8	J2		1,800 00	11,800 00	

Accts. Rec./Karen Louis — Account No. 102

DATE		EXPLANATION	POST. REF.	DEBIT	CREDIT	BALANCE DEBIT	BALANCE CREDIT
19—							
Oct.	1	Opening entry.........	J1	1,000 00		1,000 00	
	5	Remittance Slip RS-104 ...	J1		1,000 00	— 00	
	27	Invoice 111...........	J1	1,000 00		1,000 00	

Accts. Rec./Rose Shops — Account No. 103

DATE		EXPLANATION	POST. REF.	DEBIT	CREDIT	BALANCE DEBIT	BALANCE CREDIT
19—							
Oct.	1	Opening entry.........	J1	700 00		700 00	
	27	Invoice 112...........	J1	800 00		1,500 00	

Furniture — Account No. 111

DATE		EXPLANATION	POST. REF.	DEBIT	CREDIT	BALANCE DEBIT	BALANCE CREDIT
19—							
Oct.	1	Opening entry.........	J1	3,000 00		3,000 00	
	7	Invoice 9822..........	J1	600 00		3,600 00	
	8	Credit Memorandum CM-67	J1		200 00	3,400 00	

Office Equipment — Account No. 112

DATE		EXPLANATION	POST. REF.	DEBIT	CREDIT	BALANCE DEBIT	BALANCE CREDIT
19—							
Oct.	1	Opening entry.........	J1	13,000 00		13,000 00	
	6	Check 5..............	J1	500 00		13,500 00	

Accts. Pay./Bell Products — Account No. 201

DATE		EXPLANATION	POST. REF.	DEBIT	CREDIT	BALANCE DEBIT	BALANCE CREDIT
19—							
Oct.	1	Opening entry.........	J1		1,000 00		1,000 00
	7	Invoice 9822..........	J1		600 00		1,600 00
	8	Credit Memorandum CM-67	J1	200 00			1,400 00
	12	Check 6..............	J1	1,000 00			400 00

Accts. Pay./Royal Service Shop Account No. 202

DATE		EXPLANATION	POST. REF.	DEBIT	CREDIT	BALANCE DEBIT	BALANCE CREDIT
19— Oct.	1	Opening entry	J1		200 00		200 00
	29	Invoice 212	J2		100 00		300 00

Mark Nero, Capital Account No. 301

DATE		EXPLANATION	POST. REF.	DEBIT	CREDIT	BALANCE DEBIT	BALANCE CREDIT
19— Oct.	1	Opening entry	J1		26,400 00		26,400 00
	12	Remittance Slip RS-105 . . .	J1		5,000 00		31,400 00
	21	Check 7	J1	2,000 00			29,400 00

Income Summary Account No. 399

DATE	EXPLANATION	POST. REF.	DEBIT	CREDIT	BALANCE DEBIT	BALANCE CREDIT

Sales Account No. 401

DATE		EXPLANATION	POST. REF.	DEBIT	CREDIT	BALANCE DEBIT	BALANCE CREDIT
19— Oct.	26	Invoices 106–110	J1		1,200 00		1,200 00
	27	Invoices 111–112	J1		1,800 00		3,000 00

Repairs Expense Account No. 501

DATE		EXPLANATION	POST. REF.	DEBIT	CREDIT	BALANCE DEBIT	BALANCE CREDIT
19— Oct.	29	Invoice 212	J2	100 00		100 00	

Salaries Expense Account No. 502

DATE		EXPLANATION	POST. REF.	DEBIT	CREDIT	BALANCE DEBIT	BALANCE CREDIT
19— Oct.	28	Check 8	J2	1,800 00		1,800 00	

Timeliness of Posting

The procedure of posting a transaction and computing the new balance is frequently referred to as updating the account. In general, the term **updating the account** is used in data processing systems and refers to the posting of any current data to an account or file.

The information in every account must be kept up to date. Some businesses post daily, some post once or twice a week, and others post once every two weeks. The frequency depends upon the needs of the business. Regardless of the type of business, however, most businesses update their ledger accounts at least monthly so that a set of financial statements can be prepared.

Purpose of the Balance Ledger Account Form

Now that you have posted from the journal to the ledger, you can see the advantages to using the four-column balance ledger form.

- It shows all the changes to a specific account in one place.
- It constantly shows the current account balance. Since the current balance is always shown, the accounts do not have to be balanced before the trial balance is prepared.
- It easily identifies the balances as either debit or credit balances. Thus the account does not have to be balanced at the end of the period.
- It provides the account balances for preparing the trial balance, the next step in the accounting cycle.

Some type of balance ledger form is used in most accounting systems. The ledger usually consists of loose sheets so that the accounts can be inserted in a machine for rapid posting. The machine computes and prints the new account balance as each transaction is posted.

Activity C. Arrange the following posting procedure in the correct order. Refer to the ledgers on pages 151 and 153.
Compute and record the balance
Record account number in journal
Locate ledger account

Record explanation, if needed, in account
Locate the next ledger account
Record journal page number in account
Record date in account
Record amount in account

Other Methods of Keeping the Ledger

D *Are several accounts kept on one page in a ledger?* No, in actual practice each ledger account is usually kept on a separate page or separate card. However, the accounts illustrated in this topic show several ledger accounts on one page in order to save space.

Some businesses keep their accounts in a bound "book." But many more businesses keep their accounts on individual, loose-leaf forms printed on paper or cards. The accounts can then be stored in a loose-leaf binder, a filing cabinet, a ledger tray, or an open tub file. The accounts can then be removed easily so that entries can be made manually, mechanically, or electronically. The accounts can also be rearranged to add new accounts or to remove accounts to be stored in other areas.

Some data is stored for a temporary period of time until it is needed. Other data is stored for years. Examples of equipment to store and retrieve (recover or get again) data are illustrated.

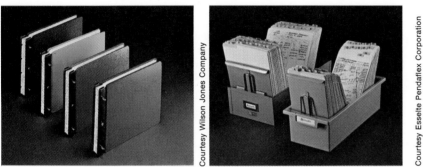

Ledgers are kept in a variety of ways. The method used depends on the needs of the business and the type of ledger.

The procedures shown for posting were those followed in posting by hand. The actual method used to post data will depend on the method of data processing used in that business. Thus posting may be done manually by machines or by computers. Remember that this just explains how it is done and the medium that is used (tape, pages, or other forms). The ledger form, however, does not vary greatly from method to method, nor does the type of data kept in the ledger account. The accounting theory is the same no matter how the posting is done.

A ledger should, therefore, be thought of as a group of accounts that can be maintained in a wide variety of ways. The way depends on the data processing system used in the business.

One last item: When you have to compute the new account balances manually, calculators are usually used (see the Working Hint on page 165). Also, modern data processing equipment automatically computes and records the new balances as the entries are posted.

A ledger is a group of accounts that can be maintained in a variety of ways.

1
Originate
data

↓

2
Journalize
transactions

↓

3
Post
entries

Accounting Cycle

The Accounting Cycle

Posting the journal entries to the ledger accounts is the third step in the accounting cycle. The steps discussed up to this point are as follows.

STEP 1. *Originating the data.* Recording the original data on a source document.

STEP 2. *Journalizing the transaction.* Recording the transactions in a journal.

STEP 3. *Posting the entries.* Transferring the journal entries to the ledger accounts.

Activity D. Answer the following questions about keeping the ledger. Refer to the text, margin notes, and illustrations on pages 154 to 156.

1. Is there a difference in the accounting data kept in manual and automated data processing?

2. Name the two ways in which posting accounting data may be completed.

3. Does the actual method used to post data depend on the method of data processing? Explain.

Accounting Concepts:

Ledger. Records of the changes caused by transactions should be available by account title and number. These records are kept in a ledger.

Audit Trail. References should be provided so that data can be traced from its origination (beginning) to its use (end).

Topic 1 Problems

6-1. Refer to the journal entries in Topic Problem 5-3. Open ledger accounts for Cash; Accts. Rec./Dolores Inski; Office Equipment; Accts. Pay./Delta Supplies; William Carrington, Capital; Sales; and Telephone Expense. Number each account according to the plan below. Post the journal entries made in Topic Problem 5-3 to the accounts.

PLAN FOR THE CHART OF ACCOUNTS

Asset accounts . . . . .101 through 199
Liability accounts . . . .201 through 299
Owner's Equity
    accounts . . . . . . .301 through 399
Revenue accounts . . .401 through 499
Expense accounts . . .501 through 599

NOTE: Save your journal from Topic Problem 5-3 and your ledger from Topic Problem 6-1 for further use in Topic Problem 6-3.

6-2. Refer to the journal entries made in Topic Problem 5-4. Open ledger accounts for Cash; Accts. Rec./Mt. Pleasant High School; Cleaning Equipment; Office Equipment; Accts. Pay./Citizen Press; Accts. Pay./Swan Company; Janet Muski, Capital; Sales; Advertising Expense; and Rent Expense. Number each account according to the plan given in Topic Problem 6-1. Post the journal entries made in Topic Problem 5-4 to the accounts.

NOTE: Save your journal from Topic Problem 5-4 and your ledger from Topic Problem 6-2 for further use in Topic Problem 6-4.

Topic 2
Preparing Accounting Proofs

A *Is there a way to check that the journal entries have been posted accurately to the ledger?* Yes, as you learned in Chapter 4, a proof is made to verify the equality of the ledger at the end of each accounting period. Proving the equality of the ledger is the fourth step in the accounting cycle. A trial balance is used to do this.

A trial balance is a proof that the ledger is in balance. As you learned in Chapter 3, the total debit balances in the ledger must always equal the total credit balances. The trial balance is used to prove this equality. In addition, it summarizes the data needed to prepare an income statement and a balance sheet.

Account Balances

When T accounts are used, the account balances have to be computed before the trial balance can be prepared. When a balance ledger form is used, the account balances are constantly updated.

The account balances on October 31 for the Globe Travel Agency are shown in the ledger (see Topic 1). Remember that the debit or credit balance an account has depends on the account itself. The process of determining the balances of a ledger account is referred to as **balancing an account.**

One of the rules for debiting and crediting given in Chapter 3 is stated as follows: The balance of an account normally appears on the same side as it is shown in the accounting equation. A review of these rules is given on page 148.

Preparing a Trial Balance

If financial statements are not prepared, a quick trial balance can be prepared. A quick trial balance is explained in Chapter 3. If, however, the financial statements are being prepared, then a formal trial balance is needed. The procedures for preparing a formal trial balance are discussed in Chapter 4. The formal trial balance for the Globe Travel Agency on October 31 is shown here.

Accounting Cycle

A trial balance is a proof that can be made in a variety of ways.

Globe Travel Agency
Trial Balance
October 31, 19—

ACCOUNT TITLE	ACCT. NO.	DEBIT	CREDIT
Cash	101	11,800 00	
Accts. Rec./Karen Louis	102	1,000 00	
Accts. Rec./Rose Shops	103	1,500 00	
Furniture	111	3,400 00	
Office Equipment	112	13,500 00	
Accts. Pay./Bell Products	201		400 00
Accts. Pay./Royal Service Shop	202		300 00
Mark Nero, Capital.	301		29,400 00
Sales	401		3,000 00
Repairs Expense	501	100 00	
Salaries Expense	502	1,800 00	
		33,100 00	33,100 00

Formal trial balance summarizes the accounts to prepare the financial statements.

Answer the following questions about account balances and the trial balance. Refer to the text, margin notes, and illustrations on pages 156 and 157.
1. What is Step 4 of the accounting cycle? When during the accounting period is this done?

2. Which form of account—T account or balance ledger—always shows the current account balance?
3. When is a formal trial balance usually needed?

Trial Balance Errors

B *How can you tell if there is an error in the trial balance?* When the debit total equals the credit total, a trial balance is in balance. However, when the two totals do not equal, the trial balance is out of balance. If the trial balance does not balance, one or more errors have been made.

To locate the error or errors, start with the last step in preparing a trial balance. Then work back, step by step through the accounting cycle until the error or errors are found. This means that you should start with the trial balance first, then the ledger, the journal, and finally the source documents.

Check-Marking

When searching for errors, follow some procedure so that you know what records you have checked and have not checked, or know what records have been checked twice. One procedure is to use a check mark ($\checkmark$), also called a tick mark, and a check mark with a line through it ($\cancel\checkmark$). Check marks are written in pencil.

• The check mark ($\checkmark$) is placed at the right of the amount or entry after it is checked for an error. The check mark shows that this item has been verified. That is, the item has been compared with its source and has been verified as being correct. The audit trail is extremely helpful in searching for errors.
• A line is made through a check mark ($\cancel\checkmark$) when an item has been checked again. This means that the item has been checked a second time and has been verified as being correct. Additional lines can be placed through the check mark if more rechecking is needed.

WRONG: $\checkmark$ 176.30
RIGHT: 176.30 $\checkmark$
Place check mark to right of amount.

When using check marks, be careful that you do not deface the accounting records. Use check marks that are small and legible. Be consistent in using them, and place them to the right of the amounts, as shown in the margin. (Placing the check marks to the right avoids running the check mark through the first digit of an amount. For example, a 1 with a line through it could be confused for a 7, and so on.)

Locating Trial Balance Errors

Follow this procedure to trace errors in the trial balance.

- *Check the addition of both money columns of the trial balance.* If an adding machine is used, check the amounts on the tape against those on the trial balance. Put check marks at the totals you checked. If there is no error, go to the next step.
- *Compare the balance of each ledger account with the amount entered for that account on the trial balance.* An account balance may have been copied incorrectly or entered in the wrong column. An account balance may have been omitted, or it may have been included more than once. Place a check mark after each item on the trial balance and in the ledger as you examine it.
- *Check that each account listed on the trial balance has a check mark beside it.* The absence of a check mark may indicate that an account was listed more than once.
- *Check entries for amount of difference.* Compute the difference between the two totals on the trial balance. Then search the ledger accounts and the journal for entries of this exact amount. For example, if difference is $50, check each entry of $50 to see whether it has been journalized and posted correctly. If only the debit entry for a $50 transaction is posted and not the credit entry, a $50 error will appear. Likewise, if a debit entry for $50 is posted twice, the debits would be $50 greater than the credits. In the journal, perhaps the $50 debit and not the credit may have been journalized.
- *Check entries for one-half of the amount of difference.* Divide the difference between the two totals on the trial balance by 2. Search the ledger accounts and the journal for an entry of this amount. For example, if the difference is $50, check entries of $25 ($50 ÷ 2). An account with a debit balance of $25 could have been placed in the credit column of the trial balance. This would throw off the trial balance by $50, twice the amount of the difference. The debit total would be $25 less than it should be, and the credit total would be $25 more.
- *Check entries for a transposition.* Divide the trial balance difference by 9. If the difference can be divided evenly by 9, two digits in an amount may have been transposed. **Transposition** means that the digits or numbers were placed in reverse order. For example, if $32 were posted as $23, there would be a difference of $9 on the trial balance. If $4,680 were posted as $4,860, there would be a difference of $180. Each of these differences can be evenly divided by 9. This method of dividing by 9 is an excellent way to uncover the possibility of transposed digits.
- *Check entries for a slide.* If the trial balance difference is divided by 9 but the error is not located, then look for a slide. A **slide** is an error

---

Trial Balance
October 31, 19—

	.00T
	11,800.00
	1,000.00
	1,500.00
	3,400.00
	13,500.00
	100.00
	1,800.00
	33,100.00T ✓
	0.00T
	400.00
	300.00
	29,400.00
	3,000.00
	33,100.00T ✓

Check addition of both money columns.

DEBIT		CREDIT	
11,800 00	✓		
1,000 00	✓		
1,500 00	✓		
3,400 00	✓		
13,500 00	✓		
		400 00	✓

Check amounts on trial balance.

Correct amount	$ 32	$4,680
Transposed amount	23	4,860
Difference	$ 9	$ 180
Differences are evenly divisible by 9.	$ 9 ÷ 9 = $ 1	$180 ÷ 9 = $20

Check for transpositions.

Correct amount	$123.40
Slide number	12.34
Difference	$111.06

Difference is evenly divisible by 9. $111.06 ÷ 9 = $12.34

Check for slides.

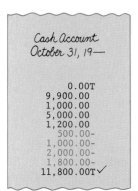

Cash Account
October 31, 19—

```
        0.00T
    9,900.00
    1,000.00
    5,000.00
    1,200.00
      500.00-
    1,000.00-
    2,000.00-
    1,800.00-
   11,800.00T✓
```

Check account balances.

Journal Proof
Page 1
October 27, 19—

```
        0.00T
    9,900.00
    1,000.00
      700.00
    3,000.00
   13,000.00
    1,000.00
      500.00
      600.00
      200.00
    1,000.00
    5,000.00
    2,000.00
    1,200.00
    1,000.00
      800.00
   40,900.00T✓

        0.00T
    1,000.00
      200.00
   26,400.00
    1,000.00
      500.00
      600.00
      200.00
    1,000.00
    5,000.00
    2,000.00
    1,200.00
    1,800.00
   40,900.00T✓
```

Check journal page proofs.

caused by the misplacement of a decimal point. For example, recording $123.40 as $12.34 will give an error of $111.06. This amount is evenly divisible by 9.

Locating Ledger Errors

If the error is not discovered by checking the trial balance, then go to the ledger. This is the next step in the reverse order of the accounting cycle.

- *Check that each account balance has a check mark.* When you checked the account balances on the trial balance, you should have put a check mark after each account that was shown correctly on the trial balance. Remember that the absence of a check mark indicates that the account balance was not listed in the trial balance.
- *Verify the balance of each ledger account.* An account balance may have been computed incorrectly. Check the addition and subtraction in each account. A method of using the calculator to check the balance of an account is given in the Working Hint on page 165.

Locating Journal Errors

If the error is not located in the ledger, go to the journal.

- *Check that each entry has been posted.* Examine the Posting Reference column in the journal to see that all entries have been posted.
- *Trace all postings back to the journal.* Remember to place a check mark after each amount in the journal and ledger. Then check for unmarked amounts in the journal or ledger. An unmarked item in the journal may indicate that an entry was not posted. An unmarked check mark in the ledger may mean that it was posted more than once.
- *Prepare a journal page proof of each journal page for the accounting period.* The total debits must equal the total credits for each page of the journal. See the Working Hint on page 141 for a suggestion of how to do this with a calculator.
- *Check journal entries with source documents.* If the entry is not found, then the source documents will have to be checked with the same journal.

Correcting Errors

A correction must be made for each error that is found. However, no erasures are made at this point. Even pencil figures should not be erased on an accounting record. To correct an error in an amount, first draw a single line through the entire incorrect amount. Then write the complete correct amount above it. Erasures are not made at this time so that the original recordings are available in case there is any question. Finally, the person making the correction should put his or her initials opposite each correction. This means that any correction can be traced to the person responsible. See the illustration in the margin and the Working Hint for Chapter 4 on page 113.

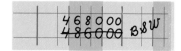

Initial all changes.

Activity B. The trial balance for the Jasmine Music Company on December 31 is shown at the right. Assume that the balance of each ledger account has been verified and that all the journal entries have been posted correctly. Thus the error or errors must be in the trial balance. Analyze each account carefully and correct any errors. Then prepare a new trial balance. (Assign appropriate account numbers to the accounts. Refer to the plan for the chart of accounts in Topic Problem 6-1.)

Jasmine Music Company Trial Balance December 31, 19—		
Cash	9,250 00	
Accts. Rec./Charles Foley	500 00	
Accts. Pay./Nashville Sound, Inc.	5,678 00	
Accts. Rec./Grand Supply	50 00	
Salaries Expense	4,121 00	
Advertising Expense	155 00	
Land	10,000 00	
Building		6,000 00
Mortgage Payable		4,000 00
Music Equipment		20,500 00
Leslie Brewer, Capital		24,898 00
Sales	16,000 00	

Errors Not Revealed by a Trial Balance

C *Are there some errors that can occur that are not shown on a trial balance?* Yes, there are such errors. The fact that a trial balance is in balance does not mean that the accounting records are completely accurate. It only proves that the totals of the debit and credit balances in the ledger accounts are equal. Thus the trial balance merely checks the mathematical accuracy of the ledger.

Some errors on the trial balance do not create a difference between the totals of the debit balances and the credit balances. Among the errors that would not throw the trial balance out of balance are these.

- A transaction that is completely omitted from a journal. Both debit and credit amounts are missing.
- A transaction that is journalized more than once. Both debits and credits increase by the same amount.
- A transaction that is correctly journalized but not posted. Both debit and credit amounts are missing.
- A transaction that is correctly journalized but posted more than once. Both debit and credit amounts increase by the same amount.
- A transaction that is correctly journalized but posted to the wrong account. For example, a debit to the Furniture account could have been posted as a debit to the Office Equipment account. The debit amount and the credit amount have been posted. The trial balance would still be in balance.
- A transaction that is incorrectly journalized because the wrong account is debited or credited. For example, a journal entry in which the

Cash account has been debited by mistake instead of the Office Equipment account. The debit amount still equals the credit amount.

• A transaction that is incorrectly journalized or posted because the wrong amount is debited and credited. Suppose a transaction for $50 is journalized as a $5 debit and a $5 credit. Both debit and credit amounts equal.

• Two errors for the same amount that cancel each other out. For example, a debit account balance that is $100 too much and a credit account balance that is $100 too much. Both the debit total and the credit total are increased by the same amount.

These errors emphasize the need for accuracy at all times in recording data, in analyzing transactions, in journalizing, and in posting. Time is lost if a person must look for errors.

Even though there are these limitations, the trial balance still serves a valuable purpose. It does show that the ledger is in balance, and it also summarizes the data for the financial statements.

The Accounting Cycle

The preparation of a trial balance is the fourth step in the accounting cycle. The steps discussed up to this point are as follows.

STEP 1. Record the original data on a source document.
STEP 2. Record the transactions in a journal.
STEP 3. Post the journal entries to the ledger accounts.
STEP 4. Prove the equality of the ledger.

The Data Processing Cycle

In Chapter 5 you learned how the first two steps of the data processing cycle—origination of data and input of data—relate to the accounting cycle. Now we will see how Step 3 of the data processing cycle relates to the accounting cycle.

Step 3. Processing of Data. After the data is put into the system, the data must be processed in order to produce the output (information) needed. **Processing** is undertaking a series of actions that will change or store data in order to bring about some result. In automated data processing, the computer will perform these actions. In manual data processing, these actions are done by hand or with the help of some equipment.

In accounting, processing data involves taking the input from the journals, sorting it according to account title and number, updating

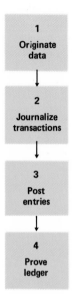

Accounting Cycle

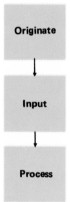

Data Processing Cycle

the account balances, storing the data until the end of the accounting cycle, and then proving the ledger. This processing involves two steps in the accounting cycle. The relationship of posting the entries and proving the ledger is shown in the chapter title ("Processing Accounting Data").

Activity C-1. Indicate which of the following errors would be revealed by the trial balance. Write "Yes" or "No" after the error, as appropriate.
EXAMPLE: Listing an incorrect account balance on the trial balance.—Yes
1. Posting a debit entry to the credit side of an account.
2. Balancing an account incorrectly.
3. Posting a journal entry (both the debit and the credit) more than once.
4. Making two errors for the same amount.
5. Failing to post a journal entry (both the debit and the credit).
6. Failing to post either a debit or a credit entry.
7. Posting an entry to the wrong account.

8. Omitting an account with a balance from the trial balance.
9. Posting a debit entry for $260 instead of $620.
10. Journalizing a debit to the wrong account.

Activity C-2. Six accounting procedures are listed here. Identify the steps of the data processing cycle in which these procedures are performed.
EXAMPLE: Writing the data on a sales invoice. Step 1—Origination of data.
1. Writing the credit account title in the journal.
2. Adding the credits on the trial balance.
3. Computing the new account balances.
4. Posting a debit amount in the Cash account.
5. Journalizing the amount in the Debit column.

Accounting Concept:
Trial Balance. The equality of the total debits and the total credits in the ledger should be verified at regular intervals.

Topic 2 Problems

6-3. Prepare a trial balance for the Midwest Data Service on December 31. Use the ledger account balances from Topic Problem 6-1.
NOTE: Save your trial balance for further use in Topic Problem 7-1.

6-4. Prepare a trial balance for Tremont Cleaners on January 31 from the ledger accounts in Topic Problem 6-2.
NOTE: Save your trial balance for further use in Topic Problem 7-2.

The Language of Business

Here are some terms that make up the language of business. Do you know the meaning of each?

posting	balance ledger	posting reference numbers	transposition
medium	form	updating the account	slide
ledger	cross-referencing in posting	balancing an account	processing
ledger account			

Chapter 6   Questions

1. Describe the procedure followed in posting an entry from the journal to the ledger.
2. Why are the journal and the ledger cross-referenced?
3. Why are audit trails used?
4. List two precautions that should be followed when posting an entry from the journal to the ledger.
5. What are the first four steps of the accounting cycle?
6. Which step of the accounting cycle—journalizing or posting—requires greater understanding of accounting principles? Why?
7. Describe four methods of keeping a ledger.
8. What kinds of accounts have debit balances after all postings are made?

9. What kinds of accounts have credit balances after all postings are made?
10. Would the following errors show up on a trial balance? Explain each answer.
a. A transaction is journalized by mistake as a debit for $50 to the Furniture account instead of to the Office Equipment account.
b. A journal entry is posted by mistake as a credit for $30 to the Cash account instead of to the Tools account.
c. A journal entry for $100 was posted as a debit for $10 and a credit for $10.
d. A $90 debit was posted as a credit.

Chapter 6   Problems

Problems for Chapter 6 are given in the *Working Papers and Chapter Problems for Part 1*. If you are using the workbook, do the problems in the space provided there.

Chapter 6   Management Cases

The Ledger and Trial Balance. Many accountants consider the ledger the heart of accounting records. In the ledger, debit and credits are posted, and accounts are kept up to date. The ledger has unique functions to perform in the accounting cycle. As a result, accuracy of the ledger data is most important because the ledger provides data to prepare financial statements. A trial balance is made to check the mathematical accuracy of the ledger. If an error is revealed by the trial balance, the source of the error must be found and corrected immediately. In many instances a quick trial balance is made to check the equality of debits and credits (see Working Hint on page 165).

Case 6M-1. The July 31 trial balance of the ledger accounts for the Royal China Restaurant shows total debits of $71,754.32 and total credits of $71,754.30. The trial balance and the account balances were readded and checked, but the error was not found. To find the error would require a check of each transaction. A detailed check would take about five hours unless the error was located early in the checking. The accounting clerk would have to work overtime at the rate of $5 per hour. Thus it might cost as much as $25 to find the error.
a. Can the manager be sure that the error is only 2 cents?
b. If you were the manager, would you want to find the error or would you ignore it?

Case 6M-2. The Interstate Moving and Storage Company owns and operates large vans that move furniture between several large cities. It also owns a number of small trucks that are used for local deliveries and pickups. In addition to the trucks, the company owns several warehouses for storing furniture, a garage for storing and repairing its trucks, and a large central office. The company owns a wide variety of loading, conveyor, and storage equipment in the warehouses. It owns tools and machines in the garage. It also owns typewriters, adding machines, calculators, and other office machines in the central office.

In the ledger, only one equipment account is used to record all costs for equipment. Thus when the balance sheet is prepared, only one amount is shown for all the equipment the company owns.

a. The president of the company believes that this plan does not provide enough detailed information. Why would the president want more detailed information about the equipment the company owns?

b. What changes in the accounting records would you suggest to provide the information the president wants?

Working Hint

Checking an Account Balance for Mathematical Accuracy. The account balances are computed immediately after posting an entry. These balances are computed horizontally (that is, across on the same line).

The final balance of an account can easily be checked vertically. Here is how to do it by using an adding machine or a calculator.

- Clear the machine; check for the clear symbol.
- Add each debit amount.
- Subtract each credit amount.
- Total the answer.

If all amounts have been entered correctly, the total should agree with the last account balance.

Cash   Account No.   101

DATE		EXPLANATION	POST. REF.	DEBIT	CREDIT	BALANCE DEBIT	BALANCE CREDIT
19—							
Oct.	1	Opening entry	J1	9,900 00		9,900 00	
	5	Remittance Slip RS-104 . . .	J1	1,000 00		10,900 00	
	6	Check 5	J1		500 00	10,400 00	
	12	Check 6	J1		1,000 00	9,400 00	
	12	Remittance Slip RS-105 . . .	J1	5,000 00		14,400 00	
	21	Check 7	J1		2,000 00	12,400 00	
	26	Invoices 106–110	J1	1,200 00		13,600 00	
	28	Check 8	J2		1,800 00	11,800 00	

Cash Account
October 31, 19—

```
      0.00T
  9,900.00
  1,000.00
  5,000.00
  1,200.00
    500.00-
  1,000.00-
  2,000.00-
  1,800.00-
 11,800.00T ✓
```

Output of Accounting Data

The trial balance provides the data to prepare the income statement and the balance sheet. The income statement is prepared first. Then the balance sheet is prepared. You will now learn how to prepare financial statements at the end of an accounting period.

Topic 1
Preparing the Financial Statements

A *What is the fifth step in the accounting cycle?* Step 5 of the accounting cycle is to prepare the financial statements at the end of the accounting period.

The trial balance provides the data for the balance sheet and the income statement. The accounts are listed according to the chart of accounts. The *balance sheet accounts* (assets, liabilities, owner's equity capital) are listed in the upper portion of the trial balance. The *income statement accounts* (revenue and expenses) are listed in the lower portion of the trial balance.

The relationship between the trial balance and the financial statements is shown as follows.

1 Originate data

2 Journalize transactions

3 Post entries

4 Prove ledger

5 Prepare financial statements

Accounting Cycle

Globe Travel Agency
Trial Balance
October 31, 19—

ACCOUNT TITLE	ACCT. NO.	DEBIT	CREDIT
Cash	101	11,800 00	
Accts. Rec./Karen Louis	102	1,000 00	
Accts. Rec./Rose Shops	103	1,500 00	
Furniture	111	3,400 00	
Office Equipment . . . . : . .	112	13,500 00	
Accts. Pay./Bell Products	201		400 00
Accts. Pay./Royal Service Shop	202		300 00
Mark Nero, Capital	301		29,400 00
Sales	401		3,000 00
Repairs Expense	501	100 00	
Salaries Expense	502	1,800 00	
		33,100 00	33,100 00

Balance Sheet Accounts

Income Statement Accounts

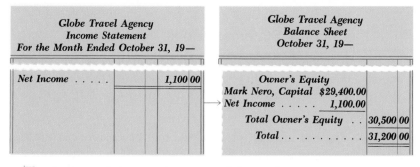

Globe Travel Agency
Income Statement
For the Month Ended October 31, 19—

Net Income	1,100 00	

Globe Travel Agency
Balance Sheet
October 31, 19—

Owner's Equity		
Mark Nero, Capital $29,400.00		
→ Net Income 1,100.00		
Total Owner's Equity . .	30,500 00	
Total	31,200 00	

Net income is obtained from income statement and shown on balance sheet.

• The income statement is prepared from the temporary accounts (400s and 500s). These accounts are listed in the lower portion of the trial balance.

- The balance sheet is prepared from the permanent accounts (100s, 200s, and 300s). These accounts are listed in the upper portion of the trial balance.
- The balance sheet is completed by obtaining the net income (or net loss) from the income statement.

The Income Statement

The income statement must be prepared before a balance sheet. The net income (or net loss) must be computed so that it can be reported on the balance sheet.

The types and amounts of the revenue and expenses are obtained from the trial balance. The income statement prepared for the Globe Travel Agency for the month ended October 31 is illustrated. It shows revenue of $3,000, expenses of $1,900, and a net income of $1,100 ($3,000 − $1,900).

Income statement shows types and amounts of revenues and expenses.

Globe Travel Agency *Income Statement* *For the Month Ended October 31, 19—*		
Revenue:		
Sales......................................		3,000 00
Expenses:		
Repairs Expense	100 00	
Salaries Expense	1,800 00	
Total Expenses		1,900 00
Net Income		1,100 00

What the Income Statement Does Not Show

The discussion about income statements has emphasized what an income statement shows. (These items are presented in Chapter 4 on pages 87 to 91.) There are a few things that an income statement does not show.

An income statement does not predict net income.

- It shows the net income (or net loss) for the current accounting period. The income statement does not predict the net income for future periods. Managers and owners use it to make decisions that should either increase or decrease the net income.

- It shows the expenses matched against the revenue. The income statement might not show all expenses for that period. For example, the expenses for an advertising campaign may have been paid in the October accounting period. However, some people will use that advertising information but will not buy the items until December. Thus the revenue will be recorded in December and the expenses in October. This does not, however, mean that the expenses are not matched against the revenue as much as is possible. (Remember the generally accepted accounting principle that revenue is matched against expenses.)

An income statement might not show all expenses.

- It shows net income (or net loss). Net income is not necessarily related to cash. Revenue includes the inflow of cash or receivables. The revenue may come in one accounting period and the cash may come in another accounting period when a customer pays his or her account. Remember that net income is the net increase to owner's equity as a result of matching revenue with expenses in an accounting period.

Net income is not necessarily related to cash.

Activity A. Answer the following questions about preparing financial statements. Refer to the trial balance, income statement, and the balance sheet of the Globe Travel Agency on pages 167 to 169.
1. What is the date of the trial balance?
2. What is the accounting period covered by the income statement?
3. What is the revenue from sales?

4. What is the source document of the net income amount shown on the balance sheet?
5. What types of expenses are incurred? What is the total amount of the expenses? Where are these amounts located on the trial balance?
6. What amount shows the increase in owner's equity as a result of business operations during October?

The Balance Sheet

B Is all the data needed to prepare the balance sheet shown on the trial balance? No, not all the data is on the trial balance. The amount of each asset and liability is on the trial balance. But the amount of owner's equity is not shown. The balance of the capital account is listed on the trial balance. However, remember that the net income must still be added to (or a net loss subtracted from) owner's equity. Net income (or net loss) is computed on the income statement, not the trial balance. Thus the total owner's equity must be computed on the balance sheet.

The balance sheet prepared for the Globe Travel Agency as of October 31, 19—, is shown on page 170. Globe Travel Agency's balance sheet shows total assets of $31,200, total liabilities of $700, and total owner's equity of $30,500. The total of the assets ($31,200) equals the total of the liabilities and owner's equity ($700 + $30,500).

Globe Travel Agency				
Balance Sheet				
October 31, 19—				
Assets			**Liabilities**	
Cash	11,800 00	Accounts Payable:		
Accounts Receivable:			Bell Products $400.00	
Karen Louis $1,000.00			Royal Service Shop . . 300.00	
Rose Shops 1,500.00	2,500 00	Total Liabilities		700 00
Furniture	3,400 00			
Office Equipment	13,500 00	**Owner's Equity**		
		Mark Nero, Capital . $29,400.00		
		Net Income 1,100.00		
		Total Owner's Equity	30,500 00	
Total	31,200 00	Total	31,200 00	

Account form balance sheet: Assets are listed on the left. Liabilities and owner's equity are listed on the right.

Report Form Balance Sheet. The balance sheets shown up to now have been presented in the account form. The **account form balance sheet** lists all assets on the left side and the liabilities and owner's equity on the right side. This format is similar to that of the accounting equation, which has asset accounts on the left and all liabilities and owner's equity accounts on the right. Another form of the balance sheet is called the report form. The **report form balance sheet** lists all assets in the upper portion and liabilities and owner's equity in the lower portion. The report form is illustrated here.

```
                            Globe Travel Agency
                               Balance Sheet
                              October 31, 19--

                                  Assets
     Cash . . . . . . . . . . . . . . . . . . . . . . . . . .    $11,800.00
     Accounts Receivable:
        Karen Louis. . . . . . . . . . . . . . $1,000.00
        Rose Shops . . . . . . . . . . . . . .  1,500.00
     Furniture  . . . . . . . . . . . . . . . . . . . . . . .      2,500.00
     Office Equipment . . . . . . . . . . . . . . . . . . . .      3,400.00
                                                                  13,500.00
                Total Assets . . . . . . . . . . . . . . . .                  $31,200.00

                                Liabilities
     Accounts Payable:
        Bell Products. . . . . . . . . . . . . . . . . . . .    $    400.00
        Royal Service Shops. . . . . . . . . . . . . . . . .         300.00
                Total Liabilities. . . . . . . . . . . . . .                  $    700.00

                              Owner's Equity
     Mark Nero, Capital . . . . . . . . . . . . . . . . . . .    $29,400.00
     Net Income . . . . . . . . . . . . . . . . . . . . . . .      1,100.00
                Total Owner's Equity . . . . . . . . . . . .                  $30,500.00
                Total Liabilities and Owner's Equity . . . . . . .            $31,200.00
```

Report form balance sheet: Assets are listed in upper portion. Liabilities and owner's equity are listed in the lower portion.

The report form is easier to prepare on a typewriter. There also is more space to write across the sheet. For example, notice that there is more space to prepare the owner's equity section. Also, there is another money column available for totals. It is much easier to identify quickly the total assets, total liabilities, and total owner's equity. All three section totals are shown in the last money column of the report form balance sheet.

Note that a double rule is drawn beneath the amount of the total assets on the report form. A double rule is also drawn beneath the amount of the total liabilities and owner's equity. The double rule indicates that the two amounts balance and that the balance sheet is completed.

Recording the Cost of Assets

A business's assets include cash, accounts receivable, and other assets such as buildings, equipment, and land. Cash is the actual dollar amount available now. Accounts receivable is the actual dollar amount that will be received when the customers pay. Thus cash and accounts receivable are recorded on the balance sheet at their actual dollar value.

Other assets such as buildings, equipment, and land are recorded on the balance sheet at their cost to the business. This means that they are recorded at the amount that the business paid or promised to pay for them. For example, the Globe Travel Agency bought office equipment for $500 on October 6 (see the journal entry on page 133). The $500 that the Globe Travel Agency (the buyer) paid the Eagle Office Corporation (the seller) is the amount recorded as the cost of the asset (office equipment).

Assets are recorded at their cost when acquired; they do not show present value.

The generally accepted accounting principle calls for assets to be recorded at their cost on the date that they were acquired. Thus the balance sheet shows assets at their cost. The assets are not shown at either their present value or the value that might be received if they are sold. **Market value** is the actual sales price for products of like type, quality, and quantity at a moment of time.

This principle means that assets are recorded on the basis of the dollars that were used to acquire them. In accounting, the cost of an asset is referred to as its **recorded value.** The recorded value of the assets on the balance sheet does not show what the assets can be sold for or what it would cost to replace them. Thus the balance sheet shows that the total recorded value of the office equipment owned by the Globe Travel Agency on October 31 is $13,500. This was the cost of the office equipment.

Language:
Value. The word *value* has many meanings. It is best to always use an adjective before the word *value,* such as recorded value, present value, market value, etc., in order to avoid any misunderstanding. If no adjective is used, *value* simply means cost of an asset.

What a Balance Sheet Does Not Show

It is important to understand what a balance sheet shows. (These items are presented on pages 91 to 98 of Chapter 4.) It also is important to understand what a balance sheet does not show.

A balance sheet does not show claims against specific assets.

- It shows the total claims of the creditors against the assets. It does not show claims against specific assets. For example, the October 31 balance sheet for the Globe Travel Agency shows total liabilities of $700. It does not indicate that these claims are against cash, furniture, office equipment, or any other specific assets.

A balance sheet does not show market value or worth.

- It shows the assets at the cost on the day they were acquired. It does not show the market value (what it could be sold for) or worth. The balance sheet shows furniture of $3,400. This was the cost when the furniture was purchased. The furniture could possibly be sold for more or less than that amount.

A balance sheet does not show how assets and liabilities changed during an accounting period.

- It shows the amount of assets and liabilities on a specific date. The balance sheet does not show how these assets and liabilities change during the accounting period. For example, the amount of cash was $11,800 on October 31. The balance sheet does not reveal whether the amount of cash increased or decreased during the period. As you know, you cannot assume that the amount of net income increased the amount of cash.
- It shows owner's equity capital on a specific date. The balance sheet does not show how capital increased or decreased during the period. For example, on October 12 Mark Nero invested an additional $5,000, and on October 21 he withdrew $2,000. These changes are not shown on the balance sheet. The balance sheet for the Globe Travel Agency does, however, show the changes to owner's equity due to the net income earned during the period.

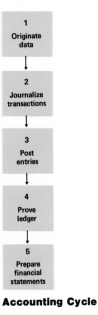

Accounting Cycle

The Accounting Cycle

The preparation of the financial statements is the fifth step in the accounting cycle. The steps discussed up to this point are as follows.

STEP 1. Record original data on a source document.
STEP 2. Record the transactions in a journal.

STEP 3. Post the journal entries to the ledger accounts.
STEP 4. Prove the equality of the ledger.
STEP 5. Prepare an income statement and a balance sheet.

Activity B. Answer the following questions about the balance sheet. Refer to the trial balance on page 167 and balance sheet of the Globe Travel Agency on page 170.
1. What is the total of the creditors' claims against the Globe Travel Agency's assets?
2. Does the total of the liabilities and owner's equity on the balance sheet equal the total of the credit balances on the trial balance? Why or why not?

3. How much money do debtors owe the Globe Travel Agency?
4. Does the total of the assets on the balance sheet equal the total of the debit balances on the trial balance? Why or why not?
5. What do the amounts shown for furniture and office equipment represent?
6. What does the amount shown for accounts receivable represent?

Accounting Concepts:
Relationship Between Financial Statements. The interrelationship between the income statement and the balance sheet is reflected in the owner's equity section of the balance sheet.
Recording Assets. Assets are recorded at their cost when acquired, not at their estimated sale or replacement value.

Accounting Principle:
Basis for Recording Assets. The generally accepted accounting principle is that a balance sheet does not presume to show either the present values of assets to the business or the values that might be realized if the assets are sold. Assets are recorded at their cost on the date when they were acquired.

Topic 1 Problems

7-1. Prepare the following financial statements for Midwest Data Service. Refer to your trial balance from Topic Problem 6-3.
a. Prepare an income statement for the two-month accounting period ended December 31.
b. Prepare a balance sheet in report form for December 31.

7-2. Use your trial balance from Topic Problem 6-4 to do the following for Tremont Cleaners.
a. Prepare an income statement for the monthly accounting period ended January 31.
b. Prepare a balance sheet in account form for January 31.

Topic 2
Updating the Owner's Equity Accounts

A | *What is the sixth step of the accounting cycle?* The sixth step of the accounting cycle is to close the ledger. *Closing the ledger*

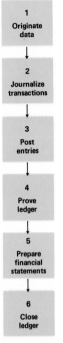

1
Originate
data

↓

2
Journalize
transactions

↓

3
Post
entries

↓

4
Prove
ledger

↓

5
Prepare
financial
statements

↓

6
Close
ledger

Accounting Cycle

involves transferring the net income (or net loss) from the temporary accounts to the capital account. This achieves two purposes.

- The temporary accounts will have zero balances.
- The capital account will contain the owner's investment plus the net income (or net loss) for the accounting period.

Remember that there are three types of temporary accounts: revenue accounts, expense accounts, and the Income Summary account.

The Closing Procedure

In Chapter 4, you learned how to update the owner's equity capital account and how to close the temporary accounts in a ledger with T accounts. The same procedure is followed in closing the ledger with balance ledger account forms. However, the entries must be journalized before the entries are posted to the ledger accounts.

1 *Close all revenue accounts.* Close all revenue accounts in the Credit column on the trial balance. (The revenue accounts have numbers in the 400s.) The balances are transferred to the Income Summary ac-

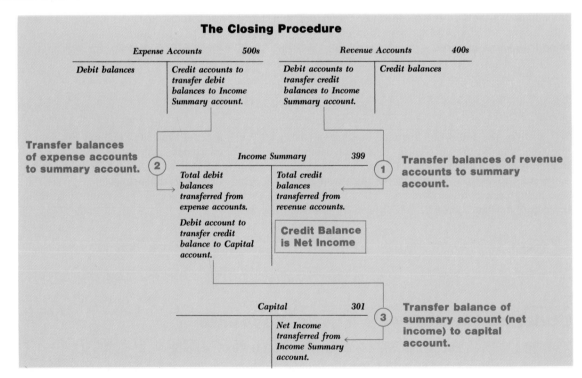

The Closing Procedure

count by debiting each revenue account and crediting the Income Summary account for the total of the balances.

Sales			401		Income Summary		399
19—		19—				19—	
Oct. 31	3,000	Oct. 31	3,000			Oct. 31	3,000

First closing entry transfers revenue account balances.

2 *Close all expense accounts.* Close all the expense accounts in the Debit column on the trial balance. (The expense accounts have numbers in the 500s.) The balances are transferred by debiting the Income Summary account for the total of the balance and crediting each expense account for the account balance.

	Repairs Expense		501		Income Summary		399
				19—		19—	
				Oct. 31	1,900	Oct. 31	3,000
19—		19—					
Oct. 29	100	Oct. 31	100				
	Salaries Expense		502				
19—		19—					
Oct. 28	1,800	Oct. 31	1,800				

Second closing entry transfers expense account balances.

3 *Close the Income Summary account.* Close the Income Summary account. After the first two closing entries are posted, the balance of the Income Summary account is the net income (or net loss). This amount must agree with the amount on the income statement. The balance of the Income Summary account is transferred to the Capital account. A net income is transferred to the Capital account by debiting the Income Summary account and crediting the Capital account for the amount of the net income. A net loss is transferred to the Capital account by debiting the Capital account and crediting the Income Summary account for the amount of the loss.

Mark Nero, Capital			301		Income Summary		399
		19—		19—		19—	
		Oct. 31	29,400	Oct. 31	1,900	Oct. 31	3,000
		31	1,100		1,100 1,100		

Third closing entry transfers Income Summary account balance.

Activity A. Answer the following questions about closing the revenue and expense accounts. Refer to the text and illustrations on pages 173 to 175.

1. What is the sixth step in the accounting cycle?

2. Which accounts are closed?

3. What does *closing an account* mean?

4. What is the entry to transfer a net loss amount?

5. What type of balances do revenue and expense accounts have at the beginning of the accounting period?

Journalizing and Posting the Closing Entries

Globe Travel Agency			
Trial Balance			
October 31, 19—			
ACCOUNT TITLE	ACCT. NO.	DEBIT	CREDIT
Cash	101	11,800 00	
Accts. Rec./Karen Louis	102	1,000 00	
Accts. Rec./Rose Shops	103	1,500 00	
Furniture	111	3,400 00	
Office Equipment	112	13,500 00	
Accts. Pay./Bell Products	201		400 00
Accts. Pay./Royal Service Shop	202		300 00
Mark Nero, Capital	301		29,400 00
Sales	401		3,000 00
Repairs Expense	501	100 00	
Salaries Expense	502	1,800 00	
		33,100 00	33,100 00

Revenue and expense account balances are obtained from the trial balance.

B *Where is the data obtained for journalizing the closing entries?* The balances of the revenue and expense accounts are obtained from the trial balance. The amount of the net income (or net loss) is obtained from the Income Summary account balance. The amount can also be obtained from the income statement.

The procedures for journalizing and posting the closing entries for the revenue, expense, and income summary accounts are discussed below. The closing entries for the Globe Travel Agency are journalized and posted on October 31.

JOURNAL					Page 2
DATE	ACCOUNT TITLE AND EXPLANATION	POST. REF.	DEBIT	CREDIT	
19—					
Oct.					
31	Sales	401	3,000 00		
	Income Summary	399		3,000 00	
	Close revenue account.				
31	Income Summary	399	1,900 00		
	Repairs Expense	501		100 00	
	Salaries Expense	502		1,800 00	
	Close expense accounts.				
31	Income Summary	399	1,100 00		
	Mark Nero, Capital	301		1,100 00	
	Transfer net income.				

Net income (or net loss) is obtained from Income Summary account.

(1) (2) (3)

1 *Closing Entries for Revenue Accounts.* The Sales account is the only source of revenue for the Globe Travel Agency for the accounting period ended October 31, 19—. The data needed for the journal entry to transfer this $3,000 credit balance from the Sales account to the Income Summary account is in the trial balance. Therefore, the trial balance is the source document for this entry.

176 **Part 1 Elements of Financial Records**

Sales | | | | | | | Account No. | 401

DATE		EXPLANATION	POST. REF.	DEBIT	CREDIT	BALANCE	
						DEBIT	CREDIT
19—							
Oct.	26	Invoices 106–110	J1		1,200 00		1,200 00
	27	Invoices 111–112	J1		1,800 00		3,000 00
	31	To Income Summary	J2	3,000 00			— 00

(Sales) balance is transferred to Summary account.

After this closing entry is posted, the Sales account has a zero balance. The total revenue of $3,000 has been transferred to the Income Summary account.

2 *Closing Entries for Expense Accounts.* The two expense accounts of the Globe Travel Agency have debit balances. A compound journal entry is required to transfer the balances of these expense accounts to the Income Summary account. This entry shows a credit to each of the two expense accounts and a debit for the total expenses to the Income Summary account.

This closing entry has reduced the expense account balances to zero and has transferred the total expenses of $1,900 to the Income Summary account. The trial balance is the source document for this entry.

Repairs Expense | | | | | | | Account No. | 501

DATE		EXPLANATION	POST. REF.	DEBIT	CREDIT	BALANCE	
						DEBIT	CREDIT
19—							
Oct.	29	Invoice 212..........	J2	100 00		100 00	
	31	To Income Summary	J2		100 00	— 00	

(Repairs) balance is transferred to Summary account.

Salaries Expense | | | | | | | Account No. | 502

DATE		EXPLANATION	POST. REF.	DEBIT	CREDIT	BALANCE	
						DEBIT	CREDIT
19—							
Oct.	28	Check 8	J2	1,800 00		1,800 00	
	31	To Income Summary	J2		1,800 00	— 00	

(Salaries) balance is transferred to Summary account.

As a result of these entries, the revenue and expense accounts of the Globe Travel Agency are now closed. They have zero balances and are ready to accumulate new revenue and expense data during the next accounting period.

3 *Closing Entry for the Income Summary Account.* The Income Summary account is a convenient device for closing the revenue and expense accounts. Moreover, it shows the essential facts about the business's revenue and expenses during its accounting period. For example, the Income Summary account for the Globe Travel Agency has a credit of $3,000 and a debit of $1,900 at this point. The account now has a credit balance of $1,100. This amount represents the net income that the Globe Travel Agency earned during the accounting period ended October 31, 19—.

Net income increases owner's equity. The net income is transferred to the Capital account as a credit. This transfer closes the Income Summary account. The Income Summary account is the source document for this entry.

(Income Summary) balance is transferred to Capital account.

Income Summary						Account No.	399	
DATE		EXPLANATION	POST. REF.	DEBIT	CREDIT	BALANCE		
						DEBIT	CREDIT	
19—								
Oct.	31	Revenue	J2		3,000 00		3,000 00	
	31	Expenses	J2	1,900 00			1,100 00	
	31	Net income	J2	1,100 00			— 00	

(Capital) account balance is identical with total owner's equity on balance sheet.

Mark Nero, Capital						Account No.	301	
DATE		EXPLANATION	POST. REF.	DEBIT	CREDIT	BALANCE		
						DEBIT	CREDIT	
19—								
Oct.	1	Opening entry	J1		26,400 00		26,400 00	
	12	Remittance Slip RS-105 . . .	J1		5,000 00		31,400 00	
	21	Check 7	J1	2,000 00			29,400 00	
	31	Net income	J2		1,100 00		30,500 00	

The Mark Nero, Capital account now has a balance of $30,500 ($29,400 + $1,100). The new balance in the Capital account is identical with the total owner's equity on the balance sheet for October 31. This is a result of closing the temporary accounts and transferring the net income into the permanent Capital account.

Globe Travel Agency			
Balance Sheet			
October 31, 19—			

Owner's Equity			
Mark Nero, Capital	29,400 00		
Net Income	1,100 00		
Total Owner's Equity		30,500 00	

Balance in Capital account is identical with total owner's equity on the balance sheet.

Two things result from closing Globe's Income Summary account.

- The Income Summary account has a zero balance.
- The Mark Nero, Capital account contains the net income for the month of October.

If the Globe Travel Agency suffered a net loss, the Income Summary account would have shown a debit balance at the end of the accounting period. A debit balance would be transferred by crediting the Income Summary account and debiting the Capital account. The debit to the Capital account would then decrease the owner's equity by the amount of the net loss. (Recall that the normal balance of the Capital account is a credit balance.)

The Accounting Cycle

Making closing entries is the sixth step in the accounting cycle. The six steps discussed up to this point are as follows.

STEP 1. Record original data on a source document.
STEP 2. Record the transactions in a journal.
STEP 3. Post the journal entries to the ledger accounts.
STEP 4. Prove the equality of the ledger.
STEP 5. Prepare an income statement and a balance sheet.
STEP 6. Journalize and post the closing entries.

Activity B-1. Answer the following questions about the October 31 closing entries for the Globe Travel Agency. Refer to the journal and the ledger accounts on pages 176 to 179.

1. Is the Sales account debited or credited to close the account? Why?

2. Is the Repairs Expense account debited or credited to close it?

3. To which account is the balance of the Repairs Expense account transferred?

4. Is the Salaries Expense account debited or credited to close it? Why?

5. What does the $1,900 debit in the Income Summary account represent?

6. What does the $1,100 debit in the Income Summary account represent?

7. What does the $3,000 credit in the Income Summary account represent?

8. Why is the Income Summary account debited to close it?

9. What does the $1,100 in the Capital account represent?

10. What is the October 31 balance of the Capital account?

11. What is the total owner's equity?

Activity B-2. The trial balance for Gatlinberg Mills on March 31 is at the right. Journalize and post the closing entries for the month ended March 31, 19—.

Gatlinberg Mills
Trial Balance
March 31, 19—

ACCOUNT TITLE	ACCT. NO.	DEBIT	CREDIT
Cash	101	11,000 00	
Equipment	102	6,100 00	
Accts. Pay./Crooker Corporation	201		1,910 00
John Knox, Capital	301		10,200 00
Sales	401		7,065 00
Miscellaneous Expense	501	275 00	
Salaries Expense	502	1,200 00	
Rent Expense	503	600 00	
		19,175 00	19,175 00

Accounting Cycle

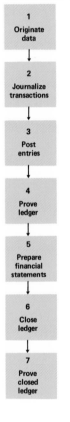

1 Originate data

2 Journalize transactions

3 Post entries

4 Prove ledger

5 Prepare financial statements

6 Close ledger

7 Prove closed ledger

Formal postclosing trial balance shows accounts and balances.

Preparing a Postclosing Trial Balance

C *What is the seventh step in the accounting cycle?* The seventh step in the accounting cycle is to prove (verify) that the debits and credits in the ledger are equal after all the closing entries have been posted. The *postclosing trial balance* is a proof that the ledger is in balance after all temporary accounts have been closed.

A postclosing trial balance is prepared like a regular trial balance. It can be prepared as a formal summary or as a quick check using a zero proof. A formal postclosing trial balance prepared for the Globe Travel Agency on October 31, 19—, is illustrated. A formal postclosing trial balance is shown so that you can easily see what accounts are included in the proof.

Globe Travel Agency
Postclosing Trial Balance
October 31, 19—

ACCOUNT TITLE	ACCT. NO.	DEBIT	CREDIT
Cash	101	11,800 00	
Accts. Rec./Karen Louis	102	1,000 00	
Accts. Rec./Rose Shops	103	1,500 00	
Furniture	111	3,400 00	
Office Equipment	112	13,500 00	
Accts. Pay./Bell Products	201		400 00
Accts. Pay./Royal Service Shop	202		300 00
Mark Nero, Capital	301		30,500 00
		31,200 00	31,200 00

The postclosing trial balance lists only those accounts that have *not* been closed. The accounts remaining open after the ledger has been closed are the permanent accounts (assets, liabilities, and owner's equity Capital). (Any account that is not closed is called an **open account.**) The permanent accounts in the ledger of the Globe Travel Agency follow.

Cash
Account No. 101

DATE		EXPLANATION	POST. REF.	DEBIT	CREDIT	BALANCE DEBIT	BALANCE CREDIT
19—							
Oct.	1	Opening entry	J1	9,900 00		9,900 00	
	5	Remittance Slip RS-104 . .	J1	1,000 00		10,900 00	
	6	Check 5	J1		500 00	10,400 00	
	12	Check 6	J1		1,000 00	9,400 00	
	12	Remittance Slip RS-105 . .	J1	5,000 00		14,400 00	
	21	Check 7	J1		2,000 00	12,400 00	
	26	Invoices 106–110	J1	1,200 00		13,600 00	
	28	Check 8	J2		1,800 00	11,800 00	

Permanent accounts are not closed.

Accts. Rec./Karen Louis
Account No. 102

DATE		EXPLANATION	POST. REF.	DEBIT	CREDIT	BALANCE DEBIT	BALANCE CREDIT
19—							
Oct.	1	Opening entry	J1	1,000 00		1,000 00	
	5	Remittance Slip RS-104 . .	J1		1,000 00	— 00	
	27	Invoice 111	J1	1,000 00		1,000 00	

Permanent accounts are not closed.

Accts. Rec./Rose Shops
Account No. 103

DATE		EXPLANATION	POST. REF.	DEBIT	CREDIT	BALANCE DEBIT	BALANCE CREDIT
19—							
Oct.	1	Opening entry	J1	700 00		700 00	
	27	Invoice 112	J1	800 00		1,500 00	

Permanent accounts are not closed.

Furniture
Account No. 111

DATE		EXPLANATION	POST. REF.	DEBIT	CREDIT	BALANCE DEBIT	BALANCE CREDIT
19—							
Oct.	1	Opening entry	J1	3,000 00		3,000 00	
	7	Invoice 9822	J1	600 00		3,600 00	
	8	Credit Memorandum CM-67	J1		200 00	3,400 00	

Permanent accounts are not closed.

Office Equipment
Account No. 112

DATE		EXPLANATION	POST. REF.	DEBIT	CREDIT	BALANCE DEBIT	BALANCE CREDIT
19—							
Oct.	1	Opening entry	J1	13,000 00		13,000 00	
	6	Check 5	J1	500 00		13,500 00	

Permanent accounts are not closed.

Accts. Pay./Bell Products						Account No.	201
DATE	EXPLANATION	POST. REF.	DEBIT	CREDIT	BALANCE		
					DEBIT	CREDIT	
19— Oct. 1	Opening entry	J1		1,000 00		1,000 00	
7	Invoice 9822	J1		600 00		1,600 00	
8	Credit Memorandum CM-67	J1	200 00			1,400 00	
12	Check 6	J1	1,000 00			400 00	

Permanent accounts are not closed.

Accts. Pay./Royal Service Shop						Account No.	202
DATE	EXPLANATION	POST. REF.	DEBIT	CREDIT	BALANCE		
					DEBIT	CREDIT	
19— Oct. 1	Opening entry	J1		200 00		200 00	
29	Invoice 212	J2		100 00		300 00	

Permanent accounts are not closed.

Mark Nero, Capital						Account No.	301
DATE	EXPLANATION	POST. REF.	DEBIT	CREDIT	BALANCE		
					DEBIT	CREDIT	
19— Oct. 1	Opening entry	J1		26,400 00		26,400 00	
12	Remittance Slip RS-105 . . .	J1		5,000 00		31,400 00	
21	Check 7	J1	2,000 00			29,400 00	
31	Net income	J2		1,100 00		30,500 00	

Permanent accounts are not closed.

Note that the accounts and the balances listed on the postclosing trial balance for the Globe Travel Agency shown in the margin now agree completely with the items on the balance sheet of October 31. As a result of the closing entries, the balance of the Mark Nero, Capital account is now identical with the total owner's equity shown on the following balance sheet.

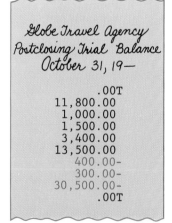

Globe Travel Agency
Postclosing Trial Balance
October 31, 19—

```
          .00T
     11,800.00
      1,000.00
      1,500.00
      3,400.00
     13,500.00
        400.00-
        300.00-
     30,500.00-
          .00T
```

Quick postclosing trial balance shows only amounts. Debits added; credits subtracted. Zero proof shows ledger is in balance.

```
                        Globe Travel Agency
                           Balance Sheet
                         October 31, 19--

                              Assets
Cash . . . . . . . . . . . . . . . . . . . . . .   $11,800.00
Accounts Receivable:
  Karen Louis. . . . . . . . . . . . . .  $1,000.00
  Rose Shops . . . . . . . . . . . . . .   1,500.00      2,500.00
Furniture . . . . . . . . . . . . . . . . . .            3,400.00
Office Equipment . . . . . . . . . . . . . . .          13,500.00
    Total Assets . . . . . . . . . . . . . . . .                   $31,200.00

                            Liabilities
Accounts Payable:
  Bell Products. . . . . . . . . . . . . . . . . .   $    400.00
  Royal Service Shops. . . . . . . . . . . . . . .        300.00
    Total Liabilities. . . . . . . . . . . . . . .                 $    700.00

                          Owner's Equity
Mark Nero, Capital . . . . . . . . . . . . . . . .   $29,400.00
Net Income . . . . . . . . . . . . . . . . . . . .     1,100.00
    Total Owner's Equity . . . . . . . . . . . . .                    30,500.00
        Total Liabilities and Owner's Equity . . . .               $31,200.00
```

The Accounting Cycle

Proving the closed ledger is the seventh step in the accounting cycle. The steps discussed up to this point are as follows.

STEP 1. Record original data on a source document.
STEP 2. Record the transactions in a journal.
STEP 3. Post the journal entries to the ledger accounts.
STEP 4. Prove the equality of the ledger.
STEP 5. Prepare an income statement and a balance sheet.
STEP 6. Journalize and post the closing entries.
STEP 7. Prove the equality of the closed ledger.

Activity C. Answer the following questions about the postclosing trial balance prepared for the Globe Travel Agency. Refer to page 180 and the accounts on pages 181 and 182.

1. What is the purpose of the postclosing trial balance?
2. Which ledger accounts are not listed on the postclosing trial balance? Why?

3. What does the debit total of the postclosing trial balance represent?
4. What does the credit total of the postclosing trial balance represent?
5. What are the amounts of the accounting equation on October 31?
6. What is the date of the postclosing trial balance?

Accounting Concepts:

Closing the Ledger. The revenue data and expense data for one accounting period must be clearly distinguished from that of another accounting period.
Postclosing Trial Balance. The equality of the total debits and the total credits in the ledger should be verified after the ledger has been closed.

Topic 2 Problems

7-3. Two Accounts Receivable accounts are illustrated. Apply the procedures for transferring amounts in accounts. Journalize and post the following entries on August 31 for the Tennessee Trucking Company. Be sure to post after every entry.
a. A sale for $600 on credit to Memphis Moving Company was incorrectly journalized as a debit to the Memphis River Boat Company.

b. A check for $900 received on account from Memphis River Boat Company was incorrectly journalized as a credit to Memphis Moving Company.
c. The Shelby Corporation purchased the business of Memphis Moving Company and requested that the balance of $600 be transferred from the Accts. Rec./Memphis Moving Company account to a new account for the Shelby Corporation.

Accts. Rec./Memphis Moving Company					Account No. 102	
DATE	EXPLANATION	POST. REF.	DEBIT	CREDIT	BALANCE DEBIT	CREDIT
19— Aug. 25		J9		900 00		900 00

Accts. Rec./Memphis River Boat Company					Account No. 103	
DATE	EXPLANATION	POST. REF.	DEBIT	CREDIT	BALANCE DEBIT	CREDIT
19— Aug. 7		J8	900 00		900 00	
9		J8	600 00		1,500 00	

7-4. Set up ledger accounts, and record the following data directly in the accounts. Journalize and post the closing entries for the year ended December 31.

Workbook accounts show data recorded.
NOTE: Save your ledger accounts for further use in Topic Problem 7-5.

Account Title	Acct. No.	Debit Entries			Credit Entries		
Cash	101	Jan. 15	J1	$ 900	Jan. 18	J1	$ 20
		Feb. 26	J1	1,250	Aug. 6	J1	50
		Dec. 6	J1	500			
Accts. Pay./Macon Brothers	201				Nov. 19	J1	30
Shane Hatley, Capital	301				Jan. 15	J1	900
Income Summary	399						
Sales	401				Feb. 26	J1	1,250
					Dec. 6	J1	500
Delivery Expense	501	Aug. 6	J1	50			
Postal Expense	502	Jan. 18	J1	20			
		Nov. 19	J1	30			

7-5. Prepare a postclosing trial balance for Shane Hatley for December 31. Use your ledger accounts from Topic Problem 7-4.

7-6. Set up ledger accounts for the Hollywood Protective Agency. Record the data below in the accounts.
NOTE: Save your ledger accounts for further use in Topic Problem 7-7.

Account Title	Acct. No.	Debit Entries			Credit Entries		
Cash	101	Mar. 1	J5	$3,000	Mar. 20	J7	$ 520
		15	J6	75	27	J7	20
		23	J7	150			
		24	J7	1,030			
Accts. Rec./Ford Grocery	102	Mar. 1	J5	500	Mar. 15	J6	75
					23	J7	150
Accts. Rec./Mom's Market	103	Mar. 22	J7	1,030	Mar. 24	J7	1,030
Tools	111	Mar. 24	J7	450	Mar. 30	J7	105
Truck	112	Mar. 12	J6	2,500			
Accts. Pay./Beaver Hardware	201	Mar. 30	J7	105	Mar. 24	J7	450
Accts. Pay./Cohen and Son	202				Mar. 1	J5	700
					12	J6	2,500
Thomas Lewis, Capital	301	Mar. 20	J7	520	Mar. 1	J5	2,800
		27	J7	20	31	J7	1,030

7-7. Prepare a postclosing trial balance for the Hollywood Protective Agency for March 31, 19—. Use the ledger accounts that you prepared in completing Topic Problem 7-6.

Topic 3
Interpreting Financial Information

A *What is the eighth step in the accounting cycle?* Interpreting (using) accounting information is the last step in the accounting cycle. Remember that the interpretation of accounting information is a process that goes on continuously. It is listed here as the last step in the accounting cycle because all statements are now available for use.

Users of Financial Statements

The financial statements provide information about the business to interested parties. Some of the persons who want this information are outsiders—those outside of the business. This includes persons such as creditors, potential investors in the business, bankers, and the state and federal tax departments. The financial statements that you have prepared are very much like these financial statements.

Other persons interested in the financial statements are insiders— those within the business. These are managers of the business. These managers are responsible for making decisions within the business.

A Comparative Income Statement

Frequently managers want to compare the results for two or more accounting periods. This is done by preparing a comparative income statement. A **comparative income statement** is an income statement that compares revenue and expense data for two or more accounting periods.

The Globe Travel Agency, for example, has been in operation two months—September and October. If Mark Nero wants to compare the revenues earned and the expenses incurred in October with those in September, he would follow these procedures.

• *What information is needed?* Mark Nero needs information about revenue and expenses for the accounting period ended September 30, 19—, and similar data for the accounting period ended October 31, 19—. This information provides Mr. Nero with data to compare revenue and expenses for one accounting period with another accounting period. As a result, he can make intelligent decisions about the operation of his business.

• *What data is required to supply this output?* Note that revenue and expense data for each accounting period must be gathered for the accounting periods ended September 30, 19—, and October 31, 19—.

• *Where is the input collected?* Data about revenue and expenses is on source documents, in the journal, in the ledger, and on the income statement. Mr. Nero can look at these. However, the income statement provides the best source of information because it summarizes all revenue and expenses during an accounting period.

• *What should be done to the input data to provide the needed output?* The income statements for the accounting period ended September 30 and the period ended October 31 and a comparative income statement are illustrated on page 186. A comparative income statement is one statement which combines income statements covering two or more accounting periods. The most recent income statement data is listed first because it shows the latest data available.

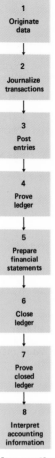

1 Originate data

↓

2 Journalize transactions

↓

3 Post entries

↓

4 Prove ledger

↓

5 Prepare financial statements

↓

6 Close ledger

↓

7 Prove closed ledger

↓

8 Interpret accounting information

Accounting Cycle

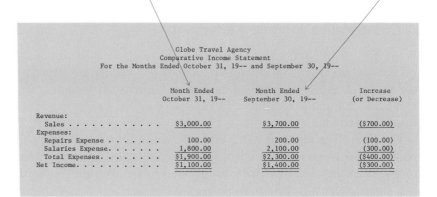

Globe Travel Agency		
Income Statement		
For the Month Ended October 31, 19—		
Revenue:		
Sales.............		3,000 00
Expenses:		
Repairs Expense	100 00	
Salaries Expense	1,800 00	
Total Expenses		1,900 00
Net Income		1,100 00

Income statement for October.

Globe Travel Agency		
Income Statement		
For the Month Ended September 30, 19—		
Revenue:		
Sales.............		3,700 00
Expenses:		
Repairs Expense	200 00	
Salaries Expense	2,100 00	
Total Expenses		2,300 00
Net Income		1,400 00

Income statement for September.

Globe Travel Agency
Comparative Income Statement
For the Months Ended October 31, 19-- and September 30, 19--

	Month Ended October 31, 19--	Month Ended September 30, 19--	Increase (or Decrease)
Revenue:			
Sales	$3,000.00	$3,700.00	($700.00)
Expenses:			
Repairs Expense	100.00	200.00	(100.00)
Salaries Expense	1,800.00	2,100.00	(300.00)
Total Expenses.	$1,900.00	$2,300.00	($400.00)
Net Income.	$1,100.00	$1,400.00	($300.00)

Comparative income statement shows increases and decreases from one accounting period to the next.

A third section has been added to the above income statement. This section shows the increases and decreases in each item reported. Parentheses were placed around each amount that decreased.

The previous four questions are related to the data processing cycle, which is discussed in Chapter 5. The next question, however, involves decision making. **Decision making** is the process of selecting a course of action from several alternatives. Thus interpreting accounting data involves answering two more questions.

• *What judgments can be made about the information?* Mark Nero compares the data on the income statements. He sees that total revenue for October ($3,000) is less than the total revenue for September ($3,700). He could interpret this as either a problem or an error. If he is concerned about accuracy, he could use an audit trail to verify the sales amount. The Sales account in the ledger would show the date and the posting reference number of each entry posted from the journal. The journal entry gives information to locate the source document. Since sales were less in the second accounting period, he should investigate the reasons. Mark Nero observes that there was a difference in expenses. Total expenses decreased during the second accounting period. On closer analysis, he observes that Repairs Expense decreased, but he is concerned about his equipment needing repair. In addition, Salaries expenses also decreased. Net income for the accounting period ended October 31 decreased $300 when compared with the net income of the previous accounting period. The decrease in net income was due to a decrease in revenue and not to expenses.

• *What decisions can be made?* Based on his interpretation of data, Mark Nero makes several decisions concerning the future operation of his business. His major decisions are to increase revenue from services, carefully use the equipment to reduce repair expenses, and supervise the work of employees.

Preparing Statements

In some accounting forms there may not be enough space to group accounts in separate columns. The amounts must be placed in one column, as the amounts were in the comparative income statement. When this is done, it is acceptable to place a single rule above a group total and also a single rule under that total. Note how a single rule was placed below the Sales amounts in the comparative income statement. This shows that these amounts are separated from those that follow.

Note that the total expenses are also enclosed by single rules. The net income is computed by subtracting the amounts in the rules.

Activity A. Answer the following questions about the interpretation of accounting information and the comparative income statement. Refer to the text, margin notes, and illustrations on pages 184 to 187.

1. Why is the interpretation of accounting information a continuous process?
2. What are the questions one answers in interpreting information?
3. Is the latest accounting period listed first on the comparative income statement? Why?

4. Is similar information shown on the comparative income statement and on the individual income statement? Explain.
5. What is the difference in net income between the accounting period ended October 31 and the period ended September 30?
6. What is the increase or decrease for each expense?
7. What is your opinion of the results of operations for the two accounting periods?

A Comparative Balance Sheet

B *How would you compare the financial position from one date to another?* The financial position of a business would be compared by preparing a comparative balance sheet. A **comparative balance sheet** is a balance sheet that compares the assets, liabilities, and owner's equity on two or more dates.

Suppose Mark Nero wants to compare his owner's equity in the Globe Travel Agency on October 31 with his equity on September 30. He needs data reported on balance sheets for those dates. He would proceed to secure the appropriate data and make the proper interpretation answering six questions discussed previously.

```
                              Globe Travel Agency
                           Comparative Balance Sheet
                For the Months Ended October 31, 19-- and September 30, 19--

                                  Month Ended        Month Ended         Increase
                                 October 31, 19--   September 30, 19--   (or Decrease)

              Assets
Cash. . . . . . . . . . . . . .    $11,800.00          $ 9,900.00        $1,900.00
Accounts Receivable . . . . . . .    2,500.00            1,700.00           800.00
Furniture . . . . . . . . . . . .    3,400.00            3,000.00           400.00
Office Equipment  . . . . . . . .   13,500.00           13,000.00           500.00
   Total Assets. . . . . . . . . .  $31,200.00          $27,600.00        $3,600.00

            Liabilities
Accounts Payable: . . . . . . . .  $    700.00          $ 1,200.00        $ (500.00)
   Total Liabilities . . . . . . . $    700.00          $ 1,200.00        $ (500.00)

           Owner's Equity
Mark Nero, Capital. . . . . . . .   $29,400.00          $25,000.00        $4,400.00
Net Income. . . . . . . . . . . .     1,100.00            1,400.00          (300.00)
   Total Owner's Equity. . . . . .  $30,500.00          $26,400.00        $4,100.00
      Total Liabilities and Owner's Equity  $31,200.00  $27,600.00        $3,600.00
```

Comparative balance sheet shows increases and decreases from one date to the next.

• *What information is needed?* Information about his financial interest in the business on September 30 and October 31 is needed. As the owner of the business, Mark Nero must evaluate his financial interest in the business. He needs to know if the operation of the business increased or decreased his financial interest.

• *What data is required to supply output?* Owner's equity data for each date is needed.

• *Where is the input collected?* Data about owner's equity is on source documents, in the journal, in the ledger, and on the balance sheet. However, balance sheets provide the best source of information about owner's equity. The balance sheet summarizes assets, liabilities, and owner's equity on a given date.

• *What should be done to the input data to provide the needed output?* A comparative balance sheet for September 30 and October 31 is illustrated above. The most recent balance sheet data is listed first because it shows the latest data available. (You can verify this data by checking the original balance sheets shown on page 92 and page 170.)

• *What judgments can be made about the data?* When Mark Nero compares the balance sheets, he notes that total owner's equity on October 31 was $4,100 higher than total owner's equity on September 30. His first interpretation is that net income was the cause of the increase in his equity. However, after further analysis, he has a second interpretation which is different than the first. On September 30 his total owner's equity was $26,400. On October 31 it was $30,500. This increase was due to two reasons. The business produced a net income *and* an additional investment in the business. A net income of $1,400 was reported for the accounting period ended September 30, 19—. A net income of only $1,100, however, was reported for the accounting period ended October 31, 19—.

• *What decisions can be made?* Based on this interpretation of data, Mark Nero makes two decisions about the future operation of his business. He decides to make better use of the business's resources to increase net income. For example, further study of the balance sheets shows that total assets increased and total liabilities decreased. This is a shift of resources. As a result, Mark Nero concludes that better use of resources might improve the operation of the business. He also decides to postpone additional cash investments until he receives balance sheet information for the next accounting period (ended November 30). You can see how the interpretation of data influences decisions that go beyond the end of an accounting cycle. Interpretation of data is in fact a continuous process.

Activity B. Answer the following questions about the comparative balance sheet. Refer to the text and illustration on pages 187 to 189.
1. Is the latest accounting period listed first on the comparative balance sheet? Why?
2. Is similar information shown on the comparative balance sheet and on the individual balance sheets? Explain.
3. Why is this form of balance sheet more helpful to managers than the regular report form?
4. State the six questions that are used in decision making and interpreting accounting information.
5. Did the amount of cash increase or decrease?
6. Did the owner's equity improve during this accounting period? Explain why or why not.

The Accounting Cycle

C *Is the accounting cycle repeated each accounting period?* The accounting cycle is repeated each accounting period.

STEP 1. Record original data on a source document.
STEP 2. Record the transactions in a journal.
STEP 3. Post the journal entries to the ledger accounts.
STEP 4. Prove the equality of the ledger.
STEP 5. Prepare an income statement and a balance sheet.
STEP 6. Journalize and post the closing entries.
STEP 7. Prove the equality of the closed ledger.
STEP 8. Interpret the accounting information.

All businesses follow the same steps of the accounting cycle to process their accounting data. However, they may use different methods, or accounting systems, to process their data. An **accounting system** is a specific method used to process data through the accounting cycle. The type of system used depends on the nature and size of the business and on the types of information needed.

Output

In the accounting cycle, the **input data** comes from transactions recorded on source documents (sales slips, purchase invoices, and so on). The input data is entered into the accounting system by journalizing the transactions. The **output data** is information about the results of business operations. This information is provided through such reports as the trial balance, the income statement, the balance sheet, and the postclosing trial balance. An accounting system takes input data from transactions. It then processes the data. Finally, an accounting system provides the desired output data to be used in making decisions.

The relationship between the data processing cycle and the accounting cycle is shown on the next page.

Activity C. Answer the following questions on the accounting cycle and data processing cycle. Refer to the text and illustration on pages 189 and 190.
1. Are the eight steps in the accounting cycle repeated each accounting period?

2. What is the source of the input data?
3. Give four examples of output data.
4. Why is interpretation of data a continuous process?
5. During which step is data put into the accounting cycle?

Accounting Concept:
Comparative Financial Statements. The information on the financial statements of a business should be compared at different times, usually in two successive accounting periods.

Topic 3 Problems

7-8. A comparative income statement for the Texas Advertising Company is illustrated below.
a. Complete the Increase (or Decrease) section of the comparative income statement.

b. What are the major factors that caused an increase in net income between the two accounting periods?

	AUGUST	JULY	INCREASE (OR DECREASE)
Revenue:			
Sales..................	50,000	47,000	
Expenses:			
Rent Expense	800	800	
Salaries Expense	30,000	31,000	
Supplies Expense	12,000	14,000	
Total Expenses	42,800	45,800	
Net Income	7,200	1,200	

Texas Advertising Company
Comparative Income Statement
For the Months Ended August 31, 19— and July 31, 19—

RELATIONSHIP OF ACCOUNTING CYCLE TO DATA PROCESSING CYCLE

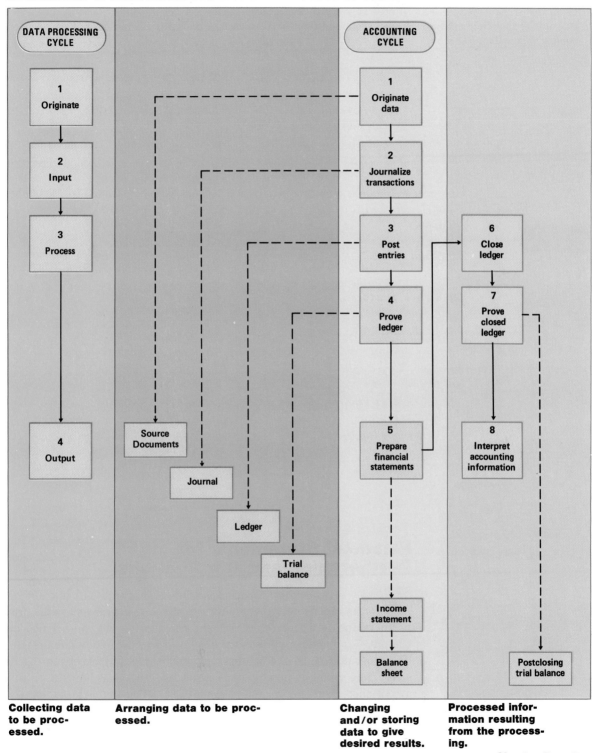

Collecting data to be processed.

Arranging data to be processed.

Changing and/or storing data to give desired results.

Processed information resulting from the processing.

7-9. A comparative balance sheet for the Florida Charter Fishing Company is illustrated below.
a. Complete the Increase (or Decrease) section of the comparative balance sheet.

b. What major factors caused a decrease in owner's equity?
c. Give an interpretation of what might have affected cash items.

Florida Charter Fishing Company Comparative Balance Sheet February 28, 19— and January 31, 19—	FEBRUARY 28, 19—	JANUARY 31, 19—	INCREASE (OR DECREASE)
Assets			
Cash	1,000 00	2,500 00	
Accounts Receivable	250 00	175 00	
Boat	65,000 00	65,000 00	
Equipment	5,800 00	6,500 00	
Supplies	770 00	830 00	
Total Assets	72,820 00	75,005 00	
Liabilities			
Bank Loan Payable	4,000 00	4,400 00	
Accounts Payable	1,820 00	1,605 00	
Total Liabilities	5,820 00	6,005 00	
Owner's Equity			
Nicholas Meko, Capital	63,000 00	64,000 00	
Net Income	4,000 00	5,000 00	
Total Owner's Equity	67,000 00	69,000 00	
Total Liabilities and Owner's Equity	72,820 00	75,005 00	

Topic 4
Financial Statements for Partnerships and Corporations

A *What are the major forms of business ownership?* The four major forms of business ownership are the single proprietorship, the partnership, the corporation, and the cooperative. As you learned in Chapter 1, a single proprietorship is a business owned by one person. The other three forms of business ownership involve two or more persons. The form of ownership determines such things as how the profits are divided, who makes management decisions, and who is legally liable for the debts of the business.

Single Proprietorships

The simplest form of business ownership to organize and operate is a single proprietorship, or sole proprietorship. This is the most common form of ownership and is found in businesses such as small retail shops, service stations, and doctors' practices. A **single proprietorship** is a business owned by one person.

A single proprietorship is owned by one person.

The single proprietorship form of business ownership has several advantages.

- *Simple to organize.* A single proprietorship is simple to organize. Only one owner is involved.
- *Owner makes all decisions.* The owner is the only one in control and makes all the management decisions.
- *Owner claims all profits.* If the business is successful, the owner enjoys all the profits.
- *Maximum personal incentive.* The owner feels a strong need to be successful. If the business is successful, the owner gets all the profits. But many businesses are not successful. If a business fails, the owner suffers all the losses.

The single proprietorship form of ownership does have disadvantages. Among them are these.

- *Unlimited liability.* The owner has unlimited liability. This means the owner is personally liable for all the debts of the business. If the business cannot pay its debts, the personal property of the owner (such as a house or an automobile) can be legally taken to pay them. Therefore, **unlimited liability** means that the owner is personally liable for all the debts of the business.
- *Limited resources.* The amount of resources that the owner can raise is limited. Additional cash, for example, is usually limited to the amount of the owner's personal savings and to the amount that can be borrowed from other sources, including the owner's bank, friends, and relatives.
- *Limited life.* A single proprietorship has a limited life. **Limited life** means that the legal life of the business ends when the owner dies or withdraws from the business.
- *Limited talent.* The success or failure of the business depends mainly on the talents of one person, the owner.

Financial Statements for Single Proprietorships

The Globe Travel Agency is a single proprietorship owned by Mark Nero. The total net income shown on the income statement is claimed by the owner. If there is a net loss, the owner suffers the entire loss.

Globe Travel Agency
Income Statement
For the Month Ended October 31, 19—

Revenue:			
Sales			3,000 00
Expenses:			
Repairs Expense	100 00		
Salaries Expense	1,800 00		
Total Expenses			1,900 00
Net Income			1,100 00

Income statement for a single proprietorship. Owner claims all net income.

Balance Sheet. The net income from the income statement is added to the owner's equity. Some of the disadvantages of the single proprietorship, however, can be seen on the balance sheet.

• The owner is liable for the liabilities of the business if it cannot pay its debts.
• The assets of the business are mainly limited by what the owner can raise.
• If the owner dies or withdraws from the business, the business ends.
• The success or failure of the business depends mainly on one person—the owner.

```
                              Globe Travel Agency
                                 Balance Sheet
                                October 31, 19--

                                    Assets
Cash . . . . . . . . . . . . . . . . . . . . . . . . . . . . . . .  $11,800.00
Accounts Receivable:
  Karen Louis . . . . . . . . . . . . . . . $1,000.00
  Rose Shops . . . . . . . . . . . . . .      1,500.00
Furniture . . . . . . . . . . . . . . . . . . . . . . . . . .        2,500.00
Office Equipment . . . . . . . . . . . . . . . . . . .               3,400.00
                                                                    13,500.00
        Total Assets . . . . . . . . . . . . . . . . . . .                       $31,200.00

                                  Liabilities
Accounts Payable:
  Bell Products . . . . . . . . . . . . . . . . . . . . .       $    400.00
  Royal Service Shops . . . . . . . . . . . . . . . .                300.00
        Total Liabilities . . . . . . . . . . . . . . . . .                      $    700.00

                                Owner's Equity
Mark Nero, Capital . . . . . . . . . . . . . . . . . .         $29,400.00
Net Income . . . . . . . . . . . . . . . . . . . . . . . . .        1,100.00
        Total Owner's Equity . . . . . . . . . . . . . .                          30,500.00
        Total Liabilities and Owner's Equity . . . . . . .                       $31,200.00
```

Balance sheet for a single proprietorship. Owner claims all net income.

Activity A. Answer the following questions. Refer to the income statement and balance sheet for the Globe Travel Agency shown above.

1. How much of the net income is claimed by Mark Nero?

2. Suppose for some reason the Globe Travel Agency

could not pay its liabilities. Mark Nero would be responsible to pay for how much from his personal property?

3. Suppose Mark Nero cannot borrow any money. How can he get more cash for the business?

4. Suppose the business had a net loss of $1,100 instead of a net income. How much of the net loss would Mark Nero suffer?

Partnerships

B *How does the ownership of a partnership differ from a single proprietorship?* A **partnership** is a business owned by two or more persons. In a partnership, ownership is divided between two or more persons who agree to share their property and skills to start and operate a business. Each owner is called a *partner.*

Among the advantages to the partnerships are these.

- *Simple to organize.* A partnership, like a single proprietorship, is simple to organize. A partnership agreement, either oral or written, is made to tell the amount of money and skill each partner will contribute, what responsibilities each will have, and how the profits and losses will be divided. A **partnership agreement** is a legal agreement expressing the terms and conditions for running a partnership.
- *Pooling of talents and skills.* The talents and skills of several owners are shared. Each owner contributes his or her specialty. Thus there is more than one person available to make decisions.
- *Resources are pooled.* Its owners can make a greater investment by pooling their property.
- *Better credit rating.* Credit is easier to get because the debt may be collected from any or all of the partners.
- *High degree of personal incentive.* Since the owners enjoy all the profits and suffer all the losses, they have a strong desire to be successful.

A partnership also has several disadvantages. Among them are these.

- *Unlimited liability.* Each partner has unlimited liability for the debts of the business. Thus a partner's personal property can be legally taken to pay these debts. In addition, one partner can be held fully responsible for all the business debts if the other partners cannot pay their shares.
- *Limited resources.* Even with several partners, the amount of money available is usually limited to what the partners can raise.
- *Limited life.* A partnership has limited life. The partnership is legally ended if one partner dies or withdraws from the business or if new partners are added.

A partnership is owned by two or more persons.

- *Divided authority.* The authority in making decisions is divided among the partners. Thus disagreements between the partners can result.

Financial Statements for Partnerships

The accounts used for a partnership are the same as in a single proprietorship, except the equity accounts. In a single proprietorship, only one Capital account is required. In a partnership, a separate Capital account is used for each partner.

Income Statement. The income statement for a partnership is the same as the one for a single proprietorship, except in the Net Income (or Net Loss) section. It shows how the net income (or net loss) is distributed to the partners. For example, assume that the Globe Travel Agency is a partnership owned by Mark Nero and Mary Trent. Assume also that the net income is shared equally by the partners. The income statement would show the net income of $1,100 being shared as in the following illustration.

<table>
<tr><td colspan="3" align="center">*Globe Travel Agency*
Income Statement
For the Month Ended October 31, 19—</td></tr>
<tr><td>*Revenue:*</td><td></td><td></td></tr>
<tr><td> *Sales*.........................</td><td></td><td>*3,000 00*</td></tr>
<tr><td>*Expenses:*</td><td></td><td></td></tr>
<tr><td> *Repairs Expense* ....</td><td>*100 00*</td><td></td></tr>
<tr><td> *Salaries Expense* ....</td><td>*1,800 00*</td><td></td></tr>
<tr><td> *Total Expenses* ....</td><td></td><td>*1,900 00*</td></tr>
<tr><td>*Net Income* ....</td><td></td><td>*1,100 00*</td></tr>
<tr><td>*Distribution of Net Income:*</td><td></td><td></td></tr>
<tr><td> *Mark Nero* ....</td><td>*550 00*</td><td></td></tr>
<tr><td> *Mary Trent*..................</td><td>*550 00*</td><td></td></tr>
<tr><td>*Net Income Allocated* ....</td><td></td><td>*1,100 00*</td></tr>
</table>

Income statement for a partnership. Distribution of net income is shown.

Balance Sheet. The balance sheet for a partnership is the same as the balance sheet for a single proprietorship, except for the Partners' Equity section. The balance sheet for the partnership shows the financial interest of each partner.

Globe Travel Agency
Balance Sheet
October 31, 19—

Assets			
Cash		11,800 00	
Accounts Receivable:			
Karen Louis $1,000.00			
Rose Shops 1,500.00		2,500 00	
Furniture		3,400 00	
Office Equipment		13,500 00	
Total Assets			31,200 00
Liabilities			
Accounts Payable:			
Bell Products		400 00	
Royal Service Shop		300 00	
Total Liabilities			700 00
Partners' Equity			
Mark Nero:			
Capital $14,700.00			
Net Income 550.00		15,250 00	
Mary Trent:			
Capital $14,700.00			
Net Income 550.00		15,250 00	
Total Partners' Equity			30,500 00
Total Liabilities and Partners' Equity			31,200 00

Balance sheet for a partnership. Partners' equity section shows the equity for each partner.

Activity B. Answer the following questions about partnerships. Refer to the text and financial statements for a partnership on pages 195 to 197.

1. What is the accounting period?
2. What amount of the net income was allocated to Mary Trent?
3. What is the total partners' equity?
4. What is the total net income shown on the balance sheet for the partnership?
5. If the Globe Travel Agency cannot pay its debts, who would be responsible for paying them?
6. Suppose that the Globe Travel Agency cannot pay its debts and that Mark Nero cannot pay his share. How much of the $700 would Mary Trent be liable for?
7. Suppose Mary Trent decided to sell her share of the business. Would the partnership still be in existence? Explain.
8. How could the partnership raise more cash without borrowing it?
9. What advantages are there to Mark Nero's being in a partnership?
10. What disadvantages are there to Mark Nero's being in a partnership?

Corporations

A corporation is usually owned by three or more persons.

C *How does a corporation differ from single proprietorships and partnerships?* A **corporation** is a business chartered under state law and owned by stockholders. A corporation may be owned by many people. It has its own name, in which it can buy, own, and sell property; make contracts; borrow money; and take court action. There are far fewer corporations than single proprietorships and partnerships combined. But corporations employ more employees than the other two and do the majority of the nation's business.

Every corporation must be chartered under state law. A **charter** is the terms and conditions for running a corporation. The corporation is supervised by a board of directors. The **board of directors** is the governing body of the corporation elected by the stockholders. The **stockholders,** or *shareholders*, are the owners of a corporation. A stockholder has one vote for each share of stock owned. The board of directors appoints officers to manage the corporation. A corporation holds at least one stockholders' meeting each year.

The corporation form of ownership has several advantages.

- *Ease of transferring ownership.* The ownership of a corporation is easily transferred. Each stockholder receives a stock certificate as evidence of ownership. This certificate is legally transferable from one person to another.
- *Continuous life.* A corporation has continuous life. **Continuous life** means that the life of the corporation does not end when stock is sold. The corporation remains intact no matter how often ownership of the stock changes.
- *Limited liability.* Stockholders have only limited liability. **Limited liability** limits the owner's liability for the debts of the business. If the corporation fails, the stockholders' losses are limited to the amount invested. They are not personally liable for the debts of the corporation. Thus a stockholder's personal property cannot be taken for these debts.
- *More resources.* Corporations are able to raise large amounts of money by selling stock to many people.
- *Professional management.* Corporations do not have to depend on the talents of their owners. The officers are usually skilled professional managers.

The corporation form of ownership also has disadvantages. Among them are these.

- *Complicated and costly to organize.* A corporation is more complicated and more costly to start.

- *More restrictions and regulations.* Many restrictions and regulations are placed upon it by state and federal laws.
- *Double taxation.* There is double taxation on a corporation's profits. A corporation pays an income tax on its profits. Then it distributes part of those profits to the stockholders as dividends. A **dividend** is a distribution of earnings to stockholders. Another tax must then be paid by the stockholders, who must declare the dividends as part of their personal income.

Financial Statements for Corporations

The major difference between the accounts for a corporation and a single proprietorship or a partnership is in the equity accounts. A capital stock account and a retained earnings account are used in a corporation. A **capital stock account** is an equity account to show the stockholders' investment. A **retained earnings account** is an equity account to show the net income kept by the corporation.

For a corporation, there is also a difference in the liability accounts. Single proprietorships and partnerships do not pay federal income taxes. The net income for the business is the owner's or partners' personal income. A corporation, however, must pay federal income taxes. Thus a corporation must have a liability account for the income taxes payable. The following illustration shows how the Income Taxes Payable would appear in the Liabilities section of the balance sheet.

Liabilities			
Accounts Payable:			
Bell Products $400.00			
Royal Service Shop 300.00	700 00		
Income Taxes Payable................	187 00		
Total Liabilities................		887 00	

A corporation that sells stock to the public must publish its financial statements for outsiders at least once a year.

Income Statement. Some of the key characteristics of an income statement for a corporation are as follows.
1 A corporation usually includes the word *Corporation* or *Incorporated* as the last word of its name. (These words may be abbreviated as *Corp.* or *Inc.*) This reminds outsiders that the stockholders have limited liability. It also reminds outsiders that the business is a legal entity. It has its own name and address, its own resources, its own continuous life, and the right to take court action. The corporation—not its owners—are responsible for its actions.

Globe Travel Agency, Inc.
Income Statement
For the Month Ended October 31, 19— ← (1)

Revenue:			
Sales..................			3,000 00
Expenses:			
Repairs Expense	100 00		
Salaries Expense	1,800 00		
Total Expenses			1,900 00
Net Income Before Income Taxes			1,100 00
Provision for Income Taxes			187 00 — (2)
Net Income After Income Taxes			913 00 — (3)

Income statement for a corporation. Provision for income taxes is shown.

Corporate Income Tax Rate
17% First $25,000
20% Second $25,000
30% Third $25,000
40% Fourth $25,000
46% Above $100,000

2 A corporation must pay income taxes. The income taxes are based on a corporation's net income. The corporation does not know the amount of the income taxes to be paid to the government until the net income is computed on the income statement. Thus the income taxes are not generally shown in the Expenses section of the income statement.

Instead, income taxes are generally listed in the Net Income section. The amount is shown as a "Provision for Income Taxes" and is subtracted from the net income. The net income after incomes taxes is the amount carried forward to the balance sheet. The income statement shown above illustrates how income taxes would be shown if the Globe Travel Agency were a corporation. As shown in the margin, the rate of the income taxes changes based on the total net income before taxes.

3 The net income in a single proprietorship or partnership is added directly to the owner's equity or partners' equity on the balance sheet. A corporation may or may not declare a dividend to the stockholders. The part of the net income that is not distributed to the owner is called *retained earnings*. To keep the illustration simple at this time, we will assume that all the net income will be retained by the corporation. The retained earnings will be used to help the business grow.

Balance Sheet. There are several differences between the balance sheet for a corporation and one for a single proprietorship or a partnership.

1 The Liabilities section of a balance sheet for a corporation shows the income taxes to be paid.

2 The Equity section of a balance sheet for a corporation shows the capital stock of $29,400. This capital stock is considered permanent capital. Normally cash is not withdrawn from the Capital Stock account. When one shareholder sells his or her shares to another, no change occurs on the balance sheet. Only the name of the owner of the shares changes.

3 The Retained Earnings account appears as the second equity item on the balance sheet. This amount represents the net income not distributed to the shareholders.

Globe Travel Agency, Inc. Balance Sheet October 31, 19—				
Assets				
Cash		11,800 00		
Accounts Receivable:				
Karen Louis	$1,000.00			
Rose Shops	1,500.00	2,500 00		
Furniture		3,400 00		
Office Equipment		13,500 00		
Total Assets			31,200 00	
Liabilities				
Accounts Payable:				
Bell Products	$400.00			
Royal Service Shop	300.00	700 00		
Income Taxes Payable		187 00		①
Total Liabilities			887 00	②
Stockholders' Equity				
Capital Stock		29,400 00		③
Retained Earnings		913 00		
Total Stockholders' Equity			30,313 00	
Total Liabilities and Stockholders' Equity . . .			31,200 00	

Balance sheet for a corporation. Liability for income taxes is shown.

Activity C. Answer the following questions about the financial statements for a corporation. Refer to the financial statements on pages 200 and 201.
1. How much money is owed by the corporation to the federal government? To the other creditors? What are the total liabilities?
2. Are the liabilities of the corporation greater than the liabilities of the partnership? Why or why not?
3. What is the total net income of the corporation before taxes? After taxes?

4. How much money is the corporation keeping from its earnings (net income)?
5. What is the amount invested by the owners of the corporation? By the owners of the partnership?
6. What are the total assets of the corporation?
7. If the corporation cannot pay its debts, are the stockholders personally liable? Explain why or why not.
8. If the corporation wants to raise more cash, how can it do so without borrowing?

Cooperatives

D *How does a cooperative differ from single proprietorships, partnerships, and corporations?* A cooperative is a special corporation that is owned by its customers. A **cooperative** is a business

A cooperative is owned by its members.

chartered under state law and owned by and operated for the benefit of its customers. Although it is organized as a corporation, it differs from the corporation in several ways. Each stockholder, usually called a *member,* has only one vote no matter how many shares the member owns. This prevents any one person from gaining control of the cooperative. The purpose of the cooperative is to provide a service to its members at a low cost, not to earn a profit. The amount of its dividends are limited by law. The profits are usually distributed to its members according to the amount each buys from the cooperative. The advantages and disadvantages of the corporation form of ownership also apply to the cooperative.

Activity D. Answer the following questions about forms of business ownership. Refer to the text and margin notes on pages 201 and 202.
1. Do all forms of business ownership have financial statements? Name the financial statements.

2. In which form of business ownership is a stockholder called a *member?*
3. Stockholders, no matter how many shares of stock they own, have only one vote in this form of business ownership. Name the form of business ownership.

Accounting Concepts:
Reporting Net Income. An income statement reports the net income. When appropriate, it should also show how the net income is distributed and the net income after income taxes.
Reporting Equity. A balance sheet reports the total equity. When appropriate, it should also show how the equity is distributed and should separate the permanent investments from the retained earnings.

Topic 4 Problems

7-10. Use a form similar to the one at the right. List the main advantages and disadvantages for each form of business ownership given in the column headings of the form.

Single Proprietorship	Partnership	Corporation
Advantages: **EXAMPLE:** **Simple to organize**	**Simple to organize**	**Limited liability of stockholers**

7-11. Robert Lipkin worked for several years in a fashion photographer's studio, and he learned a lot about the business. After he gained enough experience, he quit his job and started his own fashion advertising and photography company. He invested his savings of $35,000. The financial information at the end of his company's first year, December 31, 19—, is listed at the right.

Cash, $5,000
Accts, Rec./Bryant Supply, $3,000
Accts. Rec./Cardell Services, $2,110
Equipment, $26,000
Accts. Pay./Wayne Slasbury, $120
Accts. Pay./Roberta Northrup, $50
Capital, $20,000
Net Income Before Taxes, $15,940

Complete the equity section of the balance sheet for each of the following situations. Compute the provision for income tax. Use the tax table on page 200.

a. A single proprietorship owned by Robert Lipkin.

b. A partnership owned by Robert Lipkin and Harold Morgan if Robert Lipkin had formed a partnership with Harold Morgan. The net income is distributed evenly between Mr. Lipkin and Mr. Morgan.

c. A corporation if Robert Lipkin had formed a corpo-

ration. Compute the provision for income taxes to show total owner's equity and retained earnings. Use the tax table in the margin on page 200.

7-12. From the data in the following trial balance, prepare (a) an income statement for the month ended May 31 and (b) a balance sheet in report form for May 31 for Almont and Lisa, a law firm. The firm is a partnership, and the net income is divided equally.

Almont and Lisa
Trial Balance
May 31, 19—

ACCOUNT TITLE	ACCT. NO.	DEBIT	CREDIT
Cash	101	10,500 00	
Furniture	111	1,700 00	
Accts. Pay./Legal Books, Inc.	211		800 00
Mona Almont, Capital	301		4,000 00
Louis Lisa, Capital	302		4,000 00
Fees	401		4,220 00
Rent Expense	511	650 00	
Travel Expense	531	170 00	
		13,020 00	13,020 00

7-13. From the data in the following trial balance, prepare (a) an income statement for the year ended December 31 and (b) a balance sheet in account form for December 31 for the Prague Building Corporation.

Compute the provision for income taxes to show total owner's equity and retained earnings. Use the tax table in the margin on page 200.

Prague Building Corporation
Trial Balance
December 31, 19—

ACCOUNT TITLE	ACCT. NO.	DEBIT	CREDIT
Cash	101	17,000 00	
Accts. Rec./Aleppo Markets	102	4,000 00	
Construction Equipment	111	48,000 00	
Office Equipment	112	2,000 00	
Accts. Pay./Louvre Cement Company	201		6,800 00
Capital Stock	301		40,000 00
Sales	401		52,905 00
Maintenance Expense	501	9,730 00	
Miscellaneous Expense	502	675 00	
Salaries Expense	503	18,300 00	
		99,705 00	99,705 00

The Language of Business

Here are some terms that make up the language of business. Do you know the meaning of each?

account form balance
  sheet
report form balance
  sheet
market value
recorded value
open account

comparative income
  statement
decision making
comparative balance
  sheet
accounting system
input data

output data
single proprietorship
unlimited liability
limited life
partnership
partnership agreement
corporation
charter
board of directors

stockholders
continuous life
limited liability
dividend
capital stock account
retained earnings
  account
cooperative

Chapter 7   Questions

1. Explain why the amount for owner's equity shown on the balance sheet is not the same as the amount in the capital account before the closing entries are made.

2. What entries are needed to close the temporary owner's equity accounts at the end of the accounting period? What accounts are not affected by closing entries?

3. Why is an income summary account used?

4. Give two reasons for making closing entries.

5. Why is a postclosing trial balance prepared? How is it prepared?

6. On what statement would you find the amounts that appear on the postclosing trial balance? Why?

7. Describe the differences in the preparation of the income statements for a single proprietorship, a partnership, and a corporation.

8. Describe the differences in the preparation of the balance sheets for a single proprietorship, a partnership, and a corporation.

9. Atlanta Auto Parts had cash receipts of $45,000 and made cash payments of $37,000 during July. Can you assume that the net income for the month was $8,000? Explain.

10. Randy Curtis buys a truck for $7,000. He believes it is worth $8,800. What amount will be on the balance sheet? Why?

Chapter 7   Problems

Problems for Chapter 7 are given in the *Working Papers and Chapter Problems for Part 1.* If you are using the workbook, do the problems in the space provided there.

Chapter 7   Management Cases

Comparative Financial Statements. By looking at photographs of a person taken over a period of time, you can see changes in the person's appearance. The same is true of a business. The income statement and the balance sheet are financial pictures of a business. The income statement can be combined into one statement covering two or more accounting periods. This statement is called a *comparative income statement.*

Business managers study such statements carefully to determine (1) whether sales are increasing or decreasing, (2) whether expenses are increasing faster than sales, (3) which expense items are increasing, (4) the relationship between the amount spent for an expense and the revenue received, and (5) whether increased sales are resulting in increased net income.

The balance sheet, like the income statement, can

be combined into one statement covering two or more accounting periods. By examining several consecutive balance sheets, management is able to note changes and trends.

Case 7M-1. A comparative income statement prepared for Hilltop Cleaners is illustrated below. It contains data for three consecutive accounting periods, which cover three quarters of the year.

a. The net income has shown a steady increase. What is the main reason for this increase?

b. On July 1 the management decided to increase its advertising. It also decided to change gradually from a pickup-and-delivery service to a cash-and-carry serv-

ice. It offers a special reduced price for cleaning garments brought to and picked up at the store by the customer. What effect has this policy had upon the business?

c. On July 1 the management changed its method of paying employees from a regular weekly wage to a piece-rate plan based on the number of garments finished. This change affected approximately 75 percent of the employees. The number of employees was reduced. How has the plan affected salaries expense?

d. Is there any expense item that the management should examine more carefully?

e. What is your general opinion of the results of the operations of the business as shown on the comparative income statement?

Hilltop Cleaners
Comparative Income Statement
For the Quarters Ended September 30, June 30, and March 31, 19—

	JULY, AUG., SEPT. (THIRD QUARTER)	APR., MAY, JUNE (SECOND QUARTER)	JAN., FEB., MAR. (FIRST QUARTER)
Revenue:			
Sales..............	60,000	48,400	45,000
Expenses:			
Advertising Expense	5,500	2,700	2,000
Cleaning Supplies Used	8,500	6,100	6,000
Miscellaneous Expense	550	500	400
Pickup and Delivery Service.	2,900	6,500	6,100
Rental of Building	600	600	600
Rental of Machines.......	1,200	1,200	1,200
Salaries Expense	28,000	27,500	27,000
Total Expenses	47,250	45,100	43,300
Net Income	12,750	3,300	1,700

Case 7M-2. Michael Marino owns Marino Contractors. It is a small electrical company that installs air conditioning in homes and stores. The comparative balance sheet on page 206 shows the financial position of the business on June 30 of this year and on December 31 of last year.

a. Is the financial position better on June 30 or on December 31? Give your reasons.

b. A large number of air-conditioning units have been installed since the first of the year. Customers pay one-third of the total bill when the work is completed, and they pay the balance in six equal monthly pay-

ments. Do the amounts on the balance sheet indicate that collections are being received from the customers? Explain your answer.

c. The business owns one truck. An extra truck is often rented at a very high fee. Mr. Marino can buy a second truck for $5,000. He would have to pay $3,000 in cash now and $2,000 in six months. Could a second truck be purchased safely now? Give your reasons.

d. The general office clerk buys office supplies without getting Mr. Marino's approval. Should Mr. Marino reexamine this policy? Give your reasons.

Marino Contractors
Comparative Balance Sheet
June 30, 19—, and December 31, 19—

	JUNE 30 (THIS YEAR)		DECEMBER 31 (LAST YEAR)	
Assets				
Cash	6,500 00		2,000 00	
Notes Receivable	1,500 00		3,500 00	
Accounts Receivable	8,600 00		10,800 00	
Equipment	16,400 00		15,000 00	
Office Supplies	650 00		100 00	
Total Assets		33,650 00		31,400 00
Liabilities				
Notes Payable	2,500 00		6,000 00	
Accounts Payable	1,750 00		2,000 00	
Total Liabilities		4,250 00		8,000 00
Owner's Equity				
Michael Marino, Capital		29,400 00		23,400 00
Total Liabilities and Owner's Equity . .		33,650 00		31,400 00

Working Hint

Writing Amounts. In this textbook, the amounts in journals, ledger accounts, and statements are always written in full. That is, two zeros are used where there are no cents in the amount. To save time in recording amounts, some accountants and office workers use a dash (—) instead of the two zeros where there are no cents in the amount. For example, instead of writing $63.00, they write $63—. In financial statements, however, zeros are used. Thus $198.00 is *not* written $198— in a financial statement.

The dollar sign is not used with amounts when the figures are written in ruled columns. When zero balances occur in ledger accounts, a dash and two zeros are written in the balance column, as shown on page 150.

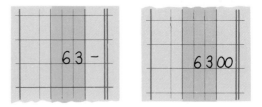

Project 1
Fortune Bus Line

On January 1 Paul Oslo started the Fortune Bus Line. At the present time the bus line is operating on a charter basis. It does not have any regularly scheduled runs. The chart of accounts is shown here.

**FORTUNE BUS LINE
CHART OF ACCOUNTS**

101	Cash	301	Paul Oslo, Capital
102	Accts. Rec./Dallas Oil Company	399	Income Summary
103	Accts. Rec./Ranch Resort	401	Sales
104	Accts. Rec./Texas Tours	501	Advertising Expense
111	Buses	502	Maintenance Expense
112	Office Equipment	503	Miscellaneous Expense
201	Accts. Pay./Lorry Trucks	504	Office Expense
202	Accts. Pay./Page Garage	505	Salaries Expense

Open the ledger accounts shown in this chart of accounts. (If you are not using the workbook, allow 13 lines for Cash; 8 lines for Paul Oslo, Capital and for Sales; and 6 lines for each of the other accounts.)

1. *Originating the data.* During the month of January, the business had the transactions listed on pages 207 and 208.

2. *Journalizing the transactions.* Record the transactions for January in the journal.

3. *Posting the transactions.* Post the journal entries.

4. *Proving the ledger.* Prepare a trial balance to prove the equality of the ledger.

5. *Preparing the financial statements.* Prepare an income statement and a balance sheet (account form).

6. *Closing the ledger.* Journalize and post the closing entries.

7. *Proving the closed ledger.* Prepare a postclosing trial balance to prove the equality of the ledger after it has been closed.

8. *Interpreting the financial information.* Based on the information in the financial records of the Fortune Bus Line, answer the following questions.

a. Mr. Oslo expects his revenue and expenses for February to be approximately the same as for January. However, he promised to pay the balance he owes to Lorry Trucks for the buses by February 28. Do you think the Fortune Bus Line will have enough cash to pay its debt by February 28?

b. If you do not think that it can pay its debt by February, where can the Fortune Bus Line obtain additional cash?

Jan. 2 Paul Oslo started the business with a cash investment of $20,500.

4 Bought 3 buses for $55,000 on credit from Lorry Trucks.

5 Paul Oslo invested an additional $15,000 in the business.

8 Paul Oslo invested a typewriter worth $550 in the business.

8 Sold services for $500 on credit to Texas Tours.

8 Owed $470 to Page Garage for maintenance on buses.

9 Paid $16.50 for an ad in the *Dallas Times*.

10 Paid $16,000 to Lorry Trucks on account.

10 Bought office equipment for $900 in cash.

15 Sold services for $300 in cash.

16 Sold services for $720 on credit to Ranch Resort.

18 Returned bus bought for $10,200 on credit from Lorry Trucks.

18 Received $150 from Texas Tours on account.

22 Sold services for $400 in cash.

23 Owed $85 to Page Garage for maintenance on the buses.

24 Returned office equipment bought for $350 in cash.

Jan. 25 Paul Oslo withdrew $3,000 from the business.

26 Paid $400 for maintenance on the buses.

26 Sold services for $2,300 on credit to Ranch Resort.

26 Paid $3,000 for salaries.

29 Paid $58 for cleaning office (Office Expense).

Jan. 29 Received $3,020 from Ranch Resort on account.

30 Sold services for $700 on credit to Dallas Oil Company.

30 Paid $15 to United Parcel for a delivery (Misc. Expense).

31 Paid $22 for an ad in the *Daily News*.

31 Received $75 from Texas Tours on account.

Banking Activities

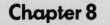

Businesses use checking accounts and other banking services to protect their cash. In accounting, *cash* refers to coins, currency (paper money), checks, and money orders, as well as money deposited in the bank. You will now learn about the handling of cash.

Topic 1
Paying by Check

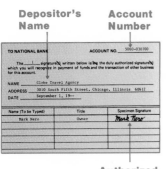

Depositor's Name **Account Number**

Authorized Signature

Signature Card

Three Parties to a Check
- Drawer
- Drawee
- Payee

A *How do businesses protect their cash?* A business uses a checking account so that it will have a safe place to deposit its cash. It will be able to use checks in the place of cash. When a checking account is opened, a signature card must be signed. A **signature card** is a card with signatures of persons authorized to draw checks on a certain bank account. Any signature on the card must be written exactly as it will appear on the checks. The bank keeps the signature on file. It can then compare the signature on the check with the signature on the card. The signature card shown in the margin was prepared when Mark Nero opened a checking account at the National Bank for the Globe Travel Agency.

Drawing Checks

A **check** is a written order to pay a specific sum from a depositor's account to a payee. The depositor tells the bank to deduct a specific sum of money from his or her checking account and to pay that amount to the person, company, or organization named on the check. A **depositor** is an individual, business, or organization in whose name money is placed in the bank.

There are three parties to a check. The depositor of the check is the **drawer.** The bank on which the check is drawn is the **drawee.** The individual, business, company, or organization to whose order the check is to be paid is the **payee.**

There are several advantages to paying all bills by check. The checkbook provides a record of cash paid out. The canceled checks provide proof that money has been paid to the person legally entitled to it. In addition, checks can be sent safely by mail. A check is safe because if it is lost or stolen, the depositor can request the bank not to pay it.

The form of a check varies with the bank and with the type of account. Checks may be written in ink or typed, but never in pencil. A variety of machines for preparing checks is available to depositors who issue many checks. One machine punches tiny holes in the check as it prints the amount. This makes it impossible to change the amount of the check. The procedure for preparing a check is as follows.

1 *When using a standard checkbook, fill in the check stub first so that you will not forget it.* If the stub is not filled in, there will be no record of the check once it is removed from the checkbook. Also, by filling in the data on the stub first, you lessen the chance of making an error when writing the check.

STANDARD STUB AND CHECK

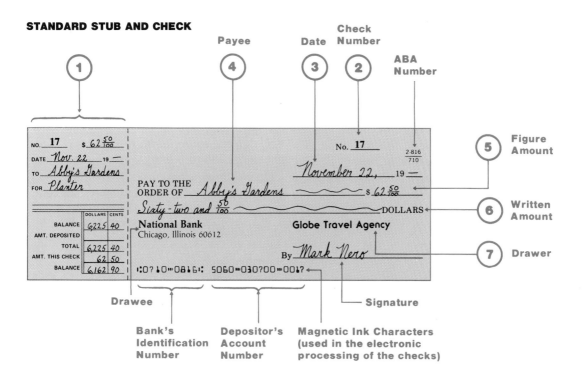

Before writing a check, first bring the checkbook balance up to date in the stub section to make sure that there is enough money on deposit to cover the check. Add the amount of each deposit to the balance previously shown. Subtract the amount of each check from the balance as it is written. Then carry the balance forward to the next check stub. If the balance is kept up to date, it will show the amount left for writing more checks.

After a check is removed from the checkbook, the check stub remains as the source document containing the data needed to journalize the transaction.

2 *Write the check number if the check has not been prenumbered by the bank.* All checks must be numbered consecutively (in numeric order). If an error is made in preparing a check, write "Void" in large letters across the face of the check as well as the stub. **Voiding a check** is the process of writing the word *void* on the check stub and the check to prevent use of the check stub and check. Do not destroy voided checks. Instead, file them until they can be sorted in numeric sequence with the canceled checks returned from the bank. In this way all checks will be available for auditing, and it can be easily proved that the voided check was not issued.

3 *Write the date on which the check is being issued.*

4 *Write the payee's name in full (starting at the extreme left), and spell it correctly.* However, omit personal titles such as *Mr., Mrs., Miss, Ms.,*

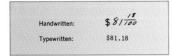

Handwritten: $81 18/100

Typewritten: $81.18

Expressing amounts in figures.

Handwritten: *Eighty-one and 18/100*

Typewritten: Eighty-one and 18/100

Expressing amounts in words.

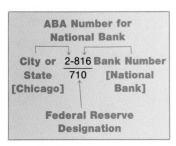

PAY
TO THE
ORDER OF *Mary Jones* ——— $ 80/100
Only Eighty Cents ——— ~~DOLLARS~~

Expressing amounts for less than $1.

ABA Number for National Bank

City or	2-816	Bank Number
State	710	[National
[Chicago]		Bank]

Federal Reserve Designation

---

or *Dr.* When making a check payable to a married woman, use her given name whenever possible. For example, write "Mary Jones" rather than "Mrs. John J. Jones." When the payee's name has been properly entered, draw a line from the name to the dollar sign so that no one can change the name. If the check is typewritten, hyphens are typed to fill the space between the end of the payee's name and the dollar sign.

5 *In the space after the name of the payee, write the amount of the check in figures.* Be sure that the first digit is placed close to the dollar sign so that no other digits can be added to increase the amount. Show the cents part of the amount as a fraction. For example, write 18 cents as "$\frac{18}{100}$." If the check is for an even dollar amount, write "$\frac{00}{100}$" or "$\frac{no}{100}$." If the check is typewritten, these amounts should be typed in the normal way—"$81.18." Amounts under $1.00 are circled, whether entered by hand or typewritten.

6 *In the space under the payee's name, write the amount in words.* Start at the extreme left of the line so that no words can be added to increase the amount. Separate the cents amount from the dollar amount by the word "and." Then write the cents as a fraction. For example, write "$\frac{18}{100}$" or "$\frac{00}{100}$." When the check is typewritten, the fraction for cents is typed as "18/100" or "00/100." Draw a line in the space between the fraction and the word "Dollars." If the check is typewritten, fill the space with hyphens. On checks for less than $1.00, write the amount as, for example, "Only Eighty Cents" and cross out the word "Dollars" at the end of the line.

The amount appears on a check twice, once in figures and once in words. This is done to make sure that the amount is stated correctly. If the amount written in figures is not the same as the amount in words, the bank will pay the amount in words. If the difference is too great, however, the bank may refuse to pay the check.

7 *The authorized person must sign the check.* A check may be filled out by anyone, but it must be signed only by a person authorized to do so. For example, at the Globe Travel Agency, the accounting clerk normally fills out the checks. However, the signature card for the account on page 210 shows that only Mark Nero is authorized to sign checks for the business. In the check shown on page 211, the name of the business has been printed above the signature line, and the signature itself reads "by Mark Nero." This emphasizes the fact that Mark Nero is acting for the business and not in his personal interest.

Processing Checks

The small fractional number in the upper right-hand corner of a check is the ABA number of the bank. (*ABA* stands for American Bankers Association.) The ABA number for the National Bank is 2-816/710.

The **ABA number** identifies the bank and the Federal Reserve district. The first part of the number (2) identifies the city or state in which the bank is located; the second part (816) identifies that bank; and the third part (710) is the Federal Reserve designation.

Most banks use checks imprinted with magnetic ink characters. **Magnetic ink** is a special ink that can be read by machines. The characters are imprinted at the bottom of the checks.

The first group of eight magnetic ink characters identifies the bank on which the check is drawn. The first four characters in this group show the Federal Reserve designation number, and the other four characters show the bank number. The first eight magnetic ink characters on the checks for the Globe Travel Agency are 0710 and 0816. Note that zeros are needed to make the Federal Reserve designation number and the bank number each contain four digits. The second group of magnetic ink characters identifies the depositor's account number. The account number of the Globe Travel Agency is 5060-030700 (the hyphen is shown by the symbol ⑩). A preprinted check number, such as 20, may also appear in magnetic ink characters following the account number (5060⑩030700⑩0020).

When a check reaches a bank, the bank imprints a third group of magnetic ink characters in the lower right corner of the check. These characters contain the amount of the check. Zeros are added to the left of an amount with less than ten digits to fill the ten spaces. No commas, decimal points, or dollar signs are used. Thus a check for $1,000 is imprinted as "0000100000."

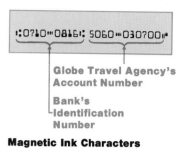

Globe Travel Agency's
Account Number

Bank's
Identification
Number

Magnetic Ink Characters

**Amount of Check
in Magnetic Ink
Characters**

To process the checks deposited, the National Bank must sort the checks. It needs to know which checks are drawn on its own accounts and which must be forwarded to other banks for collection. A machine reads the magnetic code on each check. Thus all checks with the magnetic code ⑩0710⑩0816 will automatically be sorted into one group, since they are drawn on the National Bank. The checks drawn on other banks will be sorted into separate stacks according to the bank number in the code.

The stack of checks with the number of the National Bank is then sorted according to the individual depositors' account numbers. Any check with the magnetic code 5060⑩030700⑩ will be classified as a claim against the Globe Travel Agency's checking account. The amount, which is imprinted in magnetic code, will be deducted from the account.

The machine used to read magnetic codes on checks and to sort the checks is called a **magnetic ink character recognition (MICR) machine.** This machine also transmits the data imprinted in magnetic code to other machines, which subtract the amount of the checks from the drawers' accounts and make a record of each check—the amount, the drawee's number, and the drawer's account number.

MICR Machine

Activity A. Answer the following questions about drawing and processing checks. Refer to the check and stubs illustrated below.

1. What is the ABA number of the National Bank?
2. What is the amount of Check 27?
3. Why was Check 27 drawn?
4. Who is the payee of Check 27?
5. To whom was Check 28 drawn?
6. How much was the June 26 deposit?
7. Which check was drawn on June 25? Why was it drawn?

8. What amount was brought forward on the stub of Check 29?
9. Who is the drawer of Check 29?
10. What is the total amount of the three checks?
11. Is a deposit added or subtracted on the stub? Why?
12. Is the amount of a check added or subtracted on the stub? Why?
13. Who is the drawee of Check 29?
14. What balance is carried forward from the stub of Check 29? To where is this balance carried forward?

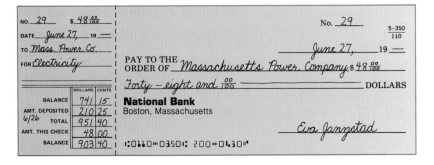

Special Types of Checks

B *What other types of checks are used by businesses?* In addition to the standard check, many businesses use what are called *voucher checks* and *certified checks.*

Voucher Checks. Many businesses use a special check form called a *voucher check.* A voucher check differs from a regular check. A **voucher check** shows the purpose for which the check is written. In one type of voucher check, the purpose of the payment is stated directly on the check.

Another type of voucher check is shown on page 215. It is perforated so that it can be separated into two parts. One part is the check itself. The other part is the voucher, on which the purpose of the payment is written. The voucher is removed by the payee before depositing the check or transferring it to another person. This type of voucher check does not have a check stub. Instead, a carbon copy of the check is kept by the drawer as a record of the transaction.

Voucher check with voucher section on check.

Certified Checks. In certain business transactions, such as those involving large sums of money, the payee of the check may want to be

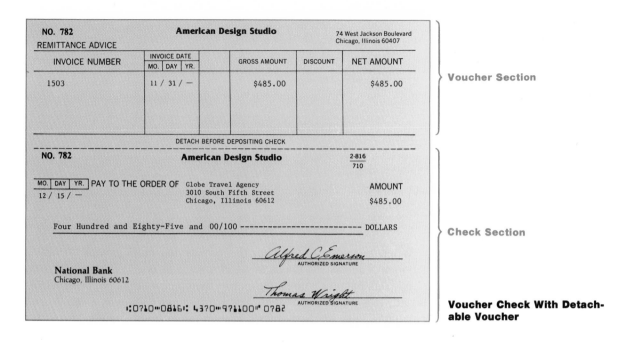

Voucher Section

Voucher Check With Detachable Voucher

Check Section

sure that the check will be paid without delay when presented to the bank. In this case the drawer obtains a certified check. A **certified check** is a depositor's check on which the bank guarantees payment. A certified check carries the guarantee of the bank that the depositor has enough funds on hand to pay the check when it is presented.

To have a check certified, the depositor writes the check in the usual way and takes it to the bank. The bank teller finds out whether the depositor has enough money in the account to meet payment of the check. If so, the teller stamps (or writes) the word "Certified" across the face of the check. The teller then signs as a bank official. Immediately the amount of that check is deducted from the depositor's account. Generally, the bank charges a fee for this service.

Stopping Payment on Checks

A **stop payment** is an authorization by the drawer to the bank to not pay a check when it is presented for payment. Occasionally, a check that has been issued is lost or stolen. When this occurs, the drawer should telephone the bank at once, giving the information about the check and the reason for stopping payment. The drawer must then give the bank a written order or a letter (with a handwritten signature) authorizing the bank not to pay the check if it is presented for payment.

```
To:     NATIONAL BANK
        Chicago, Illinois  60612                              STOP PAYMENT ORDER

                                                              DATE  December 30, 19--
          Please stop payment of check No. _____24_____    Dated  December 20, 19--
  for $ __$1,500.00__  in favor of __Barnat Garage_____

  drawn by the undersigned on you.

        Should the undersigned issue a duplicate check in place of this check bearing the same date, number, amount and payee, the undersigned agrees to
  mark such check "DUPLICATE" and such duplicate check may be honored when presented to you.


                              Globe Travel Agency        ☒ REGULAR CHECKING  ☐ SPECIAL CHECKING
        PLEASE    FROM                                   ☐ CHRISTMAS CLUB    ☐ PERSONAL MONEY ORDER
        PRINT     ADDRESS   3010 South Fifth Street       ☐ EMPLOYEE CHECKING
        CLEARLY   OR
                  LOCATION  Chicago, Illinois  60612
                   ACCOUNT No. 5060-030700               Mark Nero
                                                         AUTHORIZED SIGNATURE
  REASON: __Check lost__
```

Stop payment order telling bank not to pay Check 24 if it is presented.

When payment is stopped, the accounting clerk writes "Stopped Payment" across the check stub. The amount is added to the current checkbook balance. A new check can then be issued. If the old check is found, it is voided and filed. The bank usually charges a fee to stop payment. This fee is deducted from the depositor's account and recorded on the bank statement.

Activity B. Answer the following questions about special types of checks. Refer to the voucher check, certified check, and stop payment order above and on page 215.
1. What is the number of the invoice that the American Design Studio paid with Check 782? What was the date of the invoice?
2. What is the identification number for the National Bank?
3. What is the number of the American Design Studio's checking account?

4. Who is the payee of Check 23 issued by the Globe Travel Agency?
5. How do you know that Check 23 is certified?
6. Why was the stop payment order issued?
7. What was the number and date of the check on which the Globe Travel Agency stopped payment?
8. On what date was payment stopped?
9. Who is the payee of Check 24? The drawer? The drawee?

Accounting Concept:
Bank-Depositor Relationship. A contract exists between the bank and the depositor. The bank agrees to pay all checks drawn by the depositor as long as sufficient funds are on deposit to pay the checks.

Topic 1 Problem

8-1. Assume that you have a checking account at the National Bank, Columbus, Ohio. Your checkbook shows that after writing Check 54, you have a balance of $847. On the basis of each of the following cash transactions, record the appropriate information on the stub, carry forward the balance, write the check.

Nov. 3 Deposited $295.50 in checking account.

Nov. 4 Issued Check 55 for $250 to Mrs. Debra Palmer on account.
5 Deposited $541 in checking account.
5 Issued check for $85 to Olsen Supply Company for office supplies.
6 Deposited $484 in checking account.
7 Issued check for $614 to Mason Brothers Transport Company for delivery service.

Topic 2
Depositing Cash

A *What should a business do with the cash it receives?* A business should deposit all its cash receipts in the bank. Thus it will have an accurate record of the cash that has been received. By paying all its bills by check, the business also has an accurate record of how its cash has been spent. Two ways to control cash are to deposit all cash receipts in a bank and to pay all bills by check.

Preparing Cash for Deposit

The items to be deposited in the bank include all forms of cash—coins, currency, checks, and money orders.

The coins are sorted according to denomination (pennies, nickels, dimes, quarters, and half dollars). The coins are then counted, sorted into a specified amount, and rolled in coin wrappers supplied by the bank. If there are not enough coins of any one denomination to fill a wrapper, they may be put in small coin envelopes given by the bank.

The currency is also sorted according to denomination. Bills are placed face up with the portraits on top. All bills face the same direction. The largest denominations are placed on top of the pile. The $20 bills come first, then the $10 bills, the $5 bills, and the $1 bills. The bank supplies special paper bands to wrap the currency.

A check or money order must be endorsed before it can be deposited. To endorse either a check or a money order, write or stamp on the back the name of the person or company holding it. An **endorsement** is a signature or stamp on the back of a check that transfers ownership of a check. The person or company whose name is written or stamped on the back of the check is the **endorser.** An endorsement transfers the ownership of a check or money order. Thus an endorser endorses a check or money order for deposit so that the bank has a legal right to collect payment from the endorsee. The **endorsee** is a person or business to whom ownership of a check is transferred by endorsement. Any business paper that is a claim on cash and may be transferred legally by endorsement is a **negotiable instrument.**

The endorsement should be made across the back of the left end of checks and money orders. The illustrations in the margin here and on page 218 show the types of endorsements commonly used.

Blank Endorsement. A **blank endorsement** is endorsing a check with just the endorser's signature on the back of the check. This is the most common way of endorsing a check. A check with this type of endorsement is shown in the margin and may be cashed by anyone who holds it. To prevent an endorsed check from getting into the hands

Blank Endorsement

Full Endorsement

Restrictive Endorsement, Blank Form

Restrictive Endorsement, Full Form

Corrected Endorsement

of someone who might cash it illegally, an endorser should use a blank endorsement only when a check is being endorsed at the bank.

Full Endorsement. A full endorsement is endorsing the check with the name of the party to whom the check is to be transferred. This is a safer endorsement than the blank endorsement. As shown in the margin, only the person or firm given in the full endorsement may cash or legally transfer the check to someone else.

Restrictive Endorsement. A restrictive endorsement is endorsing the check with the purpose for which the money is to be used. This is the best endorsement for a business to use in making a deposit. A restrictive endorsement limits the use of funds to the purpose stated. Thus a check endorsed "For Deposit Only" can only be deposited. It cannot be cashed. A restrictive endorsement can be in a blank form or a full form. These forms are shown in the margin. Many businesses use a rubber stamp to endorse checks with a restrictive endorsement.

Making an Endorsement. When a check is being endorsed for deposit, the endorsement must contain the name of the depositor. Thus all checks deposited in the Globe Travel Agency's checking account must be endorsed with the name of the Globe Travel Agency, not the name of the owner, Mark Nero. Checks endorsed with the name Mark Nero would be deposited in his personal account.

An endorser's name must be signed in the exact way in which it was previously written on the instrument. If the endorser's name was written incorrectly on the instrument, the endorser's name must first be signed as it actually appears. The name must then be written correctly beneath. For example, suppose Mark Nero receives a check incorrectly made out to "Travel Agency." He must first endorse the check in the name "Travel Agency." Then he endorses it correctly in the name "Globe Travel Agency." This kind of corrected endorsement may be made only in the case of an error.

Most businesses endorse checks "For Deposit Only" as soon as they receive them. This restrictive endorsement protects the checks from being stolen or cashed by someone else.

Activity A. Assume that you are Kenneth Price and have a checking account at the National Bank. You have received a check for $85 from Edith Plate. Show how you would make the following endorsements on the check.
1. A blank endorsement.
2. A full endorsement to transfer the check to Debra Ryan.

3. A blank endorsement to correct a check made out to Kenneth Prise.
4. A blank form of restrictive endorsement to deposit the check in the National Bank.
5. A full form of restrictive endorsement to deposit the check in the National Bank.

Preparing a Deposit Ticket

B *How is a deposit ticket prepared?* After the coins and currency have been sorted and the checks and money orders have been endorsed, a deposit ticket is filled out. A **deposit ticket** is a form listing coins, currency, checks, and money orders to be deposited. The deposit ticket, supplied by the bank, shows all the details of the deposit. To show that all the cash receipts have been deposited, a duplicate copy of the deposit ticket should be made. Many banks provide deposit tickets in unit sets, which consist of two or more copies fastened together with carbon paper between the copies. The form of the deposit ticket may vary, but most deposit tickets resemble the one shown below.

The procedures for filling out a deposit ticket are as follows.

1 Write the date on the Date line.

2 Write the name and address of the depositor in the proper section. The name must appear exactly as it appears on the account.

3 Write the account number in the space provided. The number given to each account should be used on all deposit tickets to be sure that deposits will be posted quickly to the right account.

4 Record the total amount of currency on the Currency line and the total amount of coins on the Coin line. Dollar signs and decimal points are unnecessary.

5 List each check separately in the Check section. Be sure the checks are in the same order as they are listed on the deposit ticket. (Some banks require that the top portion of the ABA number be listed on the deposit ticket to identify the drawee of each check being deposited.)

If a depositor has many checks to be deposited at the same time, the bank will generally permit the checks to be itemized on an adding machine. The adding machine tape is then clipped to the deposit ticket. The total on the tape is written on the first line in the Check section of the deposit ticket with the words "See list attached."

6 Compute the amount of the deposit and record this amount on the Total line. The amount must agree with the cash value of the items to be deposited.

Activity B. Using today's date, prepare a deposit ticket for the Presto Laundry, 615 Mellon Drive, Madison, New Jersey 07940. The firm's account number at the Madison National Bank is 0814-002500. Use the information in the next column to prepare the deposit ticket.

Currency	Coins	Checks
one $20 bill	43 quarters	$48
three $10 bills	15 dimes	25
two $5 bills	28 nickels	8
thirteen $1 bills	47 pennies	

Making the Deposit

C *How are deposits made and processed?* When the deposit ticket and the cash items are presented for deposit, the bank teller gives the depositor some type of receipt as a record. Some banks provide a printed receipt that indicates the date and the amount deposited. Some banks provide a passbook. A **passbook** is a receipt in which the teller enters the date, the amount deposited (or withdrawn), and the teller's initials. The most common practice, however, is to have the deposit ticket prepared with carbon copies in unit sets. The teller stamps or initials a carbon copy and returns it to the depositor to keep as a record.

As long as a deposit does not include currency and coins, it can be safely mailed to the bank. The bank will mail back a duplicate deposit ticket or some other form of receipt. Banks generally have special forms for depositors who want to bank by mail.

Bank depositors who need to make deposits after the bank is closed can use the night depository. Deposits are placed in bank bags, and the bags are dropped through a chute into the vault.

Processing Deposits

When a depositor submits cash items for deposit, the bank uses the deposit ticket as the source document. The bank obtains from the deposit ticket the amount to be added to the account. To speed the processing of deposits and ensure accuracy, many banks now issue personalized deposit tickets, with the depositor's name and account number printed on them. The account number is imprinted in magnetic ink. The amounts of the deposits are later imprinted on these deposit tickets in magnetic ink characters. Thus the deposit tickets can be automatically sorted. The amount of each deposit can be automatically added to each depositor's account. The illustrations here show how amounts are added and subtracted in the depositor's account.

Deposit Ticket

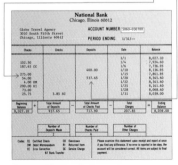

Check

Depositor's Account

Activity C. Answer the following questions about processing the data from the illustrations shown on page 220.

1. What is the number of the Globe Travel Agency's checking account?
2. Where is the account number imprinted on the deposit tickets?
3. Where is the account number imprinted on the checks?
4. Where is the account number shown on the depositor's account?
5. What is the amount of the deposit on January 20?
6. Where is the amount imprinted on a deposit ticket?
7. Where is the amount of a deposit shown in a depositor's account?
8. What source document does the bank use to add amounts to a depositor's account?

9. What source document does the bank use to deduct amounts from a depositor's account?
10. Where is the amount imprinted on a check? When is it imprinted?
11. What is the amount of the check?
12. Where is the amount of the check shown in the depositor's account?
13. Is the amount of the deposit imprinted on the deposit ticket before or after the cash items are submitted for deposit? Who does the imprinting of the deposit ticket?
14. Is the amount of a deposit added or subtracted in the depositor's account?
15. Is the amount of a check added or subtracted in the depositor's account?

Topic 2 Problem

8-2. Using today's date, prepare a deposit ticket for the Wilhelm Shop, 25 Calgore Drive, Fresno, California 93705. The shop's account number at the Golden National Bank is 0544 002837. Use the information in the next column to prepare the deposit ticket.

Currency	Coins	Checks
ten $20 bills	34 quarters	$98
twelve $10 bills	14 dimes	47
six $5 bills	43 nickels	—
thirteen $1 bills	22 pennies	—

Topic 3
Verifying the Cash Balance and the Bank Balance

A *How do depositors know if their cash records agree with the bank's records?* Periodically, each depositor should verify that the Cash account balance agrees with the checkbook balance and with the bank balance. This is usually done once a month. The Globe Travel Agency's banking activities for the month of January are described below.

Verifying the Cash Balance

When cash is received and paid out, the transactions are recorded in the journal and posted to the ledger. Thus if all cash receipts are deposited and all payments are made by check, the balance of the Cash account should agree with the balance in the checkbook.

If the balances of the Cash account and the checkbook do not agree, check that the ledger is in balance. If a trial balance shows that the ledger is in balance, the error is probably in the checkbook. The most common kinds of errors are these.

- Adding or subtracting amounts incorrectly on the check stubs.
- Carrying the wrong balance forward from one stub to another (for example, a balance of $7,350 carried forward as $7,530).
- Failing to subtract a check when it is drawn and journalized.
- Failing to deposit the cash receipts. In this case the Cash account balance equals the cash in the bank plus the cash on hand.

Any adjustments or errors in the checkbook must be corrected on the latest check stub. For example, suppose a deposit for $220.40 was recorded by mistake as $202.40 on Stub 56. On the latest check stub, Stub 79, the difference of $18 ($220.40 − $202.40) would be added to the current balance in the checkbook to correct the error. The notation "Error, see Stub 56" would also be entered. A notation would be placed on Stub 56, stating that this error was corrected on Stub 79.

As another example, suppose Check 42 was drawn for $28.75 but was recorded on the stub as $27.85. In this case, $0.90 ($28.75 − $27.85) would be subtracted on the latest check stub, Stub 79. "Error, see Stub 42" would be entered as an explanation. A notation would be placed on Stub 42 stating that the error had been corrected on Stub 79 (see the illustration in the margin).

When the balance of the Cash account and the balance in the checkbook agree, the next step is to prove that the balance in the checkbook agrees with the balance on the bank statement.

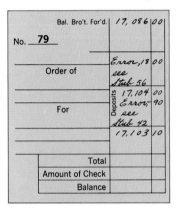

Correcting Errors

The Bank Statement

Typically, the bank sends the depositor a bank statement once a month. A **bank statement** is an itemized list of additions to and subtractions from a depositor's account.

The bank statement shows the following.

- The balance at the beginning of the monthly period.
- The deposits added during the month.
- The checks and other charges subtracted during the month.
- The balance at the end of the monthly period.

A check paid from the account and returned to the depositor is called a **canceled check.** These checks paid during the month are returned with the bank statement.

The checks that are returned with the bank statement are perforated or stamped with the word "Paid" and the date of payment. Canceled checks are valuable receipts. The endorsement on the check is evidence that the payee received the money. Therefore, canceled checks are evidence that payment has been received.

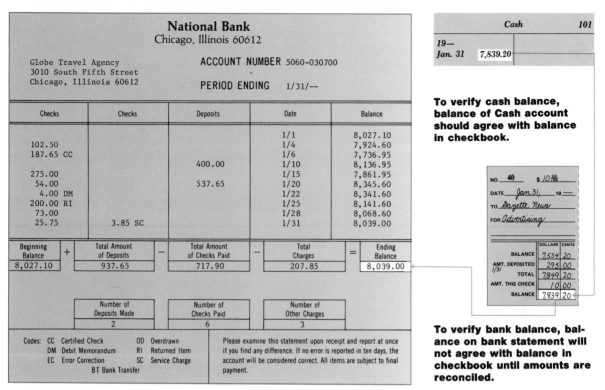

Globe Travel Agency's Bank Statement

National Bank
Chicago, Illinois 60612

Globe Travel Agency
3010 South Fifth Street
Chicago, Illinois 60612

ACCOUNT NUMBER 5060-030700

PERIOD ENDING   1/31/--

Checks	Checks	Deposits	Date	Balance
			1/1	8,027.10
102.50			1/4	7,924.60
187.65 CC			1/6	7,736.95
		400.00	1/10	8,136.95
275.00			1/15	7,861.95
54.00		537.65	1/20	8,345.60
4.00 DM			1/22	8,341.60
200.00 RI			1/25	8,141.60
73.00			1/28	8,068.60
25.75	3.85 SC		1/31	8,039.00

Beginning Balance	+	Total Amount of Deposits	−	Total Amount of Checks Paid	−	Total Charges	=	Ending Balance
8,027.10		937.65		717.90		207.85		8,039.00

Number of Deposits Made	Number of Checks Paid	Number of Other Charges
2	6	3

Codes: CC Certified Check   OD Overdrawn
DM Debit Memorandum   RI Returned Item
EC Error Correction   SC Service Charge
BT Bank Transfer

Please examine this statement upon receipt and report at once if you find any difference. If no error is reported in ten days, the account will be considered correct. All items are subject to final payment.

Cash   101

19—
Jan. 31   7,839.20

To verify cash balance, balance of Cash account should agree with balance in checkbook.

NO. 40 $ 10.00
DATE Jan.31, 19—
TO Gazette News
FOR Advertising

	DOLLARS	CENTS
BALANCE	7,554	20
AMT. DEPOSITED 1/31	295	00
TOTAL	7,849	20
AMT. THIS CHECK	10	00
BALANCE	7,839	20

To verify bank balance, balance on bank statement will not agree with balance in checkbook until amounts are reconciled.

The bank statement should be checked as soon as it is received. This is done to verify that the balance shown by the bank agrees with the balance shown in the depositor's checkbook. The January 31, 19—, bank statement shown here was sent to the Globe Travel Agency by the National Bank. The bank statement shows the following items.

- A January 1 balance of $8,027.10 (beginning balance).
- Two deposits added during January (deposits).
- Six checks subtracted during the month (checks).
- Three additional charges subtracted during the month (charges).
- A January 31 balance of $8,039.00 (ending balance).

The last checkbook stub for January (Stub 40) shows a balance of $7,839.20. This balance agrees with the balance in the Cash account on January 31. However, the balance on the bank statement does not agree with the checkbook.

This difference is not necessarily an error by either the depositor or the bank. The bank statement balance ordinarily does not agree with the checkbook balance. There usually is a delay by either the depositor or the bank in recording some of the items.

For example, a check is recorded in the checkbook when the depositor writes the check. However, the check is not subtracted from the depositor's account until the day the bank pays the check. Thus there is a delay until the bank records the check. Here are some of the factors that cause a difference between the balances.

Outstanding Checks. A check that is not yet paid by the bank is called an **outstanding check.** Outstanding checks have been drawn and subtracted from the depositor's checkbook but have not yet been presented to the bank for payment. When checks are outstanding, the bank statement will show a higher balance than the checkbook. This happens because the bank has not subtracted the checks from the depositor's account, but the depositor has subtracted them from the checkbook balance. They will be subtracted when presented to the banks for payment.

Deposits in Transit. A deposit not yet received by the bank is called a **deposit in transit.** These deposits have been added to the depositor's checkbook and mailed to the bank, but they are not listed on the monthly bank statement. When deposits are in transit, the bank statement will show a lower balance than the checkbook. This happens because the bank has not added the deposits to the depositor's account, but the depositor has added them to the checkbook balance. They will be added when received by the bank.

Dishonored Checks. A person might endorse and deposit a check and later learn that the bank cannot collect on the check. A check that is not paid when properly presented to the bank is called a **dishonored check.** There are various reasons why a check may be dishonored.

• The drawer might have "not sufficient funds" (NSF) to cover the check.
• The signature on the check might not be exactly the same as the one on the signature card.
• Payment on the check might have been stopped by the drawer.
• The check might have been altered or dated ahead.
• The endorsement might be missing or improper.

When a deposited check is dishonored, the bank subtracts the amount of the dishonored check from the depositor's account. This cancels the amount added when the check was originally deposited. The bank then returns the check to the depositor. Note that the Globe Travel Agency's bank statement shows a dishonored check for $200. This deduction is identified by the letters RI (meaning *returned item*).

Fees. Banks sometimes charge a fee for collecting payment on certain kinds of negotiable instruments. In addition, most banks charge a fee to pay for the expenses involved in stopping payment on a check. A **debit memorandum** is a document explaining fees charged to the account. Fees are explained in detail on the debit memorandum. Fees are also shown on the bank statement. The debit memorandum in the margin explains the January 22 fee of $4 on the Globe Travel Agency's bank statement.

Debit Memorandum

Service Charges. Banks also charge for many of the special services they provide. Banks may collect a service charge to cover the expense of handling a checking account. A **service charge** is a fee charged by a bank for maintaining a checking account. Service charges are usually based upon the balance of the account, the number of checks paid, and the number of items deposited. A bank might also deduct from the depositor's account a charge for the use of the night depository or for the rental of a safe-deposit box.

Service charges are deducted directly from the depositor's account. They are identified on the bank statement by the initials SC (for *service charge*). Note that the bank statement for the Globe Travel Agency shows a service charge of $3.85 for January.

Errors in Computations. The checkbook balance might agree with the Cash account balance, yet the checkbook balance might not agree with the bank statement balance. The difference might be due to one of the following errors.

- Writing a different amount on a check than on the stub.
- Issuing a check but not recording it on the stub or in the journal.
- Not recording a deposit on the stub or in the journal.

These errors in the depositor's records must be corrected.

Errors made by the bank also should be reported immediately. One bank error would be accepting a check on which someone had forged the depositor's signature (a loss to the bank, not to the depositor). Another bank error would be charging the depositor's account for another person's check by mistake.

Activity A. Answer the following questions about bank statements. Refer to the Cash account, checkbook stub 40, and bank statement on page 223.
1. What is the account number?
2. What is the last date covered by the bank statement?
3. What is the bank balance at the beginning of the month?
4. How many deposits are shown on the bank statement?
5. What is the total of the deposits?

6. How many checks are paid by the bank?
7. What is the total of the checks paid?
8. How many other charges are made by the bank? What was the total?
9. What are the other charges made by the bank?
10. What is the bank balance at the end of the month? The Cash account balance?
11. Name some of the items that may cause the difference between the bank balance and the checkbook balance.

Reconciling the Bank Statement

B *What is the procedure for determining what may be causing a difference between the checkbook balance and the bank statement balance?* You know what could cause the checkbook balance to differ from the bank statement balance. **Reconciling the bank statement** is determining what may be causing the difference between the checkbook balance and the bank statement balance. This procedure is also known as *making a bank reconciliation.*

A **bank reconciliation statement** is a statement verifying that the actual checkbook balance equals the actual bank statement balance. It is used to analyze the differences, to reconcile them, and to verify that the actual balances are equal. The bank reconciliation statement for the Globe Travel Agency as of January 31 is on the next page. The form is printed on the back of the bank statement. (Some businesses want the reconciliation statement on another sheet of paper, separate from the bank statement.)

The procedure for preparing the bank reconciliation statement is as follows.

1 Complete the heading—WHO? WHAT? WHEN?

2 Find the ending balance shown on the bank statement, and record it on the reconciliation statement. The ending balance on the January 31 bank statement for the Globe Travel Agency is $8,039.00

3 Compare the amounts of the deposits listed on the bank statement with the amounts of the deposits listed on the check stubs. Also, check last month's reconciliation statement to make sure that any deposits then in transit have been recorded on this month's statement. If any have not been recorded, notify the bank.

On the reconciliation statement, list all deposits currently in transit. These are deposits that have been added in the checkbook but do not appear on the bank statement. In the case of the Globe Travel Agency, a deposit of $295.00 is in transit. It appears on the check stub but not on the bank statement.

4 Deposits in transit are then added to the ending bank statement balance because the bank will add these deposits when they are received. The sum of the ending bank statement balance and the total deposits in transit is entered as the subtotal on the left side of the reconciliation statement.

5 Take the canceled checks and any debit memorandums that are enclosed with the bank statement. Compare the amount on each item with the amount listed on the bank statement. If an amount recorded on the bank statement is different from the amount on the check or the debit memorandum, notify the bank immediately. The statement must be corrected.

Bank reconciliation statements are used to analyze and reconcile differences and verify that the balances are equal.

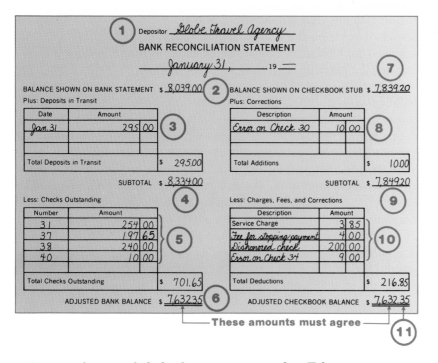

Depositor _Globe Travel Agency_

BANK RECONCILIATION STATEMENT

January 31, ___ 19 ___

BALANCE SHOWN ON BANK STATEMENT $ _8,039.00_ ②

Plus: Deposits in Transit

Date	Amount	
Jan. 31	295 00	③
Total Deposits in Transit	$ 295.00	

SUBTOTAL $ _8,334.00_ ④

Less: Checks Outstanding

Number	Amount	
31	254 00	
37	197 65	⑤
38	240 00	
40	10 00	
Total Checks Outstanding	$ 701.65	

ADJUSTED BANK BALANCE $ _7,632.35_ ⑥

⑦

BALANCE SHOWN ON CHECKBOOK STUB $ _7,839.20_

Plus: Corrections

Description	Amount	
Error on Check 30	10 00	⑧
Total Additions	$ 10.00	

SUBTOTAL $ _7,849.20_ ⑨

Less: Charges, Fees, and Corrections

Description	Amount	
Service Charge	3 85	
Fee for stopping payment	4 00	⑩
Dishonored check	200 00	
Error on Check 34	9 00	
Total Deductions	$ 216.85	

ADJUSTED CHECKBOOK BALANCE $ _7,632.35_

—— **These amounts must agree** —— ⑪

Arrange the canceled checks in numeric order. Take any stop payment orders and voided checks from the files. Insert them in numeric sequence with the canceled checks. The Globe Travel Agency stopped payment on Check 32 and voided Check 35. The stop payment check and the voided check are filed numerically with the canceled checks.

Compare each check (canceled or voided) with its stub on the checkbook. If the check agrees with the stub, make a large check mark (✓) on the stub next to the check number. This mark indicates that the check has been paid and returned by the bank or that the check, if voided, can be accounted for. In short, the mark indicates that the check is not outstanding.

On the reconciliation statement, list all the numbers and amounts of the checks that have not been checked off on the stubs. Also, check last month's reconciliation statement to make sure that any checks then outstanding have now been returned. If any of these checks are still unpaid, list them as currently outstanding.

Certified checks that have not been returned with the bank statement should not be considered outstanding checks, however. The bank deducts the amount of a certified check from the drawer's account at the time of certification. This deduction shows up on the bank statement, whether or not the canceled check is returned. The bank statement for the Globe Travel Agency shows a $187.65 deduction on January 6 for a certified check (Check 33), identified on the bank statement by the code CC.

Checks

- 29—canceled
- 30—canceled
- 31—outstanding
- 32—stop payment
- 33—canceled (certified)
- 34—canceled
- 35—voided
- 36—canceled
- 37—outstanding
- 38—outstanding
- 39—canceled
- 40—outstanding

6 Subtract the total amount of checks outstanding from the subtotal shown above it on the reconciliation statement. The difference is the adjusted bank balance. The **adjusted bank balance** is the actual balance of the account.

7 Turn to the latest checkbook stub, and record the current checkbook balance opposite "Balance Shown on Checkbook Stub" on the bank reconciliation statement.

8 List any corrections for errors that require increasing the balance of the checkbook. For example, Check 30 was issued to Bell Products on January 4 for $102.50 on account. It was recorded by mistake on the checkbook stub and in the journal as $112.50. The check was paid by the bank, returned with the January 31 bank statement, and listed correctly on the bank statement as a $102.50 deduction. The difference of $10, therefore, must be corrected in the checkbook; $10 too much was subtracted from the checkbook balance. Thus $10 is listed in the section for amounts to be added to the checkbook balance.

9 Add the total additions to the checkbook balance shown at the top of the reconciliation statement, and enter the sum as the subtotal.

10 List any charges that are shown on the bank statement but are not yet recorded in the checkbook, such as a service charge or a stop payment fee. All these charges would decrease the checkbook balance. Thus they must be deducted from the checkbook balance. List the amount of any dishonored check. Since this amount was added to the checkbook balance when it was deposited, it must now be deducted to show that the returned item cannot be collected. Also, list any errors that require decreasing the checkbook balance. For example, Check 34 was issued to pay $54 for furniture but was recorded on the check stub and in the journal as $45. The difference of $9 must be listed on the reconciliation statement as a deduction from the checkbook balance.

11 Subtract the total deductions from the subtotal shown above it. The difference is the adjusted checkbook balance. The **adjusted checkbook balance** is the actual balance of the account. This amount should be identical with the adjusted bank balance, which also represents the actual balance of the account. If the amounts do agree, the balances are said to be reconciled. **Reconciled balances** are balances that are the same. If they do not agree, all the details must be rechecked until the error has been located and the balances agree. The double rules at the end of the reconciliation statement show that the balances agree and that the statement is complete.

Making Corrections and Entries After the Reconciliation

After the reconciliation statement has been completed, the balance on the latest check stub must be brought into agreement with the adjusted checkbook balance shown on the reconciliation statement. The check stub does not have to be adjusted for deposits in transit or outstanding checks. These items have already been entered in the checkbook and will be recorded by the bank when received. However, any additions and deductions shown on the right-hand side of the reconciliation statement must now be recorded in the checkbook. (Corrections for errors on check stubs should be cross-referenced. That is, make a note on the stub containing an error that the error has been corrected.)

After these corrections have been recorded in the checkbook, the balance on the latest stub should agree with the adjusted checkbook balance on the reconciliation statement. Then these corrections must be journalized and posted.

When these entries are posted, the balance in the Cash account will agree with the adjusted balance shown in the checkbook.

After reconciliation, corrections must be recorded on latest check stub to adjust checkbook balance, and journalized and posted to adjust Cash account balance.

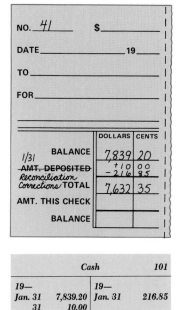

JOURNAL					Page 4
DATE		**ACCOUNT TITLE AND EXPLANATION**	**POST. REF.**	**DEBIT**	**CREDIT**
19—					
Jan.	31	Cash	101	10 00	
		Accts. Pay. / Bell Products	201		10 00
		Correct error on Check 30.			
	31	Accts. Rec./George Stevens	104	200 00	
		Furniture	111	9 00	
		Miscellaneous Expense	504	7 85	
		Cash	101		216 85
		Returned check, error on			
		Check 34, and bank charges.			

Cash			101
19—		19—	
Jan. 31	7,839.20	Jan. 31	216.85
31	10.00		
	7,849.20		
7,632.35			

Activity B. Answer the following questions about bank reconciliation. Refer to the bank reconciliation statement on page 227.

1. For what date is the reconciliation statement prepared?

2. Does $8,039 represent the bank balance at the beginning of the month or at the end of the month?

3. Why is the January 31 deposit not included in the bank balance?

4. What checks are outstanding?

5. How does the Globe Travel Agency know these checks are outstanding?

6. Are outstanding checks added to or subtracted from the bank balance? Why?

7. What does the amount $7,839.20 represent?

8. Why is $10.00 added to $7,839.20?

9. What does the amount $3.85 represent?

10. Why is a $4 fee charged?

11. Why is a $200 charge made?

12. What is the $9 correction?

13. What does the amount $7,632.35 represent?

14. What does the amount $216.85 represent?

15. Should the adjusted bank balance and the adjusted checkbook balance agree? Why or why not?

Accounting Concept:

Bank Statement. The bank must account to the depositor for all money belonging to the depositor that comes into the bank's possession.

Topic 3 Problems

8-3. Use the given data to perform the following activities for the Brooklyn Luncheonette.
a. Prepare a bank reconciliation statement as of February 28.
b. Record any corrections in the checkbook and in the journal.

Bank balance as shown on bank statement: $3,752.40.
Checkbook balance: $3,802.95.
Deposit put in night depository on last day of month recorded in checkbook but not shown on bank statement: $184.25.
Checks outstanding: Check 83, $124.60; Check 86, $55.35.
Service charge: $4.25.
Dishonored check: $42.00, received from Nate Bell on account.

8-4. Use the given data to perform the following activities for the Brooklyn Luncheonette.

a. Prepare a bank reconciliation statement as of March 31.
b. Record any corrections in the checkbook and in the journal.

Bank balance as shown on bank statement: $3,840.25.
Checkbook balance: $4,002.70.
Deposit put in night depository on last day of month, recorded in checkbook but not shown on bank statement: $256.00.
Checks outstanding: Check 128, $31.40; Check 131, $40.00; Check 132, $46.05.
Service charge: $3.90.
Dishonored check: $27.00, received from Joe Sid on account.
Fee for stopping payment on Check 126: $2.00.
Error on Check 124: Check was issued for $67, but the amount was recorded as $76 on the check stub, and the Maintenance Expense account was debited for $76 in the journal.

Topic 4
Petty Cash

A *Do businesses pay all bills by check?* For the best control of cash, all cash receipts should be deposited in the bank, and all bills should be paid by check. Sometimes, however, it is not practical to use checks for small cash transactions. As a result, most businesses usually set aside a small sum of cash. **Petty cash fund** is cash on hand to pay small amounts.

Some businesses use the petty cash fund to pay all bills of less than a certain amount, such as $5. In other businesses, all payments for such things as postage and small items of office supplies are paid out of the petty cash fund regardless of the amount.

A petty cash fund is used to pay small bills.

Establishing and Handling the Petty Cash Fund

The amount of money kept on hand as petty cash varies with the needs of the business. The fund should be large enough to cover petty cash payments for a specific period, such as two or four weeks. The fund is started by drawing a check payable to the person responsible for the petty cash fund. The check is then endorsed and cashed. The money is placed in a petty cash box or drawer, which is usually kept apart from the cash receipts. Since the petty cashier is responsible for every cent in the fund, a separate record is kept of the flow of cash into and out of the fund.

A **cash disbursement** (sometimes referred to as a *cash expenditure*) is a payment from the petty cash fund. Each disbursement must be covered by some kind of receipt as evidence that cash was paid out of the fund. The receipt may be in the form of a bill marked *Paid* by the person receiving the money. Accountants, however, prefer to have businesses use special receipt forms called petty cash vouchers. A **petty cash voucher** is a form that provides evidence of a petty cash disbursement. One is shown in the margin. The vouchers should be numbered at the time they are printed. If not, the vouchers should be numbered in sequence by the petty cashier. Normally, the voucher is signed by two persons—the person who has the authority to approve the disbursement and the person who receives the cash. The voucher is then put into the petty cash box as proof that the money was spent.

At all times, the total of the disbursements (as shown by the vouchers) plus the cash left in the fund must equal the original amount of the petty cash fund. The procedure for checking that the total disbursements plus the remaining cash equals the original amount of the fund is called **proving the petty cash fund.**

For example, the Globe Travel Agency set up a petty cash fund for $45. It requires a voucher for each disbursement. On February 15 the fund had vouchers for disbursements amounting to $42.95 and cash of $2.05. Total disbursements plus cash on hand equals $45 (the original amount of the fund). Thus the fund is proved.

After the fund is reduced by disbursements to a certain amount (for example, $5), it is built up again to the original amount ($45). This process is known as *replenishing* or *restoring*. **Replenishing the petty cash fund** is restoring the fund to the original amount. The procedure for replenishing the fund is as follows.

- Total the vouchers for disbursements from the fund.
- Prove the fund. The total of the vouchers plus the remaining cash should equal the original amount of the fund.
- Classify the type of expenses. For example, the petty cash disbursements for the Globe Travel Agency might be classified into four kinds of expenses: advertising expense, delivery expense, miscellaneous expense, and office expense.
- Draw a check payable to the order of the petty cashier for the amount of the total disbursements.
- Cancel the vouchers so that they cannot be used again.
- Attach the vouchers to the check, and submit the check to the proper person for signature.
- After the check is signed, file the vouchers in a dated envelope.

Petty Cash Voucher

Total disbursements . . .	42	95
Cash on hand	2	05
Original amount of fund	45	00

Globe Travel Agency Petty Cash Memorandum February 2 to February 15, 19—		
Advertising Expense . .	6	50
Delivery Expense	21	60
Miscellaneous Expense .	8	00
Office Expense	6	85
Total Disbursements .	42	95
Cash on Hand	2	05
Amount of Fund . . .	45	00

● Cash the check, and place the money in the petty cash fund. In this way the fund is brought back up to the original amount.

A **petty cash memorandum** is a form used to classify the petty cash disbursements according to the type of expense. The petty cash memorandum in the margin classifies the petty cash disbursements of the Globe Travel Agency over a two-week period. A petty cash memorandum is prepared unless a petty cash register is used.

The Petty Cash Register

A systematic way of handling petty cash is to keep a memorandum book. A **petty cash register** (sometimes referred to as a *memorandum* or *petty cash book*) is a record of petty cash disbursements. All cash put into and taken out of the fund is recorded in the petty cash register.

Recording the Establishment of the Fund. The amount of cash used to establish the petty cash fund is recorded in the Received column of the petty cash register. The date and an explanation are recorded in the appropriate columns. A dash is placed in the Voucher Number column because no voucher is involved.

PETTY CASH REGISTER   Page 1

PETTY CASH FUND RECEIVED	PAID OUT	DATE	EXPLANATION	VOUCHER NO.	ADV. EXPENSE	DELIVERY EXPENSE	MISC. EXPENSE	OTHER ITEMS ACCOUNT	AMOUNT
45 00		Feb. 2	Establish fund, Check 41	—					
	4 75	3	Typewriter ribbons	1				Office Expense	4 75
	8 00	4	Snow removal	2			8 00		
	2 50	5	Ad in Gazette	3	2 50				
	7 50	7	Ace Trucking	4		7 50			
	2 10	8	Stationery	5				Office Expense	2 10
	6 85	9	Ace Trucking	6		6 85			
	4 00	12	Ad in Gazette	7	4 00				
	7 25	15	Canyon Carriers	8		7 25			
45 00	42 95		Totals	—	6 50	21 60	8 00		6 85
45 00	42 95			—	6 50	21 60	8 00		6 85
	2 05	15	Cash on hand	—					
45 00	45 00								
2 05		Feb. 15	Cash on hand	—					
42 95		15	Replenish fund, Check 49	—					

Recording Disbursements. The amount of each voucher is recorded in the Paid Out column at the left. The amount is also recorded in at least one of the columns in the Distribution of Payments section at the right. The columns in the Distribution of Payments section help to classify disbursements according to the expense accounts in the ledger. The date, an explanation, and the voucher number are also recorded in the appropriate columns. The voucher is then placed in the petty cash box.

Recording the Replenishment of the Fund. When the petty cash fund is replenished, the petty cash register is totaled and ruled using the following procedures.

- Draw a single rule across all the money columns.
- Pencil-foot the totals of the columns.
- Subtract the total cash paid out from the total cash received. The difference represents the cash on hand.
- Verify the amount of cash on hand by actually counting the cash left in the box or drawer.
- Verify that the totals of the Distribution of Payments columns equal the total of the Paid Out column.
- Verify that the total of the vouchers equals the total of the Paid Out column.
- Enter all the totals in ink.
- Draw a double rule across all columns in the Distribution of Payments section.
- Enter the cash on hand balance in the Paid Out columns.
- Draw a single rule and total the Received and Paid Out columns.
- Verify that the totals of the Received column and the Paid Out column are equal. The total represents the original amount of the petty cash fund.
- Draw a double rule across the Received column, the Paid Out column, and the Date column. The double rule shows that the petty cash register is completed for this set of disbursements.
- Enter the balance of the cash on hand below the double rule in the Received column. This is the amount still in the fund.
- Enter in the Received column the amount of the check to replenish the fund.

The petty cash register is then ready for a new set of disbursements.

Advertising Expense . .	6 50
Delivery Expense	21 60
Miscellaneous Expense .	8 00
Other Items	6 85
Paid out	42 95
Cash on hand	2 05
Amount of fund	45 00

Proof of Petty Cash Register

Activity A-1. Answer the following questions about petty cash. Refer to the petty cash voucher on page 231 and the petty cash register on page 232.

1. What information is provided by the petty cash voucher?

2. Who approved the expenditure for Voucher 1? Who received the cash?

3. Why is cash paid out on Voucher 1? What expense account is affected? How much is paid out?

4. When was the petty cash fund established?

5. Where is this information given?

6. Is any money paid from petty cash on February 3? If so, for what?

7. Is every expenditure entered in more than one column in the petty cash register? Why or why not?

8. What are the total petty cash expenditures from February 2 to 15? How is this amount determined and proved?

9. How much petty cash is left in the fund on February 15? How is this amount determined and proved?

10. When is the petty cash fund replenished? For what amount?

11. Why is the petty cash fund replenished for this amount?

12. After the petty cash fund is replenished on February 15, how much is there in the fund?

Activity A-2. The petty cashier for Audio Studios had the following transactions between April 1 and April 21.

April	1	Received Check 48 for $60 to establish the petty cash fund.
	4	Paid $8.75 for advertisement in the News Herald.
	6	Paid $3.50 for parcel post delivery.
	8	Paid $5 for washing windows.
	11	Paid $7.50 to repair chair (Repairs Expense).
	14	Paid $4 for ad in football game program.
	15	Paid $5 to have leaves raked.
	18	Paid $5.50 to Town Delivery Service for delivery.
	19	Paid $3.60 for postage stamps (Office Expense).
	20	Paid $3 to United Parcel for delivery.

1. Record the transactions in the petty cash register. Number the petty cash vouchers consecutively, beginning with 1.

2. Pencil-foot the petty cash register as of April 21. Then complete a proof of the petty cash register. (There is $14.15 in the cash box on this date.)

3. Total and rule the petty cash register.

4. Record Check 63 to replenish the petty cash fund.

NOTE: Save your petty cash register for further use in Topic Problem 8-5 and Topic Problem 8-6.

Journalizing Petty Cash Entries

B *Is the information in the petty cash register posted to the ledger?* No, entries are posted from the petty cash register because the *petty cash register is not a journal.* The petty cash register is simply a memorandum record.

Because the petty cash register is not a journal, the check to establish a petty cash fund must be recorded in the journal. From the journal, this transaction is posted to the accounts in the ledger.

The next procedure to journalize petty cash entries is as follows. A Petty Cash account is opened in the ledger when a petty cash fund is established. This new account is used to show the transfer of cash from the Cash account to the Petty Cash account.

Globe Travel Agency
Chart of Accounts

Assets
101 Cash
102 Petty Cash

JOURNAL				Page	5
DATE	ACCOUNT TITLE AND EXPLANATION	POST. REF.	DEBIT	CREDIT	
19— Feb. 2	Petty Cash		45 00		
	Cash			45 00	
	Establish the petty cash fund.				

Journal entry
to establish
petty cash fund.

When the Globe Travel Agency established its petty cash fund, a check was issued for $45. This transaction is journalized as a debit to the Petty Cash account and a credit to the Cash account. To increase the fund in the future, for example, to $75, a check is issued for $30. This transaction will be journalized as a debit to the Petty Cash account and a credit to the Cash account.

Whenever a disbursement is made from the petty cash fund, an entry is recorded in the petty cash register but not in the journal.

Whenever the petty cash fund is replenished, a check must be written for the total amount that has been disbursed. This check is recorded in the journal by making a compound entry. The individual expense accounts are debited for the totals of the columns in the Disbursement of Payments section of the petty cash register. The Cash account is credited for the total amount. (The headings of the columns in the Distribution of Payments section should correspond to the titles of the expense accounts most frequently involved in the petty cash transactions.)

JOURNAL				Page	6
DATE	ACCOUNT TITLE AND EXPLANATION	POST. REF.	DEBIT	CREDIT	
19— Feb. 15	Advertising Expense		6 50		
	Delivery Expense		21 60		
	Miscellaneous Expense		8 00		
	Office Expense		6 85		
	Cash			42 95	
	Replenish petty cash fund.				

Journal entry
to replenish
petty cash fund.

A check for $42.95 was written to replenish the petty cash fund of the Globe Travel Agency. This transaction is journalized by debiting the expense accounts for the appropriate amounts and crediting Cash for the total amount.

The Petty Cash account in the ledger will have only one amount in it as long as the fund stays at the original amount. The original amount for the Globe Travel Agency was $45. The replenishment of the fund does not affect the Petty Cash account because the expense items are debited to the individual expense accounts.

The petty cash fund should be replenished whenever it falls below a certain minimum. *It must also be replenished at the end of an accounting period so that these expenditures are recorded during the accounting period in which they occur.*

The Petty Cash account is an asset account. It is listed on the balance sheet directly after Cash. Since the petty cash fund is replenished at the end of the accounting period, the amount shown on the balance sheet is the fixed amount of the fund. What this means is that this is the amount that is actually in the cash box or drawer. Replenishing the fund does *not* mean adding to the Petty Cash account in the ledger.

The following flowchart illustrates the procedure followed when a petty cash register is used. The flowchart also illustrates the entries needed to record the establishment and the replenishment of the petty cash fund. (Petty cash is an imprest fund. An **imprest fund** is a fixed amount of cash kept on hand for making small payments.)

VISUALIZING A PETTY CASH FUND SYSTEM

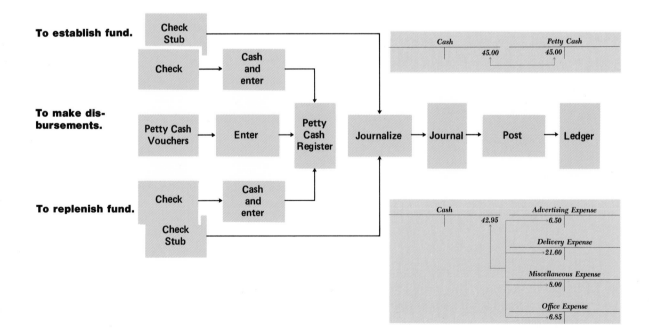

Activity B-1. Answer the following questions about journalizing petty cash entries. Refer to the petty cash register on page 232 and the related journal entries on page 235.
1. Which account was debited and which account was credited when the petty cash fund was established?
2. Which accounts were debited and credited when the fund was replenished?
3. How many petty cash expenditures are made for office expenses? How many times is the Office Expense account debited? For what amount?
4. How many petty cash expenditures are made for advertising?

5. Which account is debited on February 4 for $8?
6. How can you be sure that you have not made an error in transferring the data from the petty cash register to the journal?

Activity B-2. Answer the following questions about the petty cash register. Refer to the flowchart on page 236.
1. What items are recorded in the petty cash register?
2. What items involving petty cash are recorded in the journal?
3. What is the source of the data posted to the ledger?
4. How do the amounts of the petty cash vouchers get into the journal?

Accounting Concept:
Petty Cash Fund. A *petty cash fund* is frequently kept for expenditures made in cash. From time to time, the fund is restored to its original amount by a transfer from the Cash account of a sum equal to the total disbursements. This type of petty cash fund is called an *imprest* fund.

Topic 4 Problems

8-5. In Activity A-2 on page 234, you recorded transactions in the petty cash register for Audio Studios. Now record the journal entries needed for these petty cash transactions.
a. Make the journal entry to record Check 48, which was issued to establish the fund on April 1.
b. Make the journal entry to record Check 63, which was issued to replenish the fund on April 21.
NOTE: Save your journal and the petty cash register for further use in Topic Problem 8-6.

8-6. Use the petty cash register from Activity A-2 on page 234. Record in the journal the entries to record the following transactions for Audio Studios.
Apr. 22 Issued Check 64 for $15 to increase the fund to $75. (Debit Petty Cash. Enter amount in Received column of petty cash register.)
22 Paid $8.75 for ad in *News Herald.*
25 Issued Check 65 for $500 to pay rent for May.
27 Paid $7.50 for adding machine tapes (Office Expense).

May 4 Paid $9.50 for typewriter ribbons.
12 Paid $3.75 to United Parcel for delivery of equipment.
16 Issued Check 66 for $425 for store equipment.
18 Issued Check 67 for $220 to AKO Equipment on account.
24 Paid $6.50 to Railway Express for delivery.
26 Issued Check 68 for $125 to pay the electric bill.

a. Record these transactions in the journal or the petty cash register.
b. Pencil-foot the petty cash register on May 31, the end of the accounting period.
c. Complete a proof of the petty cash register. (The petty cash box contains the following: five $5 bills, eight $1 bills, 10 quarters, 19 dimes, 24 nickels, and 40 pennies.)
d. Record Check 69 to replenish the petty cash fund.

The Language of Business

Here are some terms that make up the language of business. Do you know the meaning of each?

signature card
check
depositor
drawer
drawee
payee
voiding a check
ABA number
magnetic ink
magnetic ink character
  recognition (MICR)
  machine

voucher check
certified check
stop payment
endorsement
endorser
endorsee
negotiable instrument
blank endorsement
full endorsement
restrictive
  endorsement
deposit ticket

passbook
bank statement
canceled check
outstanding check
deposit in transit
dishonored check
debit memorandum
service charge
reconciling the bank
  statement
bank reconciliation
  statement
adjusted bank balance

adjusted checkbook
  balance
reconciled balances
petty cash fund
cash disbursement
petty cash voucher
proving the petty cash
  fund
replenishing the petty
  cash fund
petty cash
  memorandum
petty cash register
imprest fund

Chapter 8   Questions

1. Give several reasons why businesses use checking accounts.

2. What is the purpose of the magnetic ink characters printed at the bottom of deposit tickets and checks?

3. What three records are compared to verify the cash balance at the end of the month? In what order are they compared?

4. What information appears on a bank statement?

5. On June 30 a checkbook showed a balance of $420 and the bank statement showed a balance of $410. Give four factors that may have caused this difference.

6. Why is a bank reconciliation statement prepared?

Describe in sequence the steps for preparing a bank reconciliation.

7. Which factors on the bank reconciliation statement require journal entries?

8. Explain how a petty cash fund is established and operated.

9. What is the procedure for replenishing the petty cash fund?

10. The Petty Cash account of a business has a balance of $175. At the end of the accounting period, there is still $75 in the petty cash fund. Should the fund be replenished on the last day of the period? Why or why not?

Chapter 8   Problems

Problems for Chapter 8 are given in the *Working Papers and Chapter Problems for Part 1*. If you are using the workbook, do the problems in the space provided there.

Chapter 8   Management Cases

Safeguarding Cash. Every business runs the risk of robbery, embezzlement, and fraud. Some methods a business can use to protect itself against such losses are these.
• Use source documents as evidence of cash transactions.

• Use prenumbered forms.
• Deposit cash receipts in the bank one or more times each day.
• Use the night depository for deposits after the bank is closed.
• Place cash awaiting deposit in a safe.

- Vary the time of day and routine for going to the bank.
- Employ an armed-guard service to take the cash to the bank.
- Require identification when cashing checks for customers.
- Take out insurance against burglary and robbery.

Case 8M-1. The Best Buy Sales Center is open from 9 A.M. to 9 P.M. Monday through Saturday, and 10 A.M. to 6 P.M. on Sundays. The daily cash receipts amount to several thousand dollars and are placed in an office safe at the end of the day. These receipts are then deposited in the bank the next morning. The receipts for Friday, Saturday, and Sunday are deposited on Monday morning. Over the weekend there is usually $30,000 to $35,000 in the safe.

a. What safeguards might the manager use to protect cash receipts during the day?

b. What safeguards can be taken to protect cash receipts during the evenings?

c. What safeguards can be taken to protect cash receipts during the weekends?

d. What safeguards can be taken to prevent losses due to robbery?

Case 8M-2. Adam Teran owns a parking lot that is open from 8 A.M. to 7 P.M. He charges a fee of $4 for a car, regardless of how long it is parked. Customers park their own cars and pay when they drive out of the lot. No parking ticket is issued to the customers. An attendant collects the money and deposits it in the bank once a day.

a. Mr. Teran believes that he should install some plan to ensure that each person who parks a car pays the fee. What plan do you suggest?

b. Mr. Teran also wants to ensure that all amounts collected by the attendant are deposited. What control system do you recommend?

Working Hint

Posting. Each journal entry requires a posting to the debit side of one account and a posting to the credit side of another account.

In posting a series of journal entries in sequence, many accounting clerks first post a debit, then a credit, then a debit, then a credit, and so forth. As a result of going back and forth from debit to credit, they can easily post an amount to the wrong side of an account.

The chance of making this type of error can be reduced.
- Post all the debit entries on the journal page.
- Post all the credit entries on the journal page.

Remember to fill in the Posting Reference column of the journal at the same time that you post an item. Otherwise, you will not know which items you posted and which items you did not post.

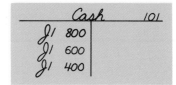

Payroll Activities

Federal laws—and some state and local laws—require employers to keep records of all salaries and wages paid to employees. You will now learn how accounting concepts, principles, and procedures are used in preparing these records.

Topic 1
Computing Gross Earnings

A *What kind of records of salaries and wages of employees must an employer keep?* A business must keep special records if it employs people. Federal laws (and some state and local laws) require that employers keep records of all salaries and wages paid to employees. How accounting is used in these activities is discussed in this chapter.

An **employer** is an individual or a business for whom an employee performs a service. An **employee** is an individual who performs a service under the direction and control of an employer. The special records on salaries and wages that an employer must keep are called **payroll records.** These records must provide several types of payroll data, including the following.

- The amount of wages or salaries paid to the employees.
- The amounts deducted from the employees' earnings.
- The expenses involved with the payroll.
- The payroll taxes owed by the employer and the employees to the government.

Employee earnings are called salaries, wages, or commissions. **Salaries** are fixed amounts paid periodically to employees for their services. **Wages** are amounts paid to employees at a certain rate per hour, day, week, or unit of production. (In practice, the terms *wages* and *salaries* often are used to mean the same thing.) **Commissions** are amounts paid to employees according to the number or price of items sold. The Internal Revenue Service uses the term *wages* to cover all types of employee earnings.

The total earnings of all the employees for a certain pay period is called the **payroll.** The pay period is usually weekly, biweekly (every two weeks), semimonthly (twice a month), or monthly.

Time Pay Plans

The amount an employee earns is known as his or her **gross earnings.** Various plans are used to determine an employee's gross earnings. The salary plan is based on the amount of time the employee works. The hourly rate plan, like the salary plan, is also based on the amount of time the employee works.

Salary Plan. The **salary plan** is a payment plan based on straight salary with a fixed amount for each pay period. Thus no computations are generally needed to find out a salaried employee's gross earnings. For example, Paul Alvarez is employed by the Globe Travel Agency. He

Salary Plan

Gross
Earnings = Salary
$212 = $212

is paid a salary of $212 per week. The amount of his gross earnings for the week is the amount of his salary—$212. The rate of pay may be stated as a certain amount of salary per week, per month, or per year. To change a yearly salary to a weekly salary, divide the yearly salary by 52 (since there are 52 weeks in a year). To change a yearly salary to a monthly salary, divide by 12 (since there are 12 months in a year). To change a weekly salary into an hourly wage, divide the weekly salary by the number of hours in the work week.

Hourly-Rate Plan

Gross
Earnings = Hours × Rate
$160 = 40 × $4

Hourly-Rate Plan. The **hourly-rate plan** is a payment plan in which the employee is paid a set amount for each hour worked. To find the employee's gross earnings, multiply the hourly rate by the number of hours worked in the pay period. For example, Doris Post, another employee at the Globe Travel Agency, is paid $4 per hour. Her gross earnings for 40 hours are $160 (40 × $4). This plan is useful when the number of hours worked varies from one pay period to another.

Incentive Pay Plans

An **incentive plan** is a pay plan based on an employee's productivity, or output. An incentive pay plan allows employees to increase their gross earnings by producing more. The piece-rate plan and the commission plan are based on the employee's output. The salary-commission plan is based on a combination of time worked and output.

Piece-Rate Plan

Gross
Earnings = Items × Rate
$225 = 2,250 × $0.10

Piece-Rate Plan. The **piece-rate plan** is a payment plan in which an employee is paid a set amount for each item produced. This plan is frequently used in factories. For example, a presser in a clothing factory is paid $0.10 for every blouse pressed. The presser's gross earnings for pressing 2,250 blouses would be $225 (2,250 × $0.10).

Commission Plan

Gross
Earnings = Percentage × Sales
$240 = 0.03 × $8,000

Commission Plan. Some businesses use the commission plan to encourage its salespeople to increase their sales. The **commission plan** is a payment plan which is based on the quantity of goods the salesperson sells. The commission is computed by multiplying the amount of sales the salesperson made during the pay period by a certain percentage. For example, suppose a salesperson receives a commission of 3 percent on all sales. If the salesperson had sales of $8,000 in a week, the gross earnings would be $240 (0.03 × $8,000).

Salary-Commission Plan

Gross
Earnings = Salary + Commission
$260 = $100 + (0.02 × $8,000)
$260 = $100 + $160

Salary-Commission Plan. The **salary-commission plan** is a payment plan in which a basic salary plus a commission is paid. For example, assume that a salesperson is paid a salary of $100 a week plus a 2 percent commission on sales. In this plan, the salesperson's gross earnings would be $260 for weekly sales of $8,000 ($100 + $160).

Activity A. Sogan Washer Corporation pays a rate of $3.50 per hour to all inexperienced employees. When employees have three months of experience, they are paid on a piece-rate basis. The employees who tap the washers receive $0.50 for each successful tap they complete. The employees who pack the tapped washers for shipment receive $0.25 for each shipment they pack. Some of the inexperienced employees, tappers, and packers for Sogan Washer Corporation are listed here. Compute the gross earnings for each employee.

Inexperienced Employees		Tapper Employees		Packer Employees	
Employee	Total Hours	Employee	Total Taps	Employee	Total Shipments
1. J. Baker	38	**4.** J. Noonan	312	**7.** P. Yung	640
2. T. Liden	40	**5.** V. Bell	285	**8.** C. Stosky	580
3. O. Malley	35	**6.** C. Dinan	270	**9.** T. Taylor	560

Wages and Hours of Work

B *What is a contract of employment?* The wages employees are paid and the number of hours employees work depend upon their contract of employment and upon government legislation. In general, an employee's rate of pay is based upon an oral or written agreement between the employer and the employee. In businesses that have many employees, a contract of employment is usually written. A **contract of employment** is an agreement between the employer and a union that covers wages, hours of work, types of benefits offered (if any), and other working conditions. Such a contract must be followed by the employer and the employee.

Overtime Pay. Certain federal and state laws regulate the number of hours employees may work and the employees' rate of pay. The Fair Labor Standards Act, also called the Wage and Hour Law, affects all firms engaged in interstate commerce. (**Interstate commerce** means that goods produced in one state are sold in other states.) Employers who are covered by the act must pay a minimum hourly rate of pay. In addition, the act requires employers to pay overtime. **Overtime pay** is wages for over 40 hours of work in any week. **Overtime rate** is a minimum rate of $1\frac{1}{2}$ times the regular rate. Thus an employee who is paid a regular rate of $4 per hour would be paid an overtime rate of $6 ($1\frac{1}{2} \times \$4$) per hour. The overtime rate of $1\frac{1}{2}$ times the regular rate is commonly called **time and a half.**

Employers who are not subject to the Fair Labor Standards Act may still pay time and a half for overtime. They may do so because of a contract of employment with the union or to keep good relations with the employees. Some contracts call for employees to be paid for work on legal holidays at double their regular rates.

Name	Ray Harris			Employee No.	2	
Week Ending	April 28, 19--					

Days	Regular				Other		Hours
	In	Out	In	Out	In	Out	
Thurs.	8 00	12 00	1 00	5 00			8
Fri.	8 58	12 00	12 59	5 00			7
Sat.							
Sun.							
Mon.	7 55	12 02	12 58	5 05	6 00	9 00	11
Tues.	8 05	12 01	12 59	5 01			8
Wed.	7 59	12 01	1 01	5 02	5 57	9 01	11

		Hours	Rate	Earnings
Extra Hours Approved	Regular	40	$ 4.00	$160.00
J. Evans	Overtime	5	$ 6.00	$ 30.00
Supervisor	Total Hours	45	Gross Earnings	$190.00

Total hours worked and gross earnings are computed on the bottom of the time card: 40 hours worked at a regular rate of $4 and 5 hours at an overtime rate of $6.

The Fair Labor Standards Act also requires that a complete record be kept of the hours worked by each employee. A **time book** is a record of the hours worked each day by the employees. Businesses with many employees frequently use a time clock. Each employee has a time card to insert in the time clock upon arrival and again upon departure. A **time card** is the source document for recording an employee's attendance at work to compute hours worked and wages. The time clock punches the time of day on the card. At the end of the pay period, the payroll clerk collects all the time cards and computes total hours worked and gross earnings for each employee.

Salaried employees are also covered by the Fair Labor Standards Act and are eligible to receive overtime pay. Thus an attendance record should be kept for salaried employees as well as for hourly employees. Such a record would show overtime hours and absences.

Payroll Clerk: DOT* 215.482-010 Computes wages and posts wages to payroll records.

Determining Hours Worked

Employers have some agreement with their employees regarding working hours. For example, employees might be required to work from 8 A.M. to noon. Noon to 1 P.M. may be set aside for lunch. Then they might work from 1 P.M. to 5 P.M. Some rules must be made regarding lateness and the computation of time worked. Although the procedure for computing time worked varies from business to business, the following procedure, which is used by the Globe Travel Agency, is common.

TIME RECORDED	CONSIDERED AS
7:55, 8:05, 7:59	8:00
8:58	9:00
12:02, 12:01	12:00
12:59, 12:58, 1:01	1:00
5:05, 5:01, 5:02	5:00

Analysis of Time

• The employee is paid only for regular hours unless extra hours have been approved by the supervisor. For example, an employee receives no pay for work before 8 A.M., between noon and 1 P.M., and after 5 P.M. unless the work has been approved.
• Daily time is computed in hours and quarter-hours. Fractions of an hour less than 15 minutes are not counted.
• The nearest quarter-hour is used to compute the time for beginning and ending work. A quarter-hour begins and ends on the hour, 15 minutes after the hour, 30 minutes after the hour, or 45 minutes after the hour. Thus, regardless of the time an employee punches in or out, the employee is given credit for working to the nearest quarter-hour.

Nearest Quarter Hour

* *Dictionary of Occupational Titles*

For example, 7:53 to 8:07 are considered as 8:00. However, 8:08 to 8:22 are considered as 8:15. Although lateness is discouraged, an employee is not penalized for being up to 7 minutes late.

Activity B. The time cards for the employees of the Masters Corporation are given here. As payroll clerk for the business, perform the following activities.
1. Find the total number of hours worked each day by Dave Cane and Josie Campbell. Regular hours are from 8 A.M. to noon and 1 to 5 P.M. Use the nearest quarter-hour to compute the beginning and ending time. Compute the daily time in hours and quarter-hours.
2. Find the total hours worked during the week for each employee.
NOTE: Save your time cards for further use in Topic Problem 9-1.

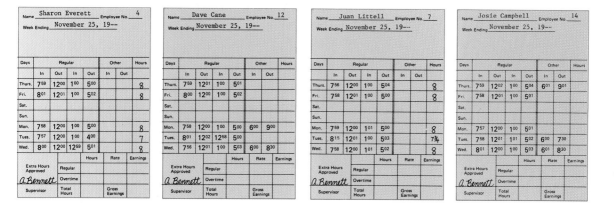

Name Sharon Everett — **Employee No.** 4
Week Ending November 25, 19--

Days	Regular In	Out	In	Out	Other In	Out	Hours
Thurs.	7:59	12:00	1:00	5:00			8
Fri.	8:01	12:01	1:00	5:02			8
Sat.							
Sun.							
Mon.	7:58	12:00	1:00	5:00			8
Tues.	7:57	12:00	1:00	4:00			7
Wed.	8:00	12:00	12:59	5:01			8

	Hours	Rate	Earnings
Extra Hours Approved *a Bennett*	Regular		
	Overtime		
Supervisor	Total Hours		Gross Earnings

Name Dave Cane — **Employee No.** 12
Week Ending November 25, 19--

Days	Regular In	Out	In	Out	Other In	Out	Hours
Thurs.	7:59	12:01	1:00	5:01			
Fri.	8:00	12:00	1:00	5:02			
Sat.							
Sun.							
Mon.	7:58	12:00	1:00	5:00	6:00	9:00	
Tues.	8:01	12:02	12:58	5:00			
Wed.	7:56	12:01	1:00	5:03	6:00	8:30	

	Hours	Rate	Earnings
Extra Hours Approved *a Bennett*	Regular		
	Overtime		
Supervisor	Total Hours		Gross Earnings

Name Juan Littell — **Employee No.** 7
Week Ending November 25, 19--

Days	Regular In	Out	In	Out	Other In	Out	Hours
Thurs.	7:56	12:00	1:00	5:04			8
Fri.	7:58	12:01	1:00	5:00			8
Sat.							
Sun.							
Mon.	7:59	12:00	1:01	5:00			8
Tues.	8:15	12:01	1:00	5:03			7¾
Wed.	7:58	12:00	1:01	5:02			8

	Hours	Rate	Earnings
Extra Hours Approved *a Bennett*	Regular		
	Overtime		
Supervisor	Total Hours		Gross Earnings

Name Josie Campbell — **Employee No.** 14
Week Ending November 25, 19--

Days	Regular In	Out	In	Out	Other In	Out	Hours
Thurs.	7:59	12:02	1:00	5:04	6:01	9:01	
Fri.	7:58	12:01	1:00	5:01			
Sat.							
Sun.							
Mon.	7:57	12:00	1:00	5:01			
Tues.	7:58	12:01	1:01	5:02	6:00	7:30	
Wed.	8:01	12:00	1:00	5:03	6:01	8:30	

	Hours	Rate	Earnings
Extra Hours Approved *a Bennett*	Regular		
	Overtime		
Supervisor	Total Hours		Gross Earnings

Topic 1 Problems

9-1. Use the time cards you prepared in Activity B above to perform the following duties as payroll clerk for the Masters Corporation.

Compute the regular, overtime, and total gross earnings for each employee. The hourly rates are as follows: Everett, $5.00; Cane, $3.50; Littell, $4.00; and Campbell, $4.00. Consider all hours in excess of 40 hours per week as overtime hours. Overtime hours are paid at the rate of 1½ times the regular hourly rate.
NOTE: Save your time cards for further use in Topic Problem 9-3.

9-2. Canyon Motors sells off-the-road vehicles and recreational vehicles (jeeps, motorcycles, and so on). The recreational vehicle salespeople are paid on a salary-commission plan. They receive a base salary of $500 per month and a 5 percent commission on their sales. The off-the-road vehicle salespeople are paid on a commission plan. They receive a 10 percent commission on their sales.
a. Compute the monthly gross earnings for each of the salespeople listed.
b. Which salespeople earn more money? Why?
c. What are the advantages and disadvantages of the two pay plans (salary-commission plan and commission plan)?

Off-the-Road Vehicle Salespeople	Total Sales	Recreational Vehicle Salespeople	Total Sales
1. B. Sampson	$10,750	**4.** T. Yee	$24,000
2. W. Harris	12,000	**5.** G. Mack	18,000
3. A. Chou	8,500	**6.** N. Wills	21,000

Topic 2
Deductions From Gross Earnings

A *Is there a difference between an employee's gross earnings and the amount actually given to an employee?* Yes, various payroll deductions must be subtracted from an employee's gross earnings. A **payroll deduction** is an amount subtracted from gross earnings. Payroll deductions include deductions required by law, such as federal income tax, state income tax, and social security tax (FICA). They may also include voluntary deductions, such as group life insurance and hospitalization insurance premiums. In addition, some union contracts call for union deductions, such as initiation fees and dues to be withheld from the employee's earnings.

Deductions Required by Law

An employer is required to withhold taxes from an employee's gross earnings. **Federal income tax** is a tax imposed by the federal government on personal or business income. Federal laws require the employer to withhold amounts for the employee's federal income tax and for the employee's share of the social security taxes. Many states and cities also require state income tax and city income tax to be withheld. In addition, courts of law can require employers to withhold money. The employer then periodically sends the amounts withheld to the proper governmental or legal agency.

Federal Income Tax Withholding

The amount of federal income tax withheld depends upon the employee's gross earnings, marital status, and number of exemptions claimed. An **exemption** is a government allowance which permits taxpayers to reduce their tax payment because they support qualified persons. In general, an employee is allowed the following exemptions.

• One exemption for the employee.
• One exemption for the employee's spouse unless he or she is working and claims a separate exemption.
• One exemption for each dependent. A **dependent** is a person supported by the taxpayer. A child under 19 or relatives receiving more than half of their support from the taxpayer are dependents. Children who are full-time students (at least five months per year) can be dependents regardless of their age or their earnings.

Each employee reports the number of exemptions claimed on an **Employee's Withholding Allowance Certificate (Form W-4).**

Form W-4 is a report by the employee of the number of exemptions. Every employee must give a Form W-4 to the employer. This is how the employer knows how many exemptions the employee is claiming.

Form **W-4** (Rev. October 1979)	Department of the Treasury—Internal Revenue Service **Employee's Withholding Allowance Certificate**	
Print your full name ▶ Ray Thomas Harris	Your social security number ▶	201 26 8341
Address (including ZIP code) ▶ 104 Second Avenue, Chicago, IL 60612		

Marital status: ☐ Single ☒ Married ☐ Married, but withhold at higher Single rate
Note: *If married, but legally separated, or spouse is a nonresident alien, check the single block.*

1 Total number of allowances you are claiming (from line F of the worksheet on page 2) 1 **3**
2 Additional amount, if any, you want deducted from each pay (if your employer agrees) . . . . 2 $
3 I claim exemption from withholding because (see instructions and check boxes below that apply):
 a ☐ Last year I did not owe any Federal income tax and had a right to a full refund of **ALL** income tax withheld, **AND**
 b ☐ This year I do not expect to owe any Federal income tax and expect to have a right to a full refund of **ALL** income tax withheld. If both
  a and b apply, enter "EXEMPT" here . . . . ▶
 c If you entered "EXEMPT" on line 3b, are you a full-time student? . . . . ☐ Yes ☐ No

Under the penalties of perjury, I certify that I am entitled to the number of withholding allowances claimed on this certificate, or if claiming exemption from withholding, that I am entitled to claim the exempt status.
Employee's signature ▶ *Ray Thomas Harris* Date ▶ January 2 , 19 --
Employer's name and address (including ZIP code) (FOR EMPLOYER'S USE ONLY) Employer identification number
Globe Travel Agency, 3010 South Fifth Street, Chicago, IL 60612 33-75091-21

Form W-4 showing three allowances.

The law requires employers to have a Form W-4 on file for each employee. Employees must file revised Form W-4s within ten days if their number of exemptions decreases. If their number of exemptions increases, they may file revised Form W-4s if they wish.

The federal income tax to be withheld from the earnings of an employee is determined by using wage-bracket tables or by computing the amount. The wage-bracket method is a one-step procedure commonly used. The Internal Revenue Service provides tables for daily, weekly, biweekly, semimonthly, monthly, and miscellaneous payroll periods. The wage-bracket table shown here is from the tax table for single persons paid weekly.

SINGLE Persons — WEEKLY Payroll Period

And the wages are—		And the number of withholding allowances claimed is—										
At least	But less than	0	1	2	3	4	5	6	7	8	9	10 or more
		The amount of income tax to be withheld shall be—										
$135	$140	$19.00	$15.30	$11.80	$8.40	$5.00	$2.10	$0	$0	$0	$0	$0
140	145	20.00	16.20	12.70	9.30	5.80	2.90	0	0	0	0	0
145	150	21.10	17.10	13.60	10.20	6.70	3.60	.70	0	0	0	0
150	160	22.60	18.60	15.00	11.50	8.10	4.70	1.80	0	0	0	0
160	170	24.70	20.70	16.80	13.30	9.90	6.40	3.30	.50	0	0	0
170	180	26.80	22.80	18.80	15.10	11.70	8.20	4.80	2.00	0	0	0
180	190	28.90	24.90	20.90	16.90	13.50	10.00	6.50	3.50	.60	0	0
190	200	31.00	27.00	23.00	18.90	15.30	11.80	8.30	5.00	2.10	0	0
200	210	33.60	29.10	25.10	21.00	17.10	13.60	10.10	6.70	3.60	.70	0
210	220	36.20	31.20	27.20	23.10	19.10	15.40	11.90	8.50	5.10	2.20	0
220	230	38.80	33.80	29.30	25.20	21.20	17.20	13.70	10.30	6.80	3.70	.80
230	240	41.40	36.40	31.40	27.30	23.30	19.20	15.50	12.10	8.60	5.20	2.30
240	250	44.00	39.00	34.00	29.40	25.40	21.30	17.30	13.90	10.40	6.90	3.80
250	260	46.60	41.60	36.60	31.60	27.50	23.40	19.40	15.70	12.20	8.70	5.30
260	270	49.20	44.20	39.20	34.20	29.60	25.50	21.50	17.50	14.00	10.50	7.10

Federal income tax wage-bracket table for single persons paid weekly.

MARRIED Persons—WEEKLY Payroll Period

And the wages are—		And the number of withholding allowances claimed is—										
At least	But less than	0	1	2	3	4	5	6	7	8	9	10 or more
		The amount of income tax to be withheld shall be—										
150	160	17.20	13.70	10.60	7.70	4.80	1.90	0	0	0	0	0
160	170	19.00	15.50	12.10	9.20	6.30	3.40	.50	0	0	0	0
170	180	20.80	17.30	13.80	10.70	7.80	4.90	2.00	0	0	0	0
180	190	22.60	19.10	15.60	12.20	9.30	6.40	3.50	.60	0	0	0
190	200	24.40	20.90	17.40	14.00	10.80	7.90	5.00	2.10	0	0	0
200	210	26.20	22.70	19.20	15.80	12.30	9.40	6.50	3.60	.80	0	0
210	220	28.10	24.50	21.00	17.60	14.10	10.90	8.00	5.10	2.30	0	0
220	230	30.20	26.30	22.80	19.40	15.90	12.50	9.50	6.60	3.80	.90	0
230	240	32.30	28.30	24.60	21.20	17.70	14.30	11.00	8.10	5.30	2.40	0
240	250	34.40	30.40	26.40	23.00	19.50	16.10	12.60	9.60	6.80	3.90	1.00
250	260	36.50	32.50	28.50	24.80	21.30	17.90	14.40	11.10	8.30	5.40	2.50
260	270	38.60	34.60	30.60	26.60	23.10	19.70	16.20	12.70	9.80	6.90	4.00
270	280	40.70	36.70	32.70	28.60	24.90	21.50	18.00	14.50	11.30	8.40	5.50
280	290	42.80	38.80	34.80	30.70	26.70	23.30	19.80	16.30	12.90	9.90	7.00
290	300	45.10	40.90	36.90	32.80	28.80	25.10	21.60	18.10	14.70	11.40	8.50

Federal income tax wage-bracket table for married persons paid weekly.

The wage-bracket table shown above is from the withholding tax table for married persons paid weekly.

To determine the amount of income tax to be deducted from each employee's gross earnings, use the following procedure.

• Locate the wage-bracket table for the pay period, such as weekly or monthly.
• Refer to the table for the employee's marital status. Different tables are provided for single (including divorced, separated, or widowed) or married persons.
• Look down the wage columns (the first two columns at the left on each table). Ranges of wages are listed in these columns, which define various wage brackets. Locate the wage bracket that covers the amount of the employee's gross earnings.
• Follow across the line to the column for the number of withholding exemptions claimed on the employee's Form W-4.
• The amount in this block of the table is the income tax to be withheld from the employee's gross earnings.

For example, Ray Harris, a Globe Travel Agency employee, had gross earnings of $190 for the week ended April 28, 19—. He is married and claims three exemptions. Use the withholding table for married persons paid weekly on page 248. Look down the wage columns for the bracket with $190 (at least $190, but less than $200). Follow this line across to the column for three exemptions. The amount in this block is $14.00.

Activity A. Find the amount to be deducted for federal income tax from the employees listed on page 249. The gross earnings are for a weekly pay period. Refer to the federal income tax withholding tables on pages 247 and 248.

Employee	Gross Earnings	Marital Status	No. of Exemp.		Employee	Gross Earnings	Marital Status	No. of Exemp.
1. B. Yannon	$190	M	3		**5.** J. Moore	$223	S	1
2. J. Reese	$172	S	1		**6.** D. Ryan	$250	M	6
3. A. Baron	$172	M	2		**7.** H. Yabski	$256	M	4
4. T. Mingo	$211	S	1		**8.** R. Williams	$255	M	3

The Federal Insurance Contributions Act (FICA)

B *What does FICA require of employers and employees?* The **Federal Insurance Contributions Act (FICA)** requires most employers and employees to pay taxes to support the federal social security programs. **FICA tax** is a social security tax paid to the federal government for use in paying old-age, survivors, disability insurance, and health insurance benefits. There are three principal federal social security programs.

- The old-age, survivors, and disability insurance program.
- The federal unemployment insurance program.
- The federal health insurance program for the aged (Medicare).

The first program provides pensions to retired persons, disability payments to disabled persons, and benefits to dependents of insured workers who are disabled or dead. This program and the Medicare program are operated by the federal government. Both programs are financed by taxes paid equally by both employers and employees. (The rate paid by self-employed persons is different from the rate paid by employers and employees.)

The tax to support the second program—the federal unemployment insurance program—is covered by the **Federal Unemployment Tax Act (FUTA)** and is often referred to as the **FUTA tax.** This program is discussed in the next topic.

The FICA tax is paid by both the employer and the employee. The tax is based only on the annual gross earnings of an employee up to a certain maximum amount paid during the calendar year (January 1 to December 31). As of this writing, the maximum amount is $29,700. Thus annual gross earnings over $29,700 are not subject to the FICA tax. The present law provides for gradual increases in the FICA tax.

Let's see how the employee's share of the FICA tax is computed. Ray Harris had gross earnings of $190 for the week ended April 28. Since Mr. Harris earned $2,688 prior to this pay period, the entire amount of his gross earnings is subject to FICA tax. He has not earned $29,700 yet this year. To compute his FICA tax, multiply his gross earnings by 6.7 percent. The FICA tax is $12.73 (0.067 × $190). The FICA rate

Employee's FICA Tax

$$\begin{array}{ccc} & & \text{Taxable} \\ \text{FICA Tax} & = & \text{Earnings} \times \text{Rate} \\ \$12.73 & = & \$190 \times 6.7\% \\ & & (0.067) \end{array}$$

may change. Therefore in this textbook a tax rate of 6.7 percent of the first $29,700 of taxable earnings is used. The FICA tax can be found on the Social Security Employee Tax Table on the next page.

The Internal Revenue Service provides a social security tax table that shows the amount of FICA tax to be deducted from various wage amounts. Sometimes these amounts differ slightly because amounts computed for individual employees are rounded. The table here is an example of a FICA tax table.

Compute the FICA tax for gross earnings not shown on the tax table. Remember that the FICA tax is levied on only $29,700 of the employee's gross earnings. Suppose Carla Jackson has earned $29,600 prior to the current pay period. Now she has gross earnings of $350 during the current pay period. Only $100 of her gross earnings will be subject to FICA tax, because she will then have reached the maximum of $29,700 ($29,600 + $100). Her FICA tax, therefore, is $6.70 (0.067 × $100). The FICA tax can be found on the social security tax table on the next page.

Every person covered by the federal social security law is required to have a social security account number. A person's social security account number is also used by the Internal Revenue Service. Taxpayers must supply their social security account numbers with their federal income tax returns. The social security account number is also used in many other ways. Some banks use it as the depositor's bank account number. Some businesses use it as the employee's identification number. Many colleges and universities use it as the student's identification number. A person can get a social security card with an account number free of charge from the Social Security Administration.

Employee's FICA Tax

Taxable

FICA Tax = Earnings × Rate

$6.70 = $100 × 6.7% (0.067)

Social Security Card

State Income Tax

In states where there is a personal income tax, state residents are taxed on their incomes. A **state income tax** is a tax imposed by a state government on personal or business income. A state may tax the income of nonresidents if the income was earned within the state.

Tax rates and laws vary greatly among states. For example, one may have a rate of less than 1% while another may have a much higher rate of over 15%. Some states have flat tax rates while others use tax tables.

Several state income tax laws permit various deductions or credits before the tax rate is applied to the income. These credits may be a personal exemption in the form of a credit against the tax. A state, therefore, may grant credits to resident taxpayers. It must also grant credits to nonresidents with taxable income in the taxing state. Nonresidents are often allowed credit for the taxes paid to their residency state. This practice, called *reciprocity*, is nearly always followed.

Social Security Employee Tax Table—Continued

6.7 percent employee tax deductions

Wages At least	But less than	Tax to be withheld	Wages At least	But less than	Tax to be withheld	Wages At least	But less than	Tax to be withheld	Wages At least	But less than	Tax to be withheld
$99.93	$100.08	$6.70	$134.26	$134.41	$9.00	$159.48	$159.63	$10.69	$210.83	$210.98	$14.13
100.08	100.23	6.71	134.41	134.56	9.01	159.63	159.78	10.70	210.98	211.12	14.14
100.23	100.38	6.72	134.56	134.71	9.02	159.78	159.93	10.71	211.12	211.27	14.15
100.38	100.53	6.73	134.71	134.86	9.03	159.93	160.08	10.72	211.27	211.42	14.16
100.53	100.68	6.74	134.86	135.00	9.04	160.08	160.23	10.73	211.42	211.57	14.17
100.68	100.83	6.75	135.00	135.15	9.05	160.23	160.38	10.74	211.57	211.72	14.18
100.83	100.98	6.76	135.15	135.30	9.06	160.38	160.53	10.75	211.72	211.87	14.19
100.98	101.13	6.77	135.30	135.45	9.07	160.53	160.68	10.76	211.87	212.02	14.20
101.13	101.28	6.78	135.45	135.60	9.08	160.68	160.83	10.77	212.02	212.17	14.21
101.28	101.42	6.79	135.60	135.75	9.09	160.83	160.98	10.78	212.17	212.32	14.22
109.93	110.08	7.37	139.93	140.08	9.38	167.84	167.99	11.25	224.56	224.70	15.05
110.08	110.23	7.38	140.08	140.23	9.39	167.99	168.14	11.26	224.70	224.85	15.06
110.23	110.38	7.39	140.23	140.38	9.40	168.14	168.29	11.27	224.85	225.00	15.07
110.38	110.53	7.40	140.38	140.53	9.41	168.29	168.44	11.28	225.00	225.15	15.08
110.53	110.68	7.41	140.53	140.68	9.42	168.44	168.59	11.29	225.15	225.30	15.09
110.68	110.83	7.42	140.68	140.83	9.43	168.59	168.74	11.30	225.30	225.45	15.10
110.83	110.98	7.43	140.83	140.98	9.44	168.74	168.89	11.31	225.45	225.60	15.11
110.98	111.12	7.44	140.98	141.12	9.45	168.89	169.03	11.32	225.60	225.75	15.12
111.12	111.27	7.45	141.12	141.27	9.46	169.03	169.18	11.33	225.75	225.90	15.13
111.27	111.42	7.46	141.27	141.42	9.47	169.18	169.33	11.34	225.90	226.05	15.14
119.48	119.63	8.01	142.02	142.17	9.52	171.72	171.86	11.51	255.15	255.30	17.10
119.63	119.78	8.02	142.17	142.32	9.53	171.86	172.01	11.52	255.30	255.45	17.11
119.78	119.93	8.03	142.32	142.47	9.54	172.01	172.16	11.53	255.45	255.60	17.12
119.93	120.08	8.04	142.47	142.62	9.55	172.16	172.31	11.54	255.60	255.75	17.13
120.08	120.23	8.05	142.62	142.77	9.56	172.31	172.46	11.55	255.75	255.90	17.14
120.23	120.38	8.06	142.77	142.92	9.57	172.46	172.61	11.56	255.90	256.05	17.15
120.38	120.53	8.07	142.92	143.06	9.58	172.61	172.76	11.57	256.05	256.20	17.16
120.53	120.68	8.08	143.06	143.21	9.59	172.76	172.91	11.58	256.20	256.35	17.17
120.68	120.83	8.09	143.21	143.36	9.60	172.91	173.06	11.59	256.35	256.50	17.18
120.83	120.98	8.10	143.36	143.51	9.61	173.06	173.21	11.60	256.50	256.65	17.19
121.73	121.88	8.16	144.11	144.26	9.66	189.93	190.08	12.73	399.33	399.48	26.76
121.88	122.03	8.17	144.26	144.41	9.67	190.08	190.23	12.74	399.48	399.63	26.77
122.03	122.18	8.18	144.41	144.56	9.68	190.23	190.38	12.75	399.63	399.78	26.78
122.18	122.33	8.19	144.56	144.71	9.69	190.38	190.53	12.76	399.78	399.93	26.79
122.33	122.48	8.20	144.71	144.86	9.70	190.53	190.68	12.77	399.93	400.08	26.80
122.48	122.63	8.21	144.86	145.00	9.71	190.68	190.83	12.78	400.08	400.23	26.81
122.63	122.78	8.22	145.00	145.15	9.72	190.83	190.98	12.79	400.23	400.38	26.82
122.78	122.93	8.23	145.15	145.30	9.73	190.98	191.12	12.80	400.38	400.53	26.83
122.93	123.08	8.24	145.30	145.45	9.74	191.12	191.27	12.81	400.53	400.68	26.84
123.08	123.23	8.25	145.45	145.60	9.75	191.27	191.42	12.82	400.68	400.83	26.85
129.03	129.18	8.65	149.78	149.93	10.04	194.71	194.86	13.05	498.74	498.89	33.42
129.18	129.33	8.66	149.93	150.08	10.05	194.86	195.00	13.06	498.89	499.03	33.43
129.33	129.48	8.67	150.08	150.23	10.06	195.00	195.15	13.07	499.03	499.18	33.44
129.48	129.63	8.68	150.23	150.38	10.07	195.15	195.30	13.08	499.18	499.33	33.45
129.63	129.78	8.69	150.38	150.53	10.08	195.30	195.45	13.09	499.33	499.48	33.46
129.78	129.93	8.70	150.53	150.68	10.09	195.45	195.60	13.10	499.48	499.63	33.47
129.93	130.08	8.71	150.68	150.83	10.10	195.60	195.75	13.11	499.63	499.78	33.48
130.08	130.23	8.72	150.83	150.98	10.11	195.75	195.90	13.12	499.78	499.93	33.49
130.23	130.38	8.73	150.98	151.12	10.12	195.90	196.05	13.13	499.93	500.08	33.50
130.38	130.53	8.74	151.12	151.27	10.13	196.05	196.20	13.14	500.08	500.23	33.51
132.76	132.91	8.90	155.00	155.15	10.39	200.98	201.12	13.47	514.71	514.86	34.49
132.91	133.06	8.91	155.15	155.30	10.40	201.12	201.27	13.48	514.86	515.00	34.50
133.06	133.21	8.92	155.30	155.45	10.41	201.27	201.42	13.49	515.00	515.15	34.51
133.21	133.36	8.93	155.45	155.60	10.42	201.42	201.57	13.50	515.15	515.30	34.52
133.36	133.51	8.94	155.60	155.75	10.43	201.57	201.72	13.51	515.30	515.45	34.53
133.51	133.66	8.95	155.75	155.90	10.44	201.72	201.87	13.52	515.45	515.60	34.54
133.66	133.81	8.96	155.90	156.05	10.45	201.87	202.02	13.53	515.60	515.75	34.55
133.81	133.96	8.97	156.05	156.20	10.46	202.02	202.17	13.54	515.75	515.90	34.56
133.96	134.11	8.98	156.20	156.35	10.47	202.17	202.32	13.55	515.90	516.05	34.57
134.11	134.26	8.99	156.35	156.50	10.48	202.32	202.47	13.56	516.05	516.20	34.58

Social security tax table to be used by married and single persons for all pay periods.

State income tax laws provide for annual reporting of income. This report is made for the preceding fiscal or calendar year by the taxpayer. Usually the state tax commission, state department of revenue, or similar state agency manages the state income tax. However, the federal income tax is managed by the United States Secretary of the Treasury through the Internal Revenue Service. In some instances, the federal government may collect a state's income tax as a service to the state. In such a case, a federal collection agreement is established between the state government and the federal government. To establish such an agreement, certain requirements must exist. For example, the state income tax must be based on a percentage of the federal tax and meet certain requirements. Or, it must be based on the federal taxable income and meet certain requirements.

The table of rates here shows three examples of how personal state income tax can be computed. The table does not show the detailed application of such rates. It is, therefore, important to note that no one state follows the exact tax rate and procedure of another state.

EXAMPLES OF STATE TAX TABLE OF RATES FOR PERSONAL STATE INCOME TAX

Oregon			Missouri			Vermont
1st	$ 500	4%	1st	$1,000	1½%	23% of federal
2nd	500	5%	2nd	1,000	$15 plus 2%	income tax.
Next	1,000	6%	3rd	1,000	35 plus 2½%	
Next	1,000	7%	4th	1,000	60 plus 3%	
Next	1,000	8%	5th	1,000	90 plus 3½%	
Next	1,000	9%	6th	1,000	125 plus 4%	
Over	5,000	10%	7th	1,000	165 plus 4½%	
			8th	1,000	210 plus 5%	
			9th	1,000	260 plus 5½%	
			Over	9,000	315 plus 6%	

For the purpose of completing the problems in this chapter, the personal state income tax withholding will be computed using the tables on the next page. These use a percentage to compute the tax. The first table is for a weekly payroll period. The second table is for a biweekly payroll period.

To compute state income tax, use the following steps and refer to the weekly table for weekly payroll or the biweekly table for biweekly payroll shown on the next page.

- *Compute gross earnings.*
- *Compute the Total Amount for Exemption.*

Multiply the number of exemptions by the deductible amount. $12.50 is the deductible amount for one exemption for a weekly payroll. $25 is the deductible amount for one exemption for a biweekly payroll.

STATE INCOME TAX WITHHOLDING FOR WEEKLY PAYROLL PERIOD

Earnings Range		Amount Withheld

Gross earnings minus $12.50 for each exemption claimed equals taxable earnings.

If taxable earnings are:

More Than	But Not Over	Amount to be withheld is:
$ 0	$ 96.15	$ .5% of such amount
96.15	192.31	.49 plus 1 % of excess over $ 96.15
192.31	288.46	1.45 plus 2 % of excess over $ 192.31
288.46	384.62	3.37 plus 2.5% of excess over $ 288.46
384.62	769.23	5.77 plus 3 % of excess over $ 384.62
769.23	—	17.31 plus 3.5% of excess over $ 769.23

STATE INCOME TAX WITHHOLDING FOR BIWEEKLY PAYROLL PERIOD

Earnings Range		Amount Withheld

Gross earnings minus $25.00 for each exemption claimed equals taxable earnings.

If taxable earnings are:

More Than	But Not Over	Amount to be withheld is:
$ 0	$ 192.31	$ .5% of such amount
192.31	384.62	.96 plus 1 % of excess over $ 192.31
384.62	576.92	2.89 plus 2 % of excess over $ 384.62
576.92	769.23	6.73 plus 2.5% of excess over $ 576.92
769.23	1,538.46	11.54 plus 3 % of excess over $ 769.23
1,538.46	—	34.62 plus 3.5% of excess over $ 1,538.46

• *Compute Taxable Earnings.*
Subtract the total amount for the exemption deduction from gross earnings.
• *Locate the taxable earnings within the earning range.*
• *Compute the amount to be withheld.*
   To compute the state income tax for Ray Harris use Table I for a weekly payroll. Ray Harris has gross earnings of $190 with three exemptions.
• *Gross earnings: $190.*
• Exemptions: 3. Amount for each exemption: $12.50. (3 × $12.50 = $37.50)
• *Total Amount for Exemptions: $37.50*

$$\begin{aligned} \text{Gross Earnings: } &\$190.00 \\ \text{Less: Total Amount for Exemptions: } &-37.50 \\ \hline \text{Taxable Earnings: } &\$152.50 \end{aligned}$$

Taxable Earnings are $152.50
• *The earnings range is: More than $96.15 but not over $192.31.*

• *For this range, the basic tax is $0.49 plus 1% of taxable earnings in excess of $96.15. ($96.15 is the lower amount in the earnings range.)* Compute the tax amount as follows:

$$
\begin{array}{rr}
\text{Taxable Earnings:} & \$152.50 \\
\text{Less: Lower Amount in Range:} & -96.15 \\ \hline
\text{Excess Amount:} & \$\ 56.35 \\
\text{Percentage:} & \times\ \ .01 \\ \hline
\text{Amount of Percent of Excess:} & \$\ .5635 \\
\text{Add Basic Tax Amount:} & +.49 \\ \hline
\text{State Income Tax for Ray Harris:} & \$1.05
\end{array}
$$

Amount of Personal State Income Tax Withheld: $1.05.

A number of cities also require employers to withhold city income taxes. There are various methods used to compute these taxes. You are not asked in this textbook to compute a city income tax. But the procedure for computing these amounts is similar to the one used for computing state income taxes.

Other Deductions Required by Law. In a few states, unemployment taxes and/or disability and sickness taxes must be deducted from an employee's gross earnings. The amounts to be deducted are specified by the laws in the various states. The procedure for computing the amounts, however, is similar to the procedure described for the other taxes.

Another possible deduction is a garnishment. A **garnishment** is an amount ordered by a court to be deducted from an employee's earnings to pay a debt owed by the employee. Each pay period the employer withholds a set amount and sends it to the court until the debt has been paid.

Voluntary Deductions

An employee may ask to have voluntary deductions made for such items as safety or protective clothing, life insurance premiums, medical and hospitalization insurance premiums, pension plans, savings, and donations to charity. These voluntary deductions are computed individually for each employee. They are handled the same way as compulsory deductions.

Union Deductions

Generally, employees who are members of a union must pay an initiation fee and union dues as a condition of employment. As part of the

---

EXAMPLES OF PAYROLL DEDUCTIONS

Deductions Required by Law
• Federal income tax withholding
• Social security tax
• State income tax (in some states)
• City income tax (in some cities)
• Garnishments

Voluntary Deductions
• Life insurance
• Medical insurance
• Hospitalization insurance
• Pension plan
• Savings bonds
• Charity donations
• Miscellaneous (for example, safety shoes)

Deductions Required by Union Agreements
• Union initiation fees
• Union dues

agreement between the employer and the union, the employer usually withholds from an employee's earnings a certain amount for union dues.

Because deductions for union dues are not covered by law, the employer must have a written authorization from the employee before making any such deduction.

Computing Net Pay

All compulsory, voluntary, and union deductions must be subtracted from the employee's gross earnings. The remainder is the employee's net pay. **Net pay** (commonly referred to as *take-home pay*) is the amount actually given to the employee.

The net pay for Ray Harris for the week ended April 28 is computed as follows. Mr. Harris's Form W-4 shows that he claims three exemptions. His time card shows that he worked 45 hours during the week. His regular rate is $4 per hour. He has a voluntary deduction of $3 for group insurance premiums and a union deduction of $2 for dues.

Gross Earnings	−	Total Deductions	=	Net Pay
Regular . . . . .40 hours × $4.00 = $160.00		Federal Income Tax Withholding . $14.00		
Overtime . . . 5 hours × $6.00 = $ 30.00		State Income Tax Withholding . . . 1.05		
		FICA Tax 12.73		
		Group Insurance Premiums 3.00		
		Union Dues 2.00		
Gross Earnings $190.00	−	Total Deductions $32.78	=	Net Pay . . $157.22

Activity B-1. Refer to the payroll information given in Activity A on pages 248 and 249 to perform the following payroll activities. Find each employee's FICA tax by using the table on page 251 or by computing it at 6.7 percent. Prior to this pay period, D. Ryan had gross earnings of $29,550 and R. Williams had gross earnings of $30,000. All other employees had gross earnings of less than $20,000. Use $29,700 as the *maximum amount of earnings subject to FICA tax*.

Activity B-2. Refer to the payroll information in Activity A on pages 248 and 249 to perform the following activity. Find each employee's state income tax by using the table on page 253.

Topic 2 Problem

9-3. Use the payroll data you computed in Topic Problem 9-1 on page 245 to continue the duties of the payroll clerk for the Masters Corporation. Compute the total deductions and net pay for the employees.
a. Use the time cards you prepared in Activity B (page 245) to obtain the information about the earnings and hours of the four hourly-rate employees. The earnings and hours of the two salaried employees are as follows: Dawn Samer earns $150 per week and works 40 hours; Bill Mix earns $225 per week and works 40 hours.
b. Use the tables on pages 247 and 248 for the federal income tax withholding to determine the tax withheld for the hourly-rate and salaried employees.

c. Compute the state income tax withholding by using the weekly tax table on page 253.
d. Compute FICA tax. (All earnings are subject to FICA tax.)

e. Each employee has a deduction of $2 for insurance.
f. Each of the four hourly-rate employees has a deduction of $4 for union dues.

Empl. No.	Name	Marital Status	No. of Exemp.
4	Sharon Everett	M	5
7	Juan Littell	S	5
12	Dave Cane	M	1

Empl. No.	Name	Marital Status	No. of Exemp.
14	Josie Campbell	S	0
20	Dawn Samer	S	1
24	Bill Mix	M	3

Topic 3
Payroll Records and Procedures

A *What payroll records does an employer keep?* By law, the employer is required to keep certain payroll data for at least four years. Three payroll records commonly used are the payroll register, employee earnings record, and employee pay statement.

The Payroll Register

The **payroll register** is a summary of payroll data for each pay period for all employees. The payroll register varies according to the needs of individual businesses. The payroll register and procedure used by the Globe Travel Agency are as follows.

Time Cards. All employees paid under the hourly-rate plan punch in and out on time cards. The time cards are collected at the end of the pay period. The payroll clerk then computes and records on each time card the number of hours worked, the regular earnings, the overtime earnings, and the total gross earnings of the employee. When the time cards are completed, the payroll data is entered in the payroll register.

Name	Ray Harris	Employee No.	2
Week Ending	April 28, 19--		

		Hours	Rate	Earnings
Extra Hours Approved	Regular	40	$ 4.00	$160.00
J. Evans	Overtime	5	$ 6.00	$ 30.00
Supervisor	Total Hours	45	Gross Earnings	$190.00

Time cards provide the hours worked and gross earnings.

PAYROLL REGISTER Page *17*

For the Week Beginning *April 22,* 19 — and Ending *April 28,* 19 — Paid _____ 19 —

	EMPLOYEE DATA				EARNINGS			DEDUCTIONS						NET PAY		
NO.	NAME	MARITAL STATUS	EXEMP.	HOURS	REGULAR	OVERTIME	TOTAL	FEDERAL INCOME TAXES PAYABLE	STATE INCOME TAXES PAYABLE	FICA TAXES PAYABLE	INSURANCE PREMIUMS PAYABLE	UNION DUES PAYABLE	TOTAL	AMOUNT	CK. NO.
1	Paul Alvarez	M	4	40	212 00		212 00	14 10	1 15	14 20	3 00		32 45	179 55	
2	Ray Harris	M	3	45	160 00	30 00	190 00	14 00	1 05	12 73	3 00	2 00	32 78	157 22	
3	David Katz	M	3	40	160 00		160 00	9 20	75	10 72	3 00	2 00	25 67	134 33	
4	Doris Post	S	1	42	160 00	12 00	172 00	22 80	1 12	11 52	3 00	2 00	40 44	131 56	
5	Ruth Sofield	S	1	40	200 00		200 00	29 10	1 40	13 40	3 00	2 00	48 90	151 10	
6	Carl Tripper	M	3	40	200 00		200 00	15 80	1 15	13 40	3 00	2 00	35 35	164 65	
					1,092 00	42 00	1,134 00	105 00	6 62	75 97	18 00	10 00	215 59	918 41	

Pay Period. The beginning and ending dates of the pay period are entered in the space at the top of the payroll register. The Paid line is not yet completed. Although the pay period ends on April 28, the payroll will not be paid until April 30. This time is needed to prepare the payroll. The data for each employee—the number, name, marital status, and withholding exemptions—is entered in the Employee Data section of the payroll register.

Earnings. The total hours, regular earnings, overtime earnings, and total (gross) earnings of each employee are copied from the time card into the Hours column and the Earnings section of the payroll register. The accuracy of this work must be proved. The totals of the regular plus overtime earnings columns must equal the amount of the total earnings columns.

Payroll Deductions. The amounts of the various payroll deductions are recorded in the appropriate columns of the Deductions section. The amount of the federal income tax withholding is entered in the first column. Ray Harris is married and has three income tax exemptions. Thus the withholding tax table for married persons paid weekly is used to determine the amount of his federal income tax ($14.00).

The amount of the state income tax withholding is entered in the second column. The state income tax for Ray Harris is $1.05.

The amount of the FICA tax is recorded in the third column of the Deductions section. It is computed by multiplying the total earnings by the tax rate. (Remember that an employee must pay FICA tax on only the first $29,700 earned in one year.) Since Ray Harris has not earned over $29,700 so far this year, he must still pay FICA tax. The amount ($12.73) is computed by multiplying the FICA tax rate of 6.7 percent by taxable earnings or by referring to the FICA tax table.

Ray Harris also has a deduction of $3 for group insurance premiums and a deduction of $2 for union dues. These amounts are entered in the appropriate columns. Some payroll registers also have an "Other" column.

The amounts of the deductions are then added. The total is entered in the Total column of the Deductions section. The employee's net pay is obtained by subtracting total deductions from total earnings. The total of the deductions for Ray Harris is $32.78. Thus his net pay is $157.22 ($190.00 − $32.78).

Proof of the Payroll Register. After the data for each employee has been entered in the payroll register, the various columns are totaled. The payroll register is then proved by adding and subtracting the column totals across the register. (See the illustration in the margin.) This process is called cross-footing. **Cross-footing** is proving that column totals equal a certain amount.

Proof of Payroll Register		
Earnings:		
Regular	$1,092 00	
Overtime	42 00	
Total		$1,134 00
Deductions:		
Fed. Inc. Tax	$ 105 00	
State Inc. Tax	6 62	
FICA	75 97	
Insurance	18 00	
Union Dues	10 00	
Total		215 59
Net Pay		$ 918 41

Activity A. The time cards for the employees of the Masters Corporation for the week ended November 25 are given in Activity B on page 245. The additional data needed to prepare the payroll is given in Topic Problem 9-1 on page 245 and Topic Problem 9-3 on page 255.

1. Record the payroll data from Topic Problem 9-3 in the payroll register. This data covers the pay period from November 19 to November 25, 19—.

2. Total and prove the payroll register.

NOTE: Save your payroll register for further use in Activity C on page 260 and in Activity D on page 262.

The Employee Earnings Record

B *What information is kept on an employee earnings record?* The details of each employee's earnings and deductions are shown on an employee earnings record. An **employee earnings record** contains cumulative data on earnings and deductions of an individual employee. As stated earlier, by federal law, some form of an earnings record must be kept for each employee for at least four years. This form contains cumulative data on all the earnings and deductions of an employee, as shown in the employee earnings record for Ray Harris. It also contains such information as the employee's number, marital status, and number of federal and state income tax exemptions. The social security number and salary or wage rate are also included.

EMPLOYEE EARNINGS RECORD FOR YEAR 19—

Name _Harris, Ray Thomas_
Address _104 Second Avenue_
Chicago, IL 60612
Telephone No. _555-5360_
Date of Birth _October 1, 1951_
Rate _$4.00 per hour_

Employee No. _2_
Social Security No. _201-26-8341_
Marital Status _Married_
Withholding Exemptions _3_
Position _Driver_
Date Employed _December 1, 1971_

DATE			EARNINGS			DEDUCTIONS							
PERIOD ENDING	PAID	HOURS	REGULAR	OVERTIME	TOTAL	FEDERAL INCOME TAX	STATE INCOME TAX	FICA TAX	INSURANCE PREMIUMS	UNION DUES	TOTAL	NET PAY	YEAR-TO-DATE EARNINGS
4/7	4/9	42	160 00	12 00	172 00	10 70	87	11 52	3 00	2 00	28 09	143 91	2,372 00
4/14	4/16	39	156 00		156 00	7 70	71	10 45	3 00	2 00	23 86	132 14	2,528 00
4/21	4/23	40	160 00		160 00	9 20	75	10 72	3 00	2 00	25 67	134 33	2,688 00
4/28	4/30	45	160 00	30 00	190 00	14 00	1 05	12 73	3 00	2 00	32 78	157 22	2,878 00

The dates for the ending of the pay period and the payment of the payroll are entered in the Date section. (Although the payroll has not been paid yet, the date it is scheduled to be paid is entered.) Note that the employee earnings record has an additional section called *Year-to-Date Earnings* that does not appear in the payroll register. **Year-to-date earnings** are total gross earnings from January 1 to the current date. This column shows the total gross earnings of the employee from the beginning of the year to the current date. The payroll clerk checks this amount before computing the deductions for taxes. The payroll clerk can then easily notice when the employee has earned the maximum amount for FICA and other taxes.

Activity B. Payroll data for five employees of the Top Machine Company is given here. Record this data on employee earnings records.

1. Jim Jackson: address, 144 Elm Street, Abilene, Texas 79601; telephone number, 555-1759; date of birth, May 8, 1942; rate, $269 per week; employee number, 1; social security number, 204–28–8623; marital status, single; withholding exemptions, 4; position, manager; date employed, August 7, 1966; year-to-date earnings, $31,000, which included incentive pay.

2. Tim O'Neal: address, 784 South Third Street, Abilene, Texas 79601; telephone number, 555-3807; date of birth, April 5, 1930; rate, $260 per week; employee number, 2; social security number, 174-91-6532; marital status, single; withholding exemptions, 5; position, supervisor; date employed, May 23, 1967; year-to-date earnings, $29,600, which included incentive pay.

3. Lance Harris: address, 614 Mohawk Ave., Abilene, Texas 79601; telephone number, 555-3605; date of birth, February 14, 1944; rate, $5.95 per hour; employee number, 3; social security number, 204-28-6107; marital status, married; withholding exemptions, 3; position, machinist 3; date employed, March 31 of the current year; year-to-date earnings, $7,300.

4. Lisa Stephens: address, 4 Grove Ct., Abilene, Texas 79601; telephone number, 555-2971; date of birth, August 23, 1956; rate, $6.40 per hour; employee number, 4; social security number, 111-18-7091; marital status, married; withholding exemptions, 2; position, machinist 2; date employed, April 15 of the current year; year-to-date earnings, $6,200.

5. Warren Gomp: address, 391 Terrace St., Abilene, Texas 79601; telephone number, 555-4382; date of birth, October 22, 1950; rate, $7.50 per hour; employee number, 5; social security number, 928-92-2200; marital status, single; withholding exemptions, 1; position, machinist 1; date employed, August 8 of the current year; year-to-date earnings, $2,700.

NOTE: Save your work for further use in Topic Problems 9-4.

Recording the Payroll

C *What information is journalized from the payroll register?* The totals of the payroll register provide the data for journalizing the payroll. The total gross earnings is an expense to the business. Thus the Salaries Expense account is debited for this amount. For example, the Salaries Expense account of the Globe Travel Agency was debited for the total gross earnings of $1,134 on April 28.

The Globe Travel Agency withheld the following from the employees' earnings: federal income taxes, $105.00; state income taxes, $6.62; FICA taxes, $75.97; group insurance premiums, $18; and union dues, $10.

At certain dates, the employer must send the amounts withheld from employees' earnings to the government, the union, and the insurance company. These amounts are liabilities until they are paid. Thus a liability account is credited for each deduction.

Until the payroll is paid, the amount of the net pay is also a liability. Therefore, the total of the Net Pay section of the payroll register is credited to the Salaries Payable account.

The entry to record the payroll for the Globe Travel Agency for the pay period ended April 28 is shown and analyzed on page 260. After this entry is journalized and posted to the ledger, the various liability

Globe Travel Agency Chart of Accounts

Liabilities
221 Federal Income Taxes Payable
222 FICA Taxes Payable
224 Group Insurance Payable
225 Salaries Payable
226 State Income Taxes Payable
228 Union Dues Payable

Costs and Expenses
502 Salaries Expense

accounts show the amount owed to the government, the union, the insurance company and the employees. The total expense is shown in the Salaries Expense account.

April 28: The Globe Travel Agency payroll expense and liabilities for the weekly pay period are recorded.

What Happens	Accounting Rule	Entry
Expense for salaries decreases owner's equity by $1,134.00.	To decrease owner's equity, debit the account.	Debit: Salaries Expense, $1,134.00.
The liability *Federal Income Taxes Payable* increases by $105.00.	To increase a liability, credit the account.	Credit: Federal Income Taxes Payable, $105.00.
The liability *State Income Taxes Payable* increases by $6.62.	To increase a liability, credit the account.	Credit: State Income Taxes Payable. $6.62.
The liability *FICA Taxes Payable* increases by $75.97.	To increase a liability, credit the account.	Credit: FICA Taxes Payable, $75.97.
The liability *Group Insurance Payable* increases by $18.	To increase a liability, credit the account.	Credit: Group Insurance Payable, $18.
The liability *Union Dues Payable* increases by $10.	To increase a liability, credit the account.	Credit: Union Dues Payable, $10.
The liability *Salaries Payable* increases by $918.41.	To increase a liability, credit the account.	Credit: Salaries Payable, $918.41.

Salaries Expense 502	Federal Income Taxes Payable 221	FICA Taxes Payable 222	Group Insurance Payable 224
1,134.00	105.00	75.97	18.00

Salaries Payable 225	State Income Taxes Payable 226	Union Dues Payable 228
918.41	6.62	10.00

Activity C. In Activity A on page 258, you prepared a payroll register for the Masters Corporation. This payroll register covered the pay period from November 19 to November 25. Now record the payroll expense and liabilities in the journal for the Masters Corporation on November 25.

NOTE: Save your working papers for further use in Activity D.

Employer Payroll Taxes

D *Are employers required to pay payroll taxes?* Federal and state laws require employers as well as employees to pay payroll taxes.

Employer FICA Tax. Employers also pay taxes to the social security program. The employer's tax is at the same rate and on the same earnings used to compute the employee's FICA tax (a maximum of $29,700 for each employee). Thus the employer pays a tax equal to the total FICA taxes deducted from the employees' earnings.

The employer's FICA tax on the April 28 payroll of the Globe Travel Agency is found by multiplying the taxable earnings ($1,134) by the tax rate (0.067). Thus the employer's FICA tax in this example is $75.98 ($1,134 × 0.067). The FICA Tax column of the payroll register shows that the total of the employees' FICA taxes is $75.97. (This is illustrated on page 256.) These amounts differ slightly because of rounding the amounts computed for individual employees.

Employer's FICA Tax

Taxable Earnings	×	Rate	=	Tax
$1,134	×	6.7% (0.067)	=	$75.98

Federal Unemployment Compensation Tax. The federal government requires some employers to provide temporary relief (money) for unemployed workers. FUTA requires most employers to pay an unemployment compensation tax for workers who become unemployed. This tax is assessed by the federal government and paid by employers. The maximum FUTA tax is 3.4 percent of the first $6,000 paid to each covered employee during a calendar year. However, the employer may take a credit against this tax of up to 2.7 percent for contributions paid to state unemployment funds. This leaves a 0.7 percent net federal tax. (No table is provided for you to compute the amounts, since the rate changes from time to time. Thus a rate of 0.7 percent is assumed to make computations easier.) The employees do not pay any FUTA tax.

None of the employees of the Globe Travel Agency earned over $6,000 before April 28. Thus the business owes FUTA tax of $7.94 (0.007 × $1,134) on the April 28 payroll.

FUTA Tax

Taxable Earnings	×	Rate	=	Tax
$1,134	×	0.7% (0.007)	=	$7.94

State Unemployment Compensation Tax. Unemployment taxes vary among states. A **state unemployment compensation tax (SUTA)** provides benefits to unemployed workers. In general, most employers are required to pay up to a 2.7 percent tax on the first $6,000 paid to each employee in a calendar year. In most states, employers who provide steady employment may earn a reduction from the maximum rate. This tax is paid by employers, although in some states employees pay this tax also.

$$\begin{array}{rcccl}
 & & \text{Taxable} & & \\
\text{Tax} & = & \text{Earnings} & \times & \text{Rate} \\
\$30.62 & = & \$1,134 & \times & 2.7\% \\
 & & & & (0.027)
\end{array}$$

At the maximum rate, the state unemployment compensation tax on the April 28 payroll of the Globe Travel Agency would be $30.62 ($0.027 \times \$1,134$).

Recording Employer Payroll Taxes

The employer's FICA tax and the federal and state unemployment compensation taxes are expenses to the employer. A separate expense account can be kept for each tax, but usually they are combined. Thus one amount is entered in one expense account, Payroll Taxes Expense. These taxes are liabilities until they are paid. A separate liability account is kept for each tax.

The entry to record the employer's payroll taxes for the Globe Travel Agency for the pay period ended April 28 is analyzed here. The entry to record the employer's payroll taxes expense is made in the journal at the end of each payroll period.

April 28: The Globe Travel Agency payroll taxes on gross earnings of $1,134.00, all of which are taxable, are recorded.

What Happens	Accounting Rule	Entry
Expense for payroll taxes decreases owner's equity by $114.54.	To decrease owner's equity, debit the account.	Debit: Payroll Taxes Expense, $114.54.
The liability *FICA Taxes Payable* increases by $75.98.	To increase a liability, credit the account.	Credit: FICA Taxes Payable, $75.98.
The liability *Federal Unemployment Taxes Payable* increases by $7.94.	To increase a liability, credit the account.	Credit: Federal Unemployment Taxes Payable, $7.94.
The liability *State Unemployment Taxes Payable* increases by $30.62.	To increase a liability, credit the account.	Credit: State Unemployment Taxes Payable, $30.62.

Payroll Taxes Expense 503	FICA Taxes Payable 222	Federal Unemployment Taxes Payable 223	State Unemployment Taxes Payable 227
114.54	75.98	7.94	30.62

Globe Travel Agency Chart of Accounts

Liabilities
223 Federal Unemployment Taxes Payable
227 State Unemployment Taxes Payable

Cost and Expenses
503 Payroll Taxes Expense

Activity D. Use the payroll register you prepared for the Masters Corporation in Activity A on page 258 to do the following.

1. Compute the employer's FICA tax at 6.7 percent. (Because of rounding, this amount may vary slightly from the total withheld from the employees.)

2. Compute the federal unemployment compensation taxes at 0.7 percent. All earnings are taxable.
3. Compute the state unemployment compensation taxes at 2.7 percent. All earnings are taxable.
4. Record the employer's payroll taxes in the journal.
NOTE: Save your working papers for further use in Activity F.

Paying the Payroll

E *What are the procedures for paying the payroll?* Most businesses set regular paydays, such as every Friday. The payday falls a few days after the end of the pay period so that the payroll can be computed and prepared.

Paying by Check. Most businesses prefer to pay their employees by check. This provides the employer with canceled checks as proof that the employees have been paid. It also avoids having a large amount of cash on hand on paydays and sorting the cash into individual pay envelopes.

Businesses usually provide an employee pay statement to each employee. An **employee pay statement** is a summary of earnings and deductions for an employee for a pay period. The statement is frequently given on the stub of a voucher check. The statement may also be separate from the check.

The Globe Travel Agency uses a voucher check that consists of two parts. The lower part is a regular check. The upper part (or voucher part) is kept by the employees as a record of gross earnings, deductions, and net pay for the pay period. As each check is written, the check number is entered in the payroll register to provide an audit trail.

Paid _April 30,_ 19 ___

| | NET PAY | |
TOTAL	AMOUNT	CK. NO.
32 45	179 55	101
32 78	157 22	102
25 67	134 33	103
40 44	131 56	104
48 90	151 10	105
35 35	164 65	106
215 59	918 41	

4/28/--	4/30	45	160.00	30.00	190.00	14.00	1.05	12.73	3.00	2.00		32.78	157.22	102
Period Ending	Date Paid	Hours Worked	Regular	Overtime	Total	Federal Withholding	State Withholding	FICA	Insurance	Union Dues	Other	Total	Amount	Ck. No.
					Earnings				Deductions				Net Pay	

Employee Pay Statement
Detach and retain for your records.

Globe Travel Agency
Chicago, Illinois 60612

- -

Globe Travel Agency
3010 South Fifth Street
Chicago, Illinois 60612

Payroll
Check

2-816
710

No. _____ 102

April 30, _____ 19 --

Pay To
The Order Of   Ray T. Harris--- $ 157.22

One hundred fifty-seven and 22/100-- Dollars

National Bank
Chicago, Illinois 60612

By_ *Mark Nero* _____

⑆0710⑆0816⑆ 5060⑆030700⑈

Voucher is employee pay statement kept by employee.

Check is cashed or deposited by employee.

Paying by Cash. When the payroll is paid in cash, the payroll clerk must determine the number of bills and coins of each denomination needed for each employee's pay envelope. A change sheet is therefore prepared. A **change sheet** is a form which lists the number and net pay for each employee and the number of bills and coins of each denomination needed to make up each employee's pay. The columns are then totaled. A change sheet is shown on page 264.

The totals of the change sheet are summarized on a currency requisition. A **currency requisition** is a form which lists the denomination,

CHANGE SHEET FOR PAYROLL		Date April 30, 19—									CURRENCY REQUISITION		Date 4/30/19—
EMPLOYEE	NET PAY	BILLS				COINS					DENOMI-NATION	QUANTITY	AMOUNT
		$20	$10	$5	$1	50¢	25¢	10¢	5¢	1¢			
1	$179 55	8	1	1	4	1			1		$20	42	$840 00
2	157 22	7	1	1	2		2			2	$10	5	50 00
3	134 33	6	1		4	1			1	3	$ 5	2	10 00
4	131 56	6	1		1	1			1	1	$ 1	16	16 00
5	151 10	7	1		1		1				50¢	3	1 50
6	164 65	8			4	1		1	1		25¢	1	25
											10¢	4	40
											5¢	4	20
											1¢	6	06
TOTALS	$918 41	42	5	2	16	3	1	4	4	6			$918 41

EARNINGS:		Name Ray T. Harris

EARNINGS:
Regular 160.00
Overtime 30.00
Total 190.00

Name Ray T. Harris
Employee No. 2   Hours Worked 45
Period Ending April 28, 19—

DEDUCTIONS:

Federal Income Tax	State Income Tax	FICA Tax	Ins. Prem.	Union Dues	Total
14.00	1.05	12.73	3.00	2.00	32.78

Date Paid April 30, 19—   Net Pay $ 157.22

Employee Pay Statement

quantity, amounts, and total cash needed. A check is then drawn for the total net pay. The check must agree with the total net pay shown in the payroll register. When the check is cashed, the payroll clerk will receive the bills and coins in the denominations needed for the payroll.

When the payroll is paid in cash, the employee pay statement is usually printed on the pay envelope and the employee may be asked to sign some kind of receipt.

Paying by Bank Transfer. Some businesses pay their employees by bank transfer. A **bank transfer** is a method of transferring funds from one account to one or more other accounts. In this method, the employer gives the bank a check for the total net pay and a list showing the net pay for each employee. On payday, the bank deposits the net pay into the employee's bank account. Each employee receives a pay statement showing the amount deposited in his or her account.

Recording the Payment of the Payroll

When the payroll is paid, the total amount of all the payroll checks is entered in the journal. The amounts are posted from the journal to the

April 30: The Globe Travel Agency payment of the April 28 payroll is recorded.

What Happens	Accounting Rule	Entry
The liability *Salaries Payable* decreases by $918.41.	To decrease a liability, debit the account.	Debit: Salaries Payable, $918.41.
The asset *Cash* decreases by $918.41.	To decrease an asset, credit the account.	Credit: Cash, $918.41.

Cash	101		*Salaries Payable*	225
	918.41		918.41	918.41

ledger accounts. The liability Salaries Payable is decreased and the asset Cash is decreased.

Activity E. The net pay for the employees of the Far West Company is given here.
1. Prepare a change sheet for the July 16 payroll.
2. Prepare a currency requisition for the payroll.

3. On July 15 prepare Check 274 payable to the Western National Bank for the amount of the payroll. The balance brought forward on the check stub is $7,824.15.

No.	Net Pay	No.	Net Pay	No.	Net Pay	No.	Net Pay
1	$241.20	3	$158.41	5	$88.74	7	$162.24
2	$184.32	4	$171.25	6	$94.00	8	$135.00

Accounting for Payroll

F *What journal entries are required to record the payroll?* The procedure for recording the payroll requires three sets of entries.

- An entry to record the expense for the payroll and the liabilities to the government, the other agencies, and the employees.
- An entry to record the employer's payroll taxes.
- An entry to record the amount paid to the employees.

The journal entries for the April 28 payroll of the Globe Travel Agency are illustrated at the top of page 266.

The checks to pay the payroll have all been recorded in one amount ($918.41). **Payday** is the date on which the payroll is paid to the employees.

					PAYROLL REGISTER									**Page** *17*	
For the Week Beginning *April 22,* **19 —** **and Ending** *April 28,* **19 —** **Paid** *April 30,* **19 —**															

	EMPLOYEE DATA				EARNINGS			DEDUCTIONS						NET PAY	
NO.	NAME	MARITAL STATUS	EXEMP.	HOURS	REGULAR	OVERTIME	TOTAL	FEDERAL INCOME TAXES PAYABLE	STATE INCOME TAXES PAYABLE	FICA TAXES PAYABLE	INSURANCE PREMIUMS PAYABLE	UNION DUES PAYABLE	TOTAL	AMOUNT	CK. NO.
					1,092 00	42 00	1,134 00	105 00	6 62	75 97	18 00	10 00	215 59	918 41	

DATE	ACCOUNT TITLE AND EXPLANATION	POST. REF.	DEBIT	CREDIT
19— Apr. 28	Salaries Expense	502	1,134 00	
	Federal Income Taxes Payable.	221		105 00
	State Income Taxes Payable	226		6 62
	FICA Taxes Payable.	222		75 97
	Group Insurance Payable	224		18 00
	Union Dues Payable	228		10 00
	Salaries Payable.	225		918 41
	April 28 payroll.			
28	Payroll Taxes Expense	503	114 54	
	FICA Taxes Payable.	222		75 98
	Federal Unemployment Taxes Payable	223		7 94
	State Unemployment Taxes Payable . .	227		30 62
	Employer's taxes on April 28 payroll.			
30	Salaries Payable	225	918 41	
	Cash	101		918 41
	April 28 payroll (Checks 101-106).			

Recorded as of date when payroll period ended.

Recorded as of date when payroll period ended.

Recorded on date payment is made.

It is not necessary to list each check on a separate line because the amounts for the individual checks are listed in the payroll register. Thus only one entry is posted to the Cash account instead of one for each employee. After the entries for the payroll are posted, the ledger accounts affected appear as follows.

Cash   Account No. 101

DATE	EXPLANATION	POST. REF.	DEBIT	CREDIT	BALANCE DEBIT	BALANCE CREDIT
19— Apr. 30		J14	8,989 41	918 41	8,071 00	

Amount of cash paid to employees.

Federal Income Taxes Payable   Account No. 221

DATE	EXPLANATION	POST. REF.	DEBIT	CREDIT	BALANCE DEBIT	BALANCE CREDIT
19— Apr. 28		J14		105 00		105 00

Amount owed to federal government.

FICA Taxes Payable Account No. 222

DATE		EXPLANATION	POST. REF.	DEBIT	CREDIT	BALANCE DEBIT	BALANCE CREDIT
19— Apr.	28	Employees'	J14		75 97		75 97
	28	Employer's	J14		75 98		151 95

Amount owed to federal government.

Federal Unemployment Taxes Payable Account No. 223

DATE		EXPLANATION	POST. REF.	DEBIT	CREDIT	BALANCE DEBIT	BALANCE CREDIT
19— Apr.	28		J14		7 94		7 94

Amount owed to federal government.

Group Insurance Payable Account No. 224

DATE		EXPLANATION	POST. REF.	DEBIT	CREDIT	BALANCE DEBIT	BALANCE CREDIT
19— Apr.	28		J14		18 00		18 00

Amount owed to insurance company.

Salaries Payable Account No. 225

DATE		EXPLANATION	POST. REF.	DEBIT	CREDIT	BALANCE DEBIT	BALANCE CREDIT
19— Apr.	28		J14		918 41		918 41
	30		J14	918 41			— 00

Amount owed to employees.

State Income Taxes Payable   Account No. 226

DATE		EXPLANATION	POST. REF.	DEBIT	CREDIT	BALANCE	
						DEBIT	CREDIT
19— Apr.	28		J14		6 62		6 62

Amount owed to state government.

State Unemployment Taxes Payable   Account No. 227

DATE		EXPLANATION	POST. REF.	DEBIT	CREDIT	BALANCE	
						DEBIT	CREDIT
19— Apr.	28		J14		30 62		30 62

Amount owed to state government.

Union Dues Payable   Account No. 228

DATE		EXPLANATION	POST. REF.	DEBIT	CREDIT	BALANCE	
						DEBIT	CREDIT
19— Apr.	28		J14		10 00		10 00

Amount owed to union.

Salaries Expense   Account No. 502

DATE		EXPLANATION	POST. REF.	DEBIT	CREDIT	BALANCE	
						DEBIT	CREDIT
19— Apr.	28		J14	1134 00		1134 00	

Amount of expense for salaries.

Payroll Taxes Expense   Account No. 503

DATE		EXPLANATION	POST. REF.	DEBIT	CREDIT	BALANCE	
						DEBIT	CREDIT
19— Apr.	28		J14	114 54		114 54	

Amount of expense for payroll taxes.

Activity F. In Activity A on page 258, you prepared the payroll register for the November 27 payroll of the Masters Corp. In Activity C on page 260, you recorded the payroll expense and liabilities in the journal. In Activity D on page 262, you recorded the employer's payroll taxes in the journal.

1. Record the payment of the payroll on November 25 in the journal.
2. Enter the check numbers and date in the payroll register. (Use Checks 419–424.)

General Office Clerk:
DOT 219.362-010. Performs variety of office duties, using knowledge of systems and procedures. May prepare payroll.

Accounting Concepts:
Payroll Records. The employer must maintain adequate *payroll records.*
Collection Agent. The employer acts as a *collection agent* for the government and for others designated by the employee or court.
Tax Records. The employer is accountable to the government and to the employees for all amounts deducted from the employees' wages. The employer, therefore, must maintain adequate records of the amounts deducted.

Topic 3 Problems

9-4. The following data covers the Top Machine Company's payroll for the week beginning October 23 and ending October 29. The payroll will be paid on October 31.
a. Record the payroll in a payroll register. The employee earnings records prepared in Activity B on page 259 show the employee data. Obtain the federal and state income tax deductions from the withholding tables on pages 247, 248, 251, and 253. Compute the FICA tax at 6.7 percent. ($29,700 is the maximum for FICA; the year-to-date earnings are shown on the employee earnings records.) Each employee has a deduction of $2.50 for insurance.
b. Total and prove the payroll register.
c. Using the payroll register, record the data for the pay period ended October 29 in the employee earnings records opened in Activity B of this topic. Compute and record the new year-to-date earnings for each employee.

NOTE: Save your working papers for further use in Topic Problem 9-5.

No.	Name	Hours	Regular Earnings	Overtime Earnings
1	Jim Jackson	40	$269.00	—
2	Tim O'Neal	40	260.00	—
3	Lance Harris	42	238.00	$17.85
4	Lisa Stephens	40	256.00	—
5	Warren Gomp	30	225.00	—

9-5. From the payroll register in Topic Problem 9-4, make the following journal entries.
a. Record the October 29 payroll expense and liabilities in the journal.

b. Compute the FICA taxes at 6.7 percent, and use $29,700 as the maximum taxable earnings. (Remember that none of Jim Jackson's earnings and only part of Tim O'Neal's earnings are taxable.)

c. Compute the federal unemployment compensation taxes at 0.7 percent, and use $6,000 as the maximum taxable earnings.

d. Compute the state unemployment compensation taxes at 2.7 percent, and use $6,000 as the maximum taxable earnings.

e. Record the employer's payroll taxes for the October 29 payroll in the journal.

f. Record the payment of the payroll in the journal on October 31. At the same time, enter the date and check numbers in the payroll register. (Use Checks 515–519.)

The Language of Business

Here are some terms that make up the language of business. Do you know the meaning of each?

employer	salary-commission plan	payroll register
employee	contract of	cross-footing
payroll records	employment	employee earnings
salaries	interstate commerce	record
wages	overtime pay	year-to-date earnings
commissions	overtime rate	state unemployment
payroll	time and a half	compensation tax
gross earnings	time book	(SUTA)
salary plan	time card	employee pay
hourly-rate plan	payroll deduction	statement
incentive plan	federal income tax	change sheet
piece-rate plan	exemption	currency requisition
commission plan	dependent	bank transfer
		payday

Employee's Withholding Allowance Certificate (Form W-4)
Federal Insurance Contributions Act (FICA)
FICA tax
Federal Unemployment Tax Act (FUTA)
FUTA tax
garnishment
state income tax
net pay

Chapter 9   Questions

1. Describe the various pay plans used to pay employees.

2. Mary Santik has weekly gross earnings of $200. Yet her take-home pay is only $150. What causes the difference?

3. Give four examples of payroll deductions required by law, five examples of voluntary deductions, and two examples of union deductions.

4. What data is needed to determine the amount of federal income tax to withhold from an employee's gross earnings?

5. Describe the procedure followed in preparing a payroll.

6. What information does the employee earnings record contain? Why are both a payroll register and an employee earnings record used?

7. Describe the various methods for paying the payroll. What journal entries are made?

8. What is a commonly used source document for recording hours worked and computing an employee's gross earnings?

9. Which source document contains information about an employee's deductions for the year?

10. What is the purpose of each of the three entries to record and pay the payroll? Which accounts are affected?

Chapter 9   Problems

Problems for Chapter 9 are given in the *Working Papers and Chapter Problems for Part 1*. If you are using the workbook, do the problems in the space provided there.

Chapter 9   Management Cases

Wage Increases. Management must decide whether or not a wage increase can be given to the employees. In making this decision, management determines whether the increase will allow the business to continue to price its products competitively. The increase in wages may make it necessary to raise prices so high that the product cannot be sold. If so, the business will soon be bankrupt. On the other hand, the increase in wages may decrease the net income enough so that it is unprofitable for the owner to keep an investment in the business. In this case, the owner will go out of business. Accounting records are used to help make decisions about wages.

9M-1. Adams Disposal Incorporated charges $10 a month for trash and garbage pickup services. The company services 1,500 residences and employs six people. The income statement for the business shows the following information.

Adams Disposal Incorporated Income Statement For the Year Ended December 31, 19—		
Revenues:		
Trash and garbage pickup service . .		180,000 00
Expenses:		
Wages Expense	90,000 00	
Truck Maintenance Expense	7,000 00	
Gas and Oil Expense	45,000 00	
Other Expenses	13,000 00	
Total Expenses		155,000 00
Net Income		25,000 00

In analyzing the costs, the accountant found that current labor costs are 50 percent of the trash service revenues. The employees have now asked for a wage increase that would total $18,000 a year. Upon studying the request, the accountant has determined that one of the following actions must be taken: (1) increase the pickup service fee, or (2) increase the number of residences that the company services without increasing the number of employees.

a. If the same number of residences are serviced, what increase in the pickup service fee is needed to absorb the wage increase? What would be the new trash pickup service fee? What would the percent of this increase be?

b. If the wage increases were granted, the pickup service fee remained the same, and all other operating expenses remained the same, how many additional residences must be serviced by the Adams Disposal Incorporated in order to maintain the same net profit?

c. As energy costs (specifically gas and oil) climb, what effects would a 20 percent increase in these costs have on Adams Disposal Incorporated?

9M-2. The Tiny Transistor Company manufactures computerized transistors. It sells the transistors at $5 each to ABN Corporation, which uses the transistors in manufacturing computers. During the past year, the Tiny Transistor Company produced and sold 85,000 transistors. The cost of goods manufactured includes labor costs of $250,000. The union is asking for a wage increase that would increase labor costs by $37,500, or 15 percent, a year. The income statement for the past year is shown here.

Tiny Transistor Company Income Statement For the Year Ended December 31, 19—		
Sales		425,000 00
Cost of Goods Manufactured		325,000 00
Gross Profit		100,000 00
Operating Expenses		40,000 00
Net Income		60,000 00

a. By approximately how much would the Tiny Transistor Company need to increase the price of its transistors to cover the wage increase and maintain its present net income (assuming that no other costs could be reduced)?

b. The ABN Corporation stated that it would stop purchasing the transistors if the Tiny Transistor Company increased the price. A competing company can supply the transistors at $5 each. Is it possible for the Tiny Transistor Company to grant the wage increase without incurring a net loss?

c. From the net income of $60,000, Clarence Nolan, the owner, should receive $40,000 as an annual salary for managing the company. The remainder of the net income, $20,000, is a return of Nolan's investment of $150,000. Is the current net income too high?

d. In your opinion, what is the maximum wage increase that the company can grant its employees if it can neither increase the selling price of the transistors nor reduce other production costs?

e. If the requested wage increase is granted and the current selling price of $5 is maintained, what must be done to maintain the present net income?

Working Hint

Finding Amounts on a Tax Table. The federal income tax withholding for each employee may be obtained from a tax table. To find the amount of income tax to be withheld, find the point on the table where the row for the employee's wages crosses the column for the number of withholding exemptions claimed. Because of the many rows and columns of figures, it is fairly easy to make an error by reading an amount from the wrong row or the wrong column.

The correct point on a table can easily be located by using a guide. Cut a "reverse" L from cardboard. Use the inside of the guide to locate the amounts. The horizontal edge makes it easy to read down from the number of exemptions. For example, to find the amount of income tax to be withheld from an employee who has wages of $137 and two exemptions, slide the horizontal edge beneath the $135–$140 row and the vertical edge to the 2-column. The amount to be withheld is $15.

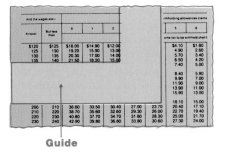

Guide

In a merchandising business, the retailer or store owner buys goods from the wholesaler and sells the merchandise to the customer.

People who use specific forms, procedures, and equipment to process data on cash receipts, cash payments, purchases on credit, sales on credit, or payroll transactions in a merchandising business work in accounting subsystems. As part of the purchases system, the receiving clerk unpacks and verifies the quantity and quality of merchandise received.

Part 2
Accounting Subsystems

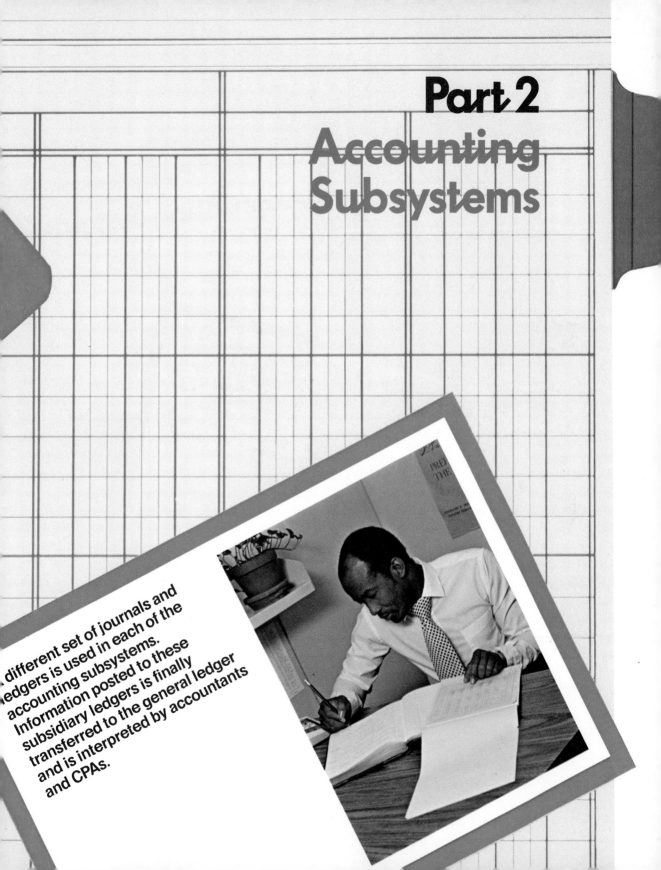

A different set of journals and ledgers is used in each of the accounting subsystems. Information posted to these subsidiary ledgers is finally transferred to the general ledger and is interpreted by accountants and CPAs.

Accounting Systems

The information about the operations of a business should be brief, complete, accurate, current, and relevant to the business decisions that must be made. You will now learn how accounting is used to provide this kind of information.

Accounts Payable Department

Topic 1
Information Processing

A *Do all businesses process data?* Yes, every business must process data to provide information about its operations. The people, forms, procedures, and equipment used to process this data make up that business's **information system.** When the information system is used to provide financial information, it is called an **accounting system.** The accounting system used by a specific business depends on the volume of data to be processed, the time available for processing the data, and the amount of money that can be spent to do so.

Accounting systems are used to provide data. *Data* means unorganized facts. Unorganized facts about business operations are called **business data.** When the data is organized, it is called **business information.** *Processing* means manipulating or handling. Broadly speaking, **information processing** is the manipulation of unorganized facts about operations to obtain organized, useful information.

Types of Accounting Systems

Once it is determined what information (output) is needed, the data (input) required to obtain this information must be located and provided.

There are two types of accounting systems used by businesses to provide financial information: manual and automated. Most businesses use both types of systems to process certain types of data.

Two Types of Accounting Systems
- Manual
- Automated

Manual Accounting Systems. In a **manual accounting system,** most data is processed manually (by hand). In recent years, minor automated devices have been developed to improve the speed and accuracy of manual accounting systems. Among these are forms registers and electronic calculators. These are discussed on pages 284 and 285.

Automated Accounting Systems. In an **automated accounting system,** sometimes referred to as an *electronic accounting system* or *computer accounting system*, data is processed at rapid speeds by computers and other automated equipment. From management's point of view, a major advantage of an automated accounting system is that fewer employees are needed to process data. Computers and other automated devices used to process data are discussed in Chapter 20.

Language
System. In general usage, *system* refers to the method for reaching a goal—providing a supply of money and credit, meeting needs for supply and demand, and providing financial information for decision making. For example, the banking system of the United States is called the Fed-

eral Reserve System. The economic system of the United States is often called the free enterprise system. In accounting usage, *system* refers to the method used to provide financial information.

Accounting Subsystems

Accounting systems vary. The system used depends on the type and size of the business, the nature of its operations, and the external and internal needs for information. No one accounting system fits the needs of every business. The people, forms, procedures, and equipment are tailored to the needs of the business.

In an accounting system there may be a number of subsystems. An **accounting subsystem** is a method used to process specific kinds of data in an accounting system. The number and types of subsystems a business uses depend on the nature of its operations. For example, the operations of a service business are rather simple. Service businesses, such as beauty salons and travel agencies, obtain revenue by charging a fee for performing services. Most transactions tend to be similar to one another. The accounting system does not have to be divided into a number of subsystems to process data about the transactions. However, the operations of a merchandising or a manufacturing business are more complex. Merchandising businesses, such as supermarkets and department stores, obtain revenue by buying finished merchandise at one price and selling it at a greater price. Manufacturing businesses, such as automobile makers and steel makers, buy raw materials, process them into finished goods, and then sell them. The accounting system must be divided into a number of subsystems to process data about the different types of transactions.

You will learn about six accounting subsystems in the chapters that follow. These subsystems are used to process data for the House of Sound for both internal and external uses. The accounting subsystems are cash receipts, cash payments, purchases on credit, sales on credit, personnel and payroll, and general accounting. These six subsystems are listed here along with the journal each uses and the types of transactions each processes.

Accounting Systems

Component	Examples
People	Accountants
	Accounting clerks
	Payroll clerks
Forms	Invoices
	Checks
	Journals
Procedures	Proving petty cash
	Handling cash receipts
	Paying invoices
Equipment	Calculators
	Cash registers
	Computers

Subsystem	Journal	Transactions Recorded
Cash receipts	Cash receipts journal	All receipts of cash
Cash payments	Cash payments journal	All payments of cash
Purchases on credit	Purchases journal	All purchases of merchandise or services on credit
Sales on credit	Sales journal	All sales of merchandise or services on credit
Personnel and Payroll	Payroll journal	All payroll and personnel expenses/liabilities
General accounting	General journal	All remaining transactions

Two other subsystems are described in Part 3. These are the perpetual inventory subsystem and the credit card subsystem.

Activity A. Indicate which accounting subsystem would be used to process each of the following transactions. Refer to the text, margin notes, and illustrations on pages 277 to 279.
EXAMPLE: Purchased equipment on credit— General Accounting
1. Sold merchandise for cash.
2. Paid telephone bill.
3. Recorded closing entries.
4. Owner withdrew money from business.
5. Recorded collections from customers.
6. Paid employees.
7. Sold merchandise on credit.
8. Purchased merchandise on credit.

Establishing Controls in an Accounting System

B *Why are controls needed in an accounting system?* An accounting system must have controls to ensure *accuracy, honesty,* and *efficiency and speed.* These three basic goals are common to all accounting systems. However, more specific controls to ensure these goals are established for processing data through each of the subsystems.

Accounting System Must Contain Controls to Ensure
- Accuracy
- Honesty
- Efficiency and speed

Accuracy. In Part 1, a number of ways to check accounting records for accuracy are discussed. For example, the trial balance and the post-closing trial balance are used to verify that the total of the debit balances agrees with the total of the credit balances in the ledger. The bank reconciliation statement verifies the accuracy of the balance shown on the bank statement against the balance shown in the checkbook.

Honesty. When a number of employees handle cash or other assets of a business, controls must be used to safeguard the assets. One control involves the *division of responsibility* so that one employee's work can be checked against another's work. The employee who handles the asset should not be the same one who keeps the records of the asset. Moreover, special procedures for storing cash and other assets may be required to reduce temptation.

Efficiency and Speed. When employees are required to process accounting data, it is efficient and essential that more than one be able to work on the records at the same time. One way to do this is to use special journals in addition to the general journal. A **special journal** is one that collects data about similar business transactions.

The types of special journals a business uses are related to the types of subsystems it has. The names and styles of the special journals differ with each business. However, the purpose of each special journal remains the same. It provides a day-to-day record of similar transactions. (See the table at the bottom of page 278.)

By using six journals, as many as six accounting clerks can be employed at one time. Each accounting clerk keeps one of the journals and journalizes only those transactions within that area of responsibility. The procedures for using each special journal are explained in later chapters.

Activity B. Answer the following questions about accounting systems and subsystems. Refer to the text, margin notes, and illustrations on pages 279 and 280.
1. What controls must be included in an accounting system?

2. How many special journals are there?
3. How does a special journal increase efficiency and speed?
4. How is cash control helped by division of responsibility?

Some Office Workers Who Deal With Accounting Terms and Concepts
Accounting clerks
Accounts payable clerks
Accounts receivable clerks
Billing clerks
Billing machine operators
Bookkeepers
Bookkeeping machine operators
Computer programmer
Credit clerks
General office clerks
Information specialist
Inventory clerks
Office cashiers
Order clerks
Payroll clerks
Purchasing clerks
Secretaries
Stenographers
Stock control clerks

Components of an Accounting System

C *What are the components (parts) of an accounting system?* The components (parts) of any accounting system are the people, forms, procedures, and equipment needed to process data and provide information. These components are described in this topic.

People

The most important part of an accounting system is the people who do the work. An accounting system can be effective only if accounting personnel are qualified to process and interpret financial information. It is also important for accounting employees to perform their duties accurately and completely, with speed and efficiency. Some of the titles of people who work with accounting information are listed in the margin.

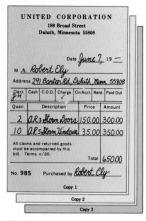

Multicopy Form

Forms

Forms are used in an accounting system to process data. A *business form* is a printed piece of paper that provides blank spaces for entering data. For example, invoices, sales slips, and tax returns are business forms. Business forms are used to assist in processing data, including accounting data. Properly designed business forms should assist the processing of data in the following ways.

• Provide blank spaces for recording the specific data required for processing.
• Provide for certain data to be preprinted.
• Provide for the data to be entered in a standard manner so that it can be easily recognized.
• Provide for the preparation of multiple copies.

Business forms may be loose forms, in which case a single sheet is used for recording data. When several copies are needed, carbon paper may be inserted between the sheets. But time can be saved by using one of the multicopy forms shown on page 282. Among these are one-time carbons, carbonless paper (NCR—No Carbon Required), or copies made on a copying machine.

Computerized Business Forms. Other types of business forms include punched cards and microforms. Punched cards are used as checks, monthly statements, and time cards. An example of a punched card used for these purposes is shown on page 282.

Microforms (microfilm) are documents in a much-reduced size. Microforms include microfiche, reels, aperture cards, and cartridges. Microforms represent an efficient way of processing, storing, and retrieving information. Large amounts of information can be stored in very little space by using microimages. For example, a page of a book is reduced to a size too small to be read without being magnified.

Paper Copier

The type of microform used to process data depends on the kind of information to be stored and how it is to be used. Microforms can be used to store information about customer accounts, payroll records, and banking records. The procedure using computers and microfilm to store information is called **computer-output-microfilm (COM).** One reason businesses use COM procedures is to reduce the space required for storing business forms. For instance, one $\frac{1}{2}$-inch (1.75-centimeter) stack of microfiche may contain as much information as is recorded on fourteen thousand $8\frac{1}{2}$- by 11-inch (21.75- by 27.5-centimeter) pages. As the use of COM procedures becomes widespread, the business office of the future may become a paperless office. A **paperless office** is an office that uses electronic technology to reduce the quantity of actual paperwork handled manually.

Procedures

Accounting procedures are the operations that must be performed, either manually or automated, to process information through the accounting system. An example of a manual procedure is the preparation of a deposit ticket. A deposit ticket is completed by an accounting clerk who writes the necessary information in the spaces provided. Two accounting procedures that have been automated in many businesses are point-of-sale (POS) and electronic funds transfer (EFT) procedures.

Microforms

Point of Sale. Procedures for capturing needed sales data and inventory data as merchandise is sold are called **point-of-sale (POS) procedures.** Many retail businesses, such as department stores and grocery stores, capture this data by using an electronic cash register equipped with an optical scanning device. Information recorded by the optical

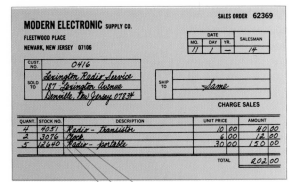

Manually processed data can be transferred to punched cards to be processed electronically.

Padded Multiple Forms. Sets of identical forms are placed in pads. The sets are glued together at the top or side.

Carbon may or may not be interleaved between the forms. Usually, however, carbon must be inserted by hand between the forms as each set is used.

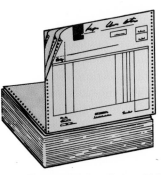

Continuous Forms. Sets of identical forms are printed on continuous strips with perforations separating each set of forms. Thus these forms are similar to the unit sets except that the bottom of each set is attached to the following set.

Carbon may or may not be interleaved between the continuous forms. The forms without carbons are generally used in a machine having a "floating carbon," which remains fixed as the forms are moved around the carbon.

Unit-Set Forms. Two or more copies are fastened together to make a single set of forms. The forms are perforated with a stub at the top, bottom, or either side. Copies may be removed easily without tearing the copies.

Usually, carbon paper is fastened to the stub. This type of form is frequently referred to as a "snap-out" form. (This can be NCR paper.)

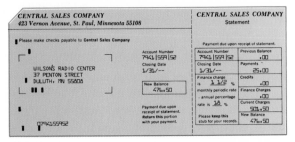

Punched card used as a statement of account.

scanner at the point of sale may include the price, size, color, style, sales department, and item number. This data is often stored on a tape cassette and later processed by computer.

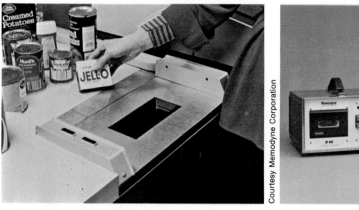

Courtesy Food Marketing Institute

Point of Sale. Electronic cash register with optical scanning device.

Courtesy Memodyne Corporation

Data Collector. Sales and inventory data recorded at point of sale on cassette tape.

Electronic Funds Transfer. Some businesses use bank transfer procedures to pay their employees. In this method the employer gives the bank a check for the total net pay and a list showing the net pay for each employee. On payday, the bank deposits the net pay for each employee into the employee's bank account. Each employee receives an employee pay statement showing the amount deposited in his or her account. When the bank uses a computer to deposit the net pay into each employee's account, the procedure is called **electronic funds transfer (EFT).**

4/28/--	4/30	45	160.00	30.00	190.00	19.30		11.12	3.00	2.00		35.42	154.58	217-48
Period Ending	Date Paid	Hours Worked	Regular	Overtime	Total	Federal Withholding	State Withholding	FICA	Insurance	Union Dues	Other	Total	Amount	Ck. No.
				Earnings				Deductions					Net Pay	
Employee Pay Statement										**Office Service Center** Portland, Oregon 97223				

Employee pay statement kept by employee.

Bank transfer procedures may also be used by retail stores in collecting accounts receivable. In this instance the customer instructs the bank to transfer the monthly payment from his or her bank account to the retail store's bank account. Again, the bank may make the transfer of funds by using a computer. This type of bank transfer eliminates the need for the customer to write a check.

Equipment

Equipment is another important accounting component. Equipment is an extremely important component of both manual and automated accounting systems. In both systems, equipment is used to increase the speed and efficiency of the employees who process and store information.

Recording Devices. Recording devices, such as forms registers, are used to record data manually. These devices aid in the recording of data at the time a transaction occurs. A **forms register** holds continuous forms in a metal box. The perforated forms are folded in a stack inside the register. After a form is completed, a new form is moved into position by pulling out the old form, by turning a hand crank, or by pressing an electronic motor button. The completed form is then detached at the perforation. Multiple copies are made by writing on forms which move across a carbon fixed within the register. One recording device used in automated accounting systems is the electronic cash register, shown on page 283.

Storage Devices. Some data is stored for a temporary period of time until it is needed. Other data is stored for years. Illustrations and brief descriptions of devices used to store data in manual and automated accounting systems are shown here and on the next page.

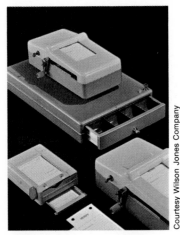

Courtesy Wilson Jones Company

Forms registers save time because the forms are positioned for use; the carbons do not have to be handled or the forms arranged. They provide a control over the use of the forms since one copy of each form usually remains locked inside the register as a record of the transactions.

Courtesy Acme Visible Records, Inc.

Vertical Shelf Files. Materials are filed on edge in a vertical position in folders on open shelves.

Courtesy Eastman Kodak Company

Film Magazines. One type of storage device for microfilm is the film magazine. Approximately 25,800 $8\frac{1}{2}'' \times 11''$ documents can be stored on one magazine. A cabinet holding 360 magazines can store 9 million documents.

Tape Library. Data processed by computers may be stored on reels of magnetic tape. Data stored on magnetic tape for a long period of time is kept in a tape library.

Courtesy 3M Company

Courtesy Wilson Jones Company

Diskettes. Diskettes (sometimes called *floppies*) are magnetic disks used as the input medium for smaller computers. Diskettes are used in place of punched cards. One diskette can hold almost as much input data as 3,000 punched cards. Each reusable diskette is sealed in an 8-inch square envelope for easier handling and weighs less than 2 ounces.

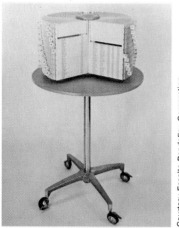

Rotary Files. Items to be stored are placed on a rotating wheel. Thus all records can be retrieved quickly.

Vertical Filing Cabinets. Materials are filed on edge in a vertical position in drawers.

Visual Record Files. Part of each record is always visible. Thus records can be retrieved quickly for updating or for reference.

Computing Devices. The calculator is probably the equipment most often used by accounting clerks and accountants in both manual and automated accounting systems. Calculators can be used for multiplication and division as well as addition, subtraction, and percentages. Three types of calculators are the electronic desk calculator, the electronic programmable printer, and the electronic hand-held calculator.

The electronic desk calculator uses electronic circuits in place of mechanical gears. In the model shown here, the answer is displayed in lighted numbers above the keyboard. It is also equipped with a voice unit that can call out entered data. There are no moving parts in an electronic calculator, and thus the computations are performed almost instantly. Electronic calculators may have storage devices in which data can be stored for future computations. Some models are listing machines. These calculators provide a paper tape containing the results.

The electronic programmable printer is an example of the listing calculator. However, the major feature of the equipment is that complete operations, such as payroll computations, can be performed automatically. This is made possible by inserting a magnetic program card into the calculator, which instructs the calculator to perform the necessary payroll computations.

The electronic hand-held calculators are available in listing and nonlisting models. These small calculators can perform simple arithmetic as well as complex mathematics. Some models are also programmable.

Electronic desk calculator equipped with a voice unit. The voice unit can be used to verify (call out) data entered into the calculator.

Electronic Hand-Held Calculator

Computers. Computers are electronic devices that come in different sizes with varying capacities for processing data. These electronic devices are very useful in performing routine accounting procedures, such as journalizing and posting. A picture of a microcomputer is shown here. Other computers and electronic devices are discussed in Chapter 20.

Courtesy The Radio Shack Division of Tandy Corporation

Microcomputer for use in schools, homes, and small business.

Activity C-1. Search your local newspapers for classified ads asking for people with a background in accounting. Make a list of the jobs available that require a knowledge of accounting. Also note the types of businesses that hire people trained in accounting.

Activity C-2. Answer the following questions about business forms. Refer to the text, margin notes, and illustrations on pages 280 to 282.

1. How do business forms assist in processing data?
2. What are some of the ways to produce multicopied business forms?
3. What is NCR paper used for?
4. Give at least two examples of punched cards being used for business forms.
5. Give at least two examples of microforms.
6. What is the advantage of COM?
7. How much information might be stored on a one-half-inch stack of microfiche?

Activity C-3. Answer the following questions about accounting procedures. Refer to the text, margin notes, and illustrations on pages 281 to 283.

1. Give an example of a procedure.

2. What types of businesses might use electronic cash registers to capture data at the point of sale?
3. What kinds of information may be processed by using an optical scanner attached to an electronic cash register?
4. How do some businesses use bank transfers to pay their employees?
5. What is the procedure called when banks use computers to transfer funds from one bank account to another?
6. How is work done in a paperless office?

Activity C-4. Answer the following questions about equipment used in accounting systems. Refer to the text, margin notes, and illustrations on pages 284 to 286.

1. How does a forms register save time in processing data?
2. List four storage devices and explain how each is used to store information.
3. Which computing device is most often used by accounting clerks and accountants?
4. Name and describe three types of electronic calculators.
5. For which routine accounting procedures are computers used?

Accounting Concepts:

Control. Procedures must be established to ensure accuracy, honesty, and efficiency and speed in handling and recording assets, liabilities, owner's equity, revenues, and expenses.

Accounting System. An *accounting system* is the method a business uses to provide information about its financial operations. An accounting system is made up of people, forms, procedures, and equipment.

Topic 1 Problem

10-1. For each job listed here, identify a form, procedure, and a piece of equipment that may be used by the individual performing the accounting duty. You may want to refer to the classified advertisements in your local newspaper. Use a form like the one shown below.

People	Form	Procedure	Equipment
EXAMPLE: Full-charge bookkeeper	**General journal**	**Recording**	**Pen**

a. Inventory clerk
b. Salesclerk
c. Accounts receivable clerk
d. Accounts payable clerk

e. Payroll clerk
f. Cashier
g. Bank teller
h. Executive secretary bookkeeper

Topic 2
Visualizing the Accounting System

A *How do flowcharts help one to visualize the accounting system?* A flowchart is often used in business to show the flow of data within a system or to show the sequence of operations needed to perform a procedure. A **flowchart** is a diagram that shows graphically the documents used to record the data, the direction in which the data and documents flow, all the operations required to perform the procedure, the relationships among the operations and procedures, and the sequence in which the operations are performed.

Two terms commonly used in flowcharts are *input data* and *output data*. Input data is the data entered into a system or procedure for processing. The information that comes out is known as output data.

In the accounting cycle, the input data comes from transactions and is recorded on source documents (sales slips, invoices, and so on). The output data is information about the results of business operations. This information is provided through such statements as the trial balance, the income statement, the balance sheet, and the postclosing trial balance. An accounting system takes input data from transactions, processes the data, and provides the desired output data to be used in making decisions.

Block Flowcharts. The simplest flowchart to draw is a block flowchart. In a **block flowchart,** a block is drawn for each operation in a procedure or for each procedure in a system. A brief description of each operation or procedure is written inside the block. The blocks are then connected by arrows to show the direction of flow. A block flowchart describing the various steps in the accounting cycle is shown in the margin.

Symbolic Flowcharts. A **symbolic flowchart** uses symbols to represent procedures or operations. The symbols are connected by arrows and may have a brief description written inside them. Symbols have several advantages. For example, they are easy to draw, and they can be standardized to mean the same thing in any flowchart.

The shape of each symbol helps to identify and communicate its meaning. Highway and traffic signs are examples of how valuable symbols are. For example, an eight-sided traffic sign always means *stop*.

The basic symbols used in flowcharts of accounting procedures in this text are shown here.

- The **input symbol** indicates the data that is to be processed or the source of the data that is to be processed.

- The **process symbol** indicates that an operation must be performed.

- The **direction-of-flow symbol** connects the other symbols and shows the direction of flow.

- The **record book symbol** indicates a book of entries, such as a journal or ledger.

- The **decision symbol** indicates that a decision must be made.

- The **document symbol** indicates that information is to appear on a paper document, such as a business form or a statement.

- The **manual operation symbol** indicates that an operation is done by hand.

- The **output symbol** indicates the information provided by the processing. Note that the input and output symbols are the same. Frequently, the symbol of the object produced is used for the output rather than the output symbol. For example, the document symbol can be used for a postclosing trial balance even though the postclosing trial balance is the output in a procedure.

The various flowchart symbols are available on a **template,** which is a pattern of the symbols. A template is helpful in preparing a flowchart because the symbols can be traced. Templates may vary, however, depending on the manufacturer. In an attempt to have standard flowchart symbols, the American National Standards Institute has approved a series of basic symbols. A standard symbol may be adapted if an appropriate symbol is not already available for an operation.

The eight steps of the accounting cycle are illustrated by the symbolic flowchart on pages 290 and 291. To read the flowchart, start at the top and follow the direction of the arrows. The input symbol is used to identify the source of the data, which is transactions. The document symbol is used to identify a variety of documents. The caption inside the symbol—source documents, trial balance, income statement, balance sheet, or postclosing trial balance—tells which document is meant. The process symbol is always used if some operation is to be performed—recording, posting, proving, preparing, balancing, ruling, or interpreting. The last output data from the accounting cycle is the postclosing trial balance. Since this is a document, the document symbol has been used rather than the output symbol.

Flowcharts are usually drawn so that they can be read from top to bottom and from left to right. Arrowheads are not always used, but they are used in the flowcharts in this text to help make the flow easier to read. Symbolic flowcharts like this one will be used throughout this text to show the steps in processing data.

Activity A. Answer the following questions about flowcharts. Refer to the symbolic flowcharts shown on pages 290 and 291.
1. What is the source of the input data?
2. What is the first operation that is performed?
3. What record book is prepared in the second operation?
4. What is the third operation that is performed?
5. What document is prepared in the fourth operation?
6. What documents are prepared in the fifth operation?
7. From what document is the data obtained for preparing the financial statements?
8. From what document is the data obtained for journalizing the closing entries?
9. What is the last operation that is performed?
10. What documents are illustrated?
11. What record books are illustrated?

Types of Flowcharts Used in Business

B *What flowcharts are used in a business?* Two basic flowcharts are used in business—system flowcharts and procedure flowcharts.

System Flowcharts. A **system flowchart** describes the procedures and the flow of data and documents through all parts of a system with little emphasis on detail. It shows what data is entered into the system, how the data is moved and processed through the system, and what output data is produced. A system flowchart presents a broad overview

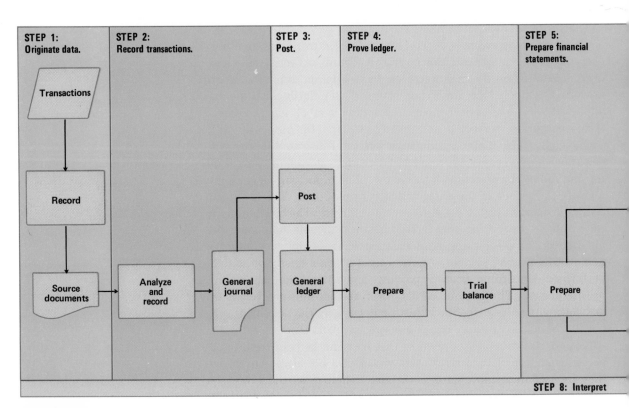

STEP 1: Originate data.	STEP 2: Record transactions.	STEP 3: Post.	STEP 4: Prove ledger.	STEP 5: Prepare financial statements.

STEP 8: Interpret

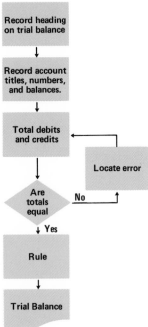

Procedure for preparing a trial balance.

of what happens within a system. The flowchart of the accounting cycle presented above and on the next page is a system flowchart. It shows the input data entering the accounting subsystems from transactions. It shows the path and sequence followed in processing the data through the accounting cycle. It also shows the output which is in the form of completed statements and other reports.

Procedure Flowcharts. A **procedure flowchart** describes the actual operations performed for a procedure and can have any degree of detail. (When a computer is used, a procedure flowchart is referred to as a *program flowchart*.) A procedure flowchart emphasizes the actual operations performed. To see how system and procedure flowcharts differ, refer to the system flowchart of the accounting cycle shown above and on the next page. The flowchart shows Step 4 as proving the ledger, but there is no description of how to prepare the trial balance that is used in proving the ledger. The procedure flowchart in the margin, however, illustrates the procedure for preparing a trial balance. Note that this flowchart shows all the operations performed, the sequence in which they are performed, and the document produced. To read the flowchart, start at the top and follow the direction of the arrows. The first process is to record the heading on the trial balance.

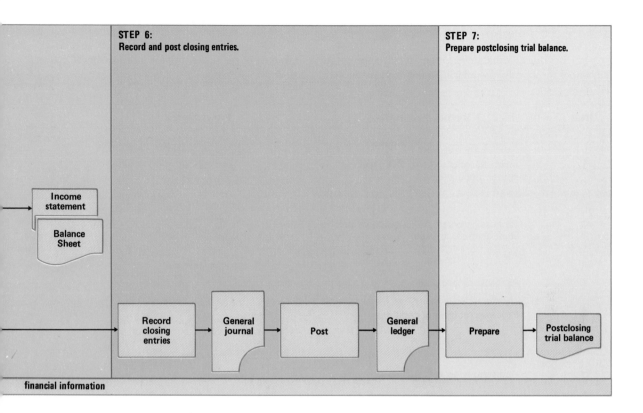

STEP 6:
Record and post closing entries.

STEP 7:
Prepare postclosing trial balance.

Income statement

Balance Sheet

Record closing entries → General journal → Post → General ledger → Prepare → Postclosing trial balance

financial information

The second process is to record the title of each account found in the general ledger. This process also involves recording the account number and balance of each account. (Accounts with no balances may be omitted from the trial balance.) The third process is to add the debits and the credits.

After the debit and credit columns are added, a decision is needed before the trial balance is completed: Do total debits equal total credits? If they do not, the error must be located before the trial balance is ruled. If they do, follow the arrow labeled "Yes." The result of this procedure is the completed trial balance. Note that the document symbol is used rather than the output symbol.

Activity B. Answer these questions about the procedures flowchart on page 290.
1. What is the first operation that is performed?
2. What is the second operation that is performed?
3. What is the third operation that is performed?

4. What is the decision that must be made?
5. If the answer to the decision is "Yes," what operation is performed?
6. If the answer to the decision is "No," what operation is performed? What is the first output?

Accounting Concept:
Flow of Information. Successful businesses establish procedures to ensure a continuous *flow of information* about business operations.

Topic 2 Problems

10-2. Provide a verbal description and an appropriate symbol for each of the missing steps in this symbolic flowchart of the procedure for journalizing illustrated below.

Step	Verbal Description	Flowchart
1	Input: transaction data taken from source documents.	Source Documents
2	Process: analyze the data and determine what account to debit.	Determine debit entry
3	Process: record date.	
4	Process: record the debit entry.	
5		
6		Is explanation needed? (Yes / No)
7	Decision: is an explanation needed?	
8		
9	Output: completed journal entry.	

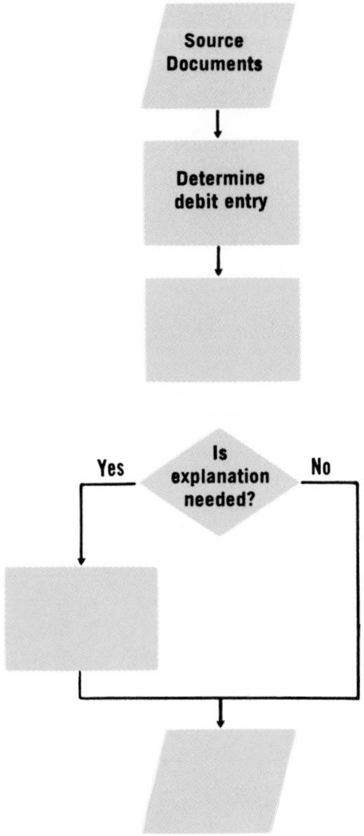

10-3. Prepare an eight-step symbolic flowchart showing the procedure for posting. The verbal descriptions for Steps 1, 2, 3, 4, 7, and 8 are listed in the table shown below.

Step	Verbal Description
1	Input: journal entry to be posted.
2	Process: locate ledger account for entry to be posted.
3	Decision: is the account to be debited?
4	Process: record the date, an explanation if needed, the journal page number, and the amount on the correct side of the account.
7	Output: journal entries posted.
8	Output: updated ledger.

The Language of Business

Here are some terms that make up the language of business. Do you know the meaning of each?

information system
accounting system
business data
business information
information processing
manual accounting
 system
automated accounting
 system

accounting subsystem
special journal
business form
microforms
computer-output-
 microfilm (COM)
paperless office
accounting procedures

point-of-sale (POS)
 procedures
electronic funds
 transfer (EFT)
forms register
flowchart
block flowchart
symbolic flowchart
input symbol
process symbol

direction-of-flow
 symbol
record book symbol
decision symbol
document symbol
manual operation
 symbol
output symbol
template
system flowchart
procedure flowchart

Chapter 10   Questions

1. What are some of the reasons that accounting systems vary?

2. What determines the number and types of subsystems a business uses?

3. Why do merchandising or manufacturing businesses use more accounting subsystems than a service business?

4. What are the components of an accounting system?

5. Name and describe the two types of accounting systems.

6. Name six major accounting subsystems used in many businesses, the journal used, and the type of transactions recorded in each subsystem.

7. List and explain the three basic goals for controls needed for an accounting system.

8. How do properly designed forms make information processing easier?

9. Give examples of POS and EFT procedures.

10. Select a business in your community that you visit regularly. Develop a list of the people, forms, and equipment used in the business's accounting system. Where possible, describe the procedures used by one of the people to process accounting information.

Chapter 10   Problems

Problems for Chapter 10 are given in the *Working Papers and Chapter Problems for Part 2.* If you are using the workbook, do the problems in the space provided there.

Chapter 10   Management Cases

Designing Accounting Systems. Accounting systems are designed to provide the information needed for making business decisions. When an accounting system is being designed, consideration must be given to the need for specific types of information. Thus the people who use the information should be involved in designing and evaluating accounting systems. Careful consideration must also be given to the need for special people, forms, procedures, and equipment. A well-designed system is one that provides people with needed information quickly, accurately, and at the least cost.

Case 10M-1. A business club has just been formed at your school, and you have been elected treasurer. Part of your responsibility will be to keep a record of the club's financial transactions and to make a treasurer's report at each meeting. Major sources of revenue for the club will be fund-raising activities, such as bake sales and car washes. Major expenditures will include financing club projects and school parties and sending representatives to state leadership conferences.

a. What kinds of forms will you need in order to keep a financial record of the club's activities?

b. What procedures will be used for controlling cash receipts and cash payments?

c. Will you need to use any equipment in preparing your treasurer's reports? List any equipment needed to prepare the reports.

d. Other than yourself, who should be involved in designing an accounting system for the business club at your school?

Case 10M-2. Harold Rose is the pharmacist and owner of the Town and Country Apothecary. In addition to filling prescriptions for his customers, Mr. Rose maintains complete records on all prescriptions filled, as required by law. He also keeps a history of prescriptions used by his regular customers. The purpose of the customer history is to make sure that each customer is following the doctor's instructions for using the medicine. The history also lets Mr. Rose determine whether the customer is allergic to certain types of medicines. However, Mr. Rose is finding it difficult to process manually all the data needed for the prescription records and histories and to bill his customers.

a. Do you believe Mr. Rose could use a microcomputer to process the data needed for the customer records and histories? Explain.

b. In what other ways could Mr. Rose use a microcomputer in his drugstore?

Working Hint

Preparing a Flowchart Template. On a heavy piece of cardboard, draw the design of each of the basic symbols you will use: input/output, process, decision, direction-of-flow, record book, and document. Then draw the designs of the eight additional symbols that are shown here: terminal, storage, com- munication, paper tape, punched tape, punched card, magnetic tape, manual, and physical asset. Cut the designs out of the cardboard, using a razor blade or a sharp knife. You can then trace the outline for a symbol by running a pencil around the edges of the opening.

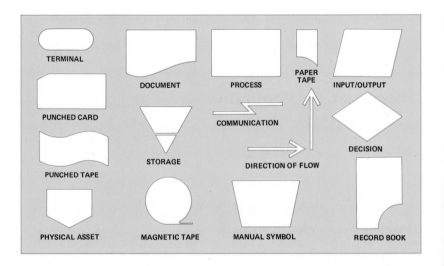

Chapter II

A Cash Receipts Subsystem

You will now learn how the people, forms, procedures, and equipment in a cash receipts subsystem are used to control cash receipts. You will also learn about the important work of the cashier in the cash receipts subsystem.

Topic 1
Controlling Cash Receipts

People, forms, procedures, and equipment are needed to process cash receipts.

A *What is a cash receipts subsystem?* The people, forms, procedures, and equipment used to process cash receipts make up a **cash receipts subsystem.** The employee who processes cash receipts receives cash, pays cash, and records the transactions on source documents is the **cashier.** There are two primary activities completed in any cash receipts subsystem. First, cash is received from customers, recorded on source documents, and proved. This activity is known as **handling cash receipts.** Second, the amounts of cash handled are journalized and posted in the accounting records. This activity is known as **recording cash receipts.** Each activity—handling and recording cash receipts—is controlled by a set of procedures. These are the procedures for the control of cash receipts. The employee who keeps the cash receipts section of the financial records is the cash receipts bookkeeper.

Procedures for Controlling Cash Receipts

The procedures for the control of cash receipts are as follows.

Control: Create source documents.
Control: Use prenumbered source documents.
Control: Prove cash frequently.
Control: Deposit all cash receipts intact.
Control: Divide responsibility.

- Source documents must be created.
- These source documents must be prenumbered.
- Cash must be proved frequently.
- All cash receipts must be deposited intact.
- The responsibilities for handling and recording cash receipts must be divided.

Creating Source Documents. When cash is received, a cashier prepares the necessary source documents to record the transaction. These source documents should mention the amount of cash, the date, why cash was received, who received the cash, and, in some cases, from whom cash was received. The source documents commonly used to record cash receipts are: cash register tapes, prenumbered sales slips, and prenumbered remittance slips.

Cash Register Tapes. A cashier usually uses a cash register to record the amount of cash received when goods or services are sold. The prices of items are entered and totaled in the cash register. The amounts are also displayed at the top of the machine, usually on a tape, as a control of the cashier's accuracy and honesty. The customer can then check the amounts entered with the price of each item. In addition, a permanent record of each cash receipt is often made on a **cash register tape,** a source document produced on a cash register.

Two copies of the tape are created. One copy is removed from the cash register and given to the customer as a receipt. A second stays in the register until it is removed and used as a source document.

Sales Slips. A **sales slip** is a source document which may also be used to record the receipt of cash. An original sales slip and one or more copies are prepared. One copy is given to the accounting department as a source document describing the sale. Another is given to the customer as a receipt. A third copy, if prepared, is kept as the record of all transactions the cashier handles.

Sales slips can be used instead of a cash register tape. There are also times when both a cash register tape and sales slips are used. A cash register tape does not include the customer's name and address. Thus a sales slip or some other receipt is used whenever names and addresses must be recorded.

In some accounting systems, prenumbered sales slips are filed in a forms register rather than in a sales book. Forms registers come with or without cash drawers. When a forms register is used, at least two copies of the sales slip are also prepared. One copy is removed from the register and given to the customer. The other copy remains locked inside the register until removed.

Remittance Slips. Checks and money orders are often received by mail. The employee who opens the mail must record the transaction. A remittance slip is the source document used to record this transaction. A **remittance slip** is used to record the amount of cash received from each customer. Completed remittance slips become source documents and are then sent to the accounting department. For control purposes, the remittance slips are prenumbered. A prenumbered remittance slip is shown in the margin.

Using Prenumbered Source Documents. A form that is numbered when printed is a **prenumbered source document.** All source documents should be prenumbered. This makes it possible to keep track of the forms used. Voided forms should be kept on file in numeric sequence to account for each form.

Prenumbered sales slips and remittance slips also provide a control for cash receipts transactions. Once either has been filled out, it is impossible to hide the fact that a transaction took place. A salesclerk must account for any slips missing from the numeric sequence.

Proving Cash. The amount of cash received should be proved frequently, usually at the end of each day. A supervisor (rather than the employee who prepares the source documents) should verify that the count of cash agrees with the total of the cash receipts recorded on the source documents. Both cash register tapes and sales slips are used in proving cash.

Cash Register Tapes. When a cash register is used, the amount of cash in the drawer at the end of the day should equal the following.

Sales slip used as receipt.

Courtesy Wilson Jones Company

Forms register with cash drawer.

Remittance Slip

- The amount of the **change fund** (the amount of cash put in the drawer to make change), plus
- The total cash sales recorded on the cash register tape, plus
- The total cash received on account from customers, less
- Any money paid out of the drawer. Usually, the only cash taken out of the drawer is the correct change given to customers. (The exception is when a customer returns goods bought for cash and wants a cash refund. The clerk must then record the amount on the cash register tape and take the cash refund from the cash drawer.)

The cash proof illustrated on the next page shows how the supervisor verifies the receipts, refunds, and change fund handled by the clerk. The cash register tape for August 3 shows that total receipts from cash sales (TCa) amounted to $180. The total cash received on account from customers (TRe) was $150. The total cash receipts (TCr) for August 3, therefore, is $330. The tape also shows that a total of $2 was paid out (TPd). The $2 must be subtracted to determine the net cash receipts for the day ($328). The supervisor counts the actual cash in the drawer ($353). The change fund ($25) is subtracted to arrive at the net cash handled ($328). The $328 agrees with the net cash receipts ($330 − $2) computed from the cash register tape.

Sales Slips. Preparing a cash proof is the next procedure followed when sales slips are used to record cash receipts. The supervisor first arranges the sales slips in numeric order (see the illustration in the margin) and makes sure that no slips are missing. A missing slip suggests that a transaction was not recorded and cash was mishandled. But the salesclerk may have an explanation for the missing slip. The supervisor then computes the total *cash sales* for the day by adding the cash sales slips on an adding machine or other calculator. The supervisor goes through the sales slips a second time and computes the total cash received on account from customers. The two totals are then added to find the total cash receipts for the day. (If cash was paid out, the supervisor would go through the sales slips a third time to find the total amount paid out. The cash paid out would be subtracted from the total cash received.)

The supervisor then counts the cash in the cash drawer and subtracts the amount of the change fund. The net amount of cash in the drawer should equal the total cash receipts recorded on the sales slips.

Remittance Slips. The cash proof is rather easy when remittance slips are used to record cash received through the mail. The total amount on the remittance slips is compared with the total amount of cash in the cash drawer. No change fund is necessary. As with sales slips, the prenumbering of remittance slips makes it easy to see if any slip is missing.

Cash proof for sales slips.

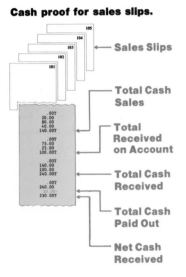

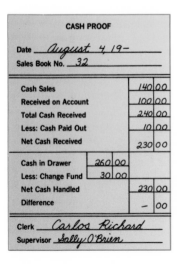

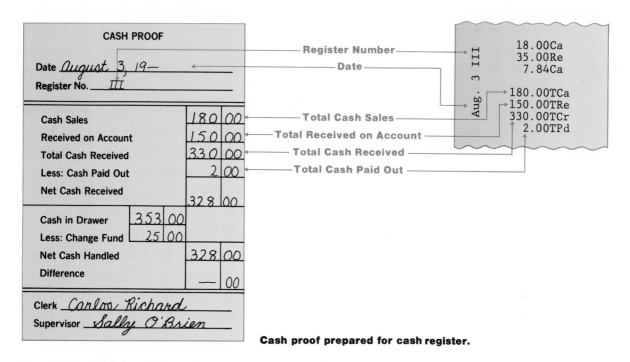

CASH PROOF			
Date August 3, 19—			
Register No. III			
Cash Sales	180	00	
Received on Account	150	00	
Total Cash Received	330	00	
Less: Cash Paid Out	2	00	
Net Cash Received			328 00
Cash in Drawer	353 00		
Less: Change Fund	25 00		
Net Cash Handled			328 00
Difference			— 00
Clerk Carlos Richard			
Supervisor Sally O'Brien			

Register Number

Date

Total Cash Sales

Total Received on Account

Total Cash Received

Total Cash Paid Out

```
        18.00Ca
III     35.00Re
         7.84Ca
  3
 Aug.  180.00TCa
       150.00TRe
       330.00TCr
         2.00TPd
```

Cash proof prepared for cash register.

Depositing All Cash Receipts Intact. All cash receipts should be deposited intact in the bank. Thus the business gains one more check on the accuracy of its cash procedures. The total bank deposits should always equal the total cash receipts.

Dividing the Responsibility. An important cash control procedure is to separate the handling of cash receipts from the recording of cash receipts. It is sometimes difficult, particularly in small businesses, to separate cash receipts procedures. But the best procedure for control, whether the business is large or small, is as follows.

Separate the handling of cash receipts from the recording of cash receipts to ensure proper controlling of cash receipts.

• The employee who prepares the cash receipts source documents should not be the employee who makes the cash proof (comparing actual cash on hand with the source documents).
• The person who prepares the actual cash receipts for deposit should not be the person who prepares the source documents.
• The person who uses the cash receipts source documents to record the cash transactions in the journal should have no contact with the actual cash receipts.

Activity A-1. Answer the following questions about procedures for proving cash receipts. Refer to the sales slip and the remittance slip on page 297.
1. From whom is cash received on August 15? How much cash is received?
2. For what purpose is the cash received?

3. Who receives the cash on August 15?
4. When is cash received from Village Notes? How much is received?
5. What is the date of the check received from Village Notes?
6. Why is the cash received from Village Notes?

7. What is the number of the cash remittance slip?

8. What would happen if the next completed sales slip was Sales Slip 103?

Activity A-2. Answer the following questions on cash proofs. Refer to the cash proof for sales slips on page 298 and the cash proof for a cash register on page 299.

1. For which cash register is the cash proof prepared?

2. What is the total amount of cash sales recorded on the cash register on August 3? How much is the last cash sale?

3. What is the total amount received on account on August 3? the last amount received on account?

4. How much is the total cash paid out on August 3?

5. What is the total cash received on August 3? How much is in the cash drawer at the end of the day? Are the two amounts different? Why?

6. Who is the clerk operating Cash Register III? Who prepares the cash proof?

7. What are the total cash sales on August 4? How much is the last cash sale?

8. Is there a difference between the total cash received and the cash in the drawer on August 4? Why or why not?

9. What would change on the cash proof for August 3 if the Cash in Drawer was $350?

Visualizing Cash Receipts

B *How are the handling and recording of cash related?* The relationship between the two procedures involved in processing cash can be illustrated by using a flowchart.

The flowchart on page 301 shows that the procedures for handling cash involve the customer, the cashier (or salesperson), and the supervisor. The procedures for recording cash involve the accounting clerk. Cash moves from the cashier to the supervisor and to the bank.

Note that all cash received in person is recorded on a cash register tape or on sales slips. All cash received in the mail is recorded on remittance slips. A cash proof is prepared daily to verify that the net cash handled equals the net cash received. The source documents are then sent to the accounting department to be journalized. All cash receipts are deposited intact in the bank. Thus at the end of the month, the total deposits must equal the total of the cash debits in the journal.

Activity B. In a table similar to the one here, indicate who prepares or sends the following forms, to whom or where they are sent, and the purpose they serve. Refer to the flowchart of a cash receipts subsystem on page 301.

1. Source document: Copy 2

2. Cash proof: Copy 1 (with source documents)

3. Cash proof: Copy 1 (with source documents after journalizing)

4. Bank statement: Copy 1

Form	Prepared or Sent By	Sent To	Purpose
EXAMPLE: Source document: Copy 1	**Cashier**	**Supervisor**	**As a record of all cash received and to provide the information needed to prepare a cash proof.**

Cashier (Office):
DOT 211.462-010. Receives cash, pays cash, and records transactions on source documents.

Cash Receipts Bookkeeper:
DOT 201.382-010. Keeps cash receipts records of the financial records.

VISUALIZING A CASH RECEIPTS SUBSYSTEM

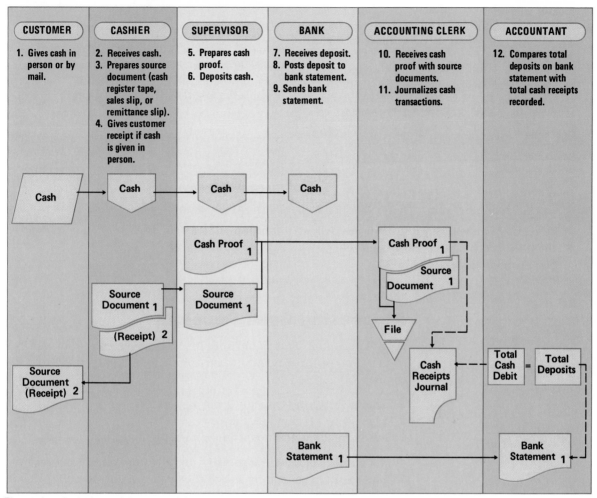

The numbers in the lower right corner of the document symbols show the copy number. The original copy is Copy 1. The duplicate copy is Copy 2.

Topic 1 Problems

11-1. From the data given here, prepare a cash proof for May 15 for Carria Hawkins, who used Cash Register IV. The change fund amounts to $40. If there is a difference between the net cash received and the net cash handled, explain what could have caused the difference.

MONEY IN CASH REGISTER DRAWER

Currency	Coins	Checks
Sixteen $20 bills	78 quarters	$100
Forty-two $10 bills	104 dimes	$ 80
Twenty-two $5 bills	46 nickels	$ 60
Eighty-two $1 bills	62 pennies	

Cash register tape totals.

May 15, IV

```
1,035.66TCa
  144.16TRe
1,179.82TCr
   15.00TPd
```

11-2. Prepare a cash proof for September 9 for Gordon Nuñez, who used Sales Book 94. Using the following information, prepare Sales Slip 258: received $26 on account from Paul Rech, 1 Poplar Road, Tucson, Arizona 85718. Data for an additional 12 sales slips and the cash in the drawer is given in the next column and below. The change fund is $25.

Prenumbered sales slips.

MONEY IN CASH REGISTER DRAWER

Currency	Coins	Checks
Seven $20 bills	14 quarters	$10
Seven $10 bills	21 dimes	$24
Thirteen $5 bills	14 nickels	$12
Thirty-three $1 bills	25 pennies	$45

11-3. Prepare Remittance Slip RS-17 using the following information: $700 was received on account from Trim-Jean, Check 180, dated July 7 and received on July 9.

Topic 2
Processing Cash Receipts

A *What kinds of transactions involve cash receipts?* In general, there are three types of cash transactions that involve cash receipts.

- Customers paying cash for goods or services.
- Debtors paying amounts they owe.
- Owners making additional investments in their businesses.

The number of cash transactions and the amount of cash received depend on the type and the size of the business. For example, a pharmacy has many cash sales. However, each sale is probably under $15. An automobile dealer, on the other hand, might have only one cash transaction a day. But this sale could involve $8,000 or more.

Source documents are prepared when cash is received, as is discussed in Topic 1. How these source documents are used to journalize and post cash receipts using the cash receipts journal is now discussed.

Journalizing Cash Receipts

Each journal entry to record a cash receipt includes a debit to the Cash account. The account credited depends on the source from which cash was received. For example, the Sales account is credited to record cash sales.

Each cash receipts entry recorded in a two-column general journal requires at least two lines. If an explanation is included, the entry requires at least three lines. Thus ten cash receipts transactions in one day require 20 to 30 lines in the general journal. Also, when the ten transactions are posted, ten separate entries in the Cash account must be made.

A special journal is often used to reduce the amount of space used in both the journal and the ledger. The **cash receipts journal** is a special journal used to record all receipts of cash. The cash receipts journal increases efficiency because all debits to the Cash account are posted in one amount at the end of the month. It also permits more than one person to work on the records at a time.

To illustrate how special journals and various methods of control are used, we will study the accounting system of House of Sound. Marcy Casey is the owner of House of Sound, which is a business that sells audio equipment.

The accounting system used by the House of Sound provides that all cash sales are recorded on a cash register. Cash received through the mail is recorded on remittance slips. Because of the large number of cash transactions, Marcy Casey proves cash and makes a bank deposit once a week. Thus the total bank deposit for any week must equal the weekly total on the cash register tape plus the weekly total of the remittance slips. The total deposit must also equal the cash receipts recorded in the journal for that week.

Using the Cash Receipts Journal Instead of the General Journal.
During August, House of Sound received $10,950. If the cash transactions were journalized in a two-column general journal, the entries would appear as shown on page 304.

Note that in this form of journal, the debit entry to the Cash account is repeated for each transaction. Cash is debited eight times to record the August transactions, and eight lines are required in the Cash account because each entry is posted separately.

The illustration on page 304 shows how the August 3 transaction to increase the owner's equity by $6,000 would be journalized in a two-column general journal. The illustration also shows the same transaction in a cash receipts journal.

When the cash receipts journal is used, the date, the account credited, the explanation, and the amount are all recorded on one line. Only the credit entry must be written. The account title *Cash* and the amount debited are not written. It is understood that there will be a debit entry to the Cash account for the *total* of all the credit entries in the cash receipts journal. Writing the amount only once saves time and reduces the chances of making an error.

The illustration on page 305 shows how the August cash receipts entries for the House of Sound would appear in a one-column cash receipts journal.

House of Sound Chart of Accounts

Assets
101 Cash
102 Petty Cash
103 Change Fund
111 Accts. Rec./Audio Shoppe
112 Accts. Rec./Newtown Music
113 Accts. Rec./Village Notes
114 Accts. Rec./Wanda's Radio
115 Accts. Rec./George Yeomans
116 Accts. Rec./Pauline Young
132 Office Equipment
133 Stockroom Equipment

Liabilities
201 Loans Payable
211 Accts. Pay./Downtown Music
212 Accts. Pay./Phelps Supply
213 Accts. Pay./Tappan Corporation
214 Accts. Pay./Viceroy, Inc.
221 Federal Income Taxes Payable
222 FICA Taxes Payable
223 Federal Unemployment Taxes Payable
224 State Unemployment Taxes Payable
225 Salaries Payable

Owner's Equity
301 Marcy Casey, Capital

Revenue
401 Sales

Expenses
511 Cash Short and Over
512 Advertising Expense
513 Delivery Expense
514 Insurance Expense
515 Miscellaneous Expense
516 Payroll Taxes Expense
517 Rent Expense
518 Salaries Expense
519 Supplies Expense

GENERAL JOURNAL   Page 1

DATE	ACCOUNT TITLE AND EXPLANATION	POST. REF.	DEBIT	CREDIT
19—				
Aug. 3	Cash	101	6,000 00	
	Marcy Casey, Capital	301		6,000 00
	Additional investment.			
6	Cash	101	800 00	
	Sales	401		800 00
	Cash sales for week.			
8	Cash	101	400 00	
	Accts. Rec./George Yeomans	115		400 00
	Received on account.			
13	Cash	101	700 00	
	Sales	401		700 00
	Cash sales for week.			
15	Cash	101	150 00	
	Accts. Rec./Audio Shoppe	111		150 00
	Received on account.			
20	Cash	101	1,500 00	
	Sales	401		1,500 00
	Cash sales for week.			
24	Cash	101	600 00	
	Accts. Rec./Village Notes	113		600 00
	Received on account.			
27	Cash	101	800 00	
	Sales	401		800 00
	Cash sales for week.			

Cash   101

6,000
800
400
700
150
1,500
600
800

Cash receipts recorded in the general journal.

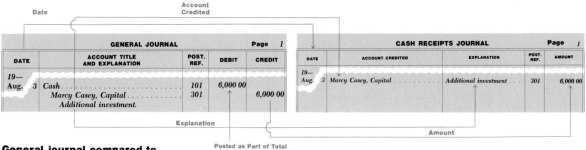

General journal compared to cash receipts journal.

Note that in the cash receipts journal on the next page, the cash balance for August 1 ($8,400) is recorded on the first line. This type of entry is commonly made at the beginning of each month. The entry for the cash balance is a memorandum entry. A **memorandum entry** is an entry that is not to be posted. Thus the balance is written in the Explanation column instead of the Amount column. Since no entry is made in the Posting Reference column, a dash is put in.

CASH RECEIPTS JOURNAL

Page 1

DATE		ACCOUNT CREDITED	EXPLANATION	POST. REF.	AMOUNT
19—					
Aug.	1	Cash Balance	$8,400	—	
	3	Marcy Casey, Capital	Additional investment . . .		6,000 00
	6	Sales	Cash sales for week		800 00
	8	Accts. Rec./George Yeomans	Received on account		400 00
	13	Sales	Cash sales for week		700 00
	15	Accts. Rec./Audio Shoppe	Received on account		150 00
	20	Sales	Cash sales for week		1,500 00
	24	Accts. Rec./Village Notes	Received on account		600 00
	27	Sales	Cash sales for week		800 00

Activity A. Answer the following questions about processing cash receipts. Refer to the two-column general journal and illustrations on page 304, and the cash receipts journal on page 305.

1. How many lines are needed to journalize cash receipts for August in the two-column general journal? How many postings to the Cash account are needed?

2. How many lines are needed to journalize one entry in the cash receipts journal? In the general journal? How many lines are saved by journalizing a cash receipts transaction in a cash receipts journal?

3. Is the entry on August 3 a debit or a credit to Marcy Casey, Capital?

4. What kind of entry is the cash balance entry on August 1? Is it posted?

5. What is the source of cash receipts journalized on August 6?

6. Why is the cash receipts journal described as a special journal?

7. How much cash is received on account for August? What are the cash sales for August?

8. Three sources of cash are recorded in August. What are the three sources?

9. What account is assumed to be debited for each entry in the cash receipts journal?

Posting the Cash Receipts

B *How are entries posted from the cash receipts journal?* The procedure for posting from a one-column cash receipts journal to the ledger is much simpler than the procedure for posting from a two-column general journal. The procedure is as follows.

• Each credit entry in the cash receipts journal is posted to the ledger account shown in the entry. The credit postings are made during the month.

• At the end of the month, the cash receipts journal is totaled and ruled.

• The total cash received during the month is then posted as a debit to the cash account.

At the end of each month, total, rule, and post the cash receipts journal.

Posting the Credit Entries. The letters *CR* are written in the Posting Reference column of the ledger account. This shows the amount was posted from the cash receipts journal. In the illustration on page 306, *CR1* shows that the $6,000 credit to the Capital account was journalized on page 1 of the cash receipts journal.

Marcy Casey, Capital					Account No.		301	
DATE	**EXPLANATION**	**POST. REF.**	**DEBIT**	**CREDIT**	**BALANCE**			
					DEBIT		**CREDIT**	
19—								
Aug. 1	Balance	—					19,000	00
3	. . . .	CR1		6,000 00			25,000	00

Totaling the Cash Receipts Journal. The amount posted to the Cash account is the total of the entries in the cash receipts journal. To find the amount, use the following procedures.

1 Draw one line under the last amount in the Amount column.
2 Write the last date of the month in the Date column.
3 Write "Cash Debit" in the Account Credited column.
4 Write "Total receipts" in the Explanation column.
5 Add the amounts in the Amount column. Write the total in small pencil-footings. Prove the addition. After proving the additions, write the total in ink beneath the single line. If an adding machine is used, clear the machine first. Then total and check the amounts on the tape against the amounts in the journal to prove the addition, or readd the column in the opposite direction. If an adding machine is not used, prove the addition by readding in the opposite direction.
6 Draw a double line under the Date, Posting Reference, and Amount columns to show that the journalizing is completed.

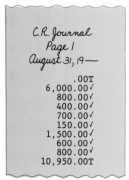

C.R. Journal
Page 1
August 31, 19—

.00T
6,000.00 ✓
800.00 ✓
400.00 ✓
700.00 ✓
150.00 ✓
1,500.00 ✓
600.00 ✓
800.00 ✓
10,950.00 T

Amounts added and checked on adding machine tape.

CASH RECEIPTS JOURNAL				Page	1
DATE	**ACCOUNT CREDITED**	**EXPLANATION**	**POST. REF.**	**AMOUNT**	
19—					
Aug. 1	Cash Balance	$8,400	—		
3	Marcy Casey, Capital	Additional investment . . .	301	6,000	00
6	Sales	Cash sales for week	401	800	00
8	Accts. Rec./George Yeomans	Received on account	115	400	00
13	Sales	Cash sales for week	401	700	00
15	Accts. Rec./Audio Shoppe	Received on account	111	150	00
20	Sales	Cash sales for week	401	1,500	00
24	Accts. Rec./Village Notes	Received on account	113	600	00
27	Sales	Cash sales for week	401	800	00
				10,950	00
31	Cash Debit	Total receipts	101	10,950	00

Posting total cash receipts.

CASH RECEIPTS JOURNAL		Page	1
DATE	**ACCOUNT CREDITED**	**POST. REF.**	**AMOUNT**
19—			
Aug. 31	Cash Debit	101	10,950 00

T Accounts

Posting the Debit to Cash. After the cash journal is totaled and ruled, the total is posted. The total amount of cash received is posted to the debit side of the Cash account. Then write the number of the Cash account in the Posting Reference column of the cash receipts journal.

After all entries for August have been posted, as shown here, the Cash account will show only one debit—$10,950—for total cash receipts from August. The total credits posted from the cash receipts journal to the various accounts in the ledger also equal $10,950. Thus the total debits posted equal the total credits posted.

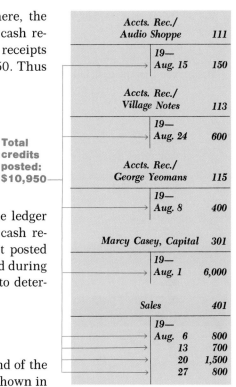

Total debits posted: $10,950 ────→

Cash		101
19—		
Aug. 31	10,950	

Total credits posted: $10,950 ────→

Accts. Rec./ Audio Shoppe		111
19—		
Aug. 15	150	

Accts. Rec./ Village Notes		113
19—		
Aug. 24	600	

Accts. Rec./ George Yeomans		115
19—		
Aug. 8	400	

Marcy Casey, Capital		301
19—		
Aug. 1	6,000	

Sales		401
19—		
Aug. 6	800	
13	700	
20	1,500	
27	800	

Suppose a trial balance is prepared during the month. The ledger would be out of balance because only the credit entries for cash receipts had been posted. The debit to the Cash account is not posted until the end of each month. Thus, if a trial balance is prepared during the month, the cash receipts journal must first be examined to determine the debits to Cash.

Recording the Memorandum Entry

The cash receipts journal is totaled, ruled, and posted at the end of the month. Thus the current balance of the Cash account will be shown in the Cash account and is available as next month's memorandum entry. The procedures for verifying the Cash account balance are explained in the next chapter.

Recording an Opening Entry

All transactions involving the receipt of cash are recorded in a cash receipts journal. Thus if an opening entry consists of a cash investment only, the opening entry is recorded in the cash receipts journal. If the owner invests other assets in addition to cash, the cash is recorded in the cash receipts journal and the other assets are recorded in the general journal.

All cash transactions are recorded in a cash receipts journal. Other assets are recorded in the general journal.

Activity B. Answer the following questions about posting cash receipts. Refer to the cash receipts journal on page 306.
1. From what other source can the August 1 cash balance be obtained?
2. Why is the amount of the August 1 cash balance shown in the Explanation column instead of in the Amount column?
3. Why is there a dash in the Posting Reference column for the cash balance?

4. What would the complete entry be if cash sales for the week of August 6 were recorded in a general journal?
5. Is the debit to the Cash account posted at the same time that the cash sale for the week of August 13 is posted? Why or why not?
6. When a $600 credit is posted from the cash receipts journal to the Village Notes ledger account, is the debit to the Cash account posted at the same time? Explain.

7. On what date is $6,000 received? From what source?

8. What amount is posted to the Cash account on August 31? Is the amount debited or credited?

9. Can you find the cash balance as of August 31 from the data in the cash receipts journal? Why or why not?

10. Is $8,400 a part of the cash debit on August 31? Why or why not?

Bank Credit Card Sales

C *How do businesses process bank credit card sales?* Businesses process bank credit card sales as a special type of cash sale.

Processing Bank Credit Card Sales

A **bank credit card** is issued through a bank and can be used at any business accepting that card. The most widely used bank credit cards are VISA and MasterCard. Illustrations of these are shown in the margin. Many businesses use credit card sales along with their cash and regular charge sales because they feel the advantages are greater than the disadvantages. Bank credit card sales have two primary advantages. First, total sales increase, for many customers prefer to purchase with this type of credit card. Second, the business receives payment immediately from the issuing or cooperating bank. The primary disadvantage of a credit card sale is that the business must pay a fee to the bank that issues the card.

The following procedure is used to process bank credit card sales.

- The customer's credit is checked
- Source documents are prepared
- Payment is obtained from the bank

Checking the Customer's Credit. Businesses that accept bank credit cards do not normally check the customer's credit for small sales. However, for larger sales the credit card system has an office that gives the needed credit information.

To check a customer's credit, the salesclerk places a telephone call to a central office. The clerk in the credit office uses a computer terminal to examine the customer's account. If the transaction is approved, the salesclerk enters a credit authorization on the credit card sales slip.

Preparing Source Documents. After the customer's credit is checked, many businesses prepare two sales slips for each credit card sale. First the salesclerk completes the sales slip that the business uses for regular cash sales. Then the salesclerk prepares a special credit

Bank Credit Cards

Sales Slip

card sales slip preprinted with the name of the credit card (such as VISA). Both are illustrated in the margins of page 308 and here.

The salesclerk places the credit card sales slip and the customer's plastic credit card in an imprinting device. This device prints the customer's name and credit card number on the sales slip. It also prints the business's name and identification number. When the sales slip is removed from the imprinting device, the customer is asked to sign the form.

Credit Card Sales Slip

Both the regular sales slip and the credit card sales slip consist of several copies. The customer receives one copy of each form. Other copies go to the accounting department. There, an accounting clerk verifies the accuracy of the amounts on the sales slips. A copy of the regular sales slip and a copy of the credit card sales slip are then filed. Another copy of the credit card sales slip is kept in the accounting department until the bank deposit is prepared.

Obtaining Payment From the Bank. When a bank deposit is prepared, an accounting clerk adds the totals of all the credit card sales slips on a calculator. The accounting clerk then lists the total on a special deposit form. This form is provided by the bank and is illustrated in the margin.

Deposit ticket for credit card sales.

The accounting clerk must also compute the processing fee. The **processing fee** is the fee that the bank deducts for handling the business's credit card sales. It is stated as a percentage of the business's credit card sales. For example, if the fee were 2 percent and total credit card sales were $618, the amount of the fee then would be $12.36 ($0.02 \times \$618.00$).

The accounting clerk then lists the fee and also the net amount of the credit card sales on the deposit form. The net amount, computed by subtracting the discount from the total of the credit card sales, is the amount the business receives from the bank. In our previous example, the net amount would be $605.64 ($618.00 − $12.36).

After the deposit form for the credit card sales is completed, the accounting clerk attaches the calculator tape and a copy of each sales slip. These items are taken to the bank along with a deposit ticket and the currency, coins, and checks that will also be deposited. When the bank records the deposit, it adds the net amount of the credit card sales to the balance of the business's checking account.

Recording Credit Card Sales

Bank credit card sales are treated as cash sales and recorded in the cash receipts journal. The entry shown at the top of page 310 would be made for the November 1 credit card sales described above.

DATE	ACCOUNT CREDITED	EXPLANATION	POST. REF.	GENERAL LEDGER CREDIT	SALES CREDIT	CREDIT CARD FEE EXPENSE DEBIT	NET CASH DEBIT
19— Nov.	1	Sales	Bank credit card sales			618 00	12 36	605 64

Recording bank credit card sales.

November 1: Recorded credit card sales of $618 less a processing fee of $12.36.

What Happens	Accounting Rule	Entry
The asset cash increases by $605.64.	To increase an asset, debit the account.	Debit: Cash, $605.64.
Credit card fee expense decreases owner's equity by $12.36.	To decrease owner's equity, debit the account.	Debit: Credit Card Fee Expense, $12.36.
Credit card sales increase owner's equity by $618.	To increase owner's equity, credit the account.	Credit: Sales, $618.

There are two items you should focus on in this transaction. First, there is a new account called Credit Card Fee Expense. The **Credit Card Fee Expense** account is an operating expense that reduces owner's equity. The $12.36 is what management is willing to pay to increase sales (revenue) by $618. Second, special columns are added to the cash receipts journal to record the credit card sales. The addition of new columns is an example of how a business can design its accounting records to meet its needs. The amounts in the Credit Card Fee Expense and Sales columns will be posted as totals at the end of the month to the proper ledger account.

Some businesses set up a separate revenue account for credit card sales. This will allow management to see the amount that credit card sales contribute to the revenues each accounting period.

Activity C. Answer the following questions about credit card sales. Refer to the text, margin notes, and illustrations on pages 308 to 310.
1. What are the two types of credit card sales?
2. What is one advantage of a credit card sale? One disadvantage?
3. What is the processing fee and the amount charged on the credit card sales illustrated on page 309?

4. How does a business obtain cash for bank credit card sales?
5. What accounts are debited when bank credit card sales are recorded? What accounts are credited?
6. What new columns have been added to the cash receipts journal to make easier the recording of bank credit card sales? How often are amounts in these columns posted?

Accounting Concepts:

Accumulating Amounts. Debit amounts and credit amounts for an account can be accumulated and posted as totals without affecting the equality of the ledger.

Posting by Total. *Posting by total* should increase accuracy and efficiency and speed because it reduces the number of times an amount is recorded.

Topic 2 Problems

11-4. Soares Motors had the transactions listed below for October.

a. Open ledger accounts and enter account balances for October 1 as follows: Cash, $1,400; Accts. Rec./Hine Corporation, $520; Accts. Rec./Roger Kraus, $310; Rental Equipment, $25,000; Anthony Soares, Capital, $27,230; and Sales. Assign a proper number to each account according to a chart of accounts.

b. In the cash receipts journal, make a memorandum entry for the October 1 cash balance. Then journalize the transactions. Post credit entries each week and on October 31.

c. Foot, prove, and rule the cash receipts journal.

d. Post the debit entry from the cash receipts journal.

e. Prepare a trial balance.

Oct. 5 Recorded cash sales of $1,020 for the week.
      5 Posted credit entries for the week ended October 5.
      8 Received $310 from Roger Kraus on account.
     12 Recorded cash sales of $1,240 for the week.
     12 Posted credit entries for the week ended October 12.
     17 Received $5,000 from Anthony Soares as additional investment.
     19 Recorded cash sales of $950 for the week.
     19 Posted credit entries for the week ended October 19.
     23 Received $180 from Hine Corporation on account.
     26 Recorded cash sales of $1,075 for the week.
     26 Posted credit entries for the week ended October 26.
     29 Received $120 from Hine Corporation on account.

Oct. 31 Received $1,200 for automobile (Rental Equipment) sold to Kern Motors.
     31 Posted credit entries for transactions October 27–31.

11-5. Adam Zak started A–Z Services on July 1. During July, the business had the transactions listed below.

a. Open the following ledger accounts: Cash; Accts. Rec./Kison Company; Land; Adam Zak, Capital; and Sales.

b. Use a cash receipts journal and a general journal to journalize the transactions listed through July 17.

c. Post the entries from the general journal. Post the credit entries from the cash receipts journal.

d. Journalize the transactions for July 20–31.

e. Post the entries from the general journal. Post the credit entries from the cash receipts journal.

f. Foot, prove, and rule the cash receipts journal.

g. Post the debit entry from the cash receipts journal.

h. Prepare a trial balance.

July 1 Mr. Zak started the business with a cash investment of $10,500.
      2 Mr. Zak invested land of $20,000.
      8 Sold shrubbery for $600 on account to Kison Company.
     10 Recorded cash proof for the register showing cash sales of $975.
     15 Received $450 from Kison Company on account.
     17 Recorded the cash proof showing cash sales of $850.
     20 Received $2,000 for land sold to Jay Berg.
     28 Received $100 from Kison Company on account.
     31 Recorded the cash proof showing cash sales of $900.

11-6. BG Motors sells auto supplies for cash and also accepts bank credit cards. On May 15 total sales were $1,600 and sales taxes were $90. Cash sales were $875.

a. Determine the bank credit card sales.

b. Compute the processing fee. (The fee is 2 percent.)

c. Prepare a bank credit card sale deposit ticket. (There were 27 credit card sales, and the checking account number is 12-7700.)

d. Record the sales, sales taxes payable, and credit card fee expense in a cash receipts journal.

The Language of Business

Here are some basic terms that make up the language of business. Do you know the meaning of each?

cash receipts
 subsystem
cashier
handling cash receipts
recording cash receipts

cash register tape
sales slip
remittance slip
prenumbered source
 document

change fund
cash receipts journal
memorandum entry

bank credit card
processing fee
Credit Card Fee
 Expense account

Chapter 11   Questions

1. List and explain the essential procedures for the control of cash receipts.

2. Explain the procedure followed for proving cash (a) when a cash register is used, (b) when sales slips are used, (c) when remittance slips are used.

3. Why should a business deposit all cash receipts intact and pay all bills by check?

4. Why should the procedure for handling cash receipts be separated from the procedure for recording cash receipts?

5. Explain how the use of a cash receipts journal simplifies the journalizing and posting of cash receipts.

6. What procedure is followed to complete the cash receipts journal at the end of the month?

7. In which journal or journals is an opening entry recorded if the investment consists of cash only? If it consists of cash and other assets?

8. What is the major advantage of bank credit card sales?

9. Is there any expense connected with bank credit card sales? Explain.

10. In what way do good control procedures for cash receipts contribute to good employer-employee relations?

Chapter 11   Problems

Problems for Chapter 11 are given in the *Working Papers and Chapter Problems for Part 2*. If you are using the workbook, do the problems in the space provided there.

Chapter 11 Management Cases

Control of Cash Receipts. A large number of the total transactions of a business involve cash receipts and cash payments. Every business should set up safeguards to control cash because this asset is more likely to be mishandled than any other.

Case 11M-1. In many large schools, the faculty members belong to the local, state, and national teachers' organizations. They pay their dues to an office clerk. The clerk issues a separate receipt for each payment of dues to any one of the three organizations. In order to reduce her work, the clerk at Manchester High School has requested that she be permitted to issue only one receipt to a person. (She would do this even when the dues are payable to more than one teacher's organization.)

a. Under the separate-receipt method, how would each of the three organizations obtain full information about the payment of dues and the members in good standing?

b. Under the one-receipt method, how would the same information be reported to each organization? How could each be sure that all dues collected were sent?

c. Design a receipt that can be used for all three organizations at one time.

Case 11M-2. Allen Manson owns the AM Service. Mr. Manson has eight employees to repair TVs, stereos, refrigerators, and similar items in the customer's home or in the shop.

Cash is received by Mr. Manson in the following ways.

a. Charge customers send checks and, occasionally, small sums of money through the mail.

b. Charge customers pay their accounts in person.

c. Cash customers pay the employees who service appliances at their homes.

d. Cash customers pay cash to the cashier for work done in Mr. Manson's shop.

e. Customers purchase tubes, extension cords, and other parts and pay the cashier in the shop.

Make suggestions that Mr. Manson might consider when reviewing his procedures for controlling cash receipts. Specifically, describe how he should do the following things. When you develop your suggestions, refer to the procedures for controlling cash receipts on pages 296 to 299.

a. Handle checks and cash received through the mail.

b. Receive and record cash paid to the cashier for appliance services.

c. Control cash received by employees in the customers' homes.

d. Control cash received for the sale of parts.

Working Hint

Errors Made in Copying Numbers. When numbers are copied, errors often occur because a number has been left out or has been mistaken for another number.

Omitting a Number. When listing a series of numbers, you can guard against accidentally omitting one of them by counting the items you copied. Then count the items in the original list. The total number in both lists must be equal.

Misreading a Number. When recording numbers, always use well-formed figures, as shown here. This will guard against misreading a number. The numbers most likely to be misread when carelessly or poorly written are these: 9 and 7; 1 and 7; 4 and 7; 2 and 0; 2 and 3; 3 and 5; 6 and 0; 8 and 0; and 2 and 7.

1 2 3 4 5 6 7 8 9 0

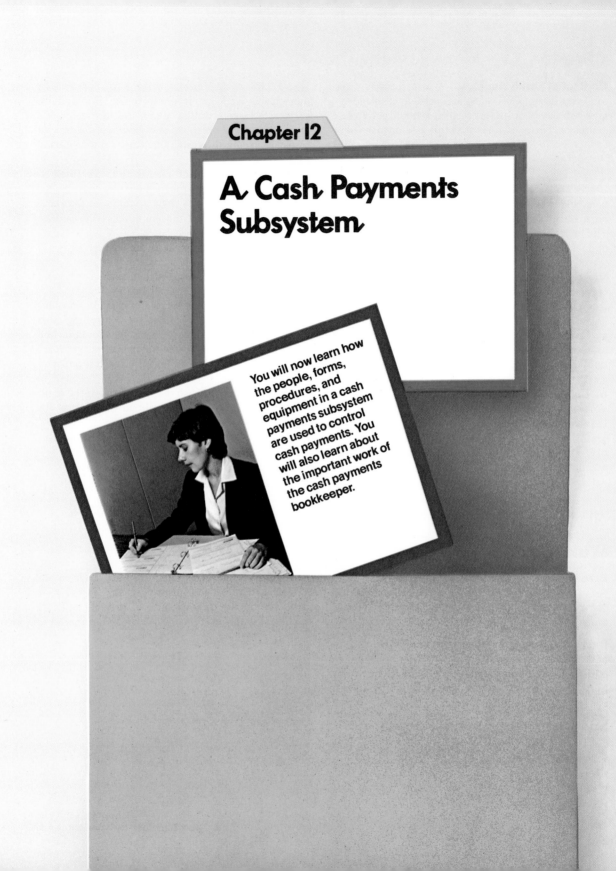

A Cash Payments Subsystem

You will now learn how the people, forms, procedures, and equipment in a cash payments subsystem are used to control cash payments. You will also learn about the important work of the cash payments bookkeeper.

Topic 1
Controlling Cash Payments

A | *What is a cash payments subsystem?* The people, forms, procedures, and equipment used to control cash payments make up a **cash payments subsystem.** As in the cash receipts subsystem, the cashier plays an important role. The employee who keeps the cash payments section of the financial records is the cash payments bookkeeper.

Cashier (Office):
DOT 211.462-010. Receives cash, pays cash, and records transactions on source documents.

Cash Payments
Bookkeeper:
DOT 210.382-018. Keeps cash payments records of the financial records.

Procedures to Control Cash Payments

The control of cash payments includes the procedures to ensure accuracy, honesty, and efficiency and speed in processing cash payments. These procedures include the following.

- Verifying and approving invoices
- Paying by check
- Using prenumbered checks
- Proving cash
- Dividing responsibilities

Control: Verify and approve invoices.
Control: Pay by check.
Control: Use prenumbered checks.
Control: Prove cash.
Control: Divide responsibility.

As you can see, some of these procedures are similar to those used in the cash receipts subsystem.

Verifying and Approving Invoices. No invoice should be paid until it has been verified. This means that the goods or services listed on the invoice must have been ordered and received and that the amount of the invoice must be accurate. If the invoice is correct, then it can be approved for payment by an authorized employee.

Paying by Check. All cash receipts should be deposited intact. No payments should be made from cash receipts. All payments (except petty cash payments) should be made by check. The check stub or a carbon copy of the voucher check becomes the source document for the data entered into the accounting system.

Using Prenumbered Checks. Prenumbered checks should be used to keep track of the checks issued. Voided checks must be kept so that every check is accounted for in numeric order.

Proving Cash. If all cash receipts are deposited in the bank and all bills are paid by check, then two separate records of cash receipts and cash payments are available. First, the business has a record of receipts in the cash receipts journal. It also has a record of payments in the checkbook, petty cash register, and cash payments journal. Second, the bank has a record of all deposits and withdrawals from the business's checking account.

When the business receives a copy of its bank statement, it prepares a bank reconciliation to verify the cash receipts and cash payments records.

Dividing the Responsibilities. It is wise to divide the responsibilities of verifying invoices, approving invoices, issuing checks, and recording checks among several employees. Thus the work of one employee can be checked against the work of another employee. The business then uses good internal control to safeguard cash payments.

Activity A. Answer the following questions about the procedures to control cash payments. Refer to the text and margin notes on page 315 and above.
1. What is meant by verifying and approving invoices?
2. What is (are) the source document(s) used when authorized payments are made by check?

3. What is the purpose of prenumbering checks?
4. When proving cash, what two records of cash are available?
5. Why do businesses divide responsibilities among employees?

Visualizing the Cash Payments Subsystem

B *How is the handling and recording of cash payments related?* The flowchart on page 317 illustrates the procedures to control the handling and recording of cash payments. The invoice is verified and approved before a check is issued. Prenumbered checks are used. The responsibilities to issue checks and journalize the payments are divided. Finally, a cash proof is prepared to verify that the total of the checks written equals the total cash paid.

Activity B. In a table similar to the one that follows, indicate who prepares or sends the following forms, to whom or where each one is sent, and the purpose each one serves. Refer to the flowchart of a cash payments subsystem on page 317.
1. Invoice (approved): Copy 1
2. Invoice (approved): Copy 1 after payment

3. Check
4. Check (to be deposited)
5. Check (deposited)
6. Check stub
7. Check stub (after journalizing)
8. Bank statement: Copy 1

Form	Prepared or Sent By	Sent To	Purpose
EXAMPLE: **Invoice: Copy 1**	*Creditor*	*Person authorized to buy*	*As a bill for the service performed or the goods supplied*

VISUALIZING A CASH PAYMENTS SUBSYSTEM

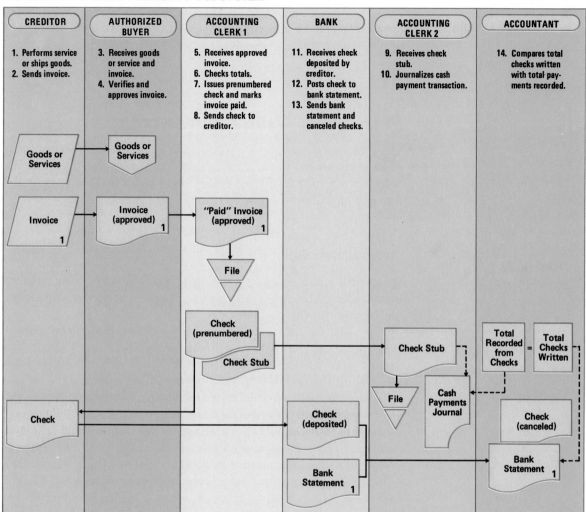

Accounting Concept:
Safeguarding Cash. A bank account safeguards cash and serves as an external record for the control of cash.

Topic 1 Problem

12-1. The Janus Company has asked you to write comments on its cash payments subsystem. A list of their procedures follows.

1. Invoices are approved and paid by one employee.
2. Most payments are made by check. However, to save time, the Janus Company makes some purchases of supplies and merchandise in cash taken from the daily cash receipts.

3. The company does not prove its cash records with the bank's records. Janus's owner feels that the bank has expensive computers to do its work without error.
4. The checks are not prenumbered by the printer. However, the person who writes each check does number the checks consecutively.

5. A general journal is used to record all cash receipts and cash payments.

6. One person handles all the accounting records for cash receipts and cash payments. This person counts the daily cash received, opens the mail, makes deposits, writes checks, makes the cash payments out of receipts, proves cash (when it is done), and files all paid checks received from the bank.

Topic 2
Processing Cash Payments

A *Why does a business make cash payments?* Cash is usually used to pay expenses, to pay creditors, and to pay for assets; cash is also withdrawn for the owner's personal use. The journalizing procedures for cash payments are now described.

Journalizing Cash Payments

When cash is paid, the asset Cash decreases. Thus every cash payment involves a credit to the Cash account. The account debited depends on the purpose for the payment.

When cash payments are recorded in a two-column general journal, every debit entry must have a credit entry to the Cash account. The August cash payments for the House of Sound would look like those recorded in the two-column general journal on page 319.

To save time when journalizing and posting, many businesses record all cash payments in a special cash payments journal. In the **cash payments journal** only the debit entries are recorded and posted individually. The entries to the Cash account are totaled and posted as one credit to the Cash account at the end of the month, as on page 319.

To see the advantages of using a one-column cash payments journal, look at the August 4 entry for rent expense in the general journal. The entry requires three lines. The same entry in a one-column cash payments journal takes only one line, and the amount is written only once. A special column for recording check numbers is also provided in the cash payments journal, to account for all checks. Note that when a check is voided (Check 203, for instance), the number is listed, a line is drawn in the Account Debited, Posting Reference, and Amount columns, and *Voided* is written in the Explanation column.

An entry that contains more than one debit is recorded in the cash payments journal like the entry to replenish petty cash on August 31. Note that the date is not repeated and a dash is placed in the Check Number column to show that no check is missing.

In addition to the above, two entries were made in the August cash payments journal that are new to you. The entries on August 25

GENERAL JOURNAL Page 1

DATE		ACCOUNT TITLE AND EXPLANATION	POST. REF.	DEBIT	CREDIT
19— Aug.	4	Rent Expense	517	600 00	
		Cash	101		600 00
		August rent, Check 201.			
	8	Accts. Pay./Downtown Music	211	400 00	
		Cash	101		400 00
		On account, Check 202.			
	18	Office Equipment	132	240 00	
		Cash	101		240 00
		New adding machine, Check 204.			
	25	Change Fund	103	35 00	
		Cash	101		35 00
		Establish fund, Check 205.			
	31	Salaries Payable	225	1,200 00	
		Cash	101		1,200 00
		August 28 payroll, Checks 206–209.			
	31	Advertising Expense	512	20 00	
		Miscellaneous Expense	515	10 00	
		Cash	101		30 00
		Replenish petty cash, Check 210.			
	31	Marcy Casey, Drawing	302	800 00	
		Cash	101		800 00
		Withdrawal, Check 211.			

Cash	101
	600
	400
	240
	35
	1,200
	30
	800

Cash payments recorded in a general journal.

(Check 205) and August 31 (Check 211) relate to change funds and personal withdrawals. The change fund is explained in Topic 3. Personal withdrawals by the owner are explained in this topic.

CASH PAYMENTS JOURNAL Page 1

DATE		ACCOUNT DEBITED	EXPLANATION	CHECK NO.	POST. REF.	AMOUNT
19— Aug.	4	Rent Expense	August rent	201		600 00
	8	Accts. Pay./Downtown Music	On account	202		400 00
	15	———————————	Voided	203	—	—..
	18	Office Equipment	New adding machine	204		240 00
	25	Change Fund	Establish fund	205		35 00
	31	Salaries Payable	August 28 payroll	206–209		1,200 00
	31	Advertising Expense	} Replenish petty	210		20 00
		Miscellaneous Expense	} cash fund	—		10 00
	31	Marcy Casey, Drawing	Withdrawal	211		800 00

← Each entry requires one line.

The Cash account is credited for the total of the debits in the cash payments journal.

Answer the following questions about journalizing cash payments. Refer to the cash payments journal on page 319.

1. What would the complete entry be if the payment of rent on August 4 was recorded in a general journal instead of in the cash payments journal?

2. When the August 4 transaction is journalized in the cash payments journal, why is no credit entry to the Cash account recorded?

3. When the office equipment transaction is posted from the cash payments journal, is the credit to the Cash account for $240 posted at the same time? Why or why not?

4. Why is a check written on August 25?

5. On what date is petty cash replenished?

6. How many checks are written on August 31? What was the total amount?

7. Why is Check 202 issued?

8. What happened to Check 203?

9. What do you think is the best reason for using a cash payments journal?

Recording Withdrawals

B *When are withdrawals made?* When cash and other assets are withdrawn from the business for the owner's personal use, the owner is said to have made a **withdrawal.** A withdrawal is made against the net income the owner expects to earn.

Withdrawals could be deducted from the owner's capital account. However, withdrawals are usually recorded in a separate owner's equity account known as a drawing account. The **drawing account** is a temporary account used to record changes in owner's equity. For instance, when the owner Marcy Casey withdraws $800 in cash for her personal use, the transaction is recorded in the cash payments journal. The Cash account is credited to show a decrease in assets. The drawing account is debited to show a decrease in owner's equity.

Credit the Cash account to show a decrease in assets. Debit the drawing account to show a decrease in owner's equity.

Temporary reduction of capital: use Drawing account.

CASH PAYMENTS JOURNAL					Page 1
DATE	ACCOUNT DEBITED	EXPLANATION	CHECK NO.	POST. REF.	AMOUNT
19—					
Aug. 4	Rent Expense	August rent	201		600 00
31	Marcy Casey, Drawing . .	Withdrawal	211		800 00

In the transaction on August 31, the owner made a withdrawal against expected net income. The entry would change if the owner planned to permanently reduce the amount of investment in the business. The reduction would be debited to the capital account (not the drawing account).

Permanent reduction of capital: use Capital account.

CASH PAYMENTS JOURNAL					Page 4
DATE	ACCOUNT DEBITED	EXPLANATION	CHECK NO.	POST. REF.	AMOUNT
19—					
Aug. 31	Marcy Casey, Capital . . .	Reduce capital . . .	211		500 00

When a drawing account is used, only the following is recorded in the capital account: the original investment, additional investments, and permanent withdrawals of investment. An additional investment is credited to the capital account. A permanent withdrawal of investment is debited to the capital account. A personal withdrawal is debited to the drawing account.

Activity B. Answer the following questions about withdrawals. Refer to the illustrations on page 320.
1. Which account is credited to record a withdrawal? Why?
2. Which account is debited to record a withdrawal? Why?

3. If the owner's withdrawal of $800 on August 31 had been a permanent withdrawal of investment, which account would have been debited?

Posting Cash Payments

C *How are entries posted from the cash payments journal?* Each debit in the cash payments journal is posted to the proper ledger account. The posting takes place at various times during the month. After an entry has been posted, the account number is entered in the Posting Reference column of the cash payments journal to show that an entry has been made. In the ledger account, the letters *CP* and the page number of the journal are written in the Posting Reference column. In the following illustration, the posting reference *CP1* shows that the $600 debit to the Rent Expense account was journalized on page 1 of the cash payments journal.

Rent Expense							Account No. 517	
DATE		EXPLANATION	POST. REF.	DEBIT	CREDIT	BALANCE		
						DEBIT	CREDIT	
19—								
Aug.	4	Rent for August.	CP1	600 00		600 00		

CASH PAYMENTS JOURNAL			Page 1	
DATE	ACCOUNT DEBI	POST. REF.	AMOUNT	
19—				
Aug.	4	Rent Expense .	517	600 00

CP: Cash payments journal

Totaling the Cash Payments Journal. The amount posted to the Cash account at the end of the month is the total of the cash payments journal. To find this, complete the procedure below and on page 322.

1 Draw a single rule under the last amount in the Amount column.
2 Write the last date of the month in the Date column.
3 Write "Cash Credit" in the Account Debited column.
4 Write "Total payments" in the Explanation column.
5 Add the amounts in the Amount column. Use an adding machine tape or the pencil-footing procedure to prove the addition. Then write the total in ink beneath the single rule.
6 Draw a double rule under the Date, Posting Reference, and Amount columns to show the journal is completed for the month.

C.P. Journal
Page 1
August 31, 19—

```
          .00T
        600.00 ✓
        400.00 ✓
        240.00 ✓
         35.00 ✓
      1,200.00 ✓
         20.00 ✓
         10.00 ✓
        800.00 ✓
      3,305.00T
```

CASH PAYMENTS JOURNAL

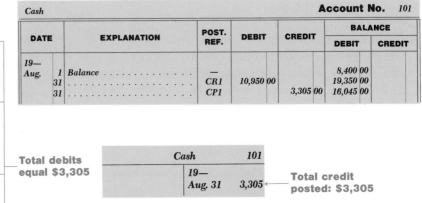

Page 1

DATE	ACCOUNT DEBITED	EXPLANATION	CHECK NO.	POST. REF.	AMOUNT
19—					
Aug. 4	Rent Expense	August rent	201	517	600 00
8	Accts. Pay./Downtown Music	On account	202	211	400 00
15		Voided	203	—	— 00
18	Office Equipment	New adding machine	204	132	240 00
25	Change Fund	Establish fund	205	103	35 00
31	Salaries Payable	August 28 payroll	206–209	225	1,200 00
31	Advertising Expense	⎫ Replenish petty	210	512	20 00
	Miscellaneous Expense	⎬ cash fund	—	515	10 00
31	Marcy Casey, Drawing	Withdrawal	211	302	800 00
					3,305 00
31	Cash Credit	Total payments	⑦	→101	3,305 00

③ ② ④ ⑦ ① ⑤ ⑥

Posting the cash payments journal.

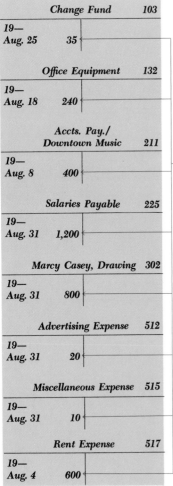

Change Fund 103

19—	
Aug. 25	35

Office Equipment 132

19—	
Aug. 18	240

Accts. Pay./Downtown Music 211

19—	
Aug. 8	400

Salaries Payable 225

19—	
Aug. 31	1,200

Marcy Casey, Drawing 302

19—	
Aug. 31	800

Advertising Expense 512

19—	
Aug. 31	20

Miscellaneous Expense 515

19—	
Aug. 31	10

Rent Expense 517

19—	
Aug. 4	600

Total debits equal $3,305

Cash   Account No. 101

DATE	EXPLANATION	POST. REF.	DEBIT	CREDIT	BALANCE DEBIT	BALANCE CREDIT
19—						
Aug. 1	Balance	—			8,400 00	
31	. . . .	CR1	10,950 00		19,350 00	
31	. . . .	CP1		3,305 00	16,045 00	

Cash	101
19—	
Aug. 31	3,305

Total credit posted: $3,305

7 Post the total credit of $3,305 to the Cash account. Enter the number of the Cash account, 101, in the Posting Reference column of the cash payments journal.

After the credit to the Cash account is posted, the account appears as above. Note that the credit of $3,305 posted to the Cash account equals the total of the debits posted from the cash payments journal to the ledger accounts. (See the illustration in the margin.)

The credit to the Cash account is not posted until the end of the month. Thus a trial balance taken during the month would be out of balance. Once the credit is posted, the trial balance should be in balance.

Cash Posting Clerk:
DOT 216.482-010. Performs a variety of computing, posting, and other accounting duties for cash receipts and/or cash payments.

Activity C. Answer the following questions about posting cash payments. Refer to the cash payments journal and Cash account on page 322.

1. What amount is posted to the Cash account from the cash payments journal on August 31? Is the account debited or credited?

2. Is $3,305 posted as a debit to any account on August 31? Why or why not?

3. Why is there a dash in the Posting Reference column of the Cash account for the August 1 entry?

4. What is the source of the August 31 debit of $10,950 in the Cash account?

5. What is the source of the August 31 credit of $3,305 in the Cash account?

6. What is the balance of the Cash account after the August 31 debit is posted?

7. Should the cash receipts or the cash payments journal be posted first? Why?

Topic 2 Problems

12-2. Karen Tak-Sun owns the Data Products Company. You have been asked to handle her accounting records for the month of September.

a. Open accounts and record the September 1 balances as follows: Cash, $7,200; Accts. Pay./Paul Horowitz, $800; Karen Tak-Sun, Capital, $6,400; Karen Tak-Sun, Drawing and Advertising Expense. Assign an appropriate number to each account.

b. Record the following transactions in a cash payments journal.

c. Post the debit entries from the cash payments journal.

d. Prove, total, and rule the cash payments journal.

e. Post the credit entry from the cash payments journal.

f. Prepare a trial balance.

Sept.
1 Issued Check 172 for $200 for advertising brochures.
2 Voided Check 173.
8 Issued Check 174 for $600 to Paul Horowitz on account.
12 Issued Check 175 for $400 to Karen Tak-Sun, the owner (withdrawal against net income).
18 Issued Check 176 for $80 to the Courier for advertisement.
27 Issued Check 177 to Paul Horowitz for the balance of the amount owed.
28 Issued Check 178 for $20 for advertisement in play program.
30 Issued Check 179 for $500 to Karen Tak-Sun. The $500 is a permanent decrease in capital.

12-3. You have recently been employed by Far Country Services, owned by Kurt Genris. As the accounting clerk, you have been asked to do the following.

a. Open accounts and record the January 1 balances as follows: Cash, $6,800; Petty Cash; Automobile, $7,200; Accts. Pay./Rita Penske, $1,200; Kurt Genris, Capital, $12,800; Kurt Genris, Drawing, Automobile Expense; Delivery Expense; Office Expense. Assign a proper number to each account.

b. Record the transactions for January 1–19 in a cash payments journal.

c. Post the debit entries from the cash payments journal.

d. Record the transactions for January 23–31.

e. Post the debit entries from the cash payments journal.

f. Prove, total, and rule the cash payments journal.

g. Post the credit entry from the cash payments journal.

h. Prepare a trial balance.

Jan.
1 Issued Check 304 for $600 to Rita Penske on account.
6 Issued Check 305 for $75 to establish a petty cash fund.
10 Voided Check 306.
11 Issued Check 307 for $3,000 for a used car.
19 Issued Check 308 for $800 to Kurt Genris, the owner (permanent withdrawal).
23 Issued Check 309 for $300 for car repairs.
25 Issued Check 310 for balance of Rita Penske account.
26 Issued Check 311 for $50 for office supplies.
27 Issued Check 312 for $6.50 for delivery expense.
31 Issued Check 313 for $400 to Kurt Genris, the owner (withdrawal against net income).
31 Issued Check 314 for $37 to replenish petty cash (Automobile Expense, $32; Office Expense, $5).

Topic 3
Proving Cash

A *What is a cash proof?* Any method used to verify that the amount of *cash recorded* equals the *cash handled* is known as a **cash proof.** You know how a cash proof is made when the total on a cash register tape (the cash recorded) is compared with the total in the cash drawer (the cash handled). Another cash proof is when the checkbook is compared with the Cash account or with the bank statement.

Verifying the Cash Account and Checkbook Balances

The balance of cash is available from three sources when cash control procedures are used. One cash balance is found in the checkbook, the second in the cash account, and the third on the monthly bank statement. The cash proof to verify the cash account balance and checkbook balance is described here.

The checkbook stub contains a record of all deposits and all checks written. Thus the balance on the checkbook stub, for any date, should be the balance of cash for that date. Also, the checkbook stub should equal the cash account balance for any date. If debits have been posted to the Cash account from the cash receipts journal and credits have been posted from the cash payments journal, the balances should be equal. If there have been no errors in the entries or computations, the cash proof is easy. Compare the checkbook stub balance to the cash account balance. If the totals are equal, the cash proof is complete.

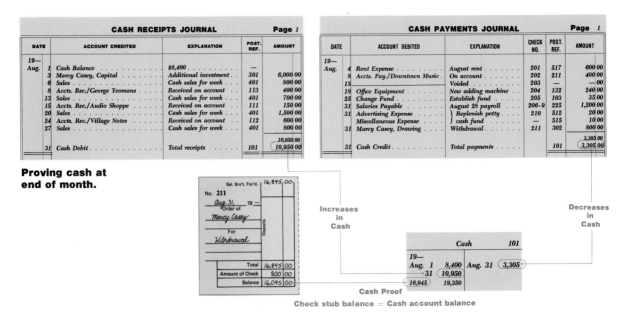

Proving cash at end of month.

Check stub balance = Cash account balance

Verifying the Checkbook and the Bank Statement Balances

Effective cash control also requires that the checkbook balance equal the bank statement balance. The two balances are seldom in agreement because of outstanding checks, deposits in transit, dishonored checks, fees, service charges, and errors. The procedures for reconciling the checkbook balance and bank statement balance are described in Chapter 8 of Part 1.

Adjustments. After the bank reconciliation is prepared, the balance on the last check stub must be brought into agreement with the "adjusted checkbook balance." This is done by transferring the adjustments from the bank reconciliation to the check stubs. Two adjustments to the checkbook balance are illustrated in the margin. The first adjustment is for a $3 service charge (SC). The second adjustment is for a $400 dishonored check (returned check or Rt. Ck.).

Adjustments that change the checkbook balance also change the Cash account balance. Thus they must be recorded and posted. An entry recording a service charge of $3 is made in the cash payments journal. The account debited is the Miscellaneous Expense account. The $3 amount is included in the credit to the Cash account, when the total of the journal is posted at the end of the month.

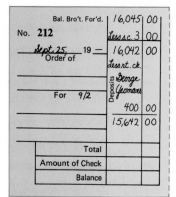

Check stub showing adjustments from bank reconciliation statement.

CASH PAYMENTS JOURNAL					Page 2	
DATE	ACCOUNT DEBITED	EXPLANATION	CHECK NO.	POST. REF.	AMOUNT	
19— Sept. 2	Miscellaneous Expense	Bank service charge . . .	—		3 00	

Entry to record bank service charge.

An entry recording the return of a dishonored check is made in the cash payments journal. The entry is not, strictly speaking, a cash payment. However, it is treated as if it were to correct the original recording of the cash receipt. The entry is shown in the cash payments journal on page 326.

The dishonored check shown on the check stub in the margin above was received from George Yeomans on August 8 in partial payment of his account. An entry was made in the cash receipts journal when the check was received. See the illustration on page 326.

When the entry was posted, the Cash account was increased by $400. Accts. Rec./George Yeomans was decreased by the same amount. Now $400 must be deducted from the Cash account and added back to the George Yeomans account. This is done by making the following entry in the cash payments journal on page 326.

CASH RECEIPTS JOURNAL				Page	1
DATE	ACCOUNT CREDITED	EXPLANATION	POST. REF.	AMOUNT	
19— Aug. 8	Accts. Rec./George Yeomans	On account	111	400 00	

Entry to record cash received on account.

CASH PAYMENTS JOURNAL					Page	2
DATE	ACCOUNT DEBITED	EXPLANATION	CHECK NO.	POST. REF.	AMOUNT	
19— Sept. 2	Accts. Rec./George Yeomans . .	Ret'd check of Aug. 8 . .	—	111	400 00	

Entry to record returned check.

Activity A. Answer the following questions about cash proofs. Refer to the cash proof illustrations on page 324, and the check stub, cash payments journal, and cash receipts journal on pages 325 to 326.
1. What does $10,950 in the cash receipts journal represent?
2. How does the House of Sound arrive at the cash balance of $16,045 for the month of August?

3. What is the cash proof amount for August 31?
4. What is the check stub balance on September 2?
5. Is a check for the $3 service charge recorded in the cash payments journal?
6. Would posting the September 2 entry increase or decrease the George Yeomans account? Why?
7. Why not accept the bank's balance for cash as the true balance and eliminate making cash proofs?

Establishing, Using, and Replenishing Change Funds

B *What is a change fund?* A change fund is the amount of cash put in the drawer to make change. The House of Sound established a change fund on August 25 for $35.

Entry to establish change fund.

CASH PAYMENTS JOURNAL					Page 7
DATE	ACCOUNT DEBITED	EXPLANATION	CHECK NO.	POST. REF.	AMOUNT
19— Aug. 25	Change Fund	Establish Change Fund	205		35 00

Establishing the Change Fund. A check establishing a change fund is drawn on the Cash account. The check is made payable to the person responsible for the fund. The check is signed and cashed, and the money is placed in the cash register. The entry for the check includes a debit to the Change Fund account and a credit to the Cash account.

Using the Change Fund. The change fund is placed in the cash register each day to make change. As cash sales are made, the salesclerks put the cash into the cash register and make change. At the end of the day, the cash in the drawer is counted and cash is proved. The amount of the change is subtracted from the total cash in the drawer to find the amount of net cash handled. This amount is then checked against the cash register tape or the net cash received on the cash proof.

Replenishing the Change Fund. No check needs to be drawn to replenish the change fund. The cash needed to replenish the fund comes from the cash drawer. Any shortage is taken from the cash received and is debited to the Cash Short and Over account. The procedures for recording cash short and over are explained in the next learning segment.

Activity B. Answer the following questions about change funds. Refer to the text, margin notes, and illustrations on pages 326 to 327.
1. Which account is debited to establish a change fund? Which account is credited?

2. What is the amount of the change fund established on August 25?
3. What are the entries to replenish the change fund?

Recording Cash Short and Over

C *What indicates that errors have been made in handling cash?* When cash is handled in making change, the cash in the drawer and the amount recorded on the cash register tape sometimes differ. The cash in the drawer might be more or less than the amount shown on the tape. When the reason for a cash difference cannot be found, it is assumed that a mistake was made in making change. These mistakes are referred to as *cash over* or *cash short*.

Cash Over. A **cash overage** is when there is more cash in the drawer than there should be (according to the cash proof). For example, the cash register tape for September 4 shows that net receipts from cash sales are $275. The supervisor copies this amount on the cash proof form. The supervisor then counts the cash in the drawer ($312) and subtracts the amount of the change fund ($35). This leaves a balance of $277. The cash proof shows the clerk should have received only $275, but $277 is in the drawer. Thus cash is over by $2. If no error is located in the records, it is assumed that a mistake was made in making change.

The cash proof is then sent to the accounting department. It becomes the source document for a journal entry. The debit entry is clear. The Cash account must be debited for $277 because this amount will be deposited in the bank. The credit entry, however, should show the Sales account credited for only $275. The debit and credit amounts must be equal. Thus, the overage of $2 must be credited to some account.

The overage could be combined with sales revenue and recorded in the Sales account. However, if this practice were followed over a period of time, the business would have incorrect sales revenue records. The solution is to set up a temporary owner's equity account, known as Cash Short and Over, to record all cash overages and cash shortages. An overage is treated as revenue because it increases owner's equity.

CASH PROOF		
Date *September 4, 19—*		
Register No. *III*		
Cash Sales	275	00
Less: Cash Paid Out	—	
Net Cash Received	275	00
Cash in Drawer	312	00
Less: Change Fund	35	00
Net Cash Handled	277	00
~~Short or~~ Over	2	00
Clerk *James Amos*		
Supervisor *L. Carson*		

Cash	?	Sales
277	2	275

Thus the overage of $2 is credited to the Cash Short and Over account. The transaction is recorded in the cash receipts journal and posted to the proper accounts as follows.

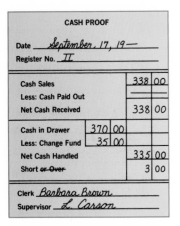

Cash	Cash Short and Over	Sales
277	2	275

CASH RECEIPTS JOURNAL				Page 2	
DATE	ACCOUNT CREDITED	EXPLANATION	POST. REF.	AMOUNT	
19— Sept. 4	Sales	Daily sales		275	00
4	Cash Short and Over	Cash overage		2	00

The T accounts in the margin show that the equality of debits and credits is kept when a cash overage is treated as revenue and properly recorded.

Cash Short. A **cash shortage** is when there is less cash in the drawer than there should be (according to the cash proof). Thus cash is short by $3, as shown in the cash proof in the margin, if the net cash received is $338 and the net amount of cash in the drawer is $335. If the money cannot be located, the shortage of $3 must be recorded.

A shortage is treated like an expense because it decreases owner's equity. Thus the $3 shortage should be debited to the Cash Short and Over account. A cash short transaction is more easily understood with the use of T accounts.

The debit to the Cash account should be only $335. This is the amount that will be deposited in the bank. However, the $338 should be credited to the Sales account. This is the true revenue that was earned. The revenue is then reduced by an expense of $3 (which is what the $3 shortage represents).

If the transaction were recorded in a general journal, it would be entered as follows.

CASH PROOF

Date _September 17, 19—_
Register No. _II_

Cash Sales		338 00
Less: Cash Paid Out		
Net Cash Received		338 00
Cash in Drawer	370 00	
Less: Change Fund	35 00	
Net Cash Handled		335 00
Short or Over		3 00

Clerk _Barbara Brown_
Supervisor _L. Carson_

Debit Cash Short and Over for a shortage.

Sept.	17	Cash	335	00		
		Cash Short and Over	3	00		
		Sales			338	00

When special cash journals are used, the transaction must be recorded in a different way. Here is the procedure the accounting clerk would follow.

1 Record a $338 credit to Sales in the cash receipts journal. (The entry assumes a $338 debit to Cash.)

CASH RECEIPTS JOURNAL　　　　　　Page 2

DATE	ACCOUNT CREDITED	EXPLANATION	POST. REF.	AMOUNT
19— Sept. 17	Sales	Daily sales		338 00

2 Record the $3 shortage as a debit to Cash Short and Over in the cash payments journal. (The entry assumes a $3 credit to Cash.) Note that a dash is placed in the Check Number column to indicate that no check was issued.

CASH PAYMENTS JOURNAL　　　　　Page 2

DATE	ACCOUNT DEBITED	EXPLANATION	CHECK NO.	POST. REF.	AMOUNT
19— Sept. 17	Cash Short and Over	Cash shortage	—		3 00

When the individual entries are posted, the balance of the Cash account would be $335. The Cash Short and Over account would have a $3 debit balance. The Sales account would have a $338 credit balance.

Uses of the Cash Short and Over Account. The Cash Short and Over account shows the shortages and overages in making change during an accounting period. Thus the balance of the Cash Short and Over account is viewed as either expense or revenue. When Cash Short and Over has a debit balance, it is shown as an expense on the income statement because it decreases owner's equity. When it has a credit balance, it is shown as revenue because it increases owner's equity.

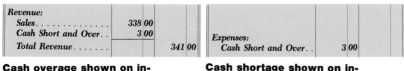

Cash overage shown on income statement as expense.　　　Cash shortage shown on income statement as expense.

The Cash Short and Over account is listed under expenses in the chart of accounts for the House of Sound. If the account has a credit balance at the end of the accounting period, the balance will be considered revenue and not an expense. In either case, it is closed into the Income Summary account at the end of the accounting period.

The Cash Short and Over account is useful for balancing accounting records when differences in cash cannot be traced. This device, however, is not a substitute for locating errors. It is used only when absolutely necessary.

Cash

338	3
335	

Cash Short and Over

3	3

②

Sales

	338

①

Cash Short and Over

Debit Balance Expense	Credit Balance Revenue

House of Sound Chart of Accounts

Expenses
511　Cash Short and Over

Activity C. Answer the following questions about cash short and over. Refer to the cash short and cash over illustrations on pages 328 and 329.
1. What might have caused the cash overage on September 4?
2. Which account is credited for cash over?
3. What are the sales for September 4?
4. How much cash is received on September 4?
5. What might have caused the cash shortage on September 17?
6. Which account is debited for cash short?
7. How much cash is received on September 17?
8. How would you react to a company policy that deducts all cash shortages from an employee's paycheck?

Accounting Concept:
Proving Assets. The accuracy of the accounting records must be verified with the actual amounts at frequent intervals.

Topic 3 Problems

12-4. Paul Marten owns the Vintage Auto Show. Visitors pay the admission price to the cashier, who records the sale on a cash register, which issues a ticket for the customer and lists the sale on a tape. You are to keep the cash records for the first two weeks of April.
a. Open balance ledger accounts and record the April 1 balances as follows: Cash, $5,200; Change Fund; Accts. Rec./Motor Tours, Inc., $600; Antique Autos, $130,000; Accts. Pay./Al's Repair Shop, $970; Paul Marten, Capital, $134,830; Paul Marten, Drawing; Admissions; Cash Short and Over; and Miscellaneous Expense.
b. Using a cash receipts journal and a cash payments journal, record the transactions below. First, record a memorandum entry for the April 1 cash balance.
c. Post the credit entries from the cash receipts journal and debit entries from the cash payments journal.
d. Prepare a cash proof for April 14. The checkbook shows a balance of $6,442.50.

April 2 Issued Check 81 for $25 to establish change fund.
 5 Received $400 from Motor Tours, Inc., on account.
 6 Recorded the cash proof, showing admissions (revenue) of $1,784 and an overage of $7.
 8 Issued Check 82 for $600 to Al's Repair Shop.
 9 Voided Check 83.
 11 Issued Check 84 for $1,600 for an antique Hudson auto (debit: Antique Autos).
 12 Issued Check 85 for $39 for tickets (Miscellaneous Expense).

13 Recorded the cash proof, showing admissions of $1,320 and a shortage of $4.50.

12-5. Use the journals and ledger prepared in Topic Problem 12-4 to keep the cash records for the Vintage Auto Show for the last two weeks of April.
a. Record the following transactions.
b. Post the individual entries from the journals.
c. Prepare a cash proof for April 30. The checkbook shows a balance of $15,159.65.
d. Rule the journals, and post the totals to the ledger.
e. Prepare a trial balance.

April 15 Received $100 from Motor Tours, Inc., on account.
 16 Issued Check 86 for $200 to Al's Repair Shop on account.
 17 Issued Check 87 for $800 to Paul Marten, the owner, for personal use.
 18 Recorded service charge of $4.75 shown on bank statement.
 18 Recorded the return by the bank of a dishonored check for $400 received from Motor Tours, Inc., on April 5.
 20 Recorded the cash proof, showing admissions of $1,750 and an overage of $18.
 26 Paul Marten invested an additional $5,000 in the business.
 27 Recorded the cash proof, showing admissions of $1,400; no shortage or overage.
 28 Received $1,200 from sale of an antique Studebaker.
 30 Recorded the cash proof, showing admissions of $657 and a shortage of $3.10.

The Language of Business

Here are some terms that make up the language of business. Do you know the meaning of each?

cash payments subsystem

cash payments journal withdrawal

drawing account
cash proof
cash overage

Cash Short and Over account
cash shortage

Chapter 12   Questions

1. List and explain the procedures for the control of cash payments.
2. What procedure is followed to complete the cash payments journal at the end of the month?
3. At the end of the accounting period, the Cash Short and Over account showed total debits of $4.80 and total credits of $3.90. Is the balance of this account considered revenue or an expense?
4. How is a cash shortage shown on the income statement? How is a cash overage shown?
5. During the past month, the Cash Short and Over account had total debits of $97 and total credits of $3. The accountant feels that the procedure for handling shortages and overages should be investigated. Do you agree? Why?
6. Explain the procedures for verifying the Cash account balance and the checkbook balance at the end of the month and during the month.
7. Explain how the monthly bank statement provides an excellent external control of cash receipts and cash payments.
8. What source documents serve as the basis for the entries in the cash payments journal?
9. How does the accountant know when to use the drawing account and when to use the capital account?

Chapter 12   Problems

Problems for Chapter 12 are given in the *Working Papers and Chapter Problems for Part 2.* If you are using the workbook, do the problems in the space provided there.

Chapter 12   Management Cases

Control of Cash Disbursements. Many businesses lose large amounts of money through the theft or embezzlement of cash. Small sums taken by dishonest employees can add up to a sizable amount over a period of time. Reports of the embezzlement of large sums of cash are frequently reported in the news. A business should set up safeguards to control cash in order to (1) remove temptations to steal and (2) protect the reputations of all employees.

Case 12M-1. The Marchand Freight Company has branches in several cities. Assume that you have been appointed manager of a branch. In addition to the drivers and their helpers, there are five people who work in the office: the manager (you), a secretary, an accounting clerk, and two office clerks. The secretary and the accounting clerk have been with the branch for a number of years. The following procedures are used in handling cash.

• Money is usually received through the mail and is opened by any office employee who has time. The person who opens the mail fills out a remittance slip for each amount received, gives the slip to the accounting clerk, and places all receipts in a locked box.
• Because the bank is a 30-minute drive from the office, deposits are usually made once a week. Any member of the office staff may be given the respon-

sibility for taking the deposit to the bank. The average weekly deposit is $4,000.

- The manager, secretary, and accounting clerk are authorized to sign checks.
- All checks are prenumbered. When an error is made in preparing a check, the check is discarded and a note is made on the checkbook stub.
- All invoices are paid by check. The invoices are verified, approved, and paid by either the accounting clerk or the secretary, whoever has time. Since both are authorized to sign checks, they and the manager have access to the checkbook.
- A cash receipts journal and a cash payments journal are used. All receipts and payments are recorded in these journals by the accounting clerk only.
- Small expenditures are made from a petty cash fund. Although a careful record is kept of the amounts put in the fund, no record is kept of the disbursements from it. The fund is kept in a small box in

the secretary's desk. Either the secretary, the accounting clerk, or the manager may take money from the box. (Each disbursement is usually less than $1, but no policy has been set as to a maximum amount.) When the money in the box is gone, cash is taken from the bank deposit and placed in the petty cash box.

What recommendations would you make to improve the controls on the following cash procedures?
a. The receipt of cash and the preparation of source documents
b. The depositing of the cash
c. The writing of checks
d. The use of prenumbered checks
e. The payment of invoices
f. The recording of cash receipts and cash payments
g. The handling of petty cash

Working Hint

Preparing a Cash Proof on an Adding Machine Tape. A cash proof can be prepared easily on an adding machine tape.
- Add the individual amounts recorded in the cash receipts journal. Obtain the total, and pencil-foot the journal.
- Add the individual amounts recorded in the cash payments journal. Obtain the total, and pencil-foot the journal.
- Clear the machine by depressing the total key. The clear symbol (.00T) will now appear on the tape for the cash proof.
- Add the balance of the Cash account at the beginning of the month (9,440.00).
- Add the total of the debits (7,475.00) recorded in the cash receipts journal.

- Obtain a subtotal (16,915.00S) by depressing the subtotal key or bar. (The subtotal device makes it possible to take a total at any point in a column of figures and to continue with the column because the accumulated amount is not cleared from the machine. The subtotal is indicated by the letter "S" or a symbol following the printed amount.) The subtotal shown on the tape is the total of the debits to the Cash account.
- Subtract the total of the credits (1,800.00) recorded in the cash payments journal.
- Obtain the total (15,115.00T). The total on the adding machine tape is the balance of the Cash account. This amount should equal the amount shown in the checkbook for the same date.

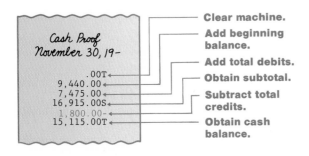

A Purchases Subsystem

You will now learn how the people, forms, procedures, and equipment in a purchases subsystem are used to control purchases on credit. You will also learn about the important jobs of the purchasing agent, inventory clerk, purchasing clerk, and receiving clerk.

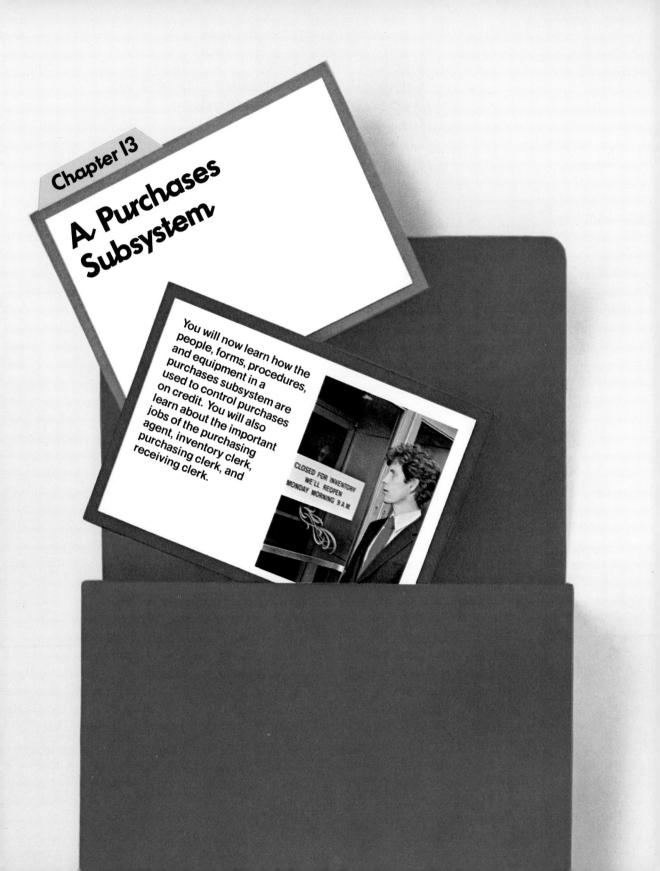

Topic 1
Controlling Purchases: Ordering, Receiving, and Accounting for Merchandise

Procedures for Controlling Purchases on Credit

A *What is a purchases subsystem?* The people, forms, procedures, and equipment used to control purchases on credit make up a **purchases subsystem.** Internal control is especially important in a purchases subsystem as purchases deal with amounts of assets. The procedures for internal control are discussed here. The purchase of merchandise involves four activities. These are as follows.

- Ordering merchandise
- Receiving merchandise
- Accounting for merchandise
- Storing merchandise

The subsystem for purchasing merchandise includes a number of procedures which ensure control over the four activities. A subsystem to control the purchase of merchandise includes the following procedures.

Control: Identify merchandise needed.
Control: Initiate purchasing by authorized personnel.
Control: Use prenumbered forms.
Control: Divide responsibility.
Control: Purchase merchandise from approved suppliers.
Control: Accept merchandise only in approved quantities and quality.
Control: Verify invoices before approving for payment.
Control: Prove inventory.
Control: Record all payables.
Control: Obtain refunds or credits for all purchase returns and allowances.
Control: Pay invoices in time to take cash discounts.

- Identify merchandise needed.
- Initiate purchasing by authorized personnel.
- Use prenumbered forms.
- Divide responsibility.
- Purchase merchandise from approved suppliers.
- Accept merchandise only in approved quantities and quality.
- Verify quantities, terms, prices, and computations on invoices before approving payment.
- Verify quantities of merchandise in stock with inventory records.
- Record data from completed purchase transactions.
- Obtain refunds or credits for all purchases returns and allowances.
- Pay invoices in time to take cash discounts.

Each of these procedures relates to ordering, receiving, storing, or accounting for purchases of merchandise. Just how they relate is discussed next.

Activity A. Answer the following questions about controlling the purchase of merchandise.
1. What activities are involved in purchasing merchandise?
2. Which procedure might be completed in the receiving department?
3. Which procedure involves the payment of cash?
4. Which procedure involves a journal entry?
5. Which procedure limits the suppliers from whom merchandise may be purchased?

Ordering Merchandise

B *How is merchandise ordered?* In a small business, merchandise may be ordered by the owner. In a large business, merchandise may be ordered by a purchasing agent in a special purchasing department. Regardless of its size, each business must decide what needs to be purchased, choose the supplier, and place the order.

Determining Needs. In a small business, a note from the owner could be the signal that some item needs to be ordered. In a large business, like the House of Sound, the signal to order comes from inventory cards. An **inventory card** is a record of the stock of one item.

The inventory card in the margin below is for Aura Portable Cassettes (A82-B). The minimum (lowest) stock for them is 10. Thus, on September 23, when the inventory drops to 10, the inventory clerk knows it is time to order additional stock. The maximum (largest) stock of Aura Cassettes (A82-B) is 28. Thus the inventory clerk can quickly determine that 18 additional cassettes must be ordered to refill the stock. The minimum (10) and the maximum (28) are based on the average volume of sales and the time needed to get new stock.

In the House of Sound, each department manager is authorized to initiate (start) purchasing for the specific department. The department manager uses a purchase requisition for this. The **purchase requisition** is a prenumbered form on which the purchasing agent orders merchandise. The purchase requisition provides the following information.

- WHO is making the request
- WHAT is to be purchased
- WHEN it is needed

The prenumbered purchase requisition is signed by an authorized employee. The requisition is the source document that starts the purchasing activity.

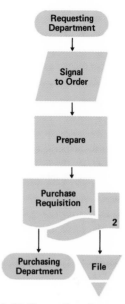

Initiating a Purchase

Control: Identify merchandise needed.
Control: Initiate purchasing by authorized personnel.
Control: Use prenumbered form.

INVENTORY CARD

No. _A82-B_
Item _Aura Portable Cassettes_
Location: Aisle _3_ Bin _4_

Maximum _28_			Minimum _10_	
Date	Quant. Rec'd	Unit Cost	Quant. Sold	Balance
19— 8/13	22	40.00		28
8/20			3	25
8/27			4	21
9/4			4	17
9/12			2	15
9/18			2	13
9/23			3	10

Inventory card showing maximum and minimum stock.

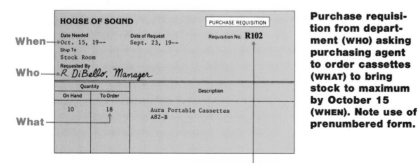

Purchase requisition from department (WHO) asking purchasing agent to order cassettes (WHAT) to bring stock to maximum by October 15 (WHEN). Note use of prenumbered form.

Prenumbered Form

Purchasing Agent:
DOT 162.157-038. Reviews requisitions, selects suppliers, and orders merchandise.

Inventory Clerk:
DOT 222.387-026. Keeps record of amount, kind, and cost of merchandise on hand. May indicate items to be reordered. May count merchandise on hand. May compare physical inventories with records.

Control: Divide responsibility
Control: Purchase merchandise from approved suppliers.

Request for quotation from House of Sound answered by Phelps Supply.

Who →
When →
What →

Selecting the Supplier. The purchasing agent has a list of suppliers for most items to be purchased. The supplier who is best able to supply the merchandise is chosen. The purchasing agent might ask for prices from new suppliers if new items are requisitioned or new suppliers are needed.

The prices and quantities of merchandise are requested on a letter or a special form called a **request for quotation.** The form provides the following information.

- WHO is making the request for a quotation
- WHAT items and quantities are wanted
- WHEN the goods are needed

The request for quotation shown in the margin was prepared by the purchasing clerk of the House of Sound. On it, Phelps Supply shows credit terms of 2/10, n/30. The term *2/10* means that the buyer can deduct 2 percent if the bill is paid within 10 days from the invoice date. In the term *n/30,* the *n* stands for *net.* Thus *n/30* means that if the discount is not taken, the buyer has 30 days in which to pay the (net) full amount. (If the terms were *n/EOM,* the buyer would have until the *end of the month* to pay the net amount.)

Phelps Supply also indicates that the goods will be shipped FOB Denver. **FOB (free on board)** is a shipping term that means that the seller pays shipping charges to that destination. Phelps Supply will pay the shipping charges from Tucson to Denver. (If the form showed FOB Tucson, House of Sound must pay the shipping charges.)

Placing the Order. The reasons vary for choosing a supplier. For example, sometimes the price is most important. Other times, delivery time matters more. Credit terms will sometimes be the deciding factor. The purchasing agent of House of Sound orders the cassettes from Phelps Supply because they quoted the lowest price.

The purchasing clerk must now prepare a purchase order. The **purchase order** is the form on which the purchasing clerk authorizes the supplier to ship merchandise and charge the purchaser the quoted prices for the merchandise. For each item, the purchase order should show the following.

1 The quantity ordered
2 A stock number, if known
3 A brief description
4 The unit price, taken either from the supplier's catalog or from the copy of the request for quotation
5 The terms
6 Shipping instructions

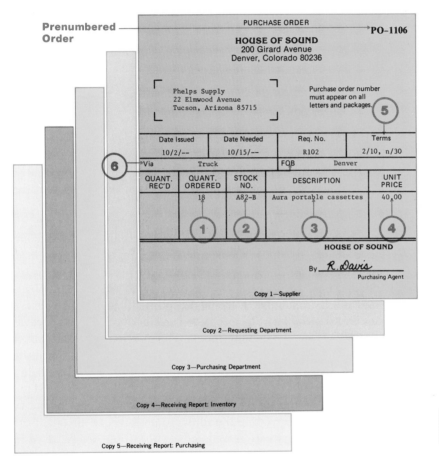

Prenumbered Order

PURCHASE ORDER

PO-1106

HOUSE OF SOUND
200 Girard Avenue
Denver, Colorado 80236

Phelps Supply
22 Elmwood Avenue
Tucson, Arizona 85715

Purchase order number must appear on all letters and packages.

5

Date Issued	Date Needed	Req. No.	Terms
10/2/--	10/15/--	R102	2/10, n/30

6 Via   Truck   FOB   Denver

QUANT. REC'D	QUANT. ORDERED	STOCK NO.	DESCRIPTION	UNIT PRICE
	18	A82-B	Aura portable cassettes	40.00

1   2   3   4

HOUSE OF SOUND

By _R. Davis_
                    Purchasing Agent

Copy 1—Supplier

Copy 2—Requesting Department

Copy 3—Purchasing Department

Copy 4—Receiving Report: Inventory

Copy 5—Receiving Report: Purchasing

The number of copies of the purchase order varies with the size of the business. The House of Sound prepares purchase orders on prenumbered forms. Each form contains five copies, as shown above. Copy 1 is the order sent to the supplier. Copy 2 is sent to the department that initiated the purchase requisition to show that the needed merchandise is now on order. Copy 3 is kept by the purchasing department as a record of all purchase orders issued. Copies 4 and 5 are sent to the receiving department until the merchandise arrives.

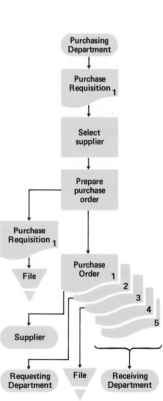

Placing an Order

Purchasing Clerk:
DOT 249.367-066. Prepares requests for quotation and purchase orders; keeps records of merchandise ordered.

Activity B. Answer the following questions about ordering merchandise. Refer to the purchase requisition, the request for quotation, and the purchase order on pages 335 to 337.

1. Where are the goods to be shipped?
2. What quantity is on hand? What quantity is requisitioned?
3. When are the cassettes needed?
4. What unit price is quoted by Phelps Supply?
5. What credit terms does Phelps Supply offer?
6. Is Phelps Supply the only supplier to receive the request for quotation?
7. What is the purchase order number?
8. When is the purchase order issued?
9. Who approved the purchase order?

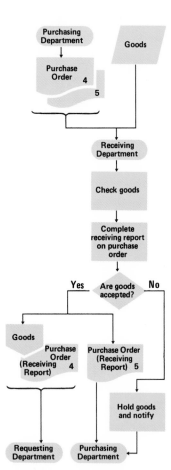

Receiving Merchandise

Receiving Merchandise

C *What happens when merchandise is received?* When merchandise is received, it first must be unpacked, inspected, and counted. Then it must be recorded as being received. Finally, it must be moved to the storage or sales area of the department that sent the purchase requisition.

The receiving clerk checks the items for any shortages, errors, or damages in shipment. The count of the items actually received is entered on Copy 4 of the purchase order. If the counts do not agree, the receiving clerk holds the shipment and asks the purchasing agent for instructions. If the counts and description agree with the purchase order and the merchandise is in good condition, the receiving clerk indicates that the shipment is accepted. The clerk initials the approval section of Copy 4—the receiving report. The merchandise and Copy 4 are then sent to the stockroom or the department that requisitioned the items. There the shipment is again counted and checked before being put into inventory.

Copy 4 serves as the source document for updating the inventory cards for the items received. In the illustration shown at the top of the next page, the inventory card is updated to show the goods received in the receiving report. The quantity received (18) is added to the balance (4). The balance is now 22. The date received (10/10) and the unit cost ($40) are also recorded on the inventory card.

Copy 5 carries the receiving clerks initials of approval and is sent to the purchasing agent to show that the shipment has been received and accepted.

Receiving Clerk:
DOT 222.387-050. Receives, unpacks, inspects, and verifies shipments; handles rejected merchandise; records merchandise and sends it to proper department.

Control: Accept merchandise in authorized quantities and quality only.

PURCHASE ORDER

PO–1106

HOUSE OF SOUND
200 Girard Avenue
Denver, Colorado 80236

Phelps Supply 22 Elmwood Avenue Tucson, Arizona 85715	Goods Received ___10/10/––___ Quantity Checked ___ℓ.n.___ Quality Checked ___J A___

Date Issued	Date Needed	Req. No.	Terms
10/2/––	10/15/––	R102	2/10, n/30

Via	Truck	FOB	Denver

QUANT. REC'D	QUANT. ORDERED	STOCK NO.	DESCRIPTION	UNIT PRICE
18	18	A82-B	Aura portable cassettes	40.00

HOUSE OF SOUND

By _R. Davis_
Purchasing Agent

Copy 4—Receiving Report: Inventory

INVENTORY CARD

No. _A-82-B_

Item _Aura Portable Cassette_

Location: Aisle ___3___ Bin ___7___

Maximum ___28___ Minimum ___10___

Date	Quant. Rec'd	Unit Cost	Quant. Sold	Balance
19— 8/13	22	40.00		28
8/20			3	25
8/27			4	21
9/4			4	17
9/12			2	15
9/18			2	13
9/23			3	10
9/28			2	8
10/2			3	5
10/8			1	4
10/10	18	40.00		22

Activity C. Answer the following questions about receiving merchandise. Refer to the receiving report and inventory card shown above.
1. When are the goods received?
2. How many cassettes are received?
3. Who checks the quantity of the goods? The quality?
4. What is the unit cost of the goods received?
5. When does the balance reach the minimum? Is a requisition issued?
6. What is the change in the unit cost?
7. What would happen if a customer wanted 5 cassettes on October 9 and would not take fewer than 5?

Accounting for Merchandise

D *What control procedures are used to account for merchandise?*
The purchasing agent must confirm that all items ordered have been received in good condition. To do so, the agent holds Copy 5 of the purchase order until an **invoice** (a bill) is received from the supplier. To the purchaser, the invoice is a **purchase invoice.** It lists the items purchased. To the supplier who has issued the bill, it is a **sales invoice.** It lists the items sold. These two invoices are checks on the accuracy of the purchaser's and supplier's records. The invoice shown on page 340 is a purchase invoice to the purchaser, House of Sound. It is a sales invoice to the supplier, Phelps Supply.

The sales invoice contains almost the same information that is on the purchase order. It shows the information listed on page 340.

- The name and address of the seller and the purchaser.
- The invoice number and the date.
- The terms.
- The purchase order number and date (for cross-reference)
- The method of shipment.
- The quantity, description, and price of each item shipped.
- The extensions.

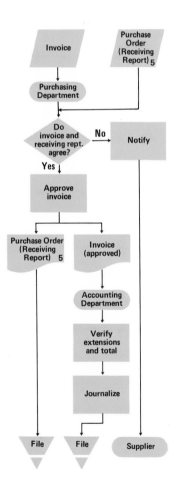

APPROVED	DATE *10/10/—*
QUANTITIES RECEIVED	*R. Davis*
PRICES CHARGED	*R. Davis*
EXTENSIONS & TOTALS	*B. Boothe*
DATE PAID	*10/18/—*
CHECK NO.	*308*

Stamp to verify invoice.

Control: Verify invoices before approving payment.

Processing a Purchase Invoice

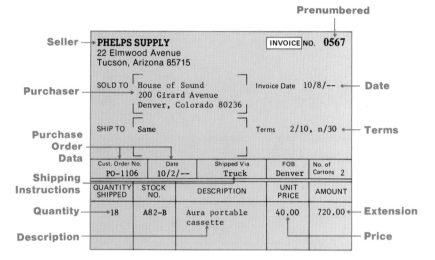

The invoice also shows how the amount owed was computed. Each amount in the Amount column is called an extension, which is found by multiplying the unit price of the item by the number of units shipped. The amount shown on the invoice above ($720) is computed by multiplying the unit price ($40) by the number of units shipped (18). If the invoice has more than one extension in the Amount column, the extensions are added to show the total amount owed.

The purpose of comparing the sales invoice with Copy 5 of the purchase order is to make sure that the business has been billed only for the items it received. If there are any differences, the purchasing agent contacts the supplier. If the invoice is correct, it is stamped with a special "Approved" stamp, as shown in the margin above. The purchasing agent initials the checked and verified items to show they are correct. The invoice is then sent to the accounting department. Copy 5 is placed in chronological sequence in the purchasing department's permanent file of completed purchase orders. (See the flowchart in the margin.)

When the accounting department receives the purchase invoice, the extensions and the total are rechecked. The invoice is then journalized. Finally, when the invoice is due, a check is issued for the correct amount. As the invoice is processed in the accounting department, the authorized employee initials the invoice to indicate the items have been checked and approved. A stamp verifying this is on page 340.

Activity D. Answer the following questions about accounting for the merchandise. Refer to the purchase invoice and the approval stamp on pages 339 and 340.
1. What is the number of the invoice?
2. What is the purchase order number?
3. How many items are shipped?
4. Is this quantity received? Who verifies that it is or is not received?

5. When is the invoice paid?
6. What is the number of the check to pay the invoice?
7. What is the total amount shown on the invoice?
8. What procedures for controlling purchases are illustrated by the approval stamp?

Visualizing a Purchases Subsystem

E | *How are the procedures in a purchases subsystem related to each other?* The flowchart on page 342 shows the procedures to control purchases in the purchases subsystem. The activities (numbered 1–22) are described briefly at the top and bottom of the flowchart. By reading the activities and following them on the flowchart, you can see how each relates to the other. You can also see that the subsystem includes all the procedures for the control of purchases that have been discussed.

Activity E. Answer the following questions about visualizing the purchases subsystem. Refer to the flowchart on page 342.
1. How many steps are completed by the supplier? What are the steps?
2. What department journalizes the purchases transactions?
3. What department prepares the purchase requisition?

4. The purchase requisition is the basis for preparing which document?
5. Does the purchasing department handle the goods?
6. Some large businesses keep the inventory cards in the accounting department. In these businesses, how do you suppose the requesting department is able to keep track of inventory balances? What is the source document for updating the inventory cards?

Accounting Concept:
Control: Procedures must be established to ensure accuracy, honesty, and efficiency and speed in handling and recording assets, liabilities, owner's equity, revenues, and expenses.

Topic 1 Problems

13-1. Home Supply uses inventory cards like the one shown on page 339.
a. Record these items on two inventory cards.
Item 35: portable sander; aisle, 12; bin, 4; maximum, 72; minimum, 18; balance of 28 on June 1; unit cost, $28.
Item 36: toaster oven; aisle, 13; bin, 8; maximum, 60;

minimum, 12; balance of 17 on June 1; unit cost, $43.
b. The following transactions were taken from receiving reports and shipping reports. Update the inventory cards.
c. List the dates on which purchase requisitions should be issued.

VISUALIZING A SUBSYSTEM FOR PURCHASES ON CREDIT

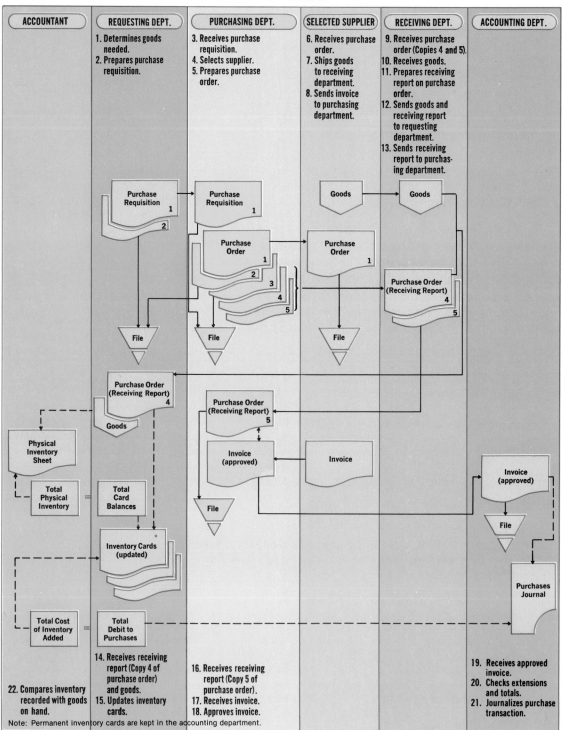

ACCOUNTANT	REQUESTING DEPT.	PURCHASING DEPT.	SELECTED SUPPLIER	RECEIVING DEPT.	ACCOUNTING DEPT.
	1. Determines goods needed. 2. Prepares purchase requisition.	3. Receives purchase requisition. 4. Selects supplier. 5. Prepares purchase order.	6. Receives purchase order. 7. Ships goods to receiving department. 8. Sends invoice to purchasing department.	9. Receives purchase order (Copies 4 and 5). 10. Receives goods. 11. Prepares receiving report on purchase order. 12. Sends goods and receiving report to requesting department. 13. Sends receiving report to purchasing department.	

Purchase Requisition 1
Purchase Requisition 1 2
Purchase Order 1 2 3 4 5
Goods
Goods
Purchase Order 1
Purchase Order (Receiving Report) 4 5
File
File
File

Purchase Order (Receiving Report) 4
Goods
Purchase Order (Receiving Report) 5
Invoice (approved)
Invoice
File

Physical Inventory Sheet
Total Physical Inventory
Total Card Balances
Inventory Cards (updated)
Invoice (approved)
File

Total Cost of Inventory Added
Total Debit to Purchases
Purchases Journal

ACCOUNTANT	REQUESTING DEPT.	PURCHASING DEPT.		RECEIVING DEPT.	ACCOUNTING DEPT.
22. Compares inventory recorded with goods on hand.	14. Receives receiving report (Copy 4 of purchase order) and goods. 15. Updates inventory cards.	16. Receives receiving report (Copy 5 of purchase order). 17. Receives invoice. 18. Approves invoice.			19. Receives approved invoice. 20. Checks extensions and totals. 21. Journalizes purchase transaction.

Note: Permanent inventory cards are kept in the accounting department.

June | 3 Sold 8 of Item 35.
4 Sold 6 of Item 36.
9 Sold 8 of Item 35.
12 Received 49 of Item 36; unit cost, $43.
13 Sold 12 of Item 36.
16 Received 60 of Item 35; unit cost, $28.
17 Sold 12 of Item 35.
17 Sold 8 of Item 36.
18 Sold 12 of Item 35.
19 Sold 12 of Item 35.
19 Sold 12 of Item 36.
23 Sold 15 of Item 35.
24 Sold 18 of Item 36.
26 Sold 6 of Item 35.

July | 1 Received 50 of Item 36; unit cost, $44.50.
3 Received 57 of Item 35; unit cost, $29.50.
6 Sold 8 of Item 36.
7 Sold 2 of Item 36.

13-2. An inventory card for one item sold by Cryder's Farm Supply is illustrated here.

INVENTORY CARD

No. _180-S_

Item _Roto-Tiller, 3-5 HP, Easy-Till_

Location: Aisle _3_ Bin _14_

Maximum _10_ Minimum _3_

Date	Quant. Rec'd	Unit Cost	Quant. Sold	Balance
19– 1/4	10	217.00		10
2/1			1	9
3/7			3	6
3/14			3	3
3/15	2	230.00		5
4/5			4	1

a. Complete Purchase Requisition R111 to increase the quantity on hand to five units. The new units should be shipped to the warehouse. The current date is April 6.

b. Complete a request for quotation. The request should be sent to the Easy-Till Company, 200 Sixth Avenue, Columbia Heights, Minnesota 55421. You need a reply by April 12 and need the items by April 20.

c. Complete a purchase order. The Easy-Till Company replies to your request for quotation and indicates that it can furnish the items by April 20 at a unit cost of $230; terms, 2/10, n/30; shipped express. Your purchase order (Purchase Order C-444) should be dated April 12.

NOTE: Save your work for further use in Topic Problem 13-3.

13-3. The invoice sent by the Easy-Till Company to Cryder's Farm Supply for the items ordered on Purchase Order C-444 is found below. If all the information on the invoice is correct, initial the invoice. If the information on the invoice is not correct, make a list of the incorrect information. Four items were received.

EASY-TILL COMPANY
200 Sixth Avenue
Columbia Heights, Minnesota 55421

INVOICE NO. **1762**

Sold to: Cryder's Farm Supply
Fairfax Road
Carol Stream, Illinois 60187

Invoice Date: April 20, 19--

Ship to: Same

Customer Order No. C-444	Date 4/12/--	Ship Via Express	Terms 2/10,n/30

QUANTITY	DESCRIPTION	UNIT PRICE	AMOUNT
5	Roto-Tiller, 3.5 HP, Easy-Till	235.00	1,175.00

13-4. In a table similar to the one below, indicate who prepares or sends the forms listed below and on page 344, to whom or where the forms are sent, and the purpose the forms serve. Base your answers on the flowchart of a purchases subsystem on page 342.

Forms

a. Copy 2 of purchase requisition
b. Copy 1 of purchase order
c. Copy 2 of purchase order
d. Copy 3 of purchase order

Form	Prepared or Sent By	Sent To	Purpose
EXAMPLE: **Purchase Requisition: Copy 1**	**Requesting department**	**Purchasing department**	**To tell the purchasing agent what is needed, when, and by whom.**

e. Copy 4 of purchase order
f. Copy 5 of purchase order
g. Copy 4 of purchase order (with receiving report)
h. Copy 5 of purchase order (with receiving report)
i. Invoice

j. Invoice (approved)
k. Invoice (approved) after journalizing
l. Inventory cards (updated)
m. Physical inventory sheet

Topic 2
Controlling Purchases: Storing Merchandise

A *How does a business control the quantity of merchandise?* The goods a merchandising business keeps on hand for resale change frequently because of purchases and sales. These goods are called **merchandise inventory.** To control merchandising inventory effectively, a business must do the following.

Control: Prove inventory.

• Know the number of items in inventory
• Keep accurate, up-to-date inventory records
• Store the merchandise properly

Quantity Control

To operate successfully, a merchandising business must maintain an adequate inventory of every item it has for resale. It must have a variety of sizes, styles, or models. If it cannot provide a broad selection and fast delivery, it will lose customers. Thus, when the inventory drops to the minimum, more merchandise must be ordered.

It is important to maintain adequate inventory. But there are also reasons why it is important for a business not to carry more of an item than it can sell in a reasonable time. First, excess inventory ties up money that could be invested in other assets. Second, storage space may have to be built or rented for the excess inventory. Third, most kinds of merchandise decrease in value after a time. For example, goods might deteriorate (food), styles may change (clothes), or new products could make the current stock obsolete (computers).

Activity A. Answer the following questions about controlling the quantity of merchandise on hand. Refer to the text above.
1. What causes the number of items in merchandise inventory to change?
2. What might happen if a business maintains too little inventory?

3. What might happen if a business maintains too much inventory?
4. What are some examples of inventory items whose value decreases?

Perpetual and Periodic Inventory Records

B *How do businesses keep track of their inventories?* Some businesses keep a daily record of each item in inventory on an inventory card. Keeping a daily record of inventory is known as the **perpetual inventory procedure.** The changes in inventory through purchases and sales are added or subtracted so that each card shows the current balance on hand for each item. At times the unit cost of each item is also recorded on the inventory card. Thus the total cost of the inventory on hand can quickly be computed.

Counting the inventory at regular intervals to find the number of items of each type in inventory at that time is called the **periodic inventory procedure.** It is used by many small retail stores which handle a large number of low-priced items. For example, in a pharmacy, it is too time-consuming and expensive for the pharmacist or inventory clerk to record on an inventory card each bottle of cold tablets sold. A bottle of cold tablets might be ordered every week. An order form like the one here might be used. The order form lists the items generally carried by the pharmacy. Next to each item on the order form is the maximum and minimum quantity that should be kept in stock. Thus, the pharmacist or inventory clerk can simply count the bottles of tablets on hand to find the quantity to be ordered.

The counting of inventory is called taking a **physical inventory.** When a physical inventory is taken, every item is counted and listed on a sheet. The inventory sheet used by the House of Sound is shown here. The total inventory cost is computed by adding the cost of each item.

ORDER FORM

BEELINE DRUGS, INC.

August 14, 19—

Description and Size	Stock No.	Number Max.	Number Min.	On Hand	Order
Cold Tablets, 100	0870	100	50	40	60
Cold Tablets, 50	0871	200	100	75	125
Cold Tablets, 25	0872	300	150	180	—

Form for identifying merchandise to be ordered.

INVENTORY SHEET

HOUSE OF SOUND
200 Girard Avenue
Denver, Colorado 80236

Date *September 30, 19—*   Sheet No. 8

Counted By *M. West*   Recorded By *J. Mann*   Figured By *D. Rice*

STOCK NO.	QUANTITY	UNIT OF COUNT	DESCRIPTION	UNIT PRICE	EXTENSION
A82-B	8	ea.	Aura Portable Cassette	40 00	320 00
937-R48	3	ea.	4-Band Receiver	125 00	375 00

| | | | | TOTAL | 4300 00 |

Total cost of inventory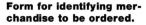

Sheet for verifying inventory.

A physical inventory serves several purposes.
- It is a check on the accuracy of the perpetual inventory records.
- It keeps track of how many items have been lost through theft or breakage by comparing the number of items on hand with the current balance in the inventory cards.
- It helps a business to have accurate financial statements. The use of inventory amounts in preparing financial statements is discussed in Chapter 16.

Activity B. Answer the following questions about inventory records. Refer to the inventory sheet and order form on page 345.
1. When is the inventory counted?
2. How many Stock A82-B cassettes are on hand?
3. What is the unit cost of each Stock A82-B cassette? What is the total cost of the cassettes in inventory?
4. What is the total cost of the inventory counted and recorded on Sheet 8 of the inventory sheets?

5. What would happen to the total cost of the inventory if the 4-band receivers were counted and recorded twice?
6. How many Stock 0871 cold tablets are on hand?
7. What is the minimum amount of Stock 0871 cold tablets that should be on hand?
8. How many Stock 0871 cold tablets must be ordered to bring the inventory up to the maximum? What is the maximum?

Inventory Loss

C *Why must merchandise be properly stored?* Merchandise inventory must be properly stored so that customers are provided with the kinds of items desired and so that inventory loss is eliminated.

Inventory loss is a term used to describe a loss of items of inventory or a loss in the resale value of merchandise inventory. The loss could be due to deterioration, obsolescence, mishandling, or theft.

Inventory losses are due to deterioration, obsolescence, mishandling, and theft.

Deterioration. **Deterioration** is the decrease in quality of goods with the passing of time. The most common examples of goods deteriorating are food and other perishable items such as cosmetics or perfume. Inventory loss due to deterioration is controlled by the regular rotating of merchandise.

Obsolescence. **Obsolescence** is the outdating of goods until they are not as useful as they were when new. Examples of goods becoming obsolete are seasonal items such as clothing fashions or high-technology items like computers. Inventory loss due to obsolescence is controlled by following sound purchasing procedures and carefully determining which goods and how many goods should be purchased.

Mishandling and Theft. Mishandling and theft are the improper handling and stealing of goods. Even though smaller goods are easier to mishandle and steal, all types of inventory are mishandled and stolen. Some statistics show that inventory is stolen every five seconds and that this costs every consumer approximately $150 a year. Inventory loss due to mishandling and theft is controlled by following strict internal control procedures. These are now discussed.

Suppose that the Major Company purchases merchandise for $150. The merchandise is a cost of doing business and thereby reduces owner's equity by $150. The Major Company now marks up the price of the inventory 50 percent and sells it to its customers for $225. The sale of merchandise increases owner's equity by $225. Thus the Major Company has a net increase in owner's equity of $75 ($225 − $150).

But now suppose that $20 of the original purchase was stolen or mishandled. The Major Company must now make an additional purchase for $20 to satisfy its customers. The total purchases are now $170 ($150 + $20 = $170), but only $150 of the merchandise is available for sale. Sales will still be $225, and the increase in owner's equity will be $55 ($225 − $170). Thus the increase in owner's equity has decreased by $20 because merchandise was mishandled or stolen.

In this example, the Major Company "absorbed" the $20 loss in inventory. They could have passed the additional cost along to the consumer. How? They could have sold the merchandise for $245 and kept their increase in owner's equity at $75 ($245 − $170). The difference is that the consumer would pay more for the merchandise.

Stolen or mishandled merchandise is a serious problem for a business. The procedures used to control mishandling and theft of merchandise include locking storage areas and prohibiting unauthorized personnel from entering them, using surveillance systems (such as television monitors and double mirrors), and dividing the responsibilities among several employees.

Activity C. Answer the following questions about inventory losses. Refer to the text on pages 346 and 347.
1. What causes inventory losses?
2. How does a business control for deterioration?
3. How are mishandling and theft controlled?

4. What is the effect of stolen merchandise on owner's equity?
5. How can a business "absorb" the cost of stolen inventory?

Topic 2 Problem

13-5. A partially completed inventory sheet for Pop N' Jay's Notions is shown here. The inventory cards are shown on page 348.
a. Complete the inventory cards.
b. Complete the inventory sheet.
c. Assuming the counts on the inventory sheet are correct, make recommendations to the owner of Pop N' Jay's Notions to improve the established system of inventory control.

Hint: Use the most recent cost prices on the cards. But if the balance on hand is greater than the quantity most recently purchased, use the cost price from the prior purchase.

INVENTORY SHEET

POP N' JAY'S NOTIONS

Date 12/31/—   Sheet No.

Counted By J. Rivera   Recorded By C. Koenig   Figured By

STOCK NO.	QUANTITY	UNIT OF COUNT	DESCRIPTION	UNIT PRICE	EXTENSION
A0-5	8	ea.	Mix Master	210 00	
A0-10	4	ea.	Mix Master	20 00	
A0-15	0	ea.	Hot Plate	38 00	
A0-20	12	ea.	Coffee Pot		
A0-25	7		Portable Radio		
SB-10	1		Cassette Player		

INVENTORY CARD

No. QO-5

Item *Mix Master*

Location: Aisle __7__ Bin __1__

Maximum __10__   Minimum __4__

Date	Quant. Rec'd	Unit Cost	Quant. Sold	Balance
19— 12/1	10	200.00		
12/2			2	
12/6			2	
12/15			3	
12/20	7	210.00		
12/25			4	
12/30	4	210.00		

INVENTORY CARD

No. QO-10

Item *Mix Master*

Location: Aisle __8__ Bin __1__

Maximum __20__   Minimum __10__

Date	Quant. Rec'd	Unit Cost	Quant. Sold	Balance
19— 12/1	20	20.00		
12/4			5	
12/8			7	
12/10			3	
12/15	15	20.00		
12/16			2	
12/18			2	
12/20			4	
12/22			6	

INVENTORY CARD

No. QO-15

Item *Hot Plate*

Location: Aisle __10__ Bin __3__

Maximum __10__   Minimum __2__

Date	Quant. Rec'd	Unit Cost	Quant. Sold	Balance
19— 12/1	1	37.00		
12/3	9	38.00		
12/7			2	
12/15			2	
12/20	4	38.00		
12/21			4	
12/22			6	

INVENTORY CARD

No. QO-20

Item *Coffee Pot*

Location: Aisle __12__ Bin __7__

Maximum __22__   Minimum __10__

Date	Quant. Rec'd	Unit Cost	Quant. Sold	Balance
19— 12/1	15	20.00		
12/10	10	20.00		
12/11			6	
12/15			10	
12/18			2	
12/20			2	
12/22	20	20.00		
12/24			10	

INVENTORY CARD

No. QO-25

Item *Portable Radio*

Location: Aisle __14__ Bin __3__

Maximum __15__   Minimum __5__

Date	Quant. Rec'd	Unit Cost	Quant. Sold	Balance
19— 12/1				
12/2	15	8.50		
12/8			4	
12/10			4	
12/17	8	9.00		
12/18			8	
12/24			3	
12/28	11	9.00		
12/29			1	
12/31			7	

INVENTORY CARD

No. SB-10

Item *Cassette Player*

Location: Aisle __14__ Bin __4__

Maximum __5__   Minimum __2__

Date	Quant. Rec'd	Unit Cost	Quant. Sold	Balance
19— 11/1	5	15.00		
12/1			2	
12/16			1	
12/17	3	15.00		
12/18			2	
12/20			2	

Topic 3
Processing Purchases on Credit

A *Does the purchase of merchandise affect a business's net income (or net loss)?* Yes, the purchase of merchandise affects a business's net income (or net loss) because it affects its costs and gross profit. A **merchandising business** earns revenue through the sale of merchandise. The amounts paid for purchases of merchandise are called **costs.** The difference between revenue and costs is called **gross profit.** A business pays its expenses from gross profit. If the gross profit is greater than the expenses, the business has a net income. If the expenses are greater than the gross profit, the business has a net loss.

Determining Cost of Goods Sold

To make a gross profit, a merchandising business must sell goods at a price higher than it pays for them. For example, the House of Sound bought tape decks for $120 and sold them for $150. In accounting terms, the revenue from the sale of goods was $150. The cost of the goods sold was $120. And the gross profit on the sale was $30. The gross profit of $30 is used to pay the expenses to operate the business.

Revenue increases owner's equity. Thus revenue from the sale of goods is credited to a temporary owner's equity account called the **Sales account.** The cost of goods purchased for resale decrease owner's equity. Expenses decrease owner's equity. Thus the cost of goods purchased is debited to a temporary owner's equity account called the **Purchases account.**

As you know, expenses are amounts spent to operate the business. Costs are amounts spent to buy merchandise for resale. The amounts in the Purchases account are costs that decrease owner's equity. Cost accounts are similar to expense accounts because both decrease owner's equity. Accountants generally group the cost and expense accounts together and call them **Cost and Expense accounts.** The Purchases account is numbered 501 in the House of Sound chart of accounts.

**House of Sound
Chart of Accounts**

Cost and Expenses
501   Purchases

Activity A. Answer the following questions about processing purchases on credit. Refer to the text on pages 348 and 349.
1. How is net income computed in a service business? In a merchandising business?
2. How is gross profit computed?

3. What is the gross profit computed on each tape deck?
4. Why are cost accounts similar to expense accounts?
5. What would the gross profit be on 10 tape decks?

Journalizing Purchases on Credit

B *How is the purchase of merchandise journalized?* The procedures for journalizing purchases depend on whether the purchase is on credit or for cash.

Purchases on Credit. When merchandise is purchased on credit, a liability is incurred. Thus the liability account, Accounts Payable, is credited because liabilities increase. The Purchases account is debited because there is a decrease in owner's equity.

The journal entry recording the purchase of merchandise on credit cannot be made until the purchasing department approves the purchase invoice. Once approved, the purchase invoice is the source document that is the basis for a debit to the Purchases account and a credit to the creditor's account.

Control: Record all payables.

October 10: The House of Sound purchases merchandise from Phelps Supply for $720 on credit.

What Happens	Accounting Rule	Entry
Cost of merchandise decreases owner's equity by $720.	To decrease owner's equity, debit the account.	Debit: Purchases, $720.
The liability *Accounts Payable* increases by $720.	To increase a liability, credit the account.	Credit: Accts. Pay./Phelps Supply, $720.

The purchase invoice from Phelps Supply could be journalized in the general journal as follows.

Purchase of merchandise on credit recorded in general journal.

GENERAL JOURNAL					Page 5
DATE	ACCOUNT TITLE AND EXPLANATION	POST. REF.	DEBIT	CREDIT	
19—					
Oct. 10	Purchases	501	720 00		
	Accts. Pay./Phelps Supply	212		720 00	
	Invoice 0567; (10/8); 2/10, n/30.				
11	Purchases	501	2,000 00		
	Accts. Pay./Downtown Music	211		2,000 00	
	Invoice 82A; (10/10); n/EOM.				

Purchases		501
19—		
Oct. 10 J5	720	
11 J5	2,000	

Accts. Pay./Downtown Music 211	
19—	
Oct. 11 J5	2,000

Accts. Pay./Phelps Supply	212
19—	
Oct. 10 J5	720

When a business has many purchases of merchandise on credit, it is more efficient to use a special journal. The **purchases journal** is a special journal used to record the purchases of merchandise on credit only.

Only *purchases of merchandise* on credit are recorded in the purchases journal. Assets other than merchandise—such as office furniture—purchased on credit are recorded in the general journal. The proper asset account (*not* the Purchases account) is debited for the amount of the invoice. If merchandise or other assets are purchased for cash, the transaction is recorded in the cash payments journal.

Assets other than merchandise purchased on credit are recorded in the general journal. Merchandise and other assets purchased for cash are recorded in the cash payments journal.

Each entry for a purchase of merchandise on credit involves a debit to the Purchases account. Only the credits to the individual creditors' accounts change. Thus a one-column purchases journal is often used to record the name of the creditor for each purchase. It is assumed that each transaction includes a debit to the Purchases account.

The purchases journal saves time and space because an entire entry is recorded on one line. The debits to the Purchases account are posted as a total at the end of the month.

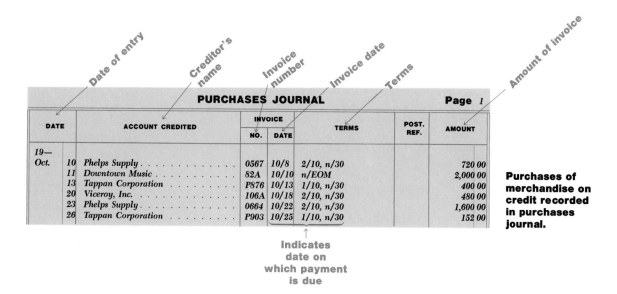

PURCHASES JOURNAL   Page 1

DATE		ACCOUNT CREDITED	INVOICE		TERMS	POST. REF.	AMOUNT
			NO.	DATE			
19—							
Oct.	10	Phelps Supply	0567	10/8	2/10, n/30		720 00
	11	Downtown Music	82A	10/10	n/EOM		2,000 00
	13	Tappan Corporation	P876	10/13	1/10, n/30		400 00
	20	Viceroy, Inc.	106A	10/18	2/10, n/30		480 00
	23	Phelps Supply	0664	10/22	2/10, n/30		1,600 00
	26	Tappan Corporation	P903	10/25	1/10, n/30		152 00

(Labels: Date of entry, Creditor's name, Invoice number, Invoice date, Terms, Amount of invoice)

↑
Indicates
date on
which payment
is due

Purchases of merchandise on credit recorded in purchases journal.

Purchases for Cash. When a business pays cash for merchandise, the asset Cash is credited because cash decreases. The Purchases account is debited because there is a decrease in owner's equity.

The check stub is the source document for journalizing the purchase of merchandise for cash. The entry is recorded in the cash payments journal because the transaction involves a credit to the Cash account.

Activity B. Answer the following questions about journalizing purchases on credit. Refer to the general journal and the purchases journal on pages 350 and 351.
1. How many lines are needed to record the October 10 and October 11 transactions in the general journal? In the purchases journal?
2. Is there a difference in your answers for questions 1? Why or why not?

3. Which columns in the purchases journal are used to find the due date of invoices?
4. What is the invoice number for the purchase on October 23?
5. What are the terms of the purchase on October 26?
6. Would you rather record purchases of merchandise on credit in a general journal or in a purchases journal? Why?

Posting Purchases on Credit

C *How is posting done from the purchases journal?* Posting entries from the purchases journal is similar to posting from other one-column journals. Each credit entry in the purchases journal is posted daily to the proper creditor's account, as shown on page 352. The credit postings are usually made daily so that the accountant will know the most current amount owed to each creditor. The account numbers placed in the Posting Reference column of the journal show that the accounts have been posted, as shown here. In the creditors' accounts, the letter "P" and the page number show that the amount has been posted from the purchases journal. The invoice number is shown in the Explanation column of the account. Thus it is easy to trace an entry to the invoice if a question arises. (The invoice date and the terms are sometimes listed in the account to show the date the invoice should be paid.)

Accts. Pay./Downtown Music					Account No.	211
DATE	EXPLANATION	POST. REF.	DEBIT	CREDIT	BALANCE DEBIT	BALANCE CREDIT
19— Oct. 11	Invoice 82A; (10/10); n/EOM	P1		2,000 00		2,000 00

Accts. Pay./Phelps Supply					Account No.	212
DATE	EXPLANATION	POST. REF.	DEBIT	CREDIT	BALANCE DEBIT	BALANCE CREDIT
19— Oct. 10	Inv. 0567; (10/8); 2/10, n/30	P1		720 00		720 00

Purchases on credit posted to creditor's account.

At the end of the month, the purchases journal is totaled. The total is the debit amount to be posted to the Purchases account. The journal is then proved and ruled. The procedure is similar to that used for the cash receipts and cash payments journals. The only difference is that the words "Purchases Debit" are written in the Account Credited column.

After the purchases journal is totaled, proved, and ruled, the total amount of the purchases is posted as a debit to the Purchases account. When the amount is posted, the number of the Purchases account (501) is written in the Posting Reference column of the journal, as shown here.

PURCHASES JOURNAL						Page 1
DATE	ACCOUNT CREDITED	INVOICE NO.	INVOICE DATE	TERMS	POST. REF.	AMOUNT
19— Oct. 10	Phelps Supply	0567	10/8	2/10, n/30	212	720 00
11	Downtown Music	82A	10/10	n/EOM	211	2,000 00
13	Tappan Corporation	P876	10/13	1/10, n/30	213	400 00
20	Viceroy, Inc.	106A	10/18	2/10, n/30	214	480 00
23	Phelps Supply	0664	10/22	2/10, n/30	212	1,600 00
26	Tappan Corporation	P903	10/25	1/10, n/30	213	152 00
						5,352 00
31	Purchases Debit				501	5,352 00

Purchases journal totaled and ruled for month.

After the entries for October are posted, the Purchases account shows only one debit of $5,352 for all credit purchases made during the entire month. The credits posted from the purchases journal to the various creditors' accounts in the ledger also equal $5,352. Thus the debit posted equals the total credits posted.

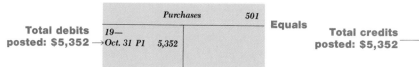

Total debits posted: $5,352 →	Purchases 501 19— Oct. 31 P1 5,352		**Equals**	Total credits posted: $5,352

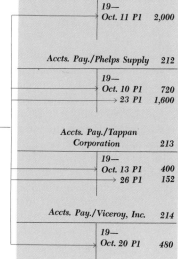

Accts. Pay./Downtown Music 211
19— Oct. 11 P1 2,000

Accts. Pay./Phelps Supply 212
19— Oct. 10 P1 720
23 P1 1,600

Accts. Pay./Tappan Corporation 213
19— Oct. 13 P1 400
26 P1 152

Accts. Pay./Viceroy, Inc. 214
19— Oct. 20 P1 480

Using the purchases journal, like using the other special journals, saves time and space in journalizing and posting. It also allows more than one person to work at one time. One person might record all invoices in the purchases journal. Another might be responsible for the cash receipts journal. Another might work on the cash payments journal, and still another on the general journal.

Activity C. Answer the following questions about posting purchases on credit. Refer to the purchases journal and accounts on pages 352 and 353.
1. When the October 11 entry is posted as a credit to Downtown Music, is a debit posted to the Purchases account at the same time? Why or why not?
2. What amount is posted to the Purchases account on October 31? Is the account debited or credited? Why?
3. Is $5,352 posted as a credit to any account on October 31? Why or why not?

4. How much is owed to Phelps Supply as of October 31? How do you know?
5. What is the meaning of the "P1" in the Posting Reference column of the Phelps Supply account?
6. How many purchases are made from Tappan Corporation during the month? From where does this information come?
7. What is the invoice number for the merchandise purchased for $480? What is the invoice date? What date is the invoice received? From whom is the merchandise purchased?

Topic 3 Problems

13-6. On January 20 Edelstein Athletics received the invoice shown here. It was checked and verified by the purchasing department and sent to the accounting department.

a. Verify the extensions and the totals. If there are any errors, give the correct amounts.
b. Which date will be used as the date for the journal entry?
c. What amount will be debited to the Purchases account?
d. What amount will be credited to Accts. Pay./Haskins Brothers?

HASKINS BROTHERS
922 South Main Street
Chicago, Illinois 60606
Invoice No. 1987

Sold to Edelstein Athletics
365 South Fourth Street
Park Forest, Illinois 60639
Date: January 19, 19—

Ship to Same

Sales Clerk	Customer Order No.	Shipped Via	Terms
B. Brown	33233	Truck	2/10, n/30

Quantity	Stock No.	Description	Unit Price	Amount
12 doz.	30A80124	Hit-more tennis balls	11.20 doz.	134.40
18	30A34801	Mercury sleds, No. 127	12.30 ea.	221.40
15	30A24506	Flex-lite casting rods	32.50 ea.	487.50
6	30A24308	Mo Hill golf sets	88.00 ea.	528.00
30	30A73502	Tru-mold sets	1.98 doz.	59.40

TOTAL AMOUNT $1,430.70
INVOICE TOTAL $1,430.70

APPROVED DATE 1/20/—
QUANTITIES RECEIVED J. Black
PRICES CHARGED K. Wern
EXTENSIONS & TOTALS

13-7. During the month of August, the purchasing agent for the Keen Shop approved the invoices shown below on the dates listed.

a. Open ledger accounts as follows: Accts. Pay./Leisure Wear, Inc.; Accts. Pay./Solar Fashions; Accts. Pay./Style Company; and Purchases. Assign an appropriate number to each account.

b. Journalize the invoices in a purchases journal on the date they were approved.

c. Post the credit entries from the purchases journal.

d. Prove and foot the purchases journal. Then rule the purchases journal.

e. Post the debit entry from the purchases journal.

Aug. 1 Invoice B73, dated July 29, from Style Company for $360; terms n/30.

10 Invoice 3637, dated August 5, from Solar Fashions for $500; terms n/60.

15 Invoice 237–846, dated August 12, from Leisure Wear, Inc., for $190; terms 2/10, n/30.

23 Invoice B114, dated August 20, from Style Company for $85; terms n/30.

27 Invoice 237–910, dated August 24, from Leisure Wear, Inc., for $230; terms 2/10, n/30.

NOTE: Save the ledger for further use in Topic Problem 13-8.

13-8. Using the ledger accounts from Topic Problem 13-7, perform the following activities and answer the questions. During September the invoices listed below were approved at the Keen Shop.

a. Journalize the invoices in the purchases journal.

b. Post the credit entries from the purchases journal.

c. Foot, prove, and rule the purchases journal.

d. Post the debit entry from the purchases journal.

e. Prepare a trial balance.

f. To which creditor is the largest balance owed on September 30?

g. What journal is used if a Keen Shop supplier requires all purchases to be made for cash?

h. What would be the effect on the number of debits to the Purchases account each month if the Keen Shop were to double its number of purchases? What would be the effect on the postings to creditors' accounts if the number of purchases were doubled?

Sept. 5 Invoice 3702, dated Sept. 1, from Solar Fashions for $241; terms n/60.

11 Invoice B173, dated Sept. 8, from Style Company for $225; terms n/30.

16 Invoice 238-004, dated Sept. 13, from Leisure Wear, Inc., for $184; terms 2/10, n/30.

24 Invoice B202, dated Sept. 21, from Style Company for $77; terms n/30.

28 Invoice 3786, dated Sept. 24, from Solar Fashions for $108; terms n/60.

Topic 4
Controlling the Accounts Payable Ledger

A *Are all accounts kept in a single ledger?* No, a single ledger is not practical for some businesses. A business may have dozens or hundreds of creditors. Thus its ledger would become very large if it contained accounts for each asset, liability, owner's equity, revenue, and expense account.

There are other problems with the single ledger. First, only one person at a time could do the posting work. Second, a trial balance prepared from the ledger would be very long. Third, if the trial balance were out of balance, it would be very difficult to find an error. All the accounts would have to be checked. The ledger is usually divided into a general ledger and subsidiary ledgers so that all these problems may be avoided.

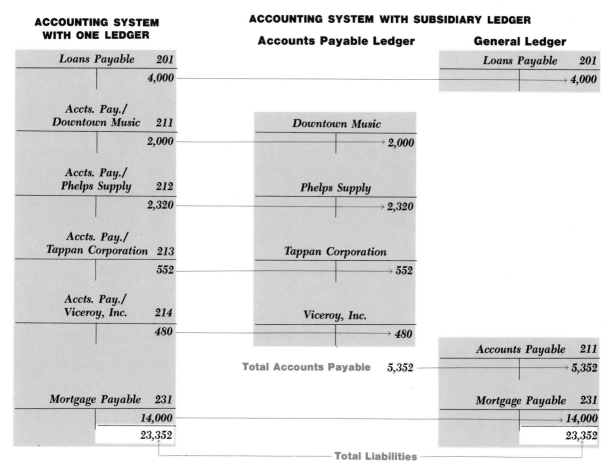

ACCOUNTING SYSTEM WITH ONE LEDGER

Loans Payable	201
	4,000

Accts. Pay./ Downtown Music	211
	2,000

Accts. Pay./ Phelps Supply	212
	2,320

Accts. Pay./ Tappan Corporation	213
	552

Accts. Pay./ Viceroy, Inc.	214
	480

Mortgage Payable	231
	14,000
	23,352

ACCOUNTING SYSTEM WITH SUBSIDIARY LEDGER

Accounts Payable Ledger

Downtown Music — 2,000

Phelps Supply — 2,320

Tappan Corporation — 552

Viceroy, Inc. — 480

Total Accounts Payable 5,352

General Ledger

Loans Payable	201
	4,000

Accounts Payable	211
	5,352

Mortgage Payable	231
	14,000
	23,352

Total Liabilities

Subsidiary Ledgers

When the ledger is divided, groups of similar accounts are removed. Each group of similar accounts kept in a separate ledger is called a **subsidiary ledger.** The accounts that are not removed make up what is called the **general ledger,** the main ledger. Two frequently used subsidiary ledgers are the accounts payable ledger and the accounts receivable ledger. The **accounts payable ledger** contains creditors' accounts. The **accounts receivable ledger** contains customers' accounts.

To understand the need for subsidiary ledgers, look at the balance sheet for the House of Sound in the margin. Only the total of the accounts payable ($5,352) is used to compute the total liabilities. Thus only one account—Accounts Payable—could be shown and the balance sheet would still be in balance. Each creditor's account is then placed in the Accounts Payable (creditor's) subsidiary ledger.

When creditors' accounts are placed in the accounts payable ledger, the Accounts Payable account in the general ledger is called a control-

House of Sound
Balance Sheet
October 31, 19—

Assets			
Cash			12,100 00
Accounts Receivable:			
Audio Shoppe	$130.00		
Newtown Music	90.00		
Village Notes	25.00		
George Yeomans	160.00	405 00	
Land		6,000 00	
Building		20,000 00	
Office Equipment		7,200 00	
Stockroom Equipment		12,100 00	
Total Assets			57,805 00
Liabilities			
Loans Payable		4,000 00	
Accounts Payable:			
Downtown Music	$2,000.00		
Phelps Supply	2,320.00		
Tappan Corporation	480.00		
Viceroy, Inc.	552.00	5,352 00	
Mortgage Payable		14,000 00	
Total Liabilities			23,352 00
Owner's Equity			
Marcy Casey, Capital			34,453 00
Total Liabilities and Owner's Equity			57,805 00

ling account. A **controlling account** is an account in the general ledger that summarizes accounts in a subsidiary ledger. Thus the Accounts Payable account summarizes the balances of all the individual creditors' accounts in the subsidiary ledger. It keeps the general ledger in balance, as shown in the illustration here.

Ledger Account Forms. Up to now, the balance ledger form with four money columns has been used. Many businesses, however, use a three-column balance ledger form for creditors' and customers' accounts, as illustrated below.

Name
Address

DATE	EXPLANATION	POST. REF.	DEBIT	CREDIT	CREDIT BALANCE

Three-column balance ledger form.

The **three-column balance ledger form** is a balance ledger which contains only one balance column. Creditors' accounts normally have a credit balance. Therefore, the three-column balance ledger form for these accounts contains a Credit Balance column. If a creditor's account has a debit balance, the balance is recorded in the Credit Balance column and circled, as shown in the margin.

The account for Phelps Supply shown here illustrates the use of the three-column balance ledger form.

CREDIT BALANCE
⟨49 50⟩

A debit balance in a creditor's account is circled.

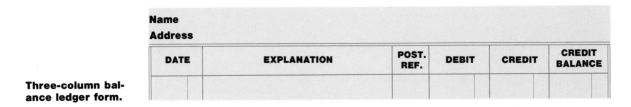

Name *Phelps Supply*
Address *22 Elmwood Avenue, Tucson, Arizona 85715*

DATE		EXPLANATION	POST. REF.	DEBIT	CREDIT	CREDIT BALANCE
19—						
Oct.	10	*Invoice 0567; (10/8); 2/10, n/30* .	P1		720 00	720 00
	18	. . . .	CP3	720 00		— 00
	23	*Invoice 0664; (10/22); 2/10, n/30* .	P1		1,600 00	1,600 00
Nov.	3	*Invoice 0703; (11/1); 2/10, n/30* .	P2		120 00	1,720 00

Three-column balance ledger form.

1 October 10: A purchase on credit for $720 is posted from the purchases journal to the Credit column of the account. The *P* in the Posting Reference column shows that the credit was posted from the purchases journal.

2 The account now has a credit balance of $720.

3 October 18: The House of Sound paid Phelps Supply $720 in cash. The payment reduces the amount owed to the creditor. The creditors' account is debited. The balance is reduced to zero.

4 October 23: A purchase on credit for $1,600 is recorded. The account now has a credit balance of $1,600.

5 November 3: A purchase on credit for $120 increases the credit balance to $1,720. Additional credits are added to the account and debits are subtracted from the account. In this way the current balance is always shown.

Note that accounts in the accounts payable ledger contain the addresses of the creditors in the heading of each account. This gives all the information needed to contact the creditor.

The creditors' accounts are usually kept on loose-leaf sheets in a binder or on file cards. This makes it easy to add or remove an account. The accounts are also placed in alphabetic order so that they can be located rapidly. Because of the alphabetic order, no account numbers are assigned to the creditors in the subsidiary ledger accounts.

House of Sound
Chart of Accounts

Assets
101 Cash
102 Petty Cash
103 Change Fund
111 Accounts Receivable
121 Land
131 Building
132 Office Equipment
133 Stockroom Equipment

Liabilities
201 Loans Payable
211 Accounts Payable
216 Sales Taxes Payable
221 Federal Employee Income Taxes Payable
222 FICA Taxes Payable
223 State Employee Income Taxes Payable
224 Federal Unemployment Taxes Payable
225 State Unemployment Taxes Payable
226 Salaries Payable
231 Mortgage Payable

Activity A. Answer the following questions about general and subsidiary ledgers. Refer to the text, margin notes, and illustrations on pages 354 to 357.
1. How many liabilities would the House of Sound have if it used only one ledger?
2. How many liabilities would it have in the general ledger if it also used an accounts payable ledger?
3. What is the dollar amount owed to the four creditors found in the subsidiary ledger?

4. What is the dollar amount of the total liabilities?
5. In what ledger will you find Phelps Supply?
6. How much is owed to Phelps Supply on October 10?
7. What is the source of the posting on October 18?
8. How much is owed to Phelps Supply on October 23?
9. How much merchandise is purchased from Phelps Supply from October 10 to November 3?

Accounts Payable Clerk:
DOT 214.362-026. Performs variety of computing, posting, and other accounting duties for accounts payable.

Posting to the Accounts Payable Ledger

B *What are the procedures for posting to the accounts payable ledger?* The use of an accounts payable ledger does not change the journalizing of approved purchase invoices in the purchases journal. However, there is a difference in posting from the purchases journal.

During the month, credit entries are posted from the purchases journal to the creditors' accounts in the subsidiary ledger, as shown in the margin. The accounts in the subsidiary ledger are not numbered. A check mark ($\checkmark$) is used in the Posting Reference column of the purchases journal to show that the amount has been posted.

No postings are made to the general ledger until the purchases journal is totaled and ruled. Then, the total purchases for the month are totaled and ruled. At that time the total purchases for the month are posted as a debit to the Purchases account and a credit to the Accounts Payable controlling account in the general ledger. The credit amounts posted to the accounts payable ledger must equal the credit posted to the controlling account in the general ledger.

When the purchases journal is totaled, "Purchases Debit/Accts. Pay Credit" is written in the Account Credited column. A diagonal line is drawn in the Posting Reference column to show that the total is posted to two accounts (the Purchases account and the Accounts Payable controlling account in the general ledger), as shown in the margin. The number of the Purchases account (501) is written above the diagonal line. The number of the Accounts Payable account (211) is written below the diagonal line. Thus an account number in the Posting Reference column of the journal shows that the amount was posted to the general ledger. A check mark ($\sqrt{}$) indicates that the amount was posted to the subsidiary ledger. This procedure is illustrated here.

Diagonal line is drawn in Posting Reference column when journal is totaled and ruled.

Accounts Payable Subsidiary Ledger

Downtown Music	
	2,000

Phelps Supply	
	720
	1,600

Tappan Corporation	
	400
	152

Viceroy, Inc.	
	480

Total credits posted: $5,325

PURCHASES JOURNAL   Page 1

DATE		ACCOUNT CREDITED	INVOICE NO.	INVOICE DATE	TERMS	POST. REF.	AMOUNT
19— Oct.	10	Phelps Supply	0567	10/8	2/10, n/30	$\sqrt{}$	720 00
	11	Downtown Music	82A	10/10	n/EOM	$\sqrt{}$	2,000 00
	13	Tappan Corporation	P876	10/13	1/10, n/30	$\sqrt{}$	400 00
	20	Viceroy, Inc.	106A	10/18	2/10, n/30	$\sqrt{}$	480 00
	23	Phelps Supply	0664	10/22	2/10, n/30	$\sqrt{}$	1,600 00
	26	Tappan Corporation	P903	10/25	1/10, n/30	$\sqrt{}$	152 00
	31	Purchases Debit/Accts. Pay. Credit .				501/211	5,352 00

General Ledger

Purchases	501
5,352	

Accounts Payable	211
	5,352

In summary, posting from the purchases journal to the subsidiary ledger and the general ledger is done in the following order.

• During the month, individual credits are posted to the creditors' accounts in the subsidiary ledger.
• At the end of the month, total purchases are posted as a debit to the Purchases account and a credit to the Accounts Payable controlling account in the general ledger.

When the balance ledger account form is used for the accounts payable ledger, the accounting clerk should post from the purchases journal before posting from the cash payments journal. Thus credits are recorded in the accounts before the debits.

Activity B. Answer the following questions about posting to the subsidiary ledger. Refer to the purchases journal, the general ledger accounts, and the subsidiary ledger accounts on pages 357 and 358.

1. What would the complete entry have been to record the October 13 purchases journal entry in a general journal?

2. When the October 13 entry is posted, is the Purchases account debited for $400 at the same time? Why or why not?

3. In which ledger is the October 13 purchase posted? What account is credited?

4. When the October 20 entry is posted, is the credit posted to both the Accounts Payable account in the general ledger and the Viceroy, Inc. account in the subsidiary ledger? Why or why not?

5. What does the check mark in the Posting Reference column of the journal for the October 20 entry mean?

6. What amount is posted to the Purchases account on October 31? Is this amount debited or credited? Why?

7. Is any account credited for $5,352 on October 31?

8. What do the 501 and 211 in the Posting Reference column of the journal on October 31 indicate?

Proving the Accounts Payable Ledger

C *When is the accounts payable ledger proved?* A proof of the equality of the subsidiary ledger and the controlling account is prepared at the end of the accounting period. The proof is done before the trial balance is prepared.

The following procedure is followed to prove the subsidiary ledger. The balances of the creditors' accounts are added. If the individual creditors' names are not needed, the proof of the subsidiary ledger can be made on an adding maching tape as shown in the margin. The total is then compared with the balance of the accounts payable controlling account.

If the total of the subsidiary ledger accounts does not agree with the balance of the controlling account, the error must be located and corrected before a trial balance is prepared. To locate the error, the accountant uses the same process used to locate an error on the trial balance, as described in Chapter 6.

Sometimes managers and owners will want a schedule of accounts payable. A **schedule of accounts payable** is a list of the names of individual creditors and the amounts owed to each creditor. A schedule of accounts payable is illustrated here.

House of Sound
Schedule of Accounts Payable
October 31, 19—

```
          .00T
     2,000.00
     2,320.00
       552.00
       480.00
     5,352.00T
```

Proof of subsidiary ledger on adding machine tape.

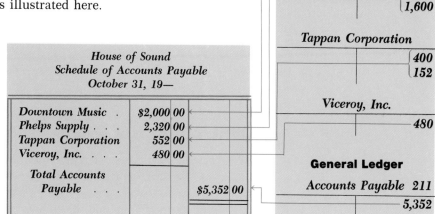

Accounts Payable Subsidiary Ledger

Downtown Music
2,000

Phelps Supply
720
1,600

Tappan Corporation
400
152

Viceroy, Inc.
480

General Ledger

Accounts Payable 211
5,352

House of Sound Schedule of Accounts Payable October 31, 19—		
Downtown Music .	$2,000 00	
Phelps Supply . . .	2,320 00	
Tappan Corporation	552 00	
Viceroy, Inc. . . .	480 00	
Total Accounts Payable . . .		$5,352 00

Proving the accounts payable ledger.

Activity C. Answer the following questions about proving the accounts payable ledger. Refer to the text and illustrations on page 359.

1. Where does the accounts payable clerk get the information for the schedule of accounts payable?

2. Is the Accounts Payable controlling account included on a trial balance? Are the individual subsidiary ledger accounts listed? Why or why not?

Accounting Concept:
Subsidiary Ledger. The equality of the *subsidiary ledger* and the controlling account must be verified at regular intervals.

Topic 4 Problems

13-9. Morgan Solomon, the owner of Solomon Surgical Supplies, has received the invoices listed for merchandise purchased for resale.
a. Open general ledger accounts for Accounts Payable and Purchases. Also open subsidiary ledger accounts for the following creditors: Druid Supply Company, 12 Muford Road, Tustin, California 70122; Fritz Mann, 27 Niles Road, Bloomington, Illinois 61701; and John Stein, 1000 Chantilly Dr., Atlanta, Georgia 30324.
b. Journalize the approved purchase invoices listed in a purchases journal.
c. Post the credit entries to the subsidiary ledger.
d. Foot, prove, and rule the purchases journal.
e. Post the total of the purchases journal to the general ledger.
f. Prepare a schedule of accounts payable. Compare the total of the schedule of accounts payable with the balance of the Accounts Payable controlling account.

Nov.   3 Invoice 3909, dated October 28, from Druid Supply Company for $600; terms 2/10, n/30.
      11 Invoice D176, dated November 6, from John Stein for $820; terms n/30.
      16 Invoice 111, dated November 13, from Fritz Mann for $584; terms n/60.
      22 Invoice D197, dated November 17, from John Stein for $844; terms n/30.

Nov. 28 Invoice 4186, dated November 23, from Druid Supply Company for $400; terms 2/10, n/30.
NOTE: Save your ledgers for further use in Topic Problem 13-10.

13-10. Perform the following activities. Use the ledger accounts from Topic Problem 13-9.
a. Journalize the approved purchase invoices listed.
b. Post the credit entries to the subsidiary ledger.
c. Foot, prove, and rule the purchases journal.
d. Post the total of the purchases journal to the general ledger.
e. Prepare a schedule of accounts payable. Compare the total of the schedule of accounts payable with the balance of the Accounts Payable controlling account.
f. Prepare a trial balance.

Dec.   5 Invoice 808, dated December 2, from Fritz Mann for $940; terms n/60.
      11 Invoice D237, dated December 6, from John Stein for $660; terms n/30.
      16 Invoice 4306, dated December 12, from Druid Supply Company for $440; terms 2/10, n/30.
      22 Invoice 882, dated December 19, from Fritz Mann for $1,004; terms n/60.
      28 Invoice D296, dated December 23, from John Stein for $236; terms n/30.

Topic 5
Controlling Net Purchases

A *Does the Purchases account show all the costs of obtaining merchandise?* No, the Purchases account does not show all the costs. It shows only the invoice cost of merchandise purchases. Other costs of the purchases might include the following.

- *Delivery costs.* Sometimes the purchaser must pay transportation costs.
- *Canceled invoices.* Sometimes part of the invoice cost is canceled because merchandise is returned or an allowance is given by the seller.
- *Discounts.* There are also times when the seller offers a discount for prompt payment. This discount reduces the amount of cash that the purchaser has to pay.

Transportation In

The cost of merchandise should include any transportation (freight) charges for delivery to the purchaser. Depending on the terms of the sale, either the seller or the purchaser may pay the transportation charges. For example, the purchasing agent for the House of Sound has the choice of buying record changers from a local wholesaler for $80 each or buying the same changers in a distant city for $75. However, if the changers are bought from the more distant seller, House of Sound must pay $5 transportation charges for each changer.

In making the decision, the purchasing agent must consider the transportation charges as part of the cost of the changers. Thus the delivered cost of the changers is the same from each supplier: $80 from the local wholesaler and $80 ($75 + $5) from the distant supplier who charges $5 for transportation.

FOB Destination. The seller may agree to pay the cost of shipping merchandise to the purchaser. For example, when the House of Sound purchased stereo speakers from Viceroy, Inc., the merchandise was shipped "FOB Denver" as shown in the invoice in the margin. The House of Sound is located in Denver. Thus the shipment was made free on board (FOB) to the destination point. In other words, the seller (Viceroy, Inc.) pays the transportation charges when merchandise is shipped **FOB destination.** The total cost of the two delivered stereo speakers is $480, the total of the invoice. When the invoice is journalized, the Purchases account will be debited for $480.

FOB Shipping Point. In some businesses it is customary for a seller to send merchandise FOB shipping point. **FOB shipping point** means that the purchaser must pay the transportation charges. For example, Downtown Music of Dallas, Texas, sent merchandise FOB shipping point to the House of Sound. The transportation charges for shipping the goods from Dallas (shipping point) to Denver (the destination) are paid by the House of Sound.

When merchandise is purchased FOB shipping point, the transportation charges are debited to a separate ledger account. Thus managers and owners can obtain information they need to control costs. Decisions can be made about using different forms of transportation (railroads, airlines, or trucks), ordering in large or small quantities, and purchasing locally or from distant suppliers.

Journalizing Transportation Costs. The House of Sound purchased merchandise from Downtown Music with the terms FOB Dallas (shipping point). The House of Sound paid $50 for the transportation charges on October 12. The payment of the transportation charges is analyzed as follows.

October 12: The House of Sound issues Check 307 for $50 to Mauro Lines for transportation charges on merchandise ordered from Downtown Music, FOB Dallas.

House of Sound Chart of Accounts

Costs and Expenses
501 Purchases
502 Transportation In
503 Purchases Returns and
      Allowances

What Happens	Accounting Rule	Entry
Cost of transportation decreases owner's equity by $50.	To decrease owner's equity, debit the account.	Debit: Transportation In, $50.
The asset *Cash* decreases by $50.	To decrease an asset, credit the account.	Credit: Cash, $50.

The entry to record the payment of transportation charges is made in the cash payments journal because cash is paid.

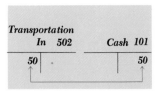

		Transportation In 502		Cash 101	
		50			50

CASH PAYMENTS JOURNAL						Page 3	
DATE	ACCOUNT DEBITED	EXPLANATION	CHECK NO.	POST. REF.	AMOUNT		
19— Oct. 12	Transportation In	Mauro Lines	307	502	50 00		

Recording transportation costs.

If transportation charges are charged to the business, the entry is made in the general journal. The Transportation In account is debited. The Accounts Payable controlling account is credited. The creditor's account in the subsidiary ledger is credited.

The account commonly used to record freight charges is the **Transportation In account** (sometimes referred to as the *Freight In* or *Freight on Purchases account*). The Transportation In account is considered an additional cost related to purchases. The total of the Purchases account and the Transportation In account is the **cost of the delivered goods.**

Special columns may be added to any journal to save time when recording and posting similar transactions. Thus some businesses add

Purchases $2,930
Add: Transportation In . .   50
Cost of Delivered Goods . $2,980

a Transportation In column to the purchases journal to record all the debits to that account.

Accounts Payable Bookkeeper:
DOT 210.382-018. Keeps accounts payable section of the financial records. May journalize accounts payable transactions, and may post to subsidiary ledger.

Activity A. Answer the following questions about the cost of merchandise. Refer to the invoice on page 361 and the entry to record transportation charges on page 362.
1. Is the merchandise purchased from Viceroy, Inc. shipped FOB destination or FOB shipping point? Explain.
2. Does Viceroy, Inc. or the House of Sound pay freight charges for the merchandise purchased on Invoice 106A?

3. What is the House of Sound's purchase order number for merchandise shipped on Invoice 106A?
4. Why is the transportation charge for merchandise purchased from Downtown Music recorded in the cash payments journal?
5. Is the merchandise from Downtown Music shipped FOB destination or FOB shipping point?
6. How is the cost of delivered goods found?
7. What is the effect on owner's equity when transportation charges are recorded?

Purchases Returns and Allowances

B *What are purchases returns and allowances? Purchases returns and allowances* refers to the procedures used when the purchaser wants to return ordered merchandise. There are many reasons why a purchaser would want to return merchandise to the supplier. The merchandise might arrive in an unacceptable condition. It might be damaged. The quantity might be more or less than was ordered. The wrong items may have been sent. In other cases, the business might find that the items received are not needed or were not ordered.

For any of these reasons, the receiving department asks the purchasing department what to do with the merchandise. The purchasing agent normally has two choices when merchandise is unacceptable: return the merchandise or keep the merchandise with a reduction in the purchase price. For example, recall the order for two stereo speakers that the House of Sound placed with Viceroy, Inc. Assume that one of the speakers was scratched in shipment. The receiving clerk notifies the purchasing agent of the damage. If the purchasing agent decides to return the speaker, the transaction is called a purchase return. Thus, a **purchases return** is merchandise sent back to the supplier.

However, Viceroy may offer to reduce the purchase price of the scratched speaker. House of Sound may then decide to keep the speaker on these terms. In this case, the difference between the original price and the reduced price is a purchases allowance. A **purchases allowance** is reductions in the purchase price for damages or other causes.

Control: Obtain refunds or credits for all purchases returns and allowances.

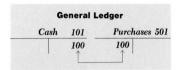

General Ledger

Cash	101	Purchases 501
	100	100

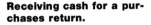

Receiving cash for a purchases return.

Purchases returns and allowances decrease cost of merchandise purchased.

Receiving Cash for Purchases Returns and Allowances.

A purchaser who has paid cash expects to have the cash returned when merchandise is returned. If a reduction is allowed in the price the purchaser has already paid, the purchaser may expect to get the allowance in cash. Suppose the supplier agrees to take back merchandise that the House of Sound purchased for $100 in cash on October 2. To understand the transaction, let's review the original entry. The merchandise was purchased for cash, and the transaction was recorded in the cash payments journal. The entry resulted in a $100 debit to the Purchases account and a $100 credit to the Cash account.

Now, with returned merchandise, the reduction in the total amount of purchases is recorded. This is done by crediting the Purchases account. (Since purchases decrease owner's equity, the return of purchases increases owner's equity.) But it is better to keep a separate record of purchases returns and allowances. Purchases are recorded in one account, and returns and allowances for purchases are recorded in another. Thus information about each activity is readily available. When the House of Sound receives $100 in cash for the returned merchandise, the Purchases Returns and Allowances account is credited. Since cash is received, the entry is in the cash payments journal.

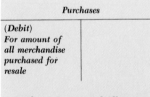

Purchases

(Debit) For amount of all merchandise purchased for resale	

Purchases Returns and Allowances

	(Credit) For amount of all returns and allowances on merchandise purchased for resale

CASH PAYMENTS JOURNAL   Page 3

DATE		ACCOUNT DEBITED	EXPLANATION	CHECK NO.	POST. REF.	AMOUNT
19— Oct.	5	Purchases	Fisher Company	304	501	100 00

The **Purchases Returns and Allowances account,** like the Purchases account, is a temporary owner's equity account. The information in the Purchases Returns and Allowances account is used to help analyze the operations of the business, as illustrated in the margin. If the amount of the returns and allowances is large, the manager or owner might want to find out why. Are errors being made on purchase orders? Is poor merchandise being bought? Is too much merchandise arriving in damaged condition? By answering these questions, managers and owners can correct poor purchasing practices.

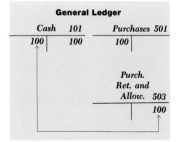

General Ledger

Cash	101	Purchases 501
100	100	100

Purch. Ret. and Allow. 503

| | 100 |

CASH RECEIPTS JOURNAL   Page 3

DATE		ACCOUNT CREDITED	EXPLANATION	POST. REF.	AMOUNT
19— Oct.	10	Purchases Returns and Allowances . .	Returns to Fisher Co. . .	503	100 00

The **Net purchases** are found by subtracting the balance of the Purchases Returns and Allowances account from the cost of delivered goods (Purchases plus Transportation In). The Purchases Returns and Allowances account number is 503 in the chart of accounts for the House of Sound.

Purchases	2,930	00
Add: Transportation In .	50	00
Cost of Delivered Goods	2,980	00
Less: Purchases Returns and Allowances . .	240	00
Net Purchases	2,740	00

Receiving Credit for Purchases Returns and Allowances.
When a purchaser has not paid for the merchandise returned, the supplier grants credit against the amount the purchaser owes. To understand the entry for a purchase return or allowance for credit, refer again to the damaged stereo speaker received from Viceroy, Inc. Suppose the purchasing agent tells Viceroy that the speaker will be returned and Viceroy agrees to take the speaker back. When the speaker is returned, Viceroy issues a credit memorandum to the House of Sound for $240, the net price of the speaker. The credit memorandum shows that the amount owed by House of Sound to Viceroy for Invoice 106A ($480) is reduced by the price of the speaker returned ($240).

House of Sound Chart of Accounts

Costs and Expenses
501 Purchases
502 Transportation In
503 Purchases Returns and Allowances

Viceroy, Inc.
16 Remington Street
Phoenix, Arizona 85711

CREDIT MEMORANDUM
Copy 1: Customer

No. **1254**

To: House of Sound
200 Girard Avenue
Denver, Colorado 80236

Date _October 27, 19--_

Sold on
Invoice No. _106A_

Your Order No. _PO1135_

We have credited your account as follows:

QUANTITY	DESCRIPTION	PRICE	AMOUNT
1	84-576 Viceroy stereo speaker Returned	240.00	240.00

A **credit memorandum** is the source document that grants credit to the purchaser for a purchase return or allowance. It also gives the reason for the credit. Thus a credit memorandum is the source document for journalizing a purchase return or allowance. A business might use a special journal to record purchases returns and allowances. If a special journal is not used, the purchases returns and allowances are journalized in the general journal.

How the credit memorandum is journalized is better understood by reviewing the purchase from Viceroy, Inc.

An entry was made in the purchases journal for the amount of the invoice, $480. Thus Viceroy's account in the accounts payable ledger was credited for $480 to show an increase in the amount owed to this creditor. Assume that this was the only entry made in the purchases journal during the month. Then, at the end of the month, a debit of $480 was posted to the Purchases account in the general ledger and a credit of $480 was posted to Accounts Payable.

Viceroy, Inc.
16 Remington Street
Phoenix, Arizona 85711

Invoice No. **106A**

Sold To: House of Sound
200 Girard Avenue
Denver, Colorado 80236

Date October 20, 19--

Terms 2/10, n/30

Salesman	Your Order No.	Shipped By		FOB
Hunt	P01135	Truck		Denver
QUANTITY	STOCK NO.	DESCRIPTION	UNIT PRICE	EXTENSION
2	84-576	Viceroy stereo speakers Less 40%	400.00	320.00

Invoice Total 480.00

PURCHASES JOURNAL

| Viceroy, Inc. . . . . | . | √ | 480 00 |
| Purch. Debit/Acc. Pay. Credit | 501/211 | | 480 00 |

Accounts Payable Subsidiary Ledger

Viceroy, Inc.

| | 480 |

General Ledger

Accounts Payable **211**

| | 480 |

Purchases **501**

| 480 | |

When the set is returned, Viceroy, Inc., sends a credit memorandum to the House of Sound. The credit memorandum shows that House of Sound now owes $240 less to Viceroy. This is the net price of one stereo speaker. The credit memorandum is then recorded in the general journal for the amount of the return, $240. Thus a debit of $240 must be posted to Viceroy's account in the accounts payable ledger to show the decrease in the amount owed. Also, two entries are needed in the general ledger: a debit to the Accounts Payable controlling account and a credit to the Purchases Returns and Allowances account. The debit entry decreases the accounts payable liability. The credit entry reduces the total amount of purchases.

October 28: The House of Sound receives a credit memorandum for $240 from Viceroy, Inc., for the return of goods purchased on credit.

What Happens	Accounting Rule	Entry
The liability *Accounts Payable* decreases by $240.	To decrease a liability, debit the account.	Debit: Accounts Payable, $240 (also the creditor's account).
The reduction in costs caused by a return of a purchase increases owner's equity by $240.	To increase owner's equity, credit the account.	Credit: Purchases Returns and Allowances, $240.

The diagonal line in the Posting Reference column of the general journal shows that the debit of $240 is posted to two accounts—the controlling account in the general ledger and the creditor's account in the subsidiary ledger. The "211" in the Posting Reference column shows that the debit has been posted to the Accounts Payable controlling account in the general ledger. The check mark ($\sqrt{}$) shows that the debit has been posted to the Viceroy, Inc., account in the subsidiary ledger. After the entries are posted, the total of the subsidiary ledger agrees with the balance of the controlling account.

Recording a credit memorandum.

GENERAL JOURNAL

Accounts Payable/Viceroy, Inc.	211/ $\sqrt{}$	240 00	
Purchases Returns and Allowances . .	503		240 00

Accounts Payable Subsidiary Ledger

General Ledger

Viceroy, Inc.

240	480

Accounts Payable 211

240	480

Purchases 501

480	

Purchases Returns and Allowances 503

	240

The credit of $240 for the returned stereo speaker is posted to the Purchases Returns and Allowances account.

The posting of an entry to the controlling account in the general ledger and to an account in the subsidiary ledger is called **double-posting.** Double-posting is illustrated above.

Activity B. Answer the following questions about purchases returns and allowances. Refer to the credit memorandum, general journal, general ledger accounts, and accounts payable subsidiary ledger account above.
1. Why is the credit memorandum issued?
2. What is the invoice number? What is the purchase order number?
3. What journal entry is made on October 28 to record the credit memorandum?
4. Why is the Viceroy, Inc., account debited on October 28 instead of credited? Why is Purchases Returns and Allowances credited?
5. What double-posting is made for the $240 debit entry of October 28?
6. What is the purpose of the check mark in the Posting Reference column of the journal for the October 28 entry?
7. Why is 211 above the check mark in the Posting Reference column of the journal?
8. How much is owed to Viceroy, Inc., after the October 28 entry is posted?

Purchase Discounts

C *When are invoices paid to the creditors?* The terms shown on the purchase order and the invoice show when an invoice is to be paid. The terms given by a seller may vary from customer to customer.

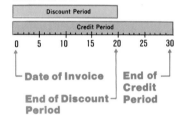

Terms: 1/20, n/30

Discount Period

Credit Period

0 5 10 15 20 25 30

Date of Invoice
End of Discount Period

End of Credit Period

Oct. 8   Oct. 18   Nov. 7

10 Days

30 Days

Date of Invoice   End of Discount Period   End of Credit Period

PHELPS SUPPLY
22 Elmwood Avenue
Tucson, Arizona 85715   INVOICE NO. 0567

SOLD TO House of Sound   Invoice Date 10/8/—
         200 Girard Avenue
         Denver, Colorado 80236

SHIP TO Same   Terms   2/10, n/30

Cust. Order No. PO-1106   FOB Denver   No. of Cartons 2

QUANTITY SHIPPED | STOCK NO. | DESCRIPTION | UNIT PRICE | AMOUNT
18 | A82-B | Aura portable cassette | 40.00 | 720.00

A customer who pays bills promptly will be given more generous credit terms than a customer who does not. A seller may demand immediate payment from some customers and offer other customers 30, 60, 90, or more days to pay an invoice. If the terms call for payment upon delivery of the merchandise, the invoice will be marked "Cash" or "Net Cash."

Credit Period. The period of time given to pay the invoice is called a **credit period.** The terms on the invoice will state the exact period of time covered in the credit period.

For most businesses, the credit period begins on the date of the invoice. If payment is due 30 days from the invoice date, the terms are shown as *n/30*. The *n* (for *net*) means that the full amount is due within 30 days after the invoice date. *N/EOM* means that the net amount on the invoice is due at the end of the month.

Cash Discounts. Many businesses try to encourage prompt payment of invoices. One method is to offer a cash discount. A **cash discount** encourages prompt payment by allowing the purchaser to deduct a certain amount from the total invoice if the invoice is paid in a specified period. The period of time in which a cash discount can be taken is the **discount period.** For example, when an invoice shows credit terms of 1/20, n/30, the purchaser has a credit period of 30 days and a discount period of 20 days. The *1/20* means that the purchaser may deduct 1 percent of the total invoice if payment is made within the 20-day discount period. The *n/30* means that if the invoice is paid within the last 10 days of the credit period, the full amount must be paid.

A cash discount on a purchase is called a **purchase discount.** A purchase discount is not recorded at the time an invoice is journalized. The purchaser obtains the cash discount *only* if payment is made within the discount period. To understand purchase discounts, refer to the October 8 invoice from Phelps Supply for $720. The terms of the purchase are 2/10, n/30, as shown in the margin. Thus, if the House of Sound mails its check on or before October 18 (10 days after the date of the invoice), it may deduct 2 percent of $720.00 ($14.40) from the invoice and pay $705.60 ($720.00 − $14.40). If House of Sound does not pay within the 10-day discount period, it must then pay the full amount of $720.00 by November 7. The business has a choice of paying early or not paying early. Thus the discount is not recorded until after the check is drawn to pay the invoice. When the purchase invoice is journalized, the creditor's account is credited for the full amount of the invoice, $720. The entry in the purchases journal appears at the top of the next page.

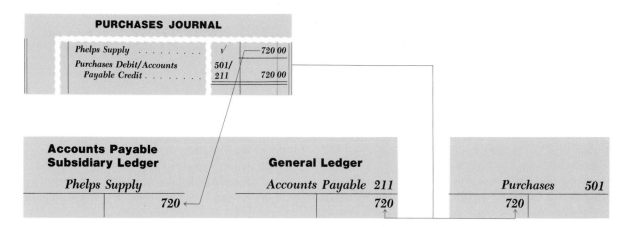

PURCHASES JOURNAL

Phelps Supply	√	—720 00	
Purchases Debit/Accounts Payable Credit	501/ 211	720 00	

Accounts Payable Subsidiary Ledger

Phelps Supply

720 ←

General Ledger

Accounts Payable 211

720

Purchases 501

720

Tickler File

To take all available discounts and to keep a good credit rating, a business must have an efficient method for keeping track of when each invoice should be paid. One method is to use a tickler file, which is illustrated in the margin. In a **tickler file,** each invoice is filed according to the date it must be considered for payment. A file folder is established for each day of the month (from 1 to 31). The accounting clerk then files each purchase invoice under the day it must be paid to obtain the cash discount. On that day the invoice is considered for payment. If the employee in charge of authorizing cash payments decides to pay the invoice, the discount is deducted from the invoice. A check is then drawn for the net amount. If it is decided not to pay the invoice, the invoice is then filed under the day that marks the end of the credit period.

Tickler File

Activity C. Answer the following questions about purchase discounts and the tickler file. Refer to the illustrations on page 368 and the tickler file shown in the margin.

1. What is the date of Invoice 0567?

2. What is the credit period given on Invoice 0567? What is the discount period?

3. What is the amount of the check if Invoice 0567 is paid before October 18? After October 18?

4. What is the amount of cash discount offered on Invoice 0567?

5. What is the amount of purchase discount offered on Invoice 0567?

6. Under what day would Invoice 0567 be filed in the tickler file to take the cash discount?

7. Under what day would Invoice 0567 be filed in the tickler file if the House of Sound did not wish to take the cash discount?

Accounting Principle:
Net Cost of Purchases. The generally accepted accounting principle is that the net cost of purchases includes the amount paid to the seller plus any transportation charges for delivery of the goods.

Accounting Concept:
Types of Accounts. The number and type of accounts used depend on how detailed the information must be.

Topic 5 Problems

13-11. During June the Sol-Way Supermarket, owned by Shaun O'Leary, received the invoices, transportation bills, and credit memorandums listed here.
a. Open general ledger accounts, assign appropriate numbers, and record the June 1 balances as follows: Cash, $6,000; Store Equipment, $14,800; Accounts Payable; Shaun O'Leary, Capital, $20,800; Shaun O'Leary, Drawing; Purchases; Transportation In; and Purchases Returns and Allowances. Open subsidiary ledger accounts for Dinan, Inc., 100 Lewis St., New Windsor, New York 12550, Florenz Supply, 850 Ellis Avenue, Houston, Texas 77007, and Makefield Markets, Post Rd., Rye, New York 10580.
b. Record the transactions listed in a purchases journal, a cash payments journal, and a general journal.
c. Post the individual entries from the purchases journal, the cash payments journal, and the general journal.
d. Prove, total, and rule the special journals.
e. Post the totals from the special journals.
f. Prepare a schedule of accounts payable.

June 2 Bought merchandise for $1,200 from Dinan, Inc.; Invoice 1250, dated June 1; terms FOB shipping point, 1/10, n/60.
2 Issued Check 192 for $19 to Lark Express for freight bill on merchandise from Dinan, Inc.
4 Bought a new refrigerator for store for $1,950 from Florenz Supply; Invoice 195, dated June 2; terms FOB destination, n/60.
5 Received Credit Memorandum 47 for $100 from Dinan, Inc., for returned goods.
9 Issued Check 193 for $130 to Maple Farms for merchandise purchased for cash.
13 Bought merchandise for $560 from Makefield Markets; Invoice 22-84, June 10; terms FOB destination, 2/10, n/60.
22 Bought merchandise for $700 from Dinan, Inc.; Invoice 711, dated June 21; terms FOB shipping point, 1/10, n/60.
22 Issued Check 194 for $52 to Pen Freight Lines for delivering merchandise from Dinan, Inc.

June 25 Received Credit Memorandum 51 for $50 from Florenz Supply as allowance for damaged goods.
30 Issued Check 195 for $650 to Equipment, Inc. for a display unit purchased for cash.
30 Issued Check 196 for $1,200 to Shaun O'Leary for personal use.

13-12. Using the general journal and the ledgers prepared in Topic Problem 13-11, a purchases journal, and a cash payments journal, perform the following activities.
a. Record the entries for the transactions listed.
b. Post the individual entries from the journals.
c. Prove, total, and rule the special journals.
d. Post the totals from the special journals.
e. Prepare a schedule of accounts payable. Compare the total of the schedule of accounts payable with the balance of the Accounts Payable account.
f. Prepare a trial balance.

July 1 Issued Check 197 for $1,100 to Dinan, Inc., on account.
5 Bought merchandise for $732 from Makefield Markets; Invoice 22-113, dated July 2; terms 2/10, n/60, FOB destination.
9 Received Credit Memorandum CM-15-2 for $100 from Makefield Markets for returned merchandise.
17 Bought merchandise for $532 from Dinan, Inc.; Invoice 802, dated July 16; terms FOB shipping point, 1/10, n/60.
17 Issued Check 198 for $64 to Star Delivery for delivering merchandise from Dinan, Inc.
21 Received Credit Memorandum CM-57 for $80 from Dinan, Inc., as allowance for scratched merchandise.
28 Bought merchandise for $360 from Makefield Markets; Invoice 22-137, dated July 25; terms FOB destination, 2/10, n/60.

370 Part 2 Accounting Subsystems

Topic 6
Controlling Cash Payments on Account

A *When are payments for purchases journalized?* The owner of the House of Sound decides when invoices are to be paid. The payment for each invoice is journalized in the cash payments journal. The procedures for paying invoices are now described.

Journalizing Cash Paid on Account

Assume the treasurer decides not to take advantage of the cash discount offered by Phelps Supply. The decision is made to pay the invoice on the last day of the credit period, which is November 7. On November 7 a check is drawn for $720, the full amount of the invoice.

Control: Pay invoices in time to avoid loss of discounts.

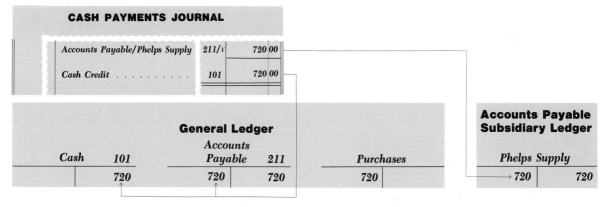

Now suppose the treasurer decides to pay the invoice within the discount period. The procedure to compute the payment is as follows.

- The rate of the cash discount is listed. In this case it is 2 percent.
- The full amount of the invoice is multiplied by the rate of the cash discount to get the amount of the discount ($0.02 \times \$720.00 = \$14.40$).
- The discount is subtracted from the full amount of the invoice to find the amount of payment ($\$720.00 - \$14.40 = \$705.60$).

Phelps Supply agrees to accept a check for $705.60 in full payment of the invoice for $720.00 if the check is sent within the discount period. On October 18, therefore, the treasurer has a check drawn for $705.60 and sends it to Phelps Supply. The transaction is described here and illustrated in the margin on page 372. (Checks should be mailed so that the creditor receives them before the end of the discount period.)

1 The creditor's account has a credit balance of $720.00 and must be debited for $720.00 to show that the account has been paid in full. The

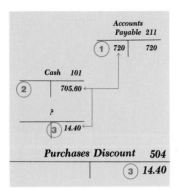

Phelps Supply account must be debited for $720.00 to reduce the credit balance to zero. The Accounts Payable account is also debited for $720.00.

2 The check drawn to pay the debt amounts to $705.60. Thus the Cash account must be credited for $705.60. This is the amount of cash paid.

3 The debit and credit amounts must be equal. The cash discount of $14.40 must be credited to some account. The discount reduces the cost of the merchandise. The cassettes are recorded at a cost of $720.00. However, House of Sound paid only $705.60 for the cassettes. Thus the purchase discount reduces the cost of the merchandise by $14.40. The reduction in cost actually increases owner's equity. Thus an owner's equity account must be credited for $14.40.

The credit entry to increase owner's equity could be made in the Purchases account. However, it is a common accounting practice to record a purchase discount in a temporary owner's equity account called the **Purchases Discount account.** This practice gives managers and owners a record of all discounts taken.

The entry to record a purchase discount of $14.40 taken on a payment of $720.00 is analyzed here.

October 18: The House of Sound issues Check 308 for $705.60 to Phelps Supply to pay an invoice for $720.00, less a cash discount of $14.40.

What Happens	Accounting Rule	Entry
The liability *Accounts Payable* decreases by $720.00.	To decrease a liability, debit the account.	Debit: Accounts Payable, $720.00 (also the creditor's account).
The asset *Cash* decreases by $705.60.	To decrease an asset, credit the account.	Credit: Cash, $705.60.
The cash discount on the purchase increases owner's equity by $14.40.	To increase owner's equity, credit the account.	Credit: Purchases Discount, $14.40.

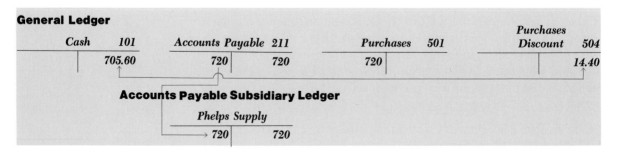

The amount of net purchases is important to a business. It shows the cost of merchandise after transportation costs, discounts, and returns and allowances have been added and subtracted from purchases. The illustration in the margin shows how the amount of net purchases is computed.

The accounts related to the cost of merchandise purchases are assigned account numbers 501, 502, 503, and 504 in the House of Sound chart of accounts.

Purchases		4,000	00
Add: Transportation In .		50	00
Cost of Delivered Goods		4,050	00
Less: Purchases			
Returns and			
Allowances . . $600			
Purchases			
Discount . . . 20		620	00
Net Purchases		3,430	00

House of Sound Chart of Accounts

Costs and Expenses
501 Purchases
502 Transportation In
503 Purchases Returns and Allowances
504 Purchases Discount

Recording Purchase Discounts in the Cash Payments Journal

All cash payments are recorded in the cash payments journal. The entry to record a payment within a discount period involves a debit to the Accounts Payable controlling account (and a debit to the individual creditor's account). The entry also involves a credit to the Purchases Discount account and a credit to the Cash account. This type of entry cannot be recorded in a one-column cash payments journal because it includes two credits. Thus most businesses adapt the cash payments journal by adding a special column for credits to the Purchases Discount account. A journal with more than one money column is known as a **multicolumn journal.**

The special columns shown in the following multicolumn cash payments journal are often added to make the recording of cash payments easier.

	CASH PAYMENTS JOURNAL								Page 3
DATE	ACCOUNT DEBITED	EXPLANATION	CHECK NO.	POST. REF.	GENERAL LEDGER DEBIT	ACCOUNTS PAYABLE DEBIT	PURCHASES DISCOUNT CREDIT	NET CASH CREDIT	
19—									
Oct. 18	Phelps Supply	Invoice 0567	308			720 00	14 40	705 60	

Recording Cash Payments.

The Net Cash Credit column is used to record the total cash paid. An entry in the Net Cash Credit column is a credit to the Cash account. The Purchases Discount Credit column is used to record the purchase discounts taken. An entry in this column is a credit to the Purchases Discount account.

The Accounts Payable Debit column is used to record all debits to creditors' accounts. The amount entered in the Accounts Payable Debit column ($720.00) must be equal to the total amount of the credits ($705.60 + $14.40). The General Ledger Debit column is used for recording debits to any account for which there is no special column in the journal.

Cash   101
                    705.60

Purchases Discount 504
                    14.40

Accounts Payable   211
720.00

Answer the following questions about journalizing payments for purchases. Refer to the text, margin notes, and illustrations on pages 371 to 373.
1. Where are payments for purchases journalized?
2. How much is the Phelps Supply willing to accept in full payment of the amount owed by House of Sound? How is the amount computed?

3. What accounts are debited and credited when the $720 invoice is paid in the discount period?
4. How many special columns are included in the cash payments journal on page 373?
5. Why is the credit entry to increase owner's equity made to the Purchases Discount account and not to the Purchases account?

Posting Cash Payments

B *Is the cash payments journal posted during or at the end of the month?* When to post the cash payments journal depends on the type of entry.

Posting the Cash Payments Journal During the Month. Each amount in the General Ledger Debit column of the cash payments journal is posted to the proper account in the general ledger. The account numbers in the Posting Reference column show that the amounts have been posted to the general ledger. These entries are posted during the month.

CASH PAYMENTS JOURNAL
Page 3

DATE		ACCOUNT DEBITED	EXPLANATION	CHECK NO.	POST. REF.	GENERAL LEDGER DEBIT	ACCOUNTS PAYABLE DEBIT	PURCHASES DISCOUNT CREDIT	NET CASH CREDIT
19—									
Oct.	2	Mortgage Payable	October mortgage	304	231	450 00			450 00
	2	Purchases	Fisher Company	305	501	100 00			100 00
	4	Office Equipment	Typewriter	306	132	700 00			700 00
	12	Transportation In	Mauro Lines	307	502	50 00			50 00
	18	Phelps Supply	Invoice 0567	308	✓		720 00	14 40	705 60
	24	Tappan Corporation . . .	Invoice P876	309	✓		400 00	4 00	396 00
	28	Downtown Music	Invoice 82A	310	✓		2,000 00		2,000 00
	31	Salaries Payable	October 29 payroll	311–314	225	1,200 00			1,200 00
	31	Advertising Expense . . .	} Replenish petty	315	512	12 25			26 00
		Miscellaneous Exp.	} cash fund	—	515	13 75			— 00

Posting the Cash Payments Journal During the Month.

Debits posted during the month to accounts in general ledger.

Debits posted during the month to creditors' accounts in subsidiary ledger.

Amounts in these two columns are not posted separately during the month.

Each of the three entries in the Accounts Payable Debit column is posted to a creditor's account in the subsidiary ledger. A check mark (✓) is placed in the Posting Reference column. The check mark shows that the amount has been posted. Note that the entries for October 18 and 24 include purchase discounts. The entry for October 28 does not include a purchase discount. None of the items in the Net Cash Credit column or Purchases Discount Credit column are posted during the month.

Posting From the Cash Payments Journal at the End of the Month. At the end of the month, all the money columns of the cash payments journal are pencil-footed. The equality of the debit and credit totals is also checked. To check the equality, add the totals of the two debit columns. Then add the totals of the two credit columns. The two sums must be equal. After the equality has been proved, the journal is totaled and ruled.

Proof of Cash Payments Journal

General Ledger Debit . .	2,526 00
Accounts Payable Debit	3,120 00
Total Debits	5,646 00
Purchases Discount Credit	18 40
Net Cash Credit	5,627 60
Total Credits	5,646 00

CASH PAYMENTS JOURNAL — Page 3

DATE		ACCOUNT DEBITED	EXPLANATION	CHECK NO.	POST. REF.	GENERAL LEDGER DEBIT	ACCOUNTS PAYABLE DEBIT	PURCHASES DISCOUNT CREDIT	NET CASH CREDIT
19—									
Oct.	2	Mortgage Payable .	October mortgage . .	304	231	450 00			450 00
	31	Advertising Expense	Replenish petty cash fund	315	512	12 25			26 00
		Miscellaneous Expense							
				—	515	13 75			— 00
	31	Totals	. . . .			2,526 00	3,120 00	18 40	5,627 60
						(—)	(211)	(504)	(101)

Posting the Cash Payments Journal at the end of the month.

The total of the General Ledger Debit column is not posted. The amounts in this column have been posted during the month. A dash is placed in the column on the line beneath the double rule to show that the total is not posted.

The total of the Accounts Payable Debit column is posted as a debit to the controlling account in the general ledger. The individual amounts in this column were posted to the subsidiary ledger during the month. The account number (211) is recorded in the column beneath the double rule.

The total of the Purchases Discount Credit column is posted as a credit to the Purchases Discount account in the general ledger. The account number (504) is then recorded in the column beneath the double rule. The total of the Net Cash Credit column is posted to the credit side of the Cash account. The account number (101) is then recorded beneath the double rule.

Summarizing Transactions Involving Purchases

The various activities involved in purchasing merchandise are discussed earlier in this chapter. As a result of these activities, an approved purchase invoice was submitted to the accounting department for journalizing. In some cases, the full amount of the invoice was paid when due. In other cases, a deduction for a return or allowance was made from the total amount of the invoice. In still other cases, a deduction for a purchase discount was also made. The flowchart on page 377 summarizes these transactions.

The flowchart on page 377

Activity B. Answer the following questions about posting from the cash payments journal. Refer to the cash payments journal on page 374.

1. What accounts and amounts are debited and credited in the entry made on October 24?

2. Why are two accounts credited in the October 24 entry?

3. Why is a check mark placed in the Posting Reference column for the October 24 entry?

4. When the October 24 entry is posted, is $4 posted as a credit to Purchases Discount? Is $396 posted as a credit to Cash? If not, how will these amounts be posted?

5. What account was debited on October 12?

6. When the October 18 entry was posted as a debit to the Phelps Supply account, was the Accounts Payable controlling account in the general ledger debited for $720 at the same time? If not, how will the amount be posted?

7. Why is a dash placed under the General Ledger Debit column?

8. Why is "(211)" placed under the Accounts Payable Debit column?

9. Is there any way to prove the amounts in the cash payments journal? How?

10. How would the following error be found? The accounting clerk posts an individual amount for $100 in the Accounts Payable Debit as $10 to the creditor's account. (Use your knowledge of controlling accounts to answer.)

Accounting Concept:
Purchase Discount. A *purchase discount* is a decrease in the cost of purchases. Costs and decreases in costs are not recorded until they are realized.

Topic 6 Problems

13-13. For each of the invoices listed in the table below, find the following: the end of the discount period, the amount of payment if the invoice is paid within the discount period, and the end of the credit period.

Invoice Date	Invoice Amount	Terms
a. 7/20	$3,000	2/10, n/30
b. 6/14	2,400	3/10, n/30
c. 11/10	1,920	1/20, n/30
d. 12/15	2,792	n/EOM

13-14. Find the cost of delivered goods and the net purchases for each of the following purchases.

Purchases	Trans. In	Purch. Ret. & Allow.	Purch. Disc.
a. $16,000	$225	$ 0	$200
b. 15,000	535	2,700	0
c. 5,500	0	700	250
d. 9,600	55	100	172

13-15. Process the following purchases data for the Richland Nursery.

a. Open the general ledger accounts, assign appropriate numbers, and record the October 1 balances as

RECORDING TRANSACTIONS INVOLVING PURCHASES OF MERCHANDISE

TRANSACTION	SOURCE DOCUMENT*	JOURNAL	GENERAL LEDGER						ACCOUNTS PAYABLE LEDGER
			Cash	Accounts Payable	Purchases	Trans-portation In	Purchases Returns & Allowances	Purchases Discount	Individual Creditor's Account
Purchase for cash.	Check Stub	Cash Payments Journal	XXXX		XXXX				
Return or allowance for cash.	Remittance Slip	Cash Receipts Journal	XXXX				XXXX		
Purchase on credit.	Purchase Invoice	Purchases Journal		XXXX	XXXX				XXXX
Transportation charge for cash.	Check Stub	Cash Payments Journal	XXXX			XXXX			
Return or allowance for credit.	Credit Memorandum	General Journal		XXXX			XXXX		XXXX
Payment with purchase discount.	Check Stub	Cash Payments Journal	XXX	XXXX				X	XXXX
Payment without purchase discount.	Check Stub	Cash Payments Journal	XXXX	XXXX					XXXX

*Only one possible source document is shown.

follows: Cash, $20,800; Accounts Payable; Dina Hertz, Capital, $20,800; Dina Hertz, Drawing; Purchases; Transportation In; Purchases Discount; Rent Expense. Open accounts payable ledger accounts for the Midas Nursery, 215 Main Street, Troy, New York 12180; and Savin Nurseries, Franklin St., Nashua, New Hampshire 03061.

b. Using a purchases journal and a cash payments journal, record the entries for the listed transactions.

c. Post the individual entries from the journals.

d. Prove, total, and rule the journals.

e. Post the totals from the journals.

f. Prepare a schedule of accounts payable. Verify the total.

Oct. 1 Issued Check 204 for $320 for October rent.

5 Bought merchandise for $500 from Savin Nurseries; Invoice 482, dated Oct. 2; terms FOB shipping point, 2/10, n/30.

5 Issued Check 205 for $52 to Van Express for delivering merchandise from Savin Nurseries.

8 Bought merchandise for $1,000 from Midas Nursery; Invoice R119, dated Oct. 5; terms FOB destination, 1/10, n/60.

11 Issued Check 206 for $490 to Savin Nurseries to pay Invoice 482, less discount.

13 Issued Check 207 for $990 to Midas Nursery to pay Invoice R119, less discount.

13 Bought merchandise for $640 from Midas Nursery; Invoice R306, dated Oct. 10; terms FOB destination, 1/10, n/60.

18 Bought merchandise for $460 from Midas Nursery; Invoice R375, dated Oct. 15; terms FOB destination, 1/10, n/60.

24 Issued Check 208 for $600 to Dina Hertz for personal use.

26 Bought merchandise for $160 from Savin Nurseries; Invoice 566, dated Oct. 23; terms FOB shipping point, 2/10, n/30.

Oct. 26 Issued Check 209 for $64 to Van Express for delivering merchandise from Savin Nurseries.

NOTE: Save your ledgers for further use in Topic Problem 13-16.

13-16. Using the ledgers prepared in Topic Problem 13-15, complete the following work.

a. Record the listed entries for November in a purchases journal and a cash payments journal.

b. Post the individual entries from the journals.

c. Prove, total, and rule the journals.

d. Post the totals from the journals.

e. Prepare a schedule of accounts payable. Verify the total.

f. Prepare a trial balance.

Nov. 1 Issued Check 210 for $320 for November rent.

3 Issued Check 211 to Midas Nursery for Invoice R306.

5 Bought merchandise for $720 from Savin Nurseries; Invoice 624, dated Nov. 2; terms FOB shipping point, 2/10, n/30.

9 Issued Check 212 for $42 to Van Express for delivering merchandise from Savin Nurseries.

9 Issued Check 213 to Savin Nurseries to pay Invoice 624.

12 Bought merchandise for $1,200 from Midas Nursery; Invoice R402, dated Nov. 9; terms FOB destination, 1/10, n/60.

18 Issued Check 214 to Midas Nursery to pay Invoice R402, less discount.

21 Issued Check 215 to Savin Nurseries to pay Invoice 566.

28 Bought merchandise for $560 from Savin Nursery; Invoice R490, dated Nov. 25; terms FOB destination, 1/10, n/60.

The Language of Business

The following terms make up the language of business. Do you know the meaning of each?

purchases subsystem	purchase order
inventory card	invoice
purchase requisition	purchase invoice
request for quotation	sales invoice
FOB (free on board)	

merchandise
  inventory
perpetual inventory
  procedure
periodic inventory
  procedure
physical inventory

inventory loss
deterioration
obsolescence
merchandising business
costs
gross profit
Sales account

Purchases account
Cost and Expense
   accounts
purchases journal
subsidiary ledger
general ledger
accounts payable
   ledger

accounts receivable
   ledger
controlling account
three-column balance
   ledger form
schedule of accounts
   payable
FOB destination
FOB shipping point
Transportation In
   account

cost of the delivered
   goods
purchases return
purchases allowance
Purchases Returns and
   Allowances account
net purchases
credit memorandum
double-posting
credit period
cash discount

discount period
purchase discount
tickler file
Purchases Discount
   account
multicolumn journal
trade discount

Chapter 13   Questions

1. How is a merchandising business different from a service business?
2. What is the purpose of the procedures for the control of purchases of merchandise?
3. Describe the four major purchasing activities.
4. What is the purpose of preparing a schedule of accounts payable? In what ways is it like a trial balance?
5. Why are transportation charges not recorded in the Purchases account?
6. Why are purchases returns and allowances not recorded in the Purchases account?

7. Why are purchase discounts not recorded in the Purchases account?
8. Name and describe the source document for journalizing each of the following: purchases for cash, purchases on credit, purchases returns and allowances, transportation charges, purchases discounts, and payments to creditors.
9. How does a four-column cash payments journal simplify journalizing and posting?
10. What would be the effect on assets, liabilities, and owner's equity if the purchase of a typewriter was recorded in the purchases journal?

Chapter 13   Problems

Problems for Chapter 13 are given in the *Working Papers and Chapter Problems for Part 2*. If you are using the workbook, do the problems in the space provided there.

Chapter 13   Management Cases

Trade Discounts. Many manufacturers and wholesalers publish catalogs showing the retail prices of their products. They frequently offer deductions from these list prices to their dealers. The reduction from list price is known as a **trade discount.** For example, a manufacturer advertises a certain $200 television set at a list price of $200 (the price to retail customers). However, it offers the same television set to dealers at a trade discount of 40 percent. This discount amounts to $80 (40 percent of $200). Thus a dealer has to pay $120 ($200 − $80) for each set.

$200   × 0.40
(List Price)   (Rate of Trade Discount)
              = $80
              (Amount of Trade Discount)
$200   − $80
(List Price) (Amount of Trade Discount)
              = $120
              (Net Price)

Trade discounts are not entered in the accounting records because they are used only to find the net purchase price. The important price is the net price that must be paid to the supplier (the list price minus the trade discount).

Case 13M-1. The Home Appliance Center buys microwave ovens for $500 each on credit terms of 1/10, n/30. The manufacturer pays the shipping cost. If the store buys a truckload of 120 ovens, a 10 percent trade discount is allowed.

Last year the store sold 100 ovens. Sales have been increasing gradually, and the store expects a 20 percent increase next year. The store manager is considering buying a truckload of ovens and has asked for your opinion.
a. What is the trade discount? What amount is recorded in the purchases journal?
b. What amount is paid for 120 ovens if the store pays within ten days? Twenty days?
c. How much money will the store be tying up in inventory if it buys the truckload?
d. Could the store lose money because of style changes or deterioration?
e. Would you recommend that the ovens be bought by the truckload? Explain.

Case 13M-2. The Creighton Shop bought a shipment of suits from the Squire Clothing Company. The invoice for the suits is for $5,000, is dated June 1, and has terms of 2/10, n/30. On June 11 the Creighton Shop does not have enough cash to pay the invoice. It will have the money by July 1. In order to take advantage of the 2 percent cash discount, the owners are considering borrowing the money from a bank to pay the invoice within the discount period. The business has a good credit rating and can borrow the necessary amount at 10 percent interest.
a. How much will the owners have to borrow to pay the invoice on June 11?
b. For how many days will they have to borrow the money?
c. How much interest will they have to pay?
d. With the interest on the loan, what will the total cost of the suits be?
e. Is there a possibility of loss due to style changes or deterioration?
f. Would you recommend that the owners borrow the money and take advantage of the cash discount or that they pay the full amount of the invoice on June 30?

Working Hint

Using the Balance Ledger Form for the General Ledger. Some accounting clerks do not take time to compute the current account balance after each posting to the general ledger. They compute and record only the ending balance for the month.

In the Cash account shown here, no balances were computed when the amounts were posted to the account during November. At the end of November, the accounting clerk balanced the account by computing and recording the balance in the Balance section of the account. The same procedure was followed in December.

Cash						Account No.	101
DATE		EXPLANATION	POST. REF.	DEBIT	CREDIT	BALANCE DEBIT	BALANCE CREDIT
19—							
Nov.	1	Opening entry	CR1	9,440 00			
	30	. . . .	CR1	7,475 00			
	30	. . . .	CP1		1,800 00	15,115 00	
Dec.	31	. . . .	CR2	5,785 00			
	31	. . . .	CP2		4,700 00	16,200 00	

Chapter 14

A Sales Subsystem

You will now learn how the people, forms, procedures, and equipment in a sales subsystem are used to control sales on credit. You will also learn about the important jobs of the accounts receivable bookkeeper, accounts receivable clerk, billing clerk, credit clerk, order clerk, and stock control clerk.

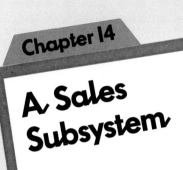

Topic 1
Controlling Sales of Merchandise

A *Are the same procedures used to control cash sales and credit sales?* No, somewhat different procedures are used. The procedures for cash sales are described in Chapter 11. Cash sales are recorded on cash register tapes or sales slips. The tapes or sales slips are then used as source documents for entries in the cash receipts journal. When a retail or wholesale business sells merchandise on credit, the procedures used cover seven sales activities. These activities are listed below and are completed in a sales subsystem. A **sales subsystem** is the people, forms, procedures, and equipment used to process sales of merchandise on credit and includes the following activities.

Control: Fill orders promptly.
Control: Use prenumbered forms.
Control: Verify data on order.
Control: Check customer's credit before shipping merchandise.
Control: Divide responsibility.
Control: Remove merchandise in authorized quantities only.
Control: Bill customers for all merchandise shipped.
Control: Record all receivables.
Control: Issue refunds and credits only for approved returns and allowances.
Control: Collect receivables as soon as possible.

- Receiving and approving the customer orders
- Shipping the merchandise
- Billing for merchandise
- Accounting for sales on credit

Procedures for Controlling Sales on Credit

Every business that sells merchandise on credit needs a subsystem to control sales. The control concept states that procedures must be established to ensure accuracy, honesty, and efficiency and speed in handling and recording assets, liabilities, owner's equity, revenues, and expenses. The subsystem must include procedures to do the following.

- Fill customers' orders promptly.
- Use prenumbered forms.
- Verify data on each order.
- Check the customer's credit before the merchandise is shipped.
- Divide responsibility among employees.
- Remove merchandise from stock only if there is proper authorization.
- Bill customers for all merchandise shipped.
- Record receivables from completed sales transactions.
- Issue refunds and credits only for approved returns and allowances.
- Collect receivables as soon as possible.

The first seven procedures for the control of sales on credit are discussed in Topic 1. The last three procedures are discussed in later topics.

Activity A. Answer the following questions about controlling sales. Refer to the control procedures above.
1. Which of the procedures above ensure accuracy?
2. Which of the procedures ensure honesty?
3. Which ensure efficiency and speed?

Receiving and Approving Customer Orders

B *What are the procedures for receiving and approving customer orders?* Customer orders must be promptly approved or disapproved when received. The procedures to do this include the following.

- Taking the order
- Preparing the shipping order
- Securing credit approval

Taking the Order. Salespeople may fill in a *sales order form.* An order may also come in on a *purchase order form* or in a customer letter. Or an order may be jotted down on a sales slip by a clerk who takes orders in person or over a telephone. Because orders are received in many ways and on many forms, some businesses find it helpful to transfer each order to standard forms. These forms are usually prenumbered and printed in multiple copies.

Order Clerk:
DOT 249.367-054. Processes orders received by mail, telephone, or in person from customers.

Preparing the Shipping Order. When a business receives an order, a clerk enters the data on a prenumbered form known as a shipping order. The shipping order below is prepared from a purchase order submitted by Wanda's Radio to the House of Sound.

Control: Fill orders promptly.

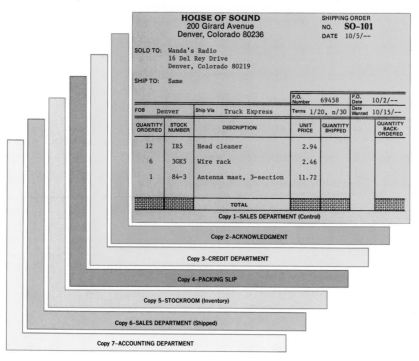

Purchase Order

Control: Use prenumbered forms.

Shipping order prepared from purchase order.

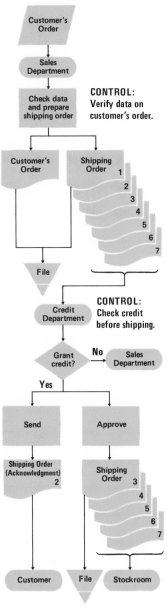

Processing a Customer's Order

Some of the information on the purchase order is transferred without change. Other information is verified. For example, the salesclerk must check the credit terms requested by the customer (1/20, n/30) before entering the terms on the shipping order. The clerk must also check the stock numbers and unit prices of items to be sure each is correct.

When the clerk completes the shipping order, Copy 1 is attached to the purchase order and is kept until the order is shipped and billed. This control copy is kept in the unshipped orders file, a file of shipping orders that have not yet been shipped. This file contains the only fixed record the company has of the order. The other copies of the shipping order (Copies 2–7) are sent to the credit department.

Securing Credit Approval. The credit department must find out if the customer is a good credit risk. That is, it must learn whether or not the customer is likely to pay the bill when it becomes due.

If the customer is a poor credit risk, the credit department usually returns the shipping order to the sales department. The salespeople must settle the problem with the customer. They either do not fill the order or work out arrangements protecting the supplier. If the customer's credit is good, the credit clerk detaches Copy 2 and sends it to the customer. The customer then knows that the order has been received and is being processed. The credit clerk then signs the panel at the top of Copy 3 to show that the order has been approved for shipment, as shown below. (By means of interleaved carbon paper or specially treated paper, the clerk's signature is transferred to the other copies. Thus anyone who uses one of the copies is sure that the customer's credit has been checked and approved.) The credit clerk then detaches Copy 3 of the shipping order for the credit department's files. Copies 4–7 are sent to the stockroom, where the merchandise is stored.

HOUSE OF SOUND
200 Girard Avenue
Denver, Colorado 80236

SHIPPING ORDER
NO. **SO-101**
DATE 10/5/--

SOLD TO: Wanda's Radio
16 Del Rey Drive
Denver, Colorado 80219

THANK YOU for your order!
This is an exact copy as we entered it.
Please notify us at once of any discrepancies

SHIP TO: Same

		P.O. Number 69458		P.O. Date 10/2/--
FOB Denver	Ship Via Truck Express	Terms 1/20, n/30		Date Wanted 10/15/--

QUANTITY ORDERED	STOCK NUMBER	DESCRIPTION	UNIT PRICE
12	IR5	Head cleaner	2.94
6	3GK5	Wire rack	2.46
1	84-3	Antenna mast, 3-section	11.72
		TOTAL	

Copy 2–ACKNOWLEDGMENT

Acknowledgment for Customer

Shipping Order With Credit Approval

Credit Signature

HOUSE OF SOUND
200 Girard Avenue
Denver, Colorado 80236

SHIPPING ORDER
NO. **SO-101**
DATE 10/5/--

SOLD TO: Wanda's Radio
16 Del Rey Drive
Denver, Colorado 80219

Credit: *J. Carson, 10/5/--*

SHIP TO: Same

		P.O. Number 69458		P.O. Date 10/2/--
FOB Denver	Ship Via Truck Express	Terms 1/20, n/30		Date Wanted 10/15/--

QUANTITY ORDERED	STOCK NUMBER	DESCRIPTION	UNIT PRICE
12	IR5	Head cleaner	2.94
6	3GK5	Wire rack	2.46
1	84-3	Antenna mast, 3-section	11.72
		TOTAL	

Copy 3–CREDIT DEPARTMENT

Activity B. Answer the following questions about receiving and approving customer orders. Refer to the text, margin notes, and illustrations on pages 383 and 384.

1. How many copies of the shipping order are prepared?

2. Which copy is sent to the customer?

3. Which department receives the customer's order?

4. What happens if credit is not approved?

5. Which copy of the shipping order is filed?

6. How many wire racks were ordered?

7. Who is the customer?

8. What credit terms are granted the customer?

Shipping Merchandise

C *What are the procedures for shipping merchandise?* After the customer's order is approved, the merchandise must be shipped. The procedures include the following.

- A shipping clerk in the stockroom assembles and packs the items.
- The shipping clerk writes on Copy 4 (the packing-slip copy) and all remaining copies whether the full quantity of each item is being sent.
- The shipping clerk fills in the shipping information on Copy 4.
- Copy 4 is then detached and separated into an address label and a packing slip. The label is attached to the outside of the package. The packing slip is enclosed in the package so that the customer can check the contents with the items listed on the packing slip.

Shipping Clerk:
DOT 222.387-050. Prepares merchandise for shipment and keeps records of the merchandise shipped.

The packing slip below shows that all the items on the purchase order are being shipped except 4 of the head cleaners. Only 8 of the 12 head cleaners ordered can be supplied. The remaining 4 are listed in the Quantity Back-Ordered column. (The quantity shipped plus the quantity back-ordered must agree with the customer's purchase order.) Thus the customer knows which items are not in the current shipment and which items will be sent when available.

- The shipping clerk then detaches Copy 5 (the inventory copy) for the stockroom's files. Copies 6 and 7 are sent back to the sales department.

Shipping Merchandise to a Customer

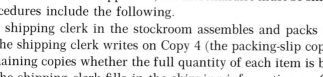

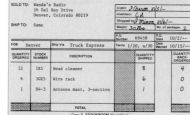

Shipping Label
Packing slip sent with goods to customer.

Inventory copy to update inventory cards.

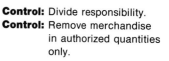

Control: Divide responsibility.
Control: Remove merchandise in authorized quantities only.

• Copy 5 is used to subtract the number of items shipped from the inventory cards.

Activity C. Answer the following questions about shipping customer orders. Refer to the text, margin notes, and illustrations on pages 385 and 386.
1. Who ships the merchandise?
2. Which of the procedures to control sales on credit is illustrated?
3. Which item is back-ordered? How many units are back-ordered?
4. What copy of the shipping order is used to update the inventory cards?
5. How are the goods being shipped?
6. Can a cash discount be received?

Control: Bill customers for all merchandise shipped.

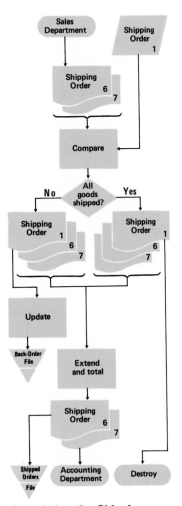

Completing the Shipping Order

Billing for Merchandise

D *What procedures are used to bill promptly customers for merchandise?* After the merchandise is shipped, the customer must be billed. Billing the customer requires that the shipping order be completed, the sales invoice be prepared, and the sales invoice be journalized. To do so, these procedures are followed.

• Copies 6 and 7 of the shipping order are returned to the sales department.
• A clerk takes Copy 1 (the control copy) out of the unshipped orders file. Copy 1 is then checked against the shipped copy (Copy 6) to see that no changes were made from the original order. If all merchandise has been shipped, Copy 1 is destroyed.
• On Copies 6 and 7, the clerk multiplies the quantity shipped by the unit price and records the extensions in the Amount column.

Orders-shipped file copy with extensions and total computed.

Copy used to prepare sales invoice.

• The clerk then totals the extensions, initials the Extensions box, and separates Copies 6 and 7.
• Copy 6 is placed in a **shipped orders file.** A shipped orders file is a file of shipping orders for orders that have been shipped. Copy 7 is sent to the accounting department. Copy 7 is used to prepare a sales invoice (the customer's bill).

This procedure changes slightly for back orders. The clerk computes the extensions and total for only those items shipped. On Copy 1 the items not shipped are checked, and Copy 1 is then filed in a back-order file. A **back-order file** is a file of shipping orders that will be filled when stock is received. A new shipping order is filled out when new stock is received. The balance of the order is then shipped to the customer. (A letter should also be sent to the customer that explains the delay and tells when delivery can be expected.)

Billing Clerk:
DOT 219.482-010. Prepares invoices. Computes amounts due. May prepare statements of account.

Preparing the Sales Invoice. The sales invoice looks like the completed shipping order, as shown here. However, it lists only the amount that the customer owes for those items actually shipped.

HOUSE OF SOUND				INVOICE NO. **101**	
200 Girard Avenue					
Denver, Colorado 80236					

SOLD TO: Wanda's Radio   Invoice Date: 10/7/--
         16 Del Rey Drive
         Denver, Colorado 80219

SHIP TO: Same   Terms: 1/20, n/30

Purchase Order No.	Date	Shipped Via	FOB	No. of. Packages
69458	10/2/--	Truck Exp.	Denver	2

QUANTITY	STOCK NUMBER	DESCRIPTION	UNIT PRICE	AMOUNT
8	IR5	Head cleaner	2.94	23.52
6	3GK5	Wire rack	2.46	14.76
1	84-3	Antenna mast, 3-section	11.72	11.72
		TOTAL		50.00
		COPY 1-CUSTOMER		

Sales invoice prepared from shipping order (Copy 7).

An accounting clerk first verifies the extensions and total amount on Copy 7 of the shipping order. At least two copies of the sales invoice are then prepared in the billing section of the accounting department. Copy 1 shown above is sent to the customer and is the customer's bill.

Copy 2 of the invoice is kept in the accounting department. It is the source document for journalizing the sales transaction. Often the sales invoice is prepared in three copies. Copy 3 is sent to the sales department and is used to analyze sales revenue.

After the invoice is prepared, the invoice date is recorded at the top of Copy 7 of the shipping order. This shows that the customer was billed for the merchandise shipped. Copy 7 is then filed in the accounting department. The billing process is illustrated in the margin.

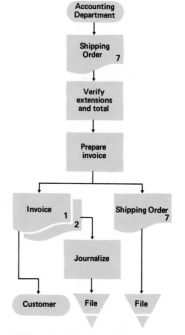

Billing for Merchandise

The subsystem for sales on credit uses multiple-copy forms. This saves retyping and recopying at each stage. If these forms were not used, the shipping labels and the packing slip, for example, would have to be prepared separately. The number of copies prepared depends on the needs of the company.

Stock-Control Clerk:
DOT 219.367-034. Processes records involving ordering, receiving, storing, and shipping merchandise, supplies, and equipment.

Credit Clerk:
DOT 205.367-022. Processes applications for loans and credit. Determines credit limit. May keep record of transactions with customers.

Activity D. Answer the following questions about billing for merchandise. Refer to the shipping orders and flowchart and the invoice on pages 386 and 387.

1. Who completed the extensions on the shipping order SO-101?
2. What is the total amount of SO-101?
3. What are the differences between Invoice 101 and the shipping order SO-101?
4. What is the last day on which Wanda's Radio can take a 1 percent discount?
5. Who will receive Copy 1 of Invoice 101?
6. Which copy of the shipping order is held in the accounting department?
7. What happens to Copy 2 of the sales invoice?
8. Which procedure for the control of sales on credit is illustrated?

Visualizing Sales on Credit

E *How are the procedures to process sales related?* The procedures for receiving and approving the customer's order, packing and shipping the merchandise, and billing for the merchandise are shown in the flowchart on the next page.

Activity E. Prepare a table to show who prepares or sends the following forms, to whom or where the forms are sent, and the purpose they serve. Refer to the flowchart on the next page.

1. Copy 1 of shipping order.
2. Copies 2–7 of shipping order.
3. Copy 2 of shipping order.
4. Copy 3 of shipping order.
5. Copies 4–7 of shipping order.
6. Copy 4 of shipping order (packing slip).
7. Copy 5 of shipping order.
8. Inventory cards (updated).
9. Copies 6 and 7 of shipping order.
10. Copy 1 of shipping order (after all merchandise is shipped).
11. Copy 6 of shipping order.
12. Copy 7 of shipping order.
13. Copy 1 of invoice.
14. Copy 2 of invoice.
15. Copy 7 of shipping order (after invoice is prepared).
16. Physical inventory sheet.

Accounting Concept:
Control. Procedures must be established to ensure accuracy, honesty, and efficiency and speed in handling and recording assets, liabilities, owner's equity, revenues, and expenses.

VISUALIZING A SUBSYSTEM FOR SALES ON CREDIT

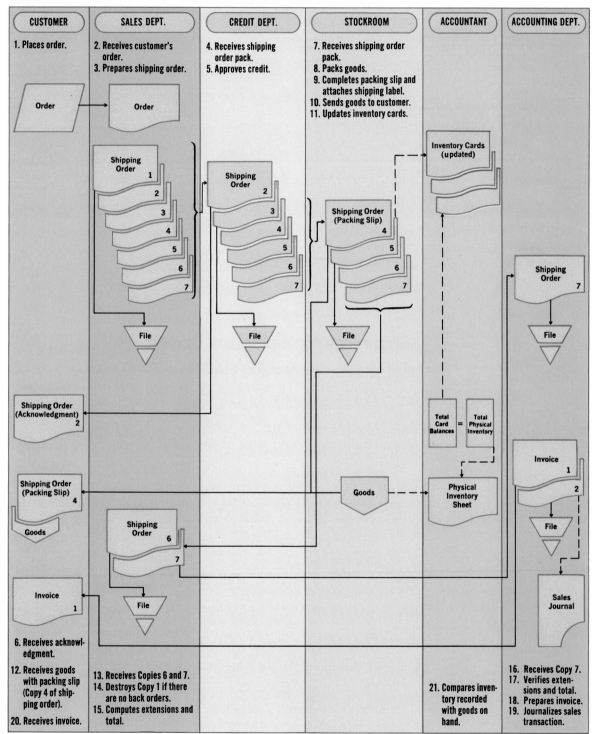

CUSTOMER	SALES DEPT.	CREDIT DEPT.	STOCKROOM	ACCOUNTANT	ACCOUNTING DEPT.
1. Places order.	2. Receives customer's order. 3. Prepares shipping order.	4. Receives shipping order pack. 5. Approves credit.	7. Receives shipping order pack. 8. Packs goods. 9. Completes packing slip and attaches shipping label. 10. Sends goods to customer. 11. Updates inventory cards.		

6. Receives acknowledgment.
12. Receives goods with packing slip (Copy 4 of shipping order).
20. Receives invoice.

13. Receives Copies 6 and 7.
14. Destroys Copy 1 if there are no back orders.
15. Computes extensions and total.

21. Compares inventory recorded with goods on hand.

16. Receives Copy 7.
17. Verifies extensions and total.
18. Prepares invoice.
19. Journalizes sales transaction.

14-1. You are employed by Richboro Manufacturing. Two purchase orders received on May 12 are shown below and at the right. Prepare a shipping order for each purchase order. The last shipping order number was 197.

Covina Hardware
East Kings Drive
West Covina, California 91791

PURCHASE ORDER NO. **E717**

Date __May 8, 19--__
Terms __2/10, n/30__
Ship Via __Express__
Required Delivery Date __5/20/--__

TO: Richboro Manufacturing
100 Almshouse Road
Richboro, Pennsylvania 18954

QUANTITY	DESCRIPTION	UNIT PRICE	AMOUNT
4	Model No. 78 dustpan	2.20	8.80
3	D-17 garden hose, 50', 3/8"	5.50	16.50
17 ctn.	30-amp fuses, H-11	2.40	40.80
	TOTAL		66.10

MOREHERD SUPPLY, Lexington, Kentucky 40505

To: Richboro Manufacturing
100 Almshouse Road
Richboro, PA 18954

Terms: 2/10, n/30

Invoice No. 206
Date: 5/10/--
Ship Via: Express
Delivery Date: 5/21/--

QUANTITY	STOCK NO.	DESCIPTION	UNIT PRICE	AMOUNT
3	176-2	Tite-Belt sander, Model 64D	40 00	120 00

14-2. In Topic Problem 14-1 you prepared two shipping orders. Each shipping order has seven copies, similar to the House of Sound. Complete a chart similar to the one at the right.

Department	Forms Received	Forms Prepared	Forms Sent To
Sales	?	?	?
Credit	?	?	?
Stockroom	?	?	?
Accounting	?	?	?

Topic 2
Processing Sales on Credit

A *What are the procedures for recording all receivables from sales transactions?* The subsystem for sales usually includes the use of a special sales journal and an accounts receivable subsidiary ledger.

Journalizing Sales on Credit

The processing of sales on credit is discussed in Topic 1. Recall that Copy 2 of the sales invoice remains in the accounting department. It is used as the source document for recording sales on credit. The invoice provides the following information.

1 The date of the transaction
2 The invoice number
3 The customer's name
4 The amount of the sale
5 The credit terms

The transaction can be recorded in the general journal. However, when a business has many sales on credit, it often uses a special journal for these transactions. The special journal saves time in journalizing and posting.

The Sales Journal. A **sales journal** is a special journal used only to record sales of merchandise on credit. The sale of any other asset sold

Control: Record all receivables.

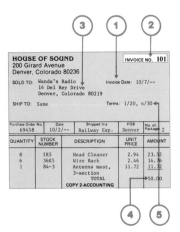

Sales Invoice

on credit is recorded in the general journal. Any cash sale (of merchandise or another asset) is recorded in the cash receipts journal.

The House of Sound makes two kinds of sales on credit. First, goods are sold to other businesses. The other businesses, in turn, sell the goods to consumers. Second, the House of Sound sells goods directly to consumers. An invoice for each type of sale on credit is shown below.

HOUSE OF SOUND				INVOICE NO. 102
200 Girard Avenue				
Denver, Colorado 80236				
SOLD TO: Village Notes			Invoice Date: 10/7/--	
17 Chaparral Boulevard				
Tucson, Arizona 85718				
SHIP TO: Same			Terms: 2/10, n/30	

Purchase Order No. G1768	Date 10/2/--	Shipped Via Railway Express	FOB Tucson	No. of Packages 4
QUANTITY	DESCRIPTION		UNIT PRICE	AMOUNT
2	G87 Vucorders		250.00	500.00
6	17 Spheral tape decks		180.00	1,080.00
1 ctn	Milar tape		20.00	20.00
		TOTAL		1,600.00
	COPY 1-CUSTOMER			

Sales invoice: goods sold to a business.

HOUSE OF SOUND				INVOICE NO. 105
200 Girard Avenue				
Denver, Colorado 80236				
SOLD TO: George Yeomans			Invoice Date: 10/15/--	
200 Hinsdale Avenue				
Englewood, Colorado 80112				
SHIP TO:			Terms: n/30	

Purchase Order No. Pick-up	Date --	Shipped Via --	FOB --	No. of Packages 1
QUANTITY	DESCRIPTION		UNIT PRICE	AMOUNT
1	Carlsbad 082 video recorder		700.00	700.00
	Sales Tax			45.50
		TOTAL		745.50
	COPY 1-CUSTOMER			

Sales invoice: goods sold to consumer.

The sales on credit here are not the same. One includes a sales tax (George Yeomans) and the other does not. Both, however, are recorded in the same sales journal. The sales journal used by the House of Sound is illustrated here.

		SALES JOURNAL					Page 1
DATE	INVOICE NO.	ACCOUNT DEBITED	TERMS	POST. REF.	ACCOUNTS RECEIVABLE DEBIT	SALES TAX PAYABLE CREDIT	SALES CREDIT
					①	②	③

Note that the sales journal used by House of Sound has three money columns. Each column is used as follows.

1 Accounts Receivable Debit: Accounts receivable is money owed by customers. Each entry in the sales journal is a debit to Accounts Receivable because each sale on credit increases the asset Accounts Receivable.

2 Sales Tax Payable Credit: Sales Tax Payable is a liability account. Businesses must often collect a sales tax on each sale. Generally, sales made directly to the consumer are subject to a sales tax. Sales made to businesses that will resell the goods are not subject to sales tax. Amounts collected as sales tax must be sent, periodically, to the government. Thus an amount in the Sales Tax Payable Credit column shows an increase in the liability Sales Tax Payable.

3 Sales Credit: Each sale on credit increases revenue. The revenue account used by many merchandising businesses is Sales. Thus the Sales Credit column shows an increase in the revenue account Sales.

Now let's analyze the two entries in the sales journal. The first is the sale on credit to Village Notes and does not include a sales tax.

October 7: The House of Sound issues Invoice 102 to Village Notes for the sale of merchandise on credit for $1,600.

What Happens	Accounting Rule	Entry
The asset *Accounts Receivable* increases by $1,600.	To increase an asset, debit the account.	Debit: Accounts Receivable, $1,600. (Also debit the customer's account.)
Revenue increases owner's equity by $1,600.	To increase owner's equity, credit the account.	Credit: Sales, $1,600.

This entry increases both assets [accounts receivable and revenue (sales)] by $1,600. Note the following.

1 The invoice number is recorded in the sales journal. Invoices are entered in numeric order to account for every invoice.

DATE	INVOICE NO.	ACCOUNT DEBITED	TERMS	POST. REF.	ACCOUNTS RECEIVABLE DEBIT	SALES TAX PAYABLE CREDIT	SALES CREDIT
19— Oct. 7	102	Village Notes	2/10, n/30	√	1,600 00		1,600 00

SALES JOURNAL — Page 1

Recording sales on credit without sales tax.

General Ledger

Accounts Receivable 111
1,600

Sales 401
1,600

Subsidiary Ledger

Village Notes
1,600

2 The credit terms are also entered in the sales journal. The credit terms will be transferred to the customers' accounts at the time of posting. For example, the sale made to Village Notes was made on terms of 2/10, n/30. By having the terms in the customer's account, the accounting clerk can quickly compute the cash discount offered and the end of the credit period. The Terms column could be eliminated if the company offers the same credit terms to each customer.

The October 15 sale on credit to George Yeomans includes sales tax and is recorded as follows.

October 15: The House of Sound issues Invoice 105 to George Yeomans for the sale of merchandise on credit for $700, plus sales tax of $45.50.

What Happens	Accounting Rule	Entry
The asset *Accounts Receivable* increases by $745.50.	To increase an asset, debit the account.	Debit: Accounts Receivable, $745.50. (Also debit the customer's account.)
The liability *Sales Tax Payable* increases by $45.50.	To increase a liability, credit the account.	Credit: Sales Tax Payable, $45.50.
Revenue increases owner's equity by $700.	To increase owner's equity, credit the account.	Credit: Sales, $700.

This entry increases assets, liabilities, and revenue. The increase in assets (Accounts Receivable) is for the amount of the sale, plus the amount of the sales tax. George Yeomans must send $745.50 to the House of Sound within 30 days. The House of Sound will then send the amount of the sales tax collected from the Yeomans account along with other sales taxes to the government. The sales journal illustrating the sales taxes is found on page 394.

Journalizing Sales Taxes

Most states and many cities collect a sales tax. A **sales tax** is a tax charged on sales of merchandise to consumers. Some states also charge sales taxes on sales of services. Typically, a sales tax is charged to the purchaser and collected by the seller. The seller then sends the collected sales taxes to the state or city government at specified times.

Sales tax collected on a cash sale is usually shown as a separate item on the cash register. At the end of the day, the cash register tape shows the total amount of sales. It also shows a separate total for the sales taxes that were collected.

House of Sound Chart of Accounts

Liabilities
201 Loans Payable
211 Accounts Payable
216 Sales Tax Payable

SALES JOURNAL

DATE	INVOICE NO.	ACCOUNT DEBITED	TERMS	POST. REF.	ACCOUNTS RECEIVABLE DEBIT	SALES TAX PAYABLE CREDIT	SALES CREDIT
19— Oct. 15	105	George Yeomans	n/30	√	745 50	45 50	700 00

Recording sale on credit with sales tax.

General Ledger

Accounts Receivable 111	Sales Tax Payable 216	Sales 401
745.50	45.50	700.00

Subsidiary Ledger

George Yeomans
745.50

Sales tax charged on a credit sale is shown separately on the invoice. When the invoice is recorded, the amount of the invoice (the sale and the sales tax) is debited to the customer's account. Thus, at the time of a credit sale, the sales tax is billed to the customer. In the entry for October 15, sales tax of $45.50 was billed to George Yeomans, as shown in the sales journal above.

Activity A. Answer the following questions about journalizing sales on credit. Refer to the text, margin notes, and illustrations on pages 390 to 394.
1. What copy of the invoice is used as the source document for an entry in the sales journal?
2. In which journal is the sale of used office equipment on account recorded?

3. An entry in the sales journal (without sales tax) means that three accounts are affected. What are these three accounts?
4. How many money columns are found in the sales journal?
5. What types of entries are recorded in the sales journal?

The Accounts Receivable Ledger

B *Is there a subsidiary ledger for customers' accounts?* Yes, there is. You learned that the creditors' accounts are often removed from the general ledger and placed in the accounts payable subsidiary ledger. It is also more efficient to remove the customers' accounts from the general ledger. They are often placed in alphabetic order in a subsidiary ledger called the accounts receivable ledger. An **accounts receivable ledger** is a subsidiary ledger for customers' accounts. The use of an accounts receivable ledger reduces the number of accounts in the general ledger. It also makes it easier to locate errors on the trial balance. The general ledger is kept in balance by including an Accounts Receivable controlling account. The balance of the Accounts Receivable controlling account must equal the total of all the customers' accounts in the accounts receivable ledger.

House of Sound Chart of Accounts

Assets
101 Cash
102 Petty Cash
103 Change Fund
111 Accounts Receivable
121 Land
131 Building
132 Office Equipment
133 Stockroom Equipment

Revenue
401 Sales

The balance ledger form is used for the accounts receivable ledger. An example of the accounts receivable ledger used by the House of Sound is illustrated here.

1 Increases in the customer's account balances are recorded in the Debit column.
2 Payments made by customers are recorded in the Credit column.
3 The customer's account balance is recorded in the Debit Balance column.

Accounts Receivable Ledger					
Name				Credit Limit	
Address				Telephone	
DATE	EXPLANATION	POST. REF.	DEBIT	CREDIT	DEBIT BALANCE
			①	②	③

Accounts Receivable Ledger Account

Order of Posting. It is important that entries from the sales journal are posted before entries from the cash receipts journal. By doing this, the debits to the accounts will be posted before the credits. This avoids having the customer's account show a credit balance until the debit amount is posted from the sales journal.

Order of posting
• Sales journal
• Cash receipts journal
• Purchases journal
• Cash payments journal
• General journal

Activity B. Answer the following questions about the accounts receivable ledger. Refer to the text, margin notes, and illustrations on pages 394 and 395.
1. Which accounts are placed in the accounts receivable ledger?
2. Which account is placed in the general ledger when a business uses an accounts receivable ledger?
3. How many money columns are included for each accounts receivable ledger account?
4. In which money column are decreases in the customers' accounts recorded?
5. How is the balance of each customer's account computed?

Posting Sales on Credit

C *What are the procedures for posting the sales journal?* Entries to the customers' accounts should be posted daily to keep each account up to date. Current account balances are especially important to the credit manager. The credit manager determines if sales on credit should be approved and make sure that payments are made on time. If payments are not made promptly, the credit manager must see that the amounts are collected. The information credit managers need to carry out their responsibilities depends on account balances being current.

Posting entries from the sales journal is similar to posting from other special journals. The procedure on page 396 is used.

SALES JOURNAL				Page 1
DATE	INVOICE NO.	ACCOUNT	POST REF.	ACCOUNTS RECEIVABLE DEBIT
19—Oct. 7	101	Wanda's Radio	✓	50 00

Name   Wanda's Radio
Address   16 Del Rey Drive, Denver, 80219

DATE	EXPLANATION	POST. REF.	DEBIT
19—Oct. 7	Invoice 101; 1/20, n/30	S1	50 00

- Each debit entry in the sales journal is posted to the customer's account in the accounts receivable ledger.
- A check mark ($\surd$) is put in the Posting Reference column of the sales journal.
- The letter "S" and the page number are then written in the Posting Reference column in the customer's account to show that the amount was posted from the sales journal.
- At the end of the month, the sales journal is totaled to find the amounts posted to the general ledger. A single rule is drawn across all money columns.
- The money columns are then pencil-footed.
- The equality of the debits and credits is proved by adding the totals of the Sales Tax Payable Credit column ($55.25) and the Sales Credit column ($4,180.00). The sum must agree with the total of the Accounts Receivable Debit column ($4,235.25).
- After the equality is proved, the totals are written in ink.
- The last line is completed by writing the word "Totals" in the Account Debited column and drawing the double lines.
- The totals of the sales journal are then posted to the proper accounts in the general ledger. The account numbers are written beneath the double rules to show that the totals have been posted.

SALES JOURNAL
Page 1

DATE	INVOICE NO.	ACCOUNT DEBITED	TERMS	POST. REF.	ACCOUNTS RECEIVABLE DEBIT	SALES TAX PAYABLE CREDIT	SALES CREDIT
19— Oct. 7	101	Wanda's Radio	1/20, n/30	$\surd$	50 00		50 00
7	102	Village Notes	2/10, n/30	$\surd$	1,600 00		1,600 00
11	103	Audio Shoppe	2/10, n/30	$\surd$	160 00		160 00
14	104	Wanda's Radio	1/20, n/30	$\surd$	800 00		800 00
15	105	George Yeomans	n/30	$\surd$	745 50	45 50	700 00
26	106	Audio Shoppe	2/10, n/30	$\surd$	320 00		320 00
26	107	Pauline Young	n/30	$\surd$	159 75	9 75	150 00
30	108	Village Notes	2/10, n/30	$\surd$	400 00		400 00
					4,235 25	55 25	4,180 00
31		Totals			4,235 25	55 25	4,180 00
					(111)	(216)	(401)

Posting the totals of the sales journal.

Accounts Receivable Ledger

| Name | Audio Shoppe | | Credit Limit | $1,000 |
| Address | 2 Camino del Oeste, Denver, Colorado 80219 | | Telephone | 369-3031 |

The telephone number and credit limit are included in the accounts receivable ledger.

DATE		EXPLANATION	POST. REF.	DEBIT	CREDIT	DEBIT BALANCE
19— Oct.	11	Invoice 103; 2/10, n/30	S1	160 00		160 00
	26	Invoice 106; 2/10, n/30	S1	320 00		480 00

Name	Newtown Music			Credit Limit	$2,000			
Address	Canyon Road, Phoenix, Arizona 85040			Telephone	248-3210			

DATE		EXPLANATION	POST. REF.	DEBIT		CREDIT	DEBIT BALANCE	
19—								
June	15	Invoice 37; n/30	S1	25	00		25	00
Aug.	10	Invoice 76; n/30	S1	17	00		42	00
Sept.	5	Invoice 89; n/30	S1	26	00		68	00

Name	Village Notes			Credit Limit	$4,000			
Address	17 Chaparral Boulevard, Tucson, Arizona 85718			Telephone	453-0701			

DATE		EXPLANATION	POST. REF.	DEBIT		CREDIT	DEBIT BALANCE	
19—								
Oct.	7	Invoice 102; 2/10, n/30	S1	1,600	00		1,600	00
	30	Invoice 108; 2/10, n/30	S1	400	00		2,000	00

Name	Wanda's Radio			Credit Limit	$2,000			
Address	16 Del Rey Drive, Denver, Colorado 80219			Telephone	293-5510			

DATE		EXPLANATION	POST. REF.	DEBIT		CREDIT	DEBIT BALANCE	
19—								
Oct.	7	Invoice 101; 1/20, n/30	S1	50	00		50	00
	14	Invoice 104; 1/20, n/30	S1	800	00		850	00

Name	George Yeomans			Credit Limit	$800			
Address	200 Hinsdale Avenue, Englewood, Colorado 80112			Telephone	261-3286			

DATE		EXPLANATION	POST. REF.	DEBIT		CREDIT	DEBIT BALANCE	
19—								
Aug.	30	Invoice 80; n/30	S1	126	00		126	00
Oct.	15	Invoice 105; n/30	S1	745	50		871	50

Name	Pauline Young			Credit Limit	$500			
Address	1 Rockview Drive, Fort Collins, Colorado 80524			Telephone	722-2232			

DATE		EXPLANATION	POST. REF.	DEBIT		CREDIT	DEBIT BALANCE	
19—								
Oct.	26	Invoice 107; n/30	S1	159	75		159	75

General Ledger

DATE		EXPLANATION	POST. REF.	DEBIT	CREDIT	BALANCE DEBIT	BALANCE CREDIT
Accounts Receivable						**Account No.**	*111*
19—							
Sept.	30					194 00	
Oct.	31		S1	4,235 25		4,429 25	

DATE		EXPLANATION	POST. REF.	DEBIT	CREDIT	BALANCE DEBIT	BALANCE CREDIT
Sales Tax Payable						**Account No.**	*216*
19—							
Oct.	31		S1		55 25		55 25

DATE		EXPLANATION	POST. REF.	DEBIT	CREDIT	BALANCE DEBIT	BALANCE CREDIT
Sales						**Account No.**	*401*
19—							
Oct.	31		S1		4,180 00		4,180 00

Often a business sells some merchandise on which sales tax is collected and other merchandise on which no sales tax is collected. In this case, two separate sales accounts could be set up. Then, at the end of the accounting period, the accountant knows on what revenue the sales taxes were collected. This information is usually needed for the sales tax returns.

Proving the Accounts Receivable Ledger

At the end of the month, a proof is made to see if the Accounts Receivable ledger agrees with the Accounts Receivable controlling account in the general ledger. The proof, called a **schedule of accounts receivable,** is a listing of the individual customers' names and the amounts owed. The owner or the credit manager will then use this information to control the amount of credit allowed each customer.

If each customer's name is not needed, the subsidiary ledger can be proved by using an adding machine. The balances of the customers' accounts are added. The total is then compared with the balance of the controlling account.

```
        .00T
     480.00
      68.00
   2,000.00
     850.00
     871.50
     159.75
   4,429.25T
```

Total
Accounts
Receivable

The proof must be prepared at the end of the accounting period before the trial balance is prepared. If the totals do not agree, the error must be located and corrected before the trial balance is prepared. To find an error on the schedule of accounts receivable, the accountant uses the same procedure used to locate an error on the trial balance.

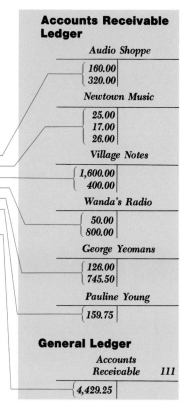

Accounts Receivable Ledger

Audio Shoppe

| 160.00 |
| 320.00 |

Newtown Music

| 25.00 |
| 17.00 |
| 26.00 |

Village Notes

| 1,600.00 |
| 400.00 |

Wanda's Radio

| 50.00 |
| 800.00 |

George Yeomans

| 126.00 |
| 745.50 |

Pauline Young

| 159.75 |

General Ledger

Accounts Receivable 111

| 4,429.25 |

House of Sound
Schedule of Accounts Receivable
October 31, 19—

Audio Shoppe	480 00
Newtown Music	68 00
Village Notes	2,000 00
Wanda's Radio	850 00
George Yeomans	871 50
Pauline Young	159 75
Total Accts. Rec. . . .	4,429 25

You cannot be sure the books are accurate even if the schedule of accounts receivable and the Accounts Receivable controlling account agree. This shows only that the total of the balances in the subsidiary ledger is equal to the controlling account in the general ledger.

Activity C. Answer the following questions about posting the sales on credit. Refer to the sales journal, subsidiary ledger accounts, and general ledger accounts shown on pages 395 to 399.

1. If the first October 7 sale had been entered in the general journal instead of the sales journal, what would the complete entry have been?

2. When the October 7 sale was posted, was the Sales account credited for $50 at the same time? Why or why not?

3. When the October 7 sale was posted, what account was debited? In which ledger is the account located?

4. What amount was posted to the Sales account on October 31? Was this amount debited or credited? Why?

5. If the Audio Shoppe wanted to pay its account on October 27, how much would it have to pay?

6. How is the accuracy of the accounts receivable subsidiary ledger proven?

7. Would proving the accounts receivable ledger identify a posting to Wanda's Radio that should have been posted to Village Notes? Why?

8. Are both the Accounts Receivable controlling account and the individual subsidiary ledger accounts listed on a trial balance? Why or why not?

Paying Sales Taxes

D *Where is the information for paying sales taxes found?* The data for the sales tax return is found in the general ledger. For example, if the House of Sound were required to file a sales tax return at the end of each month, the accountant would complete a return similar to the one shown on page 400.

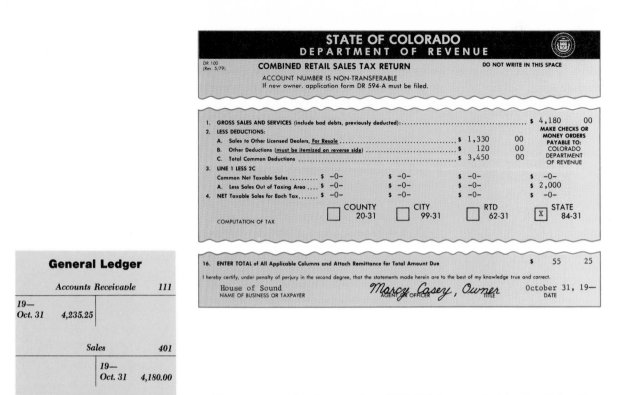

General Ledger

Accounts Receivable   111

19—	
Oct. 31	4,235.25

Sales   401

	19—
	Oct. 31 4,180.00

Sales Tax Payable   216

	19—
	Oct. 31 55.25

Sales tax return is completed from general ledger.

The amount of sales tax due ($55.25) is recorded in the Sales Tax Payable account. A check is drawn for this amount and is entered in the cash payments journal. Sales Tax Payable is debited for $55.25 because the liability account is decreased. After the entry is posted, the Sales Tax Payable account will have a zero balance.

	CASH PAYMENTS JOURNAL							Page 4
DATE	ACCOUNT DEBITED	EXPLANATION	CHECK NO.	POST. REF.	GENERAL LEDGER DEBIT	ACCOUNTS PAYABLE DEBIT	PURCHASES DISCOUNT CREDIT	NET CASH CREDIT
19—								
Nov. 8	Sales Tax Payable .	October return	313	216	55 25			55 25

Paying sales taxes.

Sales Tax Payable   216

19—		19—	
Nov. 8 CP4	55.25	Oct. 31 S1	55.25

In the sales tax illustration, only sales taxes charged on credit sales were shown. The same procedure is used for sales taxes on cash sales. Of course, the sale and the sales tax are recorded in the cash receipts journal instead of the sales journal. Two entries are required in a one-column cash receipts journal to record the amounts because there are two credits. One credit is to the Sales account. The second credit is to the Sales Tax Payable account.

CASH RECEIPTS JOURNAL				Page 4	
DATE	ACCOUNT CREDITED	EXPLANATION	POST. REF.	AMOUNT	
19—					
Nov. 15	Sales	Cash sales for week	401	300 00	
	Sales Tax Payable	Taxes on cash sales	216	19 50	

Recording sales tax on cash sales.

Activity D. Answer the following questions about paying sales taxes. Refer to the text, margin notes, and illustrations on pages 399 to 401.
1. What source of information is used to complete the sales tax return?

2. Which journal is used to record the payment of sales taxes?
3. What is the amount of sales tax due on October 31? On November 10?

Accounting Concept:
Schedule of Subsidiary Ledger. The equality of the subsidiary ledgers and the controlling accounts must be verified at regular intervals.

Topic 2 Problems

14-3. Salvia Metals issued the invoices listed below.
a. Open general ledger accounts for Accounts Receivable, Sales Tax Payable, and Sales, and open subsidiary ledger accounts for the following customers.
Bayside Repair, Jackson, Mississippi 39205; credit limit, $1,500; phone, 238-9241. Angel Mattias, Willow Dr., Jackson, Mississippi 39208; credit limit, $1,000; phone, 214-6143. Moses Simon, Company, Lorenz Dr., Jackson, Mississippi 39216; credit limit, $750; phone 555-3126.
b. Record the sales transactions in the sales journal.
c. Post the debit entries from the sales journal.
d. Prove, total, and rule the sales journal.
e. Post the totals of the sales journal.
f. Prepare a schedule of accounts receivable. (Compare the total of the schedule with the balance of the Accounts Receivable controlling account.)

Sept. 2 Invoice 710 to Bayside Repair for $400; terms 1/15, n/30.
11 Invoice 711 to Angel Mattias for $160 plus $8.00 sales tax; terms n/30.
15 Invoice 712 to Moses Simon Company for $320; terms 1/10, n/30.
23 Invoice 713 to Angel Mattias for $140 plus 5 percent sales tax; terms n/30.
28 Invoice 714 to Moses Simon Company for $220; terms 1/10, n/30.
30 Invoice 715 to Angel Mattias for $140 plus 5 percent sales tax; terms n/30.

14-4. The Village Notions Shop must collect a 4 percent sales tax on all sales of merchandise. During July the store issued the invoices listed below.
a. Open general ledger accounts for Accounts Receivable, Sales Tax Payable, and Sales. Open subsidiary ledger accounts for Aaron Evans, McCargo Fleet, Inc., and Thomas Toner.
b. Record the sales transactions in a sales journal.
c. Post the individual entries from the sales journal.
d. Prove, total, and rule the sales journal.
e. Post the totals from the sales journal.
f. Prepare a schedule of accounts receivable. (Verify the total.)
g. In a multicolumn cash payments journal, record Check 216 issued on August 2 to remit the sales taxes for the month of July. Post the debit entry to the general ledger.

July 7 Invoice 430 to Thomas Toner for $180; plus tax $7.20; terms n/30.
12 Invoice 431 to McCargo Fleet, Inc. for $150 plus $6.00 tax; terms 1/10, n/30.
16 Invoice 432 to Thomas Toner for $90 plus $3.60 tax; terms n/30.
22 Invoice 433 to McCargo Fleet, Inc. for $60 plus $2.40 tax; terms 1/10, n/30.
29 Invoice 434 to Aaron Evans for $360 plus $14.40 tax; terms 1/15, n/30.

Topic 3
Controlling Net Sales

A *What are net sales?* **Net sales** are the difference between the amounts recorded in the Sales account and the total of sales returns, sales allowances, and sales discounts. Sales returns and sales allowances are discussed in this topic.

Computing Net Sales

The amount of revenue earned by a business is often measured by the amount of gross sales. **Gross sales** is the amount found in the sales account. Thus, if a business reports its revenue as being $100,000, it might be saying that gross sales for the year were $100,000. However, a second business might also report revenue of $100,000 and be saying something different. The second business might be reporting net sales and not gross sales. The relationship between gross and net sales is illustrated in the margin.

Gross Sales		$110,000
Less: Sales Returns	$8,000	
Sales Allowances	1,000	
Sales Discounts	1,000	10,000
Net Sales		$100,000

As you view this, certain points should be clear. The company had sales of $110,000. Thus owner's equity was increased by $110,000. However, three items—returns, allowances, and discounts—reduced gross sales by $10,000. Thus, sales returns, sales allowances, and sales discounts reduced owner's equity. (In our illustration, owner's equity was reduced by $10,000.) It is important that you can define sales returns, sales allowances, and sales discounts. However, it is perhaps more important that you learn the procedures to control each of these items. A change in any one—returns, allowances, or discounts—causes a change in net sales.

Activity A. Below you will find amounts for gross sales, sales returns, sales allowances, sales discounts, and net sales. Use these amounts to complete the following chart.

	Gross Sales	Sales Returns	Sales Allowances	Sales Discounts	Net Sales
a.	$10,000	$ 100	$ 250	$ 30	$ (1)
b.	(2)	250	300	150	14,500
c.	30,000	300	300	(3)	28,800
d.	40,000	(4)	1,000	800	37,000
e.	35,000	800	700	-0-	(5)

Sales Returns and Sales Allowances

Control: Issue refunds and credits only for approved returns and allowances.

B *When are refunds and credits issued for unacceptable merchandise?* A subsystem must have controls to make sure that refunds and credits are given only for approved returns and allowances. The seller sometimes allows a customer to return unacceptable merchandise. As already stated, the reasons for returning merchandise vary. The merchandise may be damaged. The wrong items or quantities of items may have been sent. Or customers may find that the items do not meet their needs. In such cases, the seller generally allows a customer to return the items. The seller calls returned items **sales returns.**

Sometimes a customer agrees to keep the merchandise if he or she is given a reduction from the invoice price. Reductions from the sales price are called **sales allowances.**

In the previous chapter, returns and allowances are discussed from the customer's point of view as purchases returns and allowances. Now, returns and allowances are presented from the seller's point of view as *sales returns and allowances.*

Refunding Cash for Sales Returns and Allowances

Cash customers usually want returns and allowances refunded in cash. Cash refunds are made by taking the money out of the cash register or by drawing a check.

Refunds in Cash. Cash refunds made from the cash register are shown on the cash proof. For example, the cash proof illustrated in the margin shows the following.

1 $380 in cash was received from sales during the week.
2 $7 in cash was paid out of the drawer for returns and allowances. The entry to record the cash proof includes a debit for $380 to the Cash account to show the increase in assets. The Sales account is credited for $380 to show the increase in owner's equity caused by the revenue.

Cash proof is source document for recording a cash refund.

CASH RECEIPTS JOURNAL				Page 3
DATE	ACCOUNT CREDITED	EXPLANATION	POST. REF.	AMOUNT
19— Oct. 7	Sales	Cash sales for week . . .	401	380 00

Cash 101		Sales 401	
380			380

The amount of cash paid out for returns and allowances ($7) must also be recorded. Since cash is paid out, the Cash account must be credited to show the decrease in assets. Also, some of the revenue recorded in the Sales account has not been earned. Thus the total amount of sales must be reduced. Sales could be reduced by debiting the Sales account. (Since sales increase owner's equity, sales returns decrease owner's equity.) However, it is a better practice to keep a

**House of Sound
Chart of Accounts**

Revenue
401   Sales
402   Sales Returns and Allowances

record of sales returns and allowances in a separate temporary owner's equity account called a **Sales Returns and Allowances account.** In this way, information is available about the amount of sales and the amount and number of sales returns and allowances. (The Sales and the Sales Returns and Allowances accounts are closely related. Thus the Sales account number is 401 and the Sales Returns and Allowances account number is 402.)

The entry to record returns and allowances is a debit to the Sales Returns and Allowances account for $7 and a credit to the Cash account for $7. The entry is made in the cash payments journal since cash was paid out.

CASH PAYMENTS JOURNAL
Page 4

DATE	ACCOUNT DEBITED	EXPLANATION	CHECK NO.	POST. REF.	GENERAL LEDGER DEBIT	ACCOUNTS PAYABLE DEBIT	PURCHASES DISCOUNT CREDIT	NET CASH CREDIT
19—								
Oct. 7	Sales Ret. and Allow.	Returns for week ..	—	402	7 00			7 00

Recording cash paid for sales returns and allowances.

The result of posting all entries for the month, as shown here, is a net increase in the Cash account of $373 (a debit of $380 less a credit of $7). Also, there is a debit to the Sales Returns and Allowances account of $7. The credit is to the Sales account for $380.

Effect of posting cash for sales returns and allowances.

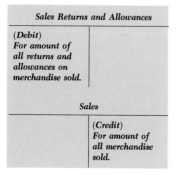

Cash	101		Sales Returns and Allowances 402		Sales	401
380	7		7			380

Cash Payments Journal

Cash Receipts Journal

Revenue From Sales:	
Sales	380 00
Less: Sales Returns	
and Allowances .	7 00
Net Sales	373 00

Sales Returns and Allowances

(Debit) For amount of all returns and allowances on merchandise sold.	
Sales	
	(Credit) For amount of all merchandise sold.

The Sales Returns and Allowances account, like the Sales account, is a temporary owner's equity account. Both accounts are included on the income statement. The amount of sales returns and allowances is subtracted from the amount of sales to find the net sales. Both the Sales Returns and Allowances and the Sales accounts are closed into the Income Summary account at the end of the accounting period.

The information in the Sales Returns and Allowances account is used to analyze the operations of the business. For example, if the amount of the returns and allowances becomes large, management should find out why. Are errors being made on shipping orders? Is the quality of the merchandise poor? Is the merchandise being packed so that damages occur in shipping?

Refunds by Check. When a check is drawn to make the refund, the check stub is the source document for the journal entry. For example, on November 8 the House of Sound issued Check 320 to refund $20 to John Wong. The entry is recorded in the cash payments journal shown below.

Check stub is source document for recording refund by check.

CASH PAYMENTS JOURNAL										Page 4
DATE	ACCOUNT DEBITED	EXPLANATION	CHECK NO.	POST. REF.	GENERAL LEDGER DEBIT		ACCOUNTS PAYABLE DEBIT	PURCHASES DISCOUNT CREDIT	NET CASH CREDIT	
19—										
Nov. 8	Sales Ret. and Allow.	J. Wong	320	402	20	00			20	00

Record check for sales returns and allowances.

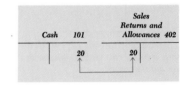

The effect of posting all the entries for the month is a debit to the Sales Returns and Allowances account and a credit to the Cash account for $20.

Activity B. Answer the following questions on sales returns and allowances. Refer to the cash proof and cash receipts journal on page 403 and the cash payments journals on pages 404 and 405.
1. What is the date of the cash proof?
2. How much are the cash sales?
3. How much cash is paid for returns and allowances?
4. What is the entry to record cash sales for the week ended October 7?

5. In which journal are the $7 cash refunds recorded? What is the entry?
6. Is the Sales Returns and Allowances account a permanent or a temporary account?
7. What are the net sales for the week of October 7?
8. Is the refund to John Wong made in cash or by check?
9. To which accounts is the entry of November 8 posted? What is the effect of the entry on net sales?

Granting Credit for Sales Returns and Allowances

C *What happens when customers are given credit for returns and allowances?* Customers who have not paid for merchandise are not given a cash refund for returns or allowances. Instead, the seller issues a credit memorandum to apply against the amount the customer owes.

Credit Memorandum. A credit memorandum is issued by the seller and shows that the customer's account is being reduced. The credit memorandum states the customer's name, the amount of the credit, and the reason for the credit. For example, on October 7, Invoice 102 was issued for $1,600 to Village Notes for stereo equipment. The tape decks arrived damaged. Village Notes got permission to repair the tape decks instead of returning them. In exchange, House of Sound reduced

Sales Invoice

the sales price by $100 for all six decks. The sales department of House of Sound then issued Credit Memorandum CM-12 for $100.

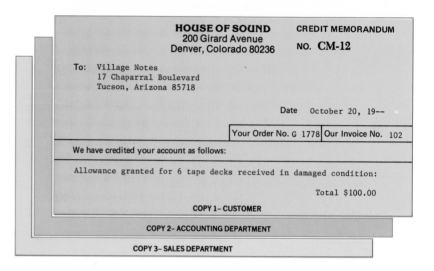

HOUSE OF SOUND
200 Girard Avenue
Denver, Colorado 80236

CREDIT MEMORANDUM

NO. **CM-12**

To: Village Notes
17 Chaparral Boulevard
Tucson, Arizona 85718

Date   October 20, 19--

Your Order No. G 1778   Our Invoice No. 102

We have credited your account as follows:

Allowance granted for 6 tape decks received in damaged condition:

Total $100.00

COPY 1 – CUSTOMER

COPY 2 – ACCOUNTING DEPARTMENT

COPY 3 – SALES DEPARTMENT

Credit memorandum is source document for recording credit for sales return or allowance.

Processing Sales Returns and Allowances

The credit memorandum is prenumbered. It is issued in three copies. One copy goes to the customer. It becomes the source document for an entry to decrease the account with the House of Sound. The second copy goes to the seller's accounting department. It becomes the source document for crediting the customer's account. The third copy is kept by the sales department for its file. After the credit memorandum has been recorded by the seller and the customer, their records should agree on the amount owed.

Recording Sales Returns and Allowances. The entry to record a credit memorandum reduces the revenue from sales and accounts receivable by the same amount. Thus, when the credit memorandum issued to Village Notes is recorded, an entry is made in the general journal to decrease the amount of the sale (a debit of $100) and the accounts receivable (a credit of $100).

October 20 The House of Sound issues Credit Memorandum CM-12 for $100 to Village Notes for allowance on merchandise sold on credit.

The debit of $100 is posted to the Sales Returns and Allowances account in the general ledger. The credit of $100 must be double-posted. It is posted both to the Accounts Receivable controlling account in the general ledger and to the customer's account in the subsidiary ledger. Thus the accounts in the general ledger are in balance, and the customer's account in the subsidiary ledger is updated.

A company that has many sales returns and allowances can use a special sales returns and allowances journal. The recording and post-

GENERAL JOURNAL				Page	3
DATE	ACCOUNT TITLE AND EXPLANATION	POST. REF.	DEBIT	CREDIT	
19— Oct. 20	Sales Returns and Allowances .... Accounts Receivable/Village Notes..... Credit Memorandum CM-12.	402 111/√	100 00	100 00	

General Ledger

Accounts Receivable 111		Sales 401		Sales Returns and Allowances 402	
1,600	100		1,600	100	

Subsidiary Ledger

Village Notes	
1,600	100

Recording and posting credit memorandum.

ing procedures used for the sales returns and allowances journal are similar to those used for the sales journal. The processing of sales returns and allowances is illustrated in the flowchart on page 406.

Sales Taxes on Sales Returns and Allowances

In states and cities where sales taxes are collected, an additional entry must be made when sales returns and allowances are recorded. Recall the transaction of October 26, in which Pauline Young bought merchandise on credit for $150 and was charged $9.75 as sales tax. The amount of the sale ($150) was credited to the Sales account. The amount of the sales tax ($9.75) was credited to the Sales Tax Payable account. The customer's account and the Accounts Receivable controlling account were debited for $159.75.

SALES JOURNAL								Page	1
DATE	INVOICE NO.	ACCOUNT DEBITED	TERMS	POST. REF.	ACCOUNTS RECEIVABLE DEBIT	SALES TAX PAYABLE CREDIT	SALES CREDIT		
19— Oct. 26	107	Pauline Young	n/30	√	159 75	9 75	150 00		

Assume that this was the only entry recorded in the sales journal during the month. The accounts would then show the amounts illustrated on page 408 at the end of the month.

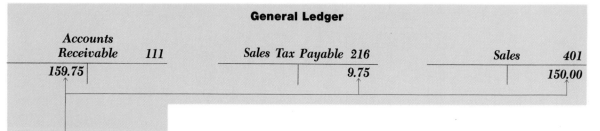

General Ledger

Accounts Receivable	111		Sales Tax Payable 216		Sales	401
159.75				9.75		150.00

Subsidiary Ledger

Pauline Young

159.75	

If the entire sale is returned, an entry must be made in the general journal to show the effect on all accounts. The necessary entries are illustrated here. The sales tax on the original sale is no longer payable to the governmental agency. Thus, the Sales Tax Payable account is reduced by the amount of the tax that was charged. Neither the customer nor the business must pay the tax.

	GENERAL JOURNAL			Page 2	
DATE	**ACCOUNT TITLE AND EXPLANATION**	**POST. REF.**	**DEBIT**	**CREDIT**
19— Oct. 29	Sales Returns and Allowances	402	150 00	
	Sales Tax Payable	216	9 75	
	Accounts Receivable/Pauline Young	111/ √		159 75
	Credit Memorandum CM-13.			

Entry is double-posted.

General Ledger

Accounts Receivable	111		Sales Tax Payable	216		Sales	401		Sales Returns and Allowances	402
159.75	159.75		9.75	9.75			150.00		150.00	

Subsidiary Ledger

Pauline Young

159.75	159.75

If Pauline Young returned only $50 of the merchandise, the following entry would be made.

Recording credit memorandum with sales tax (entire sale returned).

	GENERAL JOURNAL			Page 2	
DATE	**ACCOUNT TITLE AND EXPLANATION**	**POST. REF.**	**DEBIT**	**CREDIT**
19— Oct. 29	Sales Returns and Allowances	402	50 00	
	Sales Tax Payable	216	3 25	
	Accounts Receivable/Pauline Young	111/ √		53 25
	Credit Memorandum CM-13.			

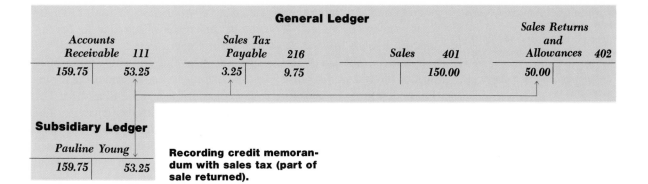

General Ledger

Accounts Receivable 111		Sales Tax Payable 216		Sales 401		Sales Returns and Allowances 402	
159.75	53.25	3.25	9.75		150.00	50.00	

Subsidiary Ledger

Pauline Young	
159.75	53.25

**Recording credit memoran-
dum with sales tax (part of
sale returned).**

In this entry, Sales Tax Payable was debited for $3.25 to cancel the amount of tax charged on $50 of merchandise (6.5 percent × $50). The balance of the Sales Tax Payable account is now $6.50, which is 6.5 percent of the actual sale ($100).

Delivery Charges

If the seller agrees to deliver the merchandise to the buyer, the shipping terms are FOB destination. If the buyer pays the cost, the terms are FOB shipping point. Thus on FOB destination sales, the seller considers any delivery payments to airlines or trucking companies as part of the expense to sell the merchandise. The amounts paid by the seller for making deliveries are debited to a separate expense account called Delivery Expense. (Remember that transportation charges on purchases are debited to Transportation In.)

> **House of Sound
> Chart of Accounts**
>
> **Costs and Expenses**
> 513   Delivery Expense
>
> Transportation charges on
> shipments of merchandise to
> customers are debited to
> Delivery Expense.

Activity C. Answer the following questions about granting credit for sales returns and allowances. Refer to the credit memorandum on page 406 and the journals on pages 407 and 408.
1. What company receives the credit memorandum? Who is the seller?
2. In which journal is the credit memorandum recorded? Why?
3. Why is the Village Notes account credited to record the sales allowance on October 20? Why is the Sales Returns and Allowances account debited?

4. How will the credit entry of October 20 be posted to the Accounts Receivable controlling account?
5. What is the effect on net sales of posting $100 to the Sales Returns and Allowances account?
6. Why is the Sales Tax Payable account debited on October 29?
7. Why is the Pauline Young account credited for $53.25 and not $50 on October 29?
8. What is the net sale to Pauline Young?
9. How much sales tax will be paid by Pauline Young?

Using Sales Discounts to Encourage Payment

D	*Why is it important to collect accounts receivable promptly?* *Money owed to a business by its customers is "tied up." That is, it*

cannot be used for other purposes. It cannot be used to purchase new

Control: Collect receivables as soon as possible.
• Record customers' accounts.
• Record payments within the discount period.
• Inform customers of status of accounts.
• Determine if payments are made promptly.

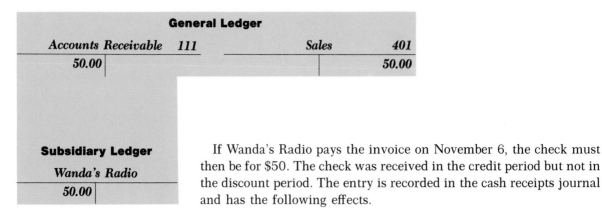

Sales invoice (prepared from shipping order Copy 3).

merchandise, to buy other assets, or to pay expenses. Thus a business that is slow in collecting accounts receivable often has to borrow money at high interest rates to continue operations.

To encourage customers to pay their invoices quickly, some businesses offer cash discounts. To the customer a cash discount is a purchase discount. To the seller, a cash discount is a **sales discount.** The procedure for recording purchase discounts was discussed earlier. The procedure the seller uses to record sales discounts is discussed here.

The October 7 sales invoice issued to Wanda's Radio for $50 is used to show how cash receipts from customers are recorded. The terms on the sale are 1/20, n/30. Thus, if Wanda's Radio pays on or before October 27 (20 days after October 7), it may deduct 1 percent of $50 ($0.50) from the invoice. Wanda's Radio would then pay $49.50 ($50 − $0.50). If Wanda's Radio does not pay within the discount period, the full amount of $50 will be due by November 6 (30 days after October 7).

Receiving Payments. A sales discount is not recorded at the time the invoice is journalized. The seller does not know if the customer will pay within the discount period. Thus, when the sales invoice is recorded, the customer's account is debited for the amount of the invoice. The entry to record the sales invoice issued to Wanda's Radio, shown here, has the following effects.

			SALES JOURNAL						Page 1
DATE	INVOICE NO.		ACCOUNT DEBITED	TERMS	POST. REF.	ACCOUNTS RECEIVABLE DEBIT	SALES TAX PAYABLE CREDIT		SALES CREDIT
19— Oct. 7	101		Wanda's Radio	1/20, n/30	√	50 00			50 00

Recording credit sales.

General Ledger

Accounts Receivable	111		Sales	401
50.00				50.00

Subsidiary Ledger

Wanda's Radio

50.00

If Wanda's Radio pays the invoice on November 6, the check must then be for $50. The check was received in the credit period but not in the discount period. The entry is recorded in the cash receipts journal and has the following effects.

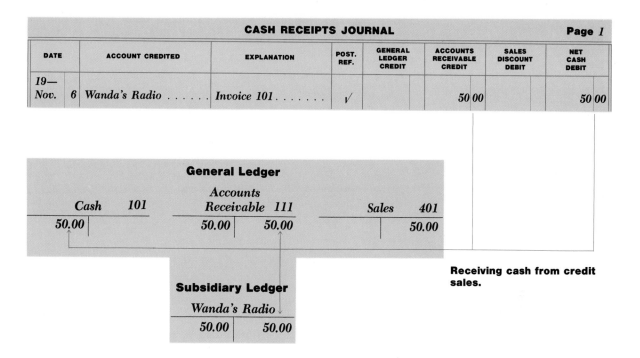

CASH RECEIPTS JOURNAL

Page *1*

DATE		ACCOUNT CREDITED	EXPLANATION	POST. REF.	GENERAL LEDGER CREDIT	ACCOUNTS RECEIVABLE CREDIT	SALES DISCOUNT DEBIT	NET CASH DEBIT
19— Nov.	6	Wanda's Radio	Invoice 101	✓		50 00		50 00

General Ledger

Cash	101		Accounts Receivable	111		Sales	401
50.00			50.00	50.00			50.00

Subsidiary Ledger

Wanda's Radio

50.00	50.00

Receiving cash from credit sales.

Suppose, however, that Wanda's Radio pays the invoice within the discount period. The check would then be for $49.50. The cash receipt is analyzed as follows.

1 The customer's account shows a debit balance of $50. The account must be credited for $50 to show that the account has been paid. Wanda's Radio account must be credited for $50 to reduce the debit balance to zero.

2 The check amounts to $49.50. Thus the Cash account must be debited for $49.50 because that is the amount of cash received.

3 The debit and credit amounts must be equal. The cash discount of $0.50 must be debited to some account. The discount reduces the revenue from sales and at the same time decreases owner's equity. For example, revenue of $50 was recorded for the merchandise sold. However, Wanda's Radio paid only $49.50 for it. Thus the sales discount reduces the revenue from the sale of merchandise by $0.50. The reduction in revenue actually decreases owner's equity.

The debit entry to decrease owner's equity could be to the Sales account. However, it is common accounting practice to record a sales discount in a temporary owner's equity account called Sales Discount. The owner or manager then has a record of all discounts allowed and can see the reduction in revenue due to the discount policy.

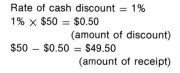

Rate of cash discount = 1%
1% × $50 = $0.50
        (amount of discount)
$50 − $0.50 = $49.50
        (amount of receipt)

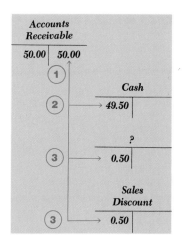

Revenue
401 Sales
402 Sales Returns and Al-
     lowances
403 Sales Discount

October 26: The House of Sound receives cash from Wanda's Radio in payment of invoice for $50 less cash discount of $0.50.

What Happens	Accounting Rule	Entry
The asset *Cash* increases by $49.50.	To increase an asset, debit the account.	Debit: Cash, $49.50.
The cash discount on the sale decreases owner's equity by $.50.	To decrease owner's equity, debit the account.	Debit: Sales Discount, $.50.
The asset *Accounts Receivable* decreases by $50.	To decrease an asset, credit the account.	Credit: Accounts Receivable, $50. (Also the customer's acccount.)

Revenue From Sales:		
Sales		4,180 00
Less: Sales Returns and		
Allowances . $120.00		
Sales Discount 30.25		150 25
Net Sales		4,029 75

To find the net revenue from sales, subtract the balance of the Sales Discount from the balance of the Sales account. If Sales Returns and Allowances has a balance, it must also be subtracted from the Sales account. These three accounts are related, and they are assigned numbers 401, 402, and 403.

General Ledger

Cash 101	Accounts Receivable 111	Sales 401	Sales Discount 403
49.50	50.00 | 50.00	50.00	0.50

Effect of a sales discount.

Subsidiary Ledger

Wanda's Radio

50.00	50.00

Activity D. Answer the following questions about encouraging payment with discounts. Refer to illustrations on pages 410 to 412.

1. What type of transaction takes place with Wanda's Radio?

2. How much cash is received?

3. Which account reduces owner's equity? By what amount is owner's equity reduced?

4. What is the net revenue from the sale to Wanda's Radio?

5. What would the net revenue be if payment was made on October 30?

14-5. Perform the following accounting activities for RP Sales.

a. Open the general ledger accounts, assign appropriate numbers, and record the February 1 balances as follows: Cash, $18,400; Accounts Receivable; Sales Tax Payable; Roger Postell, Capital, $18,400; Sales; Sales Returns and Allowances; and Delivery Expense. Open accounts for Berrios, Inc., and Elijah Gibson in the accounts receivable subsidiary ledger.

b. Record the transactions for February in a sales journal, a cash receipts journal, cash payments journal, and a general journal.

c. Post the individual entries from the sales journal, cash payments journal, cash receipts journal, and the general journal.

d. Prove, total, and rule the special journals.

e. Post the totals from the special journals.

f. Prepare a schedule of accounts receivable. (Verify that the total of the schedule of accounts receivable agrees with the Accounts Receivable controlling account.)

g. Prepare a formal trial balance.

Feb. 3 Sold merchandise for $720 on credit to Berrios, Inc.; Invoice 255; terms 2/10, n/30.

4 Recorded returns and allowances of $12 on the cash proof for the weekly cash sales. Sales were $700.

5 Issued $80 allowance to Berrios, Inc., for returned merchandise costing $80; Credit Memorandum CM-251.

13 Sold merchandise for $680 plus $13.60 sales tax on credit to Elijah Gibson; Invoice 256; terms n/30.

13 Issued Check 86 for $50 to Red-Kone Express for delivering merchandise sold to Elijah Gibson, FOB destination.

21 Sold merchandise for $600 on credit to Berrios, Inc.; Invoice 257; terms 2/10, n/30.

Feb. 25 Issued Check 87 for $40 to Kim Nisom for returned merchandise sold for cash.

26 Issued $40 allowance to Berrios, Inc., for scratched merchandise; Credit Memorandum CM-252.

14-6. During May, Fowler Network had the sales on credit listed here. (Sales tax is 4 percent.)

a. Open accounts in the general ledger for Accounts Receivable, Sales Tax Payable, Sales, and Sales Returns and Allowances. Open accounts for Calvin Childs and Major Williams in the accounts receivable subsidiary ledger.

b. Record each of the transactions for May in a sales journal or in a general journal.

c. Post the individual entries from the sales journal and the general journal.

d. Prove, total, and rule the sales journal.

e. Post the totals from the sales journal.

f. Prepare a schedule of accounts receivable. (Verify the total.)

May 6 Sold merchandise for $340 on credit to Major Williams; Invoice 896; terms 1/10, n/30; sales tax, $13.60.

7 Major Williams returned merchandise sold for $40; Credit Memorandum CM-247; sales tax, $1.60.

16 Sold merchandise for $865 on credit to Calvin Childs; Invoice 897; terms 2/10, n/30; sales tax, $34.60.

17 Issued allowance of $20 to Calvin Childs for imperfect merchandise; Credit Memorandum CM-248; sales tax, $0.80.

24 Sold merchandise for $230 on credit to Major Williams; Invoice 898; terms 1/10, n/30; sales tax, $9.20.

Topic 4
Controlling Cash Received on Account

A *How are cash receipts from sales on credit journalized?* All cash receipts from credit sales are recorded in the cash receipts journal.

Journalizing Cash Received on Account

The entry to record the receipt of cash with a sales discount involves a debit to the Cash account and a debit to the Sales Discount account. It also involves a credit to the Accounts Receivable controlling account (and the customer's account). The receipt of cash with a cash discount cannot be recorded in a one-column cash receipts journal. Two debits are involved—one to the Cash account and one to the Sales Discount account. Thus most businesses change the cash receipts journal by adding the column shown in the following illustration.

CASH RECEIPTS JOURNAL							Page 3
DATE	ACCOUNT CREDITED	EXPLANATION	POST. REF.	GENERAL LEDGER CREDIT	ACCOUNTS RECEIVABLE CREDIT	SALES DISCOUNT DEBIT	NET CASH DEBIT
19— Oct. 26	Wanda's Radio	On account	√		50 00	50	49 50

Receiving cash on account, with a sales discount.

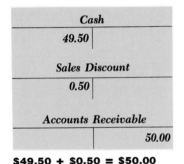

Cash

49.50

Sales Discount

0.50

Accounts Receivable

50.00

$49.50 + $0.50 = $50.00

The Net Cash Debit column is used to record the cash received. The Sales Discount Debit column is used to record the sales discount, if any. The Accounts Receivable Credit column is used to record all credits to customers' accounts from receipts. The amount entered in the Accounts Receivable Credit column ($50) must be equal to the total amount of the debits ($49.50 + $0.50). This column makes easier the double-posting that must be made to the Accounts Receivable controlling account and to the customer's account. The other credit column is the General Ledger Credit column. It is used for credits to any account for which there is no special column.

Activity A. Answer the following questions about journalizing cash received on account with a sales discount. Refer to the text and illustrations on pages 413 and 414.
1. In which journal(s) are sales discounts journalized? What accounts are involved?

2. How many amount columns are in the cash receipts journal? What are the columns?
3. Which amount column is used to record decreases in owner's equity?
4. By what amount did the sale and receipt of cash from Wanda's Radio increase owner's equity?

Posting Cash Receipts

B *How is the cash receipts journal posted during the month?* Each amount in the General Ledger Credit column of the cash receipts journal is posted during the month to the general ledger. The account numbers in the Posting Reference column of the journal indicate the following.

DATE		ACCOUNT CREDITED	EXPLANATION	POST. REF.	GENERAL LEDGER CREDIT	ACCOUNTS RECEIVABLE CREDIT	SALES DISCOUNT DEBIT	NET CASH DEBIT
19—								
Oct.	1	Cash Balance	$16,200	—				
	7	Sales	Cash sales for week .	401	720 00			766 80
		Sales Taxes Payable ..		216	46 80			— 00
	9	Office Equipment	Sold calculator	122	100 00			100 00
	11	Marcy Casey, Capital .	Additional investment	301	2,000 00			2,000 00
	14	Sales	Cash sales for week .	401	580 00			617 70
		Sales Tax Payable....		216	37 70			— 00
	21	Sales	Cash sales for week .	401	660 00			702 90
		Sales Tax Payable....		216	42 90			— 00
	24	Village Notes	On account	√		1,500 00	30 00	1,470 00
	26	Wanda's Radio	On account	√		50 00	50	49 50
	27	Audio Shoppe	On account	√		160 00		160 00
	28	Sales	Cash sales for week .	401	600 00			639 00
		Sales Tax Payable....		216	39 00			— 00

     (1)   **(2)**   **(3)**

Credits posted during the month to accounts in general ledger.	Credits posted during the month to customers' accounts in subsidiary ledger.	Amounts in these two columns are not posted during the month.

1 The amounts have been posted to the general ledger.

2 Each of the three entries in the Accounts Receivable Credit column is posted to the proper customer's account in the subsidiary ledger. A check mark (√) in the Posting Reference column means that the amount has been posted. Note that the entries for October 24 and 26 involve sales discounts. The entry for October 27 does not.

3 None of the items in the Sales Discount Debit column or the Net Cash Debit column are posted during the month.

Accounts Receivable Ledger

Name	Audio Shoppe				Credit Limit	$1,000	
Address	2 Camino del Oeste, Denver, Colorado 80219				Telephone	369-3031	

DATE		EXPLANATION	POST. REF.	DEBIT	CREDIT	DEBIT BALANCE
19—						
Oct.	11	Invoice 103; 2/10, n/30	S1	160 00		160 00
	26	Invoice 106; 2/10, n/30	S1	320 00		480 00
	27	Cash	CR3		160 00	320 00

Receipt: October 27.

Name	Village Notes			Credit Limit		$4,000	
Address	17 Chaparral Boulevard, Tucson, Arizona 85718			Telephone		453-0701	

DATE		EXPLANATION	POST. REF.	DEBIT	CREDIT	DEBIT BALANCE
19—						
Oct.	7	Invoice 102; 2/10, n/30	S1	1,600 00		1,600 00
	20	Allowance, Credit Memo. CM-12. .	J2		100 00	1,500 00
	24	Cash	CR3		1,500 00	— 00
	30	Invoice 108; 2/10, n/30.	S1	400 00		400 00

Receipt: October 24.

Name	Wanda's Radio			Credit Limit		$2,000	
Address	16 Del Rey Drive, Denver, Colorado 80219			Telephone		293-5510	

DATE		EXPLANATION	POST. REF.	DEBIT	CREDIT	DEBIT BALANCE
19—						
Oct.	7	Invoice 101; 1/20, n/30	S1	50 00		50 00
	14	Invoice 104; 1/20, n/30	S1	800 00		850 00
	26	Cash	CR3		50 00	800 00

Receipt: October 26.

Sales Taxes, Sales Returns and Allowances, and Sales Discounts

Net amount
of invoice =
$1,600 − $100 = $1,500
Rate of cash
discount = 2%
2% × $1,500 = $30 (amount of discount)
$1,500 − $30 = $1,470 (amount received)

Sales discounts are given only on the net sales price. Sales discounts are not given on any amount for which credit was given, on a return or allowance, or on any sales tax charged. For example, the entry of October 24 in the cash receipts journal shows that Village Notes was allowed a sales discount of $30. The original amount of the invoice was $1,600 (Invoice 102 of October 7). However, the customer was granted a sales allowance of $100 on October 20 (Credit Memorandum CM-12). Village Notes, therefore, was granted a discount on $1,500 ($1,600 − $100), which was the net amount of the sale.

Amount of
invoice =
$160 + $4.80 = $164.80
Rate of cash
discount = 2%
2% × $160 = $3.20 (amount of discount)
$164.80 − $3.20 = $161.60 (amount received)

Sales discounts are not given on any sales taxes. On a sale of $160 with terms of 2/10, n/30, for example, the sales tax of $6\frac{1}{2}$ percent charged to the customer would be $10.40. If the invoice is paid within the discount period, a sales discount is allowed on the $160 only—not on the $10.40. Thus the sales discount would be $3.20 (2 percent × $160). The customer would have to pay $167.20 ($160 + $10.40 − $3.20).

Posting From the Cash Receipts Journal at the End of the Month

All the money columns of the cash receipts journal are pencil-footed at the end of the month. The journal is proved by adding the two debit totals and then adding the two credit totals. These two sums must be equal. After the equality of the debits and credits has been proved, the journal is totaled and ruled.

CASH RECEIPTS JOURNAL								Page 3
DATE		ACCOUNT CREDITED	EXPLANATION	POST. REF.	GENERAL LEDGER CREDIT	ACCOUNTS RECEIVABLE CREDIT	SALES DISCOUNT DEBIT	NET CASH DEBIT
19— Oct.	1	Cash Balance	$16,200	—				
	28	Sales . . . . Sales Tax Payable. . . .	Cash sales for week .	401 216	600 00 39 00			639 00 —
	31	Totals.			4,826 40	1,710 00	30 50	6,505 90
					(—)	(111)	(403)	(101)

The total of the General Ledger Credit column is not posted. The amounts in this column were posted individually. Thus a dash is placed in the General Ledger Credit column beneath the double rules.

The total of the Accounts Receivable Credit column is posted to the credit side of the controlling account in the general ledger. Each amount in this column was posted to the subsidiary ledger during the month. The controlling account number (111) is written beneath the double rules.

The total of the Sales Discount Debit column is posted as a debit to the Sales Discount account. The total of the Net Cash Debit column is posted as a debit to the Cash account. The account numbers (403 and 101) are written beneath the double rules.

Net Cash Debit	6,505 90
Sales Discount Debit . .	30 50
Total Debits	6,536 40
General Ledger Credit .	4,826 40
Accounts Receivable Credit	1,710 00
Total Credits	6,536 40

Proof of Cash Receipts Journal

Activity B. Answer the following questions about posting cash receipts from sales on credit. Refer to the cash receipts journals on pages 414, 415, and 417.
1. What accounts and amounts are debited and credited on October 26?
2. Why is a check mark placed in the Posting Reference column of the journal for the October 26 entry?
3. Why are two debits needed in the journal entry of October 26?
4. When the October 26 journal entry is posted to the subsidiary ledger, is $0.50 posted as a debit to Sales Discount at the same time? Is $49.50 posted as a debit to Cash at the same time? If not, when will they be?
5. What account is credited on October 9?
6. When the October 9 credit is posted from the journal, is a $100 debit posted to Cash at that time? Why or why not?
7. When the Sales Discount column total is posted on October 31, is any other account credited for $30.50 at that time? Why or why not?
8. Is any account credited for $4,826.40 on October 31? Why or why not?
9. How does the accounting clerk prove the equality of debits and credits in the cash receipts journal?

14-7. Perform the following activities to process the cash receipts transactions for Instant Replay for the month of July.

a. Open general ledger accounts, assign appropriate numbers, and record the July 1 balances as follows: Cash, $14,000; Accounts Receivable; Store Equipment, $9,600; Marc Liebman, Capital, $23,600; Marc Liebman, Drawing; Sales; Sales Returns and Allowances; Sales Discount; Cash Short and Over; and Delivery Expense. Also open accounts receivable ledger accounts for Carol Optics and Regency Camera.

b. Record each of the transactions listed for July 1–14 in a sales journal, cash receipts journal, a cash payments journal, or a general journal.

c. Post the individual entries from the journals.

d. Record the transactions for July 16–31.

e. Post the individual entries from the journals.

f. Prove, total, and rule the special journals.

g. Post the totals from the special journals.

h. Prepare a trial balance.

July 1 Sold merchandise for $1,200 on credit to Regency Camera; Invoice 627; terms 2/10, n/30.

5 Sold merchandise for $1,260 on credit to Carol Optics; Invoice 628; terms 1/10, n/30.

5 Marc Liebman invested an additional $3,000.

6 Issued Check 45 for $18 to Tri-State Express for delivering merchandise sold.

9 Sold merchandise for $420 on credit to Regency Camera; Invoice 629; terms 2/10, n/30.

13 Sold merchandise for $600 on credit to Carol Optics; Invoice 630; terms 1/10, n/30.

14 Received cash from Carol Optics in payment of Invoice 628 of July 5, less discount.

14 Recorded cash proof; cash sales, $1,800; sales returns, $24.

16 Issued Check 46 to Henry Crozer to pay for returned merchandise sold for cash, $60.

18 Sold merchandise for $360 on credit to Regency Camera; Invoice 631; terms 2/10, n/30.

19 Issued allowance of $140 for damage to merchandise sold to Regency Camera on Invoice 631; Credit Memorandum CM-19.

July 22 Sold merchandise for $330 on credit to Regency Camera; Invoice 632; terms 2/10, n/30.

25 Received $625 for used store equipment sold to Knorr Brothers.

27 Received cash from Regency Camera for Invoice 631 of July 18, less allowance and discount.

29 Received cash from Regency Camera in payment of full amount of Invoice 629 of July 9.

31 Recorded cash proof: cash sales, $1,830; sales returns, $20; cash overage, $6.25.

NOTE: Save your working papers for further use in Topic Problem 14-8.

14-8. Using the working papers from Topic Problem 14-7, perform the following activities for Instant Replay during August.

a. Journalize the transactions for August 1–14.

b. Post the individual entries from the journals.

c. Record the transactions for August 15–31.

d. Post the individual entries from the journals.

e. Prove, total, and rule the special journals.

f. Post the totals from the special journals.

g. Prepare a trial balance.

Aug. 1 Received cash from Regency Camera in payment of Invoice 632 of July 22, less discount.

5 Sold merchandise for $960 on credit to Regency Camera; Invoice 633; terms 2/10, n/30.

7 Sold merchandise for $472 on credit to Carol Optics; Invoice 634; terms 1/10, n/30.

11 Received cash from Carol Optics in payment of full amount of Invoice 630 of July 13.

13 Issued Check 47 for $3,000 to Marc Liebman for withdrawal.

14 Recorded cash proof: cash sales, $2,020; sale returns, $16; cash shortage, $12.60.

15 Received cash from Regency Camera in payment of Invoice 633 of August 5, less discount.

Aug. 16 Issued Credit Memorandum 20 to Carol Optics for return of goods sold for $160 on Invoice 634.

20 Sold merchandise for $1,000 on credit to Regency Camera; Invoice 635; terms 2/10, n/30.

23 Issued Check 48 for $52 to Tri-State Express for delivering merchandise sold.

25 Sold merchandise for $20 on credit to Regency Camera; Invoice 636; terms 2/10, n/30.

Aug. 29 Sold merchandise for $160 on credit to Carol Optics; Invoice 637; terms 1/10, n/30.

31 Recorded cash proof: cash sales, $2,600.

NOTE: Save your accounts receivable ledger for further use in Topic Problem 14-10.

Topic 5
Controlling Accounts Receivable

A *What can a business do to collect accounts receivable promptly?* The use of sales discounts is discussed in Topic 3 as one way to encourage prompt payment. In this topic the use of a statement of account and aging accounts receivable are discussed. Statements of account are used to keep customers informed about their accounts. Aging accounts receivable is used by the business to keep it informed about how quickly customers are paying their accounts.

Statements of Account

In addition to the invoice, most businesses periodically send the customers a statement of account. A **statement of account** is prepared from the data in the customer's ledger account and gives the customer a summary of merchandise purchased, payments made, and other activities during the time covered by the statement. There are two types of statements of account: descriptive and nondescriptive. The statement of account may be a **descriptive statement** that shows dates, numbers, and totals. The statement of account sent to Wanda's Radio, shown here, includes the following data: beginning balance on October 1, $0.00; sales made (charges); payments made (credits); ending balance on October 26 ($800); and invoice numbers. A **nondescriptive statement** shows only the beginning balance, total charges, total credits, and the ending balance. Some nondescriptive statements show only the amount due. An example of a nondescriptive statement is shown on page 420.

Statements of account are usually sent at the end of each month. However, businesses with many customers may not send all the statements on the last day of the month. The work load that would result would be too difficult to handle at one time. Cycle billing is used to

Date	Reference	Charges	Credits	Balance
Balance Fowarded				.00
Oct. 7	101	50.00		50.00
14	104	800.00		850.00
26	Cash		50.00	800.00

Descriptive statement showing dates, numbers, invoice totals, and payments.

HOUSE OF SOUND
200 Girard Avenue, Denver, Colorado 80236

HOUSE OF SOUND
| Statement |

■ Please make checks payable to **HOUSE OF SOUND**

WANDA'S RADIO
16 DEL REY DRIVE
DENVER, CO 80219

Account Number
7941 |559 |52

Closing Date
10/31/--

New Balance
800.00

Payment due upon
receipt of statement.
Return this portion
with your payment.

0794155952

Payment due upon receipt of statement.

Account Number	Previous Balance
7941 |559 |52	.00
Closing Date	Payments
10/31/--	50.00
Finance charge	Credits
is 1 1/2 %	.00
monthly periodic rate	Finance Charges
– annual percentage	.00
rate is 18 %	Current Charges
	850.00
Please keep this	New Balance
stub for your records.	800.00

Nondescriptive statement (on a punched card) showing previous balance, ending balance, total charges (sales), and total credits (payments).

distribute the work over the month. In **cycle billing,** the customers' accounts are divided into groups, usually in alphabetic sequence of last names, and are then mailed to the different groups of customers during the month.

Last Names Beginning With	Billing Covers Charges and Payments for These Dates		Closing Date
A–F	8th of the month to 7th of the next month		7
G–K	15th	14th	14
L–R	22nd	21st	21
S–Z	29th	28th	28

Under a cycle billing plan, a statement is prepared for Brunner Services as of the 7th of the month. The statement for March would show all the charges and payments to Brunner Services account between February 8 and March 7. John Rocco's statement for March would be prepared as of March 21. It would show all charges and payments to the account between February 22 and March 21.

**Accounts Receivable Clerk:
DOT 216.482-010.** Performs variety of computing, posting, and other accounting duties for accounts receivable.

**Accounts Receivable Bookkeeper:
DOT 210.382-018.** Keeps accounts receivable section of the financial records. May journalize accounts receivable transactions, and may post to subsidiary ledger.

Activity A. Answer the following questions about collecting accounts receivable promptly. Refer to the text, margin notes, and illustrations on pages 419 and 420.

1. How do the two statements of account on pages 419 and 420 differ?
2. What is the amount of the October 26 payment?
3. How much does Wanda's Radio owe on October 26?
4. What are the total sales made to Wanda's Radio during October? (Refer to the punched-card statement for your answer.)
5. As of what date is a statement prepared for J. Molinex, under a cycle billing plan?

Aging the Accounts Receivables

B *How does a business know if customers are paying their accounts promptly?* Not all customers pay their accounts on time. To check that customers are not falling behind, businesses periodically age the accounts receivable. To age accounts receivable a schedule is prepared listing the name of each customer and the balance of the customer's account, with balances classified according to the number of days since each invoice was issued. When all the balances have been classified, the schedule's columns are added to find the total of each age group. **Aging accounts receivable** is classifying the balance of each customer's account according to the age of the claim.

The House of Sound gives every charge customer a credit period of 30 days. The schedule of accounts receivable for October 31 shows the age of the accounts according to the dates of the invoices. The schedule of accounts receivable by age is shown here.

House of Sound
Schedule of Accounts Receivable by Age
October 31, 19—

ACCOUNT WITH	BALANCE	1–30 DAYS	31–60 DAYS	61–90 DAYS	91–120 DAYS	OVER 120 DAYS
Audio Shoppe...........	320 00	320 00				
Newtown Music	68 00		26 00	17 00		25 00
Village Notes	400 00	400 00				
Wanda's Radio.........	800 00	800 00				
George Yeomans	871 50	745 50		126 00		
Pauline Young	159 75	159 75				
Totals..............	2,619 25	2,425 25	26 00	143 00		25 00

The information for aging the accounts is found in the accounts receivable ledger. The Audio Shoppe account, for example, shows a balance of $320. None of this is over the 30-day credit period. Thus the $320 balance is shown in the 1–30 Days column. The Newtown Music account shows a balance of $68. None of the $68 is current. The entire balance is past due because the credit period has expired.

The owner and credit manager use the schedule of accounts receivable by age to control the credit allowed to various customers. The credit manager, for example, should contact Newtown Music before granting more credit to see why they are not paying the invoices. It is also easy to see which accounts need special collection action. The schedule, for example, shows that George Yeomans has owed $126 for 61–90 days. The credit manager needs to take steps to collect this amount. To keep close control over customers' accounts, a business usually prepares the schedule of accounts receivable by age at the end of each month.

The Newtown Music account shown below shows how an account is aged using the dates of the invoices. To age an account receivable, begin with the most recent *unpaid* invoice. Find how many days have passed since the date the invoice was issued. Then analyze the next latest invoice. Continue in this manner until all invoices that *have not been paid* have been analyzed.

Name	Newtown Music				Credit Limit	$2,000
Address	Canyon Road, Phoenix, Arizona 85040				Telephone	248-3210

DATE	EXPLANATION	POST. REF.	DEBIT	CREDIT	DEBIT BALANCE
19—					
June 15	Invoice 37; n/30	S1	25 00		25 00
Aug. 10	Invoice 76; n/30	S1	17 00		42 00
Sept. 5	Invoice 89; n/30	S1	26 00		68 00

1 Invoice 89, the most recent invoice, is dated September 5 and has a credit period of n/30. The invoice is 56 days old (September 5 to October 31). Thus the amount of the invoice ($26) is listed in the 31–60 Days column. (See the Working Hint at the end of this chapter for help in computing the number of days since an invoice was issued.)
2 Invoice 76 is 82 days old (August 10 to October 31). Thus the invoice amount ($17) is listed in the 61–90 Days column. The invoice amount is past due because the 30-day credit period has ended.
3 Invoice 37 is 138 days old (June 15 to October 31). The invoice amount ($25) is listed in the Over 120 Days column.

Summarizing the Transactions Involving Sales

The flowchart on page 423 summarizes the various types of transactions involved with sales. In each case, the chart shows how the transaction should be recorded.

Activity B. Answer the questions below and on page 424 about aging the accounts receivable. Refer to the schedule of accounts receivable by age on page 421 and the account for Newtown Music shown above.

1. How much does Wanda's Radio owe? How much is past due?
2. What is the total amount that is past due for Newtown Music? For George Yeomans?

RECORDING TRANSACTIONS INVOLVING SALES

TRANSACTION	SOURCE DOCUMENT*	JOURNAL	GENERAL LEDGER						ACCOUNTS RECEIVABLE LEDGER
			Cash	Accounts Receivable	Sales	Sales Returns & Allowances	Sales Discount	Delivery Expense	Individual Customer's Account
Sale for cash.	Cash Proof	Cash Receipts Journal	XXXX		XXXX				
Return or allowance for cash.	Cash Proof	Cash Payments Journal	XXXX			XXXX			
Sale on credit.	Sales Invoice	Sales Journal		XXXX	XXXX				XXXX
Delivery expense for cash.	Check Stub	Cash Payments Journal	XXXX					XXXX	
Return or allowance for credit.	Credit Memorandum	General Journal		XXXX		XXXX			XXXX
Receipt without sales discount.	Remittance Slip	Cash Receipts Journal	XXXX	XXXX					XXXX
Receipt with sales discount.	Remittance Slip	Cash Receipts Journal	XXX	XXXX			X		XXXX

*Only one possible source document is shown.

3. What is the total amount owed by all customers? How much is not past due?
4. What is the total amount past due from all customers? How much was not paid within 60 days after the invoices were issued?

5. When did the credit period end for Invoice 37? For Invoice 89?

Topic 5 Problems

14-9. The account shown here is taken from the accounts receivable ledger of Pyramid Builders. Using the data in the account, age the account as of July 31 according to the dates of the invoices.

Name	Duran, Inc.				Credit Limit	$750
Address	Sky Boulevard, Cheyenne, Wyoming 80001				Telephone	614-2316

DATE		EXPLANATION	POST. REF.	DEBIT	CREDIT	DEBIT BALANCE
19—						
Apr.	1	Invoice 0971; n/30..........	S19	105 00		105 00
	15	Invoice 1121; n/30..........	S19	47 50		152 50
	21	Cash.................	CR21		47 50	105 00
	26	Invoice 2010; n/30..........	S19	132 00		237 00
May	3	Invoice 2460; n/30..........	S20	85 00		322 00
	23	Invoice 2910; n/30..........	S20	27 00		349 00
June	7	Invoice 3474; n/30..........	S20	118 00		467 00
July	25	Invoice 5609; n/30..........	S21	205 00		672 00

14.10. Using the accounts receivable ledger from Topic Problem 14-8, prepare a statement of account covering the August transactions that Instant Replay completed with Carol Optics.

The Language of Business

Here are some terms that make up the language of business. Do you know the meaning of each?

sales subsystem
unshipped orders file
shipped orders file
back-order file
sales journal

sales tax
accounts receivable
    ledger
schedule of accounts
    receivable

net sales
gross sales
sales returns
sales allowances
Sales Returns and
    Allowances account
sales discount
statement of account

descriptive statement
nondescriptive
    statement
cycle billing
aging accounts
    receivable

Chapter 14   Questions

1. List and explain the procedures for the control of sales on credit.
2. The shipping order in this chapter was prepared in seven copies. How does the use of this multicopy form save time?

3. In what way does the credit department have a powerful control over the sales department? On what department does the credit department depend heavily for its information?
4. List and explain the advantages of a special sales

journal. Describe the procedure followed in posting from the sales journal.

5. Why is a separate account used for sales returns and allowances? How is the net revenue from sales computed?

6. Describe the procedure for posting the individual amounts and the totals from the four-column cash receipts journal.

7. When a sales tax is collected from a customer, why is a liability account credited?

8. Describe the procedure to be followed in aging the accounts receivable.

9. A sale on credit to the Jay Stores was journalized correctly as $89 but was posted as $98 in the customer's account. When should this error be discovered? How might the customer detect the error?

Chapter 14 Problems

Problems for Chapter 14 are given in the *Working Papers and Chapter Problems for Part 2.* If you are using the workbook, do the problems in the space provided there.

Chapter 14 Management Cases

Returned Merchandise. It is expensive for a business to handle returned merchandise. Remember that there were many expenses from selling the merchandise the first time. Salaries were paid to salespeople. There were expenses for wrapping and delivering the merchandise and for recording the transaction. When the merchandise is returned, there are more expenses for handling the complaint, inspecting the merchandise, recording the transaction, and placing the merchandise back in stock for resale.

Case 14M-1. John Margard owns a shoe store. His net sales (sales less sales returns) for the year were $220,000. His gross profit on sales ($88,000) was 40 percent of the net sales. The expenses of handling returned items cost the store $13,200 a year.

Mr. Margard is considering adopting a policy of "All Sales Final—No Returns" and reducing the selling price of his shoes.

a. What percent of the gross profit was the $13,200 in expenses for handling returns?

b. One line of shoes sells for $20 a pair. If Mr. Margard allows no sales returns, what price would he have to charge for each pair of shoes to keep the same net income?

c. What factors should be considered before adopting an "All Sales Final—No Returns" policy?

d. Is it possible that Mr. Margard might establish a policy of "All Sales Final" yet find that he actually has to increase the selling price of his shoes? How could this happen?

Working Hints

Finding the Number of Days. In counting the number of days between two dates, begin counting from the day *after* the first date. The last day, how-ever, is counted. Thus to find the number of days between July 28 (the invoice date) and October 15 (the date the account is aged), follow this procedure.

Instruction	Procedure	Computation	
1. Find the number of days remaining in the month the invoice was issued.	Subtract the issue date from the total number of days in the month.	July (number of days) . . . . Issue date. . . . . July	31 28
		Days remaining in July. . . . . . . August. . . . . September	3 31 30
2. Find the number of full months until the month the account is aged.	Add the number of days in the months prior to the current one.		61
3. Find the number of days in the month the account is aged.	Add the number of days that have expired in the month.	October	15
4. Find the total number of days.	Add the number of days in (1), (2), and (3).	Total days	79

Chapter 15

A Personnel and Payroll Subsystem

You will now learn how the people, forms, procedures, and equipment are used to control the personnel and payroll subsystem. You will also learn about the important jobs of the payroll clerk and general office clerk.

Topic 1
Controlling Personnel and Payroll

A *What is the personnel and payroll subsystem?* The **personnel and payroll subsystem** is the people, forms, procedures, and equipment that make up the subsystem in which the payroll for a business is processed. Four primary activities are completed in any personnel and payroll subsystem.

- Hiring employees and officially terminating their employment. When an employee is hired, pay rates and deductions are fixed.
- Processing the payroll.
- Paying the payroll.
- Preparing and filing the payroll tax returns.

Procedures for Controlling Personnel and Payroll

Every business must pay its employees. Thus it is important that procedures are established to do the following.

- Hire competent and trustworthy employees.
- Pay only authorized pay rates.
- Pay employees only for time worked or services rendered.
- Deduct authorized amounts from gross earnings.
- Maintain employee earnings records.
- Divide responsibility.
- Record all data from payroll transactions.
- Use prenumbered payroll checks.
- Designate authorized employees to sign paychecks.
- Secure the check-signing machine.
- Pay only authorized employees.
- Submit tax returns promptly.

Control: Hire competent and trustworthy employees.
Control: Pay only authorized pay rates.
Control: Pay employees only for time worked or services rendered.
Control: Deduct authorized amounts from gross earnings.
Control: Maintain employee earnings records.
Control: Divide responsibility.
Control: Record payroll transactions.
Control: Use prenumbered payroll checks.
Control: Designate authorized employees to sign checks.
Control: Secure the check-signing machine.
Control: Pay only authorized employees.
Control: Submit tax returns promptly.

The first three procedures are completed as part of the activities of the personnel department. The remaining procedures are completed in the payroll department and are described in Topics 2, 3, and 4.

Activity A. Answer the following questions about the procedures for controlling personnel and payroll. Refer to the text above.
1. What are two activities completed in a personnel and payroll subsystem?
2. Which procedures are completed by the personnel department?
3. Which procedure is designed to see that the proper employees get paid?
4. Which procedure is designed to see that the proper records are kept on employee earnings?

B *What departments make up the personnel and payroll subsystem?* There are two departments in the personnel and payroll subsystem—personnel and payroll. The two departments are separate but related. That is, one must provide information for the other. The relationship of the personnel to the payroll department is now described.

Personnel Department

The personnel department is responsible for recruiting and hiring employees, authorizing pay rates and deductions, and terminating the employee's service with the employer.

Recruiting and Hiring New Employees. The recruiting and hiring of new employees is important to all businesses. The recruiting and hiring process usually begins with the request for a new employee. For instance, the accounting department might indicate the need for an accounts receivable bookkeeper. The request goes to the manager, who either agrees or disagrees that a new employee is needed. If the request is accepted, the manager will authorize the personnel department to begin the recruiting process. The authorization to recruit will usually include a job description and pay rate.

The personnel department will then advertise for an employee. The advertisement might be posted inside the business for the benefit of all employees. Or a "help-wanted ad" might be run in the newspaper. An example of a help-wanted ad is in the margin.

The process at this point will vary. Many businesses will ask each person who answers the ad to complete an employment application. Part of a sample application is shown here. Space is usually included

ACCOUNTANT *(Unusual opportunity),* assistant to head controller. Convenient center city location. Prefer person with automotive background but will consider a sincere, dependable, capable, efficient professional-type person who is seeking a permanent position with pleasant working conditions. An opportunity for advancement. We offer all major benefits; Health Ins., etc. We are an Equal Opportunity Employer (M-F). Reply in strictest confidence to Mr. James, 865-1742.

ACCOUNTANT/Adm. Asst. Wanted F/C Bookkeeper to assume responsibility for manual accounting sys. & assume add'l duties as small office grows. Should be exp'd, mature individual who works well with limited supervision. Submit resume with salary requirements to Southview Electronics, Inc., 43 Woodlawn Ave., Terre Haute, Ind. 47802.

BOOKKEEPER/Payroll Clerk able to handle payroll & payroll taxes to data company for 70 employees. Must be able to generate journal entries. Good pay with liberal fringe benefits. Call 431-9067 between 9 a.m. and 5 p.m. for appointment.

HOUSE OF SOUND
Employment Application

An Equal Opportunity Employer
House of Sound Policy and Federal Law Forbid Discrimination Because of Race, Religion, Age, Sex, Marital Status, Disability, or National Origin.

Date_____

Personal Data

Applying for position as _____ Salary required_____ Date available_____

Name: _____
    (Last)   (First)   (Middle)   (Maiden)

Present address _____
    (Street)   (City)   (State)   (Zip)   (How long at this address)

Permanent address _____
    (Street)   (City)   (State)   (Zip)   (How long at this address)

Telephone number _____ Social Security number _____
    (Area code)

Are you a U.S. Citizen? ☐ Yes ☐ No   If non-citizen, give Alien Registration No. _____

Check appropriate box for age: Under 16 ☐, 16 or 17 ☐, 18 through 64 ☐, 65 or over ☐

Person to be notified in case of emergency:
    Name_____ Telephone_____
    Address_____

Reason for terminating

Partial Job Application

for personal information, employment history, salary requirement, and references.

All applications are carefully screened and personal interviews are scheduled with potential recruits. Based on impressions made during the interview and information on the application, the most qualified person is offered the position. If the person receiving the offer finds the salary, benefits, and working conditions acceptable, the hiring process is complete. A flowchart illustrating the hiring process is in the margin.

Personnel Records. Before the new employee begins work, certain personnel records must be completed. Generally, these records are the basis for deductions that will be made from the employee's gross pay. Examples include employee income taxes, union deductions, and life insurance premiums.

Personnel's Relation to the Payroll Department. The personnel department completes a series of activities prior to and at the beginning of employment. The personnel department must forward the following information to the payroll department.

- *The date of employment.* The payroll department then will know when to begin salary payments.
- *A copy of Form W-4.* The payroll department then will know the number of exemptions to which the employee is entitled.
- *The basis for computing net pay.* The payroll department then will know the hourly wage rate, the commission or bonus plan, or the salary to be earned by the employee.
- *The conditions of employment.* The payroll department then will know if the employee is entitled to overtime pay, when to begin overtime pay, and at what rate to pay overtime.
- *Changes in the rate of pay.* The payroll department will then know when to increase or decrease an employee's gross earnings.
- *Notice of termination.* The payroll department will then know when to remove an employee from the payroll records.

The records just described form the basis for the relationship between the personnel and payroll departments. All activities in the payroll department begin with authorizations received from the personnel department.

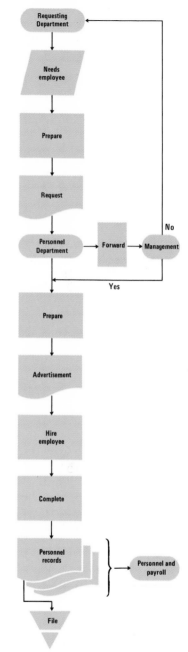

Hiring a New Employee

Activity B. Answer the following questions about activities in the personnel department. Refer to the text, margin notes, and illustrations on pages 427 to 429.
1. What begins the process for hiring a new employee?

2. Do all applicants receive a personal interview?
3. What records are completed in the personnel department for each new employee?
4. Can the payroll department operate without the personnel department?

Visualizing a Personnel and Payroll Subsystem

C *How do the four primary activities completed in a personnel and payroll subsystem relate to the personnel and payroll departments?* The flowchart on page 431 shows both the activities and relation between the personnel and payroll departments. It also shows how personnel and payroll are related to the accounting department.

Payroll Clerk
DOT 215.482-010. Computes wages and posts wages to payroll records.

Activity C. Answer the following questions about visualizing a personnel and payroll subsystem. Refer to the flowchart on page 431.
1. In what steps do you see a relation between the personnel and payroll departments?
2. How many activities are completed in the payroll department?
3. Which department prepares the paychecks? Which department prepares the Form W-2s?

4. How does the payroll department know how much to pay each employee?
5. Which journals are used in the accounting department? Which of the journals is new to you?
6. How does work completed in the payroll department act as a proof of work completed in the accounting department?

Accounting Concepts:
Payroll Records. The employer must maintain adequate *payroll records.*
Collection Agent. The employer acts as a *collection agent* for the government and for others designated by the employee or a court.

Topic 1 Problem

15-1. On a table similar to the following one, indicate who prepares or sends the following forms, to whom or where the forms are sent, and the purpose for each form. Refer to the flowchart on page 431.

Form	Prepared or Sent By	Sent To	Purpose
EXAMPLE: Request for new employee	**Requesting Department**	**Personnel Department**	**Request new employee**
a. Form W-4			
b. Deduction authorizations			
c. Help-wanted advertisement			
d. Time cards			
e. Payroll journal			
f. Paychecks			
g. Prepared payroll tax returns			
h. Checks that accompany payroll tax returns.			

VISUALIZING
A SUBSYSTEM FOR
PERSONNEL AND PAYROLL

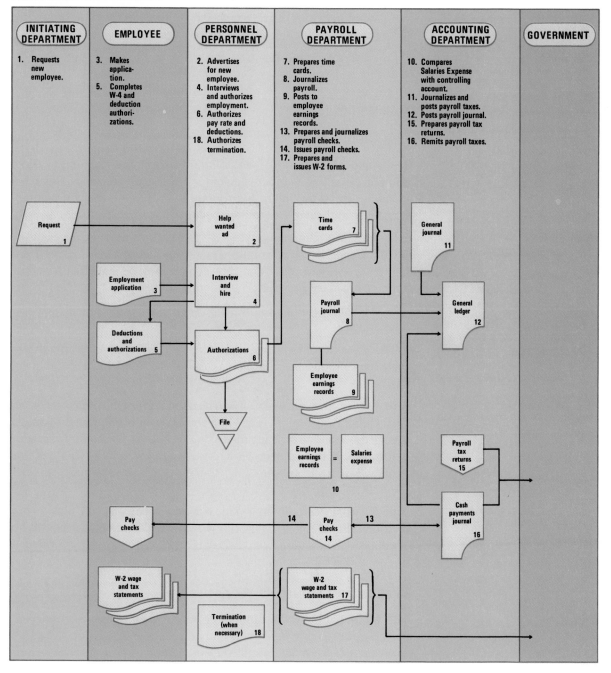

INITIATING DEPARTMENT	EMPLOYEE	PERSONNEL DEPARTMENT	PAYROLL DEPARTMENT	ACCOUNTING DEPARTMENT	GOVERNMENT
1. Requests new employee.	3. Makes application. 5. Completes W-4 and deduction authorizations.	2. Advertises for new employee. 4. Interviews and authorizes employment. 6. Authorizes pay rate and deductions. 18. Authorizes termination.	7. Prepares time cards. 8. Journalizes payroll. 9. Posts to employee earnings records. 13. Prepares and journalizes payroll checks. 14. Issues payroll checks. 17. Prepares and issues W-2 forms.	10. Compares Salaries Expense with controlling account. 11. Journalizes and posts payroll taxes. 12. Posts payroll journal. 15. Prepares payroll tax returns. 16. Remits payroll taxes.	

Topic 2
Processing the Payroll

 What are the procedures used to process the payroll? Preparing the payroll includes three procedures.

- Employees are paid for time worked or services rendered.
- Authorized amounts are deducted from gross earnings.
- Employee earnings records are maintained.
- Responsibilities are divided among the employees.

Control: Pay employees only for time worked or services rendered.
Control: Deduct authorized amounts from gross earnings.
Control: Maintain employee earnings records.
Control: Divide responsibility.

Pay Plans

The amount an employee earns is known as gross earnings. Various plans are used to compute an employee's gross earnings. Five pay plans are the salary plan, hourly-rate plan, piece-rate plan, commission plan, and salary-commission plan.

In the salary plan, employees are paid a fixed amount for each pay period. Generally no computations are needed to find a salaried employee's gross earnings. The rate of pay may be stated as a certain amount of salary per week, per month, or per year.

In the hourly-rate plan, the employee is paid a set amount for each hour worked.

The piece-rate plan involves paying an employee a set amount for each item produced. This plan is frequently used in manufacturing businesses.

In the commission plan, a salesperson's gross earnings are based on the quantity of goods sold. The commission is computed by multiplying the amount of sales made during the pay period by a certain percentage. If the salesperson had sales of $8,000 in a week and was paid a 3 percent commission, the gross earnings would be $240 ($8,000 × 0.03).

In the salary-commission plan, businesses pay a salary plus a commission. This is especially useful in a sales department. The possibility of commission in addition to salary is an incentive to the sales staff to increase its efforts.

Salary Plan
Gross Earnings = Salary
$212 = $212

Hourly-Rate Plan
Gross Earnings = Hours × Rate
$240 = 40 × $6

Piece-Rate Plan
Gross Earnings = Items × Rate
$450 = 3,000 × $0.15

Commission Plan
Gross
Earnings = Percentage × Sales
$240 = 0.03 × $8,000

Salary-Commission Plan
Gross
Earnings = Salary + Commission
$340 = $100 + ($8,000 × 0.03)
$340 = $100 + $240

Wages and Hours of Work

The wages paid and the number of hours an employee works depend on the contract of employment and government legislation. A written agreement between the employer and a union is a **contract of employment** and must be followed by the employer and the employee. You learned how to compute regular earnings, overtime, and the determining of hours worked in Chapter 9.

Computing Net Pay

Various deductions must be subtracted from an employee's gross earnings. The amount remaining after the deductions are subtracted is net pay. The deductions may be required by law or may be voluntary. Some of these are listed in the margin below.

SINGLE Persons — WEEKLY Payroll Period

| And the wages are— | | And the number of withholding allowances claimed is— | | | | | | | | | | |
At least	But less than	0	1	2	3	4	5	6	7	8	9	10 or more
		The amount of income tax to be withheld shall be—										
210	220	36.20	31.20	27.20	23.10	19.10	15.40	11.90	8.50	5.10	2.20	0
220	230	38.80	33.80	29.30	25.20	21.20	17.20	13.70	10.30	6.80	3.70	.80
230	240	41.40	36.40	31.40	27.30	23.30	19.20	15.50	12.10	8.60	5.20	2.30
240	250	44.00	39.00	34.00	29.40	25.40	21.30	17.30	13.90	10.40	6.90	3.80
250	260	46.60	41.60	36.60	31.60	27.50	23.40	19.40	15.70	12.20	8.70	5.30
260	270	49.20	44.20	39.20	34.20	29.60	25.50	21.50	17.50	14.00	10.50	7.10
270	280	51.80	46.80	41.80	36.80	31.80	27.60	23.60	19.60	15.80	12.30	8.90
280	290	54.80	49.40	44.40	39.40	34.40	29.70	25.70	21.70	17.60	14.10	10.70
290	300	57.80	52.10	47.00	42.00	37.00	32.00	27.80	23.80	19.70	15.90	12.50
300	310	60.80	55.10	49.60	44.60	39.60	34.60	29.90	25.90	21.80	17.80	14.30
310	320	63.80	58.10	52.30	47.20	42.20	37.20	32.20	28.00	23.90	19.90	16.10

MARRIED Persons — WEEKLY Payroll Period

| And the wages are— | | And the number of withholding allowances claimed is— | | | | | | | | | | |
At least	But less than	0	1	2	3	4	5	6	7	8	9	10 or more
		The amount of income tax to be withheld shall be—										
250	260	36.50	32.50	28.50	24.80	21.30	17.90	14.40	11.10	8.30	5.40	2.50
260	270	38.60	34.60	30.60	26.60	23.10	19.70	16.20	12.70	9.80	6.90	4.00
270	280	40.70	36.70	32.70	28.60	24.90	21.50	18.00	14.50	11.30	8.40	5.50
280	290	42.80	38.80	34.80	30.70	26.70	23.30	19.80	16.30	12.90	9.90	7.00
290	300	45.10	40.90	36.90	32.80	28.80	25.10	21.60	18.10	14.70	11.40	8.50
300	310	47.50	43.00	39.00	34.90	30.90	26.90	23.40	19.90	16.50	13.00	10.00
310	320	49.90	45.30	41.10	37.00	33.00	28.90	25.20	21.70	18.30	14.80	11.50
320	330	52.30	47.70	43.20	39.10	35.10	31.00	27.00	23.50	20.10	16.60	13.20
330	340	54.70	50.10	45.50	41.20	37.20	33.10	29.10	25.30	21.90	18.40	15.00
340	350	57.10	52.50	47.90	43.30	39.30	35.20	31.20	27.20	23.70	20.20	16.80

Social Security Employee Tax Table—Continued
6.7 percent employee tax deductions

Wages — At least	But less than	Tax to be withheld	Wages — At least	But less than	Tax to be withheld	Wages — At least	But less than	Tax to be withheld	Wages — At least	But less than	Tax to be withheld
$99.93	$100.08	$6.70	$134.26	$134.41	$9.00	$159.48	$159.63	$10.69	$210.83	$210.98	$14.13
100.08	100.23	6.71	134.41	134.56	9.01	159.63	159.78	10.70	210.98	211.12	14.14
100.23	100.38	6.72	134.56	134.71	9.02	159.78	159.93	10.71	211.12	211.27	14.15
100.38	100.53	6.73	134.71	134.86	9.03	159.93	160.08	10.72	211.27	211.42	14.16
100.53	100.68	6.74	134.86	135.00	9.04	160.08	160.23	10.73	211.42	211.57	14.17
100.68	100.83	6.75	135.00	135.15	9.05	160.23	160.38	10.74	211.57	211.72	14.18
100.83	100.98	6.76	135.15	135.30	9.06	160.38	160.53	10.75	211.72	211.87	14.19
100.98	101.13	6.77	135.30	135.45	9.07	160.53	160.68	10.76	211.87	212.02	14.20
101.13	101.28	6.78	135.45	135.60	9.08	160.68	160.83	10.77	212.02	212.17	14.21
101.28	101.42	6.79	135.60	135.75	9.09	160.83	160.98	10.78	212.17	212.32	14.22
109.93	110.08	7.37	139.93	140.08	9.38	167.84	167.99	11.25	224.56	224.70	15.05
110.08	110.23	7.38	140.08	140.23	9.39	167.99	168.14	11.26	224.70	224.85	15.06
110.23	110.38	7.39	140.23	140.38	9.40	168.14	168.29	11.27	224.85	225.00	15.07
110.38	110.53	7.40	140.38	140.53	9.41	168.29	168.44	11.28	225.00	225.15	15.08
110.53	110.68	7.41	140.53	140.68	9.42	168.44	168.59	11.29	225.15	225.30	15.09
110.68	110.83	7.42	140.68	140.83	9.43	168.59	168.74	11.30	225.30	225.45	15.10
110.83	110.98	7.43	140.83	140.98	9.44	168.74	168.89	11.31	225.45	225.60	15.11
110.98	111.12	7.44	140.98	141.12	9.45	168.89	169.03	11.32	225.60	225.75	15.12
111.12	111.27	7.45	141.12	141.27	9.46	169.03	169.18	11.33	225.75	225.90	15.13
111.27	111.42	7.46	141.27	141.42	9.47	169.18	169.33	11.34	225.90	226.05	15.14
119.48	119.63	8.01	142.02	142.17	9.52	171.72	171.86	11.51	255.15	255.30	17.10
119.63	119.78	8.02	142.17	142.32	9.53	171.86	172.01	11.52	255.30	255.45	17.11
119.78	119.93	8.03	142.32	142.47	9.54	172.01	172.16	11.53	255.45	255.60	17.12
119.93	120.08	8.04	142.47	142.62	9.55	172.16	172.31	11.54	255.60	255.75	17.13
120.08	120.23	8.05	142.62	142.77	9.56	172.31	172.46	11.55	255.75	255.90	17.14
120.23	120.38	8.06	142.77	142.92	9.57	172.46	172.61	11.56	255.90	256.05	17.15
120.38	120.53	8.07	142.92	143.06	9.58	172.61	172.76	11.57	256.05	256.20	17.16
120.53	120.68	8.08	143.06	143.21	9.59	172.76	172.91	11.58	256.20	256.35	17.17
120.68	120.83	8.09	143.21	143.36	9.60	172.91	173.06	11.59	256.35	256.50	17.18
120.83	120.98	8.10	143.36	143.51	9.61	173.06	173.21	11.60	256.50	256.65	17.19
121.73	121.88	8.16	144.11	144.25	9.66	189.93	190.08	12.73	275.30	275.44	18.45
121.88	122.03	8.17	144.26	144.41	9.67	190.08	190.23	12.74	275.45	275.59	18.46
122.03	122.18	8.18	144.41	144.56	9.68	190.23	190.38	12.75	275.60	275.74	18.47
122.18	122.33	8.19	144.56	144.71	9.69	190.38	190.53	12.76	275.75	275.89	18.48
122.33	122.48	8.20	144.71	144.86	9.70	190.53	190.68	12.77	275.90	276.04	18.49
122.48	122.63	8.21	144.86	145.00	9.71	190.68	190.83	12.78	276.05	276.19	18.50
122.63	122.78	8.22	145.00	145.15	9.72	190.83	190.98	12.79	276.20	276.34	18.51
122.78	122.93	8.23	145.15	145.30	9.73	190.98	191.12	12.80	276.35	276.49	18.52
122.93	123.08	8.24	145.30	145.45	9.74	191.12	191.27	12.81	276.50	276.64	18.53
123.08	123.23	8.25	145.45	145.60	9.75	191.27	191.42	12.82	276.65	276.79	18.54
129.03	129.18	8.65	149.78	149.93	10.04	194.71	194.86	13.05	299.63	299.77	20.08
129.18	129.33	8.66	149.93	150.08	10.05	194.86	195.00	13.06	299.78	299.92	20.09
129.33	129.48	8.67	150.08	150.23	10.06	195.00	195.15	13.07	299.93	300.07	20.10
129.48	129.63	8.68	150.23	150.38	10.07	195.15	195.30	13.08	300.08	300.22	20.11
129.63	129.78	8.69	150.38	150.53	10.08	195.30	195.45	13.09	300.23	300.37	20.12
129.78	129.93	8.70	150.53	150.68	10.09	195.45	195.60	13.10	300.38	300.52	20.13
129.93	130.08	8.71	150.68	150.83	10.10	195.60	195.75	13.11	300.53	300.67	20.14
130.08	130.23	8.72	150.83	150.98	10.11	195.75	195.90	13.12	300.68	300.82	20.15
130.23	130.38	8.73	150.98	151.12	10.12	195.90	196.05	13.13	300.83	300.97	20.16
130.38	130.53	8.74	151.12	151.27	10.13	196.05	196.20	13.14	300.98	301.11	20.17
132.76	132.91	8.90	155.00	155.15	10.39	200.98	201.12	13.47	514.71	514.86	34.49
132.91	133.06	8.91	155.15	155.30	10.40	201.12	201.27	13.48	514.86	515.00	34.50
133.06	133.21	8.92	155.30	155.45	10.41	201.17	201.42	13.49	515.00	515.15	34.51
133.21	133.36	8.93	155.45	155.60	10.42	201.42	201.57	13.50	515.15	515.30	34.52
133.36	133.51	8.94	155.60	155.75	10.43	201.57	201.72	13.51	515.30	515.45	34.53
133.51	133.66	8.95	155.75	155.90	10.44	201.72	201.87	13.52	515.45	515.60	34.54
133.66	133.81	8.96	155.90	156.05	10.45	201.87	202.02	13.53	515.60	515.75	34.55
133.81	133.96	8.97	156.05	156.20	10.46	202.02	202.17	13.54	515.75	515.90	34.56
133.96	134.11	8.98	156.20	156.35	10.47	202.17	202.32	13.55	515.90	516.05	34.57
134.11	134.26	8.99	156.35	156.50	10.48	202.32	202.47	13.56	516.05	516.20	34.58

EXAMPLES OF PAYROLL DEDUCTIONS

Deductions Required by Law
- Federal income tax withholding
- Social security tax
- State income tax (in some states)
- City income tax (in some cities)
- Garnishments

Voluntary Deductions
- Life insurance
- Medical insurance
- Hospitalization insurance
- Pension plan
- Savings bonds
- Charity donations
- Miscellaneous (for example, safety shoes)

Deductions Required by Union Agreements
- Union initiation fees
- Union dues

All compulsory, voluntary, and union deductions must be subtracted from the employee's gross earnings, with the remainder referred to as the employee's **net pay.** Net pay is also called *take-home pay.*

Activity A-1. Five time cards are shown here. Find the hours worked during the week for each employee. Employees are paid to the nearest quarter-hour.

NOTE: Save your work for further use in Activity A-2.

Employee No. 1 — Joseph Benedict
Week Ending July 28, 19--

Days	Regular In	Out	In	Out	Other In	Out	Hours
Thurs.	7:59	12:00	12:30	4:30			
Fri.	8:00	12:00	12:30	4:30			
Sat.							
Sun.							
Mon.	7:45	12:35	1:10	4:28			
Tues.	8:00	12:30	1:00	4:30			
Wed.	8:03	12:32	12:58	4:35			

	Hours	Rate	Earnings
Extra Hours Approved / Regular		$7.50	
Overtime			
Supervisor / Total Hours		Gross Earnings	

Employee No. 2 — Harlan Brown
Week Ending July 28, 19--

Days	Regular In	Out	In	Out	Other In	Out	Hours
Thurs.	8:00	11:58	12:31	4:30			
Fri.	8:00	11:57	12:32	4:29			
Sat.							
Sun.							
Mon.	8:00	11:59	12:30	4:28			
Tues.	8:00	12:00	12:30	4:32			
Wed.	8:00	12:00	12:30	4:35			

	Hours	Rate	Earnings
Extra Hours Approved / Regular		$7.50	
Overtime			
Supervisor / Total Hours		Gross Earnings	

Employee No. 3 — Maryann Coria
Week Ending July 28, 19--

Days	Regular In	Out	In	Out	Other In	Out	Hours
Thurs.	8:09	12:00	12:30	4:30			
Fri.	7:59	12:00	12:31	4:30			
Sat.							
Sun.							
Mon.	7:58	12:00	12:30	4:29			
Tues.	8:08	11:58	12:32	4:29			
Wed.	8:05	11:59	12:53	4:30			

	Hours	Rate	Earnings
Extra Hours Approved / Regular		$5.77	
Overtime			
Supervisor / Total Hours		Gross Earnings	

Employee No. 4 — Iris Griesbaum
Week Ending July 28, 19--

Days	Regular In	Out	In	Out	Other In	Out	Hours
Thurs.	7:58	12:00	12:31	4:30			
Fri.	7:57	12:00	12:30	4:30			
Sat.							
Sun.							
Mon.	8:00	11:59	12:29	4:35			
Tues.	8:01	12:01	12:30	4:36			
Wed.	8:04	12:00	12:31	4:31			

	Hours	Rate	Earnings
Extra Hours Approved / Regular		$5.30	
Overtime			
Supervisor / Total Hours		Gross Earnings	

Employee No. 5 — Patrick Shea
Week Ending July 28, 19--

Days	Regular In	Out	In	Out	Other In	Out	Hours
Thurs.	8:00	12:02	1:00	4:30			
Fri.	8:01	12:01	1:00	4:32			
Sat.							
Sun.							
Mon.	7:56	12:00	1:05	4:29			
Tues.	7:58	12:03	1:02	4:30			
Wed.	8:06	12:00	1:02	4:30			

	Hours	Rate	Earnings
Extra Hours Approved / Regular		$7.35	
Overtime			
Supervisor / Total Hours		Gross Earnings	

Activity A-2. Use the time cards from Activity A-1 to do the following. Compute the gross earnings for each employee. The employees are all paid on an hourly rate. Regular time is paid for the first 40 hours. Time and a half is paid on hours over 40. The hourly rates are entered on the cards.

NOTE: Save your work for further use in Activity A-3 and Activity B.

Activity A-3. Use the payroll information given in Activity A-2 to compute the Federal Income Tax Withholding and FICA Taxes for each employee. To complete this activity, use the tables on page 433 and a table similar to the one found here. No employee has reached the FICA maximum.

NOTE: Save your work for further use in Activity B.

Employee	Marital Status	No. of Exemptions	Federal Withholding	FICA Taxes
1. I. Griesbaum	S	1	?	?
2. J. Benedict	M	3	?	?
3. P. Shea	S	1	?	?
4. H. Brown	M	5	?	?
5. M. Coria	S	1	?	?

Journalizing the Payroll

B *What is the payroll journal?* The **payroll journal** is a special journal used to record payroll data for each pay period. The procedures for recording payroll data in the payroll journal are now discussed.

The Payroll Journal

Some businesses first record payroll data in a payroll register. The data in the payroll register is then used to record the payroll in the general journal. The use of the payroll register is described in Chapter 9 in Part 1. The House of Sound, like many businesses, records payroll data directly in a special payroll journal. The payroll journal used by House of Sound is illustrated here.

Control: Record all data from payroll transactions.

PAYROLL JOURNAL — Page 17

For the Week Beginning *April 21,* 19 — and Ending *April 28,* 19 — Paid *April 29,* 19 —

NO.	NAME	MARITAL STATUS	EXEMP.	HOURS	REGULAR	OVERTIME	SALARIES EXPENSE	FEDERAL INCOME TAXES PAYABLE	STATE INCOME TAXES PAYABLE	FICA TAXES PAYABLE	INSURANCE PREMIUMS PAYABLE	UNION DUES PAYABLE	TOTAL	SALARIES PAYABLE	CK. NO.
1	S. Brouse	M	3	44	240 00	36 00	276 00	28 60	8 28	18 49	5 00	4 00	64 37	211 63	
2	B. Loren	S	1	38	190 00		190 00	24 90	5 70	12 73	5 00	4 00	52 33	137 67	
3	K. Mignon	S	2	40	200 00		200 00	25 10	6 00	13 40	5 00	4 00	53 50	146 50	
4	S. O'Brien	M	2	42	200 00	15 00	215 00	21 00	6 45	14 41	5 00	4 00	50 86	164 14	
5	C. Richard	M	1	20	100 00		100 00	5 60	3 00	6 70	5 00	4 00	24 30	75 70	
6	A. Vaughn	S	0	40	280 00		280 00	54 80	8 40	18 76	5 00	4 00	90 96	189 04	
	Totals				1,210 00	51 00	1,261 00	160 00	37 83	84 49	30 00	24 00	336 32	924 68	

Remember that the payroll journal is similar to the payroll register. However, several of the column headings are new. In the Earnings section, the column Salaries Expense includes the gross earnings for

Proof of Payroll Journal

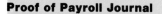

Earnings:		
Regular	1,210 00	
Overtime	51 00	
Total		1,261 00
Deductions:		
Federal Income Tax	160 00	
State Income Tax	37 83	
FICA Tax . . .	84 49	
Insurance . . .	30 00	
Union Dues . .	24 00	
Total		336 32
Net Pay		924 68

Proof of Payroll Register

each employee. The total of Salaries Expense ($1,261) is the total expense for payroll for the pay period ending on April 28.

In the Deductions section, each of the deductions is an amount withheld from the employee's earnings. Thus each deduction is a liability to the House of Sound. Each column heading in the Deductions section describes a different liability. For instance, amounts withheld for federal income taxes are recorded in the column Federal Income Taxes Payable. Similar account titles are used for the other columns in the Deductions section. The total for each of the deductions is the liability for that account for the pay period. For instance, the total liability for FICA Taxes is $84.49 for the pay period ended April 28.

The last amount column—Salaries Payable—is the employer's liability for each employee's net pay. The total of the Salaries Payable column ($924.68) is the total liability for net pay (earnings) for the pay period ended April 28.

Proving the Payroll Journal. After the data for each employee is entered in the payroll journal, the columns are pencil-footed. The payroll journal is then proved by adding and subtracting the columns as shown in the margin. When the journal is proved, write the total in ink and double-rule the journal.

Activity B. Use your work from Activities A-2 and A-3 to complete the following payroll activities.
1. Journalize the payroll for the week ended July 28 in a payroll journal. The state income tax rate is 2 percent of gross earnings. Each employee has a deduction for insurance ($5.50) and union dues ($7.00) each week. In addition, both P. Shea and H. Brown have $12.50 deducted each week for United States bonds.
2. Total and prove your payroll journal.
NOTE: Save your work for further use in Topic Problem 15-2.

Posting to Employee Earnings Records

C *What is the purpose of the employee earnings record?* After the payroll journal is totaled and proved, the payroll information is posted to the employee earnings record. An employee earnings record shows the details of an employee's earnings and deductions for the year. By federal law, some form of an earnings record must be kept for each employee for at least 4 years.

Employee Earnings Records as a Subsidiary Ledger

The last amount on the Year-to-Date Earnings column on the employee earnings record is the salaries expense for that particular employee. The last amount for all employees, when added together, is the total salaries expense for the business. Thus employee earnings records are often viewed as a subsidiary ledger. The Salaries Expense account in the general ledger is the controlling account.

EMPLOYEE EARNINGS RECORD FOR YEAR 19—

Name **Sonia Brouse**
Address **16 Carmine Drive**
　　　　Englewood, Colorado 80112
Telephone No. **277-8346**
Date of Birth **June 14, 1959**
Rate **$6.00 per Hour**

Employee No. **1**
Social Security No. **201-26-8341**
Marital Status **Married**
Withholding Exemptions **3**
Position **Accounting Department**
Date Employed **January 2, 19—**

DATE			EARNINGS			DEDUCTIONS						NET PAY	YEAR-TO-DATE EARNINGS
PERIOD ENDING	PAID	HOURS	REGULAR	OVERTIME	TOTAL	FEDERAL INCOME TAX	STATE INCOME TAX	FICA TAX	INSURANCE PREMIUMS	UNION DUES	TOTAL		
19—													
Apr. 7	4/8/—	40	240 00		240 00	23 00	7 20	14 71	5 00	4 00	53 91	186 09	3,510 00
14	4/15/—	42	240 00	18 00	258 00	24 80	7 74	15 82	5 00	4 00	57 36	200 64	3,768 00
21	4/22/—	40	240 00		240 00	23 00	7 20	14 71	5 00	4 00	53 91	186 09	4,008 00
28	4/29/—	44	240 00	36 00	276 00	28 60	8 28	18 49	5 00	4 00	64 37	211 63	4,284 00

The proof of the subsidiary ledger (employee earnings record) and the controlling account (Salaries Expense) is rather easy. The last amounts in the Year-to-Date column of each employee earnings record are added. The total is then compared to the balance of Salaries Expense in the general ledger. Any disagreement must be found and corrected.

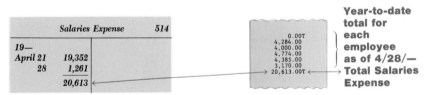

Salaries Expense 514

19—	
April 21	19,352
28	1,261
	20,613

```
         0.00T
    4,284.00
    4,000.00
    4,774.00
    4,385.00
    3,170.00
   20,613.00T
```

Year-to-date total for each employee as of 4/28/— → Total Salaries Expense

Activity C. Payroll data for five employees is given here. Record this data in employee earnings records.

1. Joseph Benedict: address, 245 North Third Street, Trenton, New Jersey 08602; telephone number, 617-3807; date of birth, June 14, 1955; rate, $7.50 per hour; employee number, 1; social security number, 174-91-6532; marital status, married; withholding exemptions, 3; position, accounting supervisor; date employed, May 23, 1975; year-to-date earnings, $10,200.

2. Harlan Brown: address, Carter Road, Yardley, Pennsylvania 19067; telephone number, 842-2891; date of birth, August 23, 1942; rate, $7.50 per hour; employee number, 2; social security number, 111-18-7091; marital status, married; withholding exemptions, 5; position, salesperson/full-charge bookkeeper; date employed, March 9, 1978; year-to-date earnings, $12,300.

3. Maryann Coria: address, P. O. Box 719, Pennington, New Jersey 08648; telephone number, 236-4382; date of birth, October 22, 1950; rate, $5.77 per hour; employee number, 3; social security number, 928-92-1100; marital status, single; withholding exemptions, 1; position, accounting clerk; date employed, March 13, 19—(current year); year-to-date earnings, $4,500.

4. Iris Griesbaum: address, 976 Carol Place, Washington Crossing, Pennsylvania 18977; telephone number, 842-1759; date of birth, June 12, 1960; rate, $5.30 per hour; employee number, 4; social security number, 204-28-8623; marital status, single; withholding exemptions, 1; position, salesperson; date employed, August 7, 1980; year-to-date earnings, $8,200.

5. Patrick Shea: address, Blytine Avenue, Lawrenceville, New Jersey 08648; telephone number, 842-

3605; date of birth, February 14, 1954; rate, $7.35 per hour; employee number, 5; social security number, 204-28-6107; marital status, single; withholding exemptions, 1; position, accounting clerk; date employed, November 5, 1977; year-to-date earnings, $10,700.

NOTE: Save your employee earnings records for further use in Topic Problem 15-2.

**House of Sound
Chart of Accounts**

Liabilities
221 Federal Income Tax
      Payable
222 FICA Taxes Payable
223 State Income Taxes
      Payable
224 Federal Unemployment
      Taxes Payable
225 State Unemployment
      Taxes Payable
226 Salaries Payable
227 Insurance Premiums
      Payable
228 Union Dues Payable

Costs and Expenses
516 Payroll Taxes Expense
517 Salaries Expense

Posting to General Ledger Accounts

D *How is the payroll journal posted?* Details in the payroll journal are posted to the employee earnings records. The totals provide the data for posting the payroll to the ledger accounts, as now described.

Posting the Payroll Journal

The date used to post the payroll journal is the end of the pay period. (In our illustration, the end of the pay period is April 28.) The amounts posted to the ledger accounts are the totals of the special columns.

"PR17" is written in the Posting Reference column for each ledger account to show that the amount was posted from page 17 of the payroll journal. (Pages in the payroll journal are numbered consecutively for each pay period.) The proper ledger account number is written beneath each special column to show that an amount was posted.

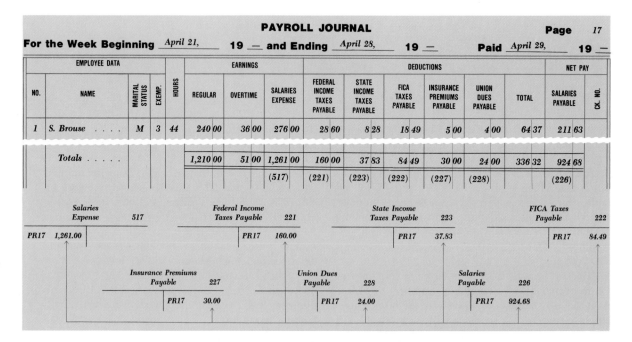

The effect of posting the payroll journal for the pay period ended April 28 is described here.

- The debit to Salaries Expense decreases owner's equity by $1,261.
- The credit to Federal Income Taxes Payable increases the liability to the federal government by $160.
- The credit to State Income Taxes Payable increases the liability to the state government by $37.83.
- The credit to FICA Taxes Payable increases the liability to the federal government by $84.49. (The amount is money withheld from the employees' earnings for social security.)
- The credit to Insurance Premiums Payable increases the liability for group and hospitalization insurance by $30. The premiums are paid periodically to the insurance company.
- The credit to Union Dues Payable increases the liability for union dues by $24. The dues are paid periodically to the proper union.
- The credit to Salaries Payable increases the liability for the employee's net earnings by $924.68.

Activity D. Answer the following questions about posting payroll information to the general ledger. Refer to the text, margin notes, and illustrations on pages 438 and 439.

1. What is the source of payroll information posted to the general ledger?

2. By what amount did posting the payroll journal decrease owner's equity?

3. By what amount did posting the payroll journal increase total liabilities?

4. To what account was the total of the regular earnings column posted? Explain.

Recording and Posting Payroll Taxes

E *Must employers pay payroll taxes?* Yes. Federal and state laws require employers as well as employees to pay payroll taxes.

Employer FICA Tax. Employers also pay taxes to the social security program. The employer's tax is at the same rate and on the same earnings used to compute the employee's FICA tax (a maximum of $29,700 for each employee).

None of the employees of the House of Sound has earned over $29,700 before April 28. Thus the business owes FICA tax of $84.49 ($1,261 × 0.067).

Employer's FICA Tax

Tax = Rate × Taxable Earnings

$84.49 = 0.067 × $1,261

Federal Unemployment Compensation Tax. The minimum FUTA tax is 0.7 percent* of the first $6,000 paid to each covered employee during a calendar year. The employees do not pay any FUTA tax. None of the employees of the House of Sound earned over $6,000 before April 28. Thus the business owes FUTA tax of $8.83 ($1,261 × 0.007) on the April 28 payroll.

FUTA Tax

Tax = Rate × Taxable Earnings

$8.83 = 0.007 × $1,261

---

* The 0.7 percent is computed as follows. The FUTA tax rate is 3.4 percent. However, the employer may take a credit against this up to 2.7 percent for contributions paid to state unemployment funds. This leaves a 0.7 percent net federal tax.

State Unemployment Compensation Tax. Unemployment taxes vary among states. In general, employers are required to pay up to a 2.7 percent tax on the first $6,000 paid to each employee in a calendar year.

SUTA Tax

Tax = Rate × Taxable Earnings

$34.05 = 0.027 × $1,261

At the maximum rate, the state unemployment compensation tax on the April 28 payroll of the House of Sound would be $34.05 ($1,261 × 0.027).

Recording Employer Payroll Taxes

The employer's FICA tax and federal and state unemployment compensation taxes are expenses to the employer. A separate expense account can be kept for each tax, but usually they are combined. Thus one amount is entered in one expense account, Payroll Taxes Expense. These individual taxes are liabilities until they are paid. A separate liability account is usually kept for each tax.

The entry to record the employer's payroll taxes for the House of Sound for the pay period ended April 28 is made in the general journal at the end of each payroll period.

	GENERAL JOURNAL			Page 17	
DATE	**ACCOUNT TITLE AND EXPLANATION**	**POST. REF.**	**DEBIT**	**CREDIT**	
19—					
Apr. 28	Payroll Taxes Expense	516	127 37		
	FICA Taxes Payable.	222		84 49	
	Federal Unemployment Taxes Payable	224		8 83	
	State Unemployment Taxes Payable . .	225		34 05	
	Record employer's payroll taxes.				

Record employer's payroll taxes.

Activity E. Answer the following questions about recording the employer's payroll taxes. Refer to the text, margin notes, and illustrations on pages 439 to 440.

1. How much does the employer owe for FICA taxes? FUTA taxes? State unemployment taxes?
2. What is the total amount the employer owes for payroll taxes? In what journal is this amount recorded?
3. How much do the employees' owe for federal unemployment taxes? State unemployment taxes? Explain.
4. Why is the employer's FICA tax described as a "matching tax"?

Topic 2 Problems

15-2. Use the payroll journal you completed in Activity B to post payroll information to the employee earnings records you completed in Activity C.
NOTE: Save your employee earnings records for further use in Topic Problem 15-4.

15-3. Use the payroll journal you completed in Activity B to post the salaries expense and payroll liabilities to the general ledger.
NOTE: Save your general ledger for further use in Topic Problems 15-4 and 15-6.

15-4. Use the payroll journal you completed in Activity B, general ledger from Topic Problem 15-3, and the employee earnings records you completed in Activity C to record and post the employer's payroll taxes.

NOTE: Save your payroll journal for further use in Topic Problem 15-6.

15-5. The totals line of the payroll journal completed for the Apex Company is given here.
a. Prove the payroll journal.
b. Post the payroll journal to the general ledger.
c. Use the payroll journal to record and post the employer's payroll taxes. None of the employees has exceeded $6,000 in total earnings on February 28.

| | | | | | | | PAYROLL JOURNAL | | | | | | | Page | 21 |

For the Week Beginning February 28, 19 — **and Ending** March 6, 19 — **Paid** March 8, 19 —

EMPLOYEE DATA					EARNINGS			DEDUCTIONS						NET PAY	
NO.	NAME	MARITAL STATUS	EXEMP.	HOURS	REGULAR	OVERTIME	SALARIES EXPENSE	FEDERAL INCOME TAXES PAYABLE	STATE INCOME TAXES PAYABLE	FICA TAXES PAYABLE	INSURANCE PREMIUMS PAYABLE	UNION DUES PAYABLE	TOTAL	SALARIES PAYABLE	CK. NO.
	Totals				2,000 00	200 00	2,200 00	300 00	20 00	147 40	40 00	36 00	543 40	1,656 60	

Topic 3
Paying the Payroll

A *What are the procedures for paying the payroll?* The procedures to control paying the payroll include the following.

- Use prenumbered payroll checks.
- Designate authorized employees to sign paychecks.
- Secure the check-signing machine.
- Pay only authorized employees.

Control: Use prenumbered payroll checks.
Control: Designate authorized employees to sign paychecks.
Control: Secure the check-signing machine.
Control: Pay only authorized employees.

Methods of Paying Employees

Typically, the payday falls a few days after the end of the pay period. Thus payroll personnel have time to compute and prepare the payroll. The method for paying employees depends on whether a business chooses to pay by check, pay by cash, or pay by bank transfer. The House of Sound pays its employees by check.

Recording a Payment of the Payroll

The following procedure is used to record payment of the payroll. When the payroll is paid, the total amount of all the payroll checks is entered in the cash payments journal. The amounts are posted from the journal to the ledger accounts. The liability Salaries Payable is decreased and the asset Cash is decreased. The last step is to enter the check numbers for individual employee paychecks in the payroll journal. The entry to pay the payroll for the House of Sound is illustrated here.

Payment of the Payroll

colspan 11 center: **CASH PAYMENTS JOURNAL** ... Page 17										

DATE	ACCOUNT DEBITED	EXPLANATION	CHECK NO.	POST. REF.	GENERAL LEDGER DEBIT	ACCOUNTS PAYABLE DEBIT	PURCHASES DISCOUNT CREDIT	NET CASH CREDIT
19— Apr. 29	Salaries Payable ..	April 28 payroll...	188-193	226	924 68			924 68

Cash	101	Salaries Payable	226
	924.68	924.68	924.68

Activity A. Answer the following questions about recording payment of the payroll. Refer to the text, margin notes, and illustrations on pages 441 to 442.
1. In what journal is the entry recorded to pay the payroll?

2. What account is debited to record payment of the payroll? What account is credited?
3. What is the source of the entry to *increase* salaries payable?

Summarizing Transactions for Payroll

B *What are the accounting entries to record and pay the payroll?* Each of the accounting entries to record and pay the payroll is presented in earlier topics. The three sets of entries follow.

• An entry to record the expense for the payroll and the liabilities to the government, other agencies, and the employees.
• An entry to record the employer's payroll taxes.
• An entry to record the amount paid to the employees.

The journal entries and related ledger accounts for the April 29 payroll of the House of Sound are illustrated here.

**PAYROLL JOURNAL** ... Page 17																

For the Week Beginning _April 21,_ **19 —** **and Ending** _April 25,_ **19 —** **Paid** _April 29,_ **19 —**

EMPLOYEE DATA					EARNINGS			DEDUCTIONS						NET PAY		
NO.	NAME	MARITAL STATUS	EXEMP.	HOURS	REGULAR	OVERTIME	SALARIES EXPENSE	FEDERAL INCOME TAXES PAYABLE	STATE INCOME TAXES PAYABLE	FICA TAXES PAYABLE	INSURANCE PREMIUMS PAYABLE	UNION DUES PAYABLE	TOTAL	SALARIES PAYABLE	CK. NO.
1	S. Brouse	M	3	44	240 00	36 00	276 00	28 60	8 28	18 49	5 00	4 00	64 37	211 63	188
	Totals				1,210 00	51 00	1,261 00	160 00	37 83	84 49	30 00	24 00	336 32	924 68	
							(517)	(221)	(223)	(222)	(227)	(228)		(226)	

Record payroll.

GENERAL JOURNAL

DATE		ACCOUNT TITLE AND EXPLANATION	POST. REF.	DEBIT	CREDIT
19—					
Apr.	29	Payroll Taxes Expense	516	127 37	
		FICA Taxes Payable	222		84 49
		Federal Unemployment Taxes Payable	224		8 83
		State Unemployment Taxes Payable . .	225		34 05
		Record payroll taxes.			

Record employer's payroll taxes.

CASH PAYMENTS JOURNAL

DATE		ACCOUNT DEBITED	EXPLANATION	CHECK NO.	POST. REF.	GENERAL LEDGER DEBIT	ACCOUNTS PAYABLE DEBIT	PURCHASES DISCOUNT CREDIT	NET CASH CREDIT
19—									
Apr.	29	Salaries Payable . .	April 28 payroll . . .	188–193	226	924 68			924 68

Pay payroll.

Cash — Account No. 101

DATE	EXPLANATION	POST. REF.	DEBIT	CREDIT	BALANCE DEBIT	BALANCE CREDIT
19—						
Apr. 29		CP17		924 68	3,786 80	

Amount of cash paid to employees.

Federal Unemployment Taxes Payable — Account No. 224

DATE	EXPLANATION	POST. REF.	DEBIT	CREDIT	BALANCE DEBIT	BALANCE CREDIT
19—						
Apr. 29		J17		8 83		35 08

Amount owed to federal government.

Federal Income Taxes Payable — Account No. 221

DATE	EXPLANATION	POST. REF.	DEBIT	CREDIT	BALANCE DEBIT	BALANCE CREDIT
19—						
Apr. 29		PJ17		160 00		650 00

Amount owed to federal government.

State Unemployment Taxes Payable — Account No. 225

DATE	EXPLANATION	POST. REF.	DEBIT	CREDIT	BALANCE DEBIT	BALANCE CREDIT
19—						
Apr. 29		J17		34 05		135 30

Amount owed to state government.

FICA Taxes Payable — Account No. 222

DATE	EXPLANATION	POST. REF.	DEBIT	CREDIT	BALANCE DEBIT	BALANCE CREDIT
19—						
Apr. 29		PR17		84 49		537 68
29		J17		84 49		622 17

Amount owed to federal government.

Salaries Payable — Account No. 226

DATE	EXPLANATION	POST. REF.	DEBIT	CREDIT	BALANCE DEBIT	BALANCE CREDIT
19—						
Apr. 29		PJ17		924 68		924 68
29		CP17	924 68			— 00

Amount owed to employees.

State Income Taxes Payable — Account No. 223

DATE	EXPLANATION	POST. REF.	DEBIT	CREDIT	BALANCE DEBIT	BALANCE CREDIT
19—						
Apr. 29		PR17		37 83		150 33

Amount owed to state government.

Insurance Premiums Payable — Account No. 227

DATE	EXPLANATION	POST. REF.	DEBIT	CREDIT	BALANCE DEBIT	BALANCE CREDIT
19—						
Apr. 29		PJ17		30 00		120 00

Amount owed to insurance company.

Union Dues Payable					Account No. 228	
DATE	EXPLANATION	POST. REF.	DEBIT	CREDIT	BALANCE DEBIT	BALANCE CREDIT
19— Apr. 29		PJ17		24 00		144 00

Amount owed to union.

Payroll Taxes Expense					Account No. 516	
DATE	EXPLANATION	POST. REF.	DEBIT	CREDIT	BALANCE DEBIT	BALANCE CREDIT
19— Apr. 29		J17	127 37	1,018 96		

Amount of expense for payroll taxes.

Salaries Expense					Account No. 517	
DATE	EXPLANATION	POST. REF.	DEBIT	CREDIT	BALANCE DEBIT	BALANCE CREDIT
19— Apr. 29		J17	1,261 00		5,011 00	

Amount of expense for salaries.

Activity B. Answer the following questions about summarizing transactions for payroll. Make whatever entries are necessary to complete the payment of the payroll. Refer to the text and illustrations on pages 442 to 444.

1. In which journal is the payroll recorded?
2. In which journal is the entry to record the employer's payroll taxes recorded?
3. How many checks are necessary to pay the payroll?

Topic 3 Problem

15-6. Refer to the payroll journal completed in Topic 2, Activity B and the general ledger accounts completed in Topic Problem 15-4.
a. Record the payment of the payroll. The next available check is 78.

b. Make whatever entries you feel are necessary in the payroll journal and employee earnings record.

Topic 4
Preparing Payroll Tax Returns

Control: Submit tax returns promptly.

A *What is the employer's responsibility for payroll taxes?* Payroll tax returns must be prepared promptly. These payroll tax returns must be submitted on time. The federal and state governments have time schedules for all employers to report and pay payroll taxes. The time schedules are based on the calendar year. What this means is that a business must use the calendar year for payroll tax purposes.

Paying Federal Taxes

The federal income taxes and the employees' and employer's share of the FICA taxes must be paid to the Internal Revenue Service. The employer pays the taxes by depositing the amount in a Federal Reserve bank. Or the employer may deposit the taxes in an approved commercial bank.

Federal Tax Deposit (Form 501). Form 501 is a tax form used to deposit federal income taxes and FICA taxes. The due dates for depositing the federal income taxes and the FICA taxes depend on the amount of the undeposited taxes.

SCHEDULE OF DEPOSITS FOR FEDERAL INCOME TAX WITHHOLDING AND FICA TAXES

Effective Date	Amount	Deposit Due	Example
7th, 15th, 22nd, or last day of any month	$2,000 or more	Within 3 banking days after effective date.	Undeposited taxes on April 22 are $2,100. Must deposit within 3 banking days after April 22.
Last day of first or second month of a quarter (Jan., Feb., Apr., May, July, Aug., Oct., Nov.)	$200 or more but less than $2,000	Within 15 days after end of month.	Undeposited taxes on February 28 are $300. Must deposit by March 15.
	Less than $200	Hold till end of quarter. Then follow dates below.	Undeposited taxes on February 28 are $170. Hold until March 31. Rule below then shows April 30.
Last day of third month of a quarter (Mar., June, Sept., Dec.)	$200 or more but less than $2,000	By the last day of next month.	Undeposited taxes on June 30 are $225. Must deposit by July 31.
	Less than $200	May make deposit by last day of next month, or may file with quarterly tax return (Form 941).	Undeposited taxes on March 31 are $170. May either deposit or pay with tax return by April 30.

The undeposited taxes for the House of Sound on April 30 are $1,272.17, as shown in the table in the margin. (The calendar quarter is April, May, and June.) The quarter ends on June 30. The undeposited amount is more than $200 but less than $2,000 for the first month of the quarter. Thus the taxes must be deposited by May 15. The deposit must include a Federal Tax Deposit (Form 501). A Form 501 is illustrated here.

UNDEPOSITED PAYROLL TAXES ON APRIL 30

Employees': Federal Income Taxes	$ 650.00
FICA Taxes	311.09
Employer's: FICA Taxes	311.08
Total	$1,272.17

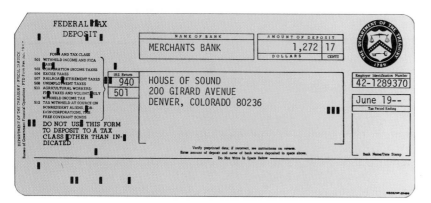

Form 501 showing deposit of taxes on April payrolls. (Note that this tax deposit form can be used to deposit other types of taxes.)

On May 5, $1,272.17 was deposited in the Merchants Bank, which is a commercial bank qualified as a depository for federal taxes. The entry to journalize the check includes debits to the liability accounts because the liabilities are decreased. The Federal Income Taxes Payable account is debited for the amount of income taxes withheld ($650). The FICA Taxes Payable account is debited for $622.17. This is the total of the employees' FICA taxes withheld ($311.09) and the employer's FICA tax ($311.08). The Cash account is credited for $1,272.17.

Entry for May 5 deposit of income taxes withheld and FICA taxes for April.

CASH PAYMENTS JOURNAL

Page 18

DATE	ACCOUNT DEBITED	EXPLANATION	CHECK NO.	POST. REF.	GENERAL LEDGER DEBIT	ACCOUNTS PAYABLE DEBIT	PURCHASES DISCOUNT CREDIT	NET CASH CREDIT
19—								
May 5	Fed. Inc. Taxes Pay.	Deposit for April ..	217	221	650 00			1,272 17
	FICA Taxes Payable			222	622 17			— 00

Cash	101		Federal Income Taxes Payable	221		FICA Taxes Payable	222
19—		19—	19—		19—	19—	
May 5	1,272.17	May 5	650.00	Apr. 30	650.00	May 5	622.17	Apr. 30	622.17

Employer's Quarterly Federal Tax Return (Form 941). The employer must file an Employer's Quarterly Federal Tax Return (Form 941) with the Internal Revenue Service. The **Form 941** return shows the total federal income tax withheld and the total FICA taxes (employees' and employer's share) for the quarter. The Form 941 must be filed by the last day of the month following the end of the calendar quarter. The amounts of the Federal Tax Deposits (Form 501) are shown on the record of federal tax deposits of Form 941.

Activity A-1. Answer the following questions about preparing payroll tax returns. Refer to the Form 501 on page 445 and the journal above.
1. Which form is sent along with the deposit for federal income taxes withheld and FICA taxes?
2. How much is the total deposit?
3. The total balances of what ledger accounts equal the amount of the deposit?
4. What is the employer identification number of the House of Sound?

5. What journal entry is made to record the deposit?
6. The deposit covers income taxes for what period of time?

Activity A-2. Answer the following questions about the Form 941. Refer to the text, margin notes, and illustrations on pages 444 to 446.
1. What form does the House of Sound file to give information about all the federal income taxes withheld and FICA taxes for the quarter?

Form **941** (Rev. April 19--) Department of the Treasury Internal Revenue Service		**Employer's Quarterly Federal Tax Return**				

Form 941
(Rev. April 19--)
Department of the Treasury
Internal Revenue Service

Employer's Quarterly Federal Tax Return

Your name, address, employer identification number, and calendar quarter of return. (If not correct, please change)

			T	
			FF	
Name (as distinguished from trade name)	Date quarter ended		FD	
MARCY CASEY	JUNE 30, 19--		FP	
Trade name, if any	Employer identification number		I	
HOUSE OF SOUND	42-1289370		T	
Address and ZIP code				
200 GIRARD AVENUE, DENVER, COLORADO 80236				

If address is different from prior return, check here ▶ ☐

1 Number of employees (except household) employed in the pay period that includes March 12th (complete for first quarter only)		6	
2 Total wages and tips subject to withholding, plus other compensation . . . . ▶		15,800	00
3 Total income tax withheld from wages, tips, annuities, gambling, etc.		2,100	00
4 Adjustment of withheld income tax for preceding quarters of calendar year			
5 Adjusted total of income tax withheld . . . . ▶		2,100	00
6 Taxable FICA wages paid . . . . $ 15,800.00 . . . . . multiplied by 13.40%=TAX .		2,117	20
7 Taxable tips reported . . . . $ . . . . multiplied by 6.70%=TAX .			
8 Total FICA taxes (add lines 6 and 7) . . . . ▶		2,117	20
9 Adjustment of FICA taxes (see instructions)			
10 Adjusted total of FICA taxes . . . . ▶		2,117	20
11 Total taxes (add lines 5 and 10)		4,217	20
12 Advance earned income credit (EIC) payments, if any (see instructions)			
13 Net taxes (subtract line 12 from line 11)		4,217	20

Record of Federal Tax Deposits (See instructions on page 4)

Deposit period ending:		I. Tax liability for period	II. Date of deposit	III. Amount deposited
	Overpayment from previous quarter			
First month of quarter	1st through 7th day	1,272.17	May 5, 19--	1,272.17
	8th through 15th day			
	16th through 22d day			
	23d through last day			
	A First month total . . . . A	1,272.17		1,272.17
Second month of quarter	1st through 7th day	1,550.50	June 6, 19--	1,550.50
	8th through 15th day			
	16th through 22d day			
	23d through last day			
	B Second month total . . . . B	1,550.50		1,550.50
Third month of quarter	1st through 7th day	1,394.53	July 5, 19--	1,394.53
	8th through 15th day			
	16th through 22d day			
	23d through last day			
	C Third month total C	1,394.53		1,394.53
	D Total for quarter (add items A, B, and C) .	4,217.20		4,217.20
	E Final deposit made for quarter. (Enter zero if the final deposit made for the quarter is included in item D) . . .			-0-

14 Total deposits for quarter (including final deposit made for quarter) and overpayment from previous quarter. (See instructions for deposit requirements on page 4.)		4,217	20
Note: If undeposited taxes at the end of the quarter are $200 or more, deposit the full amount with an authorized financial institution or a Federal Reserve bank according to the instructions on the back of the Federal Tax Deposit Form 501. Enter this deposit in the Record of Federal Tax Deposits and include it on line 14.			
15 Undeposited taxes due (subtract line 14 from line 13—this should be less than $200). Pay to Internal Revenue Service and enter here . . . . ▶		-0-	
16 If line 14 is more than line 13, enter overpayment here ▶ $ and check if to be: ☐ Applied to next return, or ☐ Refunded.			
17 Number of Forms W-4 enclosed. Do not send originals. (See General and Specific Instructions.) . . . ▶			
18 If you are not liable for returns in the future, write "FINAL" (see instructions) ▶ Date final wages paid ▶			

Under penalties of perjury, I declare that I have examined this return, including accompanying schedules and statements, and to the best of my knowledge and belief it is true, correct, and complete.

Date ▶ July 17, 19-- Signature ▶ *Marcy Casey* Title ▶ Owner

Please file this form with your Internal Revenue Service Center (see instructions on "Where to File"). Form **941** (Rev. 4----)

Form 941 reporting income taxes withheld and FICA taxes for calendar quarter ending June 30. Quarter covers the April, May, and June payrolls.

If employer owes less than $200 at the end of the quarter, amount may be sent with Form 941.

2. What are the total taxable wages paid from April 1 to June 30?

3. How much is withheld from employees during the quarter for federal income tax?

4. How much is the total FICA tax for the 3 months? How much is withheld from the employees? How much does the employer have to pay?

5. How many employees does the House of Sound have?

6. What is the total deposit for the April payroll taxes? The May payroll taxes? The June payroll taxes? The payroll taxes for the quarter? Where does this information come from?

7. Why is the balance of taxes due zero for the quarter?

8. What journal entry is made when Form 941 is filed? Why?

Preparing Wage and Tax Statements

Form W-2 due by January 31 to employees or within 30 days if employee leaves.

B *How are employees informed of yearly earnings?* By January 31, the employer is required to give each employee a Wage and Tax Statement (Form W-2). If an employee leaves the job, the employer must give the employee the Form W-2 within 30 days after the last payday. The **Form W-2** is a federal tax form which shows the following for the previous year.

- Federal income tax information, including the amount of the federal income tax withheld from the employee and the total amount of the employee's earnings.
- Social security information, including the FICA tax withheld from the employee's earnings and the total amount of the employee's earnings subject to FICA taxes.
- State or local income tax information, including information regarding the wages paid and tax withheld for state or local taxes.

The information for the Form W-2 (below) is obtained from the employee earnings records. The Yearly Totals section on the employee earnings record for Sonia Brouse provided the information reported on the Form W-2 prepared by the House of Sound.

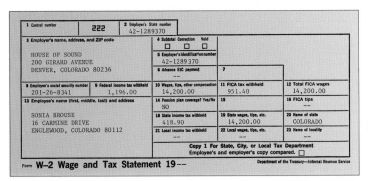

Form W-2 showing data obtained from employee earnings record.

EMPLOYEE EARNINGS RECORD FOR YEAR 19—

Name _Sonia Brouse_

Address _16 Carmine Drive_
Englewood, Colorado 80112

Telephone No. _277-8346_
Date of Birth _June 14, 1959_
Rate _$6.00 per Hour_

Employee No. _1_
Social Security No. _201-26-8341_
Marital Status _Married_
Withholding Exemptions _3_
Position _Accounting Department_
Date Employed _January 2, 19—_

DATE			EARNINGS			DEDUCTIONS						NET PAY	YEAR-TO-DATE EARNINGS
PERIOD ENDING	PAID	HOURS	REGULAR	OVERTIME	TOTAL	FEDERAL INCOME TAX	STATE INCOME TAX	FICA TAX	INSURANCE PREMIUMS	UNION DUES	TOTAL		
12/29	12/30	40	240 00		240 00	23 00	7 20	15 96	5 00	4 00	53 91	186 09	14,200 00
Totals			12,480 00	1,720 00	14,200 00	1,196 00	418 90	951 40	260 00	208 00	3,034 30	11,165 70	14,200 00

At least six copies of each Form W-2 are prepared. Three copies are given to the employee. (One is sent with the employee's federal income tax return. The second one is sent with the state income tax return. The third is for the employee's file.) Another copy is for the employer's records. The employer sends a fifth copy to the federal government along with a Form W-3, described next. (A sixth copy is sent to the state government.)

Transmittal of Income Tax Statements (Form W-3). The employer must file a Transmittal of Income and Tax Statements **(Form W-3)** with the Internal Revenue Service by February 28 of each year. A copy of each employee's Wage and Tax Statement (Form W-2) is sent with the yearly Form W-3. No payment is made with this return because the deposits have been made and reported on the quarterly Form 941s. The House of Sound filed the Form W-3 shown here at the end of the year.

Form W-3 due by February 28.

1 Control number	33333				
☐	Kind of Tax Statements Transmitted ▷	2 941/941E ☐ CT–1 ☐	Military ☐ 942 ☐	943 ☐ Section 218 ☐	3 W–2 ☒ W–2P ☐	4 Original ☒ Corrected ☐	5 With TIN ☒ Without TIN ☐

6 State SSA number 42-1289370	7 Advance EIC payments –0–	8 Number of statements attached 6
9 Federal income tax 7,200.00	10 Wages, tips, and other compensation 86,134.00	11 FICA tax withheld 5,770.98
12 Employer's State number	13 FICA wages 86,134.00	14 FICA tips –0–
15 Employer's identification number 42-1289370		16 Establishment number 746-D31
17 Employer's name MARCY CASEY		18 Gross annuity, pension, retired pay, or IRA payment –0–
HOUSE OF SOUND 200 GIRARD AVENUE DENVER, COLORADO 80236		20 Taxable amount 86,134.00
19 Employer's address and ZIP code		

Under penalties of perjury, I declare that I have examined this return, including accompanying documents, and to the best of my knowledge and belief, it is true, correct, and complete. In the case of documents without recipients' identifying numbers, I have complied with the requirements of the law by requesting such numbers from the recipients, but did not receive them.

Signature ▶ *Marcy Casey* Title ▶ Owner Date ▶ 1/29/–-

Form **W-3** Transmittal of Income and Tax Statements **19--** Department of the Treasury Internal Revenue Service

Form W-3, showing amount of income tax withheld during year, must be filed on or before February 28 of the following year.

Activity B. Answer the following questions about the tax returns. Refer to the text, margin notes, and illustrations on pages 448 and 449.

1. Which form does the House of Sound give to Sonia Brouse?

2. How many copies of Form W-2 are prepared, and who gets them?

3. What are Sonia Brouse's total wages for the year? What are her total FICA taxable wages for the year? Are these amounts the same? When would the amounts be different?

4. How much is withheld from Sonia Brouse's earnings during the year for federal income taxes? For FICA taxes?

5. Which journal entry is made when the Form W-2 was filed? Why?

6. Which form does the House of Sound send to the Internal Revenue Service with the Form W-2s?

7. How many Form W-2s does the House of Sound send to the Internal Revenue Service?

8. When must employers give Form W-2 to current employees? To former employees?

Paying Unemployment Compensation Taxes

C *When are unemployment compensation taxes paid?* The state unemployment compensation tax is paid quarterly. The date for paying the federal unemployment compensation tax depends on the amount of tax to be paid.

State Unemployment Compensation Taxes. The form for the state unemployment compensation taxes return varies with the state. Usually the form asks for the names of the employees and their taxable earnings during the quarter.

The employer's payroll taxes are recorded when the payroll is paid. On June 30 the State Unemployment Taxes Payable account for the House of Sound has a balance of $340.50. This amount is 2.7 percent of the taxable salaries and wages paid during the quarter ($12,611). The quarter covers the months of April, May, and June.

During the quarter, the employees of the House of Sound had gross earnings of $15,800. However, all employees passed the $6,000 maximum gross earnings for these taxes. Thus the taxable earnings are less than the gross earnings.

A payment of $340.50 was sent for the state unemployment tax on July 17. The liability account State Unemployment Taxes Payable is debited because the liability is decreased. The asset account Cash is credited because the asset is decreased.

State Unemployment	
Taxes Payable **225**	
	340.50

Balance of account on June 30 is amount due for quarter.

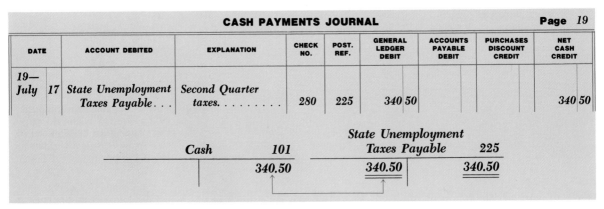

CASH PAYMENTS JOURNAL — Page 19

DATE	ACCOUNT DEBITED	EXPLANATION	CHECK NO.	POST. REF.	GENERAL LEDGER DEBIT	ACCOUNTS PAYABLE DEBIT	PURCHASES DISCOUNT CREDIT	NET CASH CREDIT
19— July 17	*State Unemployment Taxes Payable*...	*Second Quarter taxes*.........	280	225	340 50			340 50

Cash 101	*State Unemployment Taxes Payable* 225
340.50	*340.50* | *340.50*

Entry for second quarter's state unemployment taxes deposited on July 17.

Federal Unemployment Compensation Taxes. Federal unemployment compensation taxes must be paid if the amount owed is more than $100 for any quarter. The amount must be deposited by the last day of the month following the quarter. The deposit must be made in a federal depository bank. A Federal Tax Deposit **(Form 508)** must be sent with each deposit.

Amounts of $100 or less do not have to be deposited until the quarter when the tax owed exceeds $100. The table here lists the schedule of deposits for federal unemployment taxes.

SCHEDULE OF DEPOSITS FOR FEDERAL UNEMPLOYMENT TAXES

Amount	Effective Day	Deposit Due
More than $100	Last day of quarter	Last day of following month
More than $100	Last day of year	January 31
Less than $100	Last day of quarter	Quarter when tax exceeds $100
Less than $100	Last day of year	January 31 or pay with Form 940

During the first quarter, the House of Sound paid taxable salaries and wages of $22,300. None of the employees passed the maximum gross earnings during the quarter. Thus all salaries and wages paid were subject to the federal unemployment compensation tax of 0.7 percent. The House of Sound owed $156.10 ($22,300 × 0.007) for the first quarter. This exceeded $100, and the tax must be deposited.

The deposit is made in a federal depository bank. The balance of the Federal Unemployment Taxes Payable account on March 31 shows the amount to be deposited.

Because the amount of taxes owed in the first quarter exceeds $100, the federal unemployment compensation taxes must be deposited in April, the first month following the quarter. A Federal Tax Deposit (Form 508) must accompany the deposit.

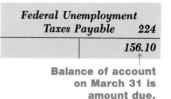

Federal Unemployment Taxes Payable	224
	156.10

Balance of account on March 31 is amount due.

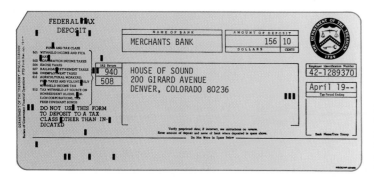

Form 508 showing deposit of federal unemployment compensation taxes for second quarter. (Note that this tax deposit form was also used to deposit payroll taxes.)

The payment is recorded in the cash payments journal. The liability account Federal Unemployment Taxes Payable is debited because the liability is decreased. The asset account Cash is credited because the asset is decreased. The entry to record the deposit of federal unemployment compensation taxes on April 19 is presented on page 452.

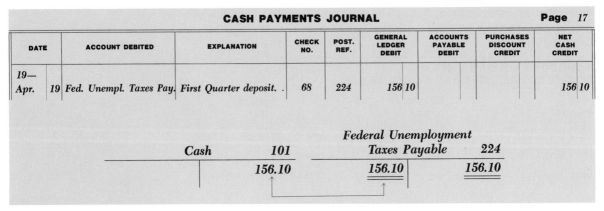

CASH PAYMENTS JOURNAL

Page 17

DATE		ACCOUNT DEBITED	EXPLANATION	CHECK NO.	POST. REF.	GENERAL LEDGER DEBIT	ACCOUNTS PAYABLE DEBIT	PURCHASES DISCOUNT CREDIT	NET CASH CREDIT
19— Apr.	19	Fed. Unempl. Taxes Pay.	First Quarter deposit. .	68	224	156 10			156 10

Cash   101

156.10

Federal Unemployment Taxes Payable   224

156.10   156.10

Entry for federal unemployment taxes deposited on April 19.

By January 31, an employer of four or more employees covered by unemployment compensation must file an Employer's Annual Federal Unemployment Tax Return **(Form 940).** (See the illustration on page 453.) At the same time, the employer must deposit or pay the balance of the tax for the year.

Activity C. Record the entries for depositing the taxes listed in the next column for the first quarter. Refer to the text, margin notes, and illustrations on pages 450 to 452.

April 7 Deposited state unemployment compensation taxes of $567 (Check 451).

7 Deposited federal unemployment compensation taxes of $105 (Check 452).

Topic 4 Problems

15-7. Prepare a Form 941 for Exeter Products Company for the fourth quarter. Prepare the form on January 10 for Gordon Du Clare, the owner. (Do not sign the form.) There are no taxable tips. The additional data needed to prepare the form is given here. (**NOTE:** You must complete the Taxable FICA Wages for Quarter column.)
The Federal Employee Income Taxes Payable account

shows that the total federal income taxes withheld from earnings for the quarter ended December 31 were $3,959.80.

Federal tax deposits were made as follows: October, $1,428.45; November, $2,189.90; December, $3,317.59. Complete the taxable FICA wages for the quarters here.

Employee	Social Security Number	Year-to-Date Earnings (Dec. 31, 19—)	Total Wages Paid During Quarter	Taxable FICA Wages for Quarter
Bettie Ellis	201-35-4461	$30,200	$6,800	?
Michael Hennings	246-78-2311	16,800	4,230	?
Joanne Herring	997-87-9531	26,000	7,000	?
Shirley Mitchell	548-74-3857	19,920	4,680	?

15-8. The credit balances on several dates are shown here for the FICA Taxes Payable account, the Federal

Employee Income Taxes Payable account, and the Federal Unemployment Taxes Payable account.

Form **940**
Department of the Treasury
Internal Revenue Service

Employer's Annual Federal Unemployment Tax Return

19--

			T	
			FF	
			FD	
			FP	
			I	
			T	

If incorrect, make any necessary change. ▶

Name (as distinguished from trade name)
MARCY CASEY

Calendar Year
19--

Trade name, if any
HOUSE OF SOUND

Employer identification number
42-1289370

Address and ZIP code
200 GIRARD AVENUE, DENVER, COLORADO 80236

A Did you pay all required contributions to your State unemployment fund by the due date of Form 940? . . . . . . ☒ Yes ☐ No
If you check the "Yes" box, enter amount of contributions timely paid to your State unemployment fund . . . ▶ $ 972 | 00
B Are you required to pay contributions to only one State? . . . . ☐ Yes ☒ No
If you checked the "Yes" box, (1) Enter the name of the State where you are required to pay contributions . . . ▶ Colorado
(2) Enter your State reporting number as shown on State unemployment tax return . . . . ▶

Part I Computation of Taxable Wages and Credit Reduction (To Be Completed by All Taxpayers)		
1 Total payments (including exempt payments) during the calendar year for services of employees		36,000 | 00
2 Exempt payments. (Explain each exemption shown, attaching additional sheets if necessary) ▶	Amount paid	
3 Payments for services in excess of $6,000. Enter only the excess over the first $6,000 paid to individual employees exclusive of exempt amounts entered on line 2. Do not use State wage limitation		
4 Total exempt payments (add lines 2 and 3)		
5 Total taxable wages (subtract line 4 from line 1). (If any portion is exempt from State contributions, see instructions). . ▶		36,000 | 00

6 State wages included on line 5, Part I

(a) CT..........× .007
(b) DE..........× .006
(c) DC..........× .006
(d) IL..........× .003
(e) ME..........× .003
(f) NJ..........× .003
(g) PA..........× .006
(h) PR..........× .003
(i) RI..........× .006
(j) VT..........× .006
(k) VI..........× .003

7 Add lines 6(a) through 6(k). (Enter total on line 2, Part II or line 4, Part III, as appropriate) . . . . ▶

Part II Tax Due or Refund (Complete if You Checked the "Yes" boxes in Both Items A and B Above)	
1 FUTA tax. Multiply the wages on line 5, Part I, by .007 and enter here	252 | 00
2 Credit reduction. Enter amount from line 7, Part I	
3 Total FUTA tax (add lines 1 and 2)	
4 Less: Total FUTA tax deposited from line 5, Part IV	252 | 00
5 Balance due (subtract line 4 from line 3—if over $100, see Part IV instructions). Pay to IRS . . . . . ▶	252 | 00
6 Overpayment (subtract line 3 from line 4) . . . . ▶	

Part III Tax Due or Refund (Complete if You Checked the "No" Box in Either Item A or Item B Above)		
1 Gross FUTA tax. Multiply the wages on line 5, Part I, by .034		1,224 | 00
2 Maximum credit. Multiply the wages on line 5, Part I, by .027	972 | 00	
3 Enter the smaller of the amount on line 11, Part V, or line 2, Part III . . .	252 | 00	
4 Credit reductions. Enter amount from line 7, Part I		972 | 00
5 Credit allowable (subtract line 4 from line 3)		252 | 00
6 Net FUTA tax (subtract line 5 from line 1)		252 | 00
7 Less: Total FUTA tax deposited from line 5, Part IV		
8 Balance due (subtract line 7 from line 6—if over $100, see Part IV instructions). Pay to IRS . . . . . ▶		
9 Overpayment (subtract line 6 from line 7) . . . . ▶		

Part IV Record of Federal Tax Deposits for Unemployment Tax (Form 508) (Do not include contributions paid to State)

	a. Quarter	b. Liability for quarter	c. Date of deposit	d. Amount of deposit
1	First	156.10	April 19, 19--	156 | 10
2	Second	95.90	July 17, 19--	95 | 90
3	Third			
4	Fourth			
5 Total FUTA tax deposited (add column d, lines 1 through 4) . . . . ▶				

If you will not have to file returns in the future, write "Final" here (see general instruction "Who Must File") . . ▶

Under penalties of perjury, I declare that I have examined this return, including accompanying schedules and statements, and to the best of my knowledge and belief, it is true, correct, and complete, and that no part of any payment made to a State unemployment fund claimed as a credit was or is to be deducted from the payments to employees.

Date ▶ January 17, 19-- Signature ▶ *Marcy Casey* Title (Owner, etc.) ▶ Owner

Form 940 reporting amount of federal unemployment taxes withheld during the year.

---

a. For each date, determine the amount that must be deposited for the FICA taxes and income taxes and for the federal unemployment compensation taxes.

b. Determine the deadlines for making the deposits.
c. Tell which forms must be included with the deposits.

	FICA Taxes Payable	Employee Income Taxes Payable	Federal Unemployment Taxes Payable
Feb. 28	$ 832.00	$ 560.00	$ 80
Mar. 31	1,040.00	700.00	130
Apr. 7	1,560.00	1,550.00	75
July 31	41.60	145.60	8
Dec. 31	104.00	38.40	30

15-9. Part of the June 30 trial balance for Rios Enterprises is given here.

ACCOUNT TITLE	ACCT. NO.	DEBIT	CREDIT
Federal Employee Income Taxes Pay. .	221		789 00
FICA Taxes Pay.	222		813 56
Federal Unemployment Taxes Pay. . . .	223		120 00
Group Insurance Pay.	224		19 20
State Unemployment Taxes Pay.	225		648 00
Union Dues Pay.	226		48 00

Rios Enterprises
Trial Balance
June 30, 19—

a. Compute the amount to be deposited in a federal depository for the employee income taxes and the FICA taxes for the month of June.
b. Record the entry to journalize Check 181, which was drawn on July 5 to make the federal employee income taxes and FICA withholding deposit.
c. Record the entry to journalize Check 182 drawn on July 5 to remit the amount of the state unemployment compensation taxes.
d. Record the entry to journalize Check 183 drawn on July 5 to remit the amount of the federal unemployment compensation taxes.
e. Record the entry to journalize Check 184 drawn on July 5 to remit the amount of the insurance premiums to the Shield Insurance Company.
f. Record the entry to journalize Check 185 drawn on July 5 to remit the amount of the union dues to the United Union Local 18.

15-10. The payroll journal for the March 29 payroll of the Career Planning Institute shows the following totals: salaries expense, $2,500; withheld for federal income taxes, $350; withheld for FICA taxes, $167.50; withheld for group insurance premiums, $20; withheld for union dues, $40. No maximum for FICA, FUTA, or SUTA has been reached by any employee.
a. Post the payroll journal.
b. Record and post the following transactions.

March 29 Record the employer's payroll taxes: FICA taxes (6.7 percent), federal unemployment compensation taxes (0.7 percent), and state unemployment compensation taxes (2.7 percent).
29 Post the employer's payroll taxes.
31 Record payment of March 29 payroll (Checks 323–326).
April 1 Deposited federal income taxes withheld and FICA taxes for the month of March (Check 354). Obtain amounts from the general ledger.
12 Deposited federal unemployment compensation taxes for the first quarter (Check 355).
12 Deposited state unemployment compensation taxes for the first quarter (Check 356).
12 Remitted group insurance premiums for the month of March (Check 357).
12 Remitted union dues for the month of March (Check 358).

The Language of Business

Here are some terms that make up the Language of Business. Do you know the meaning of each?

personnel and payroll subsystem
contract of employment
net pay
payroll journal
employee earnings record
Form 501
Form 941
Form W-2
Form W-3
Form 508
Form 940

Chapter 15 Questions

1. What activities are completed in a personnel and payroll subsystem?

2. How does the personnel department relate to the payroll department?

3. How does the payroll department relate to the accounting department?

4. What information is contained in the employee earnings records? How can the employee earnings records be used as a subsidiary ledger?

5. What data is needed to determine the amount of federal income tax to be withheld from an employee's gross earnings?

6. What is the purpose of the entries to record and pay the payroll? The entries to record and pay the payroll taxes?

7. Contrast the use of a payroll journal (discussed in Chapter 15) and a payroll register (discussed in Chapter 9).

Chapter 15   Problems

Problems for Chapter 15 are given in the *Working Papers and Chapter Problems for Part 2.* If you are using the workbook, do the problems in the space provided there.

Chapter 15   Management Cases

Fringe Benefits. Fringe benefits are benefits received by employees *in addition to their wages.* The kind and amount of fringe benefits received are often the subject of much discussion between employees and employers.

Case 15M-1. Using a business in your community that is willing to cooperate with you, obtain a description of their "fringe benefit package."

a. Describe the kinds of fringe benefits offered to employees.

b. Determine the cost to employers of the fringe benefits.

c. Make a decision whether it is better for the employees to receive both wages and fringe benefits or to receive additional wages equal to the cost of the fringe benefits.

d. Discuss whether it matters to employers whether they pay both wages and offer fringe benefits or just offer additional wages (in place of fringe benefits) to employees.

e. Discuss whether older employees would agree with your decision in c above.

Case 15M-2. Jay's Brite Wash charges $3 to wash a car. The business washed 20,000 cars last year. The income statement for the business is shown in the next column.

In analyzing the costs, the accountant found that current labor costs are 60 percent of the selling price of each car wash. The employees have now asked for a wage increase that would total $5,000 a year. A com-

Jay's Brite Wash Income Statement For the Year Ended December 31, 19—		
Revenue:		
Sales		60,000 00
Expenses:		
Salaries	36,000 00	
Other Expenses	15,000 00	
Total Expenses		51,000 00
Net Income		9,000 00

mittee representing management and labor reviewed the request. They decided that in order to grant the wage increase, one of the following actions must be taken: (1) increase the selling price of a car wash, or (2) increase the number of cars that are washed without increasing the number of employees.

a. If the same number of car washes are sold, what increase in the selling price is necessary to absorb the wage increase? What would be the new selling price?

b. If the selling price of a car wash is increased, what would be the percent of increase?

c. At one time, the government requested businesses not to increase their prices by more than 7 percent. This was an attempt to curb inflation. Do you think that the management of Jay's Brite Wash should simply refuse the wage increase because it exceeds 7 percent?

d. How many more car washes must be sold each year if the selling price is not raised, the labor force remains the same, and the other expenses and net income remain at $24,000 ($15,000 for other expenses and $9,000 for net income)?

Working Hint

Schedule of Employer's Duties for Payroll Taxes. Once the employee is hired, the employer is responsible for filing the correct tax forms for the employee and collecting the correct amount of taxes from the employee's paycheck each pay period. To keep track of all the due dates and taxes due, an employer should prepare a chart like the one below.

	Type of Payroll Tax				
Due Date	**Fed. Inc. Tax Withhold.**	**FICA Tax**	**Fed. Unempl. Comp. Tax**	**State Unempl. Comp. Tax**	**Employer's Duties**
Upon hiring an employee	X				Have employee fill out Form W-4.
		X			Record employee's account number and name from social security card.
On each payment of wages to an employee	X				Withhold correct tax according to employee's Form W-4 and current rate.
		X			Withhold correct tax according to current rate.
On the fifteenth of each month	X	X			Deposit tax due.
By April 30, July 31, October 31, and January 31	X	X			Deposit taxes due. File Form 941.
			X		Deposit taxes due. Deposit full amount by January 31.
Quarterly (date depends on state)				X	File state unemployment tax return. Deposit taxes due.
Before December 1 of each year	X				Request new Form W-4 from each employee whose withholding exemptions will change from previous year.

Chapter 16

A General Accounting Subsystem

Cash receipts, cash payments, purchases, sales, and personnel and payroll are known as *special subsystems* because special information is processed in each. You will now learn how the *general accounting subsystem* is used to process general ledger information in order to update the accounts and prepare financial reports.

Topic 1
Controlling Internal Transactions

A *What are the special and general accounting subsystems?* The cash receipts, cash payments, purchases, sales, and personnel and payroll subsystems are the special subsystems. The **general accounting subsystem** is used to process general ledger information in order to update the accounts and prepare financial reports. The steps in the accounting cycle are listed in the margin. The first three steps—originate data, journalize transactions, and post transactions—are completed as part of the work in the five special accounting subsystems. These steps are summarized in the illustration on page 459. Steps 4 through 8 in the accounting cycle are completed in the general accounting subsystem.

Steps in Accounting Cycle
1. Originate data
2. Journalize transactions
3. Post transactions
4. Prove ledgers and prepare worksheet
5. Prepare financial statements
6. Make closing entries
7. Prepare postclosing trial balance
8. Interpret financial information

Procedures for Controlling Internal Transactions

Internal transactions are those completed by a business within the accounting cycle. The majority of the procedures to control internal transactions were studied as part of the cash receipts, cash payments, purchases, sales, and personnel and payroll subsystems. Each control was designed to ensure accuracy, honesty, and efficiency and speed in handling and recording assets, liabilities, owner's equity, revenues, and expenses. Likewise, there must be procedures to control the activities within the general accounting subsystem.

Control: Prove the equality of debits and credits in the ledger.

Control: Prove the agreement of accounting records and actual amounts.

Control: Properly match revenue and expenses.

Control: Use proper cutoff date.

Control: Accurately report the results of operations.

Control: Accurately report financial position.

Control: Separate revenue and expenses for accounting periods.

Control: Divide responsibility.

Procedures to Control the General Accounting Subsystem. There are two primary activities in the general accounting subsystem. The first activity is to prepare the accounts for the next accounting period. The second is to prepare the financial reports (statements) needed to make management decisions. It is important that special procedures are used to ensure the following.

- Prove equality of debits and credits in the ledger
- Prove agreement of accounting records and actual amounts
- Properly match revenue and expenses
- Use proper cutoff date
- Accurately report the results of operations
- Accurately report financial position
- Separate revenue and expenses for accounting periods
- Divide responsibility

Activity A. Answer the following questions about the procedures for controlling the general accounting subsystem. Refer to the text and margin notes above.
1. What are the special subsystems you have studied?
2. What does the general accounting subsystem do?

3. Which steps in the accounting cycle are completed primarily in the special subsystems? Which are completed in the general accounting subsystem?
4. What is the purpose of internal transactions?

Visualizing the Accounting System

B *How does financial data flow from the special subsystems through the general accounting subsystem?* The flowchart on pages 460 to 461 shows how financial data flows through an accounting system—the eight steps of the accounting cycle. The first three steps in the accounting cycle include steps to do the following.

1 Originate data.

2 Record transactions in journals.

3 Post to ledgers.

These three steps are completed, primarily, in the special accounting subsystems you studied in Chapters 10–15. The flowchart shown here indicates how accounting information flows from the special subsystems to the general ledger.

VISUALIZING AN ACCOUNTING SYSTEM THROUGH POSTING

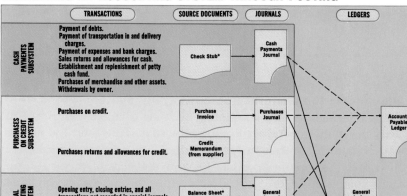
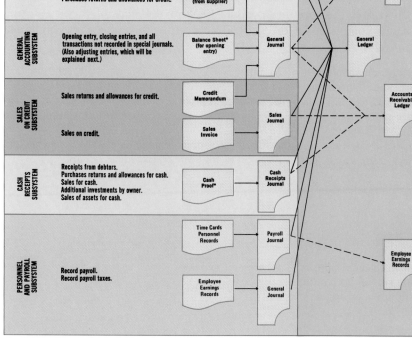

*Only one possible source document is showing.

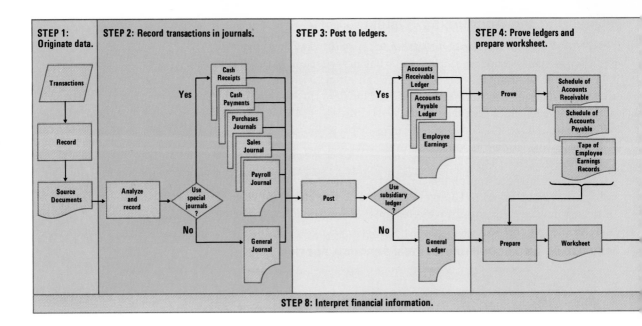

STEP 1: Originate data.	STEP 2: Record transactions in journals.	STEP 3: Post to ledgers.	STEP 4: Prove ledgers and prepare worksheet.

STEP 8: Interpret financial information.

Visualizing the General Accounting Subsystem (Steps 4–8).

Steps 4 through 8 of the accounting cycle are completed as part of the activities in the general accounting subsystem. Thus Step 4 in the general accounting subsystem (prove ledgers and prepare worksheet) is Step 4 in the accounting cycle. Each of the steps of the accounting cycle completed in the general accounting subsystem are explained next.

Activity B. Answer the following questions about visualizing the accounting system. Refer to the flowchart of an accounting system on pages 460 to 461.

1. What types of transactions are journalized in the general journal?

2. In this accounting system, entries are posted to the accounts payable subsidiary ledger from which journals?

3. What types of transactions are journalized in the cash payments journal?

4. What types of transactions are recorded on cash proofs?

5. Is the cash proof the only source document for entries in the cash receipts journal? Can you name others?

6. On what source documents can sales returns and allowances for cash be recorded?

Topic 1 Problem

16-1. In a chart similar to the one in the next column, summarize information about the special accounting subsystems and the general accounting subsystem.

			Type of Subsystem		
Subsystem	Source Documents	Journal Used	Special	General	Ledgers Posted to
Cash Receipts	?	?	?	?	?
Cash Payments	?	?	?	?	?
Purchases	?	?	?	?	?
Sales	?	?	?	?	?
Personnel and Payroll	?	?	?	?	?
General Accounting	?	?	?	?	?

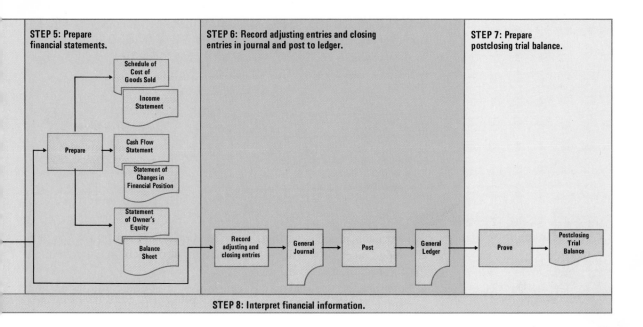

STEP 5: Prepare financial statements.	STEP 6: Record adjusting entries and closing entries in journal and post to ledger.	STEP 7: Prepare postclosing trial balance.

STEP 5: Prepare financial statements.

- Schedule of Cost of Goods Sold
- Income Statement
- Prepare → Cash Flow Statement
- Statement of Changes in Financial Position
- Statement of Owner's Equity
- Balance Sheet

STEP 6: Record adjusting entries and closing entries in journal and post to ledger.

Record adjusting and closing entries → General Journal → Post → General Ledger

STEP 7: Prepare postclosing trial balance.

Prove → Postclosing Trial Balance

STEP 8: Interpret financial information.

Topic 2
Updating the Trial Balance

A *What happens after information is posted to the general ledger?* Information posted to the general ledger is processed to prepare financial statements and prepare the accounts for the next accounting period. The first step after posting is Step 4 in the accounting cycle—proving the ledgers and preparing the worksheet. Proving the ledgers is explained in this topic. Preparing the worksheet is discussed in Topic 3.

Step 4: Proving the Ledgers

After all entries are posted, a proof must be made of the accuracy of the postings. First, a schedule of accounts receivable is prepared, as shown in the margin. The total on this schedule is proved with the balance of the Accounts Receivable controlling account in the general ledger. A similar schedule is prepared for the accounts payable ledger. The total is compared with the balance of the Accounts Payable controlling account. The subsidiary ledgers are usually proved daily or monthly even if the accounting period is longer.

The next step is to prove the amounts related to payroll. The proof involves comparing amounts in the employee's earnings records with amounts in the general ledger. First, a calculator tape is run of each employee's gross earnings. The total of this tape must equal the bal-

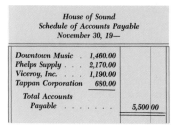

House of Sound
Schedule of Accounts Receivable
November 30, 19—

Audio Shoppe . . .	1,000 00	
Newtown Music . .	280 00	
Village Notes . . .	750 00	
George Yeomans . .	— 00	
Pauline Young . .	970 00	
Total Accounts Receivable . .		3,000 00

House of Sound
Schedule of Accounts Payable
November 30, 19—

Downtown Music .	1,460.00	
Phelps Supply . . .	2,170.00	
Viceroy, Inc.	1,190.00	
Tappan Corporation	680.00	
Total Accounts Payable		5,500 00

```
 560.00
 600.00
 470.00
 663.00
 276.00
 231.00
2,800.00
```

ance of the Salaries Expense account in the general ledger. Businesses can also use the amounts withheld for FICA taxes and employee's income taxes to verify the related credits to FICA Taxes and the Federal and State Income Taxes Payable accounts.

Proof	Ledger
Schedule of accounts receivable	Accounts receivable ledger
Schedule of accounts payable	Accounts payable ledger
Tape of gross earnings	Employee earnings record
Trial balance	General ledger

**House of Sound
Chart of Accounts**

Assets
112 Merchandise Inventory
113 Prepaid Insurance
114 Supplies on Hand

Owner's Equity
399 Income Summary

Expenses
514 Insurance Expense
518 Supplies Expense

After each proof is verified, a trial balance is prepared for the general ledger accounts. It shows that the total of the debit balances equals the total of the credit balances.

Note that the trial balance for the House of Sound contains six new accounts: Merchandise Inventory (112); Prepaid Insurance (113); Supplies on Hand (114); Income Summary (399); Insurance Expense (514); and Supplies Expense (518). Each account will be explained in the following sections. Also note that Insurance Expense, Supplies Expense, and Income Summary do not have balances at the time the trial balance is prepared.

Activity A. Answer the following questions about proving the ledgers. Refer to the text, margin notes, and illustrations on pages 461 to 462.
1. What subsidiary ledgers are maintained by the House of Sound?

2. What are the total accounts receivable?
3. From what source does the accountant obtain the $2,800 for Salaries Expense?
4. What would the accountant do if the balances for any one of the proofs did not agree?

Updating Merchandise Inventory

B *What happens after the trial balance is prepared?* Managers, owners, and outsiders use the financial statements of a business to judge both financial position and the results of operations. The trial balance must be analyzed and updated as a first step in the preparation of accurate financial statements. To analyze and update the trial balance, the accountant asks this question about every account: Is the amount of the account on the trial balance accurate? If it is, the account is not changed. If it is not accurate, the account balance must be adjusted to update the trial balance.

An adjustment is a change that must be made in an account to have the account show the correct balance.

House of Sound
Trial Balance
November 30, 19—

ACCOUNT TITLE	ACCT. NO.	DEBIT	CREDIT
Cash	101	9,500 00	
Petty Cash	102	30 00	
Change Fund	103	35 00	
Accounts Receivable	111	3,000 00	
Merchandise Inventory	112	7,000 00	
Prepaid Insurance	113	480 00	
Supplies on Hand	114	350 00	
Land	121	8,000 00	
Building	131	22,000 00	
Office Equipment	132	1,800 00	
Stockroom Equipment	133	2,700 00	
Loans Payable	201		4,000 00
Accounts Payable	211		5,500 00
Sales Taxes Payable	216		200 00
Federal Income Taxes Payable	221		360 00
FICA Taxes Payable	222		220 00
State Income Taxes Payable	223		140 00
Federal Unemployment Taxes Payable	224		48 00
State Unemployment Taxes Payable	225		176 00
Salaries Payable	226		— 00
Mortgage Payable	231		14,000 00
Marcy Casey, Capital	301		29,232 00
Marcy Casey, Drawing	302	1,200 00	
Income Summary	399	— 00	— 00
Sales	401		12,600 00
Sales Returns and Allowances	402	190 00	
Sales Discount	403	45 00	
Purchases	501	6,800 00	
Transportation In	502	80 00	
Purchases Returns and Allowances	503		185 00
Purchases Discount	504		50 00
Advertising Expense	511	100 00	
Cash Short and Over	512	6 00	
Delivery Expense	513	120 00	
Insurance Expense	514	— 00	
Miscellaneous Expense	515	40 00	
Payroll Taxes Expense	516	195 00	
Salaries Expense	517	2,800 00	
Supplies Expense	518	— 00	
Utilities Expense	519	240 00	
		66,711 00	66,711 00

Merchandise Inventory

The House of Sound keeps audio equipment in inventory to sell to its customers. The inventory increases and decreases when goods are purchased and sold. A successful business always has merchandise on hand to satisfy its customers' needs. Thus the business begins and ends each accounting period with merchandise in its inventory.

The merchandise on hand at the beginning of an accounting period is known as the **beginning inventory.** Inventory on hand at the end of a period is known as the **ending inventory.** Accounting periods follow each other. Therefore, the ending inventory of one period is the beginning inventory of the next period.

The income statement and the balance sheet cannot be prepared until the accountant finds the *cost* of the goods remaining on hand at the end of the accounting period and the cost of the goods sold during the period.

Computing the Cost of Goods on Hand. At the end of the accounting period, all businesses—those using the perpetual inventory and the periodic inventory procedures—must take a physical inventory. The **physical inventory** verifies the perpetual inventory records for businesses using the perpetual inventory procedure. For businesses using the periodic inventory procedure, the physical inventory is taken to find the cost of the inventory on hand. Periodic inventory accounting is discussed in this chapter.

The House of Sound, for example, uses periodic inventory accounting. A physical inventory on October 31 showed the cost of the unsold merchandise to be $7,000. The cost of inventory on October 31 was computed by the following procedure.

- The items in the inventory were physically counted and recorded on an inventory sheet.
- The quantity of each item was multiplied by the unit cost. For example, the unit cost of the A82-B portable cassettes was $40.00. Then this amount was multiplied by the number of cassettes in stock (8) to find the total cost of $320.
- The total cost for the entire inventory was found by adding the costs of all the items. The total cost of the ending inventory for the House of Sound on October 31 was $7,000. The $7,000 is also the beginning inventory of the next accounting period, which starts on November 1.

The total cost of the inventory is recorded in an account called Merchandise Inventory. The merchandise inventory owned by a business is an asset. Thus it is shown in the Assets section of the balance sheet.

Inventory Clerk:
DOT 222.387-026. Keeps record of amount, kind, and cost of merchandise on hand. May count merchandise on hand. May compare physical inventories with records. May indicate items to be reordered.

Computing the Cost of Goods Sold.

The dollar amounts of sales of merchandise are revenue. The dollar amounts of purchases of merchandise are costs. The difference between revenue and costs is known as *gross profit*. A business pays its expenses from the gross profit. A business can determine whether it has a net income or net loss by subtracting expenses from the gross profit for the accounting period.

The costs for merchandise purchased are recorded in the Purchases account and the Transportation In account. Amounts for items returned or allowances are recorded as credits in the Purchases Returns and Allowances account to offset the debit to the Purchases account. Also, the cash discounts during the period are credited to the Purchases Discount account. The cost accounts are temporary owner's equity accounts, showing the cost of the merchandise purchased *during* the accounting period.

During the accounting period ended November 30, the House of Sound purchased merchandise for $6,800. Transportation charges were $80. The total amount of purchases returns and allowances was $185, and there were purchases discounts of $50. The amount of net purchases for November was $6,645 ($6,800 + $80 − $185 − $50).

No entries were made to the Merchandise Inventory account *during the accounting period.* All entries were made to the four temporary cost accounts. Thus, at the end of the accounting period, the Merchandise Inventory account still shows the inventory for the beginning of the period ($7,000). The physical inventory taken by the House of Sound on November 30 shows the total cost of unsold merchandise as $6,400. Obviously, the $7,000 in the Merchandise Inventory account is incorrect. The Merchandise Inventory account must be adjusted to show the actual inventory at the end of the period on November 30. To offset the decrease in the debit balance from $7,000 to $6,400, the Merchandise Inventory account must be credited for $600. What account should be debited?

Increases and decreases in owner's equity due to cost of merchandise are transferred to Income Summary.

Revenue (from goods sold)
− Cost (of goods sold)

Gross Profit (on sales)
− Expenses (to operate business)

Net Income
or Net Loss

Purchases		6,800 00
Add: Transportation In		80 00
Cost of Delivered Goods		6,880 00
Less: Purchases Returns		
and Allowances	$185.00	
Purchases Discount	50.00	235 00
Net Purchases		6,645 00

Cost of merchandise purchased during November.

Beginning of Period

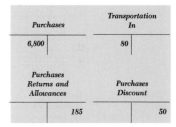

Merchandise Inventory

19—
Nov. 1   7,000

During Period

Purchases
6,800

Transportation In
80

Purchases Returns and Allowances
185

Purchases Discount
50

End of Period

Merchandise Inventory
6,400 | 600

?
600

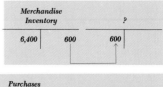

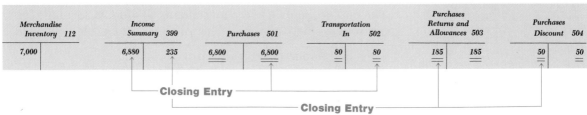

Merchandise Inventory 112		Income Summary 399		Purchases 501		Transportation In 502		Purchases Returns and Allowances 503		Purchases Discount 504	
7,000		6,880	235	6,800	6,800	80	80	185	185	50	50

—————Closing Entry—————

—————Closing Entry—————

At the *end of the accounting period,* the House of Sound has $600 less merchandise on hand than it had at the beginning of the period. This means that $600 more merchandise was sold than was purchased during the period. The entry to record the cost of the merchandise sold from the inventory is made by debiting the Income Summary account.

Remember that at the end of the accounting period, the temporary owner's equity accounts are closed into the Income Summary account. The balances of the Purchases, Transportation In, Purchases Returns and Allowances, and Purchases Discount accounts will be transferred to the proper side of the Income Summary account.

The additional cost of $600 also affects owner's equity. The $600 is transferred from the Merchandise Inventory account to the Income Summary account.

November 30: The House of Sound makes an adjusting entry to decrease the Merchandise Inventory account by $600.

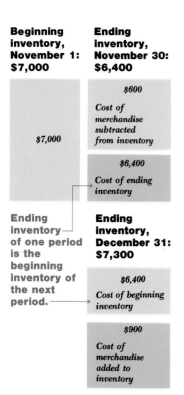

Beginning inventory, November 1: $7,000

Ending inventory, November 30: $6,400

$600
Cost of merchandise subtracted from inventory

$7,000

$6,400
Cost of ending inventory

Ending inventory of one period is the beginning inventory of the next period.

Ending inventory, December 31: $7,300

$6,400
Cost of beginning inventory

$900
Cost of merchandise added to inventory

What Happens	Accounting Rule	Entry
The increase in the cost of merchandise decreases owner's equity by $600.	To decrease owner's equity, debit the account.	Debit: Income Summary, $600.
The asset *Merchandise Inventory* decreases by $600.	To decrease an asset, credit the account.	Credit: Merchandise Inventory, $600.

Merchandise Inventory 112

7,000	600

Income Summary 399

① 6,880	③ 235
② 600	

GENERAL JOURNAL   **Page 6**

DATE	ACCOUNT TITLE AND EXPLANATION	POST. REF.	DEBIT	CREDIT
19—				
Nov. 30	Income Summary	399	600 00	
	Merchandise Inventory	112		600 00
	Adjust inventory.			

The Income Summary account contains all the data about the cost of goods sold during November. The following are on the debit side.

1 Costs due to purchases and transportation charges.
2 Costs due to a reduction in the inventory.
The following is on the credit side.
3 Reductions in costs due to returns, allowances, and discounts.

The cost of goods sold during the period is $7,245 ($6,880 + $600 − $235).

The merchandise counted on the last day of an accounting period is the merchandise inventory on the first day of the next period. On December 1 the balance of the Merchandise Inventory account is $6,400. Suppose the business has purchases of $8,400 during December and an ending inventory of $7,300. Since the ending inventory is $900 more than the beginning inventory ($6,400), more merchandise was purchased than sold. An adjusting entry must be made to increase the Merchandise Inventory account by $900.

December 31: The House of Sound makes an adjusting entry to increase the Merchandise Inventory account by $900.

What Happens	Accounting Rule	Entry
The asset *Merchandise Inventory* increases by $900.	To increase an asset, debit the account.	Debit: Merchandise Inventory, $900.
The reduction in the cost of merchandise increases owner's equity by $900.	To increase owner's equity, credit the account.	Credit: Income Summary, $900.

Merchandise Inventory 112	Income Summary 399	Purchases 501
6,400	900	8,400
900		

— Adjusting Entry —

When the closing entries are made, all temporary owner's equity accounts are closed into the Income Summary account. The credit of $900 to owner's equity is posted directly to the temporary Summary account. As a result, the Merchandise Inventory account shows the cost of the merchandise inventory at the end of the period ($7,300). The cost of merchandise that has been sold during the month is shown in the Income Summary account ($8,400 − $900 = $7,500).

Merchandise Inventory 112	Income Summary 399	Purchases 501
6,400	8,400 900	8,400 8,400
900		

— Closing Entry —

Merchandise Inventory Decreased			Merchandise Inventory Increased		
Ending inventory *less* than beginning inventory.			Ending inventory *more* than beginning inventory.		
Sold *more* merchandise than purchased.			Sold *less* merchandise than purchased.		
Decrease Merchandise Inventory account balance.			*Increase* Merchandise Inventory account balance.		
Adjusting entry for amount of decrease:			Adjusting entry for amount of increase:		
Income Summary	xxx		*Merchandise Inventory*	xxx	
Merchandise Inventory		xxx	*Income Summary*		xxx

Activity B-1. Answer the following questions about updating merchandise inventory. Refer to the text, margin notes, and illustrations on pages 462 to 468.

1. Why is the Merchandise Inventory account credited for $600?

2. What effect does the $600 adjustment have on owner's equity?

3. If the merchandise inventory had been larger on November 30 than it was on November 1, what adjusting entry would have been required?

Activity B-2. Answer the following questions about updating merchandise inventory. Refer to the illustrations on page 467.

1. Why is merchandise inventory debited for $900?
2. What effect does the $900 have on owner's equity?
3. Why is Purchases credited for $8,400?
4. What effect does the $8,400 debit to Income Summary have on owner's equity?
5. What is the cost of merchandise sold for the month?
6. What type of entry is the $8,400 debit to Income Summary and the $8,400 credit to Purchases?
7. What is the balance of merchandise inventory on the first day of the new accounting period?

Updating Prepaid Expenses

C *What are prepaid expenses?* The costs of items and services bought for use in operating the business but not used at the end of the accounting period are called **prepaid expenses.** Supplies on hand and prepaid insurance are examples of prepaid expenses.

Some business transactions cover more than one accounting period. For example, a business usually buys enough office supplies to last for several months. Accountants follow a principle called the "matching principle." The matching principle means that the income statement for a business should show all expenses incurred in earning the revenue during that accounting period. Only the supplies used should be considered an expense. Unused supplies are not an expense until used in a future accounting period.

Supplies on Hand

Supplies are considered assets at the time of purchase. Supplies become an expense of doing business as they are used. The accounting procedure for supplies is as follows.

- When supplies are purchased, the cost of supplies is debited to an asset account called Supplies on Hand.
- At the end of the accounting period, supplies on hand are counted.
- The amount of the supplies used in the accounting period is transferred from the asset account to an expense account. The asset account Supplies on Hand is decreased for the amount of supplies used.

November 4: The House of Sound draws a check for $350 to pay for supplies, which will last for several months.

What Happens	Accounting Rule	Entry
The asset *Supplies on Hand* increases by $350.	To increase an asset, debit the account.	Debit: Supplies on Hand, $350.
The asset *Cash* decreases by $350.	To decrease an asset, credit the account.	Credit: Cash, $350.

Cash	*101*	*Supplies on Hand*	*114*
		350	*350*

Purchasing Supplies

At the end of the accounting period on November 30, the supplies on hand are counted. The physical inventory shows supplies on hand of $300. This means that supplies of $50 ($350 − $300) were used during November. An adjusting entry is made to transfer the amount of the used supplies ($50) from the asset account to the Supplies Expense account. The entry is made in the general journal.

November 30: A physical count of the supplies on hand shows unused supplies of $300.

What Happens	Accounting Rule	Entry
Expense decreases owner's equity by $50.	To decrease owner's equity, debit the account.	Debit: Supplies Expense, $50.
The asset *Supplies on Hand* decreases by $50.	To decrease an asset, credit the account.	Credit: Supplies on Hand, $50.

Cash	*101*	*Supplies on Hand*	*114*	*Supplies Expense*	*518*
	350	*350*	*50*	*50*	

Adjusting Supplies

- Debit asset account when items are purchased.
- Determine unused portion at end of period.
- Debit expense account for portion used. Credit asset account for portion used.

The effect of the adjusting entry is that Supplies on Hand now has a debit balance of $300. This is the amount of the asset shown on the balance sheet. In addition, the Supplies Expense account has a debit balance of $50. This is the amount of supplies used during the accounting period. Thus the financial statements will show accurate amounts for the asset and the expense.

Prepaid Insurance

Assets of a business, such as equipment and buildings, are usually insured against loss due to theft, fire, flood, or storm. The total premium on an insurance policy is paid at the beginning of the insurance period, or paid in advance.

The amount paid for an insurance premium covering more than one accounting period is a prepaid expense. The amount of the premium is debited to the asset account Prepaid Insurance. As the insurance premium expires, that portion becomes an expense.

November 1: The House of Sound issues a check for $480 to pay the annual premium for fire insurance covering its equipment and building.

What Happens	Accounting Rule	Entry
The asset *Prepaid Insurance* increases by $480.	To increase an asset, debit the account.	Debit: Prepaid Insurance, $480.
The asset *Cash* decreases by $480.	To decrease an asset, credit the account.	Credit: Cash, $480.

Cash	101	*Prepaid Insurance*	113
	480	480	

Purchasing Insurance

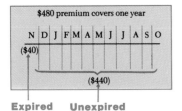

Expired   Unexpired

The premium of $480 provides a year's fire insurance coverage. However, each accounting period must be charged for the portion of the premium that expires during that period. The House of Sound has an accounting period of one month. The cost of the insurance for the month of November would be one-twelfth of the annual premium of $480, or $40. At the end of November, an entry is made in the general journal to transfer one month's insurance premium ($40) from the Prepaid Insurance account to the Insurance Expense account.

The balance of the Prepaid Insurance account on December 1 will be $440. This $440 represents the premium for 11 months' insurance

November 30: The House of Sound records the amount of insurance expired during the month of November.

What Happens	Accounting Rule	Entry
Expense decreases owner's equity by $40.	To decrease owner's equity, debit the account.	Debit: Insurance Expense, $40.
The asset *Prepaid Insurance* decreases by $40.	To decrease an asset, credit the account.	Credit: Prepaid Insurance, $40.

Cash 101	Prepaid Insurance 113	Insurance Expense 514
480	480 | 40	40 |

Adjusting Prepaid Insurance

that has not expired ($40 × 11). At the end of each month an adjusting entry is made. The asset Prepaid Insurance will contain the amount of the unexpired insurance, and the Insurance Expense account will contain the amount of insurance that expired during the accounting period.

House of Sound Chart of Accounts

Assets
113 Prepaid Insurance

Costs and Expenses
514 Insurance Expense

Other Prepaid Expenses

A business may have other prepaid expenses that are adjusted at the end of the accounting period. Examples would include prepaid advertising, prepaid subscriptions, and prepaid membership fees.

Activity C. Answer the following questions on updating prepaid expenses. Refer to the transaction analyses and accounts shown on pages 468 to 471.
1. Why is it necessary to adjust the Supplies on Hand account on November 30?
2. What is the effect of the $50 credit to Supplies on Hand on November 30?
3. What is the effect on owner's equity of the debit to Supplies Expense?
4. Why is it necessary to adjust the Prepaid Insurance account on November 30?
5. What effect does the $40 credit to the Prepaid Insurance account have on the total assets of the business?

Accounting Clerk:
DOT 216.482-010. Performs variety of computing, posting, and other accounting duties. May be classified according to type of accounting performed, as accounts receivable clerk.

Accounting Concepts:
Schedule of Subsidiary Ledgers. The equality of the subsidiary ledgers and the controlling accounts must be verified at regular intervals.

Trial Balance. The equality of the total debits and the total credits in the general ledger should be verified at regular intervals.

Accounting Principles:

Cutoff Date. The generally accepted accounting principle is that there must be a proper cutoff date for the recording of revenues, costs, and expenses in the accounting period.

Matching Revenue and Expenses. The generally accepted accounting principle is that revenue must be matched against the expenses incurred in obtaining that revenue. The result of matching revenue and expenses is net income (or net loss) for the accounting period.

Prepaid Expenses. The generally accepted accounting principle is that prepaid expenses—items or services that benefit more than one accounting period—are assets at first and become expenses only as they are used. Thus prepaid expenses should be charged as expenses to future periods in which they are used.

Topic 2 Problems

16-2. For each of the adjustments listed below, give the following information: (1) the amount of the adjustment, (2) the account debited and the account credited, (3) the account balance after the adjustment is posted, (4) whether the new account balance is a debit or credit balance.

a. Merchandise inventory at the beginning of the accounting period: $16,920. Merchandise inventory at the end of the accounting period: $19,370.

b. Merchandise inventory at the beginning of the accounting period: $10,280. Merchandise inventory at the end of the accounting period: $7,170.

c. Supplies on hand at the beginning of the period: $560. Supplies on hand at the end of the period: $85.

d. Supplies on hand at the beginning of the period: $30. Supplies purchased during the period: $25. Supplies on hand at the end of the period: $35.

16-3. For each of the adjustments listed below, give the following information: (1) the amount of the adjustment, (2) the account debited and the account credited, (3) the account balance after the adjustment is posted, and (4) whether the new account balance is a debit or credit balance.

a. Prepaid insurance at the beginning of the period: $580. Insurance purchased during the period: $120. Insurance expired during the period: $180.

b. Prepaid insurance at the beginning of the period: $960. Unexpired insurance at the end of the period: $320.

c. Prepaid insurance at the beginning of the period: $1,800. Insurance purchased during the period: $600. Unexpired insurance at the end of the period: $2,200.

d. Supplies on hand at the beginning of the period: $720. No supplies were purchased during the period. Supplies on hand at the end of the period: $730. (*HINT*: Discuss what could have caused this situation.)

Topic 3
Completing the Worksheet

A *How does completing the worksheet relate to the accounting cycle?* Completing the worksheet is a part of Step 4 of the accounting cycle—prove ledgers and prepare worksheet. Steps 5 and 6 of the accounting cycle include the preparation of financial statements and the recording of adjusting and closing entries. The worksheet—Step 4—relates to Steps 5 and 6 in that it provides the accountant with a handy tool to do the following.

- Prepare the trial balance.
- Prepare the adjusting entries.
- Prepare the financial statements.

Format of the Worksheet

The **worksheet** is a columnar form on which the accountant gathers data at the end of the accounting period. There are columns for preparing the unadjusted trial balance. Columns are provided for preparing the adjustments. Columns are also provided for sorting and classifying account balances before preparing the financial statements.

The worksheet in this chapter has ten money columns. It consists of five main sections: the Unadjusted Trial Balance, the Adjustments, the Adjusted Trial Balance, the Income Statement, and the Balance Sheet.

Ten-Column Worksheet Sections
- Unadjusted Trial Balance
- Adjustments
- Adjusted Trial Balance
- Income Statement
- Balance Sheet

House of Sound
Worksheet
For the Month Ended November 30, 19—

	ACCOUNT TITLE	ACCT. NO.	UNADJUSTED TRIAL BALANCE		ADJUSTMENTS		ADJUSTED TRIAL BALANCE		INCOME STATEMENT		BALANCE SHEET		
			DEBIT	CREDIT	DEBIT	CREDIT	DEBIT	CREDIT	DEBIT	CREDIT	DEBIT	CREDIT	
1													1
2													2
3													3
4													4
5													5
6													6
7													7
8													8

The worksheet is not a financial statement. The worksheet is prepared in pencil so that amounts can be erased and changed. It is designed so that a proof is provided for each part of the work.

The worksheet prepared for the House of Sound on November 30 will be used to show how the worksheet is prepared.

The heading of the worksheet answers three questions.
- WHO? (the name of the business)
- WHAt? (a worksheet)
- WHEN? (the accounting period)

WHO ⟶ *House of Sound*
WHAT ⟶ *Worksheet*
For the Month Ended November 30, 19—
↑
WHEN

The worksheet covers the accounting period because it is used to compute the net income (or net loss) for the period. After the heading is completed, the procedures described on the following pages are used to complete the five sections of the worksheet.

Activity A. Answer the following questions about the format of a worksheet. Refer to the text, margin notes, and illustrations on pages 472 to 473.
1. What is the purpose of the worksheet?
2. Is the worksheet a statement?

3. What three pieces of information are found in the heading of the worksheet?
4. How many money columns are found on the worksheet?

Updating the Unadjusted Trial Balance

B *What is the unadjusted trial balance?* The **unadjusted trial balance** is a proof of the equality of debits and credits in the ledger before the adjusting entries have been recorded on the worksheet. The steps to complete the unadjusted Trial Balance columns are:

Step 4a: Completing the Unadjusted Trial Balance. The unadjusted trial balance is prepared directly on the worksheet. Each account is listed, just as it appears in the ledger. The account title and number are listed. The account balance is entered in the proper Debit or Credit column. If an account does not have a balance, a dash is placed in the money columns. After the balances are entered, a single rule is drawn across both money columns and the amounts are totaled. If the unadjusted trial balance is in balance, draw double rules across both money columns. If it is out of balance, locate the error before completing the worksheet.

Step 4b: Completing the Adjustments Section. Some trial balance accounts must be adjusted to show the correct balances. Three accounts must be adjusted on November 30: Merchandise Inventory, Prepaid Insurance, and Supplies on Hand. In practice, the adjustments are computed on the worksheet before being journalized. (Follow the discussion by looking at the worksheet on page 475.)

Adjustment for Merchandise Inventory (a). The beginning inventory was $7,000 (the unadjusted trial balance). The ending inventory is $6,400. Therefore, the Merchandise Inventory account must be decreased by $600 ($7,000 − $6,400). The Merchandise Inventory account has a debit balance and must be credited to decrease the balance. The $600 is entered in the Credit column of the Adjustments section on the same line as the Merchandise Inventory account (line 5). This amount is identified by the letter (a). The debit and credit amounts for each adjustment are labeled (a), (b), or (c) so the complete entry can be identified for journalizing. The $600 adjustment is also entered as a debit in the Adjustments section opposite the Income Summary account (line 24). The adjustment to Income Summary is also identified by the letter (a).

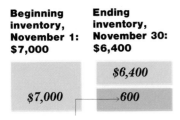

Beginning inventory, November 1: $7,000

Ending inventory, November 30: $6,400

$6,400

$7,000 →600

Cost of merchandise subtracted from inventory.

Adjustment for Expired Insurance (b). A review of the insurance policy shows that it is dated November 1 and runs for 1 year. On November 30, 1 month of the policy has expired. The balance of $480 in the Prepaid Insurance account on the unadjusted trial balance is the payment for 1 year's coverage. The monthly insurance expense is therefore $40 (one-twelfth of $480). On November 30 an adjustment is made to show that $40 of the prepaid expense has expired. The adjustment transfers the amount expired from the asset account (Prepaid

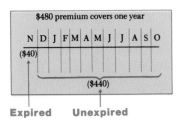

$480 premium covers one year

N D J F M A M J J A S O

($40)

($440)

Expired   Unexpired

Insurance) to the expense account (Insurance Expense). Thus $40 is entered in the Credit column of the Adjustments section on the same line as Prepaid Insurance. The amount is identified by the letter (b). The adjustment for $40 is also entered on the same line as the Insurance Expense account. Insurance Expense is debited and is identified with the letter (b).

House of Sound
Worksheet
For the Month Ended November 30, 19—

	ACCOUNT TITLE	ACCT. NO.	UNADJUSTED TRIAL BALANCE		ADJUSTMENTS		ADJUSTED TRIAL BALANCE		INCOME STATEMENT		BALANCE SHEET		
			DEBIT	CREDIT	DEBIT	CREDIT	DEBIT	CREDIT	DEBIT	CREDIT	DEBIT	CREDIT	
1	Cash	101	9,500										1
2	Petty Cash	102	30										2
3	Change Fund	103	35										3
4	Accounts Receivable	111	3,000										4
5	Merchandise Inventory	112	7,000			(a) 600							5
6	Prepaid Insurance	113	480			(b) 40							6
7	Supplies on Hand	114	350			(c) 50							7
8	Land	121	8,000										8
9	Building	131	22,000										9
10	Office Equipment	132	1,800										10
11	Stockroom Equipment	133	2,700										11
12	Loans Payable	201		4,000									12
13	Accounts Payable	211		5,500									13
14	Sales Taxes Payable	216		200									14
15	Fed. Inc. Taxes Pay.	221		360									15
16	FICA Taxes Payable	222		220									16
17	State Inc. Taxes Pay.	223		140									17
18	Federal Unempl. Taxes Pay. .	224		48									18
19	State Unempl. Taxes Pay. . . .	225		176									19
20	Salaries Payable	226		—									20
21	Mortgage Payable	231		14,000									21
22	Marcy Casey, Capital	301		29,232									22
23	Marcy Casey, Drawing	302	1,200										23
24	Income Summary	399	—	—	(a) 600								24
25	Sales	401		12,600									25
26	Sales Returns and Allowances	402	190										26
27	Sales Discount	403	45										27
28	Purchases	501	6,800										28
29	Transportation In	502	80										29
30	Purchases Returns and Allow.	503		185									30
31	Purchases Discount	504		50									31
32	Advertising Expense	511	100										32
33	Cash Short and Over	512	6										33
34	Delivery Expense	513	120										34
35	Insurance Expense	514	—		(b) 40								35
36	Miscellaneous Expense	515	40										36
37	Payroll Taxes Expense	516	195										37
38	Salaries Expense	517	— 00										38
39	Supplies Expense	518	— 00		(c) 50								39
40	Utilities Expense	519	240										40
41			66,711	66,711	690	690							41

(4a)   (4b)

NOTE: The cents columns have been omitted in order to show the entire worksheet.

Supplies Available	350 00
Less: Supplies on Hand . .	300 00
Supplies Used	50 00

Adjustment for Supplies Used (c). The trial balance shows a balance of $350 for Supplies on Hand. The supplies on hand were counted on November 30, and the unused supplies amounted to only $300. Thus the Supplies on Hand account must be decreased to show that $50 ($350 − $300) of the prepaid expense has been used. The $50 amount is entered in the Credit column of the Adjustments section on the same line as Supplies on Hand. The letter (c) is used to identify the adjustment. The expense for the supplies used is recorded by debiting the Supplies Expense account. The amount ($50) is entered in the Debit column of the Adjustments section and is identified by the letter (c).

Totaling the Adjustments Section. After all the adjustments have been entered on the worksheet, a single rule is drawn across the money columns. Then the columns are totaled. The two totals must be equal to prove the equality of the debit and credit entries. If there is an error, it must be located before completing the worksheet. When the two amounts agree, double rules are drawn under the totals.

Step 4c: Completing the Adjusted Trial Balance Section. The new balances for the accounts that have been adjusted are found by completing the Adjusted Trial Balance section of the worksheet. Each account balance in the Unadjusted Trial Balance section is combined with the adjustment, if any, in the Adjustments section. The new balance is moved to the Adjusted Trial Balance section. The cross-footing requires either adding or subtracting the adjustment from the balance.

The balance in the Unadjusted Trial Balance section is simply moved to the Adjusted Trial Balance section for accounts that were not adjusted. For example, the first four accounts (Cash, Petty Cash, Change Fund, and Accounts Receivable) were not adjusted. Thus the balances were moved to the Debit column of the Adjusted Trial Balance section. However, Merchandise Inventory (line 5) was adjusted. The Unadjusted Trial Balance section shows a debit of $7,000. The Adjustments section shows a credit adjustment of $600. The new balance is found by subtracting the $600 credit from the $7,000 debit, leaving a debit balance of $6,400. The adjusted balance is then entered in the Debit column of the Adjusted Trial Balance section. The same procedure is followed for the Prepaid Insurance and the Supplies on Hand accounts.

The Income Summary account had no balance in the Unadjusted Trial Balance section. However, there is a $600 debit in the Adjustments section. The amount moved to the Adjusted Trial Balance section is, therefore, a debit balance of $600. The same procedure is used for the Insurance Expense and the Supplies Expense accounts.

After all the account balances are entered in the Adjusted Trial Balance section, the columns are totaled. If the total debits equal the total

Obtaining Adjusted Trial Balance Amounts

Merchandise Inventory:
$7,000 − $600 = $6,400
Prepaid Insurance:
$480 − $40 = $440
Supplies on Hand:
$350 − $50 = $300

credits, the columns are ruled. The accountant can then assume that there are no mathematical errors. The adjusted trial balance is the second trial balance prepared. It is used to check the equality of the debit and credit balances after the adjustments are made.

House of Sound
Worksheet
For the Month Ended November 30, 19—

	ACCOUNT TITLE	ACCT. NO.	UNADJUSTED TRIAL BALANCE DEBIT	UNADJUSTED TRIAL BALANCE CREDIT	ADJUSTMENTS DEBIT	ADJUSTMENTS CREDIT	ADJUSTED TRIAL BALANCE DEBIT	ADJUSTED TRIAL BALANCE CREDIT	INCOME STATEMENT DEBIT	INCOME STATEMENT CREDIT	BALANCE SHEET DEBIT	BALANCE SHEET CREDIT	
1	Cash	101	9,500				9,500						1
2	Petty Cash	102	30				30						2
3	Change Fund	103	35				35						3
4	Accounts Receivable	111	3,000				3,000						4
5	Merchandise Inventory	112	7,000			(a) 600	6,400						5
6	Prepaid Insurance	113	480			(b) 40	440						6
7	Supplies on Hand	114	350			(c) 50	300						7
8	Land	121	8,000				8,000						8
9	Building	131	22,000				22,000						9
10	Office Equipment	132	1,800				1,800						10
11	Stockroom Equipment	133	2,700				2,700						11
12	Loans Payable	201		4,000				4,000					12
13	Accounts Payable	211		5,500				5,500					13
14	Sales Taxes Payable	216		200				200					14
15	Fed. Inc. Taxes Pay.	221		360				360					15
16	FICA Taxes Payable	222		220				220					16
17	State Inc. Taxes Pay.	223		140				140					17
18	Federal Unempl. Taxes Pay.	224		48				48					18
19	State Unempl. Taxes Pay.	225		176				176					19
20	Salaries Payable	226		—				—					20
21	Mortgage Payable	231		14,000				14,000					21
22	Marcy Casey, Capital	301		29,232				29,232					22
23	Marcy Casey, Drawing	302	1,200				1,200						23
24	Income Summary	399	—	—	(a) 600		600						24
25	Sales	401		12,600				12,600					25
26	Sales Returns and Allowances	402	190				190						26
27	Sales Discount	403	45				45						27
28	Purchases	501	6,800				6,800						28
29	Transportation In	502	80				80						29
30	Purchases Returns and Allow.	503		185				185					30
31	Purchases Discount	504		50				50					31
32	Advertising Expense	511	100				100						32
33	Cash Short and Over	512	6				6						33
34	Delivery Expense	513	120				120						34
35	Insurance Expense	514	—		(b) 40		40						35
36	Miscellaneous Expense	515	40				40						36
37	Payroll Taxes Expense	516	195				195						37
38	Salaries Expense	517	2,800				2,800						38
39	Supplies Expense	518	—		(c) 50		50						39
40	Utilities Expense	519	240				240						40
41			66,711	66,711	690	690	66,711	66,711					41
42													42
43	Net Income												43
44				(4a)		(4b)		(4c)					44

NOTE: The cents columns have been omitted in order to show the entire worksheet.

Answer the following questions about updating the trial balance. Refer to the worksheet on page 477.

1. What is the debit and credit for the (a) adjustment?
2. What is the adjusted trial balance amount for Prepaid Insurance? How was it found?
3. What is the adjusted trial balance amount for Mortgage Payable?
4. What is the effect of the credit to the Supplies on Hand account?
5. What is the total amount of the adjustments?
6. How are the amounts in the Adjusted Trial Balance columns computed?

Completing the Financial Statement Sections

C *How does the accountant sort the balances in the Adjusted Trial Balance columns?* Each balance in the Adjusted Trial Balance columns is moved to one of the four remaining columns. Balance sheet accounts are moved to the Balance Sheet columns. Temporary owner's equity accounts are moved to the Income Statement columns.

Step 4d: Completing the Financial Statement Sections. The balances of the assets, liabilities, and the owner's capital and drawing accounts are moved to the proper Debit or Credit column in the Balance Sheet section. For example, Cash, the first account, has a debit balance of $9,500. Since Cash is an asset, the balance of the account will appear on the balance sheet. Thus the adjusted trial balance amount of $9,500 for Cash is moved into the Debit column of the Balance Sheet section. The next ten accounts in the Adjusted Trial Balance section are also assets. These balances are also moved to the Debit column of the Balance Sheet section.

The balances of the liability accounts (lines 12–21) and the Marcy Casey, Capital account (line 22) are moved to the Credit column of the Balance Sheet section. The Marcy Casey, Drawing account has a debit balance and is moved to the Debit column of the Balance Sheet section. (Note that November 30 is a Friday, and thus Salaries Payable has no balance.)

The balances of the revenue, cost, and expense accounts (including the Income Summary account) are moved to the proper Debit or Credit column in the Income Statement section. For example, Sales (line 25) is a revenue account and has a credit balance. Sales appears on the income statement, and the balance of $12,600 is moved to the Credit column of the Income Statement section. The remainder of the account balances (lines 26 to 40) are moved to the proper columns of the Income Statement section.

The numbering system for the chart of accounts is helpful in classifying the accounts. The accounts are listed in the Unadjusted Trial Balance section of the worksheet in the same order in which they appear in the ledger.

House of Sound Chart of Accounts

Asset accounts:	101–199
Liability accounts:	201–299
Owner's equity accounts:	301–399
Revenue accounts:	401–499
Cost and expense accounts:	501–599

	ACCOUNT TITLE	ACCT. NO.	UNADJUSTED TRIAL BALANCE DEBIT	CREDIT	ADJUSTMENTS DEBIT	CREDIT	ADJUSTED TRIAL BALANCE DEBIT	CREDIT	INCOME STATEMENT DEBIT	CREDIT	BALANCE SHEET DEBIT	CREDIT	
1	Cash	101	9,500				9,500				9,500		1
2	Petty Cash	102	30				30				30		2
3	Change Fund	103	35				35				35		3
4	Accounts Receivable	111	3,000				3,000				3,000		4
5	Merchandise Inventory	112	7,000			(a) 600	6,400				6,400		5
6	Prepaid Insurance	113	480			(b) 40	440				440		6
7	Supplies on Hand	114	350			(c) 50	300				300		7
8	Land	121	8,000				8,000				8,000		8
9	Building	131	22,000				22,000				22,000		9
10	Office Equipment	132	1,800				1,800				1,800		10
11	Stockroom Equipment	133	2,700				2,700				2,700		11
12	Loans Payable	201		4,000				4,000				4,000	12
13	Accounts Payable	211		5,500				5,500				5,500	13
14	Sales Taxes Payable	216		200				200				200	14
15	Fed. Inc. Taxes Pay.	221		360				360				360	15
16	FICA Taxes Payable	222		220				220				220	16
17	State Inc. Taxes Pay.	223		140				140				140	17
18	Federal Unempl. Taxes Pay.	224		48				48				48	18
19	State Unempl. Taxes Pay.	225		176				176				176	19
20	Salaries Payable	226		—				—					20
21	Mortgage Payable	231		14,000				14,000				14,000	21
22	Marcy Casey, Capital	301		29,232				29,232				29,232	22
23	Marcy Casey, Drawing	302	1,200				1,200				1,200		23
24	Income Summary	399	—	—	(a) 600		600		600				24
25	Sales	401		12,600				12,600		12,600			25
26	Sales Returns and Allowances	402	190				190		190				26
27	Sales Discount	403	45				45		45				27
28	Purchases	501	6,800				6,800		6,800				28
29	Transportation In	502	80				80		80				29
30	Purchases Returns and Allow.	503		185				185		185			30
31	Purchases Discount	504		50				50		50			31
32	Advertising Expense	511	100				100		100				32
33	Cash Short and Over	512	6				6		6				33
34	Delivery Expense	513	120				120		120				34
35	Insurance Expense	514	—		(b) 40		40		40				35
36	Miscellaneous Expense	515	40				40		40				36
37	Payroll Taxes Expense	516	195				195		195				37
38	Salaries Expense	517	2,800				2,800		2,800				38
39	Supplies Expense	518	—		(c) 50		50		50				39
40	Utilities Expense	519	240				240		240				40
41			66,711	66,711	690	690	66,711	66,711	11,306	12,835	55,405	53,876	41
42										11,306			42
43	Net Income									1,529		1,529	43
44											55,405	55,405	44

NOTE: The cents columns have been omitted in order to show the entire worksheet.

By completing the worksheet, the accountant has also classified each account according to the financial statement on which it will appear. The financial statements can then be prepared easily from the worksheet.

Determining the Net Income or Net Loss. After each account balance has been moved to either the Income Statement or the Balance Sheet section, a single rule is drawn across all money columns and the amounts are totaled. At this point the total debits in the Income Statement section do not equal the total credits because the business has a net income (increases in owner's equity are greater than decreases) or a net loss (decreases in owner's equity are greater than increases).

Net Income. To find the net income (or net loss), begin with the Income Statement section. If the total of the Credit column is greater than the total of the Debit column, there is a net income. To find the amount of net income, follow this procedure.

1 Place the total of the Debit column beneath the total of the Credit column and subtract. The amounts entered in the Debit column of the Income Statement section are decreases in owner's equity. The amounts entered in the Credit column are increases in owner's equity. The increases in owner's equity (credits) are greater than the decreases (debits). The difference between the two totals is a net income.

2 Move the amount of the net income to the Credit column of the Balance Sheet section. This is done because a net income increases owner's equity. Owner's equity is increased on the credit side. The net income is now shown on the balance sheet.

3 Add the net income to the total of the Credit column because a net income increases owner's equity. If all computations are correct, the total of the Credit column will now equal the total of the Debit column in the Balance Sheet section. The amounts must be equal after the net income is transferred to the Capital account because the total debits must equal the total credits.

If the totals agree, complete the worksheet. Draw double rules across the Income Statement and Balance Sheet sections. If the totals do not agree, recheck until the error is found. If the adjusted trial balance was correct, the error was made in moving the balances or computing the totals.

Net Loss. If the total of the Debit column of the Income Statement section is greater than the Credit column total, the business has a net loss. To find the amount of the net loss, follow this procedure.

1 Place the total of the Credit column under the total of the Debit column and subtract. The difference is the net loss.

2 Extend the amount of the net loss to the Debit column of the Balance Sheet section. This is done because a net loss decreases owner's equity, and owner's equity is decreased on the debit side.

3 Add the net loss to the total of the Debit column. If no errors were made, the totals of the Debit and Credit columns will be equal.

INCOME STATEMENT		BALANCE SHEET	
DEBIT	CREDIT	DEBIT	CREDIT
11,306	12,835	55,405	53,876
	11,306		
	1,529	②	1,529
	①	55,405	55,405

Computing Net Income on the Worksheet

INCOME STATEMENT		BALANCE SHEET	
DEBIT	CREDIT	DEBIT	CREDIT
27,000	24,000	89,000	92,000
24,000		②	
3,000		3,000	
①		92,000	92,000

Computing Net Loss on the Worksheet

Activity C. Answer the following questions about completing the financial statements sections of the worksheet. Refer to the completed worksheet on page 479.
1. Is every balance in the Unadjusted Trial Balance section moved to the Adjusted Trial Balance section? If so, are the balances for the same account always identical? Why or why not?
2. When Merchandise Inventory is credited for $600 in the Adjustments section, what account is debited? Why is this entry made?
3. What is the purpose of the small letters in the Adjustments section?

4. What is the amount of the net income? How is it determined?
5. Why is the $1,529 net income added to the total of the Credit column in the Balance Sheet section?
6. Does the amount of net income in the Income Statement section always have to be the same as the amount of net income in the Balance Sheet section? Why or why not?
7. How can you tell that the $1,529 is net income and not net loss?
8. Why is the $7,000 for Merchandise Inventory not moved to the Balance Sheet section?

Topic 3 Problems

16-4. The accounts in the general ledger of Jeter's Farm Bureau showed the balances listed below on July 31. (Mr. Jeter has only one employee.)

The physical inventory on July 31 showed (1) merchandise on hand amounting to $9,870 and (2) unused supplies amounting to $140. The amount of unexpired insurance as of July 31 is $450. Complete a worksheet for the month ended July 31.
NOTE: Save your worksheet for further use in Topic Problems 16-6.

16-5. The accounts in the general ledger of the Richelieu Outfitters showed the balances listed below on December 31. (Mr. Richelieu has no employees.)

The physical inventory on December 31 showed merchandise on hand amounting to $7,520. The cost of the supplies used was $30, and the amount of expired insurance for December is $75. Complete a worksheet for the month ended December 31.
NOTE: Save your worksheet for further use in Topic Problems 16-8 and 16-10.

ACCOUNT TITLE	ACCT. NO.	DEBIT	CREDIT
Cash	101	9,240 00	
Accounts Receivable	111	3,875 00	
Merchandise Inventory	112	12,653 00	
Prepaid Insurance	113	540 00	
Supplies on Hand	114	160 00	
Land	121	6,900 00	
Building	131	20,000 00	
Equipment	132	6,040 00	
Accounts Payable	211		1,783 00
Employee Income Taxes Payable	221		70 00
FICA Taxes Payable	222		62 00
Mortgage Payable	231		20,000 00
Mark Jeter, Capital	301		32,567 00
Mark Jeter, Drawing	302	800 00	
Income Summary	399	— 00	— 00
Sales	401		10,346 00
Sales Returns and Allowances	402	138 00	
Sales Discount	403	183 00	
Purchases	501	3,765 00	
Transportation In	502	45 00	
Purchases Returns and Allowances	503		87 00
Purchases Discount	504		76 00
Insurance Expense	511		— 00
Miscellaneous Expense	512	21 00	
Payroll Taxes Expense	513	31 00	
Salaries Expense	514	600 00	
Insurance Expense	515	— 00	— 00

ACCOUNT TITLE	ACCT. NO.	DEBIT	CREDIT
Cash	101	3,521 00	
Change Fund	102	35 00	
Accounts Receivable	111	283 00	
Merchandise Inventory	112	6,213 00	
Prepaid Insurance	113	300 00	
Supplies on Hand	114	45 00	
Office Equipment	131	800 00	
Store Equipment	132	2,429 00	
Accounts Payable	201		86 00
Sales Taxes Payable	211		242 00
Carl Richelieu, Capital	301		14,696 00
Carl Richelieu, Drawing	302	140 00	
Income Summary	399	— 00	
Sales	401		4,930 00
Sales Returns and Allowances	402	90 00	
Sales Discount	403	70 00	
Purchases	501	5,800 00	
Transportation In	502	23 00	
Purchases Returns and Allowances	503		45 00
Purchases Discount	504		120 00
Advertising Expense	511	140 00	
Insurance Expense	512	— 00	— 00
Miscellaneous Expense	513	60 00	
Rent Expense	514	170 00	
Supplies Expense	515	— 00	— 00

Topic 4
Preparing Financial Statements

A *What is the source of data that the worksheet supplies to prepare financial statements?* The account balances have been sorted on the worksheet according to the statements on which the accounts appear. Also, the net income (or net loss) has been computed. It is now easy to prepare the financial statements—Step 5 in the accounting cycle.

Step 5a: Preparing the Schedule of Cost of Goods Sold and the Income Statement

Schedule of Cost of Goods Sold. The **schedule of cost of goods sold** is a statement showing the computation of cost of goods sold during the accounting period. The schedule of cost of goods sold is prepared before the income statement because the amount of the cost of goods sold is needed to complete the income statement.

The schedule of cost of goods sold that was prepared for the House of Sound for the month of November is shown on page 483. Note that the heading indicates that the schedule covers a period of time.

1 *Merchandise Inventory, November 1.* The inventory for November 1 is the cost of merchandise inventory on hand as of the beginning of the accounting period. The amount ($7,000) is found on the Unadjusted Trial Balance.

2 *Net Purchases.* The data needed to compute the net purchases is found in the Income Statement section of the worksheet. During the month of November, House of Sound purchased merchandise costing $6,800. It also paid transportation charges of $80. The cost of delivered goods was $6,880 ($6,800 + $80). During the month, the business returned merchandise costing $185. It also took cash discounts of $50 offered by the suppliers. The two amounts reduced the net cost of the merchandise by $235 ($185 + $50). The amount of net purchases was $6,645 ($6,880 − $235).

3 *Cost of Goods Available for Sale.* This amount ($13,645) is the total of the inventory on hand at the beginning of the accounting period ($7,000), plus the net purchases ($6,645). The cost of goods available for sale is the total cost of goods that could have been sold if all the beginning inventory and purchases were sold. In practice one would not expect to see all the beginning inventory and purchases sold.

4 *Merchandise Inventory, November 30.* The amount of the merchandise inventory at the end of the accounting period on November 30 is $6,400 and is found in the balance sheet section. This amount must be subtracted from the cost of goods available for sale in order to arrive at the cost of goods sold. Why must the ending inventory be subtracted

Purchases		6,800	00
Add: Transportation In . . .		80	00
Cost of Delivered Goods . .		6,880	00
Less: Purchases Returns			
and Allowances . . $185.00			
Purchases Discount . 50.00		235	00
Net Purchases		6,645	00

Computing Net Purchases

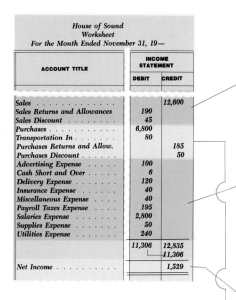

House of Sound
Worksheet
For the Month Ended November 31, 19—

ACCOUNT TITLE	INCOME STATEMENT	
	DEBIT	CREDIT
Sales		12,600
Sales Returns and Allowances	190	
Sales Discount	45	
Purchases	6,800	
Transportation In	80	
Purchases Returns and Allow.		185
Purchases Discount		50
Advertising Expense	100	
Cash Short and Over	6	
Delivery Expense	120	
Insurance Expense	40	
Miscellaneous Expense	40	
Payroll Taxes Expense	195	
Salaries Expense	2,800	
Supplies Expense	50	
Utilities Expense	240	
	11,306	12,835
		11,306
Net Income		1,529

House of Sound
Income Statement
For the Month Ended November 30, 19—

Revenue From Sales:			
Sales.		12,600 00	
Less: Sales Returns and			
Allowances	$190.00		
Sales Discount	45.00	235 00	
Net Sales			12,365 00
Cost of Goods Sold (See Schedule)			7,245 00
Gross Profit on Sales.			5,120 00
Operating Expenses:			
Advertising Expense		100 00	
Cash Short and Over.		6 00	
Delivery Expense.		120 00	
Insurance Expense.		40 00	
Miscellaneous Expense		40 00	
Payroll Taxes Expense		195 00	
Salaries Expense		2,800 00	
Supplies Expense		50 00	
Utilities Expense		240 00	
Total Operating Expenses			3,591 00
Net Income			1,529 00

House of Sound
Schedule of Cost of Goods Sold
For the Month Ended November 30, 19—

(1)	Merchandise Inventory, November 1			7,000 00
	Purchases.		6,800 00	
	Add: Transportation In		80 00	
	Cost of Delivered Goods		6,880 00	
	Less: Purchases Returns and			
	Allowances	$185.00		
	Purchases Discount	50.00	235 00	
(2)	Net Purchases.			6,645 00
(3)	Cost of Goods Available for Sale.			13,645 00
(4)	Less: Merchandise Inventory, November 30 . .			6,400 00
(5)	Cost of Goods Sold			7,245 00

from the cost of goods available for sale? An actual count of the inventory revealed that unsold merchandise costing $6,400 was still sitting on the shelves and in storage at the House of Sound. Since it was not sold, it cannot be included in the cost of goods sold.

5 *Cost of Goods Sold.* This amount ($7,245) is the dollar value of goods actually transferred to customers through business activity. It is found by subtracting the ending inventory ($6,400) from the cost of goods available for sale ($13,645). In practice, the amount of "inventory losses" (discussed in Chapter 14) is also included in the cost of goods sold.

Income Statement for Merchandising Business Contains Five Sections

- Revenue
- Cost of Goods Sold
- Gross Profit
- Operating Expenses
- Net Income (or Net Loss)

Income Statement. The income statement for a merchandising business contains five sections: revenue, cost of goods sold, gross profit, operating expenses, and net income (or net loss). The two new sections—cost of goods sold and gross profit—are important. The net income (or net loss) of a merchandising business is found by subtracting both the cost of goods sold and expenses from revenue.

The income statement prepared for the House of Sound for the month of November is an example of an income statement for a merchandising business. The amounts of the revenue, operating expenses, and net income are obtained directly from the Income Statement section of the worksheet. The cost of goods sold and the gross profit must be computed.

Revenue From Sales:			
Sales		$12,600	00
Less: Sales Returns and			
Allowances . .	$190.00		
Sales Discount	45.00	235	00
Net Sales		12,365	00

Revenue From Sales. The total sales for the month ($12,600) is found in the Income Statement section of the worksheet. From this amount, the sales returns and allowances ($190) and sales discounts ($45) are deducted to obtain the net sales of $12,365.

Cost of Goods Sold. The total cost of goods sold is shown on the income statement. The computation of the cost of goods sold is usually shown on a schedule that goes with the income statement. When a schedule of cost of goods sold supports the income statement, only the amount of the cost of goods sold ($7,245) appears on the income statement.

Net Sales	12,365	00
Cost of Goods Sold . . .	7,245	00
Gross Profit on Sales . .	5,120	00

Gross Profit on Sales. A gross profit on sales is made by selling merchandise for a higher price than was paid by the business. The amount of gross profit on sales ($5,120) is found by subtracting the cost of goods sold ($7,245) from the net sales ($12,365).

Operating Expenses. Each expense and the total expenses of operating the business for the month of November ($3,591) is found in the Income Statement section of the worksheet.

Gross Profit on Sales . .	5,120	00
Operating Expenses . . .	3,591	00
Net Income	1,529	00

Net Income. The net income is the amount remaining after total operating expenses are subtracted from the gross profit on sales. During November, the House of Sound has a gross profit on sales of $5,120, operating expenses of $3,591, and a net income of $1,529 ($5,120 − $3,591). This is the same amount as the net income computed on the worksheet. If expenses had been greater than the gross profit on sales, there would have been a net loss.

Activity A. Answer the following questions about the schedule of cost of goods sold and the income statement. Refer to the schedule of cost of goods sold and income statement on page 483.

1. How much is total purchases?

2. How much is net purchases?

3. What is the difference between total purchases and net purchases?

4. How much is the cost of goods sold? How is it obtained?

5. Where is the data obtained for preparing the income statement?

6. What is the total amount of sales?

7. What is the amount of net sales?

8. What is the difference between total sales and net sales?

9. How much is the gross profit on sales?

10. How much is the net income?

Step 5b: Preparing the Statement of Owner's Equity and the Balance Sheet

B *What are the procedures for preparing the statement of owner's equity and the balance sheet?* The financial position of a business is shown on two statements—the statement of owner's equity and the balance sheet. The statement of owner's equity is prepared first because it is needed to complete the balance sheet.

Statement of Owner's Equity

Frequently, the owner desires more information about the changes in owner's equity during the accounting period than is shown on the balance sheet. In this case, a **statement of owner's equity** is a financial statement to report investments and withdrawals, as well as the net income (or net loss) for the period. The statement of owner's equity is prepared before the balance sheet.

The owner's equity on November 1, the beginning of the accounting period, was $27,732. On November 30, the end of the accounting period, the owner's equity increased to $29,561. The increase of $1,829 was due to an additional investment of $1,500 and the net income of $1,529, less withdrawals of $1,200.

House of Sound Statement of Owner's Equity For the Month Ended November 30, 19—		
Capital, November 1....................		27,732 00
Additional Investments		1,500 00
Total Investments		29,232 00
Net Income for the Month..............	1,529 00	
Less: Withdrawals	1,200 00	
Increase in Capital		329 00
Capital, November 30		29,561 00

If a statement of owner's equity is prepared, the owner's capital at the end of the accounting period is the only amount shown in the Owner's Equity section of the balance sheet. The November 30 balance sheet for the House of Sound shows just one amount in the Owner's Equity section ($29,561).

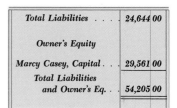

Total Liabilities	24,644 00
Owner's Equity	
Marcy Casey, Capital . .	29,561 00
Total Liabilities and Owner's Eq. . .	54,205 00

If the House of Sound had a net loss, a decrease in capital would be shown on the statement of owner's equity. For example, if there had been a net loss of $1,500 for November, the capital would decrease by $2,700 (net loss of $1,500 plus withdrawals of $1,200).

Not all the information to prepare the statement of owner's equity is shown on the worksheet. The balance of the capital account at the beginning of the accounting period and the additional investments are found in the owner's capital account in the general ledger. The withdrawals and the net income (or net loss) are found in the Balance Sheet section of the worksheet.

Balance Sheet

The balance sheets up to this point have shown all assets in one group. All liabilities have also been shown in one group. For accounting purposes, however, assets and liabilities are usually classified into these groups: current assets, plant and equipment assets, current liabilities, and long-term liabilities.

House of Sound Chart of Accounts

Current Assets
101 Cash
102 Petty Cash
103 Change Fund
111 Accounts Receivable
112 Merchandise Inventory
113 Prepaid Insurance
114 Supplies on Hand

Current Assets. Cash, assets that will be changed into cash, and assets that will be used in the normal operations of the business within a year of the date of the balance sheet are classified as **current assets.** The four major types of current assets are cash, receivables, merchandise inventory, and prepaid expenses. The order on the balance sheet is determined by liquidity—that is, by how quickly each asset is expected to be changed into cash or used.

Cash is always listed first because it is available to pay debts. Petty Cash and Change Fund are listed next. Next are the *receivables*, such as Notes Receivable and Accounts Receivable. These are the amounts that customers owe the business. (Notes Receivable is usually listed before Accounts Receivable because notes are negotiable.)

Merchandise Inventory is listed next. It shows the cost of items the business has on hand and hopes to sell within the accounting period. Then come the *prepaid expenses*, such as Prepaid Insurance and Supplies on Hand. Prepaid expenses are current assets because each will be used, and the business will not have to use cash to buy them in the near future.

The total current assets are used for many purposes. For example, when a business applies for a loan, the bank often reviews the current assets to see if there will be cash to repay the loan. Also, the business may review its current assets to see if it can pay debts as they become due.

Plant and Equipment. Assets that are expected to be useful to the business for a number of years are known as plant and equipment.

Examples are land, buildings, furniture, and machinery. One way of listing plant and equipment on the balance sheet is to list the more permanent assets such as land and buildings first. Land has unlimited life. All other plant and equipment assets gradually lose their usefulness because they wear out and need replacement, become obsolete, or because more efficient items are needed.

**House of Sound
Balance Sheet
November 30, 19—**

Assets			
Current Assets:			
Cash	9,500 00		
Petty Cash	30 00		
Change Fund	35 00		
Accounts Receivable	3,000 00		
Merchandise Inventory	6,400 00		
Prepaid Insurance	440 00		
Supplies on Hand	300 00		
Total Current Assets		19,705 00	
Plant and Equipment:			
Land	8,000 00		
Building	22,000 00		
Office Equipment	1,800 00		
Stockroom Equipment	2,700 00		
Total Plant and Equipment		34,500 00	
Total Assets		54,205 00	
Liabilities			
Current Liabilities:			
Loans Payable	4,000 00		
Accounts Payable	5,500 00		
Sales Taxes Payable	200 00		
Federal Income Taxes Payable	360 00		
FICA Taxes Payable	220 00		
State Income Taxes Payable	140 00		
Federal Unemployment Taxes Payable	48 00		
State Unemployment Taxes Payable	176 00		
Total Current Liabilities		10,644 00	
Long-Term Liabilities:			
Mortgage Payable		14,000 00	
Total Liabilities		24,644 00	
Owner's Equity			
Marcy Casey, Capital		29,561 00	
Total Liabilities and Owner's Equity		54,205 00	

Current Liabilities. **Current liabilities** are debts that must be paid within a year of the balance sheet date. Current liabilities are listed in the order that they must be paid. Those that must be paid first are shown first. (Loans Payable is generally listed before Accounts Payable because loans have a definite due date.)

Long-Term Liabilities. Debts that are not due within a year are considered **long-term liabilities** (sometimes referred to as *fixed liabilities*). An example of a long-term liability is a mortgage on land and buildings.

A classified balance sheet prepared for the House of Sound on November 30 is shown on page 487. (If a business does not have each group of assets or liabilities, it simply omits any group that it does not have from the balance sheet.)

Activity B. Answer the following questions about preparing the statement of owner's equity and the balance sheet. Refer to the statement of owner's equity on page 485 and the balance sheet on page 487.

1. Does Marcy Casey make any additional investments during the month? If so, how much?

2. Where is the net income obtained for the statement of owner's equity? Owner's withdrawals? Total investments?

3. Where is the data obtained for preparing the balance sheet and the statement of owner's equity?

4. Is the beginning or the ending merchandise inventory recorded on the balance sheet? Why?

5. Are there any prepaid expenses on the balance sheet? If so, what are the account titles and balances?

6. What is the total amount of current assets? Of plant and equipment? What is the total of the assets?

Statement of Changes in Financial Position

C *What is the Statement of Changes in Financial Position?* The statement of changes in financial position details changes in assets and liabilities by focusing on changes in *working capital.* **Working capital** is the difference between the total current assets and total current liabilities. By focusing on changes in current assets and current liabilities, the accountant is also able to provide the details of changes in other asset and liability accounts.

The balance sheet prepared for the House of Sound on November 30 shows the balance of assets, liabilities, and owner's equity. By comparing the balance sheets for October 31 and November 30, it is easy to see that the assets, liabilities, and owner's equity have changed. The statement of owner's equity provides the details of changes in the owner's equity. However, the details of changes in assets and liabilities are not shown on any statement prepared to this point. The **statement of changes in financial position** is the statement that details changes in assets and liabilities.

Preparing the Statement of Changes in Financial Position.
The statement of changes in financial position prepared for the House of Sound has four sections, as shown in the statement.

	House of Sound Statement of Changes in Financial Position For the Month Ended November 30, 19—			
Sources of Working Capital:				
From Current Operations:				
Net Income	1,529 00			
From Additional Investment	1,500 00			
Total Sources of Working Capital			3,029 00	
Uses of Working Capital:				
Payments on Mortgage	150 00			
Withdrawals	1,200 00			
Total Uses of Working Capital			1,350 00	
Net Increase in Working Capital			1,679 00	

1 *Heading.* The heading has three lines and answers this question: For what time period was the statement prepared? The statement prepared for the House of Sound details the changes for the month of November.

2 *Sources of Working Capital.* The House of Sound had two sources of working capital: net income ($1,529) and an additional cash investment by the owner ($1,500).

A net income increases working capital in the following manner. All revenue transactions increase working capital by increasing either cash or accounts receivable. All cost and expense transactions decrease working capital by decreasing cash (paying for purchases and expenses) or increasing liabilities (purchasing on credit or incurring expenses on credit). For the House of Sound, the difference in the revenue and cost and expense transactions was a net increase in working capital of $1,529.

3 *Uses of Working Capital.* This section shows what caused working capital to leave the business. The House of Sound had two uses of working capital: a payment on the mortgage ($150) and a withdrawal by the owner ($1,200).

4 *Net Increase in Working Capital.* This section shows what the increase (or decrease) in working capital was for the month of November. The increase ($1,679) is found by subtracting the total uses of working capital ($1,350) from the total sources of working capital ($3,029).

Verifying the Net Increase in Working Capital. The increase in working capital is computed on the statement of changes in financial position. The increase in working capital is also computed by subtracting the working capital at the end of November from the working capital at the end of October. The computation is shown in the following table.

CHANGES IN WORKING CAPITAL

	October 31	November 30	Change
Current Assets	$17,980	$19,705	$1,725
Current Liabilities	−10,598	−10,644	− 46
Working Capital	$ 7,382	$ 9,061	$1,679

As the owner of the House of Sound reviews the statement of changes in financial position, certain facts are clear. First, the source of working capital to run the business is evenly divided between operations and an additional investment made during the month. Without the additional investment, working capital would have changed very little during November.

In addition, the owner also knows that the only asset, liability, and owner's equity accounts that changed during the month were the working capital accounts, mortgage payable, and owner's equity. None of the plant and equipment accounts for the House of Sound changed during the month.

Activity C. Answer the following questions about the statement of changes in financial position. Refer to the text, margin notes, and illustrations on pages 488 to 490.

1. Would you describe the statement of changes in financial position as a summary statement or a status statement?

2. What are the total uses of working capital? The total sources of working capital?
3. By what amount did working capital increase during the month of November? What was the source of your answer?
4. What would have been the increase (or decrease) in working capital if the owner had not made an additional investment?

Accounting Principles:
Classifying Assets. The generally accepted accounting principle is that the assets reported on the balance sheet should be classified into at least two groups: current assets and plant and equipment.

Classifying Liabilities. The generally accepted accounting principle is that liabilities reported on the balance sheet should be classified into at least two groups: current liabilities and long-term liabilities.

16-6. Using the data from the worksheet prepared in Topic Problem 16-4 on page 481, complete the following work for Jeter's Farm Bureau for the month ended July 31.

a. Prepare a schedule of cost of goods sold and an income statement.

b. Prepare a statement of owner's equity and a classified balance sheet.

Mr. Jeter made additional investments of $5,000 during the period.

16-7. Complete the following schedule of goods sold.

16-8. Using the data from the worksheet prepared in Topic Problem 16-5, complete the following work for Richelieu Outfitters for the month ended December 31, 19—.

a. Prepare a schedule of cost of goods sold and an income statement.

b. Prepare a statement of owner's equity and a classified balance sheet.

Mr. Richelieu made additional investments of $4,000 during the period.

NOTE: Save your worksheet for further use in Topic Problem 16-10.

Feldman Company
Schedule of Cost of Goods Sold
For the Quarter Ended March 31, 19—

Merchandise Inventory, January 1			7,000 00
Purchases	7,315 00		
Add: Transportation In	60 00		
Cost of Delivered Goods			
Less: Purchases Returns and Allow. . . $185.00			
Purchases Discount 120.00			
Net Purchases			
Cost of Goods Available for Sale			
Less: Merchandise Inventory, March 31			6,000 00
Cost of Goods Sold			

16-9. Supply the missing amounts in the table below.

	Purchases	Transp. In	Cost of Delivered Goods	Purch. Ret.	Purch. Disc.	Net Purch.	End. Inv.	Cost of Goods Available for Sale	Cost of Goods Sold
Beg. Inv.									
a. $6,500	$8,000	$400	?	$700	$ 800	?	$7,000	?	?
b. $8,500	$4,800	?	$5,000	$100	?	$ 600	$8,700	?	?
c. $3,800	$7,600	$100	?	$240	$ 160	?	?	?	$6,600
d. $7,000	?	$800	$7,200	$160	$ 240	?	$3,000	?	?
e. ?	?	$180	?	$280	$ 120	$6,800	$6,400	?	$8,600
f. $3,800	$7,100	?	$8,200	?	$ 160	$7,800	$3,900	?	?

Topic 5
Adjusting and Closing the Ledger

A *Are the adjustments shown on the worksheet also recorded in the ledger?* Yes, the ledger accounts—the permanent records—must be adjusted to contain the same balances shown on the worksheet. The procedure for bringing the ledger accounts up to date is known as

adjusting the ledger. Also, a procedure known as *closing the ledger* is completed so that the ledger accounts for the next accounting period are prepared. Adjusting and closing the ledger is completed as a part of Step 6 in the accounting cycle.

Step 6a: Recording and Posting the Adjusting Entries

The end-of-period adjustments are computed on the worksheet to provide correct account balances for the financial statements.

In the example of the House of Sound, adjustments were needed for (a) Merchandise Inventory, (b) Prepaid Insurance, and (c) Supplies on Hand. These accounts in the general ledger, however, still show the incorrect balances. Thus it is necessary to journalize the adjustments in the general journal and post the entries to the ledger. After journalizing and posting the adjustments, the accounts in the general ledger will agree with the amounts on the financial statements. The data for the adjusting entries is found in the Adjustments section.

Worksheet: Source of Adjustments

House of Sound Worksheet For the Month Ended November 30, 19—		
	ADJUSTMENTS	
ACCOUNT TITLE	DEBIT	CREDIT
Merchandise Inventory . . .		(a) 600
Prepaid Insurance		(b) 40
Supplies on Hand		(c) 50
Income Summary	(a) 600	
Insurance Expense	(b) 40	
Supplies Expense	(c) 50	

Adjustments recorded in general journal.

GENERAL JOURNAL				Page 6	
DATE		ACCOUNT TITLE AND EXPLANATION	POST. REF.	DEBIT	CREDIT
19— Nov.	30	Income Summary	399	600 00	
		Merchandise Inventory	112		600 00
		Adjust inventory.			
	30	Insurance Expense	514	40 00	
		Prepaid Insurance	113		40 00
		Record expired insurance.			
	30	Supplies Expense	519	50 00	
		Supplies on Hand	114		50 00
		Record supplies used.			

Ledger accounts after posting adjustments.

Merchandise Inventory   Account No. 112

DATE		EXPLANATION	POST. REF.	DEBIT	CREDIT	BALANCE DEBIT	BALANCE CREDIT
19— Nov.	1	Balance	—			7,000 00	
	30	Adjustment	J6		600 00	6,400 00	

Income Summary   Account No. 399

DATE		EXPLANATION	POST. REF.	DEBIT	CREDIT	BALANCE DEBIT	BALANCE CREDIT
19— Nov.	30	Inventory adjustment	J6	600 00		600 00	

Prepaid Insurance   Account No. 113

DATE		EXPLANATION	POST. REF.	DEBIT	CREDIT	BALANCE DEBIT	BALANCE CREDIT
19— Nov.	1	. . . .	CP6	480 00		480 00	
	30	Expired	J6		40 00	440 00	

Insurance Expense   Account No. 514

DATE		EXPLANATION	POST. REF.	DEBIT	CREDIT	BALANCE DEBIT	BALANCE CREDIT
19— Nov.	30	. . . .	J6	40 00		40 00	

Supplies on Hand   Account No. 114

DATE		EXPLANATION	POST. REF.	DEBIT	CREDIT	BALANCE DEBIT	BALANCE CREDIT
19— Nov.	3	. . . .	CP6	350 00		350 00	
	30	Used	J6		50 00	300 00	

Supplies Expense   Account No. 519

DATE		EXPLANATION	POST. REF.	DEBIT	CREDIT	BALANCE DEBIT	BALANCE CREDIT
19— Nov.	30	. . . .	J6	50 00		50 00	

Activity A. Answer the following questions. Refer to the adjusting entries on page 492.
1. Where is the data obtained for making the adjusting entries?
2. Why is Prepaid Insurance credited for $40? What is the new balance?
3. Why is Supplies on Hand credited for $50? What is the new balance?

4. Is the ending inventory less than the beginning inventory? By how much?
5. Why is the difference between the beginning inventory and the ending inventory transferred to the Income Summary account?

Step 6b: Recording and Posting the Closing Entries

B *What is the purpose of the closing entries?* The closing entries are necessary to close the ledger. Closing the ledger is preparing the accounts for the next accounting period. The first part of Step 6 is to journalize and post the adjusting entries. Next, all temporary owner's equity accounts—revenue, cost and expense, income summary, and drawing accounts—have to be closed. This is done by transferring the temporary account balances to other accounts. The temporary accounts then have zero balances and are ready for the next period's revenue and cost and expense data.

Four journal entries are made to transfer the balances of the temporary accounts. The procedures to do this are as follows.

• Close all the revenue and cost accounts in the Credit column of the Income Statement section of the worksheet. The balances are transferred to the Income Summary account by debiting each account for the account balance and crediting Income Summary for the total of the balances.

Transfer temporary accounts with credit balances in the Income Statement section to the Income Summary account.

GENERAL JOURNAL					Page 6
DATE	ACCOUNT TITLE AND EXPLANATION	POST. REF.	DEBIT	CREDIT	
19—					
Nov. 30	Sales	401	12,600 00		
	Purchases Returns and Allowances .	503	185 00		
	Purchases Discount	504	50 00		
	Income Summary	399		12,835 00	
	Close accounts with credit balances.				

House of Sound
Worksheet
For the Month Ended November 30, 19—

ACCOUNT TITLE	INCOME STATEMENT	
	DEBIT	CREDIT
Sales		12,600
Purchases Ret. and Allow.		185
Purchases Discount		50
		12,835

• Close all the accounts (except the Income Summary account) in the Debit column of the Income Statement section of the worksheet. The balances are transferred by crediting each account for the account balance and debiting the Income Summary account for the total of the balances. (The $600 debit was already transferred to the Income Summary account through an adjusting entry.)

Transfer temporary accounts with debit balances (except Income Summary) in Income Statement section to Income Summary account.

House of Sound
Worksheet
For the Month Ended November 30, 19—

ACCOUNT TITLE	INCOME STATEMENT	
	DEBIT	CREDIT
Income Summary	600	
Sales Ret. and Allow.	190	
Sales Discount	45	
Purchases	6,800	
Transportation In	80	
Advertising Expense	100	
Cash Short and Over	6	
Delivery Expense	120	
Insurance Expense	40	
Miscellaneous Expense . . .	40	
Payroll Taxes Expense . . .	195	
Salaries Expense	2,800	
Supplies Expense	50	
Utilities Expense	240	
	11,306	12,835
Net Income		1,529

GENERAL JOURNAL — Page 6

DATE	ACCOUNT TITLE AND EXPLANATION	POST. REF.	DEBIT	CREDIT
19—				
Nov. 30	Income Summary	399	10,706 00	
	Sales Returns and Allowances . . .	402		190 00
	Sales Discount	403		45 00
	Purchases	501		6,800 00
	Transportation In	502		80 00
	Advertising Expense	511		100 00
	Cash Short and Over	512		6 00
	Delivery Expense	513		120 00
	Insurance Expense	514		40 00
	Miscellaneous Expense	515		40 00
	Payroll Taxes Expense	516		195 00
	Salaries Expense	518		2,800 00
	Supplies Expense	519		50 00
	Utilities Expense	520		240 00
	Close accounts with debit balances.			

Income Summary — Account No. 399

DATE	EXPLANATION	POST. REF.	DEBIT	CREDIT	BALANCE DEBIT	BALANCE CREDIT
19—						
Nov. 30	Inventory adjustment	J6	600 00		600 00	
30	Closing entry	J6		12,835 00		12,235 00
30	Closing entry	J6	10,706 00			1,529 00

• Close the Income Summary account. After the first two closing entries are posted, the balance of the Income Summary account is the net income (or net loss). Income Summary is then transferred to the capital account by debiting the Income Summary account and crediting the capital account for the amount of the net income. A net loss is transferred to the capital account by debiting the capital account and crediting the Income Summary account for the amount of the net loss.

Transfer Income Summary account balance to capital account.

GENERAL JOURNAL — Page 6

DATE	ACCOUNT TITLE AND EXPLANATION	POST. REF.	DEBIT	CREDIT
19—				
Nov. 30	Income Summary	399	1,529 00	
	Marcy Casey, Capital	301		1,529 00
	Transfer net income.			

Income Summary Closed

Income Summary — Account No. 399

DATE	EXPLANATION	POST. REF.	DEBIT	CREDIT	BALANCE DEBIT	BALANCE CREDIT
19—						
Nov. 30	Inventory adjustment	J6	600 00		600 00	
30	Closing entry	J6		12,835 00		12,235 00
30	Closing entry	J6	10,706 00			1,529 00
30	Transfer net income	J6	1,529 00			— 00

Balance of Capital: Investment and Net Income

House of Sound
Worksheet
For the Month Ended November 30, 19—

ACCOUNT TITLE	INCOME STATEMENT	
	DEBIT	CREDIT
	11,306	12,835
		11,306
Net Income		1,529

Marcy Casey, Capital — Account No. 301

DATE	EXPLANATION	POST. REF.	DEBIT	CREDIT	BALANCE DEBIT	BALANCE CREDIT
19—						
Nov. 1	Balance	—				27,732 00
2	Additional investment	CR5		1,500 00		29,232 00
30	Net income	J6		1,529 00		30,761 00

• Close the drawing account. The owner makes withdrawals against expected net income by debiting the drawing account. At the end of the accounting period, the withdrawals are transferred to Capital. Thus the withdrawals can be offset against the net income or loss. The $1,200 in the drawing account is transferred to Capital. This data is in the Balance Sheet section of the worksheet.

Transfer drawing account balance to capital account.

House of Sound
Worksheet
For the Month Ended November 30, 19—

| ACCOUNT TITLE | BALANCE SHEET | |
	DEBIT	CREDIT
Marcy Casey, Drawing	1,200	

GENERAL JOURNAL   **Page** 6

DATE	ACCOUNT TITLE AND EXPLANATION	POST. REF.	DEBIT	CREDIT
19—				
Nov. 30	Marcy Casey, Capital	301	1,200 00	
	Marcy Casey, Drawing	302		1,200 00
	Transfer to capital.			

Marcy Casey, Capital   **Account No.** 301

| DATE | EXPLANATION | POST. REF. | DEBIT | CREDIT | BALANCE | |
					DEBIT	CREDIT
19—						
Nov. 1	Balance	—				27,232 00
2	Additional investment	CR5		1,500 00		29,232 00
30	Net income	J6		1,529 00		30,761 00
30	Transfer from drawing	J6	1,200 00			29,561 00

Capital account contains net income and withdrawals.

Marcy Casey, Drawing   **Account No.** 302

| DATE | EXPLANATION | POST. REF. | DEBIT | CREDIT | BALANCE | |
					DEBIT	CREDIT
19—						
Nov. 23	Withdrawal	CP5	1,200 00		1,200 00	
30	Transfer to capital	J6		1,200 00	— 00	

Drawing account closed.

Full-Charge
Bookkeeper:
DOT 210.382-014. Keeps complete records of financial transactions. A Bookkeeper II may keep one section of the records, as accounts receivable bookkeeper.

Activity B. Answer the following questions about recording and posting the closing entries. Refer to the closing entries shown on pages 493 to 495.
1. Where is the data obtained for making the closing entries?
2. How is the $12,835 credit to the Income Summary account obtained? Why is this entry made?
3. How is the $10,706 debit to the Income Summary account obtained? What is the purpose of this entry?

4. What is the Income Summary balance after the transfer of debit balances from temporary accounts? What does this amount represent?
5. What is the purpose of the $1,529 credit to the capital account?
6. Why is the drawing account credited for $1,200?
7. What makes up the $29,561 balance of the capital account?

Step 7: Preparing a Postclosing Trial Balance

C | *What is the purpose of the postclosing trial balance?* At the end of the accounting period, an unadjusted trial balance was prepared to prove the equality of the debits and credits in the general ledger. After the adjustments were made on the worksheet, an adjusted trial balance was prepared to verify the equality of the debits and credits. Now, a postclosing trial balance is prepared to verify the equality of debits and credits in the general ledger after the adjusting and closing entries have been posted.

The postclosing trial balance prepared for the House of Sound on November 30 is shown on page 496. (Notice that the postclosing trial balance shows the same balances for the asset, liability, and owner's equity accounts as the balance sheet.) When the postclosing trial balance is in balance, the accounts are ready for the next period.

House of Sound
Postclosing Trial Balance
November 30, 19—

ACCOUNT TITLE	ACCT. NO.	DEBIT	CREDIT
Cash	101	9,500 00	
Petty Cash..................	102	30 00	
Change Fund	103	35 00	
Accounts Receivable...........	111	3,000 00	
Merchandise Inventory	112	6,400 00	
Prepaid Insurance..............	113	440 00	
Supplies on Hand	114	300 00	
Land	121	8,000 00	
Building....................	131	22,000 00	
Office Equipment	132	1,800 00	
Stockroom Equipment	133	2,700 00	
Loans Payable	201		4,000 00
Accounts Payable.............	211		5,500 00
Sales Taxes Payable	216		200 00
Federal Income Taxes Payable......	221		360 00
FICA Taxes Payable	222		220 00
State Income Taxes Payable........	223		140 00
Federal Unemployment Taxes Payable	224		48 00
State Unemployment Taxes Payable ..	225		176 00
Mortgage Payable..............	231		14,000 00
Marcy Casey, Capital	301		29,561 00
		54,205 00	54,205 00

Activity C. Answer the following questions about preparing the postclosing trial balance. Refer to the postclosing trial balance above and the worksheet on page 479.
1. Why is the capital account balance not the same on the postclosing trial balance and worksheet?

2. What other items differ on the postclosing trial balance and in the Balance Sheet section of the worksheet? Why do they differ?
3. The balance of the Income Statement section of the worksheet appears in what account on the postclosing trial balance?

Accounting Concepts:
Closing the Ledger. The revenue data and the cost and expense data for one accounting period must be clearly distinguished from that of another accounting period.
Postclosing Trial Balance. The equality of the total debits and the total credits in the general ledger should be verified after the ledger has been closed.
Accounting Principle:
Matching Revenue and Expenses. The generally accepted accounting principle is that revenue must be matched against the expenses incurred in obtaining that revenue. The result of matching revenue and expenses is net income (or net loss) for the accounting period.

16-10. Using the data from the worksheet prepared in Topic Problem 16-5 and the financial statements prepared in Topic Problem 16-8, complete the following. **a.** Journalize the adjusting entries and the closing entries.

b. During December, Richelieu Outfitters suffered a net loss. In analyzing the financial statements, what are some factors that should be considered in attempting to make a net income in January?

Topic 6
Interpreting Financial Information

A *When does the interpretation of financial information take place?* The interpretation of financial data takes place any time that owners and managers use the accounting records to make business decisions. Interpreting financial information is listed as the last step in the accounting cycle. However, owners and managers might compare salaries or sales for one month in the accounting period with similar data for another month. You have already learned how the accounts receivable ledger is used to age receivables and to analyze the due dates for accounts payable. These are only some examples of how owners and managers interpret financial information whenever they have the need.

Financial information is interpreted at any time during or at the end of the accounting period.

Topic 4 discusses a statement that is used to interpret financial position—the statement of changes in financial position. Another statement that is extremely important to management—the cash-flow statement—and the use of ratios and budgets as tools for decision making are now discussed.

Analyzing Cash Flow

On October 31 the House of Sound had a cash balance of $6,700. On November 30 the cash balance was $9,500. The cash balance increased $2,800 for the month.

$9,500	Cash balance, Nov. 30
6,700	Cash balance, Oct. 31
$2,800	Net increase in cash for Nov.

Knowing that cash increased $2,800 is important to management. However, the increase in cash for the month is only a part of the picture. Cash has been received and paid daily. Thus it is important to find out where cash comes from and how it is spent. The receipts and payments of cash for a period of time are known as **cash flow.** Cash-flow information enables owners and managers to plan for the future. A cash-flow statment is prepared to provide this information.

Cash-Flow Statement. A **cash-flow statement** is a summary of cash receipts (sources of cash) and cash payments (uses of cash) for an accounting period. The cash-flow statement is similar to the statement of changes in financial position. However, it explains the flow of cash rather than working capital.

The cash-flow statement contains four sections: heading, sources of cash, uses of cash, and net increase (or net decrease) in cash during the accounting period.

A transaction that increases the amount of cash is called a **source of cash.** A transaction that decreases the amount of cash is called a **use of cash.** If more cash was received than was paid during the accounting period, there is a **net increase in cash.** If more cash was paid than received, there is a **net decrease in cash.** The following sections describe the cash-flow statement prepared for the House of Sound on November 30.

House of Sound Cash-Flow Statement For the Month Ended November 30, 19—		
Sources of Cash:		
From Current Operations.............	2,650 00	
From Additional Investment	1,500 00	
Total Sources of Cash..............		4,150 00
Uses of Cash:		
Payment on Mortgage	150 00	
Withdrawals......................	1,200 00	
Total Uses of Cash...............		1,350 00
Net Increase in Cash		2,800 00

1 *Heading.* The heading answers this question: For what time period does the cash-flow statement cover? The statement prepared for the House of Sound gives cash information for the month of November.
2 *Sources of Cash.* This section answers this question: What caused cash to increase? The House of Sound had two sources of cash for November: operations ($2,650) and a cash investment ($1,500) by the owner.

The operations of the business increase cash in the following manner. At the beginning of November, customers owed the House of Sound for sales on credit. Some of these customers paid their accounts during the month. Also, other charge customers bought and paid for goods during the month. The House of Sound also had cash sales that were a source of cash.

The House of Sound had to make payments on accounts payable during the month, pay expenses, and make cash purchases. Each of these payments is a use of cash. When the difference between cash receipts and cash payments due to operations was computed, the House of Sound had a *net* source of cash of $2,650.

3 *Uses of Cash.* This section answers this question: What caused cash to decrease? The House of Sound had two uses of cash during the month. (Keep in mind that all the uses of cash due to operations have already been included when figuring sources of cash.) The first was a cash payment for the mortgage ($150), and the second was a $1,200 withdrawal by the owner.

4 *Net Increase in Cash.* This section answers this question: What was the net increase in cash for November? The answer is found by subtracting the total uses of cash ($1,350) from the total sources of cash ($4,150). The net increase in cash was $2,800 ($4,150 − $1,350).

A review of the cash-flow statement for the House of Sound provides managers and owners with certain information. First, cash receipts from operations are exceeding cash payments. Second, there was only one cash payment other than the withdrawal—the mortgage payment. Finally, managers and owners also know that cash would have increased even if the additional investment had not been made.

Activity A. Answer the following questions about cash flow. Refer to the text, margin notes, and illustration on pages 497 to 499.
1. What are the total sources of cash?
2. What is meant by cash due to operations?

3. What would the net increase (or net decrease) in cash be if the owner had not made the additional investment?
4. What are two ways to compute the net increase (or net decrease) in cash?

Using Ratios

B *How are ratios used to interpret financial information?* Many financial interpretations are between two amounts on the financial statements for one accounting period. For example, managers and owners might want to compare the amount of debts owed with the business's ability to pay the debts.

The numeric relation of one amount to another is called a **ratio.** A ratio may be expressed as a number, a percent, or a fraction. For example, if sales are $400,000 and net income is $40,000, the ratio can be expressed as follows.

$$\text{Sales} \div \text{Net Income} = \text{Number Ratio}$$
$$\$400,000 \div \$40,000 = 10$$

You can say that the ratio of sales to net income is 10 to 1, often written 10:1. A ratio can also be expressed as a percent.

$$\text{Net Income} \div \text{Sales} = \text{Percent Ratio}$$
$$\$40,000 \div \$400,000 = .10, \text{ or } 10\%$$

In this case you say that net income is 10 percent of sales. Ratios can also be expressed as fractions.

$$\text{Net Income} \div \text{Sales} = \text{Fraction Ratio}$$
$$\$40,000 \div \$400,000 = \tfrac{1}{10}$$

This ratio means that net income is one-tenth of sales.

The problem with interpreting financial information is deciding what ratio is satisfactory. Accountants look to different sources for comparative ratios. Sources include comparing current results with previous accounting periods, comparing results with similar businesses, and comparing results with government or investment guides.

Ratios computed for the House of Sound follow. These ratios can be computed for any business and compared with the sources mentioned previously.

Ratios That Measure Current Position. For accounting purposes, as you know, working capital is the difference between current assets and current liabilities. The working capital for the House of Sound is computed in the margin.

A company has an idea of its ability to pay current debts by computing working capital. If there are more current assets than current liabilities, the company may be able to pay current debts and is described as **solvent.** If there are more current liabilities than current assets, the company will not be able to pay current debts and is described as **insolvent.**

Computing working capital is one way to determine debt-paying ability. The working capital can also be further interpreted.

The **current ratio** (sometimes referred to as *working capital ratio*) is the number relation between current assets and current liabilities. The current ratio for the House of Sound appears here.

$$\frac{\text{Current Assets}}{\text{Current Liabilities}} = \text{Current Ratio}$$

$$\frac{\$19,705}{\$10,644} = 1.85:1$$

The current ratio for the House of Sound is expressed as 1.85:1. This means that the business owns $1.85 of current assets for each $1 of current liabilities. The House of Sound is in a better position than a company with a ratio of 1.20:1 ($1.20 to $1).

Generally, the higher the current ratio, the more favorable the financial position of the business. A 2:1 current ratio has been generally accepted as satisfactory. But this varies from business to business. Some businesses require a much higher ratio, and some can operate with a smaller ratio.

$19,705	Current Assets
− 10,644	Current Liabilities
$ 8,061	Working Capital

Ratios are used to measure current position.

Ratios That Measure Operating Results

Ratios such as the current ratio can be used to measure current position. Ratios can also be used to measure operating results. Two ratios used to determine a business's ability to earn a satisfactory net income are described here.

Ratios are used to measure operating results.

Return on Total Assets Ratio. The House of Sound earns a net income by putting assets to work. A **return on total assets ratio** is computed to see how effectively the assets are being used. The return on total assets ratio is computed by dividing net income by the total assets. The computation of this ratio for the House of Sound for November is shown here.

$$\frac{\text{Net Income}}{\text{Total Assets}} = \text{Return on Total Assets}$$

$$\frac{\$1,529}{\$54,205} = 2.8\%$$

The net income ($1,529) and total assets ($54,205) were taken from the House of Sound financial statements for November. In this case, the House of Sound earned 2.8 cents for each $1 in assets for 1 month—November. On a yearly basis, the return would be 33.6 percent (2.8% × 12 months = 33.6%, or $0.336 on each $1 of assets).

To interpret whether this is a sufficient return, the return must be compared with other investments. If the owner could earn more with another investment, then the second investment might be considered.

Return on Owner's Equity Ratio. Perhaps the most important ratio for owners is the return on owner's equity. The **return on owner's equity ratio** shows the return on the owner's investment and is found by dividing net income by total owner's equity. The resulting percent is used to indicate profitability. The November return on owner's equity for the House of Sound is illustrated here.

$$\frac{\text{Net Income}}{\text{Owner's Equity}} = \text{Return on Owner's Equity}$$

$$\frac{\$1,529}{\$29,561} = 5\%$$

The net income ($1,529) was taken from the income statement for November. The total owner's equity ($29,561) was taken from the balance sheet. The return on owner's equity is viewed as follows: The owner has invested cash and other resources, plus past earnings, of $29,561 in the House of Sound. In return, the owner has earned 5 percent on the investment for one month. When deciding to continue operating the House of Sound, the owner must compare the return on the investment, plus the advantages of business ownership, with other investment choices.

Activity B. Answer the following questions about using ratios. Refer to the text, margin notes, and illustrations on pages 499 to 502.

1. Do the ratios illustrated compare financial information from one accounting period to information from another period? Explain.

2. How does working capital differ from the current ratio?

3. Could a company have a current ratio of 0.8:1? Explain.

4. What is the source of information used to compute the current ratio?

5. What does a return of 12 percent on total assets mean?

6. What is the source of information used to compute the return on total assets for the House of Sound?

7. Why is the return on owner's equity ratio so important?

8. Someone commented that the 5 percent return on owner's equity for the House of Sound was not very good. The owner can get 10 percent in savings certificates. Do you agree that the 5 percent is not very good? Explain.

Budgeting

C *What is a budget?* A **budget** is a plan for a future period, stated in money terms. The preparation of a budget has two purposes. First, it can act as a guide for operating a business. Second, it can be used to compare the actual results of business activity with the planned operations (the budget).

Marcy Casey is the owner of the House of Sound. She notes that the net income for November was $1,529. She also notes that December is the best sales month for a business like the House of Sound. With November as a base month, she feels that the House of Sound should double its net income for December. To do so requires three things. The first is a plan. She decides to prepare a budget.

The second is a commitment to the budget, once prepared. She is committed to do what is necessary to make the budget work. The right kinds of merchandise must be purchased, overtime must be paid to employees, advertising must be purchased, and other expenditures must be met to make the budget work.

The third is a commitment of human resources. The budget is only a piece of paper. People must make it work. The commitment of human resources is very personal and is not included in a budget.

Preparing a Budget

Preparing a Budget
- Set goals.
- Prepare expected sales amounts.
- Prepare expected cost and expense amounts.
- Prepare the budget.

The budget prepared by Marcy Casey is shown on the next page. It was necessary to do the following to prepare the budget.

- Set goals for December.
- Prepare expected sales amounts.
- Prepare expected cost and expense amounts.
- Prepare the actual budget.

House of Sound
Projected Income Statement
For the Month of December, 19—

Revenue From Sales:			
Sales..................................	31,500 00		
Less: Sales Returns and			
Allowances $1,000.00			
Sales Discounts.......... 100.00	1,100 00		
Net Sales		30,400 00	
Cost of Goods Sold...................		18,000 00	
Gross Profit on Sales.................		12,400 00	
Operating Expenses:			
Advertising Expense	1,000 00		
Cash Short and Over..............	20 00		
Delivery Expense.................	400 00		
Insurance Expense................	40 00		
Miscellaneous Expense	50 00		
Payroll Taxes Expense	450 00		
Salaries Expense	6,000 00		
Supplies Expense	400 00		
Utilities Expense	500 00		
Total Operating Expenses		8,860 00	
Net Income		3,540 00	

House of Sound Income Statement For the Month Ended November 30, 19—

Revenue From Sales:			
Sales.		12,600 00	
Less: Sales Returns and			
Allowances $190.00			
Sales Discount 45.00	235 00		
Net Sales		12,365 00	12,365 00
Cost of Goods Sold (See Schedule)			7,245 00
Gross Profit on Sales..............			5,120 00
Operating Expenses:			
Advertising Expense		100 00	
Cash Short and Over................		6 00	
Delivery Expense .		120 00	
Insurance Expense		40 00	
Miscellaneous Expense .		40 00	
Payroll Taxes Expense		195 00	
Salaries Expense		2,800 00	
Supplies Expense		50 00	
Utilities Expense .		240 00	
Total Operating Expenses			3,591 00
Net Income			1,529 00

As you review the budget, note the following.

• The budget is actually an income statement with *projected* amounts.

• The projected net income is achieved because the expected sales amount ($31,500) is approximately $2\frac{1}{2}$ times the November sales amount ($12,600).

• The projected cost of goods sold ($18,000) is approximately $2\frac{1}{2}$ times the November amount.

• Certain of the expenses are projected to increase much more than sales or cost of goods sold. For instance, advertising expense has increased 10 times over the November amount. This increase is a way of saying that the House of Sound must advertise to increase sales. Note also that the salaries expense ($6,000) has a large projected increase. This increase indicates that the employees will be working long hours or that part-time help will be hired.

• The projected net income ($3,540) is approximately 2.3 times the November net income ($1,529). This means that it is projected to take $2\frac{1}{2}$ times the amount of sales to produce 2.3 times the net income.

Comparison of Actual and Projected Amounts. On December 1 the budget prepared by Marcy Casey was a guide to operations for December. On December 31 the budget is used to evaluate performance for the month of December. Evaluation of performance is done by comparing the projected amounts with the actual amounts for December. These figures are found here in the comparison of actual and projected operations.

House of Sound
Comparison of Projected and Actual Operations
For the Month of December 19—

	PROJECTED				ACTUAL	
Revenue From Sales:						
Sales.....................	31,500 00				30,100 00	
Less: Sales Ret. and Allow.....$1,000.00				$1,100.00		
Sales Discounts........ 100.00	1,100 00			120.00	1,220 00	
Net Sales		30,400 00				28,880 00
Cost of Goods Sold..............		18,000 00				16,200 00
Gross Profit on Sales.............		12,400 00				12,680 00
Operating Expenses:						
Advertising Expense	1,000 00			990 00		
Cash Short and Over.............	20 00			40 00		
Delivery Expense...............	400 00			460 00		
Insurance Expense.............	40 00			40 00		
Miscellaneous Expense...........	50 00			45 00		
Payroll Taxes Expense	450 00			440 00		
Salaries Expense	6,000 00			5,880 00		
Supplies Expense..............	400 00			600 00		
Utilities Expense	500 00			560 00		
Total Operating Expenses		8,860 00				9,055 00
Net Income		3,540 00				3,625 00

The comparison of actual and projected operations is prepared from the projected income statement (budget) for December and the actual income statement prepared at the end of December. The columns labeled Projected are the budgeted figures. The columns labeled Actual are the results of operations for the month of December.

How would the performance for the month of December be evaluated? It appears that all the commitments and goals were realized. Actual sales ($30,100) fell a little short of the budget ($31,500). However, the gross profit ($12,680) exceeded the budget ($12,400) because Marcy Casey was able to take advantage of some quantity purchases.

The advertising expense was right on the budget because the House of Sound committed itself to spending $1,000 and would not exceed that commitment. As the rest of the expenses are reviewed, note that those that could be controlled did not exceed the budget. In a few instances, expenses over which there is little control slightly exceeded the budget (for example, the Utilities Expense).

Activity C. Answer the following questions about budgeting. Refer to the text, margin notes, and illustrations on pages 502 to 505.
1. What are the two purposes of a budget? Which of the two do you feel is most important?
2. What steps are completed to prepare the budget?
3. What is the source of the projected sales, costs, and expenses?
4. What is the source of the actual sales, costs, and expenses?
5. By what amount did the projected net income exceed or fall short of the actual net income?

Topic 6 Problem

16-11. The balance sheet prepared for Aaron Bryce on June 30 is illustrated. The net income for Bryce Falls was $16,800 for the year ended June 30.
a. Compute the following.
   1. A current ratio
   2. Working capital
   3. Return on total assets
   4. Return on owner's equity
b. Do you think Bryce Falls is a profitable business? Explain.

Bryce Falls Balance Sheet June 30, 19—		
Assets		
Current Assets:		
Cash	5,600 00	
Petty Cash	40 00	
Change Fund	30 00	
Accounts Receivable	1,600 00	
Merchandise Inventory	24,510 00	
Prepaid Insurance	2,200 00	
Store Supplies on Hand	280 00	
Total Current Assets		34,260 00
Plant and Equipment:		
Land	7,700 00	
Building	30,000 00	
Equipment	17,000 00	
Total Plant and Equipment		54,700 00
Total Assets		88,960 00
Liabilities		
Current Liabilities:		
Accounts Payable	18,000 00	
Sales Tax Payable	340 00	
Employee Income Taxes Payable	170 00	
FICA Taxes Payable	160 00	
Total Current Liabilities		18,670 00
Long-Term Liabilities:		
Mortgage Payable		16,000 00
Total Liabilities		34,670 00
Owner's Equity		
Aaron Bryce, Capital		54,290 00
Total Liabilities and Owner's Equity		88,960 00

The Language of Business

Here are some terms that make up the language of business. Do you know the meaning of each?

general accounting
    subsystem
internal transactions
beginning inventory
ending inventory
physical inventory
prepaid expenses
worksheet
unadjusted trial
    balance

schedule of cost of
    goods sold
statement of owner's
    equity
current assets
current liabilities
long-term liabilities
working capital
statement of changes
    in financial position

adjusting the ledger
cash flow
cash-flow statement
source of cash
use of cash
net increase in cash
net decrease in cash
ratio

solvent
insolvent
current ratio
return on total assets
    ratio
return on owner's
    equity ratio
budget

Chapter 16   Questions

1. What is merchandise inventory?

2. What procedure is followed to record the purchase of a prepaid expense item? When and how is the expense recorded?

3. What is meant by the principle for matching revenue with expenses?

4. Describe the sequence that is followed in preparing the worksheet.

5. If no adjustment is made to transfer $50 from the Prepaid Insurance account to the Insurance Expense account, what will be the effect on net income? On total assets? On owner's equity?

6. Why does the total of the debits not equal the total of the credits in the Income Statement section of the worksheet? In the Balance Sheet section?

7. Describe the procedure that is followed to find the cost of goods sold.

8. Describe the sequence of steps for journalizing the closing entries.

9. What is the difference between a cash-flow statement and a statement of changes in financial position?

10. How does the work of the accounting clerk affect the accountant's ability to interpret financial information?

Chapter 16   Problems

Problems for Chapter 16 are given in the *Working Papers and Chapter Problems for Part 2*. If you are using the workbook, do the problems in the space provided there.

Chapter 16   Management Cases

Plant and Equipment. Business managers must maintain a relation between the amount invested in plant and equipment and the amount of current assets. One of the mistakes often made by a person going into business for the first time is to put too much money into plant and equipment (buildings and equipment). Usually too little money is left for buying merchandise and supplies, for carrying accounts receivable, and for paying expenses. As a guide for small businesses, the United States Department of Commerce has compiled figures that show what percent of total assets successful small businesses have invested in plant and equipment. An example follows.

Type of Business	Plant and Equipment as a Percent of Total Assets
Automobile agencies	12%
Department stores	8%
Food and beverage stores	14%
Furniture stores	9%
Lumber and fuel companies	24%

Case 16M-1. Michael Paulsen, the owner of Paulsen Beverages, has had difficulty in paying his debts when they become due. As a result, he has a poor credit rating and cannot get additional credit. The balance sheet for his business on December 31 is shown here.

a. What percent of the company's total assets is invested in plant and equipment?
b. What would you suggest the owner do to improve his credit situation?
c. Which of the assets are current assets? Plant and equipment?
d. Which of the liabilities are current liabilities? Long-term liabilities?

Paulsen Beverages
Balance Sheet
December 31, 19—

Assets		Liabilities	
Cash	3,000 00	Accounts Payable	37,600 00
Accounts Receivable	27,000 00	Mortgage Payable	50,000 00
Inventory	24,000 00	Total Liabilities	87,600 00
Materials and Supplies	6,000 00		
Buildings and Storage Facilities	116,000 00	Owner's Equity	
Trucks	54,000 00	Michael Paulsen, Capital	142,400 00
Total	230,000 00	Total	230,000 00

Case 16M-2. Carla Amidon has worked for a number of years in a delicatessen and now wants to open her own business. She has found a house with an attached store in a residential section where she believes a

small store would be successful. To meet the competition of other chain stores, she plans to purchase directly from suppliers in the area. She then expects to resell the products at lower prices than her competitors. To meet the competition of supermarkets, she plans to deliver telephone orders and to sell on credit. Miss Amidon believes that she will have to make an initial investment of $63,000 to start the business. A breakdown of the initial investment is as follows.

$45,000	Building
4,000	Remodeling
12,000	Store fixtures
2,000	Used delivery truck
$63,000	Total

Miss Amidon has total resources of $75,000 as follows.

$30,000	Savings
20,000	Bank mortgage
15,000	Small business loan from bank
10,000	Personal loan from relative
$75,000	Total cash resources

After the initial investment, Ms. Amidon will have $12,000 ($75,000 − $63,000) cash to meet additional costs and expenses as she tries to get her business started.
a. Do you think that Ms. Amidon will have sufficient funds to start the business as planned?
b. What would you suggest she do to improve her financial situation?

Case 16M-3. Pat George works in the stockroom of Ski-Slope, Inc. Early in December a fellow employee saw her steal a ski sweater that cost the employer $120. When asked why she stole the sweater, Ms. George replied that Ski-Slope has an inventory of at least 80 dozen sweaters and wouldn't miss just one.

The income statement for Ski-Slope, Inc., as of December 31, 19—, is illustrated here.

Ski-Slope, Inc.
Income Statement
For the Year Ended December 31, 19—

Sales	280,000 00
Cost of Goods Sold	168,000 00
Gross Profit on Sales	112,000 00
Operating Expenses	85,000 00
Net Income	27,000 00

Using the above situation and financial information, determine the effect of Ms. George's theft. Your decision should include the effect on net income, plus other possible outcomes of this theft of one sweater.

Working Hint

Using the Worksheet Efficiently. The worksheet is a time-saving device because the account titles need to be written only once. The amounts, not the titles, are extended to the appropriate columns. This arrangement can, however, present a problem in preparing the financial statements. The account titles appear at the extreme left side of the worksheet. The account balances in the statement columns appear at the extreme right side. Because of the distance between the account title column and the statement columns, it is fairly easy to look at the wrong line for the balance and then copy an incorrect amount.

This error can frequently be avoided by folding the worksheet so that the statement columns line up next to the account title column.

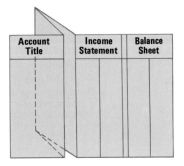

Project 2
Reno Appliances

You have been hired to keep the financial records of the Reno Appliances, owned by Renee Blum. The records used, the chart of accounts, and the balance sheet prepared on May 31 are shown here and on page 510.

Reno Appliances
Chart of Accounts

Assets
101 Cash
102 Petty Cash
103 Change Fund
111 Accounts Receivable
112 Merchandise Inventory
113 Prepaid Insurance
114 Store Supplies on Hand
121 Land
131 Building
132 Equipment

Liabilities
211 Accounts Payable
216 Sales Tax Payable
221 Federal Income Taxes Payable
222 FICA Taxes Payable
223 Salaries Payable
224 State Income Taxes Payable
225 Insurance Premiums Payable
226 Federal Unemployment Taxes Payable
227 State Unemployment Taxes Payable
231 Mortgage Payable

Owner's Equity
301 Renee Blum, Capital
302 Renee Blum, Drawing
399 Income Summary

Revenue
401 Sales
402 Sales Returns and Allowances
403 Sales Discount

Expenses
501 Purchases
502 Transportation In
503 Purchases Returns and Allowances
504 Purchases Discount
511 Cash Short and Over
512 Advertising Expense
513 Delivery Expense
514 Insurance Expense
515 Miscellaneous Expense
516 Payroll Taxes Expense
517 Salaries Expense
518 Store Supplies Expense
519 Telephone Expense

Reno Appliances
Records

Cash receipts journal
Cash payments journal
Payroll journal
Purchases journal
Sales journal
General journal
Petty cash register
General ledger
Accounts payable ledger
Accounts receivable ledger
Employee earnings records

The subsidiary ledgers have the following accounts: Roland Long and Worrall Supply are in the accounts receivable ledger, and Ford Brothers and Grupp, Inc., are in the accounts payable ledger. If you are not using the workbook, establish the general ledger and subsidiary ledger accounts and enter the June 1 balances.

Payroll Information
Employees are paid biweekly.
FICA tax rate—6.7 percent.
FUTA tax rate—0.7 percent.
SUTA tax rate—2.7 percent.
State income tax rate—2 percent.
Insurance premiums are $12.50 for each biweekly pay period. Employees are paid 1½ their hourly rate for

hours in excess of 40 per week. All employees' wages are subject to FICA, FUTA, and SUTA taxes.

Maxine Gray is single, claims one exemption, and is paid $7.25 per hour. Paul Krause is single, claims two exemptions, and is paid $6 per hour. Marvis Nolan is single, claims one exemption, and is paid $7.80 per hour.

1. *Originating the Data.* During June, the business had the transactions listed on pages 511 to 512.

2. *Journalizing the Transactions.* Record the transactions for June in the appropriate journal or petty cash journal. On the dates indicated, prepare cash proofs to verify the checkbook balance. Also, post the individual entries from the journals after the cash proof is prepared. Prove, total, and rule the special journals at the end of the month.

3. *Posting the Transactions.* Post the totals from the special journals to the appropriate ledger accounts. (*Remember:* to post the payroll journal for June 14 and June 28.)

4. *Proving the Ledgers.* Prove the ledgers as follows.
   a. Prepare a schedule of accounts receivable by age. Verify the total.
   b. Prepare a schedule of accounts payable. Verify the total.
   c. Prepare a trial balance on a worksheet.

5. *Preparing the Financial Statements.* Prepare the financial statements for the accounting period as follows.
   a. Complete the worksheet. A physical count of the merchandise on June 30 showed an inventory of $24,510, and a count of the store supplies showed an inventory of $280. An examination of the insur-

	Reno Appliances		
	Balance Sheet		
	May 31, 19—		
Assets			
Current Assets:			
Cash	8,600 00		
Merchandise Inventory	28,050 00		
Store Supplies on Hand	270 00		
Total Current Assets			36,920 00
Plant and Equipment:			
Land	15,400 00		
Building	50,000 00		
Equipment	17,000 00		
Total Plant and Equipment			82,400 00
Total Assets			119,320 00
Liabilities			
Current Liabilities:			
Sales Tax Payable	440 00		
Federal Employee Income Taxes Payable	176 00		
FICA Taxes Payable	165 00		
State Employee Income Taxes Payable	58 00		
Federal Unemployment Taxes Payable	19 00		
State Unemployment Taxes Payable	73 00		
Total Current Liabilities			931 00
Long-Term Liabilities:			
Mortgage Payable			16,300 00
Total Liabilities			17,231 00
Owner's Equity			
Renée Blum, Capital			102,089 00
Total Liabilities and Owner's Equity			119,320 00

SINGLE Persons— BIWEEKLY Payroll Period

And the wages are—		And the number of withholding allowances claimed is—		
At least	But less than	0	1	2
		The amount of income tax to be withheld shall be—		
460	480	82.70	72.70	62.70
480	500	87.90	77.90	67.90
500	520	93.10	83.10	73.10
520	540	98.30	88.30	78.30
540	560	103.70	93.50	83.50
560	580	109.70	98.70	88.70
580	600	115.70	104.20	93.90
600	620	121.70	110.20	99.10
620	640	127.70	116.20	104.60
640	660	133.70	122.20	110.60
660	680	140.00	128.20	116.60
680	700	146.80	134.20	122.60
700	720	153.60	140.60	128.60

ance policies showed unexpired insurance of $2,200.

b. Prepare a schedule of cost of goods sold and an income statement.

c. Prepare a statement of owner's equity and a classified balance sheet.

6. *Adjusting and Closing the Books.* Complete the books for the accounting period as follows.

a. Journalize and post the adjusting entries.

b. Journalize and post the closing entries.

7. *Proving the Accuracy of the Ledger.* Prepare a postclosing trial balance.

8. *Interpreting the Financial Information.* Based on the information in the financial records of the Reno Appliances, answer the following questions.

a. Ms. Blum wonders whether the accounts give her all the detailed information she needs. Do you think additional accounts are needed?

b. Are the accounts receivable being collected on time?

c. Are the current assets sufficiently greater than the current liabilities to pay current debts? (Bankers suggest that current assets should be approximately twice as large as the current liabilities.)

June 1 Recorded a memorandum entry for the cash balance in the cash receipts journal.

1 Issued Check 212 for $2,400 to pay annual insurance premium.

June 1 Received Invoice 516, dated May 31, from Ford Brothers for merchandise purchased for $680 on credit: terms 2/10, n/30.

1 Issued Check 213 for $30 to establish change fund.

2 Issued Invoice 402 to Roland Long for merchandise sold for $500 plus $25 sales tax on credit: terms 2/10, n/30.

2 Issued Check 214 for $440 to remit sales tax collected during May.

2 Deposited cash in bank; checkbook balance is $5,730. Prepare a cash proof to compare checkbook balance with Cash account balance. (Remember that the entries have not been posted to the Cash account. Post the individual entries.)

4 Issued Check 215 for $40 to establish petty cash fund.

4 Received Invoice L15, dated June 2, from Grupp, Inc., for merchandise purchased for $925 on credit; terms 1/10, n/30.

5 Received Credit Memorandum CM-CO9 for $50 from Grupp, Inc., for merchandise returned to them.

8 Issued Check 216 for $200 to Ms. Blum for personal use.

8 Paid $8 from petty cash for ad in baseball program.

8 Issued Check 217 to deposit federal income taxes withheld of $176 and FICA taxes of $165 for month of May.

9 Issued Invoice 403 to Worrall Supply for merchandise sold for $940 on credit; terms 2/10, n/30. (No sales tax since Worrall is out of state.)

9 Issued Check 218 for $666.40 to Ford Brothers to pay Invoice 516, less discount.

9 Paid $5 from petty cash for store supplies.

9 Issued Check 219 for $52.20 to pay telephone bill.

9 Recorded cash proof showing weekly cash sales of $1,650.50, sales tax of $82.53, and an overage of $3.50.

9 Deposited all cash in bank; the balance in the checkbook is now $6,166.93. Prepare a cash proof. (Post the individual entries.)

11 Received Invoice 44405, dated June 10, from Ford Brothers for merchandise purchased for $980 on credit; terms 2/10, n/30.

June 11 Received check for $515 from Roland Long in payment of Invoice 402 of June 2, less discount (sales tax not included in computing discount).

11 Issued Check 220 to remit state income taxes withheld for May.

14 Recorded the biweekly payroll in the payroll journal. Maxine Gray and Paul Krause worked 80 hours, and Marvis Nolan worked 84 hours.

14 Recorded the employer's payroll taxes (FICA, FUTA, and SUTA).

14 Issued Checks 221–223 in payment of the June 14 payroll.

15 Paid $6.50 from petty cash to Wing Trucking for delivering merchandise to customers.

15 Issued Invoice 404 to Roland Long for merchandise sold for $960 plus $48 sales tax on credit; terms 2/10, n/30.

15 Issued Check 224 for $92 to pay electric bill.

16 Issued Credit Memorandum CM-41 to Roland Long for returned merchandise of $30 plus $1.50 sales tax.

16 Paid $4.60 from petty cash to Wing Trucking for delivering merchandise to customers.

16 Recorded cash proof showing weekly cash sales of $2,005, sales tax of $100.25, and a shortage of $5.

16 Deposited all cash in bank; checkbook balance is $7,389.76. Prepare a cash proof. (Post the individual entries. Post to the employees earnings records.)

18 Received a $2,000 check from Ms. Blum as additional investment.

18 Issued Check 225 for $60 to M-R Supplies for store supplies.

19 Received a check for $921.20 from Worrall Supply in payment of Invoice 403 of June 9, less discount.

19 Paid $0.75 from petty cash for phone call from pay phone.

22 Paid $3.10 from petty cash for coffee (Misc. Expense).

22 Received Invoice L371, dated June 20, from Grupp, Inc., for merchandise purchased for $635 on credit; terms 1/10, n/30.

June 23 Issued Check 226 for $480 to Pine Barren, Inc., for merchandise purchased for cash.

23 Issued Check 227 for $15 to Penn Trucking for transportation of purchases from Pine Barren, Inc.

23 Issued Check 228 for $250 to Ms. Blum for personal use.

23 Recorded cash proof showing weekly cash sales of $1,407, sales tax of $70.35, and sales returns of $27.

23 Deposited all cash in bank; checkbook balance is $10,956.31. Prepare a cash proof. (Post the individual entries.)

25 Issued Invoice 405 to Worrall Supply for merchandise sold for $390 on credit; terms 2/10, n/30.

26 Received a check for $23 from Pine Barren, Inc., for return of merchandise purchased for cash.

28 Issued Check 229 for $226.60 to Ryan's Express for delivering merchandise to customers.

28 Issued Invoice 406 to Roland Long for merchandise sold for $720 plus $36 sales tax on credit; terms 2/10, n/30.

28 Received Invoice L795, dated June 26, from Grupp, Inc., for equipment (office chairs) purchased for $320 on credit; terms 1/10, n/30.

28 Recorded the biweekly payroll. Maxine Gray worked 90 hours, Paul Krause worked 87 hours, and Marvis Nolan worked 85 hours.

28 Recorded the employer's payroll taxes.

29 Issued Checks 230–232 in payment of the June 28 payroll.

29 Issued Check 233 for $5,000 to Ms. Blum as a permanent withdrawal of investment.

30 Issued Check 234 for $875 to Grupp, Inc., to pay Invoice L15, less returns.

30 Recorded cash proof showing weekly cash sales of $1,908.30, sales tax of $95.42, a shortage of $3, and sales returns of $8.

30 Issued Check 235 to replenish petty cash fund. Amount in petty cash box is $12.05. Prove the petty cash fund.

30 Deposited all cash in bank; checkbook balance is $5,484.18. Prepare a cash proof. (Post the individual entries. Post to the employees earnings records.)

The cost of plant and equipment assets are written off over a period of time.

A daily record of inventory is called perpetual inventory control. Another method is the periodic inventory control, which is conducted after predetermined periods of time.

Part 3
Special Accounting Systems and Procedures

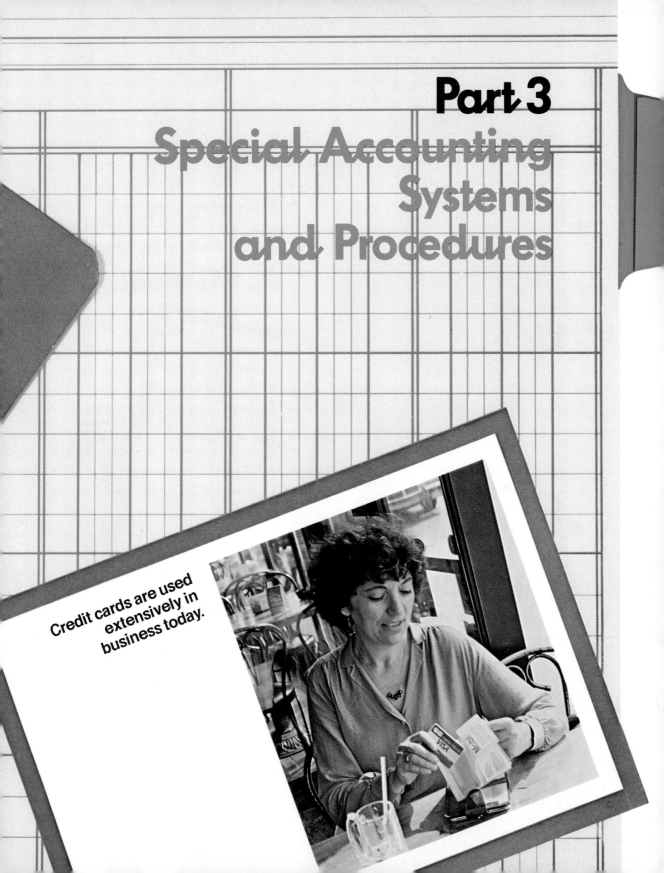

Credit cards are used extensively in business today.

Updating Accounts/ Uncollectible Accounts and Depreciation

Certain account balances, such as expenses, must be updated before the financial statements are prepared. In some cases, however, the amounts of expenses can only be estimated. You will now learn how adjustments are made to estimate expenses.

Topic 1
Updating Accounts Receivable

A *Why are adjustments to accounts receivable necessary?* The adjustment to record a decrease in the Accounts Receivable account is needed so that the assets on the balance sheet and the expenses on the income statement are reported accurately.

For most expenses, the accountant can report the actual amount paid for items or services used. For example, the amount for utilities expense is taken from the meter billings. The amount for insurance expense is determined by the time expired on the insurance policy. In some cases, however, the accountant can only *estimate* the amounts of expenses. In Topic 1 you will learn about a new adjustment. The adjustment is to record a decrease in the current asset Accounts Receivable because some accounts will be uncollectible. An account that cannot be collected is called an **uncollectible account** (sometimes referred to as a *bad debt* or *doubtful account*).

Losses From Uncollectible Accounts

A business wants to give credit only to those customers who can pay their debts. Yet despite the business's effort to do this, some of its accounts receivable will prove uncollectible. The reasons that credit customers do not pay their accounts vary. But the important point for the creditor is that the balance of the Accounts Receivable account is not the realizable value of this account. The **realizable value of accounts receivable** is the amount a business can actually expect to receive from credit customers.

An uncollectible account usually cannot be identified in the accounting period in which the sale is made. In fact, a year or more may pass before an account becomes uncollectible. One of two methods is used to record losses due to uncollectible accounts.

• The direct write-off method
• The allowance method

In the **direct write-off method,** an uncollectible account expense is recorded at the time the customer's account is found to be uncollectible. In the **allowance method,** an estimate of uncollectible accounts expense is recorded before accounts are actually proven to be uncollectible.

To show the difference between the two methods, we now discuss a sales transaction that proved to be uncollectible. Let's begin with the sale and the account receivable. The Allen Cox Company sold merchandise for $200 on credit to Lewis Vano on December 1, 19X3. The transaction was recorded in the sales journal.

General Ledger

	Accounts Receivable	121			Sales	401
Lewis Vano						
19X3					19X3	
Dec. 1 S75 200	Dec. 31 S75 14,500				Dec. 31 S75 14,500	

Included in $14,500 debited to the controlling account.

The $200 is posted as a debit to the customer's account in the accounts receivable ledger. It is included in the total of $14,500 debited to the Accounts Receivable controlling account and credited to the Sales account. Since the amount is not paid on December 31, 19X3, the $200 appears on the balance sheet as part of the amount of Accounts Receivable in the Current Assets section. It is at this point the two methods of recording uncollectible accounts differ.

The Direct Write-Off Method

Allen Cox Company Chart of Accounts

Costs and Expenses
511 Uncollectible Accounts Expense

Lewis Vano did not pay his $200 account when it came due on December 31, 19X3. An attempt was made to collect the amount due, but Mr. Vano still did not pay. The decision was made on June 15, 19X4, when the customer's account was found to be uncollectible, to write off the $200 balance of Mr. Vano's account as an uncollectible accounts expense. The direct write-off method was to be used.

The entry made to record the write-off consists of a credit of $200 to Accounts Receivable and a debit of $200 to an account called the Uncollectible Accounts Expense account. An **Uncollectible Accounts Expense account** is used to record the amounts *not* expected to be received from customers to whom sales were made on credit. Also, when the entry is posted, Mr. Vano's account in the subsidiary ledger is reduced to zero, and the Accounts Receivable controlling account in

Accounts Receivable Subsidiary Ledger

Lewis Vano

19X3		19X4	
Dec. 1 S75	200	June 15 J36	200
		Uncollectible	

Entry made to write off an uncollectible account using the direct write-off method.

GENERAL JOURNAL				Page 36	
DATE	**ACCOUNT TITLE AND EXPLANATION**	**POST. REF.**	**DEBIT**	**CREDIT**	
19X4					
June 15	Uncollectible Accounts Expense . . .	511	200 00		
	Accounts Receivable/Lewis Vano	121/√		200 00	
	Write off the account as				
	uncollectible.				

General Ledger

	Accounts Receivable	121			Uncollectible Accounts Expense	511
19X3		19X4		19X4		
Dec. 31 S75 14,500		June 15 J36 200		June 15 J36 200		

the general ledger is decreased by $200. The Uncollectible Accounts Expense account is increased by $200.

When the original sale to Lewis Vano was recorded, owner's equity was increased by crediting the Sales account for $200. When it is found that an account receivable cannot be collected, owner's equity must then be *decreased* for the amount of the sale ($200). Thus the Uncollectible Accounts Expense account is debited to decrease owner's equity. The uncollectible account is an expense to the business.

The direct write-off method of recording uncollectible accounts expense is often criticized by accountants because the revenue from the sale is recorded in one accounting period but the expense for the uncollectible account is recorded in another period. As a result, the income statement and the balance sheet show incorrect amounts.

The net income shown on the income statement is incorrect for the accounting period in which the sale is made and is incorrect for the accounting period in which the account is written off. The net income is overstated for the period in which the sale is made because the uncollectible account expense was omitted from the income statement. No subtraction was made from gross profit for this expense.

On the other hand, the net income is understated for the period in which the uncollectible accounts expense is recorded because an expense from a prior accounting period is deducted from the gross profit of the current period. Assume that the Allen Cox Company had the same amount of sales and gross profit for the years 19X3 and 19X4. Also assume that the only expense the company had was for uncollectible accounts. Then you can see from the income statements in the margin how the overstatement and understatement of net income occurs.

The amount of the Accounts Receivable shown on the balance sheet is overstated until the account is written off. For example, the Current Assets section of the Allen Cox Company's balance sheet for December 31, 19X3, includes Lewis Vano's $200 account. Because the amount was uncollectible, the assets were overstated by $200. The overstatement of assets appears on each balance sheet prepared prior to writing off the account.

If overstatements and understatements on the balance sheet and the income statement are to be avoided, each accounting period must be charged with its probable uncollectible accounts expense for sales on credit. Thus the Allen Cox Company balance sheet should show the net amount that probably will be collected from the accounts receivable, and the income statement will include an uncollectible accounts expense.

Income statement and balance sheet show incorrect amounts in direct write-off method.

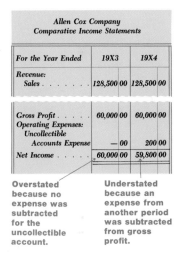

Allen Cox Company Comparative Income Statements		
For the Year Ended	19X3	19X4
Revenue:		
Sales	128,500 00	128,500 00
Gross Profit	60,000 00	60,000 00
Operating Expenses:		
Uncollectible		
Accounts Expense	— 00	200 00
Net Income	60,000 00	59,800 00

Overstated because no expense was subtracted for the uncollectible account.

Understated because an expense from another period was subtracted from gross profit.

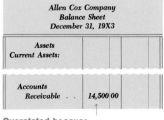

Allen Cox Company Balance Sheet December 31, 19X3			
Assets Current Assets:			
Accounts Receivable . .	14,500 00		

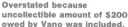

Overstated because uncollectible amount of $200 owed by Vano was included.

Activity A. Answer the following questions about uncollectible accounts. Refer to the text, margin notes, and illustrations on pages 517 to 519.

1. What accounts are debited and credited to record the uncollectible accounts expense? For what amounts?

2. Are the sales reported correctly for 19X3, or are they overstated or understated? Explain.
3. Is the gross profit reported correctly for 19X4? Explain.
4. Are the operating expenses recorded correctly for 19X3? Explain.

5. Is the net income reported correctly for 19X4? Explain.
6. Is the amount of the Accounts Receivable reported correctly for 19X3? Explain.

The Allowance Method

B *When is the amount of uncollectible accounts determined using the allowance method?* The actual expense caused by an uncollectible account can be found only after all attempts to collect the account have failed. The decision is usually not made until some future accounting period. Therefore, the only way to record an expense for an uncollectible account in the same accounting period as the revenue from sales is recorded is to *estimate* what the expense from uncollectible accounts will be. As a result, the uncollectible accounts expense in the allowance method will be related to the sales transactions from which the accounts receivable were obtained.

Recording the Estimate. At the end of each accounting period, an estimate is made of the uncollectible accounts expense likely to result from making sales on credit. The estimated expense is then recorded through an adjusting entry. The amount of the estimated expense is debited to the Uncollectible Accounts Expense account. This decreases owner's equity. The expense for uncollectible accounts is as much an operating expense as supplies used, expired insurance, and utilities.

The amount of the estimated expense is credited to an account called **Allowance for Doubtful Accounts account.** The account is called Allowance for Doubtful Accounts because the accountant does not know at this time which—if any—of the customers' accounts will be uncollectible. The accountant usually *estimates* the amount of uncollectible accounts for each accounting period. The accountant cannot know which customers' accounts will actually be uncollectible. If the Accounts Receivable controlling account were credited for the estimated expense resulting from uncollectible accounts, the controlling account would no longer be in balance with the total of the customers' accounts in the subsidiary ledger.

The Allowance for Doubtful Accounts account, used to find the realizable value (book value) of the asset Accounts Receivable, is known as a contra account. A **contra account** is an account used to record deductions in the balance shown in some other account. (*Contra* means contrary to the normal balance.) An **asset contra account** (sometimes called a *valuation account, minus asset account,* or *asset reduction account*) always has a credit balance because it represents

Adjusting Entry for Uncollectible Accounts
Debit: Uncollectible
          Accounts Expense
Credit: Allowance for
          Doubtful Accounts

the credit side of the asset account. The credit balance of the asset contra account is always subtracted from the asset account on the balance sheet to show the estimated value of the asset. The accountant for the Allen Cox Company assigned the number 122 to the Allowance for Doubtful Accounts account so that it would directly follow the Accounts Receivable account (121) in the Current Assets section of the chart of accounts.

Using the contra account to record uncollectible accounts makes it possible to maintain the equality of the Accounts Receivable controlling account in the general ledger and the total of the customers' accounts in the accounts receivable ledger. The balance of the Allowance for Doubtful Accounts account shows the part of the total accounts receivable estimated to be uncollectible. The difference between the balances of the Accounts Receivable account and the Allowance for Doubtful Accounts account is the realizable value of the accounts receivable.

The Accounts Receivable account (in the margin below) shows the total of the customers' accounts ($14,500). Allowance for Doubtful Accounts account shows the estimated amount of the accounts that will not be paid by the customers ($600). The Uncollectible Accounts Expense account shows the estimated expense recorded for the period ($600).

December 31, 19X3: The Allen Cox Company records an estimated loss from uncollectible accounts of $600 for the accounting period.

What Happens	Accounting Rule	Entry
The expense for uncollectible accounts decreases owner's equity by $600.	To decrease owner's equity, debit the account.	Debit: Uncollectible Accounts Expense, $600.
The realizable value of *Accounts Receivable* decreases by $600.	To decrease an asset, credit the account.	Credit: Allowance for Doubtful Accounts, $600.

Accounts Receivable 121	Allowance for Doubtful Accounts 122	Uncollectible Accounts Expense 511
14,500	600	600

Both Accounts Receivable and Allowance for Doubtful Accounts must be shown on the balance sheet to provide the correct information about the current assets. Allowance for Doubtful Accounts shows the estimated decrease in the value of the asset Accounts Receivable. The difference between the accounts shows the realizable value of the accounts receivable.

Allowance Method

Realizable Value of the Accounts Receivable

Accounts Receivable . .	$14,500	
Less: Allowance for Doubtful Accounts . . .	600	13,900 00

Uncollectible Accounts on the Worksheet

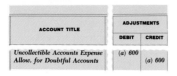

ACCOUNT TITLE	ADJUSTMENTS	
	DEBIT	CREDIT
Uncollectible Accounts Expense	(a) 600	
Allow. for Doubtful Accounts		(a) 600

The estimated uncollectible accounts expense for an accounting period is recorded at the *end* of that period. The expense is computed and entered in the Adjustments section of the worksheet. For example, the Allen Cox Company estimates its uncollectible accounts expense as being $600. The adjustment to record the estimate involves a debit to the Uncollectible Accounts Expense account for $600 and a credit to the Allowance for Doubtful Accounts account for $600.

The adjustment is recorded in the Adjustments section of the worksheet below and shown as adjustment (a). When the trial balance was prepared, the Uncollectible Accounts Expense account and the Allowance for Doubtful Accounts account had zero balances.

After adjustment (a) is made, the Allowance for Doubtful Accounts account has a credit balance of $600. The amount is moved to the Adjusted Trial Balance section and then to the Balance Sheet section of the worksheet. The contra account is a minus asset account and always appears with its related asset account. The realizable value of accounts receivable is $13,900 (14,500 − $600).

The amount of the Uncollectible Accounts Expense account ($600) is an operating expense and is extended to the Adjusted Trial Balance section and then to the Income Statement section of the worksheet.

Allen Cox Company
Worksheet
For the Year Ended December 31, 19X3

	ACCOUNT TITLE	ACCT NO.	UNADJUSTED TRIAL BALANCE		ADJUSTMENTS		ADJUSTED TRIAL BALANCE		INCOME STATEMENT		BALANCE SHEET		
			DEBIT	CREDIT	DEBIT	CREDIT	DEBIT	CREDIT	DEBIT	CREDIT	DEBIT	CREDIT	
1	Cash	101	18,400				18,400				18,400		1
2	Petty Cash	102	50				50				50		2
3	Notes Receivable	111	2,000				2,000				2,000		3
4	Accounts Receivable	121	14,500				14,500				14,500		4
5	Allow. for Doubtful Accounts	122				(a) 600		600				600	5
23	Sales	401		128,500				128,500		128,500			23
24	Sales Returns and Allowances	402	7,000				7,000		7,000				24
25	Sales Discount	403	1,500				1,500		1,500				25
36	Uncollectible Accounts Expense	511			(a) 600		600		600				36

NOTE: The cents columns have been omitted in order to show the entire worksheet.

Uncollectible Accounts on the Financial Statements

The amount of the Uncollectible Accounts Expense account for the current accounting period is shown as an operating expense on the income statement. The amount of the Allowance for Doubtful Accounts account is shown on the balance sheet as a subtraction from Accounts Receivable.

Allen Cox Company Income Statement For the Year Ended December 31, 19X3		
Sales		128,500 00
Gross Profit on Sales		60,000 00
Operating Expenses:		
Uncollectible Accounts Expense	600 00	

Allen Cox Company Balance Sheet December 31, 19X3		
Assets		
Current Assets:		
Cash		18,400 00
Petty Cash		50 00
Notes Receivable		2,000 00
Accounts Receivable $14,500.00		
Less: Allow. for Doubtful Accounts 600.00		13,900 00

Uncollectible Accounts in Closing the Ledger

The adjusting entry to record the uncollectible accounts expense is journalized at the same time other adjusting entries are journalized.

GENERAL JOURNAL   Page 30

DATE	ACCOUNT TITLE AND EXPLANATION	POST. REF.	DEBIT	CREDIT
19X3 Dec. 31	Uncollectible Accounts Expense	511	600 00	
	Allowance for Doubtful Accounts ...	122		600 00
	Record estimated loss.			

Adjusting entry to journalize uncollectible accounts expense for the period.

The balance of the Uncollectible Accounts Expense account is transferred to the Income Summary account by the closing entries. The closed contra account and the expense account appear as follows.

Close Uncollectible Accounts Expense account into Income Summary.

Allowance for Doubtful Accounts   Account No. 122

DATE	EXPLANATION	POST. REF.	DEBIT	CREDIT	BALANCE DEBIT	BALANCE CREDIT
19X3 Dec. 31	....	J30		600 00		600 00

Uncollectible Accounts Expense   Account No. 511

DATE	EXPLANATION	POST. REF.	DEBIT	CREDIT	BALANCE DEBIT	BALANCE CREDIT
19X3 Dec. 31	....	J30	600 00		600 00	
31	To Income Summary	J31		600 00	— 00	

At the beginning of the new accounting period, the Allowance for Doubtful Accounts account of the Allen Cox Company has a credit balance of $600, and the Uncollectible Accounts Expense account has a zero balance. Allowance for Doubtful Accounts appears on the post-closing trial balance, but Uncollectible Accounts Expense does not because it has been closed for the period.

Activity B. Answer the following questions about the allowance method. Refer to the text, margin notes, and illustrations on pages 520 to 524.
1. In what section of the worksheet is the estimated uncollectible accounts expense for the current accounting period first recorded?
2. What accounts are debited and credited for the estimated uncollectible accounts expense? Why?
3. What general journal entry is made to record the estimated uncollectible accounts expense?
4. What is the previous balance of the Allowance for Doubtful Accounts account?

5. Why is there no previous balance for the Uncollectible Accounts Expense account?
6. To what worksheet column is the Allowance for Doubtful Accounts amount extended from the Adjusted Trial Balance section? Why?
7. What is the amount of Allowance for Doubtful Accounts?
8. To what worksheet column is the amount of the Uncollectible Accounts Expense account extended from the Adjusted Trial Balance section? Why is the amount extended?

Accounting Principles:
Matching Revenue and Expenses. The generally accepted accounting principle is that revenue must be matched against the expenses incurred in obtaining that revenue. The result of matching revenue and expenses is net income (or net loss) for the accounting period.
Reporting Receivables. The generally accepted accounting principle is that accounts receivable should be reported on the balance sheet as the total amount billed and that the allowance for accounts estimated to be uncollectible should be subtracted from that amount.

Topic 1 Problem

17-1. Parts of the trial balance of December 31 for the Bike Shop are given here.
a. Enter this data on a worksheet for the month ended December 31.
b. Make the adjustments for the following items: estimated loss from uncollectible accounts, $210; ending merchandise inventory, $5,300; insurance expired, $50; supplies used, $40.

c. Extend all amounts to their proper columns in the Income Statement or Balance Sheet sections.
d. Prepare an income statement. The cost of goods sold is $10,400.
e. Using the data given, show how the current assets would appear on the Bike Shop balance sheet.
f. Record the general journal entries that would be made on December 31 for the adjustments.

ACCOUNT TITLE	ACCT. NO.	DEBIT	CREDIT
Cash	101	4,200 00	
Notes Receivable	111	350 00	
Accounts Receivable	121	2,800 00	
Merchandise Inventory	131	4,000 00	
Prepaid Insurance.	141	600 00	
Supplies on Hand	142	200 00	
Sales	401		20,000 00
Sales Returns and Allowances	402	300 00	
Miscellaneous Expense	513	780 00	
Rent Expense	514	1,200 00	

Topic 2
Estimating and Writing Off Uncollectible Accounts

A | *How is the amount of the uncollectible accounts estimated?* The portion of Accounts Receivable estimated to be uncollectible is usually found by taking a percentage of the net sales, or a percentage of the aged accounts receivable.

Estimating Uncollectible Accounts
• Net sales method.
• Aged accounts receivable method.

Percentage of Net Sales Method

In the **percentage of net sales method** of estimating the uncollectible accounts expense, the business assumes that a percent of net sales will not be collected. The percent used is usually based on the business's past experience with uncollectible accounts. If the business has many cash sales, only credit sales should be used to determine the expense resulting from uncollectible accounts.

Suppose that during the present year a business has gross sales of $128,500, sales returns and allowances of $7,000, and sales discounts of $1,500. Its net sales for the year, therefore, are $120,000. From past experience, the accountant estimates the uncollectible accounts expense will be 0.5 percent of the net sales. Thus the amount of the uncollectible accounts expense for the year is estimated to be $600 ($120,000 $\times$ 0.005).

When the estimate of the uncollectible accounts expense is based on a percentage of net sales, the amount of the adjustment is the amount computed *regardless* of any balance in Allowance for Doubtful Accounts. Thus if Allowance for Doubtful Accounts has a credit balance of $300 and the estimated uncollectible accounts expense for the current period is $600, the amount of the adjustment is $600. The new balance of Allowance for Doubtful Accounts is then $900 ($300 + $600).

Sales	. . . .	128,500 00
Less: Sales Returns		
and Allowances $7,000.00		
Sales Discounts 1,500.00	8,500 00	
Net Sales		120,000 00

Net Sales Method: Amount of adjustment is amount computed regardless of balance in Allowance for Doubtful Accounts.

Percentage of Aged Accounts Receivable Method

In the more accurate **percentage of aged accounts receivable method,** the estimated uncollectible accounts expense is determined by *aging* the accounts receivable. **Aging the accounts receivable** means assigning the balance of each customer's account to a group

Allen Cox Company
Schedule of Accounts Receivable by Age
December 31, 19X3

ACCOUNT WITH	BALANCE	1–30 DAYS	31–60 DAYS	61–90 DAYS	91–120 DAYS	OVER 120 DAYS
Adams Roller Company ..	300 00	300 00				
Lewis Vano	200 00	200 00				
Charles Bakkus	250 00				250 00	
Ross and Needham	1,700 00	1,500 00		200 00		
Sorrell Corporation	2,400 00	1,800 00	400 00		200 00	
Joseph Tanno, Inc.	400 00					400 00
Totals	14,500 00	12,400 00	800 00	200 00	600 00	500 00

according to the age of the receivable. Thus the accountant prepares a schedule of accounts receivable by age.

The schedule of accounts receivable by age shows a breakdown of the total accounts receivable by age groups. The estimated expense from uncollectible accounts is then found by taking a percentage of the total of each age group. The percentage varies from group to group because the older an account is, the less likely it is to be collected. For example, 50 percent of the accounts that are more than 120 days past due might be viewed as uncollectible, while only 1 percent of accounts with a current balance might be viewed as uncollectible. The uncollectible accounts estimated for the Allen Cox Company is $560, as shown in the table below.

PERCENTAGE OF PROBABLE LOSSES

1–30 Days	1%
31–60 Days	2%
61–90 Days	10%
91–120 Days	25%
Over 120 Days	50%

Age Group (in days)	Total	Estimated Percentage	Estimated Loss
1–30	$12,400	1%	$124
31–60	800	2%	16
61–90	200	10%	20
91–120	600	25%	150
Over 120	500	50%	250
	$14,500		$560

The adjusted balance of Allowance for Doubtful Accounts must equal the amount of the estimated expense. Thus, if Allowance for Doubtful Accounts has a credit balance of $400 before the adjustment, the adjusting entry must credit Allowance for Doubtful Accounts for $160 and debit Uncollectible Accounts Expense for the same amount.

Accounts Receivable 121	Allowance for Doubtful Accounts 122	Uncollectible Accounts Expense 511
14,500	Balance 400	160
	160	
	560	

If the Allowance for Doubtful Accounts account has a debit balance of $300 before the adjustment, the adjusting entry must credit the account for $860 ($300 + $560). The Uncollectible Accounts Expense account must be debited for the same amount. Allowance for Doubtful Accounts will have a debit balance any time the actual amount of uncollectible accounts written off is greater than the estimated allowance for doubtful accounts.

Allowance for Doubtful Accounts 122	Uncollectible Accounts Expense 511
Balance 300 860	860

Activity A. Answer the following questions about estimating uncollectible accounts expense. Refer to the text, margin notes, and illustrations on pages 525 to 527.
1. How can the estimate of uncollectible accounts expense be computed?
2. Refer to the estimate of uncollectible accounts expense computed as a percentage of net sales. What amount is credited to the Allowance for Doubtful Accounts account when it has no balance? When it has a credit balance of $300?

3. When the estimate of uncollectible accounts expense is computed as a percentage of aged accounts receivable, what amount is credited to the Allowance for Doubtful Accounts account when it has a credit balance of $400? What amount would be credited if the account had a debit balance of $300?
4. What percentage of accounts receivable over 120 days past due is estimated to be uncollectible?

Recording Actual Uncollectible Accounts Expense

B *How is a customer's account written off?* When a customer's account is found to be uncollectible, an entry is made to reduce the account to zero. The entry consists of a credit to the Accounts Receivable controlling account and a debit to the Allowance for Doubtful Accounts account. The entry to write off the account of Lewis Vano ($200) under the allowance method is shown on page 528.

It is important to note that writing off a customer's account under the allowance method does not affect the Uncollectible Accounts Expense account for the period. It does not establish an expense. It shows that part of the estimate for uncollectible accounts expense has occurred.

To Write Off Uncollectible Account
Debit: Allowance for Doubtful Accounts
Credit: Accounts Receivable/Customer's Account

GENERAL JOURNAL

Page 36

DATE		ACCOUNT TITLE AND EXPLANATION	POST. REF.	DEBIT	CREDIT
19X4 June	15	Allowance for Doubtful Accounts	122	200 00	
		Accounts Receivable/Lewis Vano . . .	121/√		200 00
		Write off account as uncollectible.			

Entry to write off uncollectible account using allowance method.

General Ledger

Accounts Receivable

Account No. 121

DATE		EXPLANATION	POST. REF.	DEBIT	CREDIT	BALANCE DEBIT	BALANCE CREDIT
19X4 June	1	Balance	—			17,000 00	
	15	. . . .	J36		200 00	16,800 00	

Amount written off this period as uncollectible.

Amount of estimated uncollectible account expense estimated at end of previous period.

Amount still estimated after Vano's account was written off.

Allowance for Doubtful Accounts

Account No. 122

DATE		EXPLANATION	POST. REF.	DEBIT	CREDIT	BALANCE DEBIT	BALANCE CREDIT
19X4 Jan.	1	Balance	—				600 00
June	15	Lewis Vano	J36	200 00			400 00

Amount written off does not appear as an expense of this period; it was recorded at end of previous period.

Uncollectible Accounts Expense

Account No. 511

DATE	EXPLANATION	POST. REF.	DEBIT	CREDIT	BALANCE DEBIT	BALANCE CREDIT

Accounts Receivable Ledger

Name	Lewis Vano	Credit Limit	$300
Address	1132 Peabody Street, Nashville, Tennessee 37203	Telephone	555-1121

DATE		EXPLANATION	POST. REF.	DEBIT	CREDIT	DEBIT BALANCE
19X3 Dec.	1	. . . .	S75	200 00		200 00
19X4 June	15	Uncollectible	J36		200 00	— 00

Customer's account in subsidiary ledger after posting the write-off.

Collecting Accounts Written Off

If an account written off as uncollectible is later collected, the write-off entry must be reversed. For example, when Lewis Vano's account was written off on June 15, 19X4, the entry consisted of a $200 debit to the Allowance for Doubtful Accounts account and a $200 credit to the Accounts Receivable account. If Lewis Vano pays his account on May 31, 19X5, the entry shown below will be made.

		GENERAL JOURNAL			Page 46
DATE		ACCOUNT TITLE AND EXPLANATION	POST. REF.	DEBIT	CREDIT
19X5 May	31	Accounts Receivable/Lewis Vano	121/√	200 00	
		Allowance for Doubtful Accounts . . .	122		200 00
		Reverse entry of June 15, 19X4,			
		writing off this account, which			
		was collected in full today.			

After the entry is posted, the customer's account once again shows the original balance. The check is then recorded in the cash receipts journal in the usual manner.

		CASH RECEIPTS JOURNAL						Page 80
DATE	ACCOUNT CREDITED	EXPLANATION	POST. REF.	GENERAL LEDGER CREDIT	ACCOUNTS RECEIVABLE CREDIT	SALES DISCOUNT DEBIT	NET CASH DEBIT	
19X5 May 31	Lewis Vano	On account	√		200 00		200 00	

As a result of reversing the original write-off entry, the customer's account in the accounts receivable subsidiary ledger contains a complete record of all transactions and entries affecting the account.

Accounts Receivable Ledger

Name Lewis Vano   **Credit Limit** $300

Address 1132 Peabody Street, Nashville, Tennessee 37203   **Telephone** 273-1121

DATE		EXPLANATION	POST. REF.	DEBIT	CREDIT	DEBIT BALANCE
19X3 Dec.	1	. . . .	S75	200 00		200 00
19X4 June	15	Uncollectible	J36		200 00	— 00
19X5 May	31	Reverse write-off	J46	200 00		200 00
	31	. . . .	CR80		200 00	— 00

Activity B. Answer the following questions about recording uncollectible accounts expense. Refer to the text, margin notes, and illustrations on pages 527 to 529.
1. Whose account is written off as being uncollectible? What amount is written off?
2. What entry is made to write off the account?
3. After Mr. Vano's account is written off on June 15, 19X4, what is the total amount billed but not yet paid by customers? How much is still estimated to be uncollectible? What is the estimated realizable value of the accounts receivable?
4. When Mr. Vano's account is written off, what amount appears in the Uncollectible Accounts Expense account for 19X4?
5. What is the purpose of the general journal entry made on May 31, 19X5?
6. What is the purpose of the cash receipts journal entry of May 31, 19X5?

Topic 2 Problems

17-2. The Wiggs Company estimates its uncollectible accounts expense to be 1 percent of its net sales. The trial balance on December 31 shows these account balances: Sales, $55,600; Sales Returns and Allowances, $1,000; and Sales Discount, $300.
a. Record the adjusting entry for the uncollectible accounts expense in the general journal. The Allowance for Doubtful Accounts account has a zero balance.
b. Record the adjusting entry if the Allowance for Doubtful Accounts account has a credit balance of $60.
c. Record the adjusting entry if the Allowance for Doubtful Accounts account has a debit balance of $20.

17-3. The Patterson Fuel Company estimates its uncollectible accounts expense as a percentage of the aged accounts receivable. The aging of the accounts receivable on October 31 shows the following breakdown.

Age Group	Total of Group
1–30 days	$11,000
31–60 days	6,300
61–90 days	2,200
91–120 days	1,700
Over 120 days	700
Total Accounts Receivable	$21,900

a. Compute the total amount of the expected uncollectible accounts expense. Use the percentages of probable losses shown on page 526.
b. Record the adjusting entry for uncollectible accounts expense in the general journal. The Allowance for Doubtful Accounts account has a zero balance.

c. Record the appropriate adjusting entry for uncollectible accounts expense. The Allowance for Doubtful Accounts account of the Patterson Fuel Company has a credit balance of $200.
d. Record the adjusting entry if the Allowance for Doubtful Accounts account has a debit balance of $65.

17-4. Perform the following activities involving the percentage of net sales method for estimating uncollectible accounts for the Music Center.
a. Open general ledger accounts, and record the May 31 balances as follows: Cash, $8,600; Accounts Receivable, $12,000; Allowance for Doubtful Accounts, $67 (credit); Income Summary; Uncollectible Accounts Expense. Also open accounts receivable ledger accounts and record the following debit balances: Jack Kelley, $210; Tania Davis, $50.
b. Record an entry in the general journal on May 31 for an estimated expense of $290 from uncollectible accounts for the month. Then post the entry.
c. Record an entry on May 31 to close the Music Center's Uncollectible Accounts Expense account into the Income Summary account, and then post the entry. NOTE: Save your working papers for use in Topic Problems 17-5 and 17-6.

17-5. Using the working papers from Topic Problem 17-4, journalize and post the following transactions of the Music Center for June.

June 10 Tania Davis' account for $50 is determined uncollectible.
15 Jack Kelley's account for $210 is determined uncollectible.
30 Record estimated uncollectible accounts expenses of $260 for the month.

June 30 Close the expense account into the Income Summary account.

NOTE: Save your working papers for use in Topic Problem 17-6.

17-6. Using the working papers from Topic Problems 17-4 and 17-5 and a multicolumn cash receipts journal, journalize and post the following transactions of the Music Center for July.

July 5 Tania Davis paid her account, which had been written off on June 10.

31 Record estimated uncollectible accounts expense of $125 for the month.

31 Close the expense account into the Income Summary account.

Topic 3
Updating Plant and Equipment Accounts

A *Are there other areas besides uncollectible accounts in which the accountant must estimate the amount of the expense?* Yes, another adjustment that must be estimated is one to *decrease* the recorded value of plant and equipment assets.

Allocating the Cost of Plant and Equipment Assets

A plant and equipment asset is an asset that will be used in the operation of the business over a number of years. For example, land, furniture, and machinery are plant and equipment assets. Most plant and equipment assets have a limited useful life. That is, the asset will be of use to the business only for a limited number of accounting periods. The useful life of a plant and equipment asset is limited because it gradually *deteriorates* (wears out), becomes *obsolete,* or becomes *inadequate* because more efficient equipment is needed. The one exception is land. Land has unlimited useful life because it can always be used for some purpose.

A business purchases a plant and equipment asset to produce revenue. As the plant and equipment asset produces revenue, a portion of the asset's cost should be matched against the revenue. Thus a portion of the plant and equipment asset's cost should be charged as expense in each period in which the asset is used. The portion of the cost of a plant and equipment asset that is allocated to each accounting period in which revenue is produced is called **depreciation.**

We can illustrate depreciation with an example. Allen Cox, the owner of the Allen Cox Company, purchased a building at a cost of $150,000. He acquired the building to provide a place to operate his business and earn revenue. The useful life of the building will be limited by deterioration from use, exposure to the sun and wind, and obsolescence. Mr. Cox estimates the total useful life of the building to be 30 years. He believes that the cost of the building should be charged to expense over a 30-year period.

**DEPRECIATION OF BUILDING DURING FIRST
5 YEARS OF 30-YEAR USEFUL LIFE**

Time of Purchase

Original cost. . . . . $150,000   Unexpired Cost—$150,000

End of 1 Year   1

Original cost. $150,000
Expired cost. . . . . $5,000   Unexpired Cost—$145,000

End of 5 Years   1 2 3 4 5

Original cost. $150,000
Expired cost. . . . . $25,000   Unexpired Cost—$125,000

In effect, Allen Cox has purchased the use of the building for 30 years at an original cost of $150,000. A portion of the cost will expire in each accounting period in which service is received from the asset. If the owner assumes that each year's operations should bear an equal share of the original cost of the building, the annual charge against revenue for depreciation will amount to $\frac{1}{30}$ of $150,000, or $5,000. In other words, $5,000 of the original cost of the building will expire each year for 30 years. The table above shows how the original cost is spread over the first five years of the building's estimated useful life.

Depreciation is a process of allocating the cost of a plant and equipment asset over its useful life. Depreciation has nothing to do with any loss in the value of a plant and equipment asset that may have occurred. A part of the original cost of a plant and equipment asset must be matched with the revenue earned in each accounting period in which the asset is used. Failure to record depreciation expense causes the total operating expenses for the period to be understated and thus causes the net income to be overstated.

Net income is overstated if depreciation expense is not recorded.

Estimating Depreciation

When a plant and equipment asset is purchased, the accountant does not know exactly how long the asset will be useful. Nor is it known whether the asset will be sold, traded in for a new model, or scrapped because it is no longer useful. Thus, to estimate the amount of the depreciation, the accountant must make an estimate of the useful life of the asset and also of its disposal value. The **disposal value** (sometimes referred to as *salvage value* or *trade-in value*) is the value of the asset at the end of its useful life. The estimates of the useful life and the disposal value are needed because the depreciation of a plant and equipment asset is figured in advance.

Three amounts are needed to estimate the depreciation on a plant and equipment asset.

- The cost of the plant and equipment asset.
- The number of years the asset is expected to be useful.
- The estimated disposal value of the asset.

The accountant may use depreciation guidelines published regularly by the Internal Revenue Service in estimating useful life.

To see how the annual depreciation of a plant and equipment asset is computed, let's assume that an electronic programmable calculator is purchased for $860. It has an estimated useful life of five years and an estimated disposal value of $110. The procedure to compute annual depreciation is as follows.

- Subtract the estimated disposal value from the cost to obtain the total depreciation.
- Divide the total depreciation by the years of estimated useful life to obtain the annual depreciation. To determine depreciation for less than a year, find the annual depreciation and then divide that amount by the part of the year being considered. Thus monthly depreciation would be determined by dividing annual depreciation by 12.

It is also important to know how many months to use in calculating depreciation for less than a year. For example, if the calculator is purchased on May 7, eight months of depreciation will be recorded on December 31 (May through December). However, if the calculator is purchased on May 16, only seven months of depreciation will be recorded as the adjusting entry on December 31 (June through December). Thus if a plant and equipment asset is purchased during the first half of the month depreciation is computed from the first of that month. If, on the other hand, the asset is purchased during the second half of the month, depreciation is computed beginning with the first day of the following month.

After the electronic programmable calculator has been used for five years, it will have an estimated disposal value of $110, which is $750 ($860 − $110) less than its purchase price. In effect, the business has purchased five years' use of the electronic programmable calculator at a total cost of $750. The $750 is depreciation that should be spread over the five years that the electronic programmable calculator is used. Thus the electronic programmable calculator has an annual depreciation of $150 ($750 ÷ 5), or a monthly depreciation of $12.50 ($150 ÷ 12).

The method just shown for computing depreciation is called the **straight-line method** because an equal amount of the cost of the plant and equipment asset is estimated as being used each year. There are several other methods that accountants can use to compute the amount of depreciation for each year. Among them are the sum-of-the-years'-digits method and the declining-balance method. These methods are discussed in more advanced accounting courses.

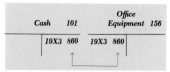

Purchase of a Plant and Equipment asset.

Needed to Compute Depreciation
- Cost (actual)
- Useful life (estimated)
- Disposal value (estimated)

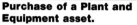

	Disposal	Total
Cost −	Value	= Depr.
$860 −	$110	= $750

Total	Years of	Annual
Depr. ÷	Use	= Depr.
$750 ÷	5	= $150

Annual		Monthly
Depr.	÷ 12 =	Depr.
$150	÷ 12 =	$12.50

1. What is the original cost of the building?
2. What is the annual depreciation charge?
3. What are the expired and unexpired costs after five years?

4. What are expired and unexpired costs after 30 years?
5. What is needed to compute depreciation?
6. What is the cost of the electronic programmable calculator? What is the disposal value? the total depreciation?
7. What method is used to compute the depreciation on the electronic programmable calculator?

Recording Depreciation

Adjusting Entry for Depreciation

Debit: Depreciation Expense
Credit: Accumulated Depreciation

B *How often is depreciation recorded?* A portion of the total depreciation should be charged against revenue earned in each accounting period. The electronic programmable calculator is being used to earn revenue during the year, and $150 ($750 ÷ 5) should be charged against that annual revenue.

The amount of depreciation expense is recorded at the *end* of each accounting period. At that time, adjusting entries are made for all plant and equipment asset accounts except land. The adjusting entry for depreciation is similar to the one for uncollectible accounts. The debit is to an expense account (for depreciation expense). The credit is to an asset contra account (for accumulated depreciation).

A plant and equipment asset account is not credited directly because the amount of the depreciation is only an estimate. Furthermore, if the plant and equipment asset account were credited, it would appear as though the business had disposed of part of the plant and equipment asset. The accumulated depreciation account will always show the total expired cost of the asset to that time. The difference between the balance of the plant and equipment asset account and the balance of the accumulated depreciation account is the book value of the plant and equipment asset. The **book value** represents that portion of the cost of the asset that has not been recorded as a depreciation expense.

For example, assuming the Allen Cox Company purchased an electronic programmable calculator on January 2, 19X3, for $860, the first year's depreciation would be recorded as follows.

December 31, 19X3: The Allen Cox Company records depreciation of $150 on the calculator for the first year.

What Happens	Accounting Rule	Entry
The expense for depreciation decreases owner's equity by $150.	To decrease owner's equity, debit the account.	Debit: Depreciation Expense— Office Equipment, $150.
The book value of the asset *Office Equipment* decreases by $150.	To decrease an asset, credit the account.	Credit: Accumulated Depreciation— Office Equipment, $150.

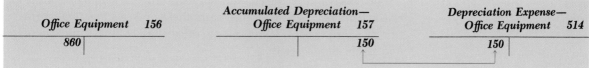

Office Equipment 156	Accumulated Depreciation—Office Equipment 157	Depreciation Expense—Office Equipment 514
860	150	150

Depreciation for first year.

The Depreciation Expense—Office Equipment account is an expense account and is debited to record the decrease in owner's equity. At the end of the accounting period, it is closed with the other expense accounts into the Income Summary account.

The Office Equipment account shows the original cost of the plant and equipment asset ($860) and is not affected by the adjusting entry. The Accumulated Depreciation—Office Equipment account shows the total amount of depreciation estimated and recorded for the first year ($150).

Both the plant and equipment asset account and the accumulated depreciation account must be shown on the balance sheet to provide all information about the asset. If the electronic programmable calculator were the only piece of office equipment owned by the Allen Cox Company, it would be listed under plant and equipment assets, as shown in the margin.

Depreciation in succeeding years is recorded as follows. At the end of the second year, an adjusting entry is made to record the year's depreciation. Office Equipment and the related accounts would appear as shown here.

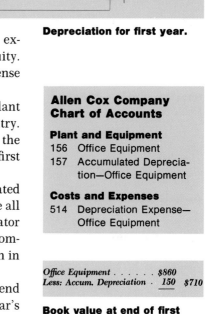

Allen Cox Company Chart of Accounts

Plant and Equipment
156 Office Equipment
157 Accumulated Depreciation—Office Equipment

Costs and Expenses
514 Depreciation Expense—Office Equipment

Office Equipment $860
Less: Accum. Depreciation . 150 $710

Book value at end of first year.

Office Equipment 156	Accumulated Depreciation—Office Equipment 157	Depreciation Expense—Office Equipment 514
19X3 860	19X3 150 19X4 150 300	19X4 150

Depreciation for second year.

Office Equipment $860
Less: Accum. Depreciation . 300 $560

Book value at end of second year.

The Office Equipment account still shows the cost of the electronic programmable calculator ($860). The Accumulated Depreciation—Office Equipment account now has a balance of $300 ($150 × 2). The book value is now $560 ($860 − $300).

If similar entries are made for each year, at the end of the fifth year the accounts will appear as follows.

Office Equipment 156	Accumulated Depreciation—Office Equipment 157	Depreciation Expense—Office Equipment 514
19X3 860	19X3 150 19X4 150 19X5 150 19X6 150 19X7 150 750	19X7 150

Depreciation for fifth year.

The book value of the electronic programmable calculator at the end of the fifth year is $110 (office equipment of $860 less total depreciation of $750). The $110 represents the disposal value of the calculator and is not depreciated.

When a plant and equipment asset is sold, the cost of the asset must be removed from the plant and equipment asset account. Also the accumulated depreciation must be removed from the contra account. Assume that the Allen Cox Company sells the calculator for $110 in cash on January 2, 19X8. The transaction would require the following entry. The Cash account is debited for $110, the amount of cash received. The contra account is debited for $750, the total accumulated depreciation at the time of the sale. The asset account is credited for $860, the cost of the asset. After the entry is posted, the balance of Office Equipment is reduced to zero (if the calculator is the only equipment), and the Accumulated Depreciation—Office Equipment account is closed because the equipment is no longer owned.

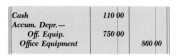

| Office Equipment . . . . . | $860 | |
| Less: Accum. Depreciation . | 750 | $110 |

Book value at end of fifth year

Cash	110 00	
Accum. Depr.—		
Off. Equip.	750 00	
Office Equipment		860 00

General journal entry.

	Cash	101			Office Equipment	156			Accumulated Depreciation—Office Equipment	157
19X8	110			19X3	860	19X8	860	19X8	750	19X3 150
										19X4 150
										19X5 150
										19X6 150
										19X7 150
									750	750

Subsidiary Ledger for Plant and Equipment Assets. To determine the amount of depreciation for each accounting period, the accountant needs information about each plant and equipment asset the business owns. The accountant needs to know the cost, purchase date, number of years of useful life, and estimated disposal value of each item. This information is necessary not only for estimating depreciation but also for completing the required federal tax forms.

It is not practical to open an account in the general ledger for each piece of furniture or machinery the business owns. The needed details are usually kept in a subsidiary ledger called the **plant and equipment ledger.** Each item is recorded on a separate card, similar to the plant and equipment record card shown on page 537. The cards support the general ledger accounts for plant and equipment assets, which now become controlling accounts.

The plant and equipment record card on page 537 was prepared for a Compak calculator with the serial number X-9114. The title "Office Equipment" was written on the General Ledger Account line to show that this card supplements the Office Equipment account. When the calculator was purchased, the $860 debit was posted to the Plant and

Equipment Account section because the Office Equipment account in the general ledger was debited for $860, the cost.

PLANT AND EQUIPMENT RECORD

Item __Calculator__ General Ledger Account __Office Equipment__
Serial No. __X-9114__ Purchased From __Eagle Office Supply__
Description __Compak__ Location __Accounting Department__
Cost When Acquired __$860__ Age When Acquired __New__
Estimated Life __5 yrs.__ Estimated Scrap or Trade-In Value __$110__ Annual Depreciation __$150__

| DATE | | | EXPLANATION | PLANT AND EQUIPMENT ACCT. | | | ACCUMULATED DEPRECIATION | | | BOOK VALUE |
MO.	DAY	YR.		DEBIT	CREDIT	BALANCE	DEBIT	CREDIT	BALANCE	
1	2	X3	Purchased	860 00		860 00				860 00
12	31	X3						150 00	150 00	710 00
12	31	X4						150 00	300 00	560 00
12	31	X5						150 00	450 00	410 00
12	31	X6						150 00	600 00	260 00
12	31	X7						150 00	750 00	110 00
1	2	X8	Sold		860 00	— 00	750 00		— 00	— 00

Sold, Traded, or Scrapped to: Elaine Spradlin 1/2/X8   Amount Received: $110

Entries Affecting Plant
and Equipment Account
in General Ledger
(Original Cost)

Entries Affecting
Contra Account in
General Ledger
(Expired Cost)

Balance of
Plant and
Equipment
Account
Minus
Accumulated
Depreciation
(Current
Unexpired
Cost or
Book Value)

The entries recorded in the Accumulated Depreciation section of the plant and equipment record card were made each time the depreciation entry was posted to the contra account in the general ledger. The book value of the asset was computed after each entry was posted.

When the calculator was sold, a credit of $860 was posted to the Plant and Equipment Account section of the card for the cost and a debit of $750 was posted to the Accumulated Depreciation section for the total accumulated depreciation. Both the Plant and Equipment account and the Accumulated Depreciation account balances became zero. Thus the book value is zero. At the time of disposal, the plant and equipment record card is removed from the subsidiary ledger.

To prove the subsidiary ledger for a plant and equipment account (such as Office Equipment), the accountant adds the balance column of the Plant and Equipment Account section on each card for that asset. The total of all the balances must equal the balance of the asset account in the general ledger. The contra account is proved by adding the balance column of the Accumulated Depreciation section on each card.

The total of all the balances must equal the balance of the contra account in the general ledger. The book value on all the cards is equal to the difference between the balance of the asset account and the balance of the contra account.

Depreciation on the Worksheet

The entries to record the depreciation for an accounting period are completed after the trial balance has been prepared on the worksheet. The amount of depreciation must be found for each plant and equipment asset except land. Then the necessary adjustments are made in the Adjustments section of the worksheet. Adjustments for depreciation on the worksheet are shown below.

No depreciation is recorded for land.

Allen Cox Company
Worksheet
For the Year Ended December 31, 19X5

	ACCOUNT TITLE	ACCT. NO.	UNADJUSTED TRIAL BALANCE		ADJUSTMENTS		ADJUSTED TRIAL BALANCE		INCOME STATEMENT		BALANCE SHEET		
			DEBIT	CREDIT	DEBIT	CREDIT	DEBIT	CREDIT	DEBIT	CREDIT	DEBIT	CREDIT	
8	Land	151	60,000				60,000				60,000		8
9	Building	152	150,000				150,000				150,000		9
10	Accumulated Depr.—Building	153		10,000		(e) 5,000		15,000				15,000	10
11	Delivery Equipment	154	19,500				19,500				19,500		11
12	Accumulated Depr.—Del. Eq. .	155		6,000		(f) 3,000		9,000				9,000	12
13	Office Equipment	156	12,000				12,000				12,000		13
14	Accumulated Depr.— Off. Eq.	157		2,000		(g) 1,000		3,000				3,000	14
41	Depr. Expense—Building . . .	512			(e) 5,000		5,000		5,000				41
42	Depr. Expense—Delivery Equip.	513			(f) 3,000		3,000		3,000				42
43	Depr. Expense—Office Equip. .	514			(g) 1,000		1,000		1,000				43

NOTE: The cents columns have been omitted in order to show the entire worksheet.

Cost of building	150,000 00
Less: Disposal value	0 00
Total depreciation	150,000 00

Building. The Allen Cox Company owns land that cost $60,000 and a building that cost $150,000. The useful life of the building is estimated to be 30 years. At the end of that time, the building will be worthless. Therefore, the yearly depreciation of the building is $5,000 ($150,000 ÷ 30). The contra account, Accumulated Depreciation—Building, has a credit balance of $10,000 on the trial balance ($5,000 depreciation was recorded in each of the previous two years).

Yearly depr. = $150,000 ÷ 30
Yearly depr. = $5,000

Adjustment (e) is made to record the depreciation for the current year. The Depreciation Expense—Building account is debited for $5,000 and the Accumulated Depreciation—Building account is credited for $5,000. The Adjusted Trial Balance section shows that the contra account now has a credit balance of $15,000 (the amount of depreciation for three years' use). The book value of the building is, therefore, $135,000 ($150,000 − $15,000).

Delivery Equipment. The business owns three delivery trucks, each purchased for $6,500. Each truck is estimated to have a useful life of six years and a trade-in value (disposal value) of $500. Thus each truck has annual depreciation of $1,000 ($6,500 − $500 = $6,000; $6,000 ÷ 6 = $1,000). The contra account on the trial balance shows a $6,000 credit balance for the previous two years. The adjustment (f) to record present depreciation ($3,000) debits the expense account and credits the contra account. The Adjusted Trial Balance section shows a $9,000 credit balance for the contra account (depreciation for three years' use). Thus the book value of the three trucks is $10,500 ($19,500 − $9,000).

Cost of truck	6,500	00
Less: Trade-in value . .	500	00
Total depreciation . .	6,000	00

Yearly depr. for each truck
= $6,000 ÷ 6 = $1,000
Yearly depr. for 3 trucks
= $3,000

Office Equipment. The cost of the office equipment is $12,000, and the depreciation recorded for past periods is $2,000. The book value of the office equipment is now $10,000 ($12,000 − $2,000). The plant and equipment record cards for the office equipment show the business owns several kinds of office equipment. The cards also indicate that the equipment was purchased at various times. To know what depreciation should be charged during this accounting period, the accountant must add the various amounts on the cards. Total depreciation for office equipment is $1,000 and is adjustment (g) in the Adjustments section of the worksheet. Depreciation Expense—Office Equipment is debited for $1,000, and Accumulated Depreciation—Office Equipment is credited for $1,000.

As shown on the worksheet for the Allen Cox Company (page 538), there are contra accounts for each plant and equipment asset except land. The accumulated depreciation account remains as an open account as long as the plant and equipment asset is owned by the business. The book value of each group of plant and equipment assets is shown on the balance sheet by subtracting each contra account from its plant and equipment asset account.

Depreciation expense accounts are also set up for each group of plant and equipment assets, such as Depreciation Expense—Building, Depreciation Expense—Delivery Equipment, and Depreciation Expense—Office Equipment. The depreciation expenses are charged against current operations and are reported on the income statement. At the end of the period, depreciation expenses are closed into the Income Summary account.

Depreciation expense accounts are closed into Income Summary account.

Depreciation on the Financial Statements

The amounts of estimated depreciation for the current accounting period are reported as operating expenses on the income statement. On the balance sheet, three items are shown for each group of plant and equipment assets: cost, accumulated depreciation, and book value.

Allen Cox Company Income Statement For the Year Ended December 31, 19X5		
Revenue From Sales		200,000 00
Gross Profit on Sales		110,000 00
Operating Expenses:		
Uncollectible Accounts Expense . .	670 00	
Depreciation Expense—Building .	5,000 00	
Depreciation Exp.—Del. Equip. . .	3,000 00	
Depreciation Exp.—Office Equip. .	1,000 00	

Allen Cox Company Balance Sheet December 31, 19X5		
Assets		
Current Assets:		
Cash	18,600 00	
Total Current Assets		53,000 00
Plant and Equipment Assets:		
Land	60,000 00	
Building $150,000.00		
Less: Acc. Depr. . 15,000.00	135,000 00	
Delivery Equipment $ 19,500.00		
Less: Acc. Depr. . 9,000.00	10,500 00	
Office Equipment . . $ 12,000.00		
Less: Acc. Depr. . 3,000.00	9,000 00	
Total Plant and Equipment		214,500 00
Total Assets		267,500 00

If no plant and equipment assets are sold during the next accounting period (19X6) and no additional plant and equipment assets are purchased, the cost of the plant and equipment assets will remain the same. However, the amount of the accumulated depreciation will increase each year. As a result, the book value of the assets will decrease each year. Assume that no plant and equipment assets are sold or purchased during a four-year period and that the amount of the depreciation remains the same. The amounts shown for plant and equipment assets on the successive balance sheets will appear as follows.

	19X3		19X4		19X5		19X6	
Plant and Equipment Assets:								
Land		60,000		60,000		60,000		60,000
Building	150,000		150,000		150,000		150,000	
Less: Accumulated Depreciation . .	5,000	145,000	10,000	140,000	15,000	135,000	20,000	130,000
Delivery Equipment	19,500		19,500		19,500		19,500	
Less: Accumulated Depreciation . .	3,000	16,500	6,000	13,500	9,000	10,500	12,000	7,500
Office Equipment	12,000		12,000		12,000		12,000	
Less: Accumulated Depreciation . .	1,000	11,000	2,000	10,000	3,000	9,000	4,000	8,000
Total Plant and Equipment		232,500		223,500		214,500		205,500

Building	5,000 00
Delivery Equipment . .	3,000 00
Office Equipment	1,000 00
	9,000 00

The total of the plant and equipment assets decreases each year by $9,000 (from $232,500 to $223,500 to $214,500 to $205,500), the amount of the depreciation recorded each year. The computation for recording depreciation each year is shown in the margin.

Depreciation in Closing the Ledger

After the financial statements are prepared, the adjusting and closing entries are journalized in the general journal. When the entries are posted, the plant and equipment asset accounts, accumulated depreciation accounts, and the depreciation expense accounts appear as shown below and on page 542.

	GENERAL JOURNAL			Page 46
DATE	**ACCOUNT TITLE AND EXPLANATION**	**POST. REF.**	**DEBIT**	**CREDIT**
19X5				
Dec. 31	Depreciation Expense—Building	512	5,000 00	
	Accumulated Depreciation—Building . . .	153		5,000 00
	Record depreciation for year.			
31	Depreciation Expense—Delivery Equipment	513	3,000 00	
	Accumulated Depr.—Delivery Equip. . . .	155		3,000 00
	Record depreciation for year.			
31	Depreciation Expense—Office Equipment . .	514	1,000 00	
	Accumulated Depreciation—Office Equip.	157		1,000 00
	Record depreciation for year.			

Adjusting entries for recording depreciation.

Debited for cost of land when purchased.

Land		151
19X3		
Jan. 1 Balance √ 60,000		

No depreciation is recorded on land.

Debited for cost of building when purchased.

Building		152
19X3		
Jan. 1 Balance √ 150,000		

To be credited for cost at time of disposal.

Debited for total amount of accumulated depreciation at time of disposal.

Accumulated Depreciation—Building		153
	19X5	
	Jan. 1 Balance √ 10,000	
	Dec. 31 J46 5,000	

Credited for depreciation each accounting period until time of disposal or until book value equals disposal value.

Debited for cost of delivery equipment when purchased.

Delivery Equipment		154
19X3		
Jan. 1 Balance √ 19,500		

To be credited for cost at time of disposal.

To be debited for total amount of accumulated depreciation at time of disposal.

Accumulated Depreciation— Delivery Equipment		155
	19X5	
	Jan. 1 Balance √ 6,000	
	Dec. 31 J46 3,000	

Credited for depreciation each accounting period until time of disposal or until book value equals disposal value.

Debited for cost of office equipment when purchased.	Office Equipment	156	To be credited for cost at time of disposal.

	Office Equipment		156
19X3 Jan. 1 Balance √ 12,000			

Debited for cost of office equipment when purchased. · **To be credited for cost at time of disposal.**

	Accumulated Depreciation— Office Equipment		157
		19X5 Jan. 1 Balance √ 2,000	
		Dec. 31 J46 1,000	

To be debited for total amount of accumulated depreciation at time of disposal. · **Credited for depreciation each accounting period until time of disposal or until book value equals disposal value.**

	Depreciation Expense—Building		512
19X5 Dec. 31 J46 5,000			

Debited at end of accounting period for estimated depreciation for period. · **To be closed to Income Summary account.**

	Depreciation Expense— Delivery Equipment		513
19X5 Dec. 31 J46 3,000			

Debited at end of accounting period for estimated depreciation for period. · **To be closed to Income Summary account.**

	Depreciation Expense— Office Equipment		514
19X5 Dec. 31 J46 1,000			

Debited at end of accounting period for estimated depreciation for period. · **To be closed to Income Summary account.**

The balances of the depreciation expense accounts are transferred to the Income Summary account by the closing entries. The plant and equipment asset accounts and the accumulated depreciation accounts appear on the postclosing trial balance. The depreciation expense accounts will not appear on the postclosing trial balance because each has been closed for the period.

Activity B. Answer the following questions about recording depreciation. Refer to the text, margin notes, and illustrations on pages 534 to 542.

1. Are the entries to record depreciation made first on the worksheet or in the general journal?

2. In what section of the worksheet is the estimated annual depreciation of the building first entered?

3. When the adjustment is made for depreciation, which account is debited?

4. What journal entry must be made to record the annual depreciation of the building?

5. Why is there no previous balance for Depreciation Expense—Building?

6. To what column is the new total of Accumulated Depreciation—Building extended from the Adjusted Trial Balance section? Why?

7. What is the new book value of the building?

8. What is the amount of Depreciation Expense—Building?

9. To what worksheet column is the amount of Depreciation Expense—Building extended from the Adjusted Trial Balance section? Why?

10. In what worksheet section is the estimated annual depreciation of the office equipment first recorded?

11. Which account is debited and which is credited to adjust for depreciation of office equipment? Why?

12. What general journal entry is made to record the estimated annual depreciation of office equipment?
13. To what worksheet column is the new total of Accumulated Depreciation—Office Equipment extended from the Adjusted Trial Balance section? Why?

14. What is the new total of Accumulated Depreciation—Office Equipment? How is this computed?
15. What is the new book value of Office Equipment?
16. What is the purpose of the small (f) before the amount in the Adjustments section of the worksheet?

Accounting Principles:
Depreciation. The generally accepted accounting principle is that *depreciation* is a process of allocating (distributing) the cost of a plant and equipment asset over its expected useful life. Depreciation is a process of allocation, not of valuation.
Reporting Depreciation. The generally accepted accounting principle is that accumulated depreciation should be shown as a deduction from plant and equipment.
Cost. The generally accepted accounting principle is that plant and equipment assets are recorded on the balance sheet at their original cost.
Matching Revenue and Expenses. The generally accepted accounting principle is that revenue must be matched against the expenses incurred in obtaining that revenue. The result of matching revenue and expenses is net income (or net loss) for the accounting period.

Topic 3 Problems

17-7. Instead of keeping plant and equipment record cards, the Somwang Corporation keeps a list of its plant and equipment assets. The list for the second year of the business's operations is shown here.

a. Supply the missing amounts.
b. Make the estimated semiannual entries in the general journal to record the estimated depreciation of the listed plant and equipment assets on June 30.

Asset	Cost	Disposal Value	Estimated Useful Life (in years)	Annual Depreciation	Monthly Depreciation	Current Book Value
(1) Automobile	$ 8,500	$ 1,000	5	$1,500	$125	$5,500
(2) Building	115,000	10,000	25	?	?	?
(3) Furniture	26,000	2,000	10	?	?	?
(4) Office Equipment	5,400	-0-	5	?	?	?
(5) Tools	2,016	-0-	6	?	?	?
(6) Truck	24,400	1,000	3	?	?	?

17-8. Parts of the trial balance prepared by Mitch Kern, an accountant, follow.

ACCOUNT TITLE	ACCT. NO.	DEBIT	CREDIT
Cash	101	6,230 00	
Accounts Receivable	111	4,920 00	
Allowance for Doubtful Accounts ...	112		140 00
Prepaid Insurance................	113	600 00	
Building........................	121	80,000 00	
Accumulated Depreciation—Building.	122		3,000 00
Furniture......................	123	3,000 00	
Accumulated Depreciation—Furniture	124		600 00
Miscellaneous Expense	505	2,560 00	

a. Enter this data on a worksheet for the year ended December 31.
b. Make the adjustments for the following: estimated uncollectible accounts, $60 (based on a percentage of net sales); expired insurance, $450; estimated depreciation of building, $3,000; and estimated depreciation of furniture, $300.
c. Extend all amounts to the proper columns of the worksheet.
d. Record the adjusting entries in the general journal.
e. Show how each current asset and plant and equipment asset and the asset contra accounts would appear on the balance sheet.

The Language of Business

Here are some basic terms that make up the language of business. Do you understand the meaning of each?

uncollectible
  account
realizable value of
  accounts
  receivable
direct write-off
  method

allowance method
Uncollectible
  Accounts Expense
  account
Allowance for
  Doubtful Accounts
  account

contra account
asset contra account
percentage of net
  sales method
percentage of aged
  accounts
  receivable method
aging the accounts
  receivable

depreciation
disposal value
straight-line method
book value
plant and equipment
  ledger

Chapter 17 Questions

1. What are two methods for writing off uncollectible accounts? Briefly describe each method.
2. If no allowance is made for uncollectible accounts, what effect does this have on revenue? On expenses? On net income? On assets? On owner's equity?
3. Why is the amount of uncollectible accounts credited to an asset contra account rather than to the Accounts Receivable controlling account?
4. Describe two methods of estimating uncollectible accounts.
5. How is the amount of the debit to the Uncollectible Accounts Expense account obtained when the estimate is based on a percentage of net sales? On a percentage of the aged accounts receivable?

6. Two years ago, the balance of the customer's account for Joanna Peck was written off as an uncollectible account. Describe the procedure used to record the check received from her today.
7. For which plant and equipment asset is no depreciation recorded?
8. Why must the amount of depreciation on plant and equipment assets be recorded on the financial statements?
9. Why is the amount of depreciation credited to a contra account rather than to the plant and equipment asset account?
10. What is the effect upon owner's equity if no adjustment is made for depreciation? Why?

Chapter 17 Problems

Problems for Chapter 17 are given in the *Working Papers and Chapter Problems for Part 3*. If you are using the workbook, do the problems in the space provided there.

Chapter 17 Management Cases

Credit Policies. Some businesses find it necessary to sell on credit to their customers. In businesses that sell furniture, for example, about 90 percent of the sales are made on credit. Thus a furniture business may not be able to survive if it does not give credit.

A new business must determine what is the best credit policy for it to follow in order to sell its products. With a strict credit policy, uncollectible accounts expense is low, but sales may also be low. With a lenient credit policy, both sales and uncollectible accounts expense will probably be high. Each business must decide which credit policy will yield the greater net income—more sales with more uncollectible accounts or fewer sales with fewer uncollectible accounts.

Case 17M-1. Andy Vetter owns the Colonial Furniture Store. If the business follows an extremely liberal policy of giving credit to customers, Mr. Vetter estimates that the total credit sales will be $300,000 during the year but that uncollectible accounts will be 5 percent of the credit sales. He figures that the gross profit after deduction of the uncollectible accounts expense would be as follows.

Credit Sales	$300,000
Gross Profit (25% of Sales)	$75,000
Uncollectible Accounts Expense (5% of Credit Sales)	15,000
Gross Profit After Uncollectible Accounts Expense	$60,000

Mr. Vetter estimates that the business will have the following credit sales and uncollectible accounts expense if less liberal credit policies are used.

Very strict:	Sales, $150,000; losses $\frac{1}{4}$%
Strict:	Sales, $175,000; losses, $\frac{1}{2}$%
Moderate:	Sales, $250,000; losses, 1%
Lenient:	Sales, $275,000; losses, 3%

a. Based on each of Mr. Vetter's estimates, what gross profit would the business have after the uncollectible accounts are deducted?
b. What credit policy do you recommend that Mr. Vetter follow?

Case 17M-2. The Sunshine Laundry Service owns a truck that it uses for picking up and delivering laundry. Last year, the truck traveled 60,000 miles and made 29,500 stops. Operating expenses were as follows: fuel, $7,500; repairs, $1,700; depreciation, $1,300; insurance, $560; license, $80; storage, $650; and driver's salary, $15,000. Madge O'Leary, the owner, is thinking of selling the truck and either leasing a truck from the E-Z Drive Company or using the Quick Delivery Service.

The E-Z Drive Company charges $400 per month for the truck. In addition to the monthly charge, the Sunshine Laundry Service must pay for the fuel, insurance, storage, and driver's salary. The E-Z Drive Company pays for repairs and the license.

The Quick Delivery Service will pick up and deliver the laundry in each delivery area once daily, at $1.20 per stop.
a. What decision would you make regarding the truck?
b. Are there other factors that should be considered besides the cost?

Working Hint

Depreciation Guidelines. A new system for computing depreciation was signed into law as part of the Economic Recovery Act of 1981. The system—called the Accelerated Cost Recovery System (ACRS)—classifies all plant and equipment assets as three-, five-, ten-, or fifteen-year property.

The ACRS eliminates the need to determine estimated life, salvage value, or the method of depreciation to use. In other words, the total cost of a plant and equipment asset will be depreciated over a three-, five-, ten-, or fifteen-year period. For example, an automobile that cost $10,000 is classified as a three-year property. The depreciation for each of the three years is computed as shown in the table below.

Year	Cost	×	Rate	=	Depreciation
First Year	$10,000	×	25%	=	$2,500
Second Year	$10,000	×	38%	=	$3,800
Third Year	$10,000	×	37%	=	$3,700
Total			100%		$10,000

Chapter 18

Updating Accounts for Accruals and Deferrals

Some transactions affect more than one accounting period. To have accurate financial statements, all revenues and expenses must be recorded in the accounting period when revenues are earned and expenses are used. You will now learn how unrecorded expenses and revenue affect financial information.

Topic 1
Unrecorded Expenses and Liabilities

A *How are most expenses paid and recorded?* Most expenses, such as utilities and rent, are paid and recorded as expenses during the accounting period in which they are incurred. However, some expenses may be incurred during the accounting period but not recorded because they will not be paid until a future accounting period. Adjusting entries must be made at the end of each accounting period for any unrecorded expenses.

Accrued Expenses

An expense item incurred during the accounting period but not paid and recorded is known as an **accrued expense.** For example, interest on a loan is charged for each day the borrower has the use of the money. However, the borrower does not pay the interest each day, and the interest is not recorded each day. In many cases interest is not paid and recorded until the due date of the loan. Thus if an interest-bearing promissory note will not be paid until a future accounting period, the amount of the interest expense incurred during the present period has not been recorded. An adjusting entry must be made to record the accrued interest expense.

A promissory note is a written promise to pay a sum of money at a fixed time in the future.

Accrued Interest Expense. On November 1, 19X3, the Allen Cox Company gives a creditor a 90-day, 12 percent promissory note for $10,000 in payment of its account payable. The general journal entry made to record the transaction is shown here.

GENERAL JOURNAL		Page	30		
DATE	ACCOUNT TITLE AND EXPLANATION	POST. REF.	DEBIT		CREDIT
19X3 Nov. 1	Acc. Pay./Best Equipment, Inc.	211/√	10,000	00	
	Notes Payable	201			10,000 00
	Gave 90-day, 12% note.				

In counting the number of days a note has to run, begin counting the day after the note is issued since the note states "after date." The last day, however, is counted. The calendars in the margin show 90 days after November 1 as January 30.

The interest on the note adds up day by day over the 90-day period but is not paid or recorded each day. When the note is due on January 30, 19X4, a total of $10,300 will be paid: $10,000 for the note and $300 for the interest.

19X3

November						
S	M	T	W	T	F	S
			1	2	3	4	5
6	7	8	9	10	11	12
13	14	15	16	17	18	19
20	21	22	23	24	25	26
27	28	29	30			

December						
S	M	T	W	T	F	S
					1	2	3
4	5	6	7	8	9	10
11	12	13	14	15	16	17
18	19	20	21	22	23	24
25	26	27	28	29	30	31

19X4

January						
S	M	T	W	T	F	S
1	2	3	4	5	6	7
8	9	10	11	12	13	14
15	16	17	18	19	20	21
22	23	24	25	26	27	28
29	30	31				

Nov.	30	days
	-1	
	29	days
Dec.	31	days
Jan.	30	days
Total	90	days

12% Interest on $10,000

$200 for 60 days
 100 for 30 days
$300 for 90 days

Since the Allen Cox Company has an annual accounting period that ends on December 31, the interest that accrues in the 60-day period from November 1 to December 31, 19X3, is an expense for the year 19X3. However, no expense is recorded in November or December. No payment of interest is recorded in November or December because no payment of interest is made in either month. If this interest expense is not recorded in 19X3, the following will happen.

- The net income for the year will be overstated.
- As a result, owner's equity will also be overstated.
- The financial statements for the following year will also be affected because the interest expense for 19X3 will be deducted from the revenue earned in 19X4.

An adjusting entry is necessary to record expenses that have been incurred but not yet paid so that financial statements are accurate.

Adjusting Interest Expense. The amount of interest accrued on the $10,000 note payable for the last 60 days of 19X3 is $200. Since none of the interest has been recorded, the Interest Expense account must be debited for $200 to show the actual interest expense for 19X3. The $200 will not be paid until January 30, 19X4, when the entire $300 in interest becomes due and the amount of the note is paid. As a result, the $200 is interest owed. Thus it is a liability. The $200 is credited to a liability account called Interest Payable to show the increase in liabilities.

Nov. 1 to Dec. 31		Jan. 1 to Jan. 30		
Previous Period $200	+	Present Period $100	=	Total Interest $300
Interest Payable		Interest Expense		

December 31, 19X3: The Allen Cox Company records interest expense of $200 accrued for 60 days on a note payable.

What Happens	Accounting Rule	Entry
The expense for interest decreases owner's equity by $200.	To decrease owner's equity, debit the account.	Debit: Interest Expense, $200.
The liability *Interest Payable* increases by $200.	To increase a liability, credit the account.	Credit: Interest Payable, $200.

Notes Payable 201	Interest Payable 202	Interest Expense 516
19X3 Nov. 1 10,000	19X3 Dec. 31 200	19X3 Dec. 31 200

Allen Cox Company Chart of Accounts

Current Liabilities
201 Notes Payable
202 Interest Payable

Other Expenses
516 Interest Expense

After the adjusting entry is posted, the three accounts related to notes payable show these items. The Notes Payable account shows the amount of the note owed ($10,000). The Interest Payable account shows the liability for interest incurred but not yet paid ($200). The Interest Expense account shows the interest expense incurred during the accounting period ($200).

After the closing entries are made on December 31, Interest Expense will be closed. The Interest Payable remains open until the liability is paid.

Paying the Interest. When the note is paid on January 30, 19X4, the Allen Cox Company sends $10,300 to the payee ($10,000 to pay the note and $300 to pay the interest from November 1 to January 30). Of the total interest being paid, $200 (the amount from November 1 to December 31) has been recorded as an expense of the previous accounting period (19X3). The remainder ($100) is an expense of the 19X4 accounting period. Therefore, the Interest Expense account must be debited for $100 to record the expense of the present period, and the Interest Payable account must be debited for $200 to decrease the liability recorded in the previous period.

Entry to Pay Accrued Expense

Debit: Liability account
Debit: Expense account
Credit: Cash

January 30, 19X4: The Allen Cox Company sends $10,300 to Best Equipment, Inc., to pay promissory note of $10,000 and interest of $300 for 90 days.

What Happens	Accounting Rule	Entry
The liability *Notes Payable* decreases by $10,000.	To decrease a liability, debit the account.	Debit: Notes Payable, $10,000.
The liability *Interest Payable* decreases by $200.	To decrease a liability, debit the account.	Debit: Interest Payable, $200.
The expense for interest decreases owner's equity by $100.	To decrease owner's equity, debit the account.	Debit: Interest Expense, $100.
The asset *Cash* decreases by $10,300.	To decrease an asset, credit the account.	Credit: Cash, $10,300.

Since cash is being paid, the entry is recorded in the cash payments journal. Three lines are needed since there are no special columns for Notes Payable, Interest Payable, or Interest Expense.

CASH PAYMENTS JOURNAL									Page 81
DATE	ACCOUNT DEBITED	EXPLANATION	CHECK NO.	POST. REF.	GENERAL LEDGER DEBIT	ACCOUNTS PAYABLE DEBIT	PURCHASES DISCOUNT CREDIT	NET CASH CREDIT	
19X4									
Jan. 30	Notes Payable	Note dated Nov. 1 .	275	201	10,000 00			10,300 00	
	Interest Payable . .	Interest for 60 days.	—	202	200 00			—	
	Interest Expense . . .	Interest for 30 days.	—	516	100 00			—	

After the entry is posted, the balance in both the Notes Payable and Interest Payable accounts will be zero. Interest Expense will show the amount of interest that is an expense for the current period.

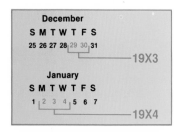

Notes Payable 201		Interest Payable 202		Interest Expense 516		Cash 101	
19X4	19X3	19X4	19X3	19X4			19X4
Jan. 30 10,000	Nov. 1 10,000	Jan. 30 200	Dec. 31 200	Jan. 30 100			Jan. 30 10,300

Activity A. Answer the following questions about accrued interest. Refer to the text, margin notes, and illustrations on pages 547 to 550.

1. Why is Interest Expense debited for $200?

2. What account is credited for $200? Why?

3. What adjusting entry is made to record the accrued interest?

4. What is the amount of Check 275? Why is it issued?

5. What is the relationship between the entry for Interest Payable on January 30 in the cash payments journal and the adjusting entry for Interest Payable on December 31 in the general journal?

6. What is the relationship between the entry for the Interest Expense account on January 30 in the cash payments journal and the adjusting entry for the Interest Expense account on December 31 in the general journal?

Accrued Salaries Expense

B *Does salary expense accrue the same as interest expense does?* Yes, employees earn salaries day by day, but the salary expense is not recorded until the end of the pay period. For example, the pay period for the Allen Cox Company ends each Wednesday. The total salaries are $300 a day, or $1,500 for five working days. Suppose that December 31 (the end of the accounting period) falls on a Saturday. Then salaries for two days have been earned during the current accounting period but will not be paid until Wednesday, January 4, which is in the next accounting period.

Adjusting Salaries Expense. The salaries for Thursday and Friday, December 29 and 30, amount to $600 (2 × $300). The accrued expense is recorded in the same manner as the accrued interest expense was recorded. It is an expense for the current accounting period that will be paid in the next accounting period. The adjusting entry for $600 is a debit to Salaries Expense to record the expense and a credit to Salaries Payable to record the liability.

Salaries Payable 221		Salaries Expense 519	
	19X3	19X3	
	Dec. 31 600	Dec. 31 600	

When the closing entries are made on December 31, the Salaries Expense account is closed into the Income Summary account. The Salaries Payable account remains open until the liability is paid.

Paying the Salaries. When the salaries are paid on January 4 of the next accounting period, the Salaries Payable account is debited for

December

S M T W T F S

25 26 27 28 29 30 31 ──── 19X3

January

S M T W T F S

1 2 3 4 5 6 7 ──── 19X4

Allen Cox Company Chart of Accounts

Current Liabilities
221   Salaries Payable

Costs and Expenses
519   Salaries Expense

$600 to record the decrease in the liability recorded in the previous period (for the salaries earned on December 29 and 30). The Salaries Expense account is debited for $900 to record the amount of the salaries that is an expense for the new accounting period (the salaries earned on January 2, 3, and 4). The Cash account is credited for the total amount of salaries paid ($1,500).

Entry to Pay Accrued Expense
Debit: Liability account
Debit: Expense account
Credit: Cash

Cash		101	Salaries Payable			221	Salaries Expense		519
	19X4		19X4		19X3		19X4		
	Jan. 4	1,500	Jan. 4	600	Dec. 31	600	Jan. 4	900	

Accounting for Accrued Expenses

Adjusting entries are needed for accrued expenses for the following reasons.

• To report all expenses incurred during the accounting period so that the correct net income will appear on the income statement.
• To report all liabilities on the balance sheet.
• To report the correct owner's equity on the balance sheet.

To record an accrued expense, debit the expense account to decrease owner's equity for the current accounting period. Credit the liability account to increase the liabilities. (Since these amounts are both expenses and liabilities, accrued expenses are also referred to as *accrued liabilities*.)

The entry to record the payment of an expense item that was recorded as an accrued expense is made by debiting the liability account for the amount recorded as accrued in the previous period, debiting the expense account for the amount incurred in the current period, and crediting Cash for the total amount paid.

Adjusting Entry for Accrued Expense
Debit: Expense account
Credit: Liability account

Activity B. Answer the following questions about accrued salaries. Refer to the text, margin notes, and illustrations on pages 550 to 551.
1. Why is Salaries Expense debited for $600?
2. What account is credited for $600? Why?
3. What adjusting entry is made to record the accrued salaries?

Accrued Expenses on the Worksheet

C *When are accrued expenses recorded?* The entries to record the accrued expenses for an accounting period are made as adjustments at the end of the accounting period. At that time, the amounts of the accrued expenses are computed and entered in the Adjustments section of the worksheet.

	ACCOUNT TITLE	ACCT. NO.	UNADJUSTED TRIAL BALANCE		ADJUSTMENTS		ADJUSTED TRIAL BALANCE		INCOME STATEMENT		BALANCE SHEET		
			DEBIT	CREDIT	DEBIT	CREDIT	DEBIT	CREDIT	DEBIT	CREDIT	DEBIT	CREDIT	
26	Interest Payable	202				(h) 200		200				200	26
27	Salaries Payable	221				(i) 600		600				600	27
30	Interest Expense	516	500		(h) 200		700		700				30
33	Salaries Expense	519	29,000		(i) 600		29,600		29,600				33

The Unadjusted Trial Balance section shows Interest Expense of $500 and Salaries Expense of $29,000 paid during the year. Interest Expense of $500 does not include the interest of $200 accumulated from November 1 to December 31 on the $10,000 note due January 30, 19X4. Salaries Expense of $29,000 does not include $600 for salaries earned on December 29 and 30.

The adjustments to record the accrued expenses require debits to the expense accounts and credits to the liability accounts. The adjustments are shown as (h) and (i) on the worksheet illustrated.

Accrued Interest Expense. The amount of the interest expense paid during the accounting period was $500. To this amount must be added the accrued interest of $200. Therefore, the adjustment includes a debit to the Interest Expense account for $200 and a credit to the Interest Payable account for the same amount. The Interest Payable account had no balance when the trial balance was prepared.

The Adjusted Trial Balance section shows that the actual amount of interest expense for the period is $700 ($500 interest paid plus $200 interest accrued). This amount is moved to the Income Statement section of the worksheet. The Adjusted Trial Balance section also shows interest payable of $200. The $200 is extended to the Balance Sheet section because interest payable is a liability.

Accrued Salaries Expense. As shown on the trial balance, the amount of salaries paid during the period was $29,000. The adjustment of $600 for the accrued salaries is added to the $29,000, and the total salaries expense ($29,600) is entered in the Adjusted Trial Balance section. The $29,600 is then extended to the Income Statement section. Salaries Payable now shows $600, the amount of salaries incurred during the period but not yet paid. The $600 is extended to the Balance Sheet section because salaries payable is a liability.

Interest Expense

Interest Paid	$500
Accrued Interest	200
Total Interest Expense	$700

Salary Expense

Salaries Paid	$29,000
Accrued Salaries	600
Total Salary Expense	$29,600

Accrued Expenses on the Financial Statements

Accrued expenses are reported on the income statement. Salaries expense appears in the Operating Expenses section. The expense for interest, however, is not considered an operating expense because it is not incurred in the day-to-day operations of the business. As a result, interest expense is reported in the Other Expenses section of the income statement.

If the accrued expenses are to be paid within a year, the liability accounts are listed in the Current Liabilities section of the balance sheet. If the accrued expenses are not due within a year, the liability accounts are listed in the Long-Term Liabilities section.

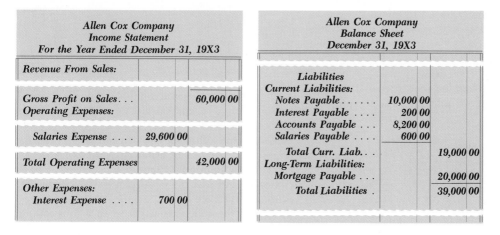

Allen Cox Company Income Statement For the Year Ended December 31, 19X3		
Revenue From Sales:		
Gross Profit on Sales. . .		60,000 00
Operating Expenses:		
Salaries Expense	29,600 00	
Total Operating Expenses		42,000 00
Other Expenses:		
Interest Expense	700 00	

Allen Cox Company Balance Sheet December 31, 19X3		
Liabilities		
Current Liabilities:		
Notes Payable.	10,000 00	
Interest Payable	200 00	
Accounts Payable . . .	8,200 00	
Salaries Payable	600 00	
Total Curr. Liab.. . .		19,000 00
Long-Term Liabilities:		
Mortgage Payable . . .		20,000 00
Total Liabilities .		39,000 00

Accrued Expenses in Closing the Ledger

The adjusting entries to record the accrued expenses are journalized in the general journal with the other adjusting entries.

The closing entries transfer the balances of the Interest Expense account and the Salaries Expense account to the Income Summary account. Thus the expense accounts have zero balances. The Interest Payable account and the Salaries Payable account have credit balances. These liability accounts will appear on the postclosing trial balance. However, the expense accounts will not appear on the postclosing trial balance because they have been closed for the accounting period.

Expense accounts are closed into Income Summary account.

Activity C. Answer the following questions about accrued expenses on the worksheet. Refer to the worksheet on page 552.
1. Has the $500 debited to Interest Expense in the Unadjusted Trial Balance section been paid?
2. Has the $200 debited to Interest Expense in the Adjustments section of the worksheet been paid? Explain.

3. Has the $29,000 debited to Salaries Expense in the Unadjusted Trial Balance section of the worksheet been paid?
4. Has the $600 debited to Salaries Expense in the Adjustments section of the worksheet been paid? Explain.

Topic 1 Problems

18-1. Perform the following activities for Lena's Restaurant.

a. Open general ledger accounts and record the September 1 balances as follows: Notes Payable, $8,000; Interest Payable, $0; Income Summary, $0; and Interest Expense, $0.

b. Record the adjusting entry in the general journal for accrued interest expense of $80 on September 30. Post the entry.

c. Record and post the closing entry for Interest Expense on September 30.

d. Record the following payment in a four-column cash payments journal: Check 210 for $8,120 was issued on October 15 to pay an $8,000 note payable dated September 1 and $120 in interest. Post the debit entries.

18-2. Parts of the trial balance prepared for the Cracraft Corporation on June 30 of the current year are shown here.

Purchases.....................	501	69,450 00	
Purchases Returns and Allowances ..	502		925 00
Interest Expense	525	110 00	
Salaries Expense	527	2,300 00	

a. Enter this data on a worksheet for the year ended June 30.

b. Make the adjustments for accrued interest of $30 on notes payable and accrued salaries of $150.

c. Extend all amounts to the proper columns of the Income Statement section or the Balance Sheet section of the worksheet.

d. Record the adjusting entries in the general journal.

18-3. The Salaries Expense account below appeared in the general ledger of the Ansley Company on April 30 of the current year.

Salaries Expense   **Account No.** 527

DATE	EXPLANATION	POST. REF.	DEBIT	CREDIT	BALANCE DEBIT	BALANCE CREDIT
19—						
Apr. 7		CP18	650 00		650 00	
14		CP18	700 00		1,350 00	
21		CP19	700 00		2,050 00	
28		CP19	700 00		2,750 00	

a. Open general ledger accounts for Salaries Payable, Income Summary, and Salaries Expense. (Include the entries just given.)

b. Record the adjusting entry in the general journal for accrued salaries of $360 on April 30. Post the entry to the appropriate accounts.

c. Record and post the closing entry for Salaries Expense on April 30.

d. Record the following payment in a four-column cash payments journal: Check 1500 for $700 was issued on May 4 to pay total salaries. Post the debit entries.

Topic 2
Unrecorded Revenue and Assets

A *Are all revenue transactions recorded during the accounting period in which they are earned?* Most revenue items, such as sales, are recorded during the accounting period in which they are earned. However, there are some revenue items that may be earned during the accounting period but are not recorded in that accounting period. The reason that they are not recorded in that accounting period is because the revenue will not be received until a future accounting period.

How and when to record revenue earned in one accounting period but received in a future accounting period are discussed in this topic.

Accrued Revenue

A revenue item earned during the current accounting period but not received until a future accounting period is known as **accrued revenue.** One example of accrued revenue is the interest that accumulates on a note receivable. The interest is revenue to the payee (receiver) of the note and should be recorded as revenue for the accounting period in which it is earned.

When a note is received and due in the same accounting period, the interest revenue is recorded when the payee receives the cash for the note and the interest. If the note is received in one accounting period, but is not due until a future accounting period, an adjusting entry must be made at the end of the current accounting period. This is done to record the interest earned but not yet received. Accrued interest revenue will be used to show the procedure to account for accrued revenue.

Accrued Interest Revenue. On December 1, 19X3, Karen Botham gives the Allen Cox Company a 120-day, 12 percent note for $1,000 in payment of her account. The transaction is recorded as follows.

	GENERAL JOURNAL			Page 30
DATE	**ACCOUNT TITLE AND EXPLANATION**	**POST. REF.**	**DEBIT**	**CREDIT**
19X3 Dec. 1	Notes Receivable	111	1,000 00	
	Accounts Receivable/Karen Botham	121/√		1,000 00
	Received 120-day, 12% note.			

Notes Receivable   111

19X3
Dec. 1 J30   1,000

Date of Note		Due Date
Dec. 1	Dec. 31	Mar. 31
	19X3	19X4

The note receivable is recorded at its **face value** (the principal) of $1,000 and remains as a debit in the Notes Receivable account until it is due. The interest on the note is earned day by day but is not recorded each day. No interest will be received until the note is due. Thus on March 31, 19X4, when the note is due, the Allen Cox Company will receive $1,040 ($1,000 to pay the note and $40 to pay the interest) from Karen Botham (the **maker** of the note). In this case, the interest has been earned in two accounting periods because the Allen Cox Company has an accounting period that ends on December 31. Therefore, an adjusting entry must be made on December 31 to record the accrued interest revenue for 19X3.

The amount of interest that has accrued on the $1,000 note receivable during the last 30 days of 19X3 is $10. If the interest revenue is not recorded in the 19X3 accounting period, both the net income and the

December	31
	−1
	30 days
January	31 days
February	28 days
March (due)	31 days
	120 days

12% interest on $1,000 for 30 days = $10

owner's equity will be understated. In the next accounting period, the net income will be overstated because all the interest received on the note will be recorded as revenue for 19X4. An adjusting entry must be made in order to have the accrued revenue recorded in the accounting period in which it is earned.

Adjusting Interest Revenue. The amount of interest accrued on the $1,000 note receivable during 19X3 is $10. The Interest Revenue account must be credited for $10 in order to report all the interest earned during the period. Since none of the interest will be received until the note is due, the $10 is a claim against the maker of the note until the maker pays the interest. Thus the accrued interest of $10 is a receivable, which is an asset.

A separate asset account, called Interest Receivable, is used to record the interest accrued on notes receivable. The asset account is debited to show the increase in assets. Because of its relationship with Notes Receivable, Interest Receivable is listed immediately after Notes Receivable in the Current Assets section of the Allen Cox Company's chart of accounts.

December 31, 19X3: The Allen Cox Company records interest revenue of $10 accrued for 30 days on a note receivable.

What Happens	Accounting Rule	Entry
The asset *Interest Receivable* increases by $10.	To increase an asset, debit the account.	Debit: Interest Receivable, $10.
The revenue from interest increases owner's equity by $10.	To increase owner's equity, credit the account.	Credit: Interest Revenue, $10.

Notes Receivable 111		*Interest Receivable* 112		*Interest Revenue* 491	
19X3		19X3		19X3	
Dec. 1 1,000		Dec. 31 10		Dec. 31 10	

Balance of Notes Receivable account is total amount to be received from notes.

Balance of Interest Receivable account is total amount of interest earned but not yet received.

Balance of Interest Revenue account is total amount of revenue earned from interest.

After the adjusting entry is posted, the three accounts related to notes receivable show the following amounts. The Notes Receivable account shows the amount of the Note Receivable ($1,000). The Interest Receivable account shows the amount of the interest earned but not yet received ($10). The Interest Revenue account shows the amount of the interest earned during the current accounting period ($10).

When the closing entries are made, Interest Revenue is closed into the Income Summary account. Interest Receivable is a permanent account and remains open until the accrued interest has been received.

(Since the amounts of the accrued items are both revenue and assets, accrued revenue is also referred to as an **accrued asset**.)

Receiving the Interest. When the note comes due on March 31, 19X4, the Allen Cox Company receives $1,040 in cash from Karen Botham ($1,000 for the note receivable and $40 for the interest from December 1 to March 31). Of the total interest received, $10 (the amount for December 1 to December 31) has been recorded as revenue for the previous accounting period (19X3).

The remainder of the interest ($30) is revenue for the accounting period of 19X4. Therefore, the Interest Revenue account must be credited for $30. This must be done to record the revenue for the present period. The Interest Receivable account must also be credited for $10. This must be done to decrease the asset that was recorded in the previous period.

Dec. 1 to Dec. 31		Jan. 1 to Mar. 31		
Previous Period $10	+	Present Period $30	=	Total Interest $40
Interest Receivable		Interest Revenue		

March 31, 19X4: The Allen Cox Company receives $1,040 in cash from Karen Botham for a note receivable of $1,000 and interest of $40.

What Happens	Accounting Rule	Entry
The asset *Cash* increases by $1,040.	To increase an asset, debit the account.	Debit: Cash, $1,040.
The asset *Notes Receivable* decreases by $1,000.	To decrease an asset, credit the account.	Credit: Notes Receivable, $1,000.
The asset *Interest Receivable* decreases by $10.	To decrease an asset, credit the account.	Credit: Interest Receivable, $10.
The revenue from interest increases owner's equity by $30.	To increase owner's equity, credit the account.	Credit: Interest Revenue, $30.

Notes Receivable 111		Interest Receivable 112		Interest Revenue 491		Cash 101	
19X3 Dec. 1 1,000	19X4 Mar. 31 1,000	19X3 Dec. 31 10	19X4 Mar. 31 10		19X4 Mar. 31 30	19X4 Mar. 31 1,040	

The entry to record the receipt of cash by the Allen Cox Company for the note receivable and the interest covering two accounting periods is shown at the top of page 558. The entry is recorded in the cash receipts journal. Three lines are required to record the transaction in the cash receipts journal.

DATE	ACCOUNT CREDITED	EXPLANATION	POST. REF.	GENERAL LEDGER CREDIT	ACCOUNTS RECEIVABLE CREDIT	SALES DISCOUNT DEBIT	NET CASH DEBIT
19X4							
Mar. 31	*Notes Receivable*	*Karen Botham, Dec. 1*	*111*	*1,000 00*			*1,040 00*
	Interest Receivable...	*Interest for 30 days* .	*112*	*10 00*			*— 00*
	Interest Revenue	*Interest for 90 days* .	*491*	*30 00*			*— 00*

After the entry is posted, the balance of the Notes Receivable account is zero because the cash has been received for the note. The Interest Receivable account balance is also zero because the interest earned during the previous accounting period has now been received. The revenue account Interest Revenue shows the amount of interest that is revenue for the current accounting period.

Activity A. Answer the following questions about accrued revenue and accrued assets. Refer to the text, margin notes, and illustrations on pages 554 to 558.
1. What adjusting entry is made on December 31?
2. What is the effect of the December 31 entry on current assets? On owner's equity?
3. What entry is made on March 31?

4. What is the effect of the March 31 entry on receivables? On cash?
5. What amount of the $40 interest is earned in 19X3? What amount of the interest is earned in 19X4?
6. What would be the effect on net income for 19X3 and 19X4 if $40 were recorded as interest earned in 19X4?

Deferred Revenue

B *Do businesses ever receive payment in advance?* Yes, sometimes a business receives payments for goods or services before the goods are delivered or the services are performed. Part of the payment may be revenue for the current accounting period, and part may represent revenue for future accounting periods.

Revenue received before it is earned is known as **deferred revenue** (sometimes referred to as *unearned revenue*). The term *deferred revenue* is used because recording the revenue must be deferred (postponed) until it is earned. Until then, the amount received is shown in the accounting records as a liability. It is shown as a liability until then because cash has been received, and the business is now "liable" either for providing the product or service or for refunding the cash received.

Deferred revenue is first recorded as a liability.

The following are examples of deferred revenue.

• A tenant pays rent in advance for December, January, and February. If the property owner has an annual accounting period that ends on December 31, only one month of the rent received will be earned in the current accounting period. The other two months' rent will be revenue of the next accounting period.

- A magazine publisher receives payment for a subscription in advance. This is deferred revenue until the magazines are sent to the subscriber.
- An insurance company requires the policyholder to pay the premiums on a policy months or years in advance. The premiums are deferred revenue until actually earned.

Recording Deferred Revenue. To see how deferred revenue is recorded, assume that the Allen Cox Company permits the Castle Inn to install an advertising billboard on its property for two years, from July 1, 19X3, to June 30, 19X5. In return for the use of the land, the Castle Inn agrees to pay $1,200 rent for the entire two-year period. On July 1, 19X3, the Castle Inn pays the Allen Cox Company the $1,200 rent in advance for the two-year period. Since the Allen Cox Company has received the money, it is obligated to rent the property to the Castle Inn for the entire two-year period.

Receiving Deferred Rental Revenue. When the $1,200 in cash is received for the rent, the transaction is recorded in the cash receipts journal. The Cash account is debited for $1,200. The amount covers more than one accounting period. Therefore, since the rent cannot be recorded as revenue earned because the Allen Cox Company has collected the rent but has not yet earned it, the $1,200 is credited to a liability account called **Unearned Rental Revenue account.** The entry to record the receipt of deferred revenue in the cash receipts journal is as follows.

CASH RECEIPTS JOURNAL   Page 65

DATE		ACCOUNT CREDITED	EXPLANATION	POST. REF.	GENERAL LEDGER CREDIT	ACCOUNTS RECEIVABLE CREDIT	SALES DISCOUNT DEBIT	NET CASH DEBIT
19X3								
July	1	Unearned Rent. Rev. . .	Castle Inn, 2 yrs.' rent	231	1,200 00			1,200 00

At the end of the accounting period, an adjusting entry is needed to transfer the amount of the revenue earned from the liability account to a revenue account. If the adjustment is not made, the liabilities will be overstated and the revenue will be understated. As a result, the owner's equity will be understated.

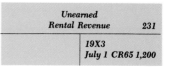

Unearned Rental Revenue	231
	19X3
	July 1 CR65 1,200

Adjusting Deferred Rental Revenue. At the end of the accounting period on December 31, 19X3, the Allen Cox Company has earned six months' rent (July through December). Since the rent for two years is $1,200, the amount for one month is $50 ($1,200 ÷ 24). The revenue earned for six months is $300 ($50 × 6).

The adjusting entry to transfer the revenue earned ($300) from the liability account to a revenue account, called the Rental Revenue account, requires a debit to the liability account and a credit to the revenue account. (The **Rental Revenue account** is used to record rental revenue earned.) Since the revenue from the rental of the property is not connected directly with the operations of the business, Rental Revenue is assigned the number 492 in the Allen Cox Company's chart of accounts. The account is considered as Other Revenue.

December 31, 19X3: The Allen Cox Company records $300 of deferred rental revenue as rent earned for six months.

What Happens	Accounting Rule	Entry
The liability *Unearned Rental Revenue* decreases by $300.	To decrease a liability, debit the account.	Debit: Unearned Rental Revenue, $300.
The revenue from rent increases owner's equity by $300.	To increase owner's equity, credit the account.	Credit: Rental Revenue, $300.

Unearned Rental Revenue 231		*Rental Revenue* 492	
19X3	*19X3*	*19X3*	
Dec. 31 300	*July 1* *1,200*	*Dec. 31* *300*	
	900		

After the adjusting entry is posted, the two accounts show the following amounts. The Unearned Rental Revenue account shows the amount of deferred revenue ($900) not yet earned. The Rental Revenue account shows the amount of revenue earned during the current accounting period ($300).

When the closing entries are made, Rental Revenue is closed into the Income Summary account. Unearned Rental Revenue is a liability account. It is open until all the deferred revenue has been earned.

Accrued Revenue and Deferred Revenue on the Worksheet

The adjustments to record the amounts of the accrued revenue and the deferred revenue earned during the accounting period are computed and entered in the Adjustments section of the worksheet before each is journalized. The adjustment to record accrued interest revenue is identified as adjustment (j), and the adjustment to record deferred rental revenue is identified as adjustment (k).

Allen Cox Company
Worksheet
For the Year Ended December 31, 19X3

	ACCOUNT TITLE	ACCT. NO.	UNADJUSTED TRIAL BALANCE		ADJUSTMENTS		ADJUSTED TRIAL BALANCE		INCOME STATEMENT		BALANCE SHEET		
			DEBIT	CREDIT	DEBIT	CREDIT	DEBIT	CREDIT	DEBIT	CREDIT	DEBIT	CREDIT	
15	Interest Receivable	112			(j) 10		10				10		15
19	Unearned Rental Revenue . .	231		1,200	(k) 300			900				900	19
26	Interest Revenue	491		56		(j) 10		66		66			26
44	Rental Revenue	492				(k) 300		300		300			44

NOTE: The cents columns have been omitted in order to show the entire worksheet.

Accrued Revenue—Interest Revenue. The amount of the interest revenue received during the accounting period was $56. It is shown in the Unadjusted Trial Balance section. To this amount is added the accrued interest of $10. As a result, the Adjusted Trial Balance section shows the actual amount of Interest Revenue for the accounting period as $66 ($56 interest received plus $10 interest accrued). The revenue amount ($66) is extended to the Income Statement section. The adjustment for accrued interest revenue contains a debit ($10) to Interest Receivable, which is extended to the Balance Sheet section.

Deferred Revenue—Rental Revenue. As shown on the trial balance, the unearned rental revenue received during the accounting period amounted to $1,200. When the amount was received, it was credited to the liability account Unearned Rental Revenue because the amount received has not been earned.

The adjustment of $300 for the revenue earned is subtracted from the amount of Unearned Rental Revenue. The balance of Unearned Rental Revenue is now $900 ($1,200 − $300) and is entered in the Adjusted Trial Balance section and then extended to the Balance Sheet section. Rental Revenue shows $300 as rent earned during the period. The amount is extended to the Income Statement section.

Accrued Revenue and Deferred Revenue on the Financial Statements

The amounts of the revenue earned are reported on the income statement. Both Interest Revenue and Rental Revenue appear in the Other Revenue section because they are not considered as being earned from the regular operations of the business. Other Expenses is generally shown as a subtraction from Other Revenue. Thus only one amount appears on the income statement—either Net Other Revenue or Net Other Expense.

The amount of Interest Receivable ($10) is reported as a current asset on the balance sheet because the amount will be received within a year. The amount of Unearned Rental Revenue ($900) is reported as a current liability because the major part of it will be earned within the next year.

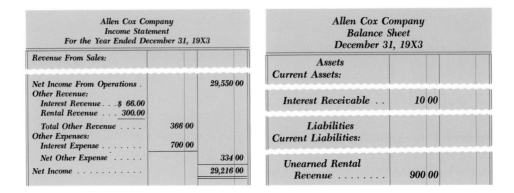

Accrued Revenue and Deferred Revenue in Closing the Ledger

The adjusting entries for accrued revenue and deferred revenue are journalized in the general journal with the other adjustments.

The closing entries for accrued revenue and deferred revenue are journalized in the general journal with the other closing entries.

Revenue accounts are closed into Income Summary account.

The closing entries transfer the balances of the Interest Revenue account ($66) and the Rental Revenue account ($300) to the Income Summary account. The revenue accounts then have zero balances. The Interest Receivable account has a debit balance of $10. The Unearned Rental Revenue account has a credit balance of $900. The Interest Receivable account and the Unearned Rental Revenue account will appear on the postclosing trial balance. The revenue accounts will not appear on the postclosing trial balance because they have been closed for the period.

Summary of Accruals and Deferrals

Accrued expenses and accrued revenue are known as **accruals.** Deferred revenues and prepaid expenses are known as **deferrals.**

Accounts	Accruals	Deferrals
Revenue	Accrued Revenue: revenue earned but not yet received.	Deferred Revenue: revenue received but not yet earned.
Expense	Accrued Expense: expense incurred but not yet paid.	Prepaid (Deferred) Expense: expense paid but not yet incurred.

Cash Basis or Accrual Basis

A business can choose one of two procedures to process financial data: the cash basis of accounting or the accrual basis of accounting. The primary difference between the two is when the business records (recognizes) revenue and expenses.

Under the **cash basis of accounting,** revenue is recorded in the accounting period when cash is received from customers and expenses are recorded in the accounting period when cash is actually paid.

Many service businesses and professional people use the cash basis of accounting. For example, if a lawyer uses the cash basis, the recorded revenues are only those fees actually collected from clients during the year. The lawyer may have performed services for other clients. But until that revenue is received, the fees are not recorded as revenue.

Under the **accrual basis of accounting,** revenue is recorded in the accounting period in which merchandise is sold or a service is performed, and expenses are recorded in the accounting period in which they are incurred. Thus revenue is recorded whether or not cash has been received. Expenses are recorded whether or not cash has been paid. Businesses that have inventories to sell generally use the accrual basis of accounting.

From an accounting point of view, the accrual basis is preferred over the cash basis. This is because the accrual basis complies with the matching principle. In other words, the accrual basis records all expenses—paid or not paid—that were incurred in earning the revenue of each accounting period. Thus businesses using the accrual basis of accounting must update their accounts each period by making adjusting entries.

Activity B. Answer the following questions about deferred revenue. Refer to the cash receipts journal on page 559 and the worksheet and T accounts on pages 559 to 561.
1. Has the $1,200 credited to the Unearned Rental Revenue account in the Unadjusted Trial Balance section of the worksheet already been received?
2. Why is the balance of Unearned Rental Revenue extended to the Balance Sheet section of the worksheet?
3. What adjusting entry is made to record earned rental revenue?
4. What is the relationship between the July 1 entry in the cash receipts journal for Unearned Rental Revenue and the $1,200 amount for that account in the Unadjusted Trial Balance section of the worksheet?

Accounting Concepts:

Accrual Basis of Accounting. Under the *accrual basis of accounting,* revenue is recorded in the accounting period in which it is earned, whether or not cash is received. Expenses are recorded in the account-ing period in which they are incurred, whether or not cash has been paid.

Cash Basis of Accounting. Under the *cash basis of accounting,* reve-nue is recorded in the accounting period in which cash is actually col-lected. Expenses are recorded in the accounting period in which they are actually paid.

Accounting Principles:

Matching Revenue and Expenses. The generally accepted account-ing principle is that revenue must be matched against the expenses in-curred in obtaining that revenue. The result of matching revenue and expenses is net income (or net loss) for the accounting period.

Updating Accounts. The generally accepted accounting principle is that certain accounts must be updated at the end of each accounting period. This procedure requires the recording of adjusting entries in order to reflect current account balances.

Topic 2 Problems

18-4. Parts of the trial balance prepared for the Newby Publishing Co. on June 30 are given here.

Notes Receivable	111	3,000 00	
Interest Receivable	112		
Accounts Payable	211		2,340 00
Unearned Subscription Revenue	215		15,110 00
Subscription Revenue	401		24,000 00
Miscellaneous Expense	526	248 00	

a. Enter this data on a worksheet for the year ended June 30.

b. Make the adjustments for accrued interest of $30 on notes receivable and $1,500 of subscription reve-nue that was previously recorded as unearned but is now earned.

c. Extend all amounts to the proper columns of the Income Statement section or the Balance Sheet sec-tion of the worksheet.

d. Record the adjusting entries in the general journal.

From the following information, record adjust-ing entries in the general journal of TMW Enterprises for the year ended December 31.

a. *Merchandise Inventory:* The trial balance shows a debit balance of $12,400 for Merchandise Inventory. An actual count of the merchandise inventory showed $10,300.

b. *Prepaid Expenses:* The trial balance shows a debit balance of $170 for Prepaid Insurance. The amount of insurance paid in advance is now $30.

c. *Uncollectible Accounts:* The estimated uncollect-ible accounts loss is $220.

d. *Depreciation:* The estimated depreciation is $1,600/year on a building and $800/year on a truck.

e. *Accrued Revenue:* The accrued revenue from inter-est is $25.

f. *Accrued Expense:* The accrued expense for salaries is $90.

g. *Deferred Revenue:* The trial balance shows a credit balance of $1,200 for Unearned Rental Revenue. Dur-ing the current accounting period, $400 of this rent has been earned.

18-6. Union College collects tuition from its students on a quarterly basis: in September, December, March, and June. On September 21 the Unearned Tuition Revenue account in the general ledger contained the information shown on the next page.

a. Open general ledger accounts for Cash, Unearned Tuition Revenue (include the entries shown on the next page), Income Summary, and Tuition Revenue. Enter the balance of $7,800 in the cash account as of September 1.

b. On September 28, $9,600 in cash was received from tuition payments. Record this transaction in a four-column cash receipts journal.

Unearned Tuition Revenue					Account No.	207	
DATE	EXPLANATION	POST. REF.	DEBIT	CREDIT	BALANCE		
					DEBIT	CREDIT	
19—							
Sept. 1	Balance	—				45,000	00
7		CR42		10,000 00		55,000	00
14		CR42		12,000 00		67,000	00
21		CR43		11,000 00		78,000	00

c. Tuition earned for the month ended September 30 was $29,200. Record the adjusting entry for this deferred revenue item in a general journal.
d. Post the entries from the journals to the ledger.
e. Record and post the closing entry for Tuition Revenue on September 30.
NOTE: Save your general journal and the ledger for further use in Topic Problem 18-7.

18-7. Use the general journal and the ledger from Topic Problem 18-6 to do the following work.
a. Tuition earned for the month ended October 31 is $29,200. Record and post the adjusting entry on October 31.

b. Record and post the closing entry for Tuition Revenue on October 31.
NOTE: Save your general journal and the ledger for further use in Topic Problem 18-8.

18-8. Use your general journal and the ledger from Topic Problem 18-7 to do the following.
a. Tuition earned for the month ended November 30 is $29,200. Record and post the adjusting entry.
b. Record and post the closing entry for Tuition Revenue on November 30.

The Language of Business

Here are some terms that make up the language of business. Do you know the meaning of each?

accrued expense
accrued revenue
face value
maker
accrued asset
deferred revenue
Unearned Rental
  Revenue account
Rental Revenue account
accruals
deferrals
cash basis of
  accounting
accrual basis of
  accounting

Chapter 18 Questions

1. What type of account is Interest Payable? On which financial statement does it appear?
2. What is the difference between prepaid expenses and accrued expenses?
3. What is the difference between accrued revenue and deferred revenue?
4. In what respect are accrued expenses like accrued revenue? Prepaid expenses like deferred revenue?
5. How do the adjusting entries for accrued expenses relate to the matching principle?
6. Why is a deferred revenue item credited to a liability account rather than to a revenue account?

7. If no adjustment is made to record the accrued expenses for the current period, what effect does this have on the net income? On the balance sheet accounts?
8. If no entry is made to adjust the deferred revenue for the current period, what effect does this have on the net income? On the balance sheet accounts?
9. If no adjustment is made to record the accrued revenue for the current period, what effect does this have on the net income? On the balance sheet accounts?

Chapter 18 Problems

Problems for Chapter 18 are given in the *Working Papers and Chapter Problems for Part 3.* If you are using the workbook, do the problems in the space provided there.

Chapter 18 Management Cases

Cash Basis vs. Accrual Basis. Federal income tax regulations give the individual taxpayer the option of reporting revenue and expenses on a cash basis or on an accrual basis.

If the *cash basis* is used, the taxpayer reports as revenue only those amounts actually received and deducts as expenses only those amounts actually paid.

When the taxpayer uses the *accrual basis,* the reported revenue for the period is all revenue earned whether or not it has actually been received during the period. The taxpayer reports as expenses for the period all expenses incurred whether or not they have actually been paid during the period.

The taxpayer must be consistent from one year to the next in the method of reporting. A change cannot be made from the cash basis to the accrual basis or vice versa without the consent of the Internal Revenue Service. Furthermore, the taxpayer must report tax data in the manner in which the records are kept.

Case 18M-1. Gwen Engles plans to start a medical practice in a small rural community. She will be the only doctor in the area and will be expected to handle all calls and treat all patients. Some patients will be unable to pay any of her fee. Others will pay only part of her fee. She expects to accumulate a large number of accounts receivable, many of which she will never collect. Dr. Engles also knows she will receive payments from her patients on an irregular basis. Some patients will pay immediately. Others will wait before paying.

Would you advise Dr. Engles to keep her accounting records on a cash or accrual basis? Why?

Case 18M-2. The Watson Advertising Agency specializes in preparing videotape advertisements. The agency prepares the tapes under contracts with various businesses that advertise their products on television. The standard contract provides for the agency to be paid in full upon the completion and delivery of each series of tapes. Frequently, the tapes are in process for several months before they are ready and can be delivered. The accounting records for the agency have been kept on a cash basis. The tax reports have been prepared on this basis.

Do you agree with the agency's use of the cash basis? Explain why or why not.

Working Hint

Using Account Numbers When Journalizing. In automated accounting systems, account numbers are frequently used instead of account titles in journalizing transactions.

This procedure is also used for manually journalizing sales on credit. An account number is assigned to each customer. This number is recorded in the sales journal instead of under the customer's name. For example, a sale on credit to Agee, Inc., which has been assigned the Account Number 17234, would be journalized and posted as shown below.

When this procedure is used, great accuracy is necessary in recording account numbers. The accounting clerk must make sure that the correct account number is listed in the journal. Otherwise, the entry will be posted to the wrong account.

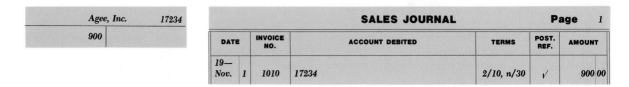

Agee, Inc.	17234
900	

		SALES JOURNAL			Page	1

DATE		INVOICE NO.	ACCOUNT DEBITED	TERMS	POST. REF.	AMOUNT
19—
Nov.	1	1010	17234	2/10, n/30	✓	900 00

Manual Accounting Systems

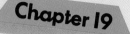

Businesses with a limited amount of data to process generally use a manual accounting system. You will now learn how these businesses record all transactions in a single journal called the combination journal. You will also learn how to use the pegboard to process sales on credit and direct-entry procedures for sales.

Topic 1
The Combination Journal

A *What is a combination journal?* A **combination journal** is a multicolumn journal that combines the features of the general journal with the features of the special journals for cash receipts, cash payments, purchases, and sales. Transactions are entered in special columns of the combination journal. Thus a combination journal saves time and space and reduces the chance of making mistakes while posting totals.

Designing a Combination Journal

The number of columns and the choice of headings in a combination journal depend upon the needs of the business. For example, if a business were to grant many sales discounts, it would require a Sales Discount column in the combination journal. Another business may not offer sales discounts, but it might have to collect sales tax. This business would include a Sales Tax Payable column in its combination journal. A business decides what special columns to use by determining which accounts are most often affected by transactions. Combination journals must include general ledger columns for debits and credits to accounts for which no special columns are provided.

The columns of the combination journal can be arranged to suit the individual business. In most businesses, the Cash account is used more than any other account. This chapter shows the Cash columns at the

COMBINATION JOURNAL

	CASH DEBIT	CASH CREDIT	DATE		ACCOUNT TITLE AND EXPLANATION	CK. NO.	POST. REF.	GENERAL LEDGER DEBIT	GENERAL LEDGER CREDIT
			19—						
1			April	1	Cash Balance, $4,080		—		
2	650 00			2	Sales		—		
3	121 50			3	Audrey Merchant		√		
4		490 00		4	Graham Electronics—Invoice 1120	211	√		
5				5	Rico Corp.—Invoice 421A; (4/1); 2/10, n/30		√		
6				6	Lindsey & Young—Invoice 140; 1/20, n/30		√		
7				8	Pur. Ret. and Allow./Rico Corp.—CM-1307		503/ √		45 00
8				9	Store Equip./Diablo Steel—Inv. 6111; (4/5); n/30 .		134/ √	90 00	
	2,000 00	*1,300 00*						*800 00*	*1,210 00*
30	**2,000 00**	**1,300 00**		19	Carried Forward		—	**800 00**	**1,210 00**

Special columns   **End of page**   **Post. ref. numbers and check marks are entered when individual amounts are posted, and dashes for amounts not posted or not posted individually.**   **General columns**

extreme left in the combination journal. Other combination journals may have more money columns at the left or all money columns at the right.

Although any number of columns can be included, the combination journal becomes hard to use if there are too many columns.

Recording Entries in the Combination Journal

Each transaction must be analyzed to determine the accounts to be debited and credited. The transaction is then recorded by entering the debit and credit amounts in the proper money columns. Thus the amounts are sorted according to the accounts affected.

To show how entries are recorded in a combination journal, we now examine the April transactions of the BEVO Products Company. The April entries are shown in the combination journal on pages 568 and 569.

April 1 At the beginning of the month, a memorandum entry is made to record the cash balance. The entry is the same as in the cash receipts journal.

DATE			ACCOUNT TITLE
19—			
1	April	1	Cash Balance, $4,080 . .

On line 1 of the combination journal, the memorandum entry is the first entry recorded for the month of April. The cash balance is shown in the Account Title and Explanation column. No amounts are written in the money columns. The dash is placed in the Posting Reference column to show that the entry is not to be posted.

For the Month of April, **19** —   **Page** 1

ACCOUNTS RECEIVABLE		ACCOUNTS PAYABLE		PURCHASES DEBIT	SALES CREDIT	PURCHASES DISCOUNT CREDIT	SALES DISCOUNT DEBIT	
DEBIT	CREDIT	DEBIT	CREDIT					
					650 00			1
	125 00						3 50	2
		500 00				10 00		3
			950 00	950 00				4
75 00					75 00			5
		45 00						6
			90 00					7
								8
1,500 00	800 00	1,000 00	1,500 00	1,500 00	2,000 00	10 00	20 00	
1,500 00	800 00	1,000 00	1,500 00	1,500 00	2,000 00	10 00	20 00	30

Proof at end of page.

Special columns

April 2 Sold merchandise for $650 in cash during the week.

The entry for this transaction involves a debit to Cash for $650 and a credit to Sales for $650. If recorded in a cash receipts journal, the entry would appear as it does as shown in the margin.

Special columns are provided in the combination journal for both the Cash and the Sales accounts. Notice on line 2 of the combination journal that $650 has been recorded in the Cash Debit column and in the Sales Credit column. The amounts in the Cash Debit column accumulate during the month just as in any special journal. Unlike the cash receipts journal, however, the combination journal provides a special column for credits to sales. At the end of the month, the amounts recorded in the Sales Credit column are posted as a total to the Sales account. The Sales Credit column contains all credits for sales transactions—both sales for cash and sales on credit. The word "Sales" is written in the Account Title and Explanation column to provide a brief explanation for the entry. Without the explanation, each money column would have to be examined to learn why the entry was made.

April 3 Received $121.50 in cash from Audrey Merchant in payment of Invoice 60 for $125, less a sales discount of $3.50.

The entry for this transaction involves three recordings: a debit to Cash for $121.50, a debit to Sales Discount for $3.50, and a credit to Accounts Receivable for $125.

The combination journal contains special columns for each of the three accounts. Thus the entry is journalized in the combination journal (see line 3) by recording $121.50 in the Cash Debit column, $125 in the Accounts Receivable Credit column, and $3.50 in the Sales Discount Debit column. The customer's name, Audrey Merchant, is recorded in the Account Title and Explanation column for use in posting the credit to the accounts receivable ledger.

April 4 Issued Check 211 for $490 to Graham Electronics in payment of Invoice 1120 for $500, less a purchase discount of $10.

The BEVO Products Company was granted a 2 percent discount of $10 because the $500 invoice was paid within the discount period. The transaction, therefore, results in a debit to Accounts Payable for $500, a credit to Purchases Discount for $10, and a credit to Cash for $490.

The combination journal has special columns for this transaction as well. The amount of $490 is recorded in the Cash Credit column, $500 is recorded in the Accounts Payable Debit column, and $10 is recorded in the Purchases Discount Credit column (see line 4). The creditor's name is recorded in the Account Title and Explanation column for use in posting the entry to the accounts payable subsidiary ledger. The invoice number (1120) is entered in the Account Title and Explanation column as a reference. The check number (211) is entered in the Check Number column to keep a record of each check.

April 5 Bought merchandise for $950 on credit from Rico Corporation, Invoice 421A.

The transaction results in a debit to Purchases and a credit to Accounts Payable.

Here again, the combination journal provides special columns for the accounts affected by this transaction. The debit to Purchases for $950 is recorded in the Purchases Debit column, and the credit to Accounts Payable for $950 is recorded in the Accounts Payable Credit column (see line 5). The creditor's name, invoice number, invoice date, and terms are entered in the Account Title and Explanation column for use in posting to the accounts payable subsidiary ledger.

April 6 Issued Invoice 140 for $75 to Lindsey and Young for a sale on credit.

The transaction includes a debit to Accounts Receivable and a credit to Sales. The debit of $75 is entered in the Accounts Receivable Debit column and the credit of $75 is entered in the Sales Credit column. Again, special columns are available for both the debit and credit amounts. The customer's name is written in the Account Title and Explanation column so that the amount can be posted to the correct account in the accounts receivable subsidiary ledger. The invoice number and terms are also entered in this column.

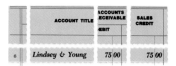

April 8 Received Credit Memorandum 1307 for $45 from Rico Corporation for the return of merchandise purchased on credit.

The entry for the transaction requires a debit to Accounts Payable for $45 and a credit to Purchases Returns and Allowances for the same amount.

When the entry is recorded in a combination journal (see line 7), the debit of $45 to Accounts Payable is recorded in the Accounts Payable Debit column. Since no special column is provided for credits to Purchases Returns and Allowances, the credit of $45 must be recorded in the General Ledger Credit column. "Pur. Ret. and Allow./Rico Corp.—CM-1307" is recorded in the Account Title and Explanation column to provide the necessary information for posting the entry. The title of the Purchases Returns and Allowances account is recorded so that the $45 credit can be posted from the General Ledger Credit column. The creditor's name is written so that the debit in the Accounts Payable Debit column can be posted to the accounts payable subsidiary ledger. A diagonal line is placed in the Posting Reference column to show that this entry is double-posted.

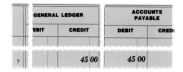

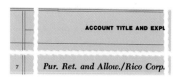

CASH		DATE		ACCOUNT TITLE AND EXPLANATION	CK. NO.	POST. REF.	GENERAL LEDGER	
DEBIT	CREDIT						DEBIT	CREDIT
		19—						
2,000 00	1,300 00	April	19	*Brought Forward*		—	800 00	1,210 00
	60 00		20	*Utilities Expense*	380	518	60 00	
			30	*Sales Ret. and Allow./Audrey Merchant—CM-27.* .		402/ √	20 00	
4,400 00	2,800 00						1,800 00	2,600 00
4,400 00	2,800 00		30	*Totals*		—	1,800 00	2,600 00
(101)	(101)						(—)	(—)

April 9 Received Invoice 6111 for $90 from Diablo Steel for store equipment bought on credit.

GENERAL LEDGER		ACCOUNTS PAYABLE
DEBIT	CREDIT	CREDIT
90 00		90 00

The transaction for the purchase of an asset includes a debit to Store Equipment and a credit to Accounts Payable for $90.

The debit of $90 is entered in the General Ledger Debit column because no special column is provided for store equipment (see line 8). The credit of $90 is entered in the Accounts Payable Credit column. The titles of two accounts (the general ledger account to be debited and the creditor's account to be credited) must be written in the Account Title and Explanation column. The invoice number and terms are also centered in this column. A diagonal line is drawn between the account titles.

Activity A. Answer the following questions about the combination journal. Refer to the combination journal on pages 568 to 569.
1. Why is the April 1 cash balance not entered in the Cash Debit column?
2. How many special money columns are there? How many specific general ledger accounts have special money columns?
3. Is each transaction recorded in more than one money column? Why or why not?
4. When is the first credit sale made? To whom is it made? How much is it?

5. Is cash received or paid out on April 3? From whom or to whom?
6. Is a sales discount recorded in the entry for April 3? If so, how much?
7. What is the difference between the April 5 transaction with Rico Corporation and the April 8 transaction?
8. In the transaction on April 8, which account(s) is (are) debited? Why?
9. Is the April 2 entry for a cash sale or a credit sale?

Proving the Combination Journal

It is easier to make errors in a combination journal because there are more columns than in a general or special journal.

B *How is the combination journal proved?* The total of the debit money columns should equal the total of the credit money columns in a combination journal. Because of the number of columns in a combination journal, it is easier to make an error when recording an

ACCOUNTS RECEIVABLE		ACCOUNTS PAYABLE		PURCHASES DEBIT	SALES CREDIT	PURCHASES DISCOUNT CREDIT	SALES DISCOUNT DEBIT	
DEBIT	CREDIT	DEBIT	CREDIT					
1,500 00	800 00	1,000 00	1,500 00	1,500 00	2,000 00	10 00	20 00	1
								2
	20 00							23
3,430 00	1,800 00	2,200 00	3,500 00	3,350 00	4,500 00	22 00	42 00	
3,430 00	1,800 00	2,200 00	3,500 00	3,350 00	4,500 00	22 00	42 00	24
(111)	(111)	(211)	(211)	(501)	(401)	(504)	(403)	

Proof at end of month.

entry in a combination journal than when recording in a general journal and separate special journals. Therefore, a proof should be made in a combination journal at least at the end of each page and always at the end of the month.

Proof at End of Page. To prove the combination journal at the end of a page (see the combination journal on pages 568 and 569), leave one blank line at the bottom of the page and follow this procedure.

• Pencil-foot all money columns. Then prove the equality of the debit columns and the credit columns (shown at the right in the margin).
• After the money columns are proved, draw a single rule under the last entry and record the current date in the Date column. Then write "Carried Forward" in the Account Title and Explanation column and place a dash in the Posting Reference column. Then enter the totals in ink on the last line.
• Bring the totals forward to the first line of the next page. (See the illustration on pages 572 and 573.) Enter the date in the Date column and write "Brought Forward" in the Account Title and Explanation column. Next place a dash in the Posting Reference column and record the amounts in the proper columns.

Follow this procedure for each page of the combination journal. To prove the journal before the end of the page, pencil-foot all money columns and prove the equality of the debits and credits.

The totals brought forward are included in the totals for each new page of the combination journal. Thus, at the end of the month, the total of each column on the last journal page for the month includes all amounts entered in the column from the beginning to the end of the month.

Proof at the End of Month. To prove the combination journal at the end of the month, follow the procedure on page 574. (See the combination journal on pages 572 and 573.)

	Debits	Credits
Cash	2,000 00	1,300 00
General Ledger . .	800 00	1,210 00
Accounts Receivable	1,500 00	800 00
Accounts Payable .	1,000 00	1,500 00
Purchases	1,500 00	
Sales		2,000 00
Purchases Discount		10 00
Sales Discount . .	20 00	
Totals	6,820 00	6,820 00

Proof of combination journal.

- Pencil-foot all money columns and prove the equality of the debit and credit columns.
- Draw a single rule in the money columns under the last entry.
- Enter the last date of the month in the Date column, write "Totals" in the Account Title and Explanation column, place a dash in the Posting Reference column, and enter the totals in ink.
- Draw double rules under all columns with the exception of the Account Title and Explanation column and the Check Number column.

Activity B. Answer the following questions about proving the combination journal. Refer to the text and illustrations on pages 572 to 574.

1. In what ways do you prove a combination journal?

2 Can the journal be proved only at the time of totaling and ruling?

3. What must be done to prove the journal before the end of the page?

4. When proving the combination journal at the end of the month, when are the totals entered in ink?

Posting From the Combination Journal

Posted During Month
- Accounts receivable ledger
- Accounts payable ledger
- General ledger debit and credit

Posted at End of Month
Special column totals

C *What is the procedure for posting from the combination journal?* The procedure for posting from the combination journal is similar to posting from the special journals. The entries in the Accounts Receivable and Accounts Payable sections of the combination journal are posted to the customers' and creditors' accounts in the subsidiary ledgers during the month. In addition, the entries in the General Ledger section of the combination journal are posted to the appropriate accounts in the general ledger during the month. At the end of the month, the totals of the special columns are posted to the general ledger after the journal is proved.

Posting From the General Ledger Columns. To post from the General Ledger columns, an accounting clerk first posts each amount in the General Ledger Debit column to the debit side of the account shown in the Account Title and Explanation column. Then the accounting clerk writes the account number in the Posting Reference column of the combination journal to show that the amount has been posted. The page number of the combination journal is then written in the Posting Reference column of the ledger account. (Letters such as CJ are not needed because this is the only journal used.) Each amount in the General Ledger Credit column is posted in the same way.

Posting From the Accounts Receivable Columns. When posting from the Accounts Receivable Debit and Credit columns of the combination journal, each amount is posted to the customer's account in the accounts receivable ledger. A check mark in the Posting Reference column of the combination journal indicates that the amount has been posted. At the month's end, the Accounts Receivable column totals are posted to the general ledger when the column totals are posted.

Posting From the Accounts Payable Columns. The accounting clerk posts each amount in the Accounts Payable Debit and Credit columns to the creditor's account in the accounts payable ledger. The check mark is placed in the Posting Reference column of the journal. The Accounts Payable column totals are then posted to the general ledger at the end of the month when the column totals are posted.

Double-Posting. Some entries in the combination journal require double-posting. For example, when the entry is journalized for merchandise a customer returns for credit, a diagonal line is drawn across the Posting Reference column (see line 23 of the journal on pages 572 to 573). When the debit is posted to the general ledger, the Sales Returns and Allowances account number is placed above the diagonal line. When the debit is posted to the accounts receivable ledger, the check mark is written below the line.

Making Other Entries. If no debit or credit amount for an entry is posted individually, place a dash in the Posting Reference column of the combination journal. This dash indicates that the amounts will be posted as part of column totals at the end of the month. The dash provides a convenient way of checking to see that all entries have been posted. It is important that a check mark, account number, or dash appears for *each* entry.

Posting the Column Totals. After the combination journal is totaled and ruled, post the totals to the proper accounts in the general ledger. The total of each column—except the General Ledger columns—is posted as a debit or credit to the account name in the column heading.

CAS...		GENERAL LEDGER	
DEBIT	CREDIT	DEBIT	CREDIT
4,400 00	2,800 00	1,800 00	2,600 00
4,400 00	2,800 00	1,800 00	2,600 00
(101)	(101)	(—)	(—)

Write the account number in parentheses below the double rule to show that the total has been posted. For example, after the totals of the Cash Debit and Credit columns are posted, the number of the Cash account (101) is recorded under each column.

The totals of the General Ledger columns are not posted because each amount in the columns has been posted individually. Dashes are put under the double rule of the two General Ledger columns. The dashes indicate that the amounts in the General Ledger columns have been posted individually and that the totals of the two columns have not been posted to any specific account.

The combination journal has the timesaving, space-saving, and error-reducing advantages of special journals because special money columns are used for similar transactions. Thus the combination journal is often used by such professionals as doctors or accountants whose businesses call for only a few types of transactions. The combination journal, however, is not adequate for a service or merchandising business unless the business's transactions are limited and do not affect a great variety of accounts. If the transactions are numerous or too varied, the special journals are more efficient.

The combination journal is extremely useful to small businesses. However, the chances of making an error by placing an amount in the wrong column are increased because of the large number of money columns. Since only one person can record an entry at one time, the use of the combination journal prevents division of responsibility.

Activity C. Answer the following questions about posting from the combination journal. Refer to the text, margin notes, and illustrations on pages 574 to 576.
1. How is the general ledger amount posted from the combination journal?
2. How is the accounts receivable amount posted from the combination journal?
3. How is the accounts payable amount posted from the combination journal?

4. Give an example of an entry in the combination journal that requires double posting.
5. What does a dash in the Posting Reference column in the combination journal indicate?
6. What are some advantages to using the combination journal? Some disadvantages?

Accounting Concept:
Posting by Total. *Posting by total* increases accuracy and efficiency and speed because it reduces the number of times an amount is recorded.

Topic 1 Problems

19-1. The Milan Flower Shop is a small business owned and operated by Ken Lang.
a. Open general ledger accounts, assign appropriate numbers, and record the May 1 balances as follows: Cash, $8,800; Accounts Receivable; Merchandise Inventory, $950; Store Equipment, $3,100; Accounts Payable; Sales Tax Payable, $150; Ken Lang, Capital, $12,700; Ken Lang, Drawing; Sales; Sales Returns and Allowances; Purchases; Purchases Returns and Allowances; Purchases Discount; Delivery Expense; and Rent Expense. Open accounts in the accounts receivable ledger for Union Club and Milan Bank. Open accounts in the accounts payable ledger for Betty's Greenhouse and Trio Sales.
b. Journalize the following transactions in a combination journal.
c. Post the individual entries from the combination journal.
d. Foot and prove the combination journal.

May   1 Recorded the memorandum entry for the cash balance.

May   2 Issued Check 69 for $600 to Mar Realty to pay May rent.
      3 Received Invoice 820, dated May 1, from Betty's Greenhouse for merchandise purchased for $500 on credit; terms 2/10, n/30.
      3 Recorded cash proof showing weekly cash sales of $600 and sales tax of $30.
      4 Received $6,000 from Ken Lang as an additional investment in the business.
      9 Received Invoice 87P, dated May 7, from Trio Sales for cash register purchased for $1,660 on credit; terms n/30.
     10 Issued Invoice 181 to Union Club for merchandise sold for $80 plus $4 sales tax on credit.
     10 Recorded cash proof showing weekly cash sales of $510 and sales tax of $25.50.
     11 Received Invoice 898, dated May 9, from Betty's Greenhouse for merchandise purchased for $210 on credit; terms 2/10, n/30.

May 12 Issued Check 70 for $490 to Betty's Greenhouse to pay Invoice 820, less discount.

15 Received Credit Memorandum CM-108 from Betty's Greenhouse for $20 as an allowance for damaged merchandise purchased on Invoice 898.

NOTE: Save your journal and ledgers for further use in Topic Problem 19-2.

19-2. Using the combination journal and the ledgers prepared in Topic Problem 19-1, perform the following activities.

a. Journalize the following transactions.

b. Post the individual entries from the combination journal.

c. Foot and prove the combination journal. Then total and rule the journal.

d. Post the totals from the combination journal.

e. Prepare a schedule of accounts receivable and a schedule of accounts payable. Prove their totals.

f. Prepare a trial balance.

May 16 Issued Invoice 182 to Milan Bank for merchandise sold for $160 plus $8 sales tax on credit.

17 Issued Credit Memorandum CM-14 to Milan Bank for allowance on merchandise sold for $10 plus $0.50 sales tax on Invoice 182.

(Show both account titles in Account Title and Explanation column.)

May 17 Recorded cash proof showing weekly cash sales of $660 and sales tax of $33.

23 Received $84 from Union Club in payment of Invoice 181.

24 Recorded cash proof showing weekly cash sales of $340 and sales tax of $17.

24 Issued Check 71 for $70 to Surfside Florists for merchandise purchased for cash.

25 Issued Check 72 for $40 to Mercury Delivery for delivery of flowers to customers.

26 Issued Invoice 183 to Milan Bank for merchandise sold for $60 plus $3 sales tax on credit.

28 Issued Check 73 for $1,600 to Ken Lang for personal use.

29 Received $157.50 from Milan Bank in payment of Invoice 182, less allowance.

29 Issued Check 74 for $190 to Betty's Greenhouse to pay Invoice 898, less allowance.

31 Recorded cash proof showing weekly cash sales of $980 and sales tax of $49.

31 Received Invoice 1078, dated May 29, from Betty's Greenhouse for merchandise purchased for $830 on credit; terms 2/10, n/30.

Topic 2
Direct-Entry Records/Pegboards

A *Why do businesses use timesaving and labor-saving methods to process data?* Most businesses have large amounts of data to process. Thus, faster and more efficient methods of processing the data are needed. This topic examines three commonly used techniques for processing sales data: batch processing, journalless accounting, and ledgerless accounting. A brief description of the pegboard is also provided.

Three Methods of Processing Data
• Batch processing
• Journalless accounting
• Ledgerless accounting

Conventional Journalizing and Posting

In order to understand how the three techniques just mentioned are applied to processing sales of merchandise on credit, it will be helpful to review quickly the conventional method for journalizing and posting a sale on credit.

1 The seller prepares a sales invoice that consists of two copies. Copy 1 is sent to the customer.

2 Copy 2 of each sales invoice is used to record the transaction in the sales journal. The sales invoices are journalized in numeric order. They are then filed in the unpaid accounts receivable file.

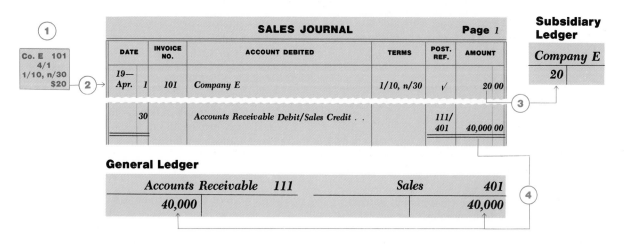

3 At certain times during the month, the entries in the sales journal are posted to the individual customers' accounts in the subsidiary ledger.

4 At the end of the month, the sales journal is totaled. The total amount of sales is then posted as a debit to the Accounts Receivable controlling account and as a credit to the Sales account in the general ledger. After all entries have been posted, the balance in the Accounts Receivable controlling account should be equal to the sum of all the balances in the customers' accounts in the subsidiary ledger.

Activity A. Answer the following questions about the conventional method for processing sales on credit when a sales journal, a general ledger, and a subsidiary ledger are used. Refer to the illustrations above.
1. What is the source document?
2. How many copies of each sales invoice are needed?
3. What is done with Copy 1 of the invoice?
4. When are the debit entries posted to the subsidiary ledger?

5. How is the total amount of sales for any one day obtained?
6. When is the total amount of sales posted from the sales journal to the accounts in the general ledger? What account is debited? What account is credited?
7. Where is the amount owed by any one customer found?
8. How can one find the total amount owed by all customers?

Journalizing Batch Totals

B *What is the batch total procedure for journalizing sales on credit?* The conventional method for journalizing and posting sales on credit is not followed by all businesses. Many firms that process a large number of sales invoices establish special methods to eliminate the time-consuming process of copying the data from each sales invoice in a journal. If a business had an average of 20 sales invoices a day, the sales journal would contain 100 entries (5 × 20) for each week, or approximately 400 entries (4 × 100) for the entire month. One method used to reduce the number of entries is to accumulate the invoices in a batch of invoices. Thus the accounting clerk would compute the total amount of the invoices in each batch and then journalize only the batch total.

A batch may consist of invoices for a part of a day, for a day, for a week, or for any other period of time, depending on the number of invoices to be processed. Consider, for example, an accounting department that receives an average of 20 sales invoices a day. If the department processes these invoices in a daily batch, only one amount, the batch total, is entered in the sales journal each day.

When batch processing is used, all sales invoices should be prenumbered in order to account for each sales transaction. Three copies of each sales invoice are prepared.

Copy 1 of Invoice. The original copy is sent to the customer.

Copy 2 of Invoice. This duplicate copy of the sales invoice is used for processing the invoices in batches and recording the transactions.

1 The accounting clerk receives Copy 2 of all the sales invoices issued during the day and sorts them in numeric order to account for each sale.

2 The amount of each invoice is listed on an adding machine tape, and the total of the credit sales is obtained. This total is referred to as the *batch total*. (The adding machine tape is an important control document because it is the only independent record at this point of the number of invoices in the daily batch and the amount of each.)

3 The accounting clerk records the batch total shown on the adding machine tape in the sales journal. The Accounts Receivable controlling account is debited for the batch total and the Sales account is

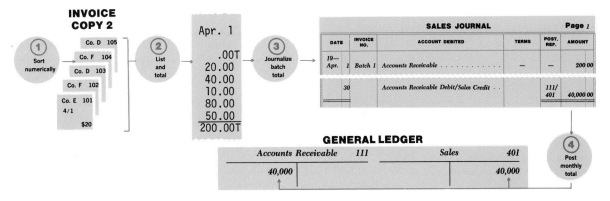

credited for the same amount. The batch of invoices with the tape is then stored for reference in case anyone wants to trace the batch total back to the specific invoices. In addition, these batches provide a numeric record of all sales invoices issued.

4 No posting to the general ledger is made until the end of the month. At that time, the sales journal is totaled and the total is posted as a debit to the Accounts Receivable controlling account and as a credit to the Sales account in the general ledger.

Direct Posting From Source Documents

When sales invoices are journalized in batches, it is impossible to post from the sales journal to the individual accounts in the subsidiary ledger. As the previous illustration shows, the journal entry does not provide enough information for posting to the subsidiary ledger. To obtain the necessary information, the accounting clerk posts directly from the individual sales invoice. In this method, called **direct posting,** data entered in the subsidiary ledger accounts is taken directly from source documents rather than from journal entries.

Copy 3 of Invoice. When sales invoices are journalized in batches, Copy 3 of each invoice is used for posting the amount of the sale directly to the subsidiary ledger account.

1 All third copies of the sales invoices are arranged in alphabetic sequence by customer name.

2 The accounting clerk then posts the amount of each invoice to the appropriate customer's account in the subsidiary ledger. A check mark ($\sqrt{}$) is made on the invoice to indicate that it has been posted. After all invoices have been posted, a check is sometimes made of the accuracy of the postings. The accounting clerk goes through the accounts in the subsidiary ledger and lists on an adding machine tape each amount that was posted that day. The total of the postings shown on this proof tape must agree with the total of the batch tape recorded in the journal. If the totals do not agree, the error must be located before going on.

3 All third copies are then placed in folders in the accounts receivable file. A separate folder is kept for each customer. The folders are filed alphabetically.

After all entries from the sales journal and the sales invoices have been posted, another proof of accuracy is made. The balance in the Accounts Receivable controlling account should equal the sum of all the balances in the customers' accounts in the subsidiary ledger.

Batch processing is much faster than the conventional method because the details of the transactions do not have to be recorded in a

April 1, 19—

```
      .00T
    10.00
    50.00
    20.00
    40.00
    80.00
   200.00T
```

Proof Tape

Details of a transaction are not recorded when batch processing is used.

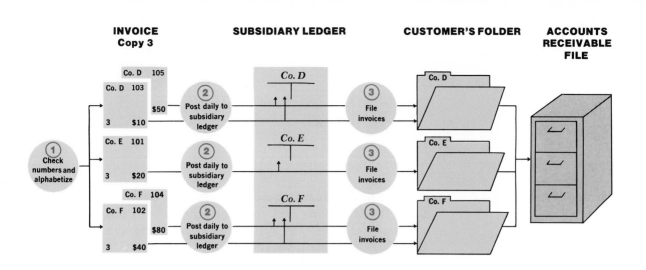

journal. Yet there is a chronological listing of the transactions. Batch processing and direct posting are widely used in manual and automated data processing.

Activity B. Answer the following questions about journalizing batch totals and direct posting sales on credit. Refer to the text and illustrations on pages 578 to 581.

1. How many copies of each sales invoice are needed?
2. What is done with Copy 1 of the invoice?
3. What is a batch of invoices?
4. Why are Copy 2s sorted in numeric order?

5. What is done with Copy 3 of each sales invoice?
6. What is a proof tape? Why is it prepared?
7. What data is posted to the general ledger? When is it posted?
8. What is the source of the data that is posted to each customer's account?
9. Are the invoices arranged alphabetically or numerically for posting? Why?

Journalless Accounting

C *Can sales on credit be journalized and posted more simply?* The method just described can be further simplified by eliminating the use of a formal journal altogether. The procedure is as follows.

Copy 1 of Invoice. The original copy of the sales invoice is sent to the customer.

Copy 2 of Invoice. As before, the invoices are sorted in numeric order and the amounts are totaled on an adding machine tape. However, the batch total for the day is *not* recorded in a sales journal. Instead, the accounting clerk simply places the daily batch of invoices in a **sales invoice binder,** which replaces the sales journal. Each batch has the adding machine tape attached.

At the end of the month, the binder contains all of the daily batches, each with its own adding machine tape attached. The accounting clerk simply adds the daily batch totals on an adding machine to get the

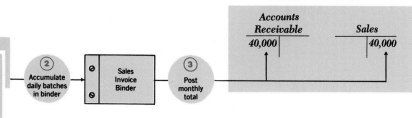

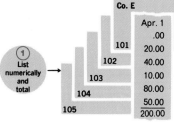

monthly total. Using this new adding machine tape as the source document, the accounting clerk then posts the monthly total as a debit to the Accounts Receivable controlling account and as a credit to the Sales account in the general ledger.

Copy 3 of Invoice. Each invoice is posted directly to the subsidiary ledger.

Obviously, the binder containing the sales invoices takes the place of the sales journal. Each invoice is posted separately to the subsidiary ledger. The total of all the invoices for the month is posted to the general ledger. This is the same procedure that is used in posting from the sales journal. This method is sometimes referred to as **journalless accounting** since a formal journal is not used to record the sales invoices.

The omission of a formal journal represents a further refinement in speeding up the recording of sales on credit. It saves time and money in making the entries. Although many accountants favor the practice of batching invoices to save time, they do not all favor eliminating the use of a journal as well. Those who do retain the practice of journalizing batch totals feel that it provides greater security than the use of a binder alone. Also, if sales taxes are charged on the invoices, a separate adding machine tape must be made to obtain the amount of the sales tax payable to the government. Thus a multicolumn sales journal may still be helpful in some cases.

Although no formal journal is used in journalless accounting, the concept of a journal still remains in the form of the binder. Also, there is no change in the double-entry principle and in the posting to the general ledger and the subsidiary ledger.

Recording Cash Receipts. When journalless accounting is used for sales on credit, no changes are required in the procedure for recording cash received on account from customers. The amount of cash received is recorded in the cash receipts journal. The credit entry is then posted from the cash receipts journal to the customer's account in the subsidiary ledger and the Accounts Receivable controlling account in the general ledger.

Journalless accounting minimizes or eliminates the use of formal journals.

Activity C. Answer the following questions about the processing of sales on credit in journalless accounting. Refer to the text and illustration on pages 581 to 582.

1. How many copies of each sales invoice are required?
2. What is done with Copy 1?
3. What is done with Copy 2?
4. What data is posted to the general ledger? From where is the data posted to the general ledger ob-

tained? What account is debited? What account is credited?
5. What is the source of the data that is posted to each customer's account?
6. What replaces the sales journal in journalless accounting?
7. Where can the amount owed by any one customer be obtained?
8. Where can the total amount owed by all customers be found?

Ledgerless Accounting

D *How can the recording of sales on credit be further simplified?* You have now seen how some businesses batch sales invoices and post directly from them, thus minimizing or omitting the use of a formal journal. All these techniques are used to speed up the recording of sales on credit. Some firms even eliminate posting to individual customers' accounts in a subsidiary ledger. Instead of a formal account, a folder is established for each customer. Instead of posting the entries from a journal or the sales invoices, the source documents themselves are placed in the customers' folders. These folders are then filed in an accounts receivable file. This file takes the place of the accounts receivable subsidiary ledger, and the individual folders take the place of the customers' accounts.

When an invoice is paid, it is removed from the customer's folder in the accounts receivable file. Thus unpaid invoices in customers' folders represent the amount they owe to the business. Since an actual subsidiary ledger is not used, this method is often referred to as **ledgerless accounting.**

When a business uses ledgerless accounting and a sales journal, a minimum of *two* copies of the sales invoice is needed. Copy 1 is sent to the customer. Copy 2 is recorded in the sales journal and then placed in the accounts receivable file. When journalless accounting and ledgerless accounting are combined, *three* copies of the sales invoice are needed. Copy 1 is for the customer, Copy 2 is for the sales invoice binder, and Copy 3 is for the customer's folder in the accounts receivable file.

One procedure for using journalless and ledgerless accounting to record sales invoices is described here.

Copy 1 of Invoice. The original copy of the sales invoice is sent to the customer.

Copy 2 of Invoice. All second copies of the sales invoices are handled as discussed on page 584.

In ledgerless accounting, the source documents are filed instead of accounts being used.

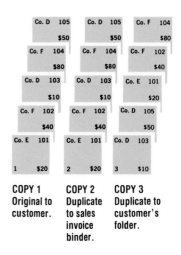

COPY 1 Original to customer. COPY 2 Duplicate to sales invoice binder. COPY 3 Duplicate to customer's folder.

1 The invoices are sorted numerically into a batch (daily or weekly), the amounts are totaled on an adding machine tape, and the tape is stapled to the top of the batch.

2 The batch of invoices is then placed in the sales invoice binder. The binder replaces the formal journal in journalless accounting.

3 At the end of the month, the total of all the batches is posted to the general ledger, which is still required although the subsidiary ledger is not. The Accounts Receivable controlling account is debited and the Sales account is credited.

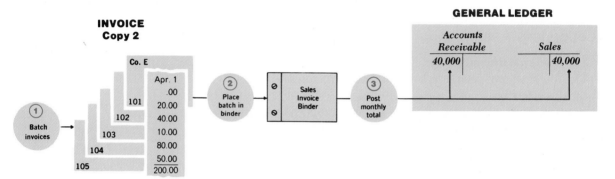

Copy 3 of Invoice. All third copies of the sales invoices are alphabetized according to customer name and placed in the customers' folders in the accounts receivable file. The accounts receivable file then contains all the unpaid sales invoices. In order to find the total owed by any customer, the customer's folder is removed from the file and the amounts of the invoices are added.

Pegboards or One-Write Systems

The pegboard is an application of the one-write technique.

The *pegboard* (*also called a* writing board, *a* posting board, *or an* accounting board) *is an application of the one-write technique.* The **one-write technique** refers to the preparation of several documents or records in one operation. Thus the **pegboard** is a device that makes it possible to record data on several forms at the same time. The pegboard has a flat writing surface and a series of evenly spaced metal pegs along the edge or in the middle of the board. Special forms with punched holes fit over the pegs. The forms are arranged on the board so that the writing line on the top form is lined up with the appropriate writing lines on the forms beneath it. When entries are written with pencil or ball-point pen, the writing is transferred from the top form to the others by carbon or NCR (no carbon required) paper. A pegboard is shown on the next page.

PEGBOARD: Holds forms in place.

JOURNAL: Journal sheet is placed on bottom.

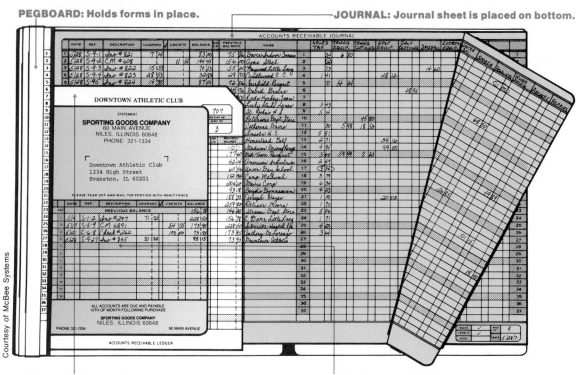

Courtesy of McBee Systems

LEDGER ACCOUNT: First customer's account is placed in position. First unused line of account is positioned over first unused line of journal.

STATEMENT OF ACCOUNT: Customer's statement of account is positioned on pegboard so that the first unused line of the statement is on top of writing line to be used on ledger account.

This topic described three techniques for processing sales data: batch processing, journalless accounting, and ledgerless accounting. These same techniques could also be used to process purchases of merchandise on credit.

Activity D. Answer the following questions about the processing of sales on credit when journalless and ledgerless accounting are used. Refer to the text and illustrations on pages 583 and 584.
1. How many sales invoice copies are required?
2. What is done with Copy 1 of the sales invoice?
3. Explain the procedure for processing Copy 2.

4. What replaces the sales journal?
5. Is the general ledger eliminated?
6. What is the source of the data that is posted to the Accounts Receivable account and the Sales account in the general ledger?
7. Explain briefly the procedure for processing Copy 3.

Topic 2 Problems

19-3. Use the partial sales slips provided in your working papers to perform the following activities for the Trendsetter Dress Shop on July 1.
a. Separate Copy 2 of each sales slip from Copy 3 by cutting along the dotted line.

b. Sort the sales slips in numeric order, and verify that all sales slips (521-538) are there.
c. Batch the Copy 2s for August 1. If an adding machine is available, list the amounts of the sales slips and obtain the batch total. If no adding machine is

available, list the amounts of the sales slips in a column on a strip of paper and compute the batch total. Attach the adding machine tape or the strip of paper to the batch of sales slips.

d. Record the batch total in the sales journal (see the illustration on page 579).

e. Sort the Copy 3s in alphabetic order by customer.

f. Post the data directly from each sales slip to the appropriate customer's account. Record the date and the slip number in the appropriate columns, a check mark in the Posting Reference column, and the amount in the Debit column. Compute and record the new balance in the Debit Balance column.

g. Prepare a schedule of accounts receivable. Since the accounts had no previous balances, the total of the schedule should equal the batch total. If it does not, locate the error.

NOTE: Save your working papers for further use in Topic Problem 19-4.

19-4. Assume that the Trendsetter Dress Shop uses the journalless and ledgerless accounting methods to process accounts receivable. Use the same sales slips you used in Topic Problem 19-3 and the remittance slips and credit memorandums in your working papers to perform the following activities.

a. Place the batch of Copy 2s for August 1 in an envelope. Mark the envelope "Sales Slip Binder." (In this procedure, the batch total on the tape represents the journal entry and the sales slip binder replaces the journal.)

b. Sort the Copy 3s in alphabetic order by customer name. Then put each customer's sales slips in numeric order and clip them together. Store each group of sales slips in an envelope marked "Open Accounts Receivable File."

c. The cash receipts and sales returns for August are listed in the right column. Update the open accounts receivable file.

Remove all sales slips paid in full from the open accounts receivable file. Write "Paid" and the date on these slips. Also remove from this file any sales slips for which credit was issued in full. Write "Credit" and the date on these slips.

Sales slips on which only partial payments were made or partial credits were issued remain in the open accounts receivable file. A notation should be made on each sales slip to record the amount paid or credited, the date, and the remaining balance.

If a sales slip has not been paid and a partial credit has been issued, attach the credit memorandum to it.

d. Sort the "Paid" and "Credit" sales slips in alphabetic order by customer name. File these slips in an envelope marked "Sales Slip File."

e. Prepare a schedule of accounts receivable on August 31. (If the total does not equal $381, locate your error.)

f. For each customer, list the number and balance of each unpaid sales slip and unused credit memorandum in the open accounts receivable file.

Aug. 12 Issued Remittance Slip RS-61 for $45 received from Karen Werner for Sales Slip 522.

20 Issued Credit Memorandum CM-49 for $18 to Jane Moss for Sales Slip 521.

21 Issued Remittance Slip RS-62 for $60 received from Kathy Zeller for Sales Slip 523.

23 Issued Credit Memorandum CM-50 for $25 to Karen Werner for Sales Slip 528.

25 Issued Credit Memorandum CM-51 for $20 to Jane Moss for Sales Slip 532.

26 Issued Remittance Slip RS-63 for $10 received from Jane Moss for Sales Slip 532.

27 Issued Credit Memorandum CM-52 for $10 to Sue Snyder for Sales Slip 529.

28 Issued Remittance Slip RS-64 for $35 received from Kathy Zeller for Sales Slip 533.

30 Issued Remittance Slip RS-65 for $117 received from Jane Moss for Sales Slips 524, 527, and 536.

The Language of Business

Here are some terms that make up the language of business. Do you know the meaning of each?

combination journal	direct posting	journalless accounting	one-write technique
	sales invoice binder	ledgerless accounting	pegboard

Chapter 19 Questions

1. What determines the number of columns in a combination journal?
2. In journalless accounting, what is used in place of the journal?
3. What are the advantages and disadvantages of using journalless accounting for sales invoices?
4. In ledgerless accounting, what is used in place of the ledger?
5. What are the advantages and disadvantages of using ledgerless accounting for sales invoices?
6. Explain why the pegboard is referred to as a one-write technique.

Chapter 19 Problems

Problems for Chapter 19 are given in the *Working Papers and Chapter Problems for Part 3*. If you are using the workbook, do the problems in the space provided there.

Chapter 19 Management Cases

Designing Journals. Journals should be adapted to meet the specific needs of a business. Thus most businesses add special columns to their journals to handle the types of transactions that occur frequently. The special columns speed up the posting process and decrease the possibility of making errors when posting. This is possible because the special columns permit posting of column totals instead of individual amounts. Special money columns can be added to any journal: the general journal, the special journals, or the combination journal.

Case 19M-1. Carla Muller owns and operates an accounting service. One of her customers is Robert Montoya, a doctor. The most frequently recurring transactions for Dr. Montoya's medical practice are the following: cash from fees received from patients, cash paid to creditors, cash paid for utilities and miscellaneous expenses, purchases of medical supplies, and cash withdrawals.

Design a combination journal with eleven special money columns that can be used to record efficiently the transactions from Dr. Montoya's medical practice.

Case 19M-2. Another of Ms. Muller's customers is Eric Schmidt, a farmer. The most frequently recurring transactions for Mr. Schmidt's farm are the following: cash received from sales of livestock and produce, purchases on credit of gasoline and oil for the truck and tractor, cash paid to creditors, and cash paid for repairs and miscellaneous expenses.

Design a combination journal with eleven special money columns that can be used to record efficiently the transactions from Mr. Schmidt's farm.

Working Hint

Improving Accuracy in Adding. When adding a long column of figures, you can improve your accuracy by following this procedure.

1 Divide the column figures into two or more groups.
2 Add each group of figures separately.
3 Then add the subtotals.

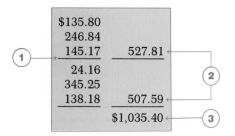

Project 3
Georgia Housewares Center

The Georgia Housewares Center uses a combination journal, a general ledger, an accounts receivable ledger, and an accounts payable ledger. The chart of accounts used and the balance sheet prepared on December 31 are shown on the next page.

The subsidiary ledgers have the accounts and balances listed here. If you are not using the workbook, establish the general ledger and subsidiary ledger accounts and record the January 1 balances.

Accounts Receivable Ledger:
Larkin Builders, $2,160 (Invoice 600 12/4);
Jack Ritter, $600 (Invoice 623 12/26)

Accounts Payable Ledger:
Norton Company and Dalton Manufacturing

1. *Originating the Data.* During January the business had the transactions listed on page 590. All sales had terms of n/30.

2. *Journalizing the Transactions.* Record the transactions for January in a combination journal. On the dates indicated prepare cash proofs to verify the checkbook balance. Also, post the individual entries from the journal after each cash proof is prepared. At the end of each page, foot and prove the journal. At the end of the month, foot, prove, total, and rule the journal.

3. *Posting the Transactions.* Post the totals from the journal.

4. *Proving the Ledgers.* Prove the ledgers as follows.
 a. Prepare a schedule of accounts receivable by age. Verify the total.
 b. Prepare a schedule of accounts payable. Verify the total.
 c. Prepare a trial balance on a worksheet.

5. *Preparing the Financial Statements.* Prepare the financial statements for the accounting period as follows.
 a. Complete the worksheet. The estimated uncollectible accounts expense for the month is $20. A physical count of the merchandise on January 31 showed an inventory of $4,300, and a physical count of the store supplies showed an inventory of $230. The estimated depreciation of the equipment

for the month is $50. Accrued interest on notes receivable is $3.00, and accrued interest on notes payable is $4.54.
 b. Prepare a schedule of cost of goods sold and an income statement.
 c. Prepare a statement of owner's equity and a classified balance sheet.

6. *Adjusting and Closing the Books.* Complete the books for the accounting period as follows.
 a. Journalize and post the adjusting entries.
 b. Journalize and post the closing entries.
 c. Foot, prove, total, and rule the journal.

7. *Preparing for the Next Accounting Period.* If a balance ledger form is used, the accounts do not need to be balanced and ruled.

8. *Proving the Accuracy of the Ledger.* Prepare a postclosing trial balance.

9. *Interpreting the Financial Information.* Based on the information in the financial records of the Georgia Housewares Center, answer the following questions.
 a. Would you have recommended that Ruth Odell, the owner of the Georgia Housewares Center, issue the note when she did?
 b. Did Ms. Odell have enough cash to take advantage of the purchase discount? If she had paid the invoice within the discount period, how much greater would her net income have been?

Georgia Housewares Center
Chart of Accounts

Assets
101 Cash
102 Notes Receivable
103 Interest Receivable
104 Accounts Receivable
105 Allowance for Doubtful Accounts
106 Merchandise Inventory
107 Supplies on Hand
108 Equipment
109 Accumulated Depreciation Equipment

Liabilities
201 Notes Payable
202 Interest Payable
203 Accounts Payable
204 Sales Tax Payable
205 Federal Income Taxes Payable
206 FICA Taxes Payable
207 Salaries Payable

Owner's Equity
301 Ruth Odell, Capital
302 Ruth Odell, Drawing
399 Income Summary

Revenue
401 Sales
402 Sales Returns and Allowances

Cost and Expenses
501 Purchases
502 Purchases Returns and Allowances
503 Purchases Discount
504 Uncollectible Accounts Expense
505 Cash Short and Over

506 Depreciation Expense—Equipment
507 Payroll Taxes Expense
508 Rent Expense
509 Salaries Expense
510 Supplies Expense

Other Revenue
601 Interest Revenue

Other Expenses
701 Interest Expense

Georgia Housewares Center
Balance Sheet
December 31, 19—

Assets			
Current Assets:			
Cash	4,210 00		
Notes Receivable	1,500 00		
Interest Receivable	70 00		
Accounts Receivable $2,760.00			
Less: Allowance for Doubtful Accounts 55.20	2,704 80		
Merchandise Inventory	7,498 00		
Supplies on Hand	120 00		
Total Current Assets		16,102 80	
Plant and Equipment:			
Equipment	12,000 00		
Less: Accumulated Depreciation—Equipment	2,350 00	9,650 00	
Total Assets		25,752 80	
Liabilities			
Current Liabilities:			
Notes Payable	800 00		
Interest Payable	6 50		
Federal Income Taxes Payable	148 30		
FICA Taxes Payable	121 70		
Total Liabilities		1,076 50	
Owner's Equity			
Ruth Odell, Capital		24,676 30	
Total Liabilities and Owner's Equity		25,752 80	

Jan. 2 Recorded memorandum entry in journal for cash balance.

2 Issued Invoice 630 to Jack Ritter for merchandise sold for $320 plus $16 sales tax on credit.

2 Issued Check 219 for $400 to pay January rent.

2 Received Invoice 4193, dated December 31, from Norton Company for merchandise purchased for $800 on credit; terms 2/10, n/30.

3 Issued Check 220 for $130 for supplies to be used in the store.

3 Issued Check 221 for $270 to federal government for monthly payment due on income tax withheld ($148.30) and FICA tax withheld ($121.70).

5 Received $600 from Jack Ritter in payment of Invoice 623 dated December 26.

6 Recorded cash proof showing weekly cash sales of $1,829.43 and sales tax of $91.47.

6 Deposited all cash; checkbook balance is $5,930.90. Prepare a cash proof. (Post the individual entries.)

8 Received $3,000 from the owner, Ruth Odell, as additional investment.

9 Issued Invoice 631 to Larkin Builders for goods sold for $620 on credit (no sales tax since appliances will be resold with house under construction).

10 Received Invoice 1412, dated January 9, from Dalton Manufacturing for merchandise purchased for $920 on credit; terms 2/10, n/30.

11 Received payment from Jack Ritter for Invoice 630 dated January 2.

11 Received Credit Memorandum CM-0091 for $50 from Dalton Manufacturing for allowance on Invoice 1412.

13 Recorded cash proof showing weekly cash sales of $2,346.10, sales tax of $117.31, and cash shortage of $7.

13 Deposited all cash; checkbook balance is $11,723.31. Prepare a cash proof. (Post the individual entries.)

15 Received $1,236 from Carl Laws in payment of 90-day, 12 percent note for $1,200 and the interest due today. ($30 of the interest has been recorded as interest receivable.)

Jan. 16 Issued Invoice 632 to Jack Ritter for merchandise sold for $480 plus $24 sales tax on credit.

17 Issued Check 222 to Dalton Manufacturing for Invoice 1412, dated January 9, less allowance and discount.

18 Issued Credit Memorandum 27 for $63 to Jack Ritter for returned merchandise of $60 and sales tax of $3.

20 Recorded cash proof showing weekly cash sales of $2,841.00 and sales tax of $142.05.

20 Deposited all cash; checkbook balance is $15,089.76. Prepare a cash proof. (Post the individual entries.)

22 Issued Check 223 for $225 to Ruth Odell for personal use.

23 Received Invoice 5062, dated January 21, from Norton Company for purchases of $550 on credit; terms 2/10, n/30.

24 Issued Check 224 to Dalton Manufacturing for $408 in payment of 60-day, 12 percent note for $400 plus interest. ($4.80 of the interest is recorded as interest payable.)

27 Recorded cash proof showing weekly cash sales of $2,634.15, sales tax of $131.71, and cash overage of $3.

27 Deposited all cash; checkbook balance is $17,225.62. Prepare a cash proof. (Post the individual entries.)

29 Issued a two-month, 12 percent note for $800 to Norton Company in payment of Invoice 4193, dated December 31.

30 Issued Invoice 633 to Jack Ritter for merchandise sold for $300 plus $15 sales tax on credit.

30 Computed and recorded the monthly payroll: salaries, $849; withheld for federal income taxes, $110.37; withheld for FICA taxes, $56.46.

30 Recorded liability of $56.46 for employer's FICA taxes.

30 Received a 90-day, 12 percent note for $441 from Jack Ritter on account for Invoice 632, less return.

31 Issued Check 225 to pay January payroll.

31 Recorded cash proof showing cash sales of $1,974 and sales tax of $98.70.

31 Deposited all cash; checkbook balance is $18,616.15. Prepare a cash proof. (Post the individual entries.)

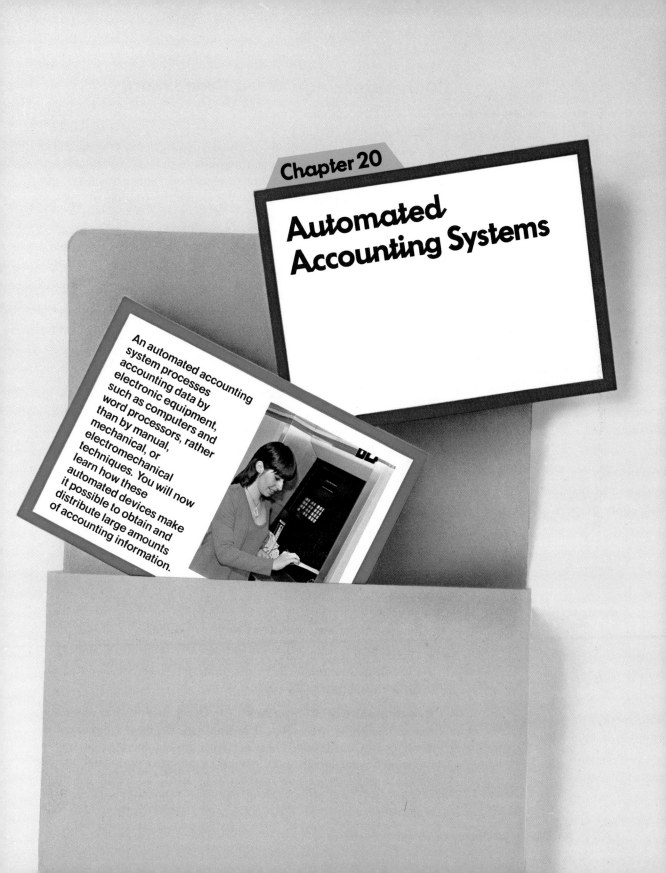

Chapter 20

Automated Accounting Systems

An automated accounting system processes accounting data by electronic equipment, such as computers and word processors, rather than by manual, mechanical, or electromechanical techniques. You will now learn how these automated devices make it possible to obtain and distribute large amounts of accounting information.

Topic 1
Computers and Word Processors

A *What are the most common types of equipment used in an auto-mated system?* The two most common types of equipment used in an automated system are computers and word processors. In the last chapter you learned how accounting data is processed manually. An **automated accounting system,** or **electronic accounting system,** processes accounting data largely by automated equipment, such as computers, word processors, and other automated devices. This method is much faster than processing data by manual, mechanical, or electromechanical techniques. These automated devices make it possible to obtain, process, and distribute large amounts of information about every facet of the business.

A **computer** is a group of electronic devices that can process data at very rapid speeds by following instructions stored in the computer. A computer includes three essential devices: an input device, a central processor, and an output device.

A **word processor** is an electronic device that may be used to prepare, duplicate, and transmit typewritten and other reports already provided by the computer. The electronic typewriter, shown in the margin, is an example of a word processor which can also automatically verify reports for spelling. Other examples of word processors are electronic typewriters, dictation equipment, text-editing typewriters, copying machines, and telecommunication devices.

Computers

Once programmed, a computer can function without human assistance and at speeds near the speed of light. For example, some processing jobs can be completed by a computer in less than three seconds. The same jobs might require about three months of constant work to process the data manually. But before a computer works so efficiently, a computer operator must first give it two things.

- The data to be processed.
- A set of instructions, called a program, that tells the computer what to do with the data.

Development of Computers. The development of modern computers had three life cycles. The first generation of computers was developed in the 1950s. These early computers operated on vacuum tubes and were large, bulky devices. Compared with later models, these computers were slow in processing data. The second generation of computers was introduced in the early 1960s and operated using

This computer consists of an input device (keyboard and screen), a central processor (large unit in rear) and an output device (printer). The central processor includes a storage device, a control unit, and an arithmetic/logic unit.

Courtesy Wang Laboratories, Inc.

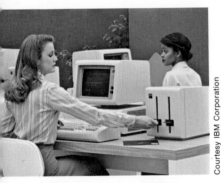

Shown here is an IBM text-editing typewriter with a 50,000-word dictionary.

Courtesy IBM Corporation

transistors. Generally these computers processed data at a faster rate than the earlier ones and had larger storage capacity. In the early 1970s the third generation of computers was developed which used small circuits, or microprocessors. These small circuits made it possible to build computers that were smaller, faster, and less expensive. A one-chip (one circuit) central processing unit is called a **microprocessor.**

Types of Computers. Today's computers are classified by cost, speed of processing data, storage capacity, and (most often) size. Generally, the larger the computer, the more it costs, the faster it can process data, and the more storage capacity it has. Types of computers classified by size are microcomputers, minicomputers, and mainframe computers.

The microcomputer is the newest and smallest computer. A **microcomputer** is a complete computer on a single circuit board. The microcomputer is sometimes referred to as a *personal computer* or a *small business computer.* Examples of the microcomputers are the IBM Personal computer, Apple III, Radio Shack TRS-80, and Texas Instruments 99/4. Microcomputers use cassette tapes, diskettes, or bubble memory devices to store data for processing.

Courtesy Ohio Scientific

Microcomputer system with color video display.

The relatively small and inexpensive minicomputer can process data faster than microcomputers. A **minicomputer** is a computer that operates with a stored program but has less storage capacity than a large computer. A minicomputer often uses a small disk, called a **diskette,** to store data. Minicomputers may be used by small- and medium-sized businesses as their main computer. Large businesses also may use minicomputers in different branch stores or production departments. When several minicomputers are used, they can be connected to a larger computer to form a computer network. See the illustration of distributed data processing on page 596.

A mainframe computer is larger than the minicomputer. A **mainframe** computer is a large full-scale computer system. It has the largest storage capacity and processes data at the greatest speeds. It may be placed in a centralized location where large volumes of data must be processed. Information processed with mainframe computers is often stored on a magnetic tape similar to that used with recording equipment.

Computer Program. A computer operates only by following a series of detailed instructions called a **program.** The program is stored in the computer. The instructions tell the computer, in a step-by-step sequence, exactly what to do and when to do it. A separate program must be prepared for each information processing job. For example, there may be a program for updating accounts receivable, a program for updating inventory records, and a program for computing the payroll.

The person who prepares a computer program is called a **programmer.** To plan the most efficient computer program, the programmer uses a diagram called a *flowchart,* sometimes referred to as a *program* or *procedure flowchart.* A flowchart shows visually the series of instructions that the computer will follow in processing data. It also can detect unnecessary operations which would otherwise use valuable computer time.

The flowchart here shows a general ledger program for maintaining a master record of customers' accounts. The program begins with reading both the master record and a customer's account card. The program ends with the output of the master record after the new customer data has been added.

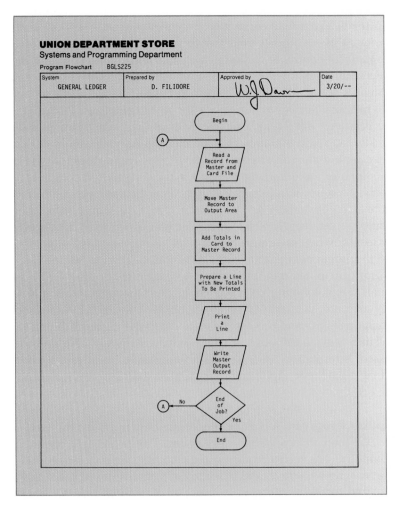

Program flowchart for keeping master records of customers' accounts.

Activity A. Answer the following questions about computers and word processors. Refer to the text, margin notes, and illustrations on pages 592 to 594.
1. Name the components of a computer.
2. What are the advantages to using automated equipment to process data?
3. What are some examples of word processors?
4. What are three common sizes of computers on the market today?
5. How is data stored for processing in a microcomputer?
6. Why is a computer program necessary?
7. How might a flowchart help to plan a computer program?

Computer Controls

B *Do automated accounting systems need to have the same basic controls as manual accounting systems?* Yes, an automated accounting system must have the same basic controls to ensure accuracy, honesty, and efficiency and speed. However, automated accounting systems must also have special controls. These are used to avoid costly computer mistakes. Two examples of these special controls are error reports and item counts.

An **error report** is a control in which the computer is instructed not to process something. For example, the computer can be instructed not to write a check for more than $500. If a check request for $600 should be processed, the computer *will not* issue the check. It *will* issue an error report and refer the request to management. This is used to control cash payments.

Error reports are also used with the automated bank tellers. These 24-hour tellers (sometimes referred to as *"intelligent" terminals*) can be programmed to allow a maximum withdrawal of only $25 for a single account in any one day. Any attempt to withdraw more than the allowed amount will result in an error message being printed on the screen or an error light flashing. An automated bank teller is illustrated in the margin.

An **item count** is a control in which the computer is programmed to allow a specified number of items to be processed. For example, in processing payroll checks, the computer can be instructed to only write a certain number of checks. This may be one for each employee. As each check (item) is written, an item count is made. If the number of checks requested is different from the number of employees, the computer will issue a warning message. This is another control for cash payments.

Two New Controls
• Error reports
• Item counts

Courtesy Citibank, N.A.

Automated bank tellers are installed at banks, shopping malls, supermarkets, office lobbies, airline terminals, and other locations.

Distributed Data Processing

Some businesses have more than one computer. For example, a large mainframe computer may be located in a centralized processing department. Several minicomputers also may be located throughout the business in various departments or branch locations. These smaller computers are usually connected to the mainframe computer by telephone lines.

Each department or branch can use its minicomputer to process data that applies only to that department or branch. This on-the-spot processing is faster and eliminates the need to send all data to a central location. At the same time, the home office can use the mainframe computer to process data that concerns the entire business. The mainframe computer can also be used to handle any excess processing needed by the departments.

The system that uses a mainframe computer connected to a network of several minicomputers is called a **distributed data processing system.** Distributed data processing often eliminates the need for businesses to buy larger and more expensive computers. It also allows departments to share information by communicating data over the network of telephone lines. This network is illustrated in the flowchart.

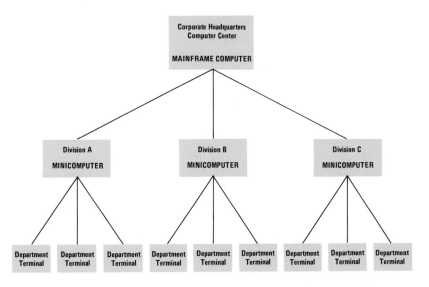

Distributed Data Processing. Computer terminals are connected to minicomputers and mainframe computer by telephone lines.

To keep down the high cost of using computers, businesses try to use them efficiently. Examples of efficient use of computers include the following.

- *Operating the computer on an around-the-clock basis.* This is especially useful with expensive mainframe computers.
- *Making the computer available to other businesses on a shared-time basis.* Even a large business, like a bank, may not have enough work to keep its computer busy all the time. When sharing the computer, the businesses pay according to the amount of computer time they use. Thus the company with the computer can reduce its own information processing expenses and can provide a service to some of its customers.

• *Purchasing or renting a keyboard terminal that is connected by telephone lines to a computer.* The computer, which may be as far as 1,000 miles away, is used by several businesses on a shared-time basis. Again, the business pays according to the amount of computer time it uses.

Data Processing Service Centers

At one time, only large businesses could afford to buy or rent computer equipment. To make automated data processing available to smaller businesses, data processing service centers were set up. A **data processing service center** is a business that processes data for other businesses for a fee. In a data processing service center, automated data processing equipment is bought or rented and then the data from other businesses is processed for a fee.

Activity B. Answer the following questions about computer controls, distributed data processing, and data processing service centers. Refer to the text, margin notes, and illustrations on pages 595 to 597.
1. How can an error report be used with an automatic 24-hour bank teller?
2. How does an item count control cash payments?

3. Where is the mainframe computer located in a business with distributed data processing? Where are the minicomputers and terminals located?
4. Why are data processing service centers used?
5. What are some ways to keep down the cost of using computers?

Word Processors

C *How are word processors used?* Word processors are used to prepare and duplicate typewritten reports such as routine correspondence, financial statements, and special management reports. Some word processors are groups of automated devices with many but not all of the capabilities of a computer. For example, most do not have an arithmetic/logic unit. Thus they do not perform computations or make decisions as computers do. The people, forms, procedures, and word processing equipment used to prepare these reports make up a **word processing system.**

Some businesses group all word processing equipment into a large word processing center. Others distribute the equipment throughout various departments. In this case only large or special reports are sent to the word processing center for preparation and duplication. An example of a word processing work station is shown in the margin.

The text-editing typewriter shown on page 592 includes a keyboard, a full-page screen, a storage unit, and a high-speed printer. When preparing reports on this text-editing typewriter, the operator first enters the manager's rough draft (the original copy) on the keyboard. As the report is keyed into the machine, the material is shown on the screen

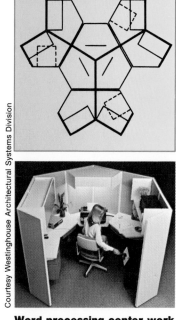

Courtesy Westinghouse Architectural Systems Division

Word processing center work station.

as well as stored on a diskette. After the complete draft of the report has been stored on the diskette, a printed copy (hard copy) can be obtained from the high-speed printer. At this time the draft of the report can be edited by the manager and returned for changes and corrections.

After the manager returns the report, the machine operator retrieves the original draft from the diskette. As each page of the report is viewed on the screen, necessary changes and corrections are made electronically. A corrected copy can then be obtained through the printer. The text-editing typewriter can also be programmed to type within certain margins and to automatically center headings, tables, and charts.

Some text-editing typewriters can also be equipped to send reports over telephone lines to distant locations. Sending reports by electronic transmission is often referred to as **electronic mail.**

Activity C. Answer the following questions about word processors. Refer to the text, margin notes, and illustrations on pages 596 and 598.
1. For what type of work is a word processor suitable?

2. What are the components of a word processing system?
3. Describe the components of a text-editing typewriter.

Accounting Concepts:
Processing Accounting Information. The method used for *processing accounting information* varies according to the type and size of the business, the volume of data to be processed, the time available for processing the data, and the amount of money that can be spent.
Information Requirements. Information about the operations of a business must be complete, accurate, current, and relevant to the decisions that must be made.

Topic 1 Problem

20-1. Check the classified section of your local newspaper for jobs using computers and word processors. List the job requirements and qualifications for each position.

Topic 2
Components of a Computer

A *What are the components of a computer?* The components of a computer include an input device, a central processor, and an output device. Once the data and the instructions are entered into the computer, this equipment processes the data and provides information for decision making.

Computer Equipment

The origination step involves collecting the data. This step usually does not involve the computer directly. After the data has been collected, it must be entered into the computer during the input step. An input device is the equipment used to enter data into the computer. The processing step is performed by a central processor. The **central processor** consists of a storage unit, arithmetic/logic unit, and control unit.

• The **storage unit** (memory) receives and stores the program, the input data, and the results of partially processed data.
• The **arithmetic/logic unit** performs computations according to the program. It can also compare data and make a decision as to the next procedure to be performed.
• The **control unit** interprets the instructions of the program and directs and coordinates all units.

The output step produces the information. The output is produced by an output device, which reports the information obtained from the data that has been processed.

The computer used by a business varies according to the needs of the business, the cost of the equipment, and the manufacturer of the equipment. However, all computers use these basic types of devices to process data.

INFORMATION PROCESSING CYCLE	COMPUTER PROCESSING
Originate	Source Document
Input	Input Device
Process	Central Processor Storage Unit Arithmetic/Logic Unit Control Unit
Output	Output Device

The components of a computer correlate with the input-process-output steps of the information processing cycle.

Input Devices

Common input media include punched cards, punched tape, magnetic tape, and documents with data printed in magnetic ink or optical type font. The coded data recorded on these media must be converted into electronic impulses for entry into the computer's central processor. Many different devices are used to provide input data to computers.

Punched-Card Reader. This input device reads punched cards one at a time and converts the data to electronic impulses. It then communicates the data to the storage unit of the central processor. There are several different types of punched-card readers. Their reading speeds vary from 100 cards per minute to 2,000 or more cards per minute.

Punched Card

Punched-Tape Reader. Punched tape is also used as an input medium. The punched-tape reader converts data into electronic impulses and communicates data to the storage unit of the central processor. Some of these readers operate at speeds up to 2,000 characters per second. Photoelectric equipment is used for the higher speeds.

Punched Tape

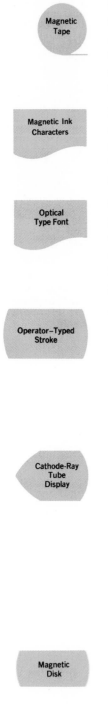

Magnetic-Tape Unit. Magnetic tape is widely used as an input medium for computers because of the rapid speed at which it can be read. Also, magnetic tape makes it possible to store large amounts of data in a small amount of space. Some magnetic-tape units can read 350,000 characters per second. The average magnetic-tape unit reads about 60,000 characters per second.

Magnetic Character Reader. This input device reads magnetic ink characters printed on paper. People can also read these characters. For example, a magnetic character reader can read the magnetic characters on a bank check and convert them into machine language. This can be done at a maximum rate of 1,600 items per minute.

Optical Scanner. The optical scanner, or optical character reader, reads the input data from source documents printed in a special optical type font. The advantage of optical scanning is that data can be converted directly from the source document into electronic impulses for entry into the central processor. Some optical scanners can also read handwritten materials.

Console Typewriter. Data can be manually entered into a computer through a console typewriter located in the computer center. As the operator types, the typewriter produces readable (hard) copy. At the same time, the typewriter converts the strokes into electronic impulses that are fed into the central processor. As a computer input device, the console typewriter is limited by the speed of the operator. It is often used to enter special instructions, to correct errors, and to ask the computer questions.

Cathode-Ray Tube Displays. A cathode-ray tube (CRT) display is similar to a typewriter with a television screen. Data is shown on the face of the tube as it is entered into the computer. The cathode-ray tube display is used by many airline ticket agents in reserving seats for passengers.

Transaction Recorders. Transaction recorders are also used as input devices. These units are connected to the computer. As a transaction is recorded, the data is transmitted directly to the computer. A cash register can be connected to a computer. When a sale is recorded, the computer updates the inventory records and posts the charge directly to the customer's account.

Magnetic-Disk Units. Magnetic-disk units can also provide input data to a computer. Magnetic disks resemble phonograph records. The data is stored on both sides of a disk in the form of magnetic spots. The data is read into the computer by the magnetic-disk unit, which converts the data into electronic impulses.

Diskettes. Diskettes (sometimes referred to as *floppies*) are small magnetic disks used as the input medium for smaller computers and word processors. A diskette is illustrated in the margin. One diskette may hold almost as much input data as 3,000 punched cards. Each diskette is sealed in an 8-inch square envelope that makes it easier to handle and store. One diskette weighs less than 2 ounces and is reusable.

Courtesy NCR Corporation

A diskette is a thin disk with one or two magnetic recording surfaces.

Telecommunication Devices. A telecommunication device can transmit data over telephone or telegraph wires directly into a computer. An example of a telecommunication device is in the margin. A voice unit may be used, on a limited basis, to enter data by talking to the computer.

Keyboard Terminal. The keyboard terminal is a typewriter-like device located at a distance from the computer. It is connected to the computer by cable or by data transmissions lines. The keyboard terminal is used mainly when there is not a lot of input data or when the computer must be asked questions. For example, a person in Portland, Oregon, may need a motel room for the next night in Dallas, Texas. The reservation clerk at the Portland Inn can ask the computer, "Is a single room available at the Dallas Inn on May 26?" The question will be entered into the reservation computer by the reservation clerk. The reply will be printed on the terminal after the computer has made its "decision."

Courtesy NCR Corp.

The portable KSB terminal is a telecommunication device that can transmit data over telephone wires into a computer. It can also receive output from a computer.

Magnetic-Card Unit. The magnetic-card unit stores data on cards with magnetic surfaces. It is recorded in tracks on the cards. When the data is needed, the magnetic-card unit reads the magnetic cards and converts the data into electronic impulses.

Activity A. Name the input device which performs each of the following activities.
1. Reads punched cards and communicates the data to the storage unit.
2. Reads input at the fastest speed.
3. Reads data printed in special type font directly from the source document.

4. Manually enters data into a computer from a distance by means of a typewriter-like device.
5. Converts characters written in magnetic ink into electronic impulses.
6. Converts data on punched tape into electronic impulses.

Central Processor

B *How is the central processor used?* This device actually processes the data. It is the heart of any computer. Its three units—the storage (memory) unit, the arithmetic/logic unit, and the control unit—may be contained in one cabinet or may be separate pieces of equipment connected by a cable.

Storage (Memory) Unit. One important characteristic of a computer is that it can store large amounts of data in its storage unit. The storage unit of the central processor receives and stores data. The data can be retrieved at a later time. When directed, the computer can rapidly retrieve any part of the data from storage. The time that it takes a computer to locate and transfer data from storage is called **access time.** The access time varies according to the storage medium used. Three types of computer storage are internal, auxiliary, and external.

Internal Storage (Memory). **Internal storage** (sometimes referred to as *primary,* or *main, storage*) is linked directly to the central processor of the computer. Instructions and data fed in by input devices are stored in internal storage. This data is then available to the arithmetic/logic unit and the control unit. An example of internal storage is the monolithic memory chip, or microprocessor.

Auxiliary Storage. **Auxiliary storage** (sometimes referred to as *secondary storage*) devices are located outside the central processor but are connected to it. As a result, auxiliary storage provides additional storage when needed by the central processor. The media commonly used for auxiliary storage are magnetic drums, magnetic film, magnetic disks, magnetic tapes, and magnetic cards. For example, a reel of tape containing data on accounts receivable would be used as auxiliary storage whenever the accounts receivable are updated.

External Storage. **External storage,** like auxiliary storage, is a device located outside the central processor, but external storage is not connected directly to the central processor. External storage is used to store data waiting to be processed or data that has been processed but will be used again. Common external storage media are punched cards, punched tape, and magnetic tape. (The videodisc is expected to become another external storage medium in the years ahead.) An advantage of videodiscs is that information can easily be viewed on a TV-type screen.

Arithmetic/Logic Unit. The arithmetic/logic unit of the central processor performs a variety of computing and decision-making functions. All computations are performed in this unit. The arithmetic/logic unit is also capable of comparing two numbers and determining the lesser or greater of the two. The computer can be instructed by a program to take alternative courses of action based on the results of the comparisons.

The arithmetic/logic unit is made up of registers, adders, and counters. A **register** is capable of receiving data, holding it, and transferring it as directed by the control unit. An **adder** receives data from two or more sources, performs the arithmetic, and sends the result to a register. A **counter** counts the number of times an operation is performed.

Control Unit. The control unit automatically directs and coordinates all units of the computer.

• It tells the input devices what data to put in storage and when to store it.
• It tells the storage unit where to store data and when to remove it.
• It tells the arithmetic/logic unit where to find data, what operations to perform, and where to store results.
• It tells the output devices what data to record and when to record it.

The control unit operates according to the stored program. The unit receives and executes its instructions one at a time until the entire program has been executed.

A computer can also be controlled externally by a computer console. The **computer console,** illustrated in the margin, is used for manual control and observation of a computer. It contains a series of lights that indicate the operations that are being performed. It also contains a number of switches and buttons that enable the operator to give certain commands, such as "start," "stop," "print," and "stop printing," and to switch from one activity to another.

The console usually contains a console typewriter that the operator can use to communicate manually with the computer.

Courtesy IBM Corporation

Central Processing Unit With Computer Console

Output Devices

The output of a computer can be in either a form that people can read or a form that a machine must interpret. For example, paychecks prepared by a printer can be read by the person receiving the check. However, a customer's file that has been updated and stored on magnetic tape can be read only by a machine. The flowchart shown on page 604 shows several output devices. Also note that a limited amount of output may be in the form of verbal responses.

Computer output can be in a form that people or equipment can read.

Printers. Printers produce a hard copy (printed copy) of the output. A printer is connected to the computer and generally prints an entire line of information at a time. When a printer prints data directly from the computer, it is said to be on-line. **On-line** means that the device is under the control of the computer. Many computers produce data faster than a printer can print it. Thus in some systems the output is recorded on magnetic tape at very high speeds. Later the magnetic tape supplies the output to a printer. This is called off-line printing. **Off-line** means that the device is not under the control of the computer. In the meantime, the computer is free to process additional data.

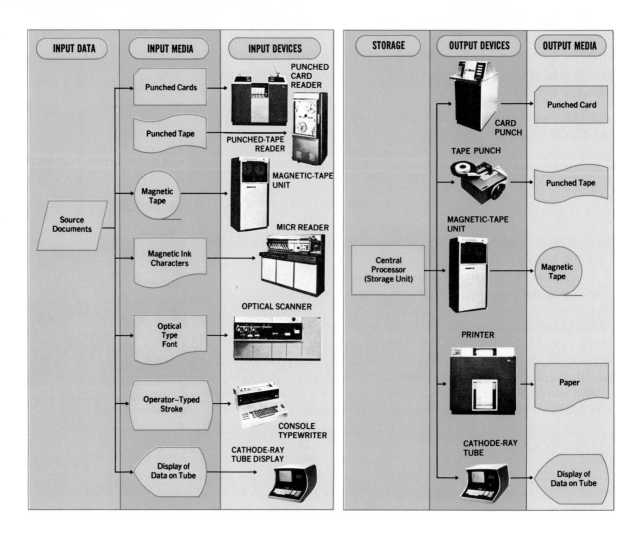

INPUT DATA	INPUT MEDIA	INPUT DEVICES		STORAGE	OUTPUT DEVICES	OUTPUT MEDIA

Console Typewriters. A console typewriter may also be used to produce output. It is much slower than a printer and is used only for printing out special information or for small computer systems.

Cathode-Ray Tube Displays. The cathode-ray tube (CRT) display can be an output as well as an input device. For example, an inventory clerk might use one to determine the number of small motors in stock. With this information the clerk knows immediately if an order for this machine can be filled.

Machine Language Output. When output is coded in machine language, output devices such as card punches, punched-tape units, and magnetic-tape units are used. For example, magnetic tape can be used to store updated accounts receivable.

Microfilm Processors. Microfilm processors are used to store computer output on microfilm. Once the data is on microfilm, it can be viewed on a microfilm display screen.

Activity B. Name the automated data processing equipment that performs each of the following activities. Also indicate whether the equipment is a unit in the central processor (name the unit) or an output device.
1. Produces the results of processing in the form of printed hard copy.
2. Automatically directs and coordinates all units of the computer.
3. Displays data on a screen.
4. Records special information from the computer; is much slower than a printer.
5. Performs computations.
6. Stores computer output on microfilm.
7. Does the decision making.
8. Controls a computer externally.

Accounting Concept:
Information Processing Cycle. The steps followed in the *information processing cycle* are to originate the data, input the data into the system, process the data, and output the information.

Topic 2 Problem

20-2. Indicate whether each of the following would be used in a manual accounting system, an automated accounting system, or both.
EXAMPLE: Pencil—Both
a. Card reader
b. CRT
c. Pegboard
d. Microfilm processor
e. Electronic typewriter
f. Transaction recorder
g. Text-editing typewriter
h. Combination journal
i. Magnetic-tape unit
j. Central processor

Topic 3
Common Language Media

A *What is machine language?* A **machine language** is a code that a machine is designed to read and understand. Machine languages are necessary because most machines cannot read the letters and numbers that people read. Thus data on source documents must usually be converted (changed) into a language that a machine can read before the data can be processed.

The material on which the coded data is recorded is called the **medium.** Some examples of common language media are described here.

The 80-Column Card

Punched cards are of uniform size so that they can be processed automatically by the various punched-card machines. Each card is divided into 80 vertical areas called **card columns.** These card columns are numbered from 1 to 80 from left to right. Each column is divided into 12 horizontal areas called **card rows.** In each row, one hole can be punched per column. The rows on the card are referred to by the numbers 12, 11, 0, 1, 2, 3, 4, 5, 6, 7, 8, and 9.

Row 12 is at the top of the card, and row 9 is at the bottom. Only rows 0 through 9 are printed on the card. Rows 11 and 12 are not printed. The top three rows (12, 11, and 0) are called **zone rows.** Rows 0 through 9 are called **numeric rows.** Row 0 can be either a zone row or a numeric row. (Sometimes row 12 is referred to as the Y-row and row 11 is referred to as the X-row.)

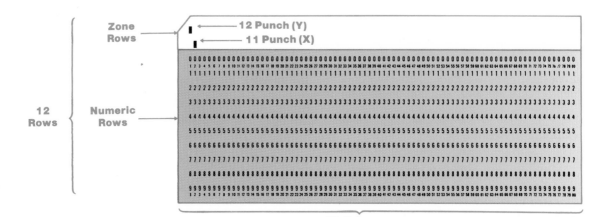

Zone Rows

12 Punch (Y)
11 Punch (X)

12 Rows

Numeric Rows

80 Columns

Corner is cropped to visually ensure that all cards are facing the same way. Cards may be cropped at any corner.

Coding

Only one letter of the alphabet, one digit, or one special character can be punched into a card column. As a result, one card can contain a maximum of 80 individual pieces of data. This data is recorded in the card by means of a code. The holes in the columns represent a code.

Numeric Data. Any digit from 0 through 9 is coded in a column by punching one hole in the appropriate row. For example, the digit zero is recorded in the first column of a card by a hole in row 0 of column 1. Since only one digit can be recorded in a card column, the number of columns needed for numeric data depends upon the number of digits involved. A one-digit number requires one column. A three-digit number requires three columns.

Alphabetic Data. A letter of the alphabet is coded by a combination of two holes in the same column. One hole is punched in a zone row (12, 11, or 0) and another hole is punched in a numeric row (1 to 9). The combinations used to code letters are given in the margin.

ALPHABETIC CHARACTERS

Letter	Punches	Letter	Punches
A	= 12 and 1	N	= 11 and 5
B	= 12 and 2	O	= 11 and 6
C	= 12 and 3	P	= 11 and 7
D	= 12 and 4	Q	= 11 and 8
E	= 12 and 5	R	= 11 and 9
F	= 12 and 6	S	= 0 and 2
G	= 12 and 7	T	= 0 and 3
H	= 12 and 8	U	= 0 and 4
I	= 12 and 9	V	= 0 and 5
J	= 11 and 1	W	= 0 and 6
K	= 11 and 2	X	= 0 and 7
L	= 11 and 3	Y	= 0 and 8
M	= 11 and 4	Z	= 0 and 9

- A through I: Zone row 12 and numeric rows 1 through 9
- J through R: Zone row 11 and numeric rows 1 through 9
- S through Z: Zone row 0 and numeric rows 2 through 9

Only one letter can be recorded in a card column. Thus the number of columns needed for alphabetic data depends upon the number of letters involved. For example, "telephone" requires nine columns. "Phone" requires only five columns.

Special Characters. Special characters, such as the dollar sign ($) and the percent symbol (%), are recorded by one, two, or three punches in a column.

The 96-Column Punched Card

Most equipment that uses punched cards is designed to use the 80-column card. However, System/3 IBM equipment uses a 96-column punched card. This card is only one-third as large as the 80-column card, yet it can hold about 20 percent more data. A punched card is shown below in the margin.

Punched Tape

Punched tape, like punched cards, contains coded data that machines can read. However, it differs from punched cards in two ways.

- Instead of a punched-card code, the common machine language of punched tape is channel code.
- Instead of being recorded in cards, the data is recorded continuously on tape.

Thus punched tape is similar to a group of punched cards joined end to end. The tape is approximately 1 inch wide and is wound on a reel. Punched tape can contain ten alphabetic and/or numeric characters per inch.

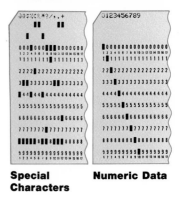

Alphabetic Data

Special Characters　　**Numeric Data**

Punched Tape

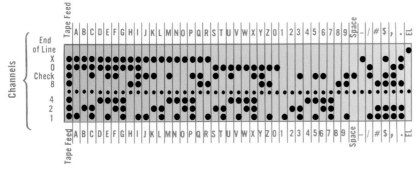

Punched Tape

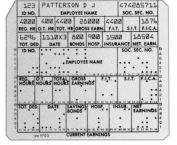

A 96-column card with complete payroll data for one employee.

Magnetic Tape

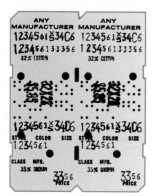

Punched Tag

Magnetic Ink Characters

Magnetic Tape

Punched cards and punched tape are important input/output media for certain types of electronic equipment. However, they have serious drawbacks for most computers. The large computers operate at such high speeds that data in punched cards and punched tape often cannot be read fast enough to keep up with the speed of the computer. **Magnetic tape** has been developed as a high-speed input/output medium for computers. A magnetic tape is illustrated in the margin.

The magnetic tape used in information processing is similar to that used in tape recorders. It is a plastic tape coated with iron oxide. Data is recorded on the tape as invisible magnetized spots placed in vertical columns. The spots, called **bits,** serve the same function as the holes in punched tape.

The Punched Tag

Another medium that uses punched holes to code data is the punched tag, illustrated in the margin. Punched tags are used primarily by retail businesses, such as department stores. Each tag generally contains some printed data as well as the data coded in small punched holes. The data is punched and printed on each tag and varies according to the business and the article to which the tag is attached.

Magnetic Ink Character Recognition (MICR)

Another method of representing data for machine processing involves the use of magnetic ink. A machine that can read data printed in magnetic ink is called a **magnetic ink character recognition (MICR) machine.** This method is used by banks in processing checks. From the time that a check is written by a depositor until it is posted to the depositor's bank account, it may be handled by many banks and processed many times. MICR equipment automates the processing of checks. An example of magnetic ink characters is in the margin.

Optical Scanning

The goal of many people in information processing is to improve optical character reading machines that can read ordinary typewritten and handwritten copy. An **optical character reading (OCR) machine** reads characters or symbols through the use of light-sensitive devices. When this is achieved, all source documents will be fed through optical character readers and processed automatically. The need to convert the data into punched cards, punched tape, magnetic tape, or some other input medium containing a code will be eliminated.

Optical scanners that can read data printed in special type (called **optical type font**) have been widely used to process charge sales made on credit cards. These scanners are machines that can identify the letters and numbers in the optical type font.

A variety of machines can be equipped to record data on a tape in optical type font. Examples are adding machines and cash registers. Recording in optical type font eliminates the need to manually re-record data in machine language. The tape produced by such a machine can then be fed directly into an optical scanner. The scanner will automatically convert the data into electrical impulses. These impulses are transmitted to other information processing equipment.

For example, a cash register can be equipped to print a detailed audit strip in optical type font. The tape can be read by an optical scanner that transmits the data to a computer. The computer can then use the data from the tape to prepare journals, update the accounts receivable, prepare an analysis of sales by department, compute the salesclerks' commissions, and prepare other reports.

Instead of reading characters, some optical scanners read a printed code. The best-known printed code is probably the bar code used to transfer data from plastic credit cards to source documents. A **bar code** uses various arrangements of short and long bars embossed on the cards to represent numeric data. The bar code is transferred from the credit cards to the source documents by an imprinting device like the data recorder shown in the margin. A special optical scanner reads the numeric data imprinted on the source documents. A data converter then punches the data into cards or tape, or it records data on magnetic tape for more processing.

Retail stores (such as food stores and department stores) use optical scanning to record sales and inventory data. Each product in a store has the manufacturer's name and the type of product (such as "tuna fish can, 567") marked on it. The data is coded in **Universal Product Code (UPC),** which consists of bars and numbers. At the checkout counter, the salesclerk passes the coded label on the product over an optical scanner. The data is automatically entered into the cash register, which is connected to a computer. The computer relays the price back to the register. Then the register records the data on the detailed audit strip, the customer's sales slip, and a cassette tape. Later the data on the tape is processed by the computer.

Optical Type Font

Optical Font Tape

Courtesy Addressograph/AM Corp.

This data recorder imprints data from embossed plastic credit cards to source documents. Customer's account number is coded in bar code on credit card.

Universal Product Code

The GIGO Principle

The accuracy of the output from automated data processing depends upon the accuracy of the input data. The automated data processing procedures eliminate the need to rewrite input data once it is recorded in machine language. They eliminate the errors that occur in recopying. However, if the input data contains errors, these errors will affect all the records that are produced from it. The relationship between the accuracy and usefulness of the output and the accuracy and completeness of the input is referred to as the **GIGO (garbage in, garbage out) principle.**

Activity A-1. Answer the following questions on machine language. Refer to the 96-column punched card for payroll shown on page 607.
1. What is the employee's name?
2. In what columns is the date punched?
3. What is the employee's identification number? The social security number?
4. How much was deducted for savings bonds? Hospitalization? Insurance?
5. What is the amount of the employee's gross earnings? Federal income tax? State income tax?

Activity A-2. Several methods of coding data are described here. For each method identify the medium used. Refer to the media shown in the illustrations on pages 606 to 609.
1. Data printed in optical type font.
2. Data coded in Universal Product Code.
3. Data coded in very small holes.
4. Data printed in magnetic ink.
5. Data coded in bar code.
6. Data coded in MICR characters.

Topic 3 Problems

20-3. Refer to the punched card in the right column to answer the following questions.
1. What month is punched?
2. How many columns are used to record the date?
3. How many columns are used to record the invoice number?
4. What invoice number is punched?
5. What is the salesclerk's number? The item number?
6. How is the item described?
7. What quantity was sold?
8. What is the price of each unit?
9. What is the cost amount? The sales amount?
10. How many columns are unassigned?

20-4. Use two 80-column cards with the same fields as those on the card in Topic Problem 20-3. Circle the punching positions that would be punched to record the following data.

1. Date: March 15, 1983
Invoice 7938
Salesclerk 371

Item 2472S
Item Description: Golf Clubs
Quantity: 6

Unit Price: $35.25
Cost Amount: $211.50
Sales Amount: $265.00

2. Date: October 14, 1984
Invoice A143M
Salesclerk 32

Item W9091
Item Description: Shoes,
  Basketball, White
Quantity: 24

Unit Price: $15.00
Cost Amount: $360.00
Sales Amount: $405.00

Topic 4
Computer Applications

A *How does the computer decrease the amount of manual operations needed to process data?* This question can best be answered by examining applications in which a computer is used to process data. One such application is described in this topic: updating accounts receivable.

Updating Accounts Receivable

A computer can decrease the amount of manual operations necessary to update accounts receivable. A computer helps in processing data from sales, remittances, and returns, and prepares monthly statements of account. A large business may have several thousand charge customers. The work involved in updating customers' accounts is highly repetitive.

Sales on Credit. The Union Department Store operates a main store and three suburban stores. Charge sales and remittances are made at all four stores. A computer center located in the central accounting office at the main store is used to keep the accounts receivable records for the 50,000 charge customers.

Origination. The four Union Department Stores are using the electronic cash register system. These cash registers record sales transactions electronically and store sales and accounts receivable data on cassette tapes for processing by the computer. Two special features of this system are the bar-coded tag and the tag reader. A **bar-coded tag** contains bars of magnetic strips containing data. The bar-coded tag contains the following numeric information for each item of merchandise: color, size, style, price, sales department, and inventory number. A bar-coded tag is attached to each item of merchandise.

A **tag reader** is an optical scanning device used to read bar-coded tags. The tag reader, shown with a bar-coded tag in the margin, is an optical scanning device that looks like a pencil with a light at one end. The tag reader unit is connected to the cash register. By passing the tag reader over the bars on the tag, the salesclerk enters the merchandise data into the cash register automatically. The need to enter sales data manually is eliminated. This speeds up the recording of sales transactions and reduces the possibility of recording the wrong information. However, sales on credit require the salesclerk to enter the customer's account number into the cash register manually.

Each sales transaction entered in the cash register is stored in three places: on the customer's receipt, on an audit tape, and on a cassette

Tag reader reading bar-coded tag.

This electronic cash register is equipped with a tag reader, which scans bar-coded tags on merchandise. At the point of sale (POS), the tag reader records such information as price, size, color, style, sales department, and item number. This data is stored on a cassette tape and is later processed by the computer.

tape. The cassette tape is in a unit called a data collector. The **data collector** is a unit for storing transactions until they are transferred to the computer center. At regular intervals during the day, sales data from the three suburban stores is transmitted by telephone lines to a cassette tape receiver in the central accounting office. The cassettes for the main store are manually carried to the central accounting office. Next the sales data from all the cassette tapes is transferred to magnetic tape for computer processing. These procedures are shown here.

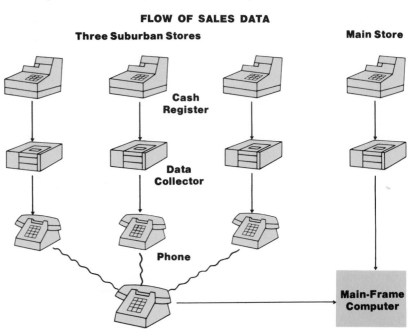

FLOW OF SALES DATA

Three Suburban Stores   Main Store

Cash Register

Data Collector

Phone

Main-Frame Computer

Input. To update accounts receivable, the computer operator feeds the program entitled "Updating Accounts Receivable—Charges to Accounts" into the computer's memory. The magnetic tape containing the information about the current balances in the customer's accounts is placed in the magnetic-tape unit. Then the cassette tape containing the data from the main store and the three suburban stores is fed into the computer.

Processing. As the magnetic-tape reader communicates the data for each charge sale to the computer, the computer does the following.
• Searches its storage, finds the customer's account, and identifies the last balance in the account.
• Records the date, sales slip number, and amount of the new charge sale to the customer's account.
• Adds the amount of the charge to the old balance.
• Records the new balance in the storage location.
• Proceeds to the next sales slip for the customer or the next account.

Output. The output of this updating procedure is the new balances and data for the customers' accounts obtained in the fourth procedure of processing. This information is stored on magnetic tape.

Remittances on Account and Returned Items. The same general procedure is followed in recording remittances from customers and credits for returned items. However, instead of adding, the computer subtracts the amount of the payment or credit from the previous balance of the customer's account to obtain the new balance.

Daily Account Positions. Each morning the computer is used to print an alphabetic listing that shows each customer's name, address, account number, credit limit, and account balance.

To keep the customers' account balances within their credit limits, the salesclerks must receive approval from the credit department for all charge sales over $50. To get this approval, the salesclerk enters the customer's account number and amount of the purchase into a cathode-ray tube (CRT) display. One is illustrated in the margin. This initiates an automatic credit check. The approval is immediately printed on the CRT display, provided the new account balance does not exceed the approved credit limit.

Courtesy NCR Corporation

A CRT display can be used to make credit status checks and get credit approval.

Monthly Statements of Account.

Another procedure involving the accounts receivable is the preparation of a statement of account for each customer at the end of the month.

Origination. The names, addresses, and account numbers of all the customers are constant data stored on magnetic tape. As the accounts receivable are updated, the variable data for the month is recorded and stored on the tape.

Input. The constant data and variable data for the month are fed into the computer by a magnetic-tape unit.

Processing. The computer sorts through the accounts and transmits to the printer the data for those accounts having a balance.

Output. The output of this procedure is a printed monthly statement for each customer which shows the following information.

1 Customer's account number, name, and address.
2 Balance of the account at the beginning of the month.
3 Date, sales or remittance slip number, and amount of each charge sale.
4 Amount of each remittance or return made.
5 Balance of the account at the end of the month.

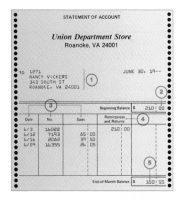

Activity A. Answer the following questions on computerized accounts receivable procedures. Refer to the accounts receivable procedures of the Union Department Store described on pages 611 to 613.

1. What types of information are included on a barcoded tag?

2. What procedure does the salesclerk follow to enter merchandise data automatically into the cash register?

3. What device is used by the salesclerk to get immediate credit approval for a customer?

4. In what three places are details of sales transactions stored?

5. What unit holds the cassette tapes?

6. How is the sales data for the three suburban stores transferred to the computer center at the main store?

7. What is the name of the program which the computer operator feeds into the computer's memory?

8. What types of information are contained in the daily account listing which the computer prints?

9. What information is included on the customer's monthly statement?

Topic 4 Problem

20-5. Christina Fashions has a medium-sized business data processing computer installation as shown in the illustration at the right.

a. Describe what procedures the computer would use to update Christina Fashions' accounts receivable.

b. Once this procedure is completed, what information would be stored on a magnetic tape?

c. How might Christina Fashions use the computer to help its customers stay within their credit limits?

Courtesy Mohawk Data Sciences Company

The Language of Business

Here are some basic terms that make up the language of business. Do you know the meaning of each?

automated accounting system	distributed data processing system	register	optical character reading (OCR) machine
electronic accounting system	data processing service center	adder	optical scanners
computer	word processing system	counter	optical type font
word processor	electronic mail	computer console	bar code
microprocessor	central processor	on-line	Universal Product Code (UPC)
microcomputer	storage unit	off-line	GIGO (garbage in, garbage out) principle
minicomputer	arithmetic/logic unit	machine language	bar-coded tag
diskette	control unit	medium	tag reader
mainframe	access time	card columns	data collector
program	internal storage	card rows	
programmer	auxiliary storage	zone rows	
error report	external storage	numeric rows	
item count		magnetic tape	
		bits	
		magnetic ink character recognition (MICR) machine	

Chapter 20   Questions

1. What is the major advantage of using an automated accounting system? The major disadvantage?
2. How are the size, speed, and storage capacity of a computer related to its cost?
3. Describe how a business might use both minicomputers and mainframe computers.

4. After what point can a computer function without people?
5. What are the purposes of error reports and item counts?
6. Describe several types of input devices. Several types of output devices.

Chapter 20   Problems

Problems for Chapter 20 are given in the *Working Papers and Chapter Problems for Part 3*. If you are using the workbook, do the problems in the space provided there.

Chapter 20   Management Cases

Selecting Computer Equipment. The selection of the right computer equipment is one of the more important decisions that management must make. Not only is a large sum of money involved, but the equipment selected will determine the types of information received from processing the data. In other words, management must consider several factors before selecting computer equipment. These factors include the following.

• Management's need for information
• Source of needed information
• Cost and capacity of equipment
• Need for computer personnel to operate equipment
• Need for special facilities
• Availability of service on equipment
• Need for support equipment to use with computer—card punches, CRT terminals, etc.

Case 20M-1. The Pecco Foodliner originated as a small grocery store serving the families in a suburb of St. Louis. Over the years the store has grown and gone through remodelings as a result of population increases and good business practices. Chris Riley, the owner, is now finalizing plans to move into a new building equipped with electronic cash registers. These cash registers will accumulate sales and inventory data on cassette tape that can be processed by a data processing service center. Each cash register will also have an optical scanner that will be built into the checkout station.

a. What types of information (reports) should Chris Riley expect to receive from the data processing service center? How often should he expect these reports?
b. What will be a major advantage of the optical scanner unit built into each checkout station?
c. Can you think of a major disadvantage of the optical scanner unit? Do you think customers might complain that the checkout lines move too fast?

Working Hint

Keyboarding Skills. Accuracy in using various types of keyboards is becoming more important as computer technology is applied to different problems. Keyboards are used on electronic devices such as typewriters, 24-hour bank tellers, calculators, computer terminals, and the ignition systems of some cars.

   The 24-hour bank teller shown at the right uses a keyboard to make deposits and withdrawals from bank accounts. The accuracy of transactions depends on following instructions.

Courtesy Citibank, N.A.

A Perpetual Inventory Subsystem

In order to maximize net income, managers and owners need information for controlling revenues and expenses. In a merchandising business, the right amount and type of merchandise must be on hand to sell. Yet too much merchandise unnecessarily ties up cash. You will now learn how special controls are used to protect merchandise inventory.

Topic 1
Inventory Management

A *What are the ways that businesses control their inventory?* One control for merchandise inventory is the use of perpetual inventory procedures. One perpetual inventory procedure is the use of inventory cards. These provide daily balances on all inventory items on hand. A **perpetual inventory procedure** updates the records of the quantities of items in inventory whenever items are added to or withdrawn from inventory. Earlier only updating the inventory cards whenever an item was sold or purchased was discussed. But the ledger accounts for Merchandise Inventory were not updated at the time of the sale. This chapter discusses methods for updating the inventory records and the Merchandise Inventory ledger account. The people, forms, procedures, and equipment used to provide continuous information about merchandise inventory make up a **perpetual inventory subsystem.** Businesses often use automated equipment to provide daily inventory reports. Large businesses may have thousands of separate items in merchandise inventory. Automated equipment such as cash registers equipped with optical scanners and computers are necessary to process their inventory data.

Point-of-sale cash registers are now commonly used in supermarkets.

Types of Inventory Methods

The two types of inventory methods are the periodic inventory method and the perpetual inventory method. As discussed in Part 2, many merchandising businesses do not update their Merchandise Inventory ledger account each time an item is purchased or sold. Nor is the cost of goods sold computed each time an item is sold. That method of accounting for inventory is called the periodic inventory method. The **periodic inventory method** involves accounting for the cost of goods sold only at the end or beginning of an accounting period.

Some businesses do not want to wait until the end of the accounting period to update the Merchandise Inventory account and to compute the cost of goods sold. Businesses that sell high-cost merchandise (like television sets) prefer to have their accounts updated each time an item is sold or purchased. Also, they want to know the cost of goods sold each time an item is sold. These businesses use the perpetual inventory method in their accounting system. A **perpetual inventory method** involves accounting for the cost of goods sold at the time of sale.

Two methods to control merchandise inventory are perpetual inventory and periodic inventory.

The Periodic Inventory Method

The accounting entries that are discussed in Part 2 are for the periodic inventory method. Let's review that method using T accounts.

Merchandise Inventory		112
19—		
July 1	6,000	

Beginning balance is 20 sets at $300 each ($6,000).

Beginning Inventory. In the periodic inventory method, the inventory on hand is recorded only at the end of the accounting period. The ending inventory for that period becomes the beginning inventory for the next period. Suppose a physical inventory was taken at the end of June and there were 20 Vista 576-19 television sets on hand at a cost of $300 each. Thus the Merchandise Inventory account would show a beginning balance of $6,000 on July 1. In this review we will use only one item—the 576-19 TVs. In actual practice, a business would have many more items.

Purchases. When new merchandise is purchased, the Purchases account is debited and either the Cash account or the Accounts Payable account is credited. Suppose that on July 15, ten TVs were purchased on credit at a cost of $300 each. Remember the Merchandise Inventory account is not used to record the purchase of merchandise. (In actual practice, the total of the purchases journal would be posted at the end of the month.)

Purchases		501	Accounts Payable		211
19—			19—		
July 15	3,000		July 15		3,000

Purchased 10 sets at $300 each ($3,000).

Cost of Goods Available for Sale. In the periodic inventory method, the cost of goods available for sale is computed only at the end of the accounting period. Two accounts are used to compute the amount: the beginning inventory amount from the Merchandise Inventory account and the additional merchandise purchased, which is shown in the Purchases account. Thus the cost of goods available for sale is $9,000 ($6,000 + $3,000). Note that no constant record of the actual amount of the merchandise inventory is available in the ledger.

Items available for sale are 30 (20 + 10). Cost of goods available for sale is $9,000 ($6,000 + $3,000).

Merchandise Inventory		112	Purchases		501
19—			19—		
July 1	6,000		July 15	3,000	

Sales. When merchandise is sold, the Sales account is credited and either the Cash account or the Accounts Receivable account is debited. Suppose that 16 TVs were sold on July 22. Assume that each set was sold for $500 and that each was sold on credit. The total amount of the sale is $8,000 ($500 × 16).

Notice that the sales price ($500) is greater than the cost price ($300). The difference is the amount needed to cover the operating

Accounts Receivable		111		Sales		401
19—				19—		
July 22	8,000			July 22		8,000

Sold 16 sets at $500 each ($8,000).

expenses and to provide a net income. (In actual practice, the total of the sales journal would be posted at the end of the month.)

Cost of Goods Sold. At the end of the accounting period (July 31), a physical inventory is taken. A total of 14 sets is on hand. The cost of each set is $300. Thus the July 31 merchandise inventory is $4,200 ($300 × 14). The July 1 Merchandise Inventory account balance and the Purchases account balance are also needed to compute the cost of goods sold. Thus the cost of goods sold is computed on the schedule of cost of goods sold. The amount of the cost of goods sold is then shown on the income statement.

Ruby Sales Company
Schedule of Cost of Goods Sold
For the Month Ended July 31, 19—

Beginning Inventory, July 1	6,000 00	← From Merchandise Inventory account
Plus: Purchases	3,000 00	← From Purchases account
Cost of Goods Available for Sale.	9,000 00	← Computed
Less: Ending Inventory, July 31.	4,200 00	← From physical inventory
Cost of Goods Sold.	4,800 00	← Computed

Gross Profit on Sales. The gross profit on sales is computed on the income statement at the end of the period. At this point, there is no record in the ledger of the gross profit on sales.

Ruby Sales Company
Income Statement
For the Month Ended July 31, 19—

Sales	8,000 00	← From Sales account
Cost of Goods Sold (See Schedule)	4,800 00	← Computed on Schedule
Gross Profit on Sales.	3,200 00	← Computed

As you can see, the Merchandise Inventory account has not been updated in the ledger. That will be done through an adjusting entry after the statements have been prepared. Also, the cost of goods sold does not appear in the ledger. The cost of goods sold is computed, rather than entered in the ledger.

Merchandise Inventory		112
19—		
July 1	6,000	

Beginning balance is 20 sets at $300 each ($6,000).

The Perpetual Inventory Method

Many of the shortcomings of the periodic inventory method are overcome by the perpetual inventory method. Let's review the perpetual inventory method by using the same transactions.

Beginning Inventory. There is no difference in showing the beginning inventory. The Merchandise Inventory account shows the beginning balance, which is the ending balance of the previous accounting period.

Purchases. In the perpetual inventory method, two differences appear.

- Purchases of merchandise are recorded in the Merchandise Inventory account. Thus additions to the inventory are now recorded as current assets, not as costs.
- No Purchases account is kept in the ledger.

On July 15, ten TVs were purchased on credit at a cost of $300 each. The total of the purchases is $3,000 ($300 × 10). The transaction would now be recorded as follows.

Merchandise Inventory		112		Accounts Payable		211
19—				19—		
July 1	6,000			July 15	3,000	
15	3,000					

Purchased 10 sets at $300 each ($3,000).

Merchandise Inventory		112
19—		
July 1	6,000	
15	3,000	
	9,000	

Items available for sale are 30 (20 + 10). Cost of goods available for sale is $9,000 (30 sets at $300 each).

Cost of Goods Available for Sale. The Merchandise Inventory account shows the cost of goods available for sale. There is no need to look at two accounts. The beginning inventory in the Merchandise Inventory account does not need to be added with the purchases recorded in the Purchases account. The balance of the Merchandise Inventory account is the cost of goods available for sale.

Sales. Under the perpetual inventory method, two entries are required for each sale.

1 The first entry records the revenue. This entry is the same as under the periodic inventory method.
2 The second entry records the cost of goods sold. A Cost of Goods Sold account is kept in the ledger. The entry transfers the cost of the items from the current asset Merchandise Inventory account to the Cost of Goods Sold account.

On July 22, 16 TVs were sold on credit for $500 each. The total sales were $8,000 ($500 × 16). The total cost of goods sold is $4,800 ($300 × 16). The transaction would be recorded as follows.

Accounts Receivable		111			Sales		401
19—						19—	
July 22	8,000					July 22	8,000

Sold 16 sets at $500 each ($8,000).

Cost of Goods Sold		501				Merchandise Inventory		112
19—				19—			19—	
July 22	4,800			July 1	6,000		July 22	4,800
				15	3,000			

The second entry would transfer the cost ($300 each) of the 16 TVs from the Merchandise Inventory account to the Cost of Goods Sold account.

Cost of Goods Sold. The second sales entry transferred the inventory cost from the asset account (Merchandise Inventory) to a cost account (Cost of Goods Sold). As a result, the cost of goods sold for each sale is shown directly in the ledger.

Cost of Goods Sold		501				Merchandise Inventory		112
19—				19—			19—	
July 22	4,800			July 1	6,000		July 22	4,800
				15	3,000			
				4,200	9,000			4,800

Cost of Goods Sold ($4,800) is shown in ledger. No schedule needs to be prepared to compute the amount.

The balance of the Cost of Goods Sold account is $4,800. The cost of the inventory on hand ($4,200) appears in the Merchandise Inventory account. You can easily check these figures. The TVs cost $300 each. There were 20 in the beginning inventory ($300 × 20 = $6,000). Then 10 additional sets were purchased ($300 × 10 = $3,000). Later, 16 were sold ($300 × 16 = $4,800). Thus 14 sets remain in inventory (20 + 10 − 16 = 14). The cost of the 14 TVs in inventory is $4,200 ($300 × 14).

Notice that a schedule of cost of goods sold is not needed. The amounts are shown in the ledger.

Perpetual inventory eliminates the need for a schedule of cost of goods sold.

Gross Profit on Sales. The gross profit on sales can easily be computed from amounts in the ledger.

A physical inventory on July 31, the end of the accounting period, showed 14 sets on hand. Since the TVs cost $300 each, the merchandise inventory is $4,200 ($300 × 14). This amount agrees with the

Ruby Sales Company
Income Statement
For the Month Ended July 31, 19—

From Sales Account ⟶
From Cost of Goods Sold Account ⟶
Computed ⟶

⟶Revenue From Sales	8,000 00	
⟶Cost of Goods Sold	4,800 00	
⟶Gross Profit on Sales		3,200 00

Gross profit on sales is computed on income statement in both periodic inventory method and perpetual inventory method.

balance in the Merchandise Inventory account. Thus the physical inventory is taken only to prove the accuracy of the inventory records.

Notice these advantages in using the perpetual inventory method.

- The cost of goods sold appears in the general ledger account. It is not computed.
- The cost of the merchandise sold is matched against the revenue from the merchandise sold.
- A physical inventory is taken. But the inventory is counted to check the accuracy of the inventory records. It is not taken to compute the ending inventory balance on the cost of goods sold.

Activity A. Explain how each of the following items would be handled in a periodic inventory method and a perpetual inventory method. Use a table like the one at the right.

1. Account containing beginning inventory?
2. Number of entries required to record sales?
3. General ledger account or accounts credited for sales on credit?
4. General ledger account or accounts debited for sales on credit?
5. Is cost of goods available for sale shown in ledger or is it computed?
6. Is amount of ending inventory shown in the general ledger?
7. Is cost of goods shown in the general ledger or is it computed?
8. Is gross profit on sales shown in the general ledger or is it computed?

9. Must a schedule of cost of goods sold be prepared?
10. On which statement is revenue from sales reported?
11. On which statement is gross profit from sales reported?
12. Is cost of goods sold reported on income statement?

Item	Periodic Inventory Method	Perpetual Inventory Method
EXAMPLE: Account debited when merchandise is purchased?	Purchases	Merchandise Inventory

Features of the Perpetual Inventory Method

B *Are the entries for sales the only differences between the perpetual inventory method and the periodic inventory method?* No, the entries for returns and allowances, discounts, and transportation are also different. The features of the perpetual inventory method are now explained.

• A **Merchandise Inventory account** is used to record *all* costs of purchases. The following accounts are *not* used in a perpetual inventory subsystem: Purchases, Purchases Returns and Allowances, Purchases Discount, and Transportation In. All these items are recorded as increases or decreases to the Merchandise Inventory account.

INVENTORY LEDGER CARD

STOCK NO. _114-2-4_
ITEM _Warm-Up Suits_
LOCATION _Department - Sportswear_
Section - Track and Field

REORDER QUANTITY _12_   REORDER POINT _5_

DATE	REF.	RECEIVED			ISSUED			BALANCE		
		UNITS	COST	TOTAL	UNITS	COST	TOTAL	UNITS	COST	TOTAL

Inventory ledger is a subsidiary ledger.

• A subsidiary inventory ledger is kept. An **inventory ledger** is a subsidiary ledger that provides a daily balance for each item in the inventory. The ledger includes accounts for each type of inventory item. The total of these accounts must always equal the balance of the Merchandise Inventory account. Thus the Merchandise Inventory account becomes a controlling account. The accounts are usually kept on cards so that they can be stored in an open tub file as shown above in the margin and are easily available for posting. The inventory ledger is updated to show daily increases and decreases in inventory items.

• The Merchandise Inventory account in the general ledger becomes a controlling account. The total of the inventory ledger cards in the subsidiary ledger must equal the balance of the Merchandise Inventory account. The balance of the Merchandise Inventory account is reported on the balance sheet.

• **A Cost of Goods Sold account** is used to record the cost of sales. The Cost of Goods Sold account has a debit balance and is reported on the income statement.

• The name of the purchases journal is changed to the merchandise inventory journal in a perpetual inventory subsystem. The **merchandise inventory journal** is used to record all purchases of merchan-

Merchandise Inventory	112
Beginning Inventory Purchases Transportation In	Purchases Returns and Allowances Purchases Discount

Open Tub File

Courtesy Esselte Pendaflex Corporation

General Ledger

Merchandise Inventory	*112*
Balance	

Subsidiary Ledger

Inventory Ledger Card	Inventory Ledger Card
Total	Total

Perpetual Inventory System
Chart of Accounts

Assets
111 Accounts Receivable
112 Merchandise Inventory

Liabilities
211 Accounts Payable
216 Sales Tax Payable

Revenue
401 Sales
402 Sales Returns and Allowances
403 Sales Discount

Costs and Expenses
501 Cost of Goods Sold
530 Merchandise Loss

dise on credit. When merchandise is purchased on credit, the Merchandise Inventory account is debited and the Accounts Payable account is credited.

• A cost of goods sold journal is used in a perpetual inventory subsystem. The **cost of goods sold journal** is used to record the costs of goods as they are sold. When goods are sold, the Cost of Goods Sold account is debited. The Merchandise Inventory account is credited.

• The perpetual inventory method eliminates the need to prepare a schedule of cost of goods sold. The amount is shown in the Cost of Goods Sold account.

• An adjusting entry is not needed to update the inventory at the end of the accounting period. The balance in the Merchandise Inventory account is updated each time purchases and sales transactions take place.

Controls

A plan for controlling inventory includes the principle for controlling both purchases and sales. The principles for controlling purchases are discussed in Chapter 13. The principles for controlling sales are discussed in Chapter 14.

Other principles for controlling inventory may also be incorporated into a perpetual inventory subsystem.

• Merchandise that is in season should be on display or stored in an area limited to authorized personnel. Merchandise that is out of season should be returned to the supplier, marked down for quick sale, or stored for next year's sales.

• A physical inventory must be taken at least once a year to verify the perpetual inventory records. This actual counting of the inventory may be completed at the end of the accounting period. Or it may also be completed on a departmental basis throughout the year.

• Inventory records should be kept by employees other than the ones responsible for selling the merchandise. Thus inventory records should be kept in the accounting department in order to ensure a division of responsibility.

• The inventory ledger should be verified at regular intervals throughout the accounting period. This is done by comparing the total of the inventory ledger cards to the balance of the Merchandise Inventory account.

Activity B. Answer the following questions about the perpetual inventory subsystem. Refer to the text, margin notes, and illustrations on pages 622 to 624.
1. What costs are debited to the Merchandise Inventory account? What costs are credited to the account?

2. On which financial statement is the Cost of Goods Sold account reported? Merchandise Inventory account?
3. What is the controlling account for the inventory ledger?

4. Which journal is used to record the purchase of merchandise on credit?
5. How often must a physical inventory be completed when perpetual inventory procedures are used?

6. How is the inventory ledger proved?
7. In which department should inventory records be kept?

Purchases Transactions

C *Are special accounting procedures needed to process purchases in a perpetual inventory subsystem?* Yes, the accounting procedures for processing purchases in a perpetual inventory subsystem are different from procedures used with the periodic inventory method. The transactions involving purchases of merchandise using periodic inventory procedures were discussed on pages 617 to 622. Purchases transactions using perpetual inventory procedures are fully described here.

Purchases for Cash

When merchandise is purchased for cash, the Merchandise Inventory account is debited. The Cash account is credited. The purchase is recorded as a debit to Merchandise Inventory in order to maintain a daily balance of inventory. (Remember that a Purchases account is not used in the perpetual inventory subsystem.) Each time the Merchandise Inventory account is debited, the inventory ledger must also be updated.

The check stub is the source document for journalizing the purchase of merchandise for cash. The entry is recorded in the cash payments journal because the transaction involved a credit to cash.

Merchandise Purchased for Cash
• Debit: Merchandise Inventory
• Credit: Cash

May 1: The Franks Department Store purchases merchandise for $500 and immediately issues Check 611 in payment.

What Happens	Accounting Rule	Entry
The asset *Merchandise Inventory* increases by $500.	To increase an asset, debit the account.	Debit: Merchandise Inventory, $500 (also the inventory ledger account).
The asset *Cash* decreases by $500.	To decrease an asset, credit the account.	Credit: Cash, $500.

Merchandise purchased for cash.

CASH PAYMENTS JOURNAL										Page	4
DATE		ACCOUNT DEBITED	EXPLANATION	CHECK NO.	POST. REF.	GENERAL LEDGER DEBIT	ACCOUNTS PAYABLE DEBIT	MERCHANDISE INVENTORY CREDIT	NET CASH CREDIT		
19— May	1	Merch. Inv.	Carleton Co. Inv. 8567	611	112/ √	500 00			500 00		

General Ledger

Cash	101		Merchandise Inventory	112
19—			19—	
May 1	500		May 1	500

Inventory Ledger

	Inventory Ledger Cards
	19—
	May 1	500

Purchases on Credit

A purchase of merchandise on credit is recorded in the merchandise inventory journal. The entry requires a debit to the Merchandise Inventory account and a credit to Accounts Payable. (Remember that the merchandise inventory journal replaces the purchases journal when a perpetual inventory method is used.)

In actual practice, the debit to the Merchandise Inventory account is posted as part of the journal total at the end of the month. The transaction is shown here as an individual amount to help you understand what is happening when merchandise is purchased on credit. The Franks Department Store's purchase on credit from the Newman Company is used to illustrate recording purchases on credit.

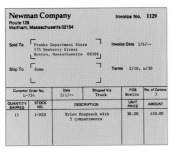

Purchase Invoice

May 8: The Franks Department Store purchases merchandise from Newman Company for $450 on credit.

What Happens	Accounting Rule	Entry
The asset *Merchandise Inventory* increases by $450.	To increase an asset, debit the account.	Debit: Merchandise Inventory, $450 (also the inventory ledger account).
The liability *Accounts Payable* increases by $450.	To increase a liability, credit the account.	Credit: Accounts Payable, $450 (also the creditor's account).

The purchase invoice is the source document for recording purchases on credit. The Franks Department Store's purchase invoice is illustrated in the margin. The table above illustrates what happens when the Franks Department Store purchases merchandise on credit from the Newman company.

The invoice data must also be posted to the merchandise inventory ledger and to the accounts payable ledger. Thus two check marks ($\sqrt{}$ / $\sqrt{}$) must be entered in the Posting Reference column of the merchandise inventory journal.

MERCHANDISE INVENTORY JOURNAL   **Page**   *4*

DATE		ACCOUNT CREDITED	INVOICE		TERMS	POST. REF.	AMOUNT
			NO.	DATE			
19—							
May	8	Newman Company	1129	5/6	2/10, n/30	211/ ✓ / ✓	450 00

General Ledger

Accounts Payable	211
	19—
	May 8 450

Merchandise Inventory	112
19—	
May 1 500	
8 450	

Accounts Payable Ledger

Newman Company

	19—
	May 8 450

Inventory Ledger

Inventory Ledger Cards	
19—	
May 1 500	
8 450	

Merchandise purchased on credit.

Transportation In

Freight paid on merchandise purchased is recorded in the cash payments journal. To record the entry in the cash payments journals, do the following: debit the Merchandise Inventory account and credit the Cash account. The reason why the Merchandise Inventory account is debited is because all costs of merchandise are summarized in this one account. It is important to note that a separate Transportation In account is not used in a perpetual inventory subsystem.

To illustrate how to record freight paid on merchandise, the Franks Department Store is once again used. A trucking company, Flyte Express, will transport the merchandise purchased to the Franks Department Store.

The invoice from the trucking company is the source document for issuing the check. The entry is recorded in the cash payments journal since it involves a credit to cash.

Since the Merchandise Inventory account is affected, the freight costs must also be added to the inventory ledger accounts.

May 9: The Franks Department Store issues Check 617 for $65 to pay transportation on merchandise ordered from Yates.

What Happens	Accounting Rule	Entry
Transportation charges increase the cost of *Merchandise Inventory* by $65.	To increase an asset, debit the account.	Debit: Merchandise Inventory, $65 (also the inventory ledger account).
The asset *Cash* decreases by $65.	To decrease an asset, credit the account.	Credit: Cash, $65.

		CASH PAYMENTS JOURNAL							Page 4
DATE		ACCOUNT DEBITED	EXPLANATION	CHECK NO.	POST. REF.	GENERAL LEDGER DEBIT	ACCOUNTS PAYABLE DEBIT	MERCHANDISE INVENTORY CREDIT	NET CASH CREDIT
19— May	1	Merchandise Inv. . . .	Carleton Co., Inv. 8567	611	112/√	500 00			500 00
	9	Merchandise Inv. . . .	Flyte Express	617	112/√	65 00			65 00

Transportation In for cash.

General Ledger

Cash   101

| 19—
May 1 | 500 |
| 9 | 65 |

Merchandise Inventory   112

19— May 1	500
8	450
9	65

Inventory Ledger

Inventory Ledger Cards

19— May 1	500
8	450
9	65

Purchases Returns and Allowances

Credit for Purchases Returns and Allowances
- Debit: Accounts Payable
- Credit: Merchandise Inventory

Transactions involving credit for merchandise returned or allowances on merchandise are recorded in the general journal. The entry is a debit to the Accounts Payable account and a credit to the Merchandise Inventory account. The creditor's account in the accounts payable ledger is also debited. The inventory ledger account is also credited.

The credit memorandum is the source document for recording a purchase return or allowance. A return or allowance involving merchandise already paid for may result in a cash refund. In this instance, the entry would be recorded in the cash receipts journal. Cash would be debited, and Merchandise Inventory would be credited. The inventory ledger would also be credited.

May 11: The Franks Department Store received Credit Memorandum CM-7 for $100 from the Newman Company as an allowance for damaged merchandise purchased on credit.

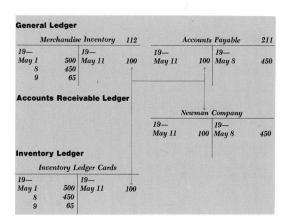

Credit Memorandum

What Happens	Accounting Rule	Entry
The liability *Accounts Payable* decreases by $100.	To decrease a liability, debit the account.	Debit: Accounts Payable, $100 (also the creditor's account).
The asset *Merchandise Inventory* decreases by $100.	To decrease an asset, credit the account.	Credit: Merchandise Inventory, $100 (also the inventory ledger account).

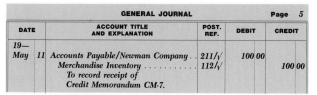

Purchases returned for credit.

Purchase Discounts

Payments to creditors not involving purchase discounts are recorded as described in Chapter 13. In the general ledger, the Accounts Payable account is debited and the Cash account is credited for the amount paid.

Payments to creditors that involve purchase discounts are recorded in the cash payments journal. The Accounts Payable account is debited for the full amount of the invoice. The Cash account is credited for the amount paid. The Merchandise Inventory account, however, is credited for the amount of the cash discount.

Note that the money column headings in the cash payments journal have been changed. The Purchase Discount Credit column is now called a Merchandise Inventory Credit column.

May 18: The Franks Department Store issues Check 624 for $343 to Newman Company to pay Invoice 1129 for $450 less returned merchandise ($100) and purchase discount of $7.

What Happens	Accounting Rule	Entry
The liability *Accounts Payable* decreases by $350.	To decrease a liability, debit the account.	Debit: Accounts Payable, $350 (also the creditor's account).
The asset *Merchandise Inventory* decreases by $7.	To decrease an asset, credit the account.	Credit: Merchandise Inventory, $7 (also the inventory ledger account).
The asset *Cash* decreases by $343.	To decrease an asset, credit the account.	Credit: Cash, $343.

CASH PAYMENTS JOURNAL								Page 4
DATE	ACCOUNT DEBITED	EXPLANATION	CHECK NO.	POST. REF.	GENERAL LEDGER DEBIT	ACCOUNTS PAYABLE DEBIT	MERCHANDISE INVENTORY CREDIT	NET CASH CREDIT
19— May 1	Merchandise Inv. . . .	Carleton Co., Inv. 8567	611	112/√	500 00			500 00
9	Merchandise Inv. . . .	Flyte Express	617	112/√	65 00			65 00
18	Accts. Pay./Newman Co.	Invoice 1129	624	211/√		350 00	7 00	343 00

Purchases Discount

General Ledger

Cash		101
19— May 1	500	
9	65	
18	343	

Accounts Payable		211	
19— May 11	100	19— May 8	450
18	350		

Merchandise Inventory		112	
19— May 1	500	19— May 11	100
8	450	18	7
9	65		

Accounts Payable Ledger

Newman Company			
19— May 11	100	19— May 8	450
18	350		

Inventory Ledger

Inventory Ledger Cards

19— May 1	500	19— May 11	100
8	450	18	7
9	65		

Summary of Transactions Involving Purchases

The flowchart on the next page summarizes the various types of transactions involved with purchases in a perpetual inventory method.

RECORDING PURCHASE TRANSACTIONS INVOLVING A PERPETUAL INVENTORY SUBSYSTEM

Transaction	General Ledger			Subsidiary Ledgers	
				Accounts Payable	Inventory
	Cash	Accounts Payable	Merchandise Inventory	Individual Creditor's Account	Individual Ledger Card
Purchase for Cash	credit: xxxx		debit: xxxx		debit: xxxx
Purchases Returns and Allowances for Cash	debit: xxxx		credit: xxxx		credit: xxxx
Purchase on Credit		credit: xxxx	debit: xxxx	credit: xxxx	debit: xxxx
Transportation In for Cash	credit: xxxx		debit: xxxx		debit: xxxx
Purchases Returns and Allowances for Credit		debit: xxxx	credit: xxxx	debit: xxxx	credit: xxxx
Payment Without Purchase Discount	credit: xxxx	debit: xxxx		debit: xxxx	
Payment With Purchase Discount	credit: xxx	debit: xxxx	credit: x	debit: xxxx	credit: x

Activity C. For each of the following transactions, indicate the accounts to be debited and credited in a perpetual inventory method.

EXAMPLE: Purchase of supplies for cash.
Debit: Supplies.   ***Credit: Cash***

1. Purchase of merchandise for cash.

2. Payment of freight on merchandise purchased.

3. Purchase of merchandise on credit.

4. Payment of merchandise bought on credit with a deduction for purchase discount.

5. Receipt of credit for merchandise returned to supplier.

Sales Transactions

D *Are special accounting procedures needed to process sales in a perpetual inventory subsystem?* Yes, the procedures are different from those used in the periodic inventory method. For example, two entries are required each time merchandise is sold. The first entry is needed to record the revenue earned on the sale. The second entry is needed to record the cost of the goods sold.

Sales for Cash

If the sale is for cash, the first entry is recorded in the cash receipts journal. Cash sales involve a debit to the Cash account and credits to the Sales account and Sales Tax Payable account.

Sales for cash are recorded in the cash receipts journal. In this instance, the Cash account is debited. The Sales account and Sales Tax Payable account are credited. The sales invoice is the source document used to record sales transactions.

Sales Invoice

May 3: The Franks Department Store sells merchandise on Invoice 315 for $400 cash plus $20 sales tax. The merchandise cost was $300.

What Happens	Accounting Rule	Entry
The asset *Cash* increases by $420.	To increase an asset, debit the account.	Debit: Cash, $420.
Revenue increases owner's equity by $400.	To increase owner's equity, credit the account.	Credit: Sales, $400.
The liability *Sales Tax Payable* increases by $20.	To increase a liability, credit the account.	Credit: Sales Tax Payable, $20.

Cash sale with sales tax.

						GENERAL	ACCOUNTS	SALES	NET
CASH RECEIPTS JOURNAL								Page	4
DATE		ACCOUNT CREDITED	EXPLANATION	POST. REF.		GENERAL LEDGER CREDIT	ACCOUNTS RECEIVABLE CREDIT	SALES DISCOUNT DEBIT	NET CASH DEBIT
19— May	3	Sales . . . . Sales Tax Payable . .	Cash sale, Invoice 315	401 216		400 00 20 00			420 00

General Ledger

Cash	101	Sales	401	Sales Tax Payable	216
19— May 3	420	19— May 3	400	19— May 3	20

The second entry to record the cost of the goods sold is recorded in a cost of goods sold journal. The Cost of Goods Sold account is debited, and the Merchandise Inventory account is credited.

The source document for recording the cost of the merchandise sold is the sales invoice. In practice, a cost accounting clerk would "cost" the sales invoice. That is, the clerk checks the ledger card for the item in the subsidiary inventory ledger. The cost of the item is listed on the inventory card. This cost is written on the invoice, and the invoice data is posted to the inventory card. The sales invoices are posted daily to the subsidiary ledger. The total of the cost of goods sold journal, however, is posted only at the end of the month. At that time, the total of the Cost of Goods Sold column is posted as a credit to the Merchandise Inventory account and a debit to the Cost of Goods Sold account.

One advantage of using the Cost of Goods Sold account is that gross profit can be easily determined. For example, the gross profit on the transaction illustrated is $100 (sales of $400 − cost of goods sold of $300).

May 3: The Franks Department Store records the $300 cost of merchandise sold on Invoice 315.

What Happens	Accounting Rule	Entry
Cost of merchandise sold decreases owner's equity by $300.	To decrease owner's equity, debit the account.	Debit: Cost of Goods Sold, $300.
The asset *Merchandise Inventory* decreases by $300.	To decrease an asset, credit the account.	Credit: Merchandise Inventory, $300 (also the inventory ledger account).

COST OF GOODS SOLD JOURNAL			Page 4
DATE	INVOICE NUMBER	POST. REF.	INVOICE COST AMOUNT
19— May 3	315		300 00
31	Cost of Goods Sold Debit/Merchandise Inventory Credit	501/ 112	300 00

Cost of merchandise sold.

General Ledger

Cost of Goods Sold	501
19— May 3 300	

Merchandise Inventory	112
	19— May 3 300

Inventory Ledger

Inventory Ledger Cards

	19— May 3 300

Sales on Credit

The first entry for a sales on credit is recorded in the sales journal. The Accounts Receivable account is debited. The Sales account and Sales Tax Payable account are credited. The second entry would be recorded in the cost of goods sold journal. The entry would also be posted to the inventory ledger card in the subsidiary ledger.

Sales Returns

Two entries are also needed when merchandise is returned by a customer. The first entry records the decrease in owner's equity caused by the decrease in revenue. The second entry records the decrease in the Cost of Goods Sold account. When a credit memorandum is issued, the two entries are recorded in the general journal.

May 5: The Franks Department Store issues Credit Memorandum CM-119 for $30 plus $1.50 sales tax for merchandise returned by Robert Berg. Cost of the goods returned is $20.

What Happens	Accounting Rule	Entry
The reduction in revenue caused by a sales return decreases owner's equity by $30.	To decrease owner's equity, debit the account.	Debit: Sales Returns and Allowances, $30.
The liability *Sales Tax Payable* decreases by $1.50.	To decrease a liability, debit the account.	Debit: Sales Tax Payable, $1.50.
The asset *Accounts Receivable* decreases by $31.50.	To decrease an asset, credit the account.	Credit: Accounts Receivable, $31.50 (also the customer's account).

May 5: The Franks Department Store records the $20 cost of merchandise returned on Credit Memorandum CM-119.

What Happens	Accounting Rule	Entry
The asset *Merchandise Inventory* increases by $20.	To increase an asset, debit the account.	Debit: Merchandise Inventory, $20 (also the inventory ledger account).
Merchandise returned reduces the *Cost of Goods Sold* and increases *Owner's Equity*.	To increase owner's equity, credit the account.	Credit: Cost of Goods Sold, $20.

		GENERAL JOURNAL			Page 4
DATE		ACCOUNT TITLE AND EXPLANATION	POST. REF.	DEBIT	CREDIT
19—					
May	5	Sales Returns and Allowances........	402	30 00	
		Sales Tax Payable	216	1 50	
		Accounts Receivable/Robert Berg ...	111/ √		31 50
		Credit Memorandum CM-119.			
	5	Merchandise Inventory..............	112/ √	20 00	
		Cost of Goods Sold..............	501		20 00
		Credit Memorandum CM-119.			

Sales return for credit.

General Ledger

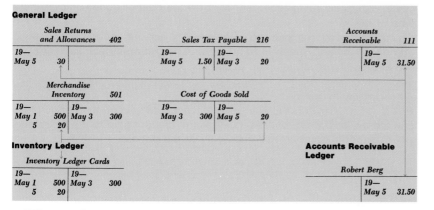

Sales Returns and Allowances		402		Sales Tax Payable			216		Accounts Receivable		111
19— May 5	30			19— May 5	1.50	19— May 3	20		19— May 5	31.50	

Merchandise Inventory		501		Cost of Goods Sold			
19— May 1 5	500 20	19— May 3	300	19— May 3	300	19— May 5	20

Inventory Ledger

Inventory Ledger Cards

19— May 1 5	500 20	19— May 3	300

Accounts Receivable Ledger

Robert Berg

19— May 5	31.50

When cash is refunded, the Cash account is credited instead of the Accounts Receivable account. Cash refunds are recorded in the cash payments journal.

Sales Allowances

When a sales allowance (reduction) is granted, only one entry is made. Since no merchandise is returned, the Merchandise Inventory account is not affected. Thus the sales allowance reduces revenue only. The cost of goods sold and the merchandise inventory are not affected.

Thus a sales allowance is recorded the same as in the periodic inventory method. The entry is recorded in the general journal. The Sales Returns and Allowances and the Sales Tax Payable accounts are debited. Either the Cash or Accounts Receivable account is credited.

Sales Discounts

Sales discounts are recorded the same under both inventory methods. Sales discounts decrease sales revenue. No merchandise was returned. Neither the Merchandise Inventory account nor the Cost of Goods Sold account is affected. Record the transaction in the cash receipts journal.

Activity D. For each of the transactions below, indicate which account is debited and which is credited. There is no sales tax.
EXAMPLE: Sold merchandise for cash.
Debit: Cash, Cost of Goods Sold.
Credit: Sales, Merchandise Inventory.
1. Sold merchandise for cash.
2. Sold merchandise on credit.
3. Returned merchandise sold for credit.
4. Returned merchandise sold for cash.
5. Granted allowance for merchandise sold on credit.
6. Issued check for allowance on merchandise sold.
7. Received cash from customer on account without sales discount.
8. Received cash from customer on account with a sales discount.

Accounting Concepts:
Perpetual Inventory Method. Procedures may be established to provide records that show the current number of items on hand and their

costs, and accounting records that show the cost of goods sold at the time of the sale.

Control. Procedures must be established to ensure accuracy, honesty, and efficiency and speed in handling and recording assets, liabilities, owner's equity, revenues, and expenses.

Accounting Principle:
Net Cost of Purchases. The generally accepted accounting principle is that the *net cost of purchases* includes the amount paid to the seller plus any transportation charges for delivery of the goods.

Topic 1 Problems

21-1. The accounting department for United Auto Parts processed the following transactions involving merchandise purchases.

June 2 Received Invoice 1137, dated May 29, from Champion, Inc., for $550; terms 2/10, n/30.
    4 Issued Check 614 for $380 to Pier Imports for merchandise purchased.
    6 Issued Check 615 for $70 to Eagle Express for freight charges on merchandise purchased from Champion, Inc.
    6 Issued Check 616 for $539 to Champion, Inc., to pay the May 29 invoice for $550 less a cash discount of $11.
    8 Received Invoice W791, dated June 5, from Packard Company for $700; terms 2/10, n/30.
    12 Received Credit Memorandum CM-C461 for $100 from Packard Company for goods returned.
    12 Issued Check 617 for $588 to Packard Company to pay Invoice W791, less merchandise returned and cash discount.

a. Open general ledger accounts for Cash, Merchandise Inventory, and Accounts Payable.
b. Using a cash payments journal, merchandise inventory journal, and general journal, record the transactions for June.

c. Prove, total, and rule the journals.
d. Post the totals from the journal.
NOTE: Save your working papers for further use in Topic Problem 21-2.

21-2. United Auto Parts processed the following transactions involving sales and cost of goods sold.

June 3 Issued Invoice 611 to Myron Rapp for cash sale of $45 plus $2.25 sales tax.
    3 Recorded cost of goods sold to Myron Rapp for $31.50.
    3 Recorded cash sales of $1,400 plus $70 sales tax for the day.
    3 Recorded cost of goods sold for $980.
    4 Refunded $10 plus sales tax ($0.50) to Myron Rapp for merchandise returned.
    4 Recorded decrease in cost of goods sold for merchandise returned of $7.00.

a. Open additional general ledger accounts for Sales, Cost of Goods Sold, Sales Tax Payable, and Sales Returns and Allowances.
b. Record the transactions in a cash receipts journal, general journal or cost of goods sold journal.
c. Prove, total, and rule the journals.
d. Post the totals from the journals.

Topic 2
The Inventory Ledger

A *Is it possible to determine the quantity of an item in stock without actually counting the item?* Yes, but only if perpetual inventory procedures are used. Perpetual inventory procedures allow a business to maintain a daily balance for each item in the inventory. The daily balances for inventory items are on cards in the inventory ledger.

As you learned previously, the inventory ledger is a subsidiary ledger that provides daily balances on all the items in the inventory. Information provided on each inventory card includes the quantity of the item purchased and sold, the cost of the item, and the balance in stock. The total of all the cards in the inventory ledger must always equal the balance in Merchandise Inventory, the controlling account.

Two other subsidiary ledgers are the accounts receivable ledger and the accounts payable ledger that are discussed in Chapters 13 and 14. A business using a perpetual inventory subsystem may have four subsidiary ledgers or more—an accounts receivable ledger, an accounts payable ledger, a plant and equipment asset ledger, and an inventory ledger.

Four Subsidiary Ledgers in the Perpetual Inventory Procedure
- Accounts receivable ledger
- Accounts payable ledger
- Plant and equipment asset ledger
- Inventory ledger

The Inventory Card

As mentioned in Part 2, inventory cards should be kept by an employee in the accounting department. This way the employee updating the inventory records is not the same employee who handles the goods—stock clerks and salesclerks handle the goods. Having an employee in the accounting department keep the inventory cards results in a division of responsibility and good internal control. An inventory card used by Franks Department Store is shown here.

INVENTORY LEDGER CARD

STOCK NO. *114-2-4*

ITEM *Warm-Up Suits*

LOCATION *Department – Sportswear*
Section – Track and Field

REORDER QUANTITY *12*   REORDER POINT *5*

DATE	REF.	RECEIVED			ISSUED			BALANCE		
		UNITS	COST	TOTAL	UNITS	COST	TOTAL	UNITS	COST	TOTAL
19-- May 3	9972	12	14 00	168 00				12	14 00	168 00
16	5114				4	14 00	56 00	8	14 00	112 00
28	5140				5	14 00	70 00	3	14 00	42 00

A separate account is kept for each type of item.

Notice that the warm-up suits have the stock number 114-2-4. The number 114 refers to all cotton warm-up suits purchased from one supplier. The number 2 refers to size (medium), and the number 4 refers to the color (red). Every size and color of each item in the inventory is assigned a stock number.

Other information recorded on the inventory card includes the name of the item and the location of the item in the store. The card also indicates the reorder point and the reorder quantity. For example, when the inventory of these medium-sized, red warm-up suits drops to five or less (the reorder point), a new order will be placed. The new order will be for the quantity identified as the reorder quantity. Thus, each additional order will be for 12 warm-up suits.

Posting to the Inventory Ledger

The inventory ledger is updated by posting purchases and sales of each inventory item.

Purchases

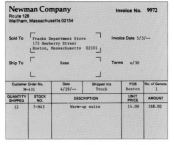

Cost of each item is posted to card in subsidiary ledger.

Purchases of a specific inventory item are posted to the inventory ledger. A copy of the purchase invoice that has been checked against the receiving report is used to do this. This invoice also shows the cost of the item. Notice that 12 warm-up suits were purchased on May 3. The following procedure is used to post to the inventory ledger.

• The quantity received is entered in the Units column of the Received section on the inventory card. During May, Franks Department Store processed one purchase of 12 warm-up suits.

• The unit cost of the item purchased is entered in the Cost column. The unit cost is found on the purchase invoice. The illustration of the inventory card on page 637 shows that the 12 warm-up suits were purchased at a unit cost of $14.

• The balance on the inventory card is computed after each purchase is posted. Thus the May 3 balance for the warm-up suits was $168.

Two checkmarks show posting to two subsidiary ledgers.

			INVOICE				
MERCHANDISE INVENTORY JOURNAL							Page 4
DATE		ACCOUNT CREDITED	NO.	DATE	TERMS	POST. REF.	AMOUNT
19— May	3	Newman Company	9972	5/3	n/30	√ / √	168 00

The total of the merchandise inventory journal is posted to the general ledger at the end of the month.

Sales

Sales of inventory items are posted to the inventory ledger using the sales invoice. The inventory card found on page 637 shows the two sales totaling nine suits during May. The following procedure is used to post to the inventory ledger.

• The sale of an inventory item is posted from the sales invoice or from merchandise tags. If tags are used, they must be removed from each item at the time of sale. The tags are then sorted for easy posting to the inventory cards. A sale of an inventory item is entered in the Issued section of the inventory card.

• After each sale is posted, a new balance is computed. For example, four warm-up suits were sold on May 16. This left a balance of eight suits at a total cost of $112. Notice that a total of nine warm-up suits were sold during May.

Cost of each item is needed in order to record cost of goods sold.

SALES JOURNAL								Page 20
DATE	INVOICE NO.	ACCOUNT DEBITED	TERMS	POST. REF.	ACCOUNTS RECEIVABLE DEBIT	SALES TAX PAYABLE CREDIT	SALES CREDIT	
19— May 16	5114	Shore Sports Shops	n/30	√	80 00			80 00

First entry records revenue.

COST OF GOODS SOLD JOURNAL				Page 4
DATE	INVOICE NUMBER	POST. REF.	INVOICE COST AMOUNT	
19— May 16	5114		56 00	

Second entry records cost of goods sold.

Postings to the Merchandise Inventory controlling account in the general ledger are made at the end of each month from the cost of goods sold journal.

Purchase Discounts and Purchases Returns and Allowances

When purchase discounts are taken, the Merchandise Inventory account is credited for the amount of the purchase discount. As a result, the inventory ledger must reflect the reduced cost of the item purchased.

Purchases returns and allowances must also be posted to the inventory ledger. Recall that purchases returns and purchases allowances are credited to the Merchandise Inventory account. Whatever entry affects the controlling account must also be posted to the inventory ledger.

In actual practice, the cash discounts are usually recorded at the same time that the invoice is recorded. This assures that all invoices will be paid in time to take the discount. This procedure is covered in advanced courses. To keep the illustration simple, assume there was no cash discount involved with the purchase of the warm-up suits.

Purchases returns and allowances would be posted as follows.

• A purchases return is posted from the credit memorandum and is entered in the Issued section of the inventory card. This is done because the item has been removed from inventory.

• The allowance granted on an item is also posted from the credit memorandum. The allowance does not affect the quantity on hand. It only affects the cost. Thus the cost in the Cost column of the Received section is corrected to show the reduced cost per unit.

Sales Discounts, Returns, and Allowances

As you know, sales discounts and sales allowances affect only revenue. They do not affect the Merchandise Inventory account. Therefore, they are not posted to the subsidiary ledger. Sales returns affect both revenue and merchandise inventory.

Activity A. Answer the following questions on the inventory card. Refer to the inventory card on page 637.
1. What is the item description?
2. Where are these items located in the store?
3. What is the reorder point? Reorder quantity?

4. How many units are in stock on May 3?
5. What is the unit cost of each item in stock on May 3? What is the total cost?
6. How many units are sold on May 16? May 28?

Proving the Inventory Ledger

B *How is the inventory ledger proved?* Two methods are used to prove the inventory ledger. One method is to compare the total of the inventory ledger to the balance in the Merchandise Inventory account—the controlling account. If all transactions have been journalized and posted correctly, these two amounts will be equal. The inventory ledger can be proved using this method at any time during the accounting period.

Another method for proving the inventory ledger is to complete a physical inventory. This method involves counting all the items in stock. Sound accounting practice requires that all businesses complete a physical inventory at least once a year.

A physical inventory should be completed at least once a year.

Counting the Inventory. Businesses usually count their inventories at the end of each accounting period. Some businesses may even close for a day or two to count the inventory without interruptions. Other businesses count their inventories at different times throughout the accounting period. In these businesses, one department may be counted in June, another department in July, and so on, until the entire inventory is verified. This procedure allows the counting to be completed without disrupting the operation of the entire business at one time.

The procedures for counting inventory will vary with different types of businesses. For example, procedures for counting the inventory in a jewelry store are different from those used in a building supply store. Each item in the jewelry store will be counted one by one. In a building supply store, the larger items will be counted one by one. However, it is not practical to count small items, such as loose nails, in this manner. These types of items will be weighed and recorded by the pound.

Specific procedures to ensure an accurate and complete count must be developed for completing a physical inventory. These procedures include the following.

- Complete instructions for counting the inventory should be developed and distributed to the employees doing the counting. These instructions should explain that *all* inventory items must be counted or weighed. This may involve unpacking boxes or cartons to count the contents of each or putting items on a scale to weigh them.
- A prenumbered **inventory tag,** illustrated here, should be used to record the stock number, quantity, price, and description of each item counted. All tags must be accounted for when the inventory is done.
- Assigned employees should count specific parts of the inventory.
- Employees counting inventory should work in pairs. As one counts the inventory items, the other writes the information on the tag. As each tag is completed, the tag is signed by the counter and left on the items counted.
- A third employee should be responsible for checking the accuracy of the counters. This employee should recount selected items to make sure the counters are doing an accurate count. This third employee also checks to make sure that all items—even those that are still packed in boxes—are being counted.
- After the inventory in each section has been counted and verified, the tags are collected. Information from these tags is recorded on an **inventory sheet,** illustrated on page 642. The employee preparing the inventory sheets also enters the cost of each merchandise item. The inventory sheet is a schedule of the inventory subsidiary ledger.
- Information on the inventory tags is also compared with the quantities and costs recorded on the inventory ledger cards.
- All costs, extensions, and totals are verified for accuracy.
- All inventory sheets are totaled to determine the amount of the merchandise inventory.

No. **75**
Description: _Warm-Up Suits_
Location: _Sportswear Dept._
Counted By: _A. Jackson_
Checked By: _J. R._

Stock No.	Quantity	Sales Price
114-2-4	6	$20.00

FRANKS DEPARTMENT STORE
175 Newberry Street
Boston, Massachusetts 02101

Date *Dec. 31, 19—*   Sheet No. *10*

Counted By *a. Jackson*		Recorded By *P. Reilly*		Figured By *L. Carr*		
STOCK. NO.	QUANTITY	DESCRIPTION		SALES PRICE	UNIT PRICE	EXTENSION
114-2-4	6	*Warm-Up Suits*		20 00	14 00	84 00
					TOTAL	2,030 00

Each type of item must be costed.

• A cutoff date must be established for the inventory. In other words, items purchased after the end of the accounting period should not be included in the inventory. Further, items sold after the end of the accounting period should not be deducted from the inventory.

• Inventory items that are damaged or out of style should be counted separately. These items will probably have to be marked down or written off as a loss.

• Merchandise purchased, but not delivered, before the end of the accounting period may have to be included in the inventory. If title (ownership) to the merchandise being shipped has already passed to the purchaser, these items must be included in the purchaser's inventory. Generally the purchaser has title to goods that are shipped FOB Shipping Point.

Costing the Inventory. The procedures used to price the inventory are these.

• The inventory items must be counted.
• Costs must be assigned to the inventory items.
• The total cost of the inventory must be computed. This is done by multiplying the items counted by the price of each item. The sum of all the items is the total cost of the inventory.

Assigning Costs to Inventory

Businesses that keep perpetual records may use several procedures to assign costs to items in the ending inventory. These procedures include average unit cost, first in, first out (FIFO), last in, first out (LIFO), average total cost, and specific identification. Only average unit cost and FIFO procedures are described in this topic. The other procedures are described in advanced accounting courses.

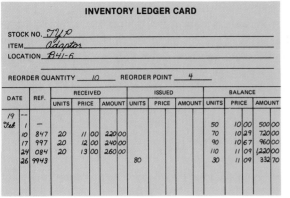

INVENTORY LEDGER CARD

STOCK NO. _TYP_
ITEM _adaptor_
LOCATION _B41-6_

REORDER QUANTITY ___10___   REORDER POINT ___4___

DATE		REF.	RECEIVED			ISSUED			BALANCE		
			UNITS	PRICE	AMOUNT	UNITS	PRICE	AMOUNT	UNITS	PRICE	AMOUNT
19 Feb.	--	--							50	10 00	500 00
	10	847	20	11 00	220 00				70	10 29	720 00
	17	997	20	12 00	240 00				90	10 67	960 00
	24	084	20	13 00	260 00				110	11 09	1,220 00
	26	9943				80			30	11 09	332 70

The Balance section shows the average unit cost.

PRODUCT TYP

Feb.	1	Balance	50 @ $10 = $500
	10	Purchased	20 @ $11 = $220
	17	Purchased	20 @ $12 = $240
	24	Purchased	20 @ $13 = $260

Total Units		
Available for Sale	110	
Number of Units Sold	−80	
February 28 Balance	30	Units in Ending Inventory

	20 @ $13 = $260
	10 @ $12 = $120
Ending Inventory:	30 $380

FIFO Procedure

Average Unit Cost. When several items are purchased at different costs, the average unit cost may be used. The **average unit cost** is computed by dividing the total cost of the units by the number of units. Thus the total cost of 110 items of product TYP is $1,220. The average cost is, therefore, $1,220 divided by 110, or $11.09. After 80 items were sold on February 26, the balance is 30 units at $11.09 each. Thus the ending inventory for product TYP is $332.70, as shown.

FIFO. Another way of computing the cost of the inventory is called the FIFO procedure. **FIFO** is a procedure by which

FIFO assumes the first units received are the first units sold.

• The ending inventory includes the most current items purchased
• The goods sold are considered as being the items purchased the longest time ago, starting with the beginning inventory

FIFO can be explained by referring to the illustration above. This illustration shows that 50 units of product TYP were in stock on February 1. It also shows that additional units were purchased on three different dates. The total units available for sale during February was 110. Further, 80 of the 110 units were sold during the month, leaving a balance of 30 units in the ending inventory.

Now the question is this: Which costs should be assigned to the 30 remaining units? Notice that the unit cost of this product goes from

$10 for the beginning balance to $13 for the units purchased on February 24. The cause of the increases in costs may be the general effects of inflation.

When FIFO is used to assign costs to inventory items, it is assumed that the units received first are sold first. This means that the 80 units sold during the month included the 50 units in inventory on February 1, the 20 units purchased on February 10, and 10 of the 20 units purchased on February 17. The 30 units in the ending inventory would then consist of 10 units purchased for $12 each ($120) and 20 units purchased for $13 each ($260). Thus the ending inventory on product TYP totals $380 ($120 + $260).

An advantage of the FIFO procedure is that the most current costs are assigned to the ending inventory. This results in the ending inventory being priced closer to market value.

Activity B-1. Describe the procedures that might be used by a business in your community to count its inventory. (Select a business that you visit on a regular basis, such as a grocery store, department store, or bookstore.)

Activity B-2. Answer the following questions about the first in, first out inventory pricing method. Refer to the table in the next column.

1. How many units of product TYP are in stock on February 1?

2. What is the total number of units that could have been sold?

3. How many units are sold during the month?

4. How many units are in the ending inventory?

5. Has the unit price of product TYP during the month increased or decreased?

6. What is the total cost of the ending inventory for this item?

PRODUCT TYP

Feb.	1	Balance	50 @ $10 = $500
	10	Purchased	20 @ $11 = $220
	17	Purchased	20 @ $12 = $240
	24	Purchased	20 @ $13 = $260

Total Units Available for Sale	110
Number of Units Sold	−80
February 28 Balance	30 Units in Ending Inventory

	20 @ $13 = $260
	10 @ $12 = $120
Ending Inventory:	30 $380

Accounting for Inventory Losses

C Will the balance in the Merchandise Inventory account always be the same as the amount of the physical inventory? No, in most instances the balance in the Merchandise Inventory account will be different from the actual count of the inventory. The difference may be due to theft or to errors in the records. When a difference exists, the Merchandise Inventory account must be corrected at the end of the accounting period to reflect the amount of the physical inventory.

Suppose the physical inventory shows items costing $500 less than the balance in the Merchandise Inventory account. In this case a correcting entry must be made in the general journal to correct the Merchandise Inventory account. The balance of the Merchandise Inventory account must equal the total physical inventory. The entry would contain a $500 debit to the Merchandise Loss account and a $500 credit to the Merchandise Inventory account. The Merchandise Loss account is an expense account. The Merchandise Inventory account is an asset account. The amount of the loss is reported on the income statement under operating expenses.

GENERAL JOURNAL				Page	6
DATE	ACCOUNT TITLE AND EXPLANATION	POST. REF.	DEBIT	CREDIT	
19— Dec. 31	Merchandise Loss............	530	500 00		
	Merchandise Inventory........	112		500 00	
	To record a loss in inventory.				

Cost of missing merchandise is an operating expense.

GENERAL JOURNAL				Page	6
DATE	ACCOUNT TITLE AND EXPLANATION	POST. REF.	DEBIT	CREDIT	
19— Dec. 31	Merchandise Inventory.........	112	200 00		
	Cost of Goods Sold..........	501		200 00	
	To adjust the merchandise inventory.				

Cost of found merchandise reduces cost of goods sold.

A correcting entry is also needed when the physical inventory total is more than the balance in the Merchandise Inventory account. Suppose the physical inventory shows $200 more than the Merchandise Inventory account. This entry contains a $200 debit to the Merchandise Inventory account and a $200 credit to the Cost of Goods Sold account. The Merchandise Inventory account is debited to reflect the increase in assets. The Cost of Goods Sold account is credited because a mistake which cannot be located was made during the year in recording the cost of sales. Or perhaps there was a mistake in counting the inventory when the previous physical inventory was taken.

These entries would be journalized before the worksheet is prepared.

The corrected Merchandise Inventory account balance is reported on the balance sheet as a current asset. Failure to correct the Merchandise Inventory account will result in errors on the financial statements. For example, total assets on the balance sheet will be incorrect. The Cost of Goods Sold account will be reported as being more than it should be. Thus the net income will be incorrect on the income statement. The net income will be less than it should be.

Corrections for merchandise inventory also require corresponding corrections on the ledger cards. The process of locating the cards with errors can be very time-consuming and is a major reason for using automated equipment.

Worksheet

Preparing a worksheet for a business using perpetual inventory procedures involves the same basic steps used in completing other worksheets. However, perpetual inventory procedures do result in some differences. These differences are as follows.

The Franks Department Store
Worksheet
For the Year Ended December 31, 19—

	ACCOUNT TITLE	ACCT. NO.	UNADJUSTED TRIAL BALANCE		ADJUSTMENTS		ADJUSTED TRIAL BALANCE		INCOME STATEMENT		BALANCE SHEET		
			DEBIT	CREDIT	DEBIT	CREDIT	DEBIT	CREDIT	DEBIT	CREDIT	DEBIT	CREDIT	
2													2
3	Merchandise Inventory	112	40,000				40,000				40,000		3
4													4
6													6
7	Cost of Goods Sold	501	55,000				55,000		55,000				7

No adjusting entries are needed for Merchandise Inventory account and Cost of Goods Sold account.

• The Merchandise Inventory account is not adjusted. The balance in this account is updated on a regular basis throughout the year. The balance is also verified and corrected to agree with the total of the physical inventory.

• The amount of merchandise inventory is extended from the Unadjusted Trial Balance section of the worksheet to the Adjusted Trial Balance section to the debit column of the Balance Sheet section.

• The balance of the Cost of Goods Sold account is extended from the Unadjusted Trial Balance section to the Adjusted Trial Balance section to the debit column of the Income Statement section. This balance is the amount of cost of goods sold reported on the income statement. The Cost of Goods Sold account is closed to the Income Summary account.

• Fewer accounts are required when using perpetual inventory procedures. Separate accounts for Purchases, Purchases Discount, Purchases Returns and Allowances, and Transportation In are *not* required. All these items are in the Merchandise Inventory account.

Financial Statements

Preparing a balance sheet when using perpetual inventory procedures is the same as preparing a balance sheet when using periodic inventory procedures. In both cases the balance of the Merchandise Inventory account is listed as a current asset. On the other hand, preparing the income statement is easier. This is because the amount of cost of goods sold does not have to be computed. The cost of goods sold is simply the balance in the Cost of Goods Sold account.

Advantages of the Perpetual Inventory Method

Perpetual inventory procedures provide several advantages to owners and managers.

Continuous Flow of Information. Management has a continuous flow of information about the inventory. Such information is important in controlling the investment in merchandise inventory. To supply this continuous flow of information requires more data to be processed. Daily balances of all inventory items, for example, must be computed.

Daily Balances. The perpetual inventory method provides information about the daily balances in the Merchandise Inventory account in the general ledger and in the subsidiary inventory ledger. The balance of the Merchandise Inventory account shows exactly how much is invested in merchandise inventory. An inventory that is too great may be reduced by special sales and fewer purchases. On the other hand, an inventory that is too low may indicate problems with suppliers or inadequate purchasing procedures.

The balances in the inventory ledger provide information about each item included in the inventory. With daily inventory reports, owners and managers can identify those items that are popular with customers and those that are not selling as expected. Daily inventory reports can also be used to identify items that should be marked down in order to sell them.

Ordering Merchandise. The use of an inventory ledger allows management to establish a reorder point and a reorder quantity for each item of merchandise. The **reorder point** is a number shown on each inventory ledger card which indicates when a particular item must be reordered.

For example, the reorder point for a specific type and size of warm-up suit is 5. When the inventory of this item decreases to 5 or fewer, a new order is placed. The reorder point reduces the chances that sales will be lost because an item was not in stock. (This is a feature that may also be used with the periodic inventory method.)

The reorder quantity is another number recorded on each inventory card. The **reorder quantity** identifies how many units of each item are to be reordered at any one time. In the illustration on page 637, the reorder quantity for warm-up suits is 12. The reorder quantity is based on past sales of the inventory item.

Reporting. Perpetual inventory procedures make it easier to prepare financial statements. For example, the amount of the merchandise inventory reported on the balance sheet is simply the balance of the Merchandise Inventory account. The cost of goods sold reported on the income statement is the balance of the Cost of Goods Sold account. Thus perpetual inventory procedures eliminate the need for a schedule of cost of goods sold.

Reduces Theft. Merchandise must be protected from theft by employees and outsiders. Perpetual inventory procedures quickly identify missing items. For example, theft may be detected by examining unexplained decreases in inventory items. When the evidence of a theft is discovered, steps can be taken to improve both store security and inventory controls.

Some retail businesses attach electronic tags to their merchandise to reduce shoplifting. These electronic tags are actually plastic clips that can be removed only with a special device. A shoplifter leaving the store is detected by the electronic tag setting off an alarm near the exit.

Adaptable to Automated Systems. Perpetual inventory procedures are based on routine procedures that can be performed by electronic equipment such as computers and point-of-sale terminals. Thus the computer makes it possible to process the data needed for inventory and sales reports.

Disadvantages of the Perpetual Inventory Method

A disadvantage of the perpetual inventory method is the work required to maintain detailed records. This work involves updating the inventory ledger and recording the cost of goods sold after each transaction. Additional time and effort are also needed to verify the inventory records. But with electronic processing equipment, this extra work is easier to do.

Activity C. Answer the following questions about the merchandise inventory account, worksheet, and financial statements. Refer to the text and illustrations on pages 644 through 648.
1. Which account is debited to record a loss of merchandise? Which account is credited?
2. Which journal is used to record correcting entries for merchandise inventory?

3. Does Merchandise Inventory require an adjusting entry at the end of the accounting period? A correcting entry?
4. What type of account is Merchandise Inventory? On which financial statement is it reflected?
5. What type of account is Cost of Goods Sold? On which financial statement is it reported?

Accounting Concepts:
Controlling Account. The equality of the ledger can be maintained by substituting a *controlling account* for a group of individual accounts.
Schedule of Subsidiary Ledger. The equality of the subsidiary ledger and the controlling account must be verified at regular intervals.

Topic 2 Problems

21-3. Complete the inventory card in your workbook by using the information provided. Be sure to determine the balance after each order received and after each sale.
Company: The Olympic Shoe Company
Product: 173-6624-10, Running Shoes
Location: Athletic Shoe Department
Reorder Point: 15
Reorder Quantity: 20
March 1 Balance: 30 pairs @ $15 each
Received: 20 pair on March 12
　　　　　20 pair on March 19
Sold:　　 6 pair on March 3
　　　　　12 pair on March 9
　　　　　20 pair on March 14
　　　　　10 pair on March 22
　　　　　11 pair on March 28

21-4. Information regarding the inventory and sales of product TL2 is listed here. Review this information and answer the following questions.

April　1　Balance 70 @ $12
　　　　5　Purchased 25 @ $14
　　　13　Purchased 25 @ $15
　　　20　Purchased 25 @ $17
　　　26　Purchased 25 @ $19
　　　　　Units Sold:145
a. How many units were available for sale?
b. How many units are in the ending inventory?
c. What is the unit cost of the units in the ending inventory using average unit cost? using FIFO?
d. What is the total cost of the ending inventory using average unit cost? using FIFO?

Topic 3
Automated Inventory Procedures

|A| *Can perpetual inventory procedures be automated?* Yes, businesses such as department stores, wholesalers, and manufacturers may rely on electronic equipment to maintain their perpetual inventory records. The electronic inventory procedures used by the Merchandise Showroom are described here.

The Merchandise Showroom is a chain of discount stores located in major cities throughout the Midwest. Merchandise sold at the showrooms includes products such as cameras, electronic calculators, jewelry, and camping equipment. All the products are priced at 20 to 35 percent below the manufacturer's suggested retail price. (In addition to the various showrooms, the company also has a central warehouse that processes catalog and telephone sales.)

The Merchandise Showroom is able to sell at discount prices for several reasons.

● All sales are made on the cash basis. By not making sales on credit, the Merchandise Showroom eliminates the cost of maintaining a credit department.

- Cash sales provide owners and managers with an immediate source of money to reinvest in the business.
- The showrooms are organized on a self-serve basis. This reduces the number of salesclerks needed.
- Purchasing for all the showrooms is centralized at the warehouse. Thus owners and managers can take advantage of special discounts given on purchases of large quantities. A special discount given on purchase of large quantities that reduce the net cost of purchases is called a **trade discount.**
- Automated equipment is used to control the merchandise inventory. By updating the inventory ledger each day, management is able to identify items that are not selling as well as items that need to be reordered.

Each Merchandise Showroom is operated by a manager with a staff consisting of salesclerks and inventory clerks.

Automating Showroom Sales

As customers enter a showroom, they pick up a clipboard that has order forms and a pencil attached to it. The customers then enter the display area where they decide what merchandise to purchase. Customers select the products to purchase by examining the samples on display or by referring to the showroom catalog. Copies of the catalog

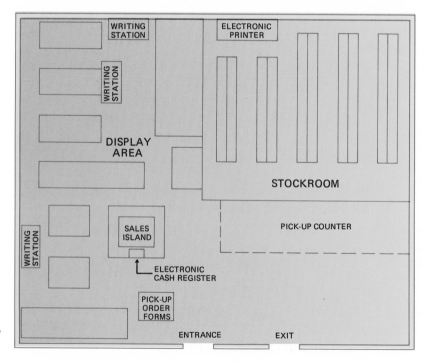

**Layout of a Merchandise
Showroom store.**

are placed on writing stations located in various parts of the showroom. Because of limited floor space, only a portion of the merchandise shown in the catalog can be displayed at one time.

When customers locate items to purchase, they complete an order form similar to the one shown below. Information needed to complete the order form is taken from the catalog or from the tag attached to the products on display. Information recorded on the order form includes the catalog number, quantity, item description, and item cost. Space is also provided for the customer's name and address. After the order form is completed, the customer takes the order to the sales island.

▶ TO PURCHASE MERCHANDISE FROM SHOWROOM OR CATALOG COMPLETE THIS FORM AND PRESENT IT TO THE SALES ISLAND. PLEASE PRINT.					**6555177**	

CUSTOMER ORDER BLANK

NAME Anna Burford
ADDRESS 2300 Terrace Drive
CITY Evansville STATE IN ZIP CODE 47704
PHONE ORDER TO BE PAID FOR BY: ☐CHECK ☐BANKCARD ☒CASH FILLED BY: DELIVERED BY: DATE

CATALOG NUMBER	SIZE	AMT.	DESCRIPTION	COST	
(1206LE)		1	ATTACHÉ CASE 5 INCH BLACK	9.77	*
450007		1	Clip-On Sunglasses	2.66	
809012		1	1-Speed Personal Fan	13.83	

Form 886 7/X2

ALL RETURNS MUST BE ACCOMPANIED BY SALES RECEIPT AND THE CUSTOMER'S CARTONS AND PACKAGING. NO RETURNS AFTER 10 DAYS.
* Your cost illustrated.

Customer fills out order form.

The cashier at the sales island enters each item on the order form into a cash register terminal. As each item is entered, the data is reflected on a CRT screen and stored temporarily in the cash register's memory unit. When all the items have been entered, the cashier depresses an inventory search key. This key instructs the computer to search the inventory for each item on the customer's order.

Determining Items in Stock

Within seconds, the cashier knows whether the items are in stock. The catalog numbers of items not in stock flash on the screen. If the customer decides not to purchase the available items, the cashier clears the cash register. This removes the data from the screen as well as from the memory unit.

However, if the customer decides to purchase those items that are in stock, the cashier depresses the sales key on the cash register. This automatically enters the available items as a completed sale. The total amount of the sale and sales tax is also computed and shown on the screen. After paying the cashier, the customer receives an electronically prepared sales slip, illustrated here.

Customer receives sales slip after paying for merchandise, but before receiving merchandise.

Merchandise Showroom

```
                                                                DATE 3/17/--

STOCK #   QTY            DESCRIPTION            PRICE    EXT-PRICE      LOCATION
450007 1          FG CLIP-ON #42 $4.00           2.66        2.66  STOCKROOM
809012 1           1-SPEED PERSONAL FAN         13.83       13.83  STOCKROOM
               CLERK 037203  16:21   SUBTOTAL=         $16.49
               SEQ 0111                  TAX=           $.66
               ORDER                   TOTAL=          $17.15
CASH--AMOUNT TENDERED ? 2000 CHANGE =      $2.85
CUSTOMER NAME: ANNA BURFORD
    RECEIPT AND ORIGINAL BOX MUST ACCOMPANY ALL REFUNDS
```

As the sales slip is being printed on the cash register, a packing slip is also being prepared on an electronic printer located in the stockroom. This packing slip, illustrated here, provides a description and the location of each item purchased. It also includes the name of the customer who purchased the items.

Packing slip shows items purchased.

Merchandise Showroom

```
                                                                DATE 3/17/--

STOCK #   QTY            DESCRIPTION            PRICE    EXT-PRICE      LOCATION
450007 1          FG CLIP-ON #42 $4.00           2.66        2.66  STOCKROOM
809012 1           1-SPEED PERSONAL FAN         13.83       13.83  STOCKROOM
               CLERK 037203  16:21   SUBTOTAL=         $16.49
               SEQ 0111                  TAX=           $.66
               ORDER                   TOTAL=          $17.15
CASH--AMOUNT TENDERED ? 2000 CHANGE =      $2.85
CUSTOMER NAME: ANNA BURFORD
    RECEIPT AND ORIGINAL BOX MUST ACCOMPANY ALL REFUNDS
```

An inventory clerk removes the packing slip from the printer and fills the customer's order. Once the order is filled, the packing slip is attached to the items and placed on a conveyor belt. The conveyor belt transports the customer's order to the pickup counter. Another inventory clerk removes the order from the conveyor belt and calls the customer's name. The customer shows the sales slip to the inventory clerk in order to verify that the items from the stockroom are the same as the items ordered. After inspecting the order, the customer leaves the showroom with the items purchased and the sales slip.

Updating Inventory

As sales data is entered in the cash register, it is stored on an audit tape and on a cassette tape. The audit tape, which is locked inside the cash register, provides a record of each sale made. The cassette tape is located inside an electronic device attached to the cash register. Data from the cassette tape is transmitted each day by telephone lines to the home office for processing on the mainframe computer. This sales data is used to update the inventory ledger for the showroom and to prepare sales and inventory reports. The next morning, the completed reports are transmitted to the showroom; a printer located in the manager's office receives the data.

Daily Sales Report

The **daily sales report** is a summary of the sales data transmitted over telephone lines from the showroom to the home office. The daily sales report provides sales information for each department in the showroom. The information includes sales, sales returns and allowances, net sales, cost of goods sold, and gross profit. The daily sales report for the Evansville showroom shows that the gross profit for March 17 was $6,800.

The daily sales report includes sales, sales returns and allowances, net sales, cost of goods sold, and gross profits.

Note that the $6,800 gross profit is the difference between net sales of $17,000 and cost of goods sold of $10,200. In other words, the Evansville showroom realized gross profit of $6,800 that can be used to cover operating expenses and to provide a net income for the day.

	1	2	3	4	5
Evansville Showroom *Daily Sales Report* *March 17, 19—*					
				Cost of	Gross Profit
Department	Sales	Sales Returns	Net Sales	Goods Sold	(Col. 3 – Col 4)
1	$ 1,100	$100	$ 1,000	$ 660	$ 340
2	2,500	100	2,400	1,440	960
3	750	-0-	750	450	300
14	3,000	150	2,850	1,710	1,140
TOTAL	$17,500	$500	$17,000	$10,200	$6,800

Daily sales report shows data of how gross profit was earned by store.

Accounting records for all the showrooms are kept at the home office. Centralizing accounting procedures make it possible to use the mainframe computer to update the inventory ledger and to journalize and post transactions. For example, entries for the sales at the Evansville showroom will be recorded as shown on page 654.

The computer would be instructed to make similar entries for each showroom. It would also be instructed to identify items that should be recorded.

CASH RECEIPTS JOURNAL Page 2

DATE	ACCOUNT CREDITED	EXPLANATION	POST. REF.	GENERAL LEDGER CREDIT	ACCOUNTS RECEIVABLE CREDIT	SALES TAX PAYABLE CREDIT	NET CASH DEBIT
19-- MAR. 17	SALES	DAILY CASH SALES ..	401	17,500 00		875 00	18,375 00

CASH PAYMENTS JOURNAL Page 4

DATE	ACCOUNT DEBITED	EXPLANATION	CHECK NO.	POST. REF.	GENERAL LEDGER DEBIT	ACCOUNTS PAYABLE DEBIT	PURCHASES DISCOUNT CREDIT	NET CASH CREDIT
19-- MAR. 17	SALES RETURNS AND ALLOW.	RETURNS ON SALES...	—	402	500 00			525 00
	SALES TAX PAYABLE			216	25 00			

COST OF GOODS SOLD JOURNAL Page 4

DATE	INVOICE NUMBER	POST. REF.	INVOICE COST AMOUNT
19-- MAR 17	BATCH SALES	501/ 112	10,200 00

Computer prints journal for each store.

Daily Inventory Report

The daily inventory report is used internally to help manage the showroom. The **daily inventory report** provides information regarding each item in each department. Specific information provided includes the beginning balance of each inventory item, the number of units received, the number of units sold, the ending balance for each item (quantity), the unit cost, and the total cost of each item.

The daily inventory report below shows that the inventory in Department 1 has a total cost of $6,800. The report also shows that 121 units

Evansville Showroom
Daily Inventory Report
March 17, 19—

Department 1 Item Number	Inventory Beginning Balance	+	Units Received	−	Units Sold	=	Units in Ending Inventory	Unit Cost	Total
315-2-4	20		0		0		20	$10	$200
315-2-5	7		12		4		15	5	75
315-2-6	14		0		2		12	12	144
Total Dept.			121		34				$6,800

Daily inventory report shows data for each item in inventory.

were received in Department 1 and that 34 units were sold. The complete daily inventory report provides the same information for all 21 departments in each showroom.

Merchandise Alert Report

The merchandise alert report is prepared once a week to identify inventory items that need the immediate attention of owners or a manager. The **merchandise alert report** lists items that are in season but are not selling as expected. The report, illustrated here, also identifies items with errors in the inventory ledger.

The merchandise alert report identifies trouble spots.

Evansville Showroom Merchandise Alert Report For the Week Ended March 20, 19—					
Department 4 Item Number	Beginning Balance	Units Received	Units Sold	Ending Balance	Action
411-5-1	30	0	0	30	Consider mark-down
471-4-3	47	12	30	27	Verify stock— 2 items missing
491-2-1	20	0	0	20	Return item to warehouse

Merchandise Alert Report lists items not selling as expected.

The merchandise alert report shown here lists three items for Department 4. Note that the balance for item 411-5-1 is the same at the end of the week as it was at the beginning of the week. This report also shows that there have been no increases or decreases in this item during the week. Thus the manager of the showroom will probably consider reducing the price of this item in order to sell it.

The second item shows an ending balance of 27 units. This is the balance shown in the inventory ledger. However, the beginning balance of 47 units, plus the 12 units received, minus the 30 units sold equals 29 units $(47 + 12 - 30)$. In other words, there should be 29 units in stock as compared with the 27 units shown in the inventory ledger. In this instance the manager is advised to verify the number of units in the Evansville stockroom.

A possible explanation of the missing two items may involve sales returns and allowances. Two units of item 471-4-3 may have been sold and then returned. When the two items were sold, the inventory ledger was updated. However, someone may have forgotten to update the inventory ledger when the items were returned.

Item 491-2-1 also has not shown any activity during the week. In this instance, however, the manager is advised to return the items to the warehouse. From the warehouse, the 20 units of this item will be sent to another showroom that has a demand for the item.

Proving the Inventory

The Merchandise Showroom maintains perpetual inventory records on all items in the various showrooms as well as in the central warehouse. These records are updated to reflect the daily balance for each inventory item. At the end of each month, the total of the inventory ledger is compared with the balance in the Merchandise Inventory account. This is done to prove the balance in the controlling account.

Another way to prove the balance in the Merchandise Inventory account is to complete a physical inventory at the beginning of each year. The physical inventory is always completed during the first two working days in January. As stated earlier, the showrooms may be closed so that the inventory can be counted without interruptions.

A special electronic device called the *ultraphase terminal* is used to count inventory in the showroom. The person counting the inventory uses an optical scanner to read the information printed in code.

Preparing Inventory Sheet

The information on each inventory tag is then entered on a CRT terminal and recorded on magnetic tape. After all tags are recorded, the magnetic tape is sent to the home office for processing on the mainframe computer. The mainframe computer is instructed to prepare a list of the complete inventory for each showroom and the warehouse. The computer is also instructed to enter the cost and sales price of each item from a product list stored on a separate magnetic tape. This information must be merged (combined) with the inventory items. Then the

INVENTORY SHEET

Evansville Showroom

Date December 31, 19--   Sheet No. 8

Counted By M. West   Recorded By T. Mann   Figured By G. Rice

STOCK NO.	QUANTITY	UNIT OF COUNT	DESCRIPTION	UNIT COST	COST EXTENSION
27-P12	8	ea.	AM/FM Portable Radio	31 50	252 00
937-R48	3	ea.	4-Band Receiver	125 00	375 00
				TOTAL	1751 50

Inventory sheet provides information about inventory.

computer performs all extensions and obtains a total of the inventory. The final instruction to the computer is to prepare a printout of the entire inventory.

Activity A-1. Answer the following questions about the automated inventory procedures used by the Merchandise Showroom. Refer to the text, margin notes, and illustrations on pages 649 through 657.
1. What are some of the products sold by the Merchandise Showroom?
2. How is the Merchandise Showroom able to sell merchandise at discount prices?
3. What do customers pick up as they enter a showroom?
4. What information do customers record on their order forms?
5. What is the memory unit on the cash register used for?
6. What is the electronic printer used for? Where is it located?
7. What items are printed on the sales slip prepared on the electronic cash register?
8. What items are listed on the packing slip prepared on the electronic printer?

Activity A-2. Answer the following questions about the sales and inventory reports for the Evansville Showroom. Refer to the text and illustrations on pages 653 to 655.
1. What are the total sales on March 17? Net sales?
2. What is the total cost of goods sold on March 17?
3. What is the total gross profit for March 17?
4. What is the cost of goods sold for Department 2 on March 17?
5. What is the gross profit for Department 2 on March 17?
6. What entry is made to record the sales for March 17? Sales returns and allowances? Cost of goods sold?
7. What are the total units received in Department 1 on March 17?
8. What are the total units sold in Department 1 on March 17?
9. What is the total cost of inventory in Department 1 on March 17?
10. What action is recommended for item 411-5-1 on the merchandise alert report? For item 471-4-3? For item 491-2-1?

Topic 3   Problem

21-5. Select a business in your community that you visit on a regular basis. Think about the types of merchandise sold by the business, and then outline procedures for counting the merchandise inventory.

The Language of Business

Here are some terms that make up the language of business. Do you know the meaning of each?

perpetual inventory
  procedure
perpetual inventory
  subsystem
periodic inventory
  method

perpetual inventory
  method
Merchandise Inventory
  account
inventory ledger
Cost of Goods Sold
  account

merchandise inventory
  journal
cost of goods sold
  journal
inventory tag
inventory sheet
average unit cost
FIFO

reorder point
reorder quantity
trade discount
daily sales report
daily inventory report
merchandise alert
  report

Chapter 21   Questions

1. Describe the features of a perpetual inventory method.

2. What are the advantages of using perpetual inventory procedures?

3. What is the purpose of the inventory ledger? What is the controlling account for the inventory ledger?

4. Describe the procedures for completing a physical inventory.

5. How is FIFO used as an inventory pricing procedure?

6. What are two ways to verify the balance in the Merchandise Inventory account?

7. What type of entry is needed when the balance in the Merchandise Inventory account is less than the total of the physical inventory? When the balance is more than the total of the physical inventory?

8. What type of adjustment is made on the worksheet for merchandise inventory when perpetual inventory procedures are used?

9. How is the cost of goods sold computed when perpetual inventory procedures are used?

Chapter 21   Problems

Problems for Chapter 21 are given in the *Working Papers and Chapter Problems for Part 3*. If you are using the workbook, do the problems in the space pro-vided there. Complete your assigned topic problems before answering the chapter problems.

Chapter 21   Management Cases

Estimating Inventory. Occasionally, the management of a business must estimate the amount of its merchandise inventory. There may not be enough time to count the inventory, or the inventory may have been stolen or destroyed by fire. Estimating the amount of merchandise inventory is also useful in verifying the total of the inventory records.

One method for estimating merchandise inventory is called the *gross profit method.* Information needed to use this method includes net sales for the period, the rate of gross profit on sales (gross profits divided by net sales), and the amount of goods available for sale.

The amount of merchandise inventory is estimated as follows.

• Multiply net sales by the gross profit rate to determine the amount of gross profit on sales.

• Subtract gross profit on sales from net sales to determine cost of goods sold. This amount should be approximately the same as the balance in the Cost of Goods Sold account.

• Subtract cost of goods sold from goods available for sale to find the amount of merchandise inventory.

Case 21M-1. The Snyder Gift Shop was totally destroyed by fire. Sue Snyder, the owner, must now esti-mate the amount of the inventory loss in order to file an insurance claim. Based on previous income statements, the gross profit rate for the gift shop is determined to be 35 percent. It is also determined that goods available for sale for the current period totaled $68,700 and net sales for the year were $50,000.

a. Estimate the amount of inventory lost in the fire.

b. Sue Snyder plans to build a new building and open a new business. Can you suggest how to make the new building "fireproof," and ways to protect the new inventory from fire and water damage?

Case 21M-2. As an accounting clerk for the Local News Bookstore, you have been asked to verify the amount of merchandise inventory reported on the balance sheet and in the inventory ledger. This information is needed in order to secure a loan from the bank. Since there is not enough time to count the inventory, you must estimate the amount of inventory using the gross profit method. You know that the gross profit rate for this bookstore is 45 percent and that the dollar value of goods available for sale is $147,000. Net sales is determined to be $160,000.

a. Estimate the amount of merchandise inventory.

b. Assume that the inventory ledger shows a total inventory that is $3,000 greater than your estimate. Can you suggest a possible reason for this difference?

Working Hint

Inventory Teams. When a physical inventory is taken, two-person teams are often assigned to count specific items in stock. Generally, each team is made up of a counter and a recorder. Procedures for counting the inventory include the following.

1. The counter counts the inventory items on each table, shelf, or rack.

2. Before an item is counted, the counter describes the item to the recorder. The recorder then writes the description (for example, item number, color, and size) on the inventory tag.

3. After an item is counted, the counter also tells the recorder how many units are in stock. At this time, the recorder enters the quantity for that item along side the item description.

4. The recorder then repeats the quantity and item description for the counter. This allows the counter to verify the data recorded on the inventory tag. In some instances, hand-held calculators and other electronic devices such as the ultraphase are used to speed up the inventory count.

Kip Peticolas/Fundamental Photographs

A Credit Card Subsystem

You have already seen how automated data processing is used to process perpetual inventory data. You will now learn how automated data processing is used to speed up processing data from credit card sales.

Topic 1
Credit Card Sales

A *What is a credit card?* Businesses that process large volumes of sales on credit often provide their customers with credit cards. These businesses include oil companies, national chain stores, airlines, and large department stores. A **credit card** is a plastic card with the customer's name and account number embossed (printed) on it. The credit card identifies the holder of the card as someone who has an account established for the holder's use.

Credit card shows name and account number.

The credit card not only identifies the person, but it also is used to process data from credit sales transactions. The data from the sales transactions provides current information about sales revenue, accounts receivable, and inventory. The people, forms, procedures, and equipment used to provide information about credit card sales make up a **credit card sales subsystem.**

There are three general types of credit cards: company cards, bank cards, and travel and entertainment cards.

A **company card** is issued by a specific company and can be used for charging sales only from the issuing company. Examples of companies that issue company credit cards are Sears, Roebuck and Company and Shell Oil Company. For example, a credit card issued by Drumlin Department Stores will be accepted only at one of the Drumlin stores. Sales processed with a company card are recorded as a sales on credit.

A company credit card can be used at any of the company's stores, stations, etc.

A **bank card** is issued through a bank and can be used at any business accepting that card. Some banks charge the holder a fee for using the card. Examples of bank cards are VISA and MasterCard. Sales processed with a bank card are recorded as cash sales. The business takes the credit card sales invoices to the bank. The bank then deposits the amount of the sales invoice, less a charge for the service, into the business's checking account. The bank collects the amount due from the customer.

A bank credit card can be used at any participating business.

The **travel and entertainment card** is issued by a private business and is often used to charge such business expenses as meals and airline tickets. In some cases the holder of a travel and entertainment card must pay an annual membership fee. This fee entitles the individual to use the card to charge goods and services and to purchase travelers checks. Examples of travel and entertainment cards are American Express and Diners Club. Sales processed with a travel and entertainment card are recorded as cash sales. The businesses send the credit card sales invoices to the credit card company. The credit card company then pays the businesses the total amount due, less a charge for the collecting service. The credit card company then collects the amount due from the customer. The accounting procedures for processing sales on credit with company cards are discussed here. The

A travel and entertainment card can be used at any participating business.

accounting procedures for processing sales on credit with bank cards are discussed in Part 2.

Controls

Controls for the sales subsystem are described in Chapter 14. The controls are outlined in the margin. Additional controls are necessary to process credit card sales.

• Credit limits are established for all customers approved for company cards. A **credit limit** (sometimes referred to as a *line of credit*) is the total amount that can be charged to a customer's account. For example, a credit limit of $600 means that an account balance cannot be more than $600. The amount of credit extended to a customer is determined by such factors as the customer's annual income, length of employment, and credit references.

• A credit card embossed with the customer's name and account number is issued to each credit card customer. The use of account numbers makes it difficult for the cards to be misused or for sales to be made without them. Credit cards also make it easier to store and retrieve sales data in electronic accounting systems.

• Store personnel are instructed on how to process credit card sales. In some businesses, training sessions are used to teach salesclerks how to process credit card sales using the electronic cash register.

• Billing procedures are established to ensure prompt collection of accounts receivable. When credit cards are used, the customers are billed once a month. The due date is not computed for each invoice. The due date is computed as a certain number of days after the monthly statement is issued. Many businesses use cycle billing. In cycle billing, customer statements are prepared and distributed over the billing period, usually one month. An example of a cycle billing schedule is shown in the margin.

• Monthly payment plans are established and explained to the customers. Two types of payment plans are the regular charge plan and the budget plan. The **regular charge plan** allows customers to pay the full balance of their accounts within a certain number of days of the billing date without finance charges, or carrying charges, added to the account balance. The customers are usually given 20 or 30 days. The **budget plan** allows customers the option of making a minimum payment or paying the full balance owed. If a minimum payment is made, finance charges will be added to the unpaid balance on the next monthly statement. A schedule of minimum payments is usually provided with each monthly statement. For example, the schedule shown on the next page shows that an account balance of $265 requires a minimum payment of $16.

SCHEDULE OF MINIMUM MONTHLY PAYMENTS

The required minimum monthly payment is based on the highest New Balance on the account.

When the Highest New Balance Reaches	The Minimum Monthly Payment Will Be	
$ 0.01 to $ 10.00	Balance	
10.01 to 160.00	$10.00	You may always pay more
160.01 to 180.00	11.00	than the required minimum
180.01 to 200.00	12.00	monthly payment.
200.01 to 220.00	13.00	The minimum payment will
220.01 to 240.00	14.00	change only if charges
240.01 to 260.00	15.00	to the account increase
260.01 to 290.00	16.00	the balance to a new high.
290.01 to 340.00	17.00	The minimum payment will
340.01 to 380.00	18.00	not decrease until the
380.01 to 410.00	19.00	New Balance is paid
410.01 to 440.00	20.00	in full.
440.01 to 470.00	21.00	
470.01 to 500.00	22.00	

Over $500 00: 1/23rd of Highest Account Balance rounded to next higher whole dollar amount.

Installment sales, another type of payment plan, are usually processed separately from credit card sales. An **installment plan** spreads the payments for large purchases over a period of several months or years.

• Procedures are needed for collecting past due accounts and for withdrawing credit privileges.

• Procedures are needed for customers to report credit cards that have been lost or stolen. These procedures also include provisions for replacing the missing credit cards. To protect their customers, some businesses provide customers with information on credit card insurance. **Credit card insurance** protects customers from having to pay for purchases made by unauthorized credit card users.

• A signed credit agreement must exist between the issuing company and the customer. A **credit agreement,** or *contract*, describes the responsibilities of the business and the credit card customers.

Activity A-1. Listed here are several statements about credit cards. Identify the type of credit card described in each statement. Use CC for the company card, BC for the bank card, and T&E for the travel and entertainment card. Some statements may apply to more than one type of credit card.

EXAMPLE: May require holder to pay membership fee—T&E and BC

1. Accepted only by the business that issued the card.
2. Accepted by many different types of businesses.
3. Sale recorded as a cash sale.

4. Used by businesses to identify customers with good credit.
5. Sale recorded as a credit sale.
6. Speeds up processing sales on credit.

Activity A-2. List 5 different credit cards that you, your friends, or your parents use to purchase goods and services. Then identify each card as a company card (CC), bank card (BC), or travel and entertainment card (T&E).

EXAMPLE: Sears, Roebuck and Company—CC

Credit Departments

B *Why do businesses have credit departments?* Businesses that sell on credit often have credit departments to determine the ability of customers to pay their bills. The credit department performs the following tasks

- Processes applications for company credit cards.
- Investigates credit references of applicants.
- Develops terms of the credit agreement.
- Issues new credit cards and replaces outdated, lost, or stolen cards.
- Maintains files on credit customers.
- Coordinates the communication between the credit department, the sales department, and accounting department of all information regarding credit card customers.

Applications for Company Credit Card

A **credit application** form contains much of the information a business needs to determine the ability of credit customers to pay their accounts. Information about the applicant's residence, jobs, credit history, and credit references must be provided.

Credit Reference Investigations

The credit application asks for names of companies that have already granted credit to the customer. The credit department may ask these other companies to supply information about the customer's credit record. At other times a credit bureau may be asked to check credit references listed on the application form. A **credit bureau** is a business that collects data on a customer's ability to pay, a customer's past performance in paying his or her bills, and a verification of the information provided on the credit application.

Terms of the Credit Agreement

Truth-in-Lending Act requires business to disclose all terms of a credit agreement.

Another responsibility of the credit department is to develop the terms of the credit agreement. When signed by the customer, these terms become a legal contract between the business and the credit card holder. The **Truth-in-Lending Act,** a federal consumer law, requires businesses to disclose all terms of the credit agreement. Terms of credit may be printed on a separate form, on the reverse side of the credit application, or on the reverse side of the credit card. The terms of credit for the Drumlin Department Stores are printed on the reverse side of the credit application, as shown on the next page.

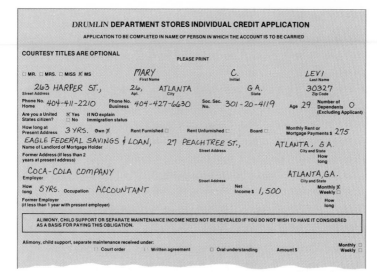

DRUMLIN **DEPARTMENT STORES INDIVIDUAL CREDIT APPLICATION**

APPLICATION TO BE COMPLETED IN NAME OF PERSON IN WHICH THE ACCOUNT IS TO BE CARRIED

COURTESY TITLES ARE OPTIONAL

PLEASE PRINT

☐ MR. ☐ MRS. ☐ MISS ☒ MS   MARY   C.   LEVI
First Name   Initial   Last Name

263 HARPER ST.,   26,   ATLANTA   G.A.   30327
Street Address   Apt.   City   State   Zip Code

Phone No. 404-411-2210   Phone No. 404-427-6630   Soc. Sec. 301-20-4119   Age 29   Number of Dependents 0
Home   Business   No.   (Excluding Applicant)

Are you a United States citizen? ☒ Yes ☐ No   If NO explain Immigration status

How long at Present Address 3 YRS.   Own ☒   Rent Furnished ☐   Rent Unfurnished ☐   Board ☐   Monthly Rent or Mortgage Payments $ 275

EAGLE FEDERAL SAVINGS & LOAN,   27 PEACHTREE ST.,   ATLANTA, G.A.
Name of Landlord or Mortgage Holder   Street Address   City and State

Former Address (if less than 2 years at present address)

COCA-COLA COMPANY   ATLANTA, GA.
Employer   Street Address   City and State

How long 5 YRS. Occupation ACCOUNTANT   Net Income $ 1,500   Monthly ☒ Weekly ☐

Former Employer (if less than 1 year with present employer)   How long

ALIMONY, CHILD SUPPORT OR SEPARATE MAINTENANCE INCOME NEED NOT BE REVEALED IF YOU DO NOT WISH TO HAVE IT CONSIDERED AS A BASIS FOR PAYING THIS OBLIGATION.

Alimony, child support, separate maintenance received under:
☐ Court order   ☐ Written agreement   ☐ Oral understanding   Amount $ Monthly ☐ Weekly ☐

DRUMLIN DEPARTMENT STORES
CREDIT AGREEMENT

Regular Charge Plan

Budget Plan

On all charges to my Drumlin Charge account I agree to the following:

1 **OPTION TO PAY IN FULL EACH MONTH TO AVOID FINANCE CHARGES.** I have the right each month to pay the total balance on my account. If I do so within 30 days (28 days for February statements) of my billing date no **Finance Charge** will be added to the account for that month. The billing date will be shown on a statement sent to me each month. The total balance on my billing date will be called the **NEW BALANCE** on my monthly statement.

2 **OPTION TO MAKE MINIMUM PAYMENTS PLUS A FINANCE CHARGE.** If I do not pay the total balance in full each month, I agree to make at least a minimum payment within 30 days (28 days for February statements) of the billing date shown on my monthly statement. The minimum payment required each month is shown in the Schedule of Minimum Monthly Payments below.

3 **SCHEDULE OF MINIMUM MONTHLY PAYMENTS.** The required minimum monthly payment is based on the highest New Balance on the account.

When the Highest New Balance Reaches	The Minimum Monthly Payment will be
$ .01 to $ 10.00	Balance
10.01 to 160.00	$10.00
160.01 to 180.00	11.00
180.01 to 200.00	12.00
200.01 to 220.00	13.00
220.01 to 240.00	14.00
240.01 to 260.00	15.00
260.01 to 290.00	16.00
290.01 to 340.00	17.00
340.01 to 380.00	18.00
380.01 to 410.00	19.00
410.01 to 440.00	20.00
440.01 to 470.00	21.00
470.01 to 500.00	22.00

You may always pay more than the required minimum monthly payment. The minimum payment will change only if charges to the account increase the balance to a new high. The minimum payment will not decrease until the New Balance is paid in full.

over $500.00 - 1/23rd of Highest Account Balance rounded to next higher whole dollar amount.

4 **FINANCE CHARGE.** If I do not pay the entire New Balance within 30 days (28 days for February statements) of the monthly billing date, a **Finance Charge** will be added to the account for the current monthly billing period. The **FINANCE CHARGE** will be either a minimum of 50¢ if the Average Daily Balance is $33.00 or less or a periodic rate of 1.5% per month (**ANNUAL PERCENTAGE RATE** of 18%) on the Average Daily Balance.

5 **HOW TO DETERMINE THE AVERAGE DAILY BALANCE.** Drumlin will determine each day's outstanding balance in the monthly billing period and divide the total of these daily balances by the number of days in the monthly billing period. The result is the Average Daily Balance. Drumlin will include the current month's charges but will not include unpaid Finance or Insurance Charge(s) if any, when determining a daily balance. All payments and other credits will be subtracted from the previous day's balance.

6 **FAILURE TO MAKE MINIMUM PAYMENT.** If I do not make at least the minimum required monthly payment when due, Drumlin may declare my entire balance immediately due and payable.

7 **SECURITY INTEREST IN GOODS.** Drumlin has a security interest under the Uniform Commercial Code in all merchandise charged to the account. If I do not make payments as agreed, the security interest allows Drumlin to repossess only the merchandise which has not been paid in full. I am responsible for any loss or damage to the merchandise until the price is fully paid. Any payments I make will first be used to pay unpaid Insurance or Finance Charge(s), if any, and then to pay for the earliest charges on the account. If more than one item is charged on the same date, my payment will apply first to the lowest priced item.

8 **CHANGE OF TERMS — CANCELLATION.** Drumlin has the right to change any term or part of this agreement by sending me a written notice. Drumlin also has the right to cancel this agreement as it relates to future purchases. I agree to return all credit cards to Drumlin upon notice of such cancellation.

9 **STATE OF RESIDENCE CONTROLS TERMS.** All terms of this agreement are controlled by the laws of my state of residence.

10 **CHANGE OF RESIDENCE.** If I change my residence, I will inform Drumlin. Drumlin has the right to transfer the account to a unit servicing my new residence. If I move to another state, the account, including any unpaid balance, will be controlled by the credit terms which apply to Drumlin credit customers in my new state of residence. Drumlin will provide me with a written disclosure of any new terms, including the amount and method of calculating the **Finance Charge.**

11 **AUTHORIZED BUYERS.** This agreement controls all charges made on the account by me or any person I authorize to use the account.

12 **CREDIT INVESTIGATION AND DISCLOSURE.** Drumlin has the right to investigate my credit, employment and income records, and has the right to verify my credit references and to report the way I pay this account to credit bureaus and other interested parties.

13 **WAIVER OF LIEN ON RESIDENCE.** Drumlin gives up any right to retain or acquire any lien which Drumlin might be automatically entitled to by law on real estate which I use as my principal residence. This does not apply to a lien created by a court judgment or acquired by a filing as provided by statute.

14 **ACCOUNT SUBJECT TO APPROVAL OF DRUMLIN CREDIT SALES DEPARTMENT.** This agreement and all charges on the account are subject to the approval of Drumlin Credit Sales Department. The agreement will be considered approved when Drumlin delivers a Drumlin credit card or other notice of approval to me.

15 **ASSIGNMENT OF ACCOUNT—PROTECTION OF BUYER'S RIGHTS.** I understand this account may be sold or assigned by Drumlin to another creditor without further notice to me. If so, the notice below, which is required by Federal law, is intended to protect any claim or right I have against Drumlin.

NOTICE: ANY HOLDER OF THIS CONSUMER CREDIT CONTRACT IS SUBJECT TO ALL CLAIMS AND DEFENSES WHICH THE DEBTOR COULD ASSERT AGAINST THE SELLER OF THE GOODS OR SERVICES OBTAINED PURSUANT HERETO OR WITH THE PROCEEDS HEREOF. RECOVERY HEREUNDER BY THE DEBTOR SHALL NOT EXCEED AMOUNTS PAID BY THE DEBTOR HEREUNDER.

16 **NOTICE TO BUYER: DO NOT SIGN THIS AGREEMENT BEFORE YOU READ IT OR IF IT CONTAINS ANY BLANK SPACES. YOU ARE ENTITLED TO AN EXACT COPY OF THE PAPER YOU SIGN. YOU HAVE THE RIGHT TO PAY IN ADVANCE THE FULL AMOUNT DUE. RECEIPT OF A COPY OF THIS AGREEMENT IS ACKNOWLEDGED.**

Drumlin Department Stores   (By)

Mary C. Levi

(Customer's Signature)   (Date) Jan. 7, 19 — —

10897 010 REV / XI
Illinois Kentucky Montana South Dakota

Issuing Credit Cards

New Credit Cards. Since credit cards can easily be misused by individuals, blank credit cards must be safeguarded much as cash is. The credit department prepares a company card for each person approved for credit. The company card will be sent to the customer along with instructions on its use. Credit card customers must also be provided with information regarding consumer rights as provided by the **Fair Credit Billing Act,** another federal consumer law. One provision of the Act is the Billing Rights Notice. Under this provision, the customer can notify the business of any problems regarding purchases on credit. If the business has been properly notified about the problem, the customer is not obligated to pay the balance owed on that purchase until the problem is corrected.

> Under the Fair Credit Billing Act, the customer does not have to pay questionable amounts until the problem is resolved if the company is notified properly.

Dated Credit Cards. Some businesses date all credit cards issued. A dated credit card which must be renewed carries an expiration date and the year the card was first issued.

This credit card shows date when account was opened and date the credit card will expire.

Terms of credit agreement are given on the back of the credit card.

For example, the card for Sarah Goble shows that she has had an account with Falcon Oil Company since 19X3. It also shows that her present company card expires in March 19X5. The year 19X3 on the card identifies Sarah Goble as being a customer with several years of good credit.

Lost or Stolen Credit Cards. Sometimes company cards are lost or stolen. When this happens, the customer must notify the business issuing the card. Upon notification, the credit department will alert all stores not to process sales using the lost or stolen cards. After a period of time, the store will issue a new card to the customer.

Credit Customer Files

The credit department also maintains two files on credit customers: a current customer file and a negative account file. The **current customer file** contains the names, addresses, and account numbers of all credit customers in good standing. Customers remain in good standing as long as they make their payments.

The **negative account file** contains the names, addresses, and account numbers of those customers who are behind in their payments. Customer accounts with reported company cards lost or stolen are also placed in this file until new cards are issued. Customers placed in the negative account file are not allowed to continue using their company cards. The negative account file eliminates the need to age accounts receivable. This is because customers must make at least the minimum payment each month or be added to the negative account file.

A customer listed in the negative account file is said to be a **delinquent account.** Delinquent accounts are often turned over to an account representative for investigation.

Coordinating the Sales, Credit, and Accounting Departments

The credit card sales subsystem requires a constant flow of information between the credit department, the sales department, and the accounting department. Salesclerks must be informed of customers who have been placed in the negative account file because of lost or stolen credit cards or because the customers have reached their credit limits. The credit department must receive updated customer account balances from the accounting department so that it can monitor the credit limits. The sales and credit departments must also be informed by the accounting department when customers have reached their credit limits. These are a few of the types of communication that must flow from one department to another.

Information must constantly flow among departments.

Activity B. Answer the following questions about the credit agreement used by Drumlin Department Stores. Refer to the text, margin notes, and illustrations on pages 664 to 667.
1. How many payment plans are described in the credit agreement for Drumlin Department Stores? Describe the plans.
2. What is the minimum payment due on an account balance of $185? On a balance of $460?
3. What is the annual percentage rate used to compute the finance charge on unpaid balances?
4. What may happen if a charge customer fails to make at least a minimum payment when due?
5. Does Drumlin have a security interest in merchandise charged to a customer's account?
6. Can Drumlin change or cancel the terms of credit described in the credit agreement? Why or why not?
7. Does Drumlin Department Stores have the right to investigate credit and income records of the person applying for credit?

Processing Credit Card Sales

C *How do company credit cards speed up the processing of sales on credit?* Company cards help by identifying customers who have already been approved for credit. Thus the salesperson does not have to check credit ratings of customers charging merchandise or services.

Electronic Cash Register

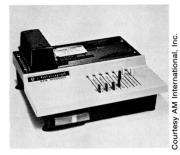

Customer name and account number imprinted from credit card.

Checking Credit Limits. Sometimes the salesperson will have to verify the credit limits. To do this, the salesperson either calls the credit department, checks a list, or uses an electronic credit check.

The printed list can be in the form of a booklet or other form. The salesperson simply looks in the list for the account number or the customer's name.

The electronic credit check may be a device with a numbered keyboard and screen. The device may be built into the cash register. After the salesperson enters the customer's account number on the keyboard an "approved" or "disapproved" message is flashed on the screen.

Preparing Sales Invoices

The sales invoice prepared for a credit card sale is a business form consisting of two or more copies separated by carbon paper. The salesperson prepares the sales invoice by inserting the form and the customer's credit card in an imprinting device. This imprinting device prints the customer's name and account number on the sales invoice.

The salesperson writes his or her number and the date on the sales invoice. Then the salesperson inserts the sales invoice in the electronic cash register. The salesperson enters his or her number. The customer's account number will be printed automatically on the invoice if credit has been approved by the electronic credit check. The register will not process a transaction if the customer's account number is disapproved. The transaction data for the merchandise purchased will be entered manually into the cash register. As the sales data is entered into the register, the details of the transaction are recorded on the sales invoice. The sales invoice describes the merchandise (usually by code number), the department or division where the merchandise is sold, the quantity and price of the items purchased, and the total of the sale. The electronic cash register is programmed to automatically compute any sales tax to be included in the total.

After the sales invoice is prepared, the customer signs it. The salesperson then gives a copy of the sales invoice to the customer as a receipt and places the other copy or copies in the cash register. The reverse side of the customer's copy may contain the terms of the credit agreement and billing procedures.

Recording Credit Card Sales. Credit card sales are recorded in the sales journal. Credit card sales are often recorded as batch totals at the end of each day. The entry involves a debit to the Accounts Receivable controlling account and credits to the Sales account and to the Sales Tax Payable account.

The amount of each transaction is posted to the customer's account in the accounts receivable ledger on a daily basis. At the end of the

May 6: The Drumlin Department Store records batch total of sales on credit for $1,200 plus $60 sales tax.

What Happens	Accounting Rule	Entry
The asset *Accounts Receivable* increases by $1,260.	To increase an asset, debit the account.	Debit: Accounts Receivable, $1,260 (also the customer's account).
The liability *Sales Tax Payable* increases by $60.	To increase a liability, credit the account.	Credit: Sales Tax Payable, $60.
Revenue increases owner's equity by $1,200.	To increase owner's equity, credit the account.	Credit: Sales, $1,200.

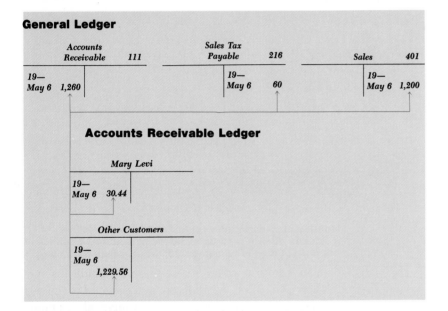

General Ledger

Accounts Receivable 111	Sales Tax Payable 216	Sales 401
19— May 6 1,260	19— May 6 60	19— May 6 1,200

Accounts Receivable Ledger

Mary Levi
19— May 6 30.44

Other Customers
19— May 6 1,229.56

SALES JOURNAL							Page 5
DATE	INVOICE NO.	ACCOUNT DEBITED	TERMS	POST. REF.	ACCOUNTS RECEIVABLE DEBIT	SALES TAX PAYABLE CREDIT	SALES CREDIT
19— May 6	Batch 6	Accounts Receivable	—	—	1,260 00	60 00	1,200 00

Credit card sales are recorded as batch totals.

month, the totals of the sales journal are posted to the accounts in the general ledger.

Preparing Monthly Statements

Customers who use company credit cards to charge goods or services are sent a **monthly statement** or *bill*.

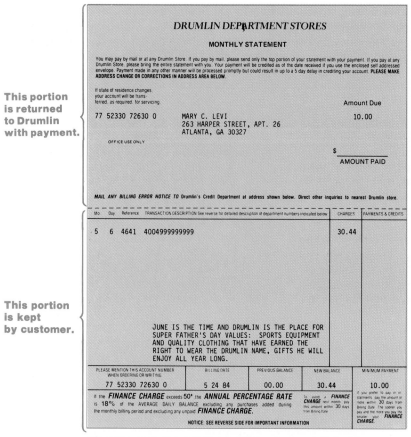

This portion is returned to Drumlin with payment.

This portion is kept by customer.

DRUMLIN DEPARTMENT STORES

MONTHLY STATEMENT

You may pay by mail or at any Drumlin Store. If you pay by mail, please send only the top portion of your statement with your payment. If you pay at any Drumlin Store, please bring the entire statement with you. Your payment will be credited as of the date received if you use the enclosed self addressed envelope. Payment made in any other manner will be processed promptly but could result in up to a 5 day delay in crediting your account. **PLEASE MAKE ADDRESS CHANGE OR CORRECTIONS IN ADDRESS AREA BELOW.**

If state of residence changes, your account will be transferred, as required, for servicing.

77 52330 72630 0

MARY C. LEVI
263 HARPER STREET, APT. 26
ATLANTA, GA 30327

OFFICE USE ONLY

Amount Due

10.00

$ _____
AMOUNT PAID

MAIL ANY BILLING ERROR NOTICE TO Drumlin's Credit Department at address shown below. Direct other inquiries to nearest Drumlin store.

Mo.	Day	Reference	TRANSACTION DESCRIPTION See reverse for detailed description of department numbers indicated below	CHARGES	PAYMENTS & CREDITS
5	6	4641	4004999999999	30.44	

JUNE IS THE TIME AND DRUMLIN IS THE PLACE FOR
SUPER FATHER'S DAY VALUES: SPORTS EQUIPMENT
AND QUALITY CLOTHING THAT HAVE EARNED THE
RIGHT TO WEAR THE DRUMLIN NAME, GIFTS HE WILL
ENJOY ALL YEAR LONG.

PLEASE MENTION THIS ACCOUNT NUMBER WHEN ORDERING OR WRITING	BILLING DATE	PREVIOUS BALANCE	NEW BALANCE	MINIMUM PAYMENT
77 52330 72630 0	5 24 84	00.00	30.44	10.00

If the **FINANCE CHARGE** exceeds 50¢ the **ANNUAL PERCENTAGE RATE** is 18% of the AVERAGE DAILY BALANCE excluding any purchases added during the monthly billing period and excluding any unpaid **FINANCE CHARGE.**

To avoid a **FINANCE CHARGE** next month pay this amount within 30 days from Billing Date.

If you prefer to pay in installments pay the amount or more within 30 days from Billing Date. The sooner you pay and the more you pay the smaller your **FINANCE CHARGE.**

NOTICE: SEE REVERSE SIDE FOR IMPORTANT INFORMATION

Monthly statement tells customer how much is due if finance charge is to be avoided, how much is due if the budget plan is followed, and when payment is due.

To make a payment on account, the customer enters the amount of the payment in the space provided in the heading. The payment with the top portion of the monthly statement is sent to the company. The Drumlin Department Stores also provides an addressed envelope for mailing the payment.

Activity C-1. Answer the following questions about processing credit card sales. Refer to the text and illustrations on pages 667 to 670.

1. How does the salesclerk at Drumlin Department Stores check the customer's credit limit?

2. What is Mary Levi's account number?

3. What journal is used to record the batch total of the credit card sales? When recording the batch totals, what account is debited? What accounts are credited?

Activity C-2. Answer the following questions about the monthly statement prepared for Mary Levi. Refer to the text and illustrations on pages 669 and 670.

1. What is the minimum amount due on the balance owed by Mary Levi?

2. What are the total charges for the month?

3. What was Mary Levi's billing date?

4. What was the previous balance?

5. What is the new balance?

Accounting Concept:

Control. Procedures must be established to ensure accuracy, honesty, and efficiency and speed in handling and recording assets, liabilities, owner's equity, revenues, and expenses.

Topic 1 Problems

22-1. Determine the billing date for customers with the following account numbers. Use the schedule on page 662.

a. 14-20091-31196-0
b. 01-41104-67155-1
c. 12-32967-00479-0
d. 09-94112-32911-4
e. 06-06679-43122-0
f. 14-00443-71931-0
g. 11-25165-60041-3
h. 12-76330-38900-0
i. 10-89406-50627-0
j. 01-54818-81132-1

22-2. Determine the minimum monthly payment required on the following account balances. Use the schedule of minimum monthly payments on page 663.

a. $337
b. $7
c. $220
d. $155
e. $379
f. $291
g. $100
h. $60
i. $560
j. $49
k. $116
l. $18

The Language of Business

Here are some basic terms that make up the language of business. Do you know the meaning of each?

credit card
credit card sales
  subsystem
company card
bank card

travel and
  entertainment card
credit limit
regular charge plan
budget plan

installment plan
credit card insurance
credit agreement
credit application
credit bureau
Truth-in-Lending-Act

Fair Credit Billing Act
current customer file
negative account file
delinquent account
monthly statement

Chapter 22   Questions

1. List and describe three types of credit cards.
2. What special controls are needed for credit card sales?
3. What is the difference between the regular charge plan and the budget plan?
4. How is the use of credit cards an advantage for a business?

5. Describe the responsibilities of a credit department.
6. List five items included in the credit agreement.
7. Do businesses increase their profitability by issuing credit cards? Why or why not?

Chapter 22   Problems

Problems for Chapter 22 are given in the *Working Papers and Chapter Problems for Part 3*. If you are using the workbook, do the problems in the space provided there.

Chapter 22   Management Cases

Consumer Credit. A large percentage of all consumer purchases is made on credit. Buying on credit allows consumers to have immediate use of goods and services and pay for them later. Buying on credit can increase the profitability of businesses because more sales can be made. However, management knows that profits will increase over a long period of time only if consumers make intelligent choices when using their credit and their credit cards. Thus, many businesses provide their credit card customers with information on the proper use of consumer credit. Such information often includes the following points.

• Don't get in over your head. Use only as much credit as you can repay comfortably.

• Consider the cost of buying now and paying later.
• Avoid buying on credit just because it is easy to say "Charge it!"
• Read any credit agreement before signing.
• Keep sales invoices and other records of purchases so that you can verify your monthly statement.
• Make payments promptly.

Case 22M-1. As credit manager for a large department store, you have been asked to prepare an advertisement on the intelligent use of credit cards. The ad will appear in several national magazines and newspapers. What will you say in your ad?

Working Hint

When you begin working and earning money, you will probably apply for one or more credit cards. Avoid getting "hooked" on the use of credit cards; charge only what you can pay for based on your net pay.

One important step to follow in using credit cards is to prepare a personal monthly budget. The budget should list your net pay minus normal monthly expenses for rent, travel, food, savings, clothes, etc. Of course, you must also include the amount of monthly payments on previous credit card purchases. Follow the procedures you would use in preparing an income statement.

Curtis Carmichael *Budget* *For the Month Ended June 30, 19—*		
Estimated Net Pay		$ ____
Estimated Expenses:		
Fixed Expenses—list expenses that remain the same every month.		
These include auto payments, insurance, and so on.	$ ____	
Variable Expenses—list expenses that change from month to month.		
These include clothes, food, gasoline, and so on.	____	
Total Expenses		____
Net amount available for savings or long-term purchases		$ ____

Index

A ABA number, *def.,* 213; *illus.,* 213
Access time, *def.,* 602
Account balance, 54–55, **60**
Account form balance sheet, *def.,* 93, 170
Account number, *def.,* 53; *illus.,* 53, 54
  chart of accounts and, 54
  using, when journalizing, 566
Account title, *def.,* 53; *illus.,* 53, 54
Accounting, *def.,* 5
  accuracy and, 16
  double-entry, 62–63, **69**
  elements of, 5–13, 14–17
    assets, 6–10
    liabilities, 10–11
    owner's equity, 11–13
  legibility and, 16
Accounting clerk (DOT 216.482-010), 471
Accounting cycle, 45–46, **46;** *def.,* 45
  data processing cycle and, 190; *illus.,* 191
  posting data to the ledger and, 155–156
  preparing accounting proofs and, 162
  preparing financial statements and, 172–173
  summarizing, 83
Accounting entity, 29; *def.,* 28
Accounting entry, 63–64; *def.,* 64
Accounting equation, 14–17, **15;** *def.,* 14; *illus.,* 14
  accuracy and, 16
  in balance, *def.,* 16
  equality in, 15–16, **29**
    proving, 39; *illus.,* 40
  legibility and, 16
  out of balance, *def.,* 16
  proving, 16, 39–46; *def.,* 16
  transactions and, 21
Accounting period, 21–22, **29;** *def.,* 21
  going concern and, 21
  summary and, 21
  time covered by, 22
Accounting principles, 37
Accounting procedures, 281, 283; *def.,* 281
  electronic funds transfer, 283

Accounting procedures (*continued*)
  point-of-sale, 281, 283
Accounting proofs, 156–165; *def.,* 16
  accounting balances and, 157, 165
  accounting cycle and, 162
  data processing cycle and, 162–163
  errors and
    check-marking and, 158
    correcting, 160–161
    journal, 160
    ledger, 160
    locating, 159–160
    not revealed by a trial balance, 161–162
    trial balance, 158–161
  trial balance and, 156–157
    errors, 158–161
    preparing a, 157–158
Accounting subsystems, 278–279; *def.,* 278 (*see also specific subsystems*)
Accounting systems, 276–294, **287;** *def.,* 277, **277–278**
  accuracy and, 279
  efficiency and speed and, 279–280
  electronic, 277
  equipment for, 284–286
    computers, 286
    computing devices, 285
    recording devices, 284
    storage devices, 284
  establishing controls in, 279–280
  forms for, 280–281
  general (*see* General accounting subsystem)
  honesty and, 279
  information system and, 277
  manual, 277
  people and, 280
  procedures for, 281, 283
    electronic funds transfer, 283
    point-of-sale, 281, 283
  subsystems of, 278–279
  visualizing (*see* Flowcharts)
Accounts, 29; *def.,* 8, **26**
  forms of, 52–61, 143–145
  permanent (*see* Permanent accounts)
  temporary (*see* Temporary accounts)
  types of, 9, **370;** *illus.,* 9 (*see also specific types of accounts*)
  updating, 154
Accounts payable, *def.,* 11
  schedule of, *def.,* 359; *illus.,* 359
Accounts payable bookkeeper (DOT 210.382-018), 363
Accounts payable clerk (DOT 214.362-026), 357
Accounts payable ledger, 354–360; *illus.,* 355
  posting to, 357–359; *illus.,* 357, 358

Accounts payable ledger (*continued*)
  proving, 359; *illus.,* 359
  subsidiary ledgers and, 355–357; *illus.,* 355, 356
Accounts receivable, 419–422; *def.,* 6
  aging the, 421–422, 425, 525–527; *illus.,* 421
  collecting, 23–24; *illus.,* 24
  as current asset, 486
  realizable value of, 521
  reporting, 524
  sales discounts and, 409–412
  statements of account and, 419–421; *illus.,* 419
    computers and, 613
  updating, 517–524 (*see also* Uncollectible accounts)
    computers and, 611–613
Accounts receivable ledger, 394–395; *def.,* 355, 394; *illus.,* 356
  posting to, 395–398; *illus.,* 396–397
  proving, 398–399; *illus.,* 399
Accounts receivable bookkeeper (DOT 210.382-018), 420
Accounts receivable clerk (DOT 216.482-010), 420
Accrual basis of accounting, 563, **564;** *def.,* 563
Accruals, *def.,* 562–563
Accrued asset, *def.,* 556
Accrued expenses, 547–554; *def.,* 547
  accounting for, 551
  in closing the ledger, 553
  on the financial statements, 553
  interest, 547–549
    adjusting for, 548–549; *illus.,* 548
    paying the, 548–549; *illus.,* 548, 549
    worksheet and, 552
  salaries, 550–551
    adjusting for, 550
    paying the, 551
    worksheet and, 552
  on the worksheet, 551–552; *illus.,* 552
Accrued liabilities, *def.,* 551
Accrued revenues, 554–558; *def.,* 555
  adjusting for, 556; *illus.,* 556
  in closing the ledger, 562
  on the financial statements, 561–562; *illus.,* 562
  receiving, 557–558; *illus.,* 557, 558
  on the worksheet, 560–561; *illus.,* 561
Accumulating amounts, 311
Accuracy, 279, 587; *def.,* 16, 19
Adder, computer, 602–603
Adjusted bank balance, *def.,* 228

Adjusted checkbook balance, *def.*, 228

Adjusting the ledger, *def.*, 491–492; *illus.*, 492

Aging accounts receivable, 421–422, 425; *illus.*, 421, 526
estimating uncollectible accounts and, 525–527

Allowance for doubtful accounts account, 520–521; *illus.*, 521

Allowance method of recording losses, 520–521; *def.*, 517; *illus.*, 521

Analyzing a transaction, 63–64, **69;** *def.*, 23; *illus.*, 23
journalizing and, 129
summary, 28

Arithmetic/logic unit, 599, 602–603

Asset accounts, 8–9
opening, 58–59; *illus.*, 59
recording changes in, 64–65; *illus.*, 65

Asset contra account, *def.*, 520–521

Asset reduction account, 520

Asset transactions, 23–24
buying an asset for cash, 23; *illus.*, 23
collecting accounts receivable, 23–24; *illus.*, 24

Assets, 6–10; *def.*, 6, **8**
buying
for cash, 23
on credit, 25
cash, 6 (*see also* Cash)
classifying, 490
current, 486
as economic resource, 5–6, 9–10
intangible, 7–8
inventories, 6–7
natural resources, 7
plant and equipment, 7, 486–487
receivables, 6
recording the cost of, 171, **173**
basis for, 173
sources of, 5–6

Audit clerk (DOT 210.382-010), 481

Audit trail, 134, **139, 156;** *def.*, 134
posting to the ledger and, 150–151

Automated accounting systems, *def.*, 277 (*see also* Computers)

Auxiliary storage, 602

Average unit cost, 643

B
Back order file, 387
Bad debt (*see* Uncollectible accounts)

Balance in an account, *def.*, 39; *illus.*, 40

Balance ledger form, 356–357, 380; *def.*, 143
four-column, 143–144; *illus.*, 144
purpose of, 154

Balance sheet, 91–98, **98;** *def.*, 91; *illus.*, 92, 97
account form, 93, 170
accrued and deferred revenue on, 562; *illus.*, 562
accrued expenses on, 553; *illus.*, 553
analyzing a, 92–93
comparative, 187–189, **190;** *def.*, 187; *illus.*, 188
for corporations, 200–201; *illus.*, 201
depreciation on, 540; *illus.*, 540
financial position and, 97
for partnerships, 196; *illus.*, 197
preparing, 93–97, 169–171, 486–488; *illus.*, 487
assets section and, 94–95
current assets and, 486
current liabilities and, 488
heading and, 94
liabilities section and, 95–96
long-term liabilities and, 488
owner's equity section and, 96–97
plant and equipment and, 486–487
purpose of, 92
relationships between income statement and, 173
report form, 170–171; *illus.*, 170
for single proprietorship, 194; *illus.*, 194
uncollectible accounts on, 522; *illus.*, 523

Balance sheet accounts, *def.*, 96–97, 167

Balancing the accounts, 77–79; *def.*, 77, 157; *illus.*, 78

Bank credit card sales, 308–310; *def.*, 308, 661; *illus.*, 308
customer's credit and, 308
payment from the bank and, 309
recording, 309–310; *illus.*, 310
source documents and, 308–309; *illus.*, 309

Bank-depositor relationship, 216

Bank reconciliation statement, *def.*, 226; *illus.*, 227

Bank statement, 222–225, **229;** *def.*, 222; *illus.*, 223
canceled checks and, 222
reconciling, 226–228; *illus.*, 227
making corrections after, 228–229; *illus.*, 229
verifying balance in checkbook and, 223–225
deposits in transit and, 224
dishonored checks and, 224
errors in computation and, 225
fees and, 224–225
outstanding checks and, 224
service charges and, 225

Bank transfer, *def.*, 264

Bar code, 609; *illus.*, 609

Bar-coded tag, 611

Batch of invoices, *def.*, 579

Batch processing, 578–581
direct posting and, 580–581; *illus.*, 581

Beginning inventory, *def.*, 464

Bill, *def.*, **117**

Billing clerk (DOT 214.482-010), 387

Billing for merchandise, 386–388
preparing invoices, 387–388

Bits, 608

Blank endorsement, 217–218; *def.*, 217; *illus.*, 217

Block flowcharts, *def.*, 288; *illus.*, 288

Board of directors, *def.*, 198

Book value, *def.*, 534

Budget charge plan, *def.*, 662

Budgeting, 502–504; *def.*, 502; *illus.*, 503, 504
comparison of actual and projected amounts, 503–504
preparing, 502–504

Business data, *def.*, 277

Business entity, 28

Business forms, 115–116, 280–281; *def.*, 116, 280; *illus.*, 280, 282
computerized, 281; *illus.*, 282

Business information, *def.*, 277

Business papers (*see* Source documents)

Buying on credit, *def.*, 10; *illus.*, 25

C
Calendar year, *def.*, 22
Canceled checks, *def.*, 222

Capital, *def.*, 12, **13**

Capital account
recording changes in, 70–72; *illus.*, 71
transferring to, 41–43; *illus.*, 43
net income, 42–43, 99–101, 103–105
net loss, 43, 99–101, 105–106

Capital stock account, *def.*, 199

Cash, *def.*, 6
buying assets for, 23; *illus.*, 23
as current asset, 486
depositing (*see* Depositing cash)
net decrease in, 498
net increase in, 498, 499
paying by
expenses, 34–35; *illus.*, 35
payroll, 263–264
receiving revenue from sales, 32; *illus.*, 32
safeguarding, 317
source of, 498–499
use of, 498, 499

Cash balance, verifying, 221–222
Cash basis of accounting, 563, **564;** *def.,* 563
Cash disbursement, *def.,* 231
Cash discounts, 368
  perpetual inventory method and, 629; *illus.,* 630
Cash expenditure, *def.,* 231
Cash flow, 497–499; *def.,* 497
Cash-flow statement, 497–499; *def.,* 497
Cash overage, 327–328; *def.,* 327; *illus.,* 327
Cash paid on account, *def.,* 26; *illus.,* 26
Cash payments bookkeeper (DOT 210.382-018), 315
Cash payments journal, 318–323; *def.,* 318; *illus.,* 319
  posting from, 321–322; *illus.,* 321, 322
    during the month, 374–375; *illus.,* 374
    at the end of the month, 375; *illus.,* 375
  recording purchase discounts in, 373; *illus.,* 373
  recording withdrawals on, 320–321; *illus.,* 320
  totaling, 321–322; *illus.,* 321, 322
Cash payments subsystem, 315–332; *def.,* 315
  on account, 371–376
    journalizing, 371–373
    posting, 374–375
    recording discounts, 373–374
  control of, 315–316
    dividing the responsibilities, 316
    paying by check, 315
    proving cash, 315–316
    using prenumbered checks, 315
    verifying/approving invoices, 315
  journalizing, 318–323; *illus.,* 319–321
  posting, 321–322; *illus.,* 321
  processing, 318–323
  recording withdrawals, 320–321; *illus.,* 320
  visualizing, 316; *illus.,* 317
Cash posting clerk (DOT 216.482-010), 322
Cash proof, 324–329; *def.,* 324
  cash account and checkbook balances and, 324; *illus.,* 324
  cash over and, 327–328; *illus.,* 327
  cash short and, 328–329; *illus.,* 328
  cash short and over account and, 327–329; *illus.,* 328, 329
  change funds and, 326–327
  checkbook and bank statement balances and, 325; *illus.,* 325, 326

Cash proof (*continued*)
  controlling cash payments and, 315–316
  controlling cash receipts and, 297–298; *illus.,* 298, 299
  preparing, on an adding machine tape, 332; *illus.,* 332
Cash receipts bookkeeper (DOT 210.382-018), 300
Cash receipts journal, 303–304; *def.,* 303; *illus.,* 304, 305
  journalizing to, 414; *illus.,* 414
  posting from, 305–307, 414–415; *illus.,* 306, 415–416
    at the end of the month, 417; *illus.,* 417
Cash receipts subsystem, 296–310; *def.,* 296
  bank credit card sales and, 308–310
  controlling, 296–300; *def.,* 296
    cash register tapes and, 296
    depositing cash receipts and, 299
    dividing responsibility and, 299
    proving cash and, 297–299
    remittance slips and, 297, 298
    source documents and, 296–298
  handling, *def.,* 296
  journalizing, 302–305; *illus.,* 304, 305
  posting, 305–307; *illus.,* 306, 307
    credit entries, 305
    the debit to cash, 306–307
    totaling the cash receipts journal and, 306
  processing, 302–310
  recording, 296, 307
  from sales on credit, 413–419
    journalizing, 414; *illus.,* 414
    posting, 414–417; *illus.,* 415–416
    taxes, returns and allowances, and discounts, 416
  visualizing, 300; *illus.,* 301
Cash received on account, *def.,* 23; *illus.,* 24
Cash refunds, 403–405
Cash register tape, *def.,* 296
  proving cash and, 297–298
Cash short and over account, *def.,* 327–328; *illus.,* 328, 329
Cash shortage, 328–329; *def.,* 328; *illus.,* 328
Cashier, office (DOT 211.462-010), 300, 315
Cathode-ray tube displays, 600, 604
Central processor, 599
Certified checks, 214–215; *def.,* 215; *illus.,* 215
Change fund, *def.,* 298, 326
  establishing, 326
  replenishing, 326–327
  using, 326

Change sheet, *def.,* 263; *illus.,* 264
Charge plans
  budget, 662
  installment, 663
  regular, 662
Chart of accounts, *def.,* 54; *illus.,* 54
Charter, corporate, *def.,* 198
Check-marking, 158
Checkbook stub, *illus.,* 118
Checks, 210–216; *def.,* 210; *illus.,* 211
  ABA number on, 213
  bank-depositor relationship and, 216
  canceled, 222
  certified, 214–215
  depositing, 217–220
  depositor and, 210
  dishonored, 224
  drawee of, 210
  drawer of, 210
  endorsements on (*see* Endorsement)
  magnetic ink on, 213
  magnetic ink character recognition machine and, 213
  outstanding, 224
  payee of, 210
  paying the payroll by, 263
  procedure for preparing, 210–212
  processing, 212–214
  signature card and, 210
  stop payment on, 215–216
  voucher, 214
Claims of creditors, 11
Claims of owner, 13
Closed account, *def.,* 101
Closing the accounts, *def.,* 106
Closing entries, *def.,* 106
Closing the ledger, 112, 183, 493–495, **496;** *def.,* 106, 173–174, 493; *illus.,* 493–495
  accrued expenses in, 553
  depreciation in, 541–542; *illus.,* 541–542
  uncollectible accounts in, 523; *illus.,* 523
Coding, *def.,* 53; *illus.,* 53, 54
Collection agent, 269, 430
Combination journal, 568–577; *def.,* 568; *illus.,* 568–569
  designing a, 568–569
  posting from, 574–576
  proving the, 572–574
  recording entries in, 569–572
Commission pay plan, *def.,* 242, 432
Commissions, *def.,* 241
Common language media, 605–610
  80-column card, 605–606
    coding on, 606–607
  magnetic ink character recognition (MICR), 608
  magnetic tape, 608

Common language media (*continued*)
  medium and, 605
  96–column card, 607
  optical scanning, 608–609
  punched tag, 608
  punched tape, 607
Company credit card, *def.*, 661
  applications for, 664
  sales, *def.*, 308
Comparative balance sheet, 187–189, **190;** *def.*, 187; *illus.*, 188
Comparative income statement, 185–187, **190;** *def.*, 185; *illus.*, 186
  preparing, 187
Compound journal entry, *def.*, 135; *illus.*, 133
Computer accounting systems, *def.*, 277
Computer-output-microfilm (COM), *def.*, 281; *illus.*, 281
Computerized business forms, 281; *illus.*, 282
Computers, 286, 598–605; *def.*, 592; *illus.*, 286, 592, 604
  access time and, 602
  adder and, 602–603
  applications of, 611–614
  arithmetic/logic unit of, 599, 602–603
  auxiliary storage and, 602
  cathode-ray tube displays and, 600, 604
  central processor and, 599, 601–603
  common language media and (*see* Common language media)
  console, 603
  console typewriter and, 600, 604
  control unit of, 599, 603
  controls for, 595
  counter and, 603
  data processing service centers and, 597
  development of, 592–593
  diskettes and, 593, 601
  distributed data processing and, 595–597
  equipment for, 599
  error report and, 595
  external storage and, 602
  GIGO principle and, 609–610
  input devices and, 599–601
  internal storage and, 602
  item count and, 595
  keyboard terminal and, 601
  machine language output and, 604
  magnetic-card unit and, 601
  magnetic character reader and, 600
  magnetic-disk units and, 600
  magnetic tape unit and, 600
  memory unit and, 602

Computers (*continued*)
  microfilm processors and, 605
  off line, 603
  on line, 603
  optical scanner and, 600
  origination step and, 599
  output devices and, 599, 603–605
  printers and, 603
  programs for, 593–594
  punched-card reader and, 599
  punched cards and (*see* Punched cards)
  punched-tape reader and, 599
  register and, 602–603
  storage unit of, 599, 602
  telecommunication devices and, 601
  transaction recorders and, 600
  types of, 593
Computing devices, 285; *illus.*, 285
Computing gross earnings, 241–245
  determining hours worked and, 244–245
  pay plans and, 241–242
    incentive, 242
  wages and hours of work and, 243–244
    overtime pay and, 243
Console typewriter, 600, 604
Continuous life, *def.*, 198
Contra account, *def.*, 520
  asset, *def.*, 520–521
Contract of employment, *def.*, 243
Control principles, **287,** 315, 334, **341,** 383–386, **388,** 390, 402, 410, 428, 437, 444, **636, 671**
Control unit, 599, 603
Controlling account, 649; *def.*, 356; *illus.*, 356
Cooperative, *def.*, 12, 201–202
Copyright, *def.*, 8
Corporation, 198–199; *def.*, 12, 198
  financial statements for, 199–201; *illus.*, 200, 201
Correcting an error, 102, 113
Cost and expense accounts, *def.*, 349
Cost of the delivered goods, *def.*, 362
Cost of goods on hand, computing, 464
  perpetual inventory method and, 620
Cost of goods sold, computing, 349, 465–468; *illus.*, 465–468
  perpetual inventory method and, 621
Cost of goods sold account, *def.*, 623
Cost of goods sold journal, *def.*, 624
Costs, *def.*, 348
Counter, computer, 603
Credit, *def.*, 6
  buying on, 10; *illus.*, 25 (*see also* Purchases, on credit)

Credit (*continued*)
  incurring expenses on, 35–36; *illus.*, 36
  line of, 662
  receiving revenue from sales on, 33; *illus.*, 33
  returning assets bought on, 25; *illus.*, 26
  selling on, 6
Credit, a, *def.*, 54, **55**
Credit agreement, 663; *illus.*, 665
  terms of, 664
Credit application, 664; *illus.*, 665
Credit approval, 384
Credit bureau, 664
Credit card fee expense, *def.*, 310
Credit card insurance, 663
Credit card sales subsystem, 661–671; *def.*, 661 (*see also* Bank credit card sales)
  charge plans and, 662–663
  controls, 662–663
  coordinating departments within, 667
  credit departments and, 664
  current customer file, 666–667
  delinquent account, 667
  issuing cards, 666
  negative account file, 667
  preparing monthly statements, 669–670; *illus.*, 670
  preparing sales invoices, 668–669; *illus.*, 669
  processing sales, 667–668
    checking credit limits, 668
  types of credit cards and, 661–662; *illus.*, 661
Credit cards, *def.*, 661; *illus.*, 308, 661
  issuing, 666
Credit clerk (DOT 205.367-022), 388
Credit customer files, 666–667
Credit department, 664
  applications and, 664; *illus.*, 665
  coordination between other departments and, 667
  customer files and, 666–667
  issuing cards, 666
  reference investigations and, 664
  terms of the credit agreement and, 664; *illus.*, 665
Credit limit, *def.*, 662
  checking, 668
Credit manager, 395
Credit memorandum, *def.*, 365; *illus.*, 119, 365
  issuing a, 405–407; *illus.*, 406, 407
  receiving a, 365–367; *illus.*, 366, 367
Credit period, *def.*, 368
Credit reference investigation, 664
Credit side of an account, *def.*, 54

Crediting the account, *def.*, 54
  decreasing accounts, 57
  increasing accounts, 57
  opening balances, 57
  permanent accounts (*see* Permanent accounts, debiting and crediting)
  rules for, 56–57; *illus.*, 56
  showing normal balances, 57
Creditor, *def.*, 10
  claims of, 11
Cross-footing, *def.*, 257
Cross-referencing, *def.*, 131
  in posting, *def.*, 150–151
Currency requisition, *def.*, 263–264
Current assets, *def.*, 486
Current customer file, 666–667
Current liabilities, *def.*, 488
Current ratio, 500
Customer letter, *illus.*, 383
Customer orders, 383–385
Cutoff date, 472
Cycle billing, 419–420; *def.*, 662; *illus.*, 420

D Daily inventory report, 654–655; *illus.*, 654
Daily sales report, 653; *illus.*, 653, 654
Data, *def.*, 277
  external, 122
  input of, 137–138
  internal, 12
  journalizing (*see* Journalizing data)
  originating (*see* Source documents)
  origination of, 137
  output of, 137–138
  processing of, 123–126
    automated, 124–126
    manual, 123
Data collector, 612
Data processing (*see* Information processing)
Data processing cycle, 137–138; *def.*, 137
  accounting cycle, 190; *illus.*, 191
  accounting proofs and, 162–163
Data processing service center, *def.*, 597
Data processing system, 595–597
Debit, *def.*, 54, **55**
Debit memorandum, *def.*, 225
Debit side of an account, *def.*, 54
Debiting the account, *def.*, 54
  decreasing accounts, 57
  increasing accounts, 57
  opening balances, 57
  permanent accounts (*see* Permanent accounts, debiting and crediting)

Debiting the account (*continued*)
  rules for, 56–57; *illus.*, 56
  showing normal balances, 57
Deductions from gross earnings, 246–256; *def.*, 246
  computing net pay, 255
  federal income tax withholding, 246–248
    tax tables for, *illus.*, 247–248
  Federal Insurance Contributions Act (FICA), 249–250
    tax table for, *illus.*, 251
  payroll register and, 257
  required by law, 246, 254
  state income tax, 250, 252–254
    tax tables for, *illus.*, 252
  union, 254–255
  voluntary, 254
Deferrals, *def.*, 562–563
Deferred revenue, 558–562; *def.*, 558
  adjusting for, 559–560; *illus.*, 560
  in closing the ledger, 562
  on the financial statements, 561–562; *illus.*, 562
  receiving, 559; *illus.*, 559
  recording, 559
  on worksheet, 560–561; *illus.*, 561
Delinquent account, 667
Delivery charges, 409
Dependent, *def.*, 246
Deposit in transit, *def.*, 224
Deposit ticket, 219–220; *def.*, 219; *illus.*, 219
Depositing cash, 217–221
  endorsements and, 217–218
  passbook and, 220
  preparing cash for deposit, 217–218
  preparing a deposit ticket, 219–220
  processing deposits, 220
  restrictive endorsement and, 218
Depositor, *def.*, 210
Depreciation, 531–543; **543;** *def.*, 531
  allocating the cost of plant and equipment and, 531–532; *illus.*, 532
  in closing the ledger, 541–542; *illus.*, 541–542
  estimating, 532–533
    disposal value and, 532–533
    IRS guidelines for, 533, 545
    straight-line method of, 533
  on the financial statements, 539–540; *illus.*, 540
  recording, 534–538; *illus.*, 535, 536
    book value and, 534
    plant and equipment ledger and, 536–538; *illus.*, 537
  reporting, 543
  on worksheet, 538–539; *illus.*, 538

Depreciation (*continued*)
  building, 538–539
  delivery equipment, 539
  office equipment, 539
Deterioration of inventory, *def.*, 346
Dictionary of Occupational Titles
  accounting clerk (DOT 216.482-010), 471
  accounts payable bookkeeper (DOT 210.382-018), 363
  accounts payable clerk (DOT 214.362-026), 357
  accounts receivable bookkeeper (DOT 210.382-018), 420
  accounts receivable clerk (DOT 216.482-010), 420
  audit clerk (DOT 210.382-010), 481
  billing clerk (DOT 214.482-010), 387
  cash payments bookkeeper (DOT 210.382-018), 315
  cash posting clerk (DOT 216.482-010), 322
  cash receipts bookkeeper (DOT 210.382-018), 300
  cashier, office (DOT 211.462-010), 300, 315
  credit clerk (DOT 205.367-022), 388
  full-charge bookkeeper (DOT 210.382-014), 495
  general office clerk (DOT 219.362-010), 269
  inventory clerk (DOT 222.387-026), 336, 465
  order clerk (DOT 249.367-054), 383
  payroll clerk (DOT 215.482-010), 430
  purchasing agent (DOT 162.157-038), 244, 336
  purchasing clerk (DOT 249.367-066), 338
  receiving clerk (DOT 222.387-050), 338
  shipping clerk (DOT 222.387-050), 385
  stock-control clerk (DOT 219.367-034), 388
Direct-entry records, 577–585
  batch processing, 578–581
  journalless accounting, 581–583
  ledgerless accounting, 583–585
Direct posting, *def.*, 580
Direct write-off method, 518–519; *def.*, 517; *illus.*, 518, 519
Discount period, *def.*, 368
Discounts
  cash, 368, 629
  credit card handling fee, 309
  purchase, 367–369
  trade, 650

Dishonored check, *def.*, 224
Diskette, 593, 601; *illus.*, 601
Disposal value, 532–533; *def.*, 532
Distributed data processing system, 595–597; *def.*, 596; *illus.*, 596
Division of responsibility, 279
Document, *def.*, 117
  source (*see* Source documents)
Double-entry accounting, 62–63, 69; *def.*, 62; *illus.*, 62
Double-posting, *def.*, 367; *illus.*, 367
Doubtful account (*see* Uncollectible accounts)
Drawee of checks, *def.*, 210
Drawer of checks, *def.*, 210
Drawing account, *def.*, 320

E Economic resources, 5–6, 10; *def.*, 5 (*see also* Assets)
  borrowing, 10
  investing, 10
Efficiency and speed, 279–280
80-column punched card, 605–606; *illus.*, 606
  coding on, 606–607
Electronic accounting systems (*see* Computers)
Electronic data processing (EDP), 124–126; *def.*, 123 (*see also* Computers)
Electronic funds transfer (EFT), *def.*, 283; *illus.*, 283
Electronic mail, *def.*, 598
Electronic typewriter, 592, 597–598; *illus.*, 592
Employee, *def.*, 241
Employee earnings record, 258–259; *def.*, 258, 436; *illus.*, 258, 437
  as a subsidiary ledger, 436–437
Employee pay statement, *def.*, 263; *illus.*, 263
Employee's Withholding Allowance Certificate (Form W-4), 246–247; *illus.*, 247
Employer, *def.*, 241
  payroll taxes paid by, 261–262
  recording, 262, 439–440
Employer FICA tax, 439
Employer's Annual Federal Unemployment Tax Return (Form 940), 452; *illus.*, 453
Employer's Quarterly Federal Tax Return (Form 941), 446; *illus.*, 447
Employment contract, *def.*, 243
Ending inventory, *def.*, 464
Endorsement, *def.*, 217
  blank, 217–218; *def.*, 217; *illus.*, 217
  full, *def.*, 218; *illus.*, 218

Endorsement (*continued*)
  making an, 218
  restrictive, *def.*, 218; *illus.*, 218
Endorser, *def.*, 217
Equality of ledger, 60
Error report, *def.*, 595
Exemption, tax, *def.*, 246
Expense accounts
  closing, 175; *illus.*, 174
  closing entries for, 177–178; *illus.*, 177
  recording changes in, 74–76; *illus.*, 75
Expense transactions, 34–36
  incurring, on credit, 35–36; *illus.*, 36
  paying, with cash, 34–35; *illus.*, 35
Expenses, 37; *def.*, 34
  accrued (*see* Accrued expenses)
Expired costs, *def.*, 34
Extensions, *def.*, 340
External data, *def.*, 122
External storage, 602

F Face value of note, 555
  Fair Credit Billing Act, 666
Fair Labor Standards Act, 243–244
Federal income tax withholding, 246–248
  computation of, 248
  tax tables for, *illus.*, 247–248
Federal Insurance Contributions Act (FICA), 249–250
  employer-paid, 261
    recording, 439, 440
  schedule of deposits for, 445–446; *illus.*, 445, 446
  tax table for, *illus.*, 251
Federal Tax Deposit (Form 501), 445–446; *illus.*, 445
Federal Tax Deposit (Form 508), 450–451; *illus.*, 451
Federal unemployment compensation taxes, 450–452
Federal Unemployment Tax Act (FUTA), 249, 261
FICA tax [*see* Federal Insurance Contributions Act (FICA)]
FIFO, 643–644
Financial Accounting Standards Board (FASB), 37
Financial information, interpreting, 497–505
  analyzing cash flow, 497–499
  budgeting and, 502–505; *illus.*, 503, 504
  using ratios, 499–502
    current ratio, 500
    return on owner's equity ratio, 501–502
    return on total assets ratio, 501

Financial position, *def.*, 97, **98**
Financial statements (*see also* Balance sheet; Income statement)
  accrued and deferred revenue on, 561–562; *illus.*, 562
  accrued expenses on, 553; *illus.*, 553
  for corporations, 199–201; *illus.*, 200, 201
  depreciation on, 539–540; *illus.*, 540
  for partnerships, 196; *illus.*, 196, 197
  perpetual inventory method and, 646–647
  preparing, 167–173, 482–491
    balance sheet and, 486–488; *illus.*, 487
    income statement and, 484; *illus.*, 483
    schedule of cost of goods sold and, 482–483; *illus.*, 483
    statement of changes in financial position, 488–490; *illus.*, 489
    statement of owner's equity, 485–486; *illus.*, 485
    worksheet and, 478–481; *illus.*, 482
  relationship between, 173
  for single proprietorships, 193–195; *illus.*, 194
  uncollectible accounts on, 522; *illus.*, 523
  users of, 185
Finished goods, *def.*, 7
Fiscal year, *def.*, 22
Fixed assets, *def.*, 7
Fixed liabilities, 488
Flow of information, 292
Flowcharts, 287–294; *def.*, 287; *illus.*, 288
  block, 288
  cash payments, 316; *illus.*, 317
  cash receipts, 300; *illus.*, 301
  computer programmers and, 594; *illus.*, 594
  credit sales, 388; *illus.*, 389, 423
  general accounting, 459–460; *illus.*, 459–461
  input data and, 287
  output data and, 287
  personnel and payroll, 430; *illus.*, 431
  preparing a template for, 289, 294; *illus.*, 289, 294
  procedure, 290–291
  purchases of merchandise, 341; *illus.*, 342
  symbolic, 288–289
  system, 289–290
FOB (free on board), *def.*, 336
  destination, *def.*, 361

FOB (free on board) (*continued*)
  shipping point, *def.*, 361
Formal trial balance, *def.*, 79
Forms register, *def.*, 284, 297; *illus.*, 284
Four-column balance ledger form, 143–144; *illus.*, 144
Franchise, *def.*, 8
Free on board (FOB), *def.*, 336, 361
Freight In account, *def.*, 362
Freight on purchases account, *def.*, 362
Full-charge bookkeeper (DOT 210.382-014), 495
Full endorsement, *def.*, 218; *illus.*, 218
FUTA tax, 249, 261

G Garbage in, garbage out (GIGO) principle, 609–610
Garnishment, *def.*, 254
General accounting subsystem, 458–512; *def.*, 458
  controlling internal transactions, 458
  financial statements and (*see* Financial statements, preparing)
  interpreting financial information and (*see* Financial information, interpreting)
  ledger and (*see* Ledger, adjusting and closing)
  procedures to control, 458
  trial balance and (*see* Trial balance, updating)
  visualizing, 459–460; *illus.*, 459–461
  worksheet and (*see* Worksheet)
General journal, 303; *illus.*, 304
General ledger, *def.*, 355
General office clerk (DOT 219.362-010), 269
Generally accepted accounting principles (GAAP), 37
GIGO principle, 609–610
Going concern, 29, *def.*, 21
Gross earnings, *def.*, 241 (*see also* Computing gross earnings; Deductions from gross earnings)
Gross profit, *def.*, 348–349, 465
  perpetual inventory method and, 621–622; *illus.*, 622
Gross sales, *def.*, 402

H Honesty, 279
Hourly-rate pay plan, *def.*, 242, 432

I Incentive pay plans, 242; *def.*, 242
Income, 31; *def.*, **31**
  net, *def.*, 41
Income statement, 87–91, **91,** 484; *def.*, 87; *illus.*, 88, 90, 483
  accrued and deferred revenue on, 561–562; *illus.*, 562
  accrued expenses on, 553; *illus.*, 553
  comparative, 185–187, **190;** *def.*, 185; *illus.*, 186
  for corporations, 199–200; *illus.*, 200
  depreciation on, 539; *illus.*, 540
  for merchandising businesses, 484; *illus.*, 483
  for partnerships, 196; *illus.*, 196
  preparing, 89–90, 168
    expense section and, 89–90
    heading and, 89
    net income or net loss section and, 90
    revenue section and, 89
  purpose of, 88
  relationship between balance sheet and, 173
  for single proprietorship, 193; *illus.*, 194
  uncollectible accounts on, 522; *illus.*, 523
  what it does not show, 168–169
Income statement accounts, *def.*, 167
Income Summary account, 32–37; *def.*, 42; *illus.*, 32
  closing, 175; *illus.*, 174
  closing entry for, 178–179; *illus.*, 178, 179
  purpose of, 103; *illus.*, 103
  as a temporary account, 36–37
  transferring
    net income, 103–105
    net loss, 105–106
Information processing, *def.*, 277 (*see also* Accounting systems)
Information processing cycle, 605 (*see also* Data processing cycle)
Information requirements, 598
Information system, *def.*, 277 (*see also* Accounting systems)
Input data, 137–138; *def.*, 137, 190
  accounting system and, 190; *illus.*, 191
  flowcharts and, 287
Input devices, 137–138; *def.*, 137
  list of, 599–601
Input medium, 137–138; *def.*, 137
Insolvency, *def.*, 500
Installment charge plan, *def.*, 663
Insurance
  adjustment for expired, 474–475
  prepaid, 470–471

Intangible assets, *def.*, 7–8
Interest expense, 547–549
  adjusting for, 548–549; *illus.*, 548
  paying the, 548–549; *illus.*, 548, 549
  worksheet and, 552
Interest revenue (*see* Accrued revenues)
Internal data, *def.*, 122
Internal storage, 602
Internal transactions, *def.*, 458
Interpreting accounting information, 44–45, 184–192; *def.*, 44; *illus.*, 45
  comparative balance sheet and, 187–189
  comparative income statement and, 185–187
  output and, 190
  preparing statements and, 187
  users of financial statements and, 185
Interstate commerce, *def.*, 243
Inventory, 6–7, 344–348; *def.*, 7, 344
  adjustment for, 474
  beginning, 464
  costing the, 642
  counting the, 640–642
  as current asset, 486
  deterioration and, 346
  ending, 464
  finished goods, 7
  mishandling and theft of, 346–347
  obsolescence and, 346
  periodic (*see* Periodic inventory method)
  perpetual (*see* Perpetual inventory subsystem)
  physical, 345–346, 464
  quantity control and, 344
  raw materials, 7
  types of, 7
  updating, 462, 464–468
    cost of goods on hand and, 464
    cost of goods sold and, 465–468
  work in process, 7
Inventory card, 335; *illus.*, 335
Inventory clerk (DOT 222.387-026), 336, 465
Inventory ledger, 636–644; *def.*, 623
  inventory card and, 637–638; *illus.*, 637
  posting to, 638–640
    purchase discounts, 639
    purchase returns and allowances, 639–640
    purchases, 638; *illus.*, 638
    sales, 639; *illus.*, 639
  proving, 640–642
    costing the inventory, 642
    counting the inventory, 640–642

Inventory ledger card, 637–638;
illus., 623, 637
Inventory loss, 346–347; *def.*, 346
accounting for, 644–646; *illus.*,
645
Inventory sheet, 641; *illus.*, 642
Inventory tag, 641; *illus.*, 641
Invoice, 115–116; *def.*, **117**
Item count, *def.*, 595

 Journal entry, *def.*, 129;
illus., 129
Journalizing data, 126–139; *def.*,
127; *illus.*, 128
audit trail and, 134
batch totals, 578–581
direct posting and, 580–581;
illus., 581
cash payments, 318–320, 371–373;
illus., 319, 371, 372
cash receipts, 302–305; *illus.*, 304,
305
from credit sales, 414; *illus.*, 414
compound journal entry and, 135
conventional, 577–578; *illus.*, 578
credit memorandum, 365–367,
405–407; *illus.*, 366, 367, 406,
407
journals and, 127–128
purpose of, 128
opening entry and, 134–135
origination and input and, 137–138
other methods of, 136–137
payroll, 435–436; *illus.*, 435
petty cash entries, 234–236
procedure for, 129–131
analyzing the transaction, 129
cross-referencing, 131
posting reference, 131
recording the credit entry, 130
recording the date, 130
recording the debit entry, 130
writing an explanation, 130–131
summarizing, 134–135
purchases on credit, 349–351;
illus., 350, 351
sales on credit, 390–393; *illus.*,
391, 392
transportation costs, 362–363;
illus., 362
two-column journal and, 135
typical transactions, 131; *illus.*,
132–134
Journalless accounting, 581–583;
def., 582
Journals, 127–128, **139;** *def.*, 127;
illus., 128
journalizing and, 127–128 (*see also*
Journalizing data)

Journals (*continued*)
locating errors in, 160
purpose of, 128
two-column, 135; *illus.*, 133

 Keyboard skills, 615
Keyboard terminal, 601

 Ledger, 60, 156, 491–497,
def., 60, 143; *illus.*, 85
adjusting entries, 492–493; *illus.*,
492
closing entries, 106, **112,** 173–
174, **183,** 493–495; *illus.*,
493–495
equality of, 60
locating errors in, 160
postclosing trial balance and, 495–
496; *illus.*, 496
posting to (*see* Posting data, to the
ledger)
proving the, 77–80
computing account balances,
77–79
preparing a trial balance, 79–80
Ledger account, *def.*, 143
forms of, 143–145, 154, 356–357
Ledgerless accounting, 583–585; *def.*,
583; *illus.*, 585
Legibility, 50; *def.*, 16
Liabilities, 10–12; *def.*, 10, **11**
accrued (*see* Accrued liabilities)
classifying, 490
current, 488
long-term, 488
paying, 26; *illus.*, 26
Liability
limited, *def.*, 198
unlimited, *def.*, 193
Liability accounts, 11
opening, 59; *illus.*, 59
recording changes in, 66–68; *illus.*,
67
Liability transactions, 25–27
buying assets on credit, 25; *illus.*,
25
paying liabilities, 26; *illus.*, 26
returning assets bought on credit,
25–26; *illus.*, 26
Limited liability, *def.*, 198
Limited life, *def.*, 193
Line of credit, *def.*, 662
Liquidity, *def.*, 94, 486
Listing (*see* Journals)
Loan payable, *def.*, 11
Long-term liabilities, *def.*, 488

 Machine language, *def.*, 605
(*see also* Common lan-
guage media)
output, 604
Magnetic-card unit, 601
Magnetic character reader, 600
Magnetic-disk units, 600
Magnetic ink, *def.*, 213; *illus.*, 213
Magnetic ink character recognition
(MICR) machine, *def.*, 213, 608;
illus., 213
Magnetic-tape unit, 600, 608
Mainframe computer, 593
Maker of the note, 555
Manual accounting systems, 567–
587; *def.*, 277 (*see also* Combina-
tion journal; Direct-entry rec-
ords)
Manual data processing, *def.*, 123
Market value, *def.*, 171
MasterCard, 308
**Matching principle, 46, 91, 472,
496, 524, 543, 564;** *def.*, 41
Measuring unit, 29
Members' equity, *def.*, 12
Memorandum book, *def.*, 232
Memorandum entry, *def.*, 304
recording, 307
Memory unit, 602
Merchandise alert report, 655; *illus.*,
655
Merchandise inventory, *def.*, 7 (*see
also* Inventory)
Merchandise inventory account, 622
Merchandise inventory journal, *def.*,
623–624
Merchandising business, *def.*, 348
Microcomputer, 593
Microfilm processors, 605
Microforms, *def.*, 281; *illus.*, 281
Microprocessor, 593
Minicomputer, 593
Minus asset account, 520
Mortgage, *def.*, 11
Mortgage payable, *def.*, 11
Multicolumn journal, 373

N Natural resources, *def.*, 7
Negative account file, 667
Negotiable instrument, *def.*, 217
Net cost of a purchase, 636
Net decrease in cash, *def.*, 498
Net income, 36, 40–41; *def.*, 41,
480; *illus.*, 41
determining, 480
reporting, *def.*, 202
for corporations, 199–201
for partnerships, 196
for single proprietorships, 193–
194

Net income (*continued*)
  revenue and, 37
  transferring, to the capital account,
    42–43, 99–101, 103–105;
    illus., 43
Net increase in cash, 499; *def.,* 498
Net loss, 40–41; *def.,* 41, 480
  determining, 480–481
  transferring, to the capital account,
    43, 99–101, 105–106; *illus.,*
    43
Net pay, *def.,* 255
  computing, 433–434; *def.,* 434;
    illus., 433, 434
96-column punched card, 607; *illus.,*
  607
Nondescriptive statements, 419;
  illus., 420
Note payable, *def.,* 11
Note receivable, *def.,* 6

O Obsolescence of inventory,
    def., 346
One-write technique, *def.,* 584; *illus.,*
  585
Opening entry, 134–135; *def.,* 134;
  illus., 133
Optical character reading (OCR) ma-
  chine, 608
Optical scanning, 600, 608–609;
  illus., 609
Optical type font, 609; *illus.,* 609
Order clerk (DOT 249.367-054), 383
Ordering merchandise, 335–338
Orders shipped file, 386
Original papers (*see* Source docu-
  ments)
Originating data, 115–126; *def.,* 115
  methods of processing data and,
    123–126
    automated, 124–125
    manual, 123
  source documents and (*see* Source
    documents)
  sources of transaction data and,
    122
Origination step, 599
Output data, *def.,* 190
  accounting system and, 190; *illus.,*
    191
  flowcharts and, 287
Output devices, 599, 603–605
Outstanding check, *def.,* 224
Overtime pay, *def.,* 243
Overtime rate, *def.,* 243
Owner, claims of, 13
Owner's equity, 11–13, 37; *def.,*
  11–12
  cooperative and, 12

Owner's equity (*continued*)
  corporation and, 12
  partnership and, 12
  single proprietorship and, 12
  statement of, 485–486
Owner's equity accounts, 12, **76**
  debiting and crediting, 70–76
    capital account, 70–72
    expense accounts, 74–76
    revenue accounts, 72–74
  opening, 59; *illus.,* 59
  temporary, 30–39
  updating, 98–112, 173–184
    account balances, 107–109
    closing the ledger and, 106,
      173–174
    closing the temporary accounts
      and, 102–103, 174–176
    income summary account and,
      103
    journalizing and posting the clos-
      ing entries, 176–179
    postclosing trial balance and,
      107, 109–110, 180–182
    transfer process and, 101
    transferring amounts and, 101–
      102
    transferring a net income, 99–
      101, 103–105
    transferring a net loss, 99–101,
      105–106
Owner's equity transactions, 27–28
  decreasing owner's investment,
    26–27; *illus.,* 27
  increasing owner's investment, 26;
    illus., 26

P Partnership, 195–196; *def.,*
    12, 195
  financial statements for, 196; *illus.,*
    196, 197
Partnership agreement, *def.,* 195
Passbook, *def.,* 220
Patent, *def.,* 8
Pay period, 257
Pay plans, 241–242
  commission, 242, 432
  hourly-rate, 242, 432
  incentive, 242
  piece-rate, 242, 243
  salary, 241–242, 432
  salary-commission, 242, 432
Payables, *def.,* 11
Payee, *def.,* 210
Paying by check, 210–216
Payroll, *def.,* 241
  accounting for, 265–269
  accrued, 550–551
  computing net pay and, 433–434

Payroll (*continued*)
  employee earnings record and, 436
    as a subsidiary ledger, 436–437
  journalizing, 435–436
  pay plans, 432
  paying the, 263–264, 441–442
    by bank transfer, 264
    by cash, 263–264
    by check, 263
    methods of, 441
    recording, 264–265, 441–442
  posting, 436–440
  processing, 432–441
  recording the, 259–260
  summarizing transactions for,
    442–444
  taxes and (*see* Payroll taxes)
  wages and hours of work and, 432
Payroll clerk (DOT 215.482-010), 430
Payroll deduction, *def.,* 246 (*see also*
  Deductions from gross earnings)
Payroll department, 429
Payroll journal, 435–436; *def.,* 435;
  illus., 435
  posting the, 438–439; *illus.,* 438
  proving the, 436; *illus.,* 436
Payroll records, 256–269, **269,**
  430; *def.,* 241
  accounting for payroll, 265–269
  employee earnings record and,
    258–259
  employer payroll taxes and, 261–262
    recording, 262
  paying the payroll, 263–265
    recording of, 264–265
  payroll register and, 256–258
  recording the payroll, 259–260
Payroll register, 256–258; *def.,* 256;
  illus., 256
  journalizing from, 259–260
  pay period and, 257
  payroll deductions and, 257
  time cards and, 256
  totaling the, 257
Payroll taxes, 444–454
  as deductions (*see* Deductions from
    gross earnings)
  employer, 261–262
    recording, 262
  paying federal taxes, 444–447
    federal tax deposit and, 445–446
    quarterly federal tax return and,
      446
  paying unemployment compensa-
    tion taxes, 450–452
    federal, 450–452
    state, 450
  recording and posting, 439–440
    employer FICA tax, 439
    state unemployment compensa-
      tion tax, 440

Payroll taxes (*continued*)
  schedule of employer's duties for, 456
  wage and tax statements, 448–449
  transmittal of income tax statements and, 449
Pegboard, *def.*, 584; *illus.*, 585
Pencil-footing, *def.*, 87
People and accounting systems, 280
Percentage of aged accounts receivable method of estimating uncollectible accounts expense, 525–527
Percentage of net sales method of estimating uncollectible accounts expense, 525
Periodic inventory method, 617–619; *def.*, 345, 617
  beginning inventory and, 618
  cost of goods available for sale and, 618
  cost of goods sold and, 619
  gross profit on sales and, 619
  purchases and, 618
  sales and, 618–619
Permanent accounts, 29; *def.*, 22 (*see also specific permanent accounts*)
  debiting and crediting, 61–70
    analyzing business transactions and, 63–64
    asset accounts and, 64–66
    double-entry accounting and, 62–63
    liability accounts and, 66–68
  increasing and decreasing, 21–30
Perpetual inventory procedure, *def.*, 617
Perpetual inventory subsystem, 616–659; *def.*, 345, 617
  accounting for inventory losses, 644–646; *illus.*, 645
  advantages of, 647–648
    adaptable to automated systems, 648
    continuous flow of information, 647
    daily balances, 647
    ordering merchandise, 647–648
    reduces theft, 648
    reporting, 648
  assigning costs to inventory, 642–644
    by average unit cost, 643
    by FIFO, 643–644
  automation of, 649–657
    customer order blank and, *illus.*, 651
    daily inventory report, 654–655; *illus.*, 654
    daily sales report, 653; *illus.*, 653, 654

Perpetual inventory subsystem, automation of (*continued*)
    determining items in stock, 651–652; *illus.*, 652
    inventory sheet, 656–657; *illus.*, 656
    merchandise alert report, 655; *illus.*, 655
    proving the inventory, 656
    showroom sales, 650–651
    updating inventory, 652–653
  controls, 624, 636
  disadvantages of, 648
  financial statements and, 646–647
  inventory ledger and (*see* Inventory ledger)
  perpetual inventory method and, 620–624, **635–636**
    beginning inventory and, 620
    cost of goods available for sale and, 620
    cost of goods sold and, 621
    gross profit on sales and, 621–622
    purchases and, 620
    sales and, 620–621
  purchase transactions and, 625–631
    cash, 625; *illus.*, 625–626
    cash discounts and, 629; *illus.*, 630
    credit, 626; *illus.*, 626–627
    purchase returns and allowances and, 628–629; *illus.*, 629
    summary of, *illus.*, 631
    transportation in and, 627; *illus.*, 628
  sales transactions and, 632–635
    cash, 632–633; *illus.*, 632, 633
    credit, 633
    sales allowances and, 635
    sales discounts and, 635
    sales returns and, 634; *illus.*, 634–635
  worksheets and, 646; *illus.*, 646
Personal computer, 593
Personnel and payroll subsystem, 427–456; *def.*, 427
  controlling, 427
  visualizing, 430; *illus.*, 431 (*see also* Payroll)
Personnel department, 428–429
  new employees and, 428–429
  personnel records and, 429
  relation to payroll department, 429
Petty cash, 230–237
  journalizing entries, 234–236; *illus.*, 235
Petty cash fund, 230–232, **237;** *def.*, 230
  establishing and handling the, 230–232
  recording, 232

Petty cash fund (*continued*)
  proving, *def.*, 231
  reimbursing, 231–232; *def.*, 231
  recording, 233
Petty cash memorandum, *def.*, 232; *illus.*, 232
Petty cash register, 232–234; *def.*, 232; *illus.*, 232
  flowchart of use of, *illus.*, 236
Petty cash voucher, *def.*, 231; *illus.*, 231
Physical inventory, *def.*, 345–346, 464
Piece-rate pay plan, *def.*, 242, 432
Plant and equipment, *def.*, 7, 486–487, 531
  cost of, 543
  updating, 531–543
Plant and equipment ledger, 536–538; *def.*, 536
Plant and equipment record card, 536–537; *illus.*, 537
Point-of-sale (POS) procedures, *def.*, 281, 283; *illus.*, 283
Postclosing trial balance, 112, 183, 496; *def.*, 107, 180, 495
  preparing, 109–110, 180–182, 495–496; *illus.*, 110, 496
  purpose of, 109
  updating account balances and, 107–109
Posting data, 239; *def.*, 143; *illus.*, 239
  batch processing and, 578–581
    direct posting and, 580–581; *illus.*, 581
  cash payments, 321–322, 374–375; *illus.*, 321, 322, 374, 375
  cash receipts, 305–307; *illus.*, 306, 307
    from credit sales, 414–415; *illus.*, 415–416
    from the cash receipts journal, 417; *illus.*, 417
    from the combination journal, 574–576
  conventional, 577–578; *illus.*, 578
  credit purchases, 351–353; *illus.*, 352, 353
  cross-referencing in, *def.*, 150–151
  double-posting, 367
  to the employee earnings record, 436; *illus.*, 437
  to the ledger, 143–156
    account cycle and, 155–156
    accounts payable ledger, 357–359; *illus.*, 357, 358
    audit trail and, 150–151
    cross-referencing and, 150–151
    inventory ledger (*see* Inventory ledger, posting to)
    ledger after posting, 151; *illus.*, 151–153

Posting data, to the ledger (*continued*)
  other methods of keeping the ledger, 154–155
  procedure for, 145–150; *illus.*, 145–148
  proving and (*see* Accounting proofs)
  reference numbers and, 151
  timeliness of, 154
  updating, 468
  to the payroll journal, 438–439; *illus.*, 438
  payroll taxes, 439–440
  reference numbers, *def.*, 151
  sales on credit, 395–398; *illus.*, 396–398
  by total, 311, 576
Prenumbered source document, *def.*, 297
Prepaid expenses, 468–471, **472;** *def.*, 468
  as current asset, 486
  insurance, 470–471
  other, 471
  supplies on hand, 469–470
  updating, 468
Prepaid insurance, 470–471
Printers, computer, 603
Procedure flowcharts, 594; *def.*, 290; *illus.*, 290, 594
Processing accounting information, 598
Processing and shipping merchandise, 385–386
Processing information, *def.*, 277
Profit, gross, *def.*, 348–349
Profit incentive, 31, **37**
Program, computer, *def.*, 593–594
Programmer, 594
Proof, *def.*, 16 (*see also* Accounting proofs)
  of accounts receivable ledger, 398–399
  of assets, 330
  of the automated inventory, 656
  cash (*see* Cash proof)
  of combination journal, 572–574
  of the equation, 16, 39–46
  of the inventory ledger, 640–642
  of ledgers (*see* Updating trial balance)
  of payroll journal, 436
Proof tape, 580
Proving (*see* Proof)
Punched-card reader, 599
Punched cards
  card columns, 605–606
  card rows, 606
  coding on, 606–607
  80-column, 605–606; *illus.*, 606
  96-column, 607
  numeric rows, 606

Punched cards (*continued*)
  zone rows, 606
Punched tape, 607; *illus.*, 607
Punched-tape reader, 599
Purchase discounts, 367–369, 376; *def.*, 368
  credit period and, 368
  discount period and, 368
  inventory ledger and, 639
  recording, in the cash payments journal, 373
  tickler file and, 369
Purchase invoice, 115–116, 339–441; *illus.*, 116, 340
Purchase order, 336–337; *illus.*, 337
Purchase order form, *illus.*, 383
Purchase requisition, 335; *illus.*, 335
Purchases account, *def.*, 349
Purchases discount account, *def.*, 372
Purchases journal, *def.*, 350; *illus.*, 351
Purchases on credit subsystem, 334–380; *def.*, 334
  accounting for merchandise, 339–341
  accounts payable ledger and (*see* Accounts payable ledger)
  cash payments on account and, 371–376
    journalizing, 371–373
    posting, 374–375
    recording discounts, 373–374
  cash purchases and, 351
  net purchases and, 360–370, **369;** *def.*, 365
    purchase discounts and, 367–369
    purchases returns and allowances and, 363–367
    tickler file and, 369
    transportation in and, 361–363
  ordering merchandise, 335–338
    determining needs, 335
    placing the order, 336–337
    selecting the supplier, 336
  processing, 348–354
    controlling, 334
    cost of goods sold and, 349
    journalizing, 349–351
    posting, 351–353
  receiving merchandise, 338–339
  storing merchandise, 344–348
  summarizing, 375–376
  visualizing, 341; *illus.*, 342
Purchases returns and allowances, 363–367; *def.*, 363
  perpetual inventory method and, 628–629; *illus.*, 629
  inventory ledger and, 639–640
  receiving cash for, 364–365; *illus.*, 364
  receiving credit for, 365–367; *illus.*, 366, 367

Purchases returns and allowances account, *def.*, 364
Purchasing agent (DOT 162.157-038), 244, 336
Purchasing clerk (DOT 249.367-066), 338

 Quantity control, 344
Quarter, *def.*, 22
Quick trial balance, *def.*, 79

R Ratios, 499–502
  current, 500
  return on owner's equity, 501–502
  return on total assets, 501
Raw materials, *def.*, 7
Real accounts, *def.*, 96–97
Realizable value of the accounts receivable, 521; *def.*, 517
Receivables (*see* Accounts receivable)
Receiving clerk (DOT 222.387-050), 338
Receiving merchandise, 338–339
Reconciled balances, *def.*, 228
Reconciling the bank statement, 226–228; *def.*, 226
  adjusted balances and, 228
  making corrections after, 228–229; *illus.*, 229
Recorded value, *def.*, 171
Recording devices, 284; *illus.*, 284
Reference numbers, posting, *def.*, 151
Register, computer, 602–603
Registers (*see* Journals)
Regular charge plan, *def.*, 662
Remittance slips, 297–298, *def.*, 122, 297; *illus.*, 118, 297
Rental revenue account, *def.*, 560; *illus.*, 560
Report form balance sheet, 170–171; *def.*, 170; *illus.*, 170
Request for quotation, *illus.*, 336
Restrictive endorsement, *def.*, 218; *illus.*, 218
Retained earnings, *def.*, 199
Return on owner's equity ratio, 501–502
Return on total assets ratio, 501
Returns and allowances (*see* Purchases returns and allowances; Sales returns and allowances)
Revenue, 37; *def.*, 32
  net income and, 37
Revenue accounts
  closing, 174–175; *illus.*, 174
  closing entries for, 176–177; *illus.*, 176, 177
  recording changes in, 72–74; *illus.*, 72

Revenue transactions, 32–34
    from cash sales, 32; *illus.*, 32
    from credit sales, 33; *illus.*, 33
Ruling, 82

S Salaries, *def.*, 241
    Salaries expense, 550–551
    adjusting for, 550
    paying the, 551
    worksheet and, 552
Salary-commission pay plan, *def.*,
    242, 432
Salary pay plan, 241–242; *def.*, 241,
    432
Sales, cash (*see* Cash receipts)
Sales account, *def.*, 349
Sales discounts, 409–412; *def.*, 410
    conditions for, 416
    perpetual inventory method and,
        635
    receiving payments and, 410–412;
        illus., 410–412
Sales invoice, 115, 386; *illus.*, 120
    preparing the, 387–388; *illus.*, 387
Sales invoice binder, 581–582
Sales journal, 390–393; *def.*, 390–
    391; *illus.*, 391, 392
Sales on credit subsystem, 382–425;
    def., 382
    accounts receivable and, 419–422
        aging, 421–422
        statement of account and, 419–
            421
    billing for merchandise, 386–388
        preparing the sales invoice, 387–
            388
    cash received on account and,
        413–419
        journalizing, 414
        posting, 414–417
        taxes, returns and allowances,
            and discounts, 416
    controlling, 382–390
        procedures for, 382
    net sales and, 402–413
        computing, 402–403
        delivery charges and, 409
        returns and allowances and (*see*
            Sales returns and allowances)
    processing, 390–401
        accounts receivable ledger and,
            394–395
        journalizing, 390–393
        paying sales taxes, 399–401
        posting, 395–398
        proving the accounts receivable
            ledger, 398–399
        sales tax and, 393–394
    processing and shipping merchan-
        dise, 385–386

Sales on credit subsystem (*continued*)
    receiving and approving orders,
        383–385
        preparing the shipping order,
            383–384
        securing credit approval, 384
        taking the order, 383
    using sales discounts to encourage
        payment, 409–412
        receiving payments and, 410–412
    visualizing, 388; *illus.*, 389, 423
Sales order form, *illus.*, 383
Sales returns and allowances, 402–
    409; *def.*, 403
    credit memorandum and, 405–406
    perpetual inventory subsystem and,
        634–635
    recording, 406–407
    refunds, 403–405
        in cash, 403–404
        by check, 405
    sales discounts and, 416
    sales tax on, 407–409
Sales returns and allowances account,
    def., 404
Sales slip, *def.*, 297; *illus.*, 297
    cash proof and, 298; *illus.*, 298
    forms register and, 297
Sales tax, 393–394; *def.*, 393; *illus.*,
    394
    paying, 399–401; *illus.*, 400, 401
    sales discounts and, 416
    on sales returns and allowances,
        407–409; *illus.*, 407–409
Salvage value, 532
Schedule of accounts payable, *def.*,
    359; *illus.*, 359
Schedule of accounts receivable,
    398–399; *illus.*, 399
Schedule of cost of goods sold, 482–
    483; *def.*, 482; *illus.*, 483
Schedule of subsidiary ledgers,
    401, 471, 649
Service charge, *def.*, 225
Shareholders, *def.*, 198
Shipping clerk (DOT 222.387-050),
    385
Shipping merchandise, 385–386
Shipping order, 383–384; *def.*, 383;
    illus., 384
Signature card, *def.*, 210; *illus.*, 210
Single proprietorship, 193; *def.*, 12,
    193
    financial statement for, 193–195;
        illus., 194
Social security programs, 249–250
    employer payroll taxes and, 261,
        439
Solvency, *def.*, 500
Source documents, 115–116, **126;**
    def., 116; *illus.*, 116
    business forms as, 116

Source documents (*continued*)
    controlling cash receipts and, 296–
        298
        cash register tapes, 296–297
        remittance slips, 297
        sales slips, 297
    prenumbered, 297
    purchase invoice as, 115–116
    purpose of, 122
    sources of, 122
    use of, 117; *illus.*, 118–121
Source of cash, 498–499; *def.*, 498
Special journal, 279–280; *def.*, 279
Special subsystems, *def.*, 458
State income tax, 250, 252–254
    computation of, 252–254
    tax tables for, *illus.*, 252
State unemployment compensation
    tax, 261–262, 450
Statement of account, 419–421;
    illus., 421
    cycle billing and, 419–420; *illus.*,
        420
    nondescriptive, 419; *illus.*, 420
Statement of changes in financial po-
    sition, 488–490; *def.*, 488; *illus.*,
    489
    preparing, 488–489
    verifying the net increase in work-
        ing capital, 489–490
Statement of earnings (*see* Income
    statement)
Statement of financial position (*see*
    Balance sheet)
Statement of operations (*see* Income
    statement)
Statement of owner's equity, 485–
    486; *def.*, 485; *illus.*, 485
Statement of profit and loss (*see* In-
    come statement)
Statement of revenue and expenses
    (*see* Income statement)
Stock-control clerk (DOT 219.367-
    034), 388
Stockholders, *def.*, 198
Stockholders' equity, *def.*, 12
Stop payment, 215–216; *def.*, 215;
    illus., 215, 216
Storage devices, 284; *illus.*, 284, 285
Storage merchandise (*see* Inventory)
Storage unit, 599, 602
Straight-line method of depreciation,
    def., 533
Subsidiary ledger, 355–356, **360;**
    def., 355; *illus.*, 355, 356
Summary, 40; *def.*, 21; *illus.*, 21
Suppliers, selecting, 336
Supplies, *def.*, 7
Supplies on hand, 469–470
    adjustment for, 476
Supporting documents (*see* Source
    documents)

Symbolic flowcharts, 288–289; *def.*, 288; *illus.*, 288
  accounting cycle and, 289; *illus.*, 290–291
  template for, 289, 294; *illus.*, 289, 294
System flowcharts, 289–290; *def.*, 289; *illus.*, 290–291
Systems, *def.*, **277–278**

T   T account, 53–56; *def.*, 53; *illus.*, 53
  account balance, 54–55
  account number, 53–54
  account title, 53
  chart of accounts and, 54
  coding and, 53
  credit side of, 54
  debit side of, 54
  disadvantages of, 143
  opening, 58–59; *illus.*, 59
  rules for debiting and crediting, 56–57
  summarizing the use of, 80
Tag reader, 611
Take-home pay, 434; *def.*, 255
Taxes (*see also* Deductions from gross earnings)
  federal income tax withholding, 246–248
  FICA [*see* Federal Insurance Contributions Act (FICA)]
  FUTA, 249, 261
  payroll (*see* Payroll taxes)
  sales (*see* Sales tax)
  state income tax, 250, 252–254
  unemployment, 440, 450–452
Telecommunication devices, 601
Temporary accounts, 36–37, **46;** *def.*, 37 (*see also specific temporary accounts*)
  closing, 102, 106
  debiting and crediting, 70–76
    capital account and, 70–72
    expense accounts and, 74–76
    revenue accounts and, 72–74
  expense transactions and, 34–36
  income and, 31
  increasing and decreasing owner's equity, 30–39
  revenue transactions and, 32–34
Three-column balance ledger form, *def.*, 356, *illus.*, 356
Tickler file, *def.*, 369; *illus.*, 369
Time-and-a-half pay, *def.*, 243
Time book, *def.*, 244
Time cards, 256
Trade discounts, 650
Trade-in value, 532
Trademark, *def.*, 8
Transaction recorders, 600

Transactions, 29; *def.*, 21
  analyzing, *def.*, 23; *illus.*, 23
    summary, 28
  asset, 23–24
    buying an asset for cash, 23
    collecting accounts receivable, 23–24
  expense, 34–36
    incurring, on credit, 35–36
    paying, with cash, 34–35
  journalizing data and (*see* Journalizing data)
  liability, 25–27
    buying assets on credit, 25
    paying liabilities, 26
    returning assets bought on credit, 25–26
  originating data and (*see* Originating data)
  owner's equity, 27–28
    decreasing owner's investment, 27–28
    increasing owner's investment, 27
  recording, 29
  revenue, 32–34
    from cash sales, 32
    from credit sales, 33
  sources of data for, 122
Transmittal of Income and Tax Statements (Form W-3), 449; *illus.*, 449
Transportation in, 361–363
  FOB destination and, 361
  FOB shipping point and, 361–362
  journalizing, 362–363; *illus.*, 362
  perpetual inventory method and, 627; *illus.*, 628
Transportation In account, *def.*, 362
Travel and entertainment credit card, *def.*, 661
Trial balance, 77–80, **80, 163, 471;** *def.*, 77, 156–157; *illus.*, 85, 90
  computing account balances and, 77–79
  errors, 158
    check-marking and, 158
    locating, 159–160
  formal, 84–87; *def.*, 79; *illus.*, 85, 157
    dollar signs and decimal points and, 86
    heading and, 86
    list of accounts and, 86
    proving, in ink, 87
    proving, in pencil, 86
  postclosing (*see* Postclosing trial balance)
  preparing, 79–80, 157
  purpose of, 84
  quick, *def.*, 79
  relationship between financial statements and, 167–168; *illus.*, 167

Trial balance (*continued*)
  updating (*see* Updating trial balance)
  zero proof and, *def.*, 79
Truth-in-Lending Act, 664
Two-column journal, *def.*, 135; *illus.*, 133

U   Ultraphase terminal, 656
  Unadjusted trial balance, 474–478; *def.*, 474
  completing the, 474
  completing the adjustments section, 474–476
  totaling the adjustments section, 476–478
Uncollectible accounts, 517–531; *def.*, 517
  allowance for doubtful accounts account and, 520
  allowance method and, 517, 520–521; *illus.*, 521
  asset contra account and, 520–521
  in closing the ledger, 523; *illus.*, 523
  collecting accounts written off, 529; *illus.*, 529
  contra account and, 520
  direct write-off method and, 517–519; *illus.*, 518, 519
  estimating, 525–527
    percentage of aged accounts receivable, method of, 525–527
    percentage of net sales, method of, 525
  expense account, 518–519; *illus.*, 518
  on financial statements, 522; *illus.*, 523
  losses from, 517–518
  realizable value of account receivable and, 517, 521
  recording actual, 527; *illus.*, 528
  on the worksheet, 522; *illus.*, 522
Uncollectible accounts expense account, 518–519; *illus.*, 518
Unearned rental revenue account, *def.*, 559; *illus.*, 559
Unearned revenue (*see* Deferred revenue)
Unemployment compensation tax
  federal, 450–452
  state, 440, 450
Unions, payroll deductions for, 254–255
Universal product code (UPC), 609; *illus.*, 609
Unlimited liability, *def.*, 193
  of partnerships, 195
  of single proprietorship, 193

Unrecorded expenses and liabilities (*see* Accrued expenses)

Unrecorded revenue and assets (*see* Accrued revenues; Deferred revenue)

Unshipped orders file, 384

Updating the account, *def.*, 154

for accruals and deferrals, 564 (*see also* Accrued expenses; Accrued revenues; Deferred revenue)

Updating trial balance, 461–472, **471**

  adjusted, 476–477

  merchandise inventory and, 464–468

    cost of goods on hand and, 464

    cost of goods sold and, 465–468

    updating, 462

  other prepaid expenses and, 471

  prepaid insurance and, 470–471

  proving the ledgers, 461–462; *illus.*, 463

  supplies on hand and, 469–470

  unadjusted (*see* Unadjusted trial balance)

  updating prepaid expenses and, 468

Use of cash, 499; *def.*, 498

Valuation account, 520

Value, *def.*, **172**

  book, *def.*, 534

Value (*continued*)

  market, *def.*, 171

  realizable, 521; *def.*, 517

  recorded, *def.*, 171, **173**

    basis for, 173

Verifying balances, 221–230

  bank statement and, 222–225

    reconciling, 226–228

  cash balance, 221–222

  making corrections, 228–229

VISA credit card, 308

Voluntary payroll deductions, 254

Voucher checks, *def.*, 214; *illus.*, 215

Wage and Hour Law, 243–244

Wage and Tax Statement (Form W-2), 448–449; *illus.*, 448

Wages, *def.*, 241

  and hours of work, 432

Wasting assets, *def.*, 7

Withdrawal, *def.*, 320

Word processors, 597–598; *def.*, 592; *illus.*, 592

  system of, 597

Work in process, *def.*, 7

Working capital, *def.*, 488

  net change in, 489

    verifying, 489–490

  sources of, 489

  uses of, 489

Working capital ratio, 500

Worksheet, 472–481; *def.*, 473; *illus.*, 473, 475

  accrued and deferred revenue on, 560–561; *illus.*, 561

  accrued expenses on, 551–552; *illus.*, 552

  completing the financial statements sections, 478–481; *illus.*, 479

  depreciation on, 538–539

    building and, 538–539

    delivery equipment and, 539

    office equipment and, 539

  determining net income or net loss, 480–481

  format of, 473

  perpetual inventory method and, 646; *illus.*, 646

  uncollectible accounts on, 522; *illus.*, 522

  updating the unadjusted trial balance, 474–478; *illus.*, 475, 477

Writing amounts, 206

Year-to-date earnings, *def.*, 258

Zero balance, *def.*, 101

Zero proof, *def.*, 79